nineteen

God's Signature in Nature and Scripture

Edip Yuksel

brainbowpress
Hundred Fourteen Books

www.19.org
www.yuksel.org
www.quranix.com
www.islamicreform.org
www.brainbowpress.com

ISBN 978-0-9796715-9-3

Cover design: Uğur Şahin

Printed in the United States of America

10 9 8 7 6 5 4 3 2

EDIP YUKSEL, American-Turkish-Kurdish author and activist, was born in Turkey in 1957 the son of late Sadreddin Yuksel, a prominent Sunni scholar. During his youth he was an internationally active Islamist who spent over four years in Turkish prisons in the 1980's for his political writings and activities that promoted an Islamic revolution in Turkey. While a popular Islamist author and youth leader, Edip adopted the Quran Alone philosophy after corresponding with Rashad Khalifa and reading his landmark book, *Quran, Hadith and Islam*. This led him to experience a paradigm change on 1st of July, 1986, transforming him from a Sunni polytheist to a reformed muslim, a peacemaker, and a rational monotheist. As a consequence, he was excommunicated and declared to be a heretic, an apostate deserving the death penalty. In 1989, he was sponsored for immigration to the USA by Rashad Khalifa and worked together for a year in Masjid Tucson, becoming a prominent member of the United Submitters International. However, shortly after the assassination of Rashad by a group of Sunni terrorists, he was *excommunicated* from the Submitters as he objected to an idol-carving gang that had infected the group with cult mentality and false ideas about Rashad.

Edip Yuksel is the author of over twenty books and hundreds of articles on religion, politics, philosophy and law in Turkish and English. His English books are recently published by Brainbow Press, which include *Quran: a Reformist Translation*, *Manifesto for Islamic Reform*, *Peacmaker's Guide to Warmongers*, and *NINETEEN: God's Signature in Nature and Scripture*. Edip is the co-editor of the annual anthology, *Critical Thinkers for Islamic Reform*.

After receiving his bachelor degrees from the University of Arizona in Philosophy and Near Eastern Studies, Edip received his law degree from the same university. Besides writing and lecturing, Edip works as an Adjunct Philosophy professor at Pima Community College. Edip is fluent in Turkish, English and Classic Arabic; proficient in Persian, and barely conversant in Kurdish, his mother tongue. Edip is the founder of Islamic Reform and co-founder of MPJP organizations. His online books, interviews, and articles are published at various Internet sites, including:

www.19.org
www.yuksel.org
www.quranix.com
www.islamicreform.org
www.quranmiracles.com
www.free-minds.org
www.quranic.org
www.quran.org
www.mpjp.org

Edip's books can be ordered at: www.amazon.com ● www.ozanyayincilik.com

I agree with Descartes: I think, therefore I am. But, I think twice: I think, therefore I do not believe.

~ Edip Yuksel

THANKS: Of course, I am grateful to God for leading my way to meet **Ahmad Deedat**, which led me meet **Dr. Rashad Khalifa**, the discoverer of the prophetic Secret, and work together with him for about a year, seven days a week at Masjid Tucson until the night of his assassination there. I am also thankful for the opportunity to communicate via snail mail and phone calls, with **Dr. Adib Cesar Majul** (Philosophy Professor) whom I benefited from his meticulous scholarship, from 1991 until his departure in 2003. I also benefited from discussing methodology and statistics with **Dr. Richard Steven Voss** (Business Professor, Troy), **Dr. Caner Taslaman** (Philosophy Professor, Istanbul), and **Cemal Aktaş** (Accountant, Istanbul). I am indebted to **Dr. Abdur Rab** (Economist, Houston), **Matthew Capiello** (Medical Student, San Diego), and **Ahamed Abdou** (Software Engineer, U.K.), for their extensive editorial assistance and feedback. I have also been very fortunate to work together and benefit from the fascinating works of **Milan Sulc** (Software Engineer, Switzerland) and **Abdullah Arik** (Mining Engineer, Tucson). I also would like to mention the chance to discuss this issue personally through snail mail and phone conversations with agnostic astronomer **Dr. Carl Sagan** (Astronomer/Author) and skeptic mathematician **Martin Gardner**. (Mathematician/Author). Both have since been teleported to another universe! Besides the names above, many people contributed, directly or indirectly, more or less, to the content of this book, in various ways such as discoveries, feedback, verification or falsification, constructive or destructive criticism on the subject. The following is a partial list in alphabetical order:

Abdurrahman Daniel Lomax (Antagonistic Critic)
Ahmet Kocagil, PhD (Quantitative Risk Manager, New York)
Ahmet Onur Durahim, PhD (Cryptologist, Turkey)
Aisha Musa, PhD (Professor of Islamic Studies, Florida Int'l Uni., Miami)
Ali Fazely, PhD (Profofessor of Physics, Southern University, Lousianna)
Amar Ourchane (Engineer, Michigan)
Arnold Mol (Reasearcher at Deen Research, Amsterdam)
Aslbek Mussin (Columnist/Entrepreneur, Almaty/Kazakhstan)
Ayman Anonymous (Antagonistic Critic)
Bahman Goherzad (Businessman, Canada)
Bapi Sengupta (Antagonistic Critic, India)
Chibuzo Casey Ohanaja (Student, Notre Dame/Texas)
Chris Moore (Theolog, United Kingdom/Turkey)
Chris Sirias (Atlanta)
Christine Frost (Editor, Boston)
Eren Canarslan (Istanbul, Turkey)
Faraydon Karim, PhD (Critic, Mathematician/Inventor, Texas)
Farhad Moeeni, PhD (Statistics Professor, Arkansas State University)
Gatut Adisoma, PhD (Engineer, Indonesia)
Gazihan Alankuş, PhD (Computer scientist, St. Lous, MO, USA)
Gerald Etienne (Telecommunication Consultant, Atlanta)
Haroon Khan (Businessman, United Kingdom)
Hasan Oezturk (Germany)
Jeff Garrisson, MD (Medical doctor, Colorado)
Kemal Shazad (Engineer, Toronto, Canada)
Mahmud Arıkan (Geologist, Turkey)
Oben Candemir, MD (Opthalmogist, Australia)
Rodeen Rahbar, MD (Medical Professor, Pennsylvania)
Serkan Canklioğlu (Engineer, Turkey)
Samir al-Imamy, PhD (Computer Programmer)
Tufan Karademir (IT expert, Turkey)

Edip Yuksel and Rashad Khalifa in front of Masjid Tucson in 1988. Because of the implications of his discovery of the Secret, as well as his strong criticism of the sectarian teachings based on Hadith and Sunna, Rashad was declared a heretic/apostate by leading Sunni scholars from 38 countries who held an emergency conference in Saudi Arabia in February 27, 1989 to discuss the Salman Rushdie controversy. While Rushdie survived the fatwa, Rashad was assassinated in this Masjid in January 31, 1990, by a terrorist group linked to al-Qaeda. The author of this book also received similar fatwas, yet he has escaped several assassination attempts, so far.

CONTENT

Appendices

Contextual Facts
on Code 19

1. *Code 19* provides a powerful evidence for God's existence, as expected, envisioned or demanded by some philosophers and scientists, such as Galileo Galilei, Isaac Newton, Gottfried Leibniz, David Hume, Paul Dirac, and Carl Sagan.

2. ***Code 19* was hidden in the 74th chapter of the Quran *The Hidden*, for 19x74 (1406) lunar years, and was discovered in 1974 by my colleague, Dr. Rashad Khalifa, an Egyptian-American biochemist. The number 19 has been a major controversy since its discovery and the number has realized all its assigned functions according to the prophetic verses of Chapter 74.**

3. **Because of the implications of his discovery of the Secret, as well as his strong criticism of the sectarian teachings based on *Hadith* and *Sunna*, Rashad was declared a heretic/apostate by leading Sunni scholars from 38 countries who held an emergency conference in Saudi Arabia in 1989 to discuss the Salman Rushdie controversy. While Rushdi survived, Rashad was assassinated in this Masjid in January 31, 1990, by a terrorist group linked to al-Qaeda. The author of this book also received similar fatwa, yet he has escaped several assassination attempts, so far.**

4. *Code 19, which was also discovered in the original portions of the* Old Testament by Judah ben Samuel in 11th century, is simple to understand but impossible to imitate.

5. ***Code 19* has little to do with numerology, since its literary-numerical (LitNu) pattern can be verified or falsified through scientific inquiry. It is radically different from the pattern demonstrated in *The Bible Code*, which has no statistical value.**

6. Unlike regular metaphysical or paranormal claims, *Code 19* can be verified or falsified by virtually anyone, since the Arabic version of the Quran is available everywhere. Besides, for the most part, the reader does not need to know Arabic but only two eyes to see, an ability to count, a critical mind, and an open mind and heart to witness extraordinary signs as the fulfillment of a great prophecy.

7. **This discovery has created a paradigm change among those who witness it: —instead of joining a religious bandwagon by blindly**

believing a holy story or hearsay, we must be critical thinkers; we must question everything and seek truth through knowledge. The code suggests a "Copernican revolution" in theology of religions. Instead of Krishna-centered, or Jesus-centered, or Muhammad-centered religions we must turn to the original center, to the God-centered model. The message of rational monotheism has sparked an ongoing controversy in countries with Muslim-majority populations, e.g., Egypt, Pakistan, Malaysia, Saudi Arabia, Turkey, etc. Internet forums are filled with heated debates regarding this code.

8. A majority of people, including many adherents of Sunni and Shiite religions so far have not been able to witness this extraordinary divine sign. *Code 19* proved one more time the Quranic maxim that the majority of people in fact do not seek nor follow the truth. It exposed billions of believers; contrary to what they pretend, they do not acknowledge the Truth but they are believers in their culture and are herds in various bandwagons (27:82).

9. *Code 19* is one the greatest discoveries in human history, since it provides an extraordinary and universal evidence for God's existence. The evidence is hundred percent objective, yet paradoxically it has a subjective pre-requisite, akin to the pre-requisite of keeping both eyes open in order to witness a 3-D picture made of random dots. This is exactly in accordance to the prophetic description in Chapter 74. As it is the case with computer generated random dot 3D stereograms, in order to witness one of the greatest miracles, some conditions need to be met.

10. By distinguishing those who regress and those who progress, *Code 19* has opened a new era. (74:37). Code 19 distinguishes rational monotheists from the blind followers of manmade hearsay collections and sectarian teachings, as well as from those who give lip service to the Quran to serve their political, financial, and personal agendas (27:82).

11. **Code 19 shed light on some multiple-meaning (*mutashabih*) and prophetic verses, in some cases enriching the meaning of many verses of the Quran. For instance, it explained the meaning and function of the combination of alphabet letters initializing 29 chapters.**

12. *Code 19* showed that the Quran is not an ordinary book, but a very interesting and unique book.

13. **Code 19 showed us that there is indeed a force, negative energy called Satan, which exerts hypnotic power over its constituents. Those who decide not to use their God-given minds to their full potentials are blinded by their masters; they cannot see and appreciate the precise and obvious divine signs and their message (7:146).**

14. The improbability and impossibility of the numerical structure of the Quran being produced by a medieval Arab genius becomes evident when we consider the following factors:

    - It includes simple elements of the Quran and goes deeper to an interlocking system of complex numerical patterns and relationships.
    - It involves not only frequencies of letters and words but also the numerical values of letters.
    - It involves not only an intricate numerical pattern but also a huge set of data consisting of units with multiple functions, such as letters that are also digits, words that are also numbers.
    - The nemeroliteral aspect of the Quran were not known by the adherents of the Quran until late 1960s and especially, 1974.
    - The literary aspect of the Quran has received praises from many literary giants throughout centuries.
    - The scientific accuracy of Quranic statements on various fields has been immaculate.
    - Muhammad was one of the busiest and greatest social and political reformists in human history.
    - The timing of the discovery of the code is precise and prophetic.
    - A series of prophetic events regarding the code has been fulfilled.

15. Whether we like it or not, the Creator of the universe decided to design creatures that could make independent decisions from their original program. For some reasons that we may not know now, the Omniscient and Omnipotent Creator, by bringing specific limitations to His powers, is testing some of these creatures with their given ability to choose. He will later discard those programs that are infected with viruses and will select those who made good and proper decisions. Put it in computer terminology, *Code 19* is one of those virus detectors. Its release year is 1974. It diagnoses the brains infected with the most destructive viruses called bigotry and polytheism, as well as the brains that are healthy. However, many people do not want to face the fact that the Hellfire and Smoke they see all over Chapter 74 is, in fact, the product of their own infected mind, their imagination.

16. You may understand nothing from the information shared in this book and you may wonder by saying "So what? What does this number mean?" You may choose to be duped by the ingrates or extreme skeptics who are good in hiding the truth and distorting the facts. Or you may witness one of the greatest miracles. If you become one of the few lucky witnesses with clear vision, nothing will be the same for you. You will experience the taste of eternal peace, love and happiness starting in this life on this lowly planet. You will respond to tragedies and miseries with resolve and dignity, and you will respond to blessings and gains with humility and appreciation. As an active peacemaker, you will stand against falsehood, superstitions,

hedonism, corruption, oppression, racism, nationalism, misogyny, intolerance and injustices without fear and hesitation. You will no longer believe in religious stories, you will no longer accept others as holy power-brokers between you and your Creator, and you will no more compromise your brain with illogical and nonsensical dogmas and taboos. You will no longer be a sheep exploited and manipulated by kings and priests, sultans and mullahs, rajahs and maharajs, politicians and pundits, atheists and polytheists. You will no more accept the claims of any "holy book" without unequivocal evidence. You will no more turn yourself into a schizophrenic character by allocating prime regions of your brain for contradictory beliefs, bizarre stories and Trojan horses. You will be a perpetual seeker of truth and submit yourself to the Truth alone. And the Truth will set you free. You will be honest; whenever your errors are shown, you will correct yourself. You will *know* that there is God, a Loving God, and you will receive God's communication through countless yet consistent signs received from multiple channels: brain, heart, nature, scripture, and your personal experience. You will be as rational as a human can be, and you will have no doubt about the purpose of life, eternity and resurrection. Though you will not find all the answers to your philosophical questions, but you will find answers to the most important ones. Of course, as a natural consequence of your appreciation and responsibility as a witness, you will share this message of rational monotheism with your friends and relatives in the best possible manner and expecting no reward from them.

17. **The author of this book challenges theologians, mathematicians, philosophers, thinkers, believers, agnostics and atheists, specifically, the living Pope, Evangelist Rick Warren, Atheist Richard Dawkins, Skeptic Michael Shermer, Mathematician Ian Stewart, professors at al-Azhar University, Ayatollahs in Qum, and other prominent scholars, including those who live in Ivory Towers, to respond to the function of *Code 19* that provides extraordinary evidence for the extraordinary claims made by the Quran. The author is ready for face-to-face public debates at the place of their choice. The author also claims right to the James Randy Educational Foundation's Million Dollar Paranormal Challenge and expects the JREF test his assertions regarding the fulfillment of the prophecies in Chapter 74 of the Quran.**

18. The author invites all mathematicians and specifically the mathematicians who have signed a petition rejecting the assertions made by the so-called *Bible Code* to examine Code 19. They rightly rejected its claims in a petition published at CalTech.

> "We refer in particular to the paper *Equidistant Letter Sequences in the Book of Genesis*, published in Statistical Science in 1994. This experiment suffers from major problems concerning both its execution and the interpretation of its conclusions. Even without these concerns, we would not take such extraordinary claims seriously without a vastly more

systematic and thorough investigation. No such investigation has been carried out, nor has the work so far established a prima facie case. In addition, word clusters such as mentioned in Witztum's and Drosnin's books and the so called messianic codes are an uncontrolled phenomenon and similar clusters will be found in any text of similar length. All claims of incredible probabilities for such clusters are bogus, since they are computed contrary to standard rules of probability and statistics."

http://math.caltech.edu/code/petition.html

Thus, I invite the same mathematicians who rejected the *Bible Code* to critically evaluate the merits of the Quranic assertion that the Quran itself is a numerically coded divine book, and the number 19 provides extraordinary evidence for its claims:

Robert E. L. Aldred, Dror Bar-Natan, Jay H. Beder, Valentina M. Borok, Robert Brooks, Mark Burgin , George M. Butler, Gary A. Chase, E. B. Davies, Percy Deift, Persi Diaconis, Laurence S. Freedman, Fritz Gesztesy, Sheldon Goldstein, Lawrence F. Gray, Rami Grossberg, Lee O. Hagglund, A. Michael Hasofer, Tim Hesterberg, Peter Hines, Svetlana Jitomirskaya, Gil Kalai, Fima Klebaner, David Klein, Richard N. Lane, Joel Lebowitz, Nati Linial, Gary Lorden, Brendan McKay, Tom Metzger, Stephen D. Miller, Paul Nevai, Amos Nevo, Eli Passow, John Allen Paulos, Yehuda Pinchover, Alexander Pruss, Maurice Rojas, Mary Beth Ruskai, Jeremy Schiff, Gideon Schwarz, Senya Shlosman, Barry Simon, Martha Simon, J. Laurie Snell, Terry Speed, Terence Tao, Ian Wanless, Thomas Ward, Herbert S. Wilf , Henry Wolkowicz, Abraham Wyner, Doron Zeilberger, Yakov I. Zhitomirskii...

Knowing that scientists and scholars too are not immune from popular prejudices, I do not expect much from mathematicians. Compared to religious communities, scientific communities provide more freedom to their members. Yet they too have their own conventions and taboos. There are red lines in each scientific community, and scientists who dare to challenge them may risk being penalized through excommunication, defamation, or loss of their jobs. For instance, questioning the atheistic spin on the theory of evolution could be considered an anathema in the biological field. Likewise, questioning the double standard in discriminating between the consumption of alcohol and other drugs might be costly for a scientist living in a world where the horrific harms of alcohol consumption to human health and morals are minimized, ignored, or even suppressed by interest groups —such as beer and wine industries, as well as the scientists and media personnel who financially benefit from them— under the mantra of beneficial effects of "drinking in moderation."

So I am not surprised if two scientist colleagues of mine, who had been supportive of this work for years, now decline to write positive reviews of my work. One of them is an accomplished mathematician and the other is a professor of statistics at a major US university. I cannot justify such fear, and

I consider it a sign of weakness in the academic and business establishment. Phillip Davis of Brown University and Reuben Hersh of University of New Mexico support my impression:

> "It is the writer's impression that most contemporary mathematicians and scientists are agnostics, or if they profess to a religious belief, they keep their science and their religion in two separate boxes. What might be described as the 'conventional scientific' view considers mathematics the foremost example of a field where reason is supreme, and where emotion is does not enter; where we know with certainty, and know that we know; where truths of today are truths forever. This view considers religion, by contrast, a realm of pure belief unaffected by reason. In this view, all religions are equal because all are equally incapable of verification and justification."[1]

Many mathematicians and scientists apparently are constrained to consider spending even a few minutes on this work, let alone studying it carefully and objectively. They may confuse the teaching of the Quran with the backwards religious teachings and practices of Sunni or Shiite sects. They may be suspicious of anything with religious connotations. They may be influenced by the political agendas and propaganda of Western imperialism against backwards countries with predominantly Muslim populations. They may have bad experience with similar claims such as the so-called *Bible Code* and confuse this work with esoteric numerology. They may also feel incompetent in assessing the value of the claims, since they assume it to be heavily dependent on the knowledge of Arabic, which is not.

As for Arabic-speaking scientists, or more generally, Muslim scientists, they may have extra impediments: the prejudices caused by Sunni and Shiite teachings, fear of violence from religious zealots who are extremely irritated when they see or hear about the number Nineteen, fear of condemnation by religious scholars who remain innumerate and ignorant, and/or fear of repressive governments that imprison and kill those who are declared as heretics…

On the other hand, I also know that critics have helped us to learn and appreciate more about this amazing evidence. Even if one of these mathematicians shows the courage and wisdom to study and then witness this prophetic sign, it might encourage their peers to get over their prejudices.

Though mathematicians are objective in their professions, when they are confronted with philosophical or theological arguments, most react skeptically, which is justifiable. However, there is a line between skepticism and dogmatism, between confidence and bigotry.

NINETEEN: God's Signature in Nature and Scripture. EXAMPLES:

The number of Arabic letters in the opening statement of the Quran, *BiSMi ALLaĤi AL-RaĤMaNi AL-RaĤYM* (1:1)	**19**	x 1
Every word in *Bismillah...* is found in the Quran in multiples of	**19**	
The frequency of the first word, Name (*Ism*)	**19**	x 1
The frequency of the second word, God (*Allah*)	**19**	x 142
The frequency of the third word, Gracious (*Raĥman*)	**19**	x 3
The fourth word, Compassionate (*Raĥym*)	**19**	x 6
Out of more than hundred attributes of God, only four has numerical values of multiple of	**19**	
One (*WAĤiD*)	**19**	x 1
Possessor of Great Bounties (*ŹuW AL-FaĎL AL-ÂŽYM*)	**19**	x 142
Glorious (*MaJYD*)	**19**	x 3
Summoner/Editor (*JAMeÂ*)	**19**	x 6
The number of chapters in the Quran	**19**	x 6
Despite its conspicuous absence from Chapter 9, Bismillah occurs twice in Chapter 27, making its frequency in the Quran	**19**	x 6
Number of chapters from the missing Ch. 9 to the extra in Ch. 27.	**19**	x 1
The total number of all verses in the Quran, including the 112 unnumbered Bismillah	**19**	x 334
29 Chapters of the Quran starts with 14 different combinations of 14 different letters. Their frequencies in the chapters that they initialize demonstrate an interlocking numerical pattern based on	**19**	
The number of all verses containing all those 14 letters.	**19**	x 6
Frequency of the letter Q in two chapters it initializes	**19**	x 6
Frequency of the letter Ŝ in three chapters it initializes	**19**	x 8
Frequency of the letters Y.S. in the chapter they initialize	**19**	x 15
Frequency of the letters K.H.Y.A.Ŝ in chapter they initialize	**19**	x 42
Frequency of the letters Ĥ.M. in seven chapters they initialize	**19**	x 113
The number of all different numbers mentioned in the Quran	**19**	x 2
The number of all numbers repeated in the Quran	**19**	x 16
The sum of all whole numbers mentioned in the Quran	**19**	x 8534
The number of lunar years in which the meaning of 19 remained hidden in Chapter 74, known *al-Muddathir* (The Hidden)	**19**	**x 74**
The year meaning of 19 in Ch. 74 (The Hidden) was unveiled	**19**	**74**
The number of letters in the first statement of Chapter 74	**19**	x 1
The numerical value of those first 19 letters in Chapter 74	**19**	**74**
The numerical value of the main message of the Quran, WAĤiD	**19**	x 1

For the curious mind:

On the Internet you will find hundreds of websites sharing the numerical and scientific miracles of the Quran. Of course, the reader should be cautious. There are many sites mixing silly and arbitrary calculations next to profound facts. So, as always, there is no free lunch. Every person must think for themselves and every person must past through critical thinking processes. This book does not contain all the significant discoveries on NINETEEN. To fit the information in a manageable and coherent book, I had to be selective. Below are the addresses of a few sites, out of many, that contain extensive information and/or discussion forums about code 19 and other scientific signs of the Quran.

19.org
quranmiracles.com
submission.org/miracle

Throughout this book I have not used the fabricated phrases of praises for Muhammad, such as *Salla Allahu Alayhi Wasallam*. In the endnotes of the *Quran: a Reformist Translation*, I have exposed and refuted the sectarian distortions on the verb *SaLlY ALA* in verse 33:56. The verse does not contain the instruction *Qul* (Say), but it instructs an action, that is, to encourage and support the prophet while he was alive. The same verb is used in verses 33.43 and 9:103, yet in order to hide their distortions it is translated differently by Sunni and Shiite clergymen. Verse 33:43 informs us that God supports/encourages (*yuSaLlY ALAkum*) us to seek the light, while verse 9:103 informs us that Muhammad was instructed to support/encourage *(SaLlY ALAyhim)* his friends. In other words, *SaLlY ALA* is not a special phrase of praise for Muhammad.

Furthermore, there is a verse instructing us how to mention the names of messengers. In verse 2:136 we are asked to mention their names without adding ostentatious words of praise. Note that the verse 2:136 uses the word *Qulu* (Say) and also warns us not to discriminate among God's messengers.

Centuries ago, the polytheists who gave lip service to rational monotheism, managed to transform the progressive message of the Quran into a backward, oppressive and superstitious culture. They accomplished this through making hearsay reports falsely attributed to Muhammad (*Hadith*) as one of the complements of the Quran in defining Islam. In order to accomplish their reprehensible act (25:30; 6:112-116; 65:35-38) they converted *La ilaha illa Allah*, the monotheistic statement (*Kalima al-Tawhid*), into a dualistic statement (*Kalima al-Tasniya*), which took more than a century after Muhammad to accomplish. The archeological evidences, gold and silver coins from Umayyad and Abbasid dynasties, provide conclusive evidence for our contention. It took four stealthy stages for backward polytheists to add Muhammad's name next to God in the *Shahada*! Verse 39:45 exposes the symptom of polytheism.

16

Pythagoras: "All things accord in number."

Plato: "The highest form of pure thought is in mathematics"

Buddha: "Do not put faith in traditions, even though they have been accepted for long generations and in many countries. Do not believe a thing because many repeat it. Do not accept a thing on the authority of one or another of the sages of old, nor on the ground of statements as found in the books. Never believe anything because probability is in its favor. Do not believe in that which you yourselves have imagined, thinking that a god has inspired it. Believe nothing merely on the authority of the teachers or the priests. After examination, believe that which you have tested for yourself and found reasonable, which is in conformity with your well being and that of others." *The Quran teaches this.*

Nicomachus: "As it appears, the universe is designed with mathematics."

Hrovista Gandersheim: "God created the world from nothingness and constructed everything with numbers."

Rene Descartes: "All intellectual issues can be united and should be united through mathematics."

Galileo Galilei: "Mathematics is the language God wrote the universe with."

David Hume: "If we take in our hand any volume of divinity or school metaphysics, for instance; let us ask, does it contain any abstract reasoning concerning quantity or number? No. Does it contain any experimental reasoning concerning matter of fact and existence? No. Commit it then to flames: for it can contain nothing but sophistry and illusion."

John Arbuthnot: "Mathematical knowledge adds vigour to the mind, frees it from prejudice, credulity, and superstition."

Arthur Schopenhauer: "All truth passes through three stages: First, it is ridiculed; Second, it is violently opposed; Third, it is accepted as self-evident."

James Jeans"The universe appears to be have been designed by a pure mathematician."

Albert Einstein "How is it possible that mathematics, a product of human thought that is independent of experience, fits so excellently the objects of physical reality?"

Paul Dirac: "If there is a God, he's a great mathematician"

0
A Brief Story

I was arrested a few days after participating in a two-week long international youth conference held in August 1980 at a campground belonging to the Turkish Ministry of Sports and Youth at a beach near Çanakkale. There, I met Ahmad Deedat and I also met the famous scholar al-Qaradawi. Though I knew al-Qaradawi from his books and I esteemed him very much, I was more interested in Ahmad Deedat and his lectures. For two weeks we shared the same camping ground. I found Ahmed very intelligent, articulate and knowledgeable in his area (more in Bible and less in Quran), devoted to the cause of promoting the message of the Quran and blessed with a great sense of humor. He was also very friendly. I heard about the mathematical miracle of the Quran for the first time from him. It was a moment that I will never forget. It was the first time I had heard about the presence and importance of the number 19 in the Quran. I was very interested in the lecture primarily for two reasons: the code was providing powerful rational and empirical evidences for the authenticity of the Quran, and it was my number. It had been about two years since I was referred to as "Mr. 19" by my friends.

At that time I was a university student, and leading member of a national youth organization called Akıncılar, the Raiders. Besides this legal organization, I decided to create a special organization without the bureaucratic paperwork and police supervision. Thus, in 1978, I decided to allocate a big room in the student dormitory, a historic domed building surrounding the Fatih mosque, for middle and high school students. I picked, organized, brainwashed, trained and mobilized 50 or 60 students to participate in our political activities promoting a theocratic revolution. I was preparing them for our bigger fight —yes literally— against other groups in the universities. A large neighborhood containing about a million people was our territory and the political graffiti, the imposed membership dues, and the numerous religious sanctions imposed on the merchants and neighborhood testified to our dominance against other rival political youth organizations.

One night, I wanted to give a name to my special illegal group. Suddenly, I thought to give them a number for a name. I decided on the number 19. I had no particular reason for choosing that number. I had no memory of its being mentioned in the Quran, nor its being the number of letters in the first verse of the Quran. I just liked that number. Thus, I called my high school group FT/19, that is Fatih/19, or Victory/19. Soon, the beautiful white marbles on the exterior of residential high buildings and stores became covered with graffiti undersigned with FT/19.

I became more dedicated to and obsessed with this group after the assassination of my younger brother in the yard of Fatih Mosque just after he exited from the congregational prayer on February 23, 1979. I was one of the leading members of the national youth organization mostly run by university students and I was also the founder of the FT/19 and the "Big Brother" of hundreds of secondary school students.

Yes, my two-year experience with the number 19 made me even more curious about its importance in the Quran. Thus, I listened to Deedat's lecture attentively. After his lecture, I met him and with my poor English I asked his permission to translate his book to Turkish. He happily gave his permission, together with many other pamphlets and posters. I fell in love with that thin book, Al-Quran, The Ultimate Miracle, which later I translated into Turkish and published it together with my additional research. Its content, physical and literal presentation, all together was fantastic.

Within days from the end of the conference I was arrested and I would spend 4 years in prison. Thank God for that. Though occasionally there was torture and very strict rules, such as not being allowed to read any book of our choice, there was a period in prison where I could find ample time to examine Deedat's book and then translate it. I added my studies on the scientific aspect of the Quran, and it was published. It became an instant best-selling book for about five years crowning the top of the best-selling list in Turkey.

I continued my communication with Deedat via Mail. But, in 1986, I discovered Rashad Khalifa. Though I had heard about him from the introduction of Deedat's book, somehow until this time I never felt the urge to communicate with him. I started communicating with Rashad... That changed my paradigm, leading me to reject Hadith and Sunna and all other sectarian teachings accept the Quran alone on the night of July 1, 1986.2

Since then I consider myself a rational monotheist, a peacemaker. It was a dramatic change that none who knew me could have envisioned and it was accomplished by the number 19. Yet, centuries before, John Arbuthnot, an English physician and mathematician, knew well the reforming and transforming power of mathematical knowledge: "Mathematical knowledge adds vigour to the mind, frees it from prejudice, credulity, and superstition."

1

"This is the Only Way"

"No, don't you see? This *would* be different. This isn't just starting the universe out with some precise mathematical laws that determine physics and chemistry. This is a *message*. Whoever makes the universe hides messages in transcendental numbers so they'll be read fifteen billion years later when intelligent life finally evolves. I criticized you and Rankin the time we first met for not understanding this. 'If God wanted us to know that he existed, why didn't he send us an unambiguous message?' I asked. Remember?"

"I remember very well. You think God is a mathematician."

"Something like that. If what we're told is true. If this isn't a wild-goose chase. If there's a message hiding in pi and not one of the infinity of other transcendental numbers. That's a lot of ifs."

"You're looking for Revelation in arithmetic. I know a better way."

"Palmer, this is the only way. This is the only thing that would convince a skeptic. Imagine we find something. It doesn't have to be tremendously complicated. Just something more orderly than could accumulate by chance that many digits into pi. That's all we need. Then mathematicians all over the world can find exactly the same pattern or message or whatever it proves to be. Then there are no sectarian divisions. Everybody begins reading the same Scripture. No one could then argue that the key miracle in the religion was some conjurer's trick, or that later historians had falsified the record, or that it's just hysteria or delusion or a substitute parent for when we grow up. Everyone could be a believer." ~ Carl Sagan[3]

The excerpts above are from *Contact*, a book by the late astronomer and author Carl Sagan. The plot is a novel expression of a philosopher's true dream—mathematical evidence for God's existence. A divine message written according to a mathematical formula seems no longer a fantasy. Interestingly, the inhabitants of this planet had received such a message 11 years before Sagan wrote *Contact*, and 23 years before the movie version of the novel was released. However, there were two differences between the fiction and the reality. The message was not hidden in π (pi), but in a prime number. And not everyone had accepted the message yet![4]

In fact, Carl Sagan, in another book had a closer idea, but this time about extraterrestrials. About six years after the discovery of the prime number in the Final Testament, he wrote the following in his book *Cosmos*: "It would be easy for extraterrestrials to make an unambiguously artificial interstellar message. For example, the first ten prime numbers—numbers divisible by only themselves and by one—are 1, 2, 3, 5, 7, 11, 13, 17, 19, 23. It is extremely unlikely that any natural physical process could transmit radio messages containing prime numbers only. If we received such a message we would deduce a civilization out there that was at least found of prime numbers."[5]

A Miracle or a Holy Hoax?

The writings some believe to be revelations of God contain narratives of miracles. For the objective researcher, those "miracles" as reported may be no more than dubious and suspicious tales. Those who hear the story of countless fabricated "holy" miracles being attributed to saints and witness appalling hoaxes by evangelical charlatans know how simple facts can be distorted among gullible rumormongers. They may consider such "narration of miracles" as of the same category as folk mythologies.

"Moses parted the Red Sea with his staff" or "Jesus cured the blind men by his prayer" is not a miracle, but merely a claim -- a hearsay that would be rejected in our judicial system if submitted as a proof of fact. If, indeed, such an extraordinary event occurred thousands of years ago, it was at best a miracle only for those who witnessed it. For us, however, it is only a narration....

Why should we believe in such a narration? Simply because others believe it? I would like to quote from Carl Sagan's book, which I highly recommend to my philosophy students: "The more we want it to be true, the more careful we have to be. No witness's say-so is good enough. People make mistakes. People play practical jokes. People stretch the truth for money or attention or fame. People occasionally misunderstand what they're seeing. People sometimes even see things that aren't there."[6]

Of course, not everyone believes this narration. Even if everyone believes it, it does not justify one's belief in it. We well know that countless of millions, throughout human history, believed fervently in many superstitions and mythologies. Many of them did not hesitate to sacrifice their lives and others' for their belief in them. When Galileo claimed the earth was round and in motion, almost everyone, including the "infallible" Pope, believed him wrong. Yet, the world did not chill flatly on top of a cow's horn, nor danced on the back of a tortoise's shell, just because the multitude believed so.

Today, there are hundreds of religions, sects, orders and denominations globally. Almost all of them introduce and promote their idiosyncratic mythologies, paranormal claims and holy hoaxes as "miracles." Millions of Catholics rejuvenate their faith in their church by the "miracle of crying Mary icons", or by that of "bleeding communion beads," while millions of Muslims witness miracles of healing powers and prophecies of the leaders of mystic orders.

21

Religious populations are filled with narration of miracles and claims, which do not provide empirical data for their scientific verification or falsification.

Forget about satisfying the reasonable standard that requires extraordinary evidence for extraordinary claims; most of the myriad claims of miracles do not have even ordinary pieces of supporting evidence.

Were These "Miracles" For Previous Generations Only?

What if the books narrating the miracles of Moses and Jesus were collections of fiction and fantasies that somehow became popular? If there is a God, and if He is sending messengers and supporting them with miracles, then why does He deprive us of similar miracles? Why does the god who showered the mostly illiterate populations of ancient villages with "miracles" fail to enable the highly educated populations of modern metropolitans to perform even a single miracle? Are modern communities less sincere and devoted than their ancient predecessors? Or do they have less doubt about God and His message?

Many people doubt miracles purportedly witnessed by previous generations. After all, they were accepted as fact by the masses in a time when people were illiterate. Some may say that those people were more gullible than those of today. Of course many people have asked the famous question, "Why don't miracles happen nowadays, huh?"

But what if there were a miracle that was not freeze-framed in the time of the people who witnessed it? What if there was a perpetual and universal miracle— something that could be viewed or acknowledged not only by modern people but also by future generations? What if in the same way such a miracle could also help distinguish the REAL miracles from the fiction, thereby proving conclusively that those miracles did truly happen?

Psychologist David Heller provides us with an amusing collection of letters written by 7 to 12 year-old kids.[7] Usually starting with "Dear God," children voice their complaints and suggestions to God. Among the letters were some that jabbered and others that demonstrated childish irreverence and rebellion toward God. A few challenged the idea of God and boldly expressed their disbelief in the existence of God in the first place. Many letters contained explicit or implicit serious criticism. One such letter relevant to our topic at hand reads as follows:

> Dear God,
>
> I read how you partered the red ocean. That was cool and unbelevable. How come you don't do things spectakquler like that any more. Hard to get up the energy? Dan B. (age 12)

22

The author, despite his use of religiously inappropriate language, makes a good point. The clergymen of various religions might ignore this question and pontificate: "there are thousands of miracles occurring everyday, but modern man is blind to them." Well, by the word "miracle" I am not referring to the incredible design in nature, which is in some measure explained by the facts supporting the theory of evolution.[8] Nor am I referring to the experiences that adherents of most religions claim to have. Surely, I am also not talking about TV evangelists who are merely charlatans whose only goal is to separate their gullible audience from their money. Muslim clerics, despite all these questions, might still continue bragging about the miracles of the Prophet Muhammad: "Muhammad did not have a shadow. He split the moon by pointing at it with his index finger and one half of the moon fell in the backyard of Ali Ben Abi Talib. Muhammad crippled a man for eating with his left hand, and he even crippled a child who walked in front of him while he prayed." Those who are interested in distinguishing fact from fiction will always ask questions.

Almost 2000 years ago, Jesus Christ began to preach to the Children of Israel to worship God alone. He warned the people against the teachings of the Pharisees, professional clergymen, who had "turned God's house into robbers' den" and forsook the spiritual aspect of religion for cleric-made legalistic formalism. Instead of reflecting on the truth-value of his message, people demanded miracles of Christ to prove his messengership.

> "Then certain of the scribes and of the Pharisees answered, saying, Master, we would see a sign from thee. But he answered and said unto them, An evil and adulterous generation seeks after a sign; and there shall no sign be given to it, but the sign of the prophet Jonas." (Matthew 12:38-39)

Though Jesus refused to comply with the challenge of disbelievers, he did, according to the Gospels, perform many miracles to support his claim of messengership. The "miracles" narrated by the Gospels were not demonstrated to persuade fanatic disbelievers to believe, but shown to those who were receptive to the message or had a healthy dose of skepticism.

> And when Jesus departed thence, two blind men followed him, crying, and saying, Thou son of David, have mercy on us. And when he came into the house, the blind men came to him: and Jesus said unto them, Believe you that I am able to do this? They said unto him, Yea, Lord. Then touched he their eyes, saying, According to your faith be it unto you. And their eyes were opened; and Jesus charged them, saying, See that no man knows it. (Matthew 9:27-30).

> Jesus answered and said unto them, Go and show John again those things which you do hear and see: The blind receive their sight, and the lame walk, the lepers are cleansed, and the deaf hear, the dead are raised up, and the poor have the gospel preached to them. (Matthew 11:4-5)

> And Jesus, when he came out, saw much people, and was moved with compassion toward them, because they were as sheep not having a shepherd:

23

and he began to teach them many things.... He says unto them, How many loaves have you? Go and see. And when they knew, they say, Five, and two fishes. And he commanded them to make all sit down by companies upon the green grass. And they sat down in ranks, by hundreds, and by fifties. And when he had taken the five loaves and the two fishes, he looked up to heaven, and blessed, and brake the loaves, and gave them to his disciples to set before them; and the two fishes divided he among them all. And they did all eat, and were filled. And they took up twelve baskets full of the fragments, and of the fishes. And they that did eat of the loaves were about five thousand men.... And he saw them toiling in rowing; for the wind was contrary unto them: and about the fourth watch of the night he comes unto them, walking upon the sea, and would have passed by them. But when they saw him walking upon the sea, they supposed it had been a spirit, and cried out: ... (Matthew 6:34, 38-44, 48-49).

The Old Testament, too, contains many references to divine "miracles," or "signs," or "wonders."

> When Pharaoh shall speak unto you, saying, Show a miracle for you: then thou shall say unto Aaron, Take thy rod, and cast it before Pharaoh, and it shall become a serpent. (Exodus 7:9)

> And Moses and Aaron did all these wonders before Pharaoh: and the LORD hardened Pharaoh's heart, so that he would not let the children of Israel go out of his land. (Exodus 11:10).

> Then thou shall say unto thy son, We were Pharaoh's bondmen in Egypt; and the LORD brought us out of Egypt with a mighty hand: And the LORD showed signs and wonders, great and sore, upon Egypt, upon Pharaoh, and upon all his household, before our eyes: (Deuteronomy 6:21-22).

As we said before, these are all hearsay reports, and their reliability is questionable. Even if the reporter claims to be an "eyewitness" of the miracle, and provides the names of others to corroborate his testimony, the narration still remains doubtful for several reasons. There is no proof that the narration was really written by that eyewitness, or was not altered after his death. Even if such a proof exists, there is no way to confirm that the eyewitness did not have a selective memory, or was not tricked by an illusion, or had pious delusions. Furthermore, any list of other witnesses to such a narration has little value as to confirmation of the very narration we seek to verify, unless we find the same list in independent sources that do not share similar religious motivations.

The Book of Mormon and numerous other religious texts rely heavily on the "testimony" of the dead. None, however, are held to any specific degree of factual reliability such as that required of evidence that is offered in any court of justice in the secular world.

Sick and Tired of Religions!

For many modern intellectuals, religions are tangled balls of contradictory teachings in dark boxes filled with metaphysical claims and assumptions that cannot be tested. The prevarication and fiction preached by dishonest clergymen to appease the gullible masses has rendered intellectuals suspicious and skeptical of everything related to religion, and reasonably so.

Many scientists are agnostics, and those who do believe in the existence of God have difficulty in accepting popular religious dogmas. Some scientists who recognize the corrupt nature of organized religions and the various problems with their teachings acknowledge the existence of the First Cause that started the universe out of nothing with the Big Bang.

The primary audience of this book is not the religious people who gullibly accept every dogma cooked and served by their clergymen, nor the fanatic atheists who have closed their mind against any message linked to God, but the agnostics.

Having previously addressed the clergymen of two major religions and their followers in my books,

- *19 Questions For Sunni and Shiite clergymen*
- *19 Questions For Christian Clergymen*

I realize that my criticism of traditional religious teachings has drawn the criticism of fanatic religious zealots whose mental conformity was disturbed by reason and critical arguments. Therefore, I might be disposed to put in a warning on this and my other books questioning the silly and contradictory teachings of clergymen: "Warning: This book might be harmful to your religious conformity."

This book will certainly not delight those professional religion-mongers who make their living out of lazy brains. Nevertheless, the only medicine of ignorance and fanaticism is to disturb the comfort of ancestor-worshiping blind viruses that block the circuits of healthy brains. The mental rehabilitation will have some side effects and may even cause shocks; I know it from my "personal experience"! I know that my name, which is already on the black list of Sunni and Shiite clergymen, will be marked worldwide and the corresponding label "apostate" will be underlined. Well, my friend who discovered Code Nineteen has already been killed by "Muslim" terrorists and I have received so many threats that they no longer increase the adrenaline in my blood.[9] I feel a responsibility to share this message written in mathematics from the Creator of the Universe with the earthlings, regardless of the risks involved, because "this is the only way."

2

The Holy Viruses
of the Brain

"Some people just can't understand that they can't understand what they can't understand." ~ Brandon Miller

"As long as the prerequisites for that shining paradise is ignorance, bigotry and hate, I say the hell with it." ~ Henry Drummond

"Do you have the same religion as your parents? Score 0 points if you do and have never doubted or questioned its teachings. Score 2 for any other answer. This is an example of dogmatism, the blind acceptance of received ideas. Religion itself is not the issue here; rather, its acceptance without question is the important matter. To adhere unflinchingly to childhood beliefs on any subject, to shut your mind to new ideas, or even to other old ideas, is death to the intellect. Besides, religions should have nothing to hide. They ought to encourage doubts and questions so that they can lay them to rest and reinforce faith." ~ Marilyn vos Savant & Leonore Fleischer[10]

"There now exists physicial evidence for a message from God to the world. This marks the advent of a new era in religion; an era where FAITH is no longer needed. There is no need to 'believe,' when one 'knows.' People of the past generations were required to believe in God, and uphold His commandments ON FAITH. With the advent of the physical evidence reported in this book, we no longer believe that God exists; we KNOW that God exists. Such knowledge is ascertained through God's final scripture, Quran, wherein overwhelming physical evidence has been encoded." ~ Rashad Khalifa[11]

Ask the people who are leaving the church after the Sunday sermon in a modern neighborhood of San Diego: "Why do you believe that Jesus is God in the flesh and was sacrificed by God for other people's sins?" As an answer, you might hear, "Because the Bible says so." If you then subject them to a follow-up question, "Well, how you do know that the Bible is the word of God?" you might hear the following answer while witnessing the smile on the face of your audience fading: "The Bible says that it is the word of God." Should you remind your audience that his/her reasoning is a circular argument the dialogue is likely to end immediately. If your audience allows you to ask more questions, you might receive the ultimate answer: "Because I believe so; I have faith in the Bible." You might not be able to hear the *reason* behind the faith of many believers; moreover, you might never hear the *real* reason. None of the

Catholics, Protestants, Baptists, or Mormons will tell you that they believe as they do because their parents and/or their immediate friends believe that way. This is, unfortunately, the reality for most believers.

If you ask the same questions to a Hindu who has just "purified" himself in the waters of the Ganges, you will receive similar answers. The answers of a Muslim praying in the Blue Mosque of Istanbul or a Buddhist chanting in a Tokyo temple will not be any different.

If you were born in India, you are most likely a Hindu, in Saudi Arabia a Muslim, in Israel a Jew, and in the USA, you are a Christian. The dominant religion of your family and your country is more likely to be adopted by you. Why? What is the relationship between religion and geography or ethnicity?

Years ago, I did some psychological experiments to explore certain common human behaviors. The most interesting one was on conformity and compliance. I wanted to find out how we, as individuals, behave under strong group pressure. How does a minority of one react against a unanimous majority? The results were incredible.

The Arrow Test

For the experiment, I gathered five persons in a room and had them sit in a line. These participants would be my confederates. I told them that we would perform an experiment on the next person who would enter the room. He would be the last in the line. In the beginning, I would ask them two warm-up questions, and trained them to give me the correct answers. But, when I would ask them the third question (the real one), my confederates would loudly give me the wrong answer, one by one.

When the real participant entered the room, I announced that we would have a test—as if I had never discussed the subject with the group before. Then, I asked two warm-up questions. I drew simple figures on the board and asked them one by one the routine question: Which one is similar to this one? After all the five participants gave the correct answer, the real participant also gave the correct answer. They were easy questions.

Then, it came to the real question, the easiest one. I asked the following question: Which figure on the right side is similar to the figure on the left side?

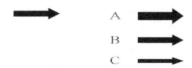

One by one, my confederates gave the wrong answer. The first said "C." The second also said "C." The third, fourth and the fifth also followed with "C." The real participant was in shock. He was amazed at the discrepancy between what he saw and what he heard. After hearing five straight C's, when his turn came, he agreed with the majority that the "C" was the right answer.

Later, I learned that I was not the first to conduct this experiment. Between 1951-56, S. E. Asch performed a series of studies on compliance and conformity. I summarize below the results of his experiments:

Asch made his experiments with different lengths of lines. He asked the participants to match the standard line with the lines on the left. Out of 123 participants, only 29 did not ever conform to the group's decision. Sixty-one participants went along with their groups on every occasion. However, 33 conformed to their groups numerous times, agreeing on the obviously wrong answer almost every time.

Some participants in the Asch study claimed to have actually seen the wrong line as a correct match. They privately accepted the belief of the majority opinion. About half of the rest of the conformists claimed that they had seen the lines correctly, but then when they heard the majority choice, became convinced they must have been wrong. They then went along with the group. The remaining conformists said they knew that the answer was not correct but that they had gone along with the group anyway.[12]

Conformity, whether in the form of compliance or private acceptance, occurs in every group. If a gang member steals a car the first time, he will most likely continue to do so. After the first criminal activity, the reluctance and moral anguish that he experienced in the first time will decrease and finally disappear with more involvement. He will probably justify his stealing in order to maintain his internal harmony. The same is true for new members of religious groups. The initial hesitation and questions are replaced by justification after participating in the first ritual or baptism ceremony.

Marilyn vos Savant, author of the popular American newspaper column *Ask Marilyn,* asked her readers whether they laugh more when watching movies in theaters rather than their homes. She then went on to evaluate the impact of a group on an individual, stating:

> "This is a good example of the human tendency to put aside one's own thinking and accept the thinking of others. Common to all of us is the pressure to go along with the group, at least to some extent. Also, we feel more comfortable, safer in a group; our opinions aren't attributable to us, and we don't stand out. It's no accident that television sitcoms come complete with laugh tracks; people feel better about laughing out loud if they can hear others laughing too. But sitcoms also come with "gasp" tracks and "awwww" tracks as well; your

responses are being subjected to professional manipulation. What we may be timid about doing or saying as individuals, we will do or say in concert with others. However, this type of behavior has a numbing effect upon the intellect. It tends to validate and maintain whatever "groupthink" is current, whether or not it's accurate or true. Worse, it puts the mind out of the habit of thinking. People who let others direct their thinking eventually stop thinking for themselves entirely."[13]

The worst place for the brain is not the theaters, since at least there you have certain control over which movie to watch. Further, movies do not control your attitude and decisions regarding issues as crucial as life and death. The worst enemy of the brain, perhaps far ahead of drugs and alcoholic beverages, is unfortunately, those places that are associated with God: churches, mosques, synagogues, and temples of any religion. Usually, these places are picked for you by your parents, even by your government. When you go there, the "sacred" dogmas and teachings in your brain are reinforced and you are told to close your eyes again in faith and condemn everyone who dares to question them. Over time, a large territory of your brain is claimed and operated by virtual religious viruses that manipulate your thought in the interest of clergymen, from whom such viruses originate. All in the name of a conventional god! There is no easy cure for this "holy" bug.

Dogmas are cannibals, brain cannibals. Jomo Kenyatta, the founding father of the Kenyan nation, once depicted the role of religion in the history of his country as the "opium of masses":

> "When the missionaries came to Africa, they had the Bible and we had the land. They said: 'Let us pray.' We closed our eyes. When we opened them, we had the Bible and they had the land."

Some religious books use an effective psychological trick to gain converts. For instance, The Book of Mormon suggests the following test for skeptics:

> "And when you shall receive these things, I would exhort you that you would ask God, the Eternal Father, in the name of Christ, if these things are not true; and if you shall ask with a sincere heart, with real intent, having faith in Christ, he will manifest the truth of it unto you, by the power of the Holy Ghost. And by the power of the Holy Ghost you may know the truth of all things."[14]

Should it come as a surprise that a good number of people who take this *test* end up experiencing transformation in their lives? The power in this so-called proof of divinity is produced by priming the gullible subject to a self-executing conversion. First, the subject must already have accepted as fact the orthodox dogma regarding the deity of Jesus and all related stories concocted by St. Paul, *the Pharisee, Son of Pharisee*. Second, the subject must believe that the verses of Moroni will lead him to find the truth about the very verses prescribing how to find the truth. Third, the subject is ready to interpret any usual or unusual event occurring in the next days in favor of these tenets! The primed mind will perhaps witness a few miracles and *feel* the Holy Ghost inside his or her mind. Fourth, the Church has won another convert who will fill its treasury with money and a potential volunteer recruiter who would use the same test to attract others to the church.

Many Sufi orders also use similar psychological tricks. For example, they ask the candidate to utter certain prayers in certain numbers and fashions while thinking about the *Sheik* before going to bed. Most of those who follow the instructions end up seeing dreams and interpreting them as expected. They become fanatic followers. Besides their night dreams, they start daydreaming. Their minds, along with their pockets, are intruded and manipulated by their religious leaders.

It may surprise many that Martin Luther, the founder of Protestant movement who has been hailed as a progressive clergyman compared to the Pope, was a bigot. Let's see his "reason" for inviting his followers to give up their reasoning faculties and discard their brains:

> "Reason is the greatest enemy that faith has; it never comes to the aid of spiritual things, but more frequently than not struggles against the divine Word, treating with contempt all that emanates from God."[15]

History is filled with tragedies created by those who gave up thinking or questioning those in power, be it of religious leaders or political heroes. No wonder millions of people accept absurd claims on faith and feel self-righteous about promoting nonsense. For instance, millions passionately reject the theory of evolution without even studying it. In the following excerpt from *Inherit the Wind*, Henry Drummond, the defense lawyer, makes a powerful point about the importance of critical thinking:

> **Matthew Harrison Brady**: We must not abandon faith! Faith is the most important thing!
> **Henry Drummond**: Then why did God plague us with the capacity to think? Mr. Brady, why do you deny the one thing that sets above the other animals? What other merit have we? The elephant is larger, the horse stronger and swifter, the butterfly more beautiful, the mosquito more prolific, even the sponge is more durable. Or does a sponge think?
> **Matthew Harrison Brady**: I don't know. I'm a man, not a sponge!
> **Henry Drummond**: Do you think a sponge thinks?
> **Matthew Harrison Brady**: If the Lord wishes a sponge to think, it thinks!
> **Henry Drummond**: Does a man have the same privilege as a sponge?
> **Matthew Harrison Brady**: Of course!
> **Henry Drummond**: [Gesturing towards the defendant, Bertram Cates] Then this man wishes to have the same privilege of a sponge, he wishes to think!

Ironically, those who have reduced their critical thinking abilities to the level of sponge show the audacity to peddle and even impose their silly stories as the ultimate truth. The audacity of arrogant believers led the movie character Henry Drummond to utter one of the most memorable statements on this point: "As long as the prerequisite for that shining paradise is ignorance, bigotry and hate, I say the hell with it."

Many followers of religions and cults stand on two horses: Ignorance and Arrogance. To protect themselves from being torn apart, they spend enormous effort to keep the two competing horses at the same speed and distance. Beware the riders of twin horses.

Before putting anything in our mouths we observe the color, sniff its smell, and then we check its taste. If a harmful bit fools all those examinations, our stomach come to rescue and throws them up. There are many other organs that function as stations for testing, examination, and modification of imported material into our bodies. They ultimately meet our smart and vigilant nano-guards: white cells. Then, it is a mystery how we put information and assertions, especially the most bizarre ones, into our brains without subjecting them to rigorous test of critical thinking. We should not turn our brains into trash cans of false ideas, holy viruses, unexamined dogmas and superstitions! We should be wise!

Carol Tavris, the author of influential books such as *The Mismeasure of Woman* and *Invitation to Psychology*, draws our attention to the psychological aspect of religious beliefs:

> "One of the problems with the skeptical movement is that it attempts to take important beliefs away from people without replacing them. People believe that skeptics and scientists are forever telling them their ideas are wrong, stupid, and naïve—"No, you cannot talk to Uncle Henry from beyond the grave; that medium is a fraud" or "No, crushed aardvark bones can't cure your cancer." One problem with the critical thinking movement, which came from philosophy, was that it missed the psychological and emotional reasons that people don't think critically and don't want to think critically. Until you understand the forces that make people want to believe something, you can't just expect people to listen rationally to a set of arguments that will skewer their deepest, most cherished ideas."[16]

Considering the prevalence of this psychological factor for most religious people, my skeptical approach to religions that are generally found to be corrupted is not likely to appeal many. It is very likely that devout members of organized religions, including the followers of Sunni and Shiite sects who give lip service to the Quran, will never be able to study the presentation of empirical and rational evidence demonstrating the authenticity of Quran's claim objectively, since their choice of religion or sect is not based on their intellect, but usually on their emotional reaction to social pressure.

No wonder many scientists, leaders, and intellectuals had negative reaction towards religion. For a sample from the Western world, see the appendices section of the book.

Religion: The Best Nest for Conformists

Organized religions may give a myriad of different answers for a single question. Dogmas attract the highest rate of conformists. Conformity, eventually, causes the private acceptance or justification of the dogma. Some people become fanatics, dedicating themselves to the dogma. The old conformists cause the newcomers to conform. This chain attraction goes on.

Why is the percentage of religious conformists and their private acceptance so high? There are many reasons. Here is my kaleidoscopic and, doubtless, incomplete list:

- We are exposed to dogmas from childhood. It is called "boiled frog syndrome." If one puts a frog in a container and pours hot water over its body, the frog will jump to save its life. But if the temperature of the water is gradually increased, the frog will not notice the heat and will boil to death. Well, we all experience the so-called "boiled frog syndrome" in many aspects of our daily lives. One of the worst examples of this syndrome is very common among religious people. Our early exposure to religion has a great impact on us. For a Hindu, thousands of human gods, the caste system, and holy cows make more sense than anything else does. For a Christian, a God with three personalities sacrificing his innocent son to criminals provides the only answer for the purpose of life. And for a Sunni Muslim, living a life according to medieval Arab culture, and glorifying Muhammad's name is the only password to heaven.

- Recent studies using Implicit Association Test or IAT show that our unconscious attitudes create strong biases. Those who do not engage in self-examination, critical thinking, and deliberate and constant struggle to be open-minded fall victim of this stealthy diabolic mental infection.

- Religious answers are not simple. On the contrary, they are mostly complex and vague. One can interpret any dogma and make it acceptable to him. The way is wide open for justification through endless speculations.

- Many answers do not have objective validity or a verifiable/falsifiable thesis. Since we cannot verify them, we can easily accept them.

- Professional priesthood survives on particular dogmas, so there will always be some well-trained holy "sales people" around. They are the most effective pitchmen ever seen in this world, and they are adept at adapting to new ways.

- The common religious norms such as "have faith without reason" or "don't question" can close all the circuits for any possible intellectual light. As long as a person has swallowed the Trojan horse of "faith without reason," with its head and tail, even the most absurd religious teachings will have access through a back door to the brain of the victim.

- Religions do not nakedly expose their false dogmas and myths. They exploit the truth and craftily amalgamate it with myths. Phraseology like "Good moral values," attracts many. For the sake of some truth, we may accept the mixture as the whole truth.

- Religious peer pressure is very strong. Because of this, the social and psychological punishment for not complying with the religion of our family and friends usually has a deterrent effect. Therefore, we may employ an intellectual censorship to avoid a possible confrontation.

- Our enigmatic brains can reinforce our private acceptance by playing odd games. Selective cognition and logical fallacies can create spiritual experiences.

- The socio-economic benefits of a religion or cult may force us to rationalize and justify their dogmas.

- The so-called third world countries that suffer from chronic economic and political problems are governed by an elite minority who exploit the resources through authoritarian repression and all that comes with it: bribery, nepotism, monopoly, and usury. In those countries, the majority of the population is condemned to struggle with unemployment, poverty, and ignorance. In such an environment of corruption and injustice, a religion or a sect that provides the oppressed and deprived with an identity and radical opposition may attract masses. In this context, the popular religion or sect is a political tool, a courage pill, and a symbol of rebellion. The suppressed hate and rage erupts with slogans colored with the name of God and religious heroes. In such an environment, religion and religious orders do not represent reason and reality, but the complex emotions caused by social and economic frustration.

- Religion, combined with Nationalistic hormones, is used with great success throughout history to send the children of the poor to wars declared by the wealthy elite who enjoy more power and obscene profits during wars. The resources of other countries are plundered in the background of holy hymns and patriotic songs. No wonder clergymen of all religions usually have been the accomplices of corrupt and oppressive kings, slave owners, the colonialists, the imperialists, the invaders, the oppressors and the greedy.

- Religion may provide the ultimate feeling of superiority for those who suffer from an inferiority complex.

- Religions promise hope to the poor and sick for eternal bliss after their miserable lives on this earth. In Karl Marx's words, "religion is the opium of masses." Ironically, to some lesser extent, the same concern becomes essential for the rich when they realize that they are aging and cannot control their rapid decline towards the grave, which will separate them from all their luxury and power. A church, a mosque, or a temple of any religion may offer them all they want: a clergyman's voice declaring their salvation and entitlement to go to heaven. Now, the poor and sick can bear their pain, and the rich can continue throwing parties and collecting luxury cars in their mansions.

- We might fall in love with the faith that we adhere to. This love affair produces hormones in our brain. Losing an established faith is scary since it threatens the current chemical structure and neurological connections of the brain. A fanatic believer may demonstrate a much stronger obsession or addiction than that of a cigarette smoker. (Surely, this is valid for fanatic disbelievers too.)

Unfortunately, most believers are ignorant of or disinterested in the intellectual and philosophical aspect and implication of religions. How many religious people do you know who changed their religion because of their intellectual inquiry? How many so-called Muslims do you know who subject their faith to a rational and empirical test, as recommended by their holy book?

> 17:36   Do not accept any information, unless you verify it for yourself. The hearing, the eyesight, and the brain are responsible for it.
>
> 10:36   Most of them follow nothing but conjecture, and conjecture is no substitute for the truth. GOD is fully aware of everything they do.

Indeed, in the Quranic terminology, the words *haq* (truth) and *zann* (conjecture) denote mutually exclusive characteristics. Unfortunately, in today's temples the former is killed and the latter is introduced as its incarnation.

3
The Book that Changed the Course of History

"Some of the Bible and much of the New Testament is polemical, but *all* of the Koran is a fierce polemic: against the pagans of Mecca, the Jews of Medina, and whatever Christians of Arabia (there cannot have been many) who were not Ebionites or Jewish Christians." ~ Herold Bloom[17]

"My choice of Muhammad to lead the list of the world's most influential persons may surprise some readers and may be questioned by others, but he was the only man in history who was supremely successful on both religious and secular levels." ~ Michael H. Hart[18]

"Of course, Arabic science was also and above all the creation of Sunni and Shiite scholars. Amongst these men were: al-Fazzari, al-Kind, al-Razi, al-Khuwarizmi, Thabit ibn Qurra, al-Battani, Abu Kamil, al-Farabi, al-Mas'udi, Abu'l Wafa, al-Karayi, al-Biruni, Ibn Sina (Avicenna), Ibn al-Haytham, 'Umar al-Khayyam, Ibn Rushd (Averros) and Ibn Khaldun ... The promotion of study and research in the Koran has already been mentioned in this chapter. This was not only a fundamental condition for the development of Arabic Islamic science, but also one of the main causes for Islam's ready acceptance of the most diverse cultures." ~ Georges Ifrah[19]

Muhammad is one of the most misrepresented leaders in the world history and his success is completely due to the Quran, which is also unfortunately mistranslated, misinterpreted, and misrepresented by ignorant and backward clergymen. Like Jesus, Muhammad was a revolutionary philosopher, a prophet. Those who followed the crowds and status-quo initially ignored him, violently opposed him, and then when his message found more support, they joined him. His ardent enemies were religious fanatics with vested interest in status quo..

It was 570 years after Christ when Muhammad was born in Mecca. At the age of 40 he made a declaration that shocked his people. During the month of Ramadan of 610, he claimed that he was visited by Holy Revelation (a.k.a. *Jibreel* or Holy Spirit) delivering him a message from God. This claim was first kept secret; he shared it only with a few close friends and relatives. A few years later he publicly declared his messengership and his opposition to the religious and political establishment of Mecca. An era of revolution and reformation that would change world history had just started.

Muhammad, a member of a powerful tribe and a successful international businessman, was not an ordinary citizen of Mecca. With his sound judgment and trustworthy personality, he had won the respect of the theocratic oligarchy. His uncles were the leaders of one of the prominent tribes and were active in social, political, economic, and religious affairs.

Arabs living in the Hijaz region were brethren of the Jews, and Abraham was their common forefather. Mecca or Bacca was the valley where Abraham had immigrated, after his exile from Babylon.[20] There is only one reference to this important city in the Old Testament:

> "Blessed is the man whose strengths in thee; in whose heart are the ways of them. Who passing through the valley of Baca make it a well; the rain also fills the pools. They go from strength to strength, every one of them in Zion appears before God. O LORD God of hosts, hear my prayer: give ear, O God of Jacob." (Psalms 84:5-8)

Meccan Arabs had deep respect for the struggle of Abraham whose courageous stand for his monotheistic belief was legendary. Therefore, they were very protective of his reputation, religious practices, and the *Kaba*. Knowing that Abraham rejected worshiping the statues besides God, contrary to common belief among Muslims, Arabs never worshiped statues or symbolic objects.[21] Nevertheless, they had holy names, such as Al-Lat, Al-Uzza, and Manat from whom they would ask intercession and help. Their association of other authorities and powers to God and their fabrication of myriad prohibitions and laws in the name of God is called *shirk*[22] and the Quran repeatedly criticizes this mindset and practice as polytheism, the source of all evil.

> 53:19-26 What do you think about Al-Lat (The Goddess), Al-Uzza? And Manat, the third one. Do you have sons, while He has daughters? What a fraudulent distribution! These are but names that you made up, you and your forefathers. God never authorized such a blasphemy. They follow conjecture, and personal desire, when the true guidance has come to them herein from their Lord. What is that the human being desires? To God belong both the Hereafter, and this world. Not even the angels in heaven possess authority to intercede. The only ones permitted by God are those who act in accordance with His will and His approval.

> 39:43-45 Have they invented intercessors to mediate between them and God? Say, "What if they do not possess any power, nor understanding?" Say, "All intercession belongs to God." To Him belongs sovereignty of the heavens and the earth, then to Him you will be returned. When God alone is mentioned, the hearts of those who do not believe in the Hereafter shrink with aversion. But when others are mentioned besides Him, they rejoice.

However, those who accept other authorities besides God never accept their crime. They vehemently deny their *shirk*. Though the majority of "believers" follow the teachings of their clergymen and assign divine authority to others besides God, they usually do not accept that they are committing *shirk*; they claim to be monotheists. If you question a Hindu who worships hundreds of gods and goddesses, you will learn that he or she is really a monotheist! A Christian who puts his full confidence in St. Paul's polytheistic teaching which was formulated in 325 CE by the Nicene Council as the Doctrine of Trinity (i.e., God with three personalities) will still claim to be a monotheist![23] Muslims who elevated Muhammad to the level of God by making him the second source of their religion and by putting his name next to God in the Statement of Testimony will also insist that they are monotheists.

> 6:22-23   On the day when we summon everyone, we will ask the *mushriks*, "Where are those whom you claimed partners?" Their only response will be, "By God our Lord, we never were *mushriks*."

> 16:35   Those who commit *shirk* say, "Had God willed, we would not have worshiped anyone besides Him, nor would our parents. Nor would we have prohibited anything besides (what was prohibited by) Him." Those before them have done the same. Can the messengers do anything but deliver the message?

Arab *mushriks* (those who accept other authorities besides God) never claimed that those holy names were gods, they were merely praying for their intercession. They believed that the saints and angels were mediators between them and God.

> 39:3   The system absolutely shall be devoted to God ALONE. Those who set up masters besides Him say, "We worship them only to bring us closer to God; they are in a good position!" God will judge them regarding their disputes. God does not guide any liar, unappreciative.

The Quran clearly rejects association of any authority besides God, whether in making religious laws or providing eternal salvation.

> 42:21   They follow those who decree for them religious laws never authorized by God. If it were not for the predetermined decision, they would have been judged immediately. Indeed, the transgressors have incurred a painful retribution.

> 9:31   They have set up their religious leaders and scholars as lords, instead of God. Others deified the Messiah, son of Mary. They were all commanded to worship only one God. There is no God except He. Be He glorified, high above having any partners.

According to the information given by the Quran, Meccan *Mushriks* preserved their forms of religious practices while losing its monotheistic and spiritual meaning. They were praying, fasting, and performed pilgrimage.[24] These were the most popular religious practices.

Mollarchy in the City State of the Arabian Peninsula

There were some characteristics of Mecca that distinguished it from other Arabian towns and cities. Mecca, with Abraham's temple, was the center of religion, politics and business. Abraham's temple, the Kaba, is described by the Quran as "People's House" or "Sacred Place of Prostration." Abraham, as I mentioned above, was a legendary ancestor for both Arabs and Jews. During the four consecutive sacred months,[25] Arabs dwelling in the region would visit Mecca for pilgrimage. Meanwhile, the occasion was also used for an international trade fair. Merchants from neighboring countries would participate in a lengthy business and cultural activity. During these religious months, besides trading, cultural and athletic competitions such as poetry and wrestling would take place. Mecca was the center for economic, political, and cultural activities of a vast land.

Prominent tribal leaders like Abu Hakem (a.k.a., Abu Jahel), Abdul Uzza (a.k.a., Abu Lahab), Abu Sufyan, Umayy Ben Halef, Nadr Ben Haris, and Valeed Ben Mugiyra could not tolerate any reformation movement that would change the status quo and risk Mecca's crucial position in the political and economic landscape. They were determined to follow the traditional religion they inherited from their ancestors who had distorted Abraham's monotheistic system to *shirk*. Preservation of the traditional religion and the status quo was vital for the theocratic government of Mecca. Questioning the orthodox belief system and the common practice could be interpreted as a foreign attack on the unity of Mecca or as a betrayal to the fabric of its society.

A teaching that rejects the idea of intercession and the sacred role of professional clergymen, a teaching that promotes the human rights of slaves and the oppressed, that seeks economic justice by objecting to monopoly and usury, that is concerned about the poor, that condemns ethnic and racial discrimination, that protects the rights of women, that advocates democratic governance through consultation, and encourages people to use their reasoning and questions tradition, surely, such a system would pose a serious threat to the economic and political interest of the ruling elite.

Social, Economic, and Political Structure Criticized

It is a well-known fact that the early revelations of the Quran use strong language in criticizing the theocratic oligarchy, which did not care about the poor, orphans and aliens; did not free the slaves; did not treat women as equal to men; and did not consult people in public affairs.

> 107:1-7 Do you know who rejects The System of God Alone? That is the one who mistreats the orphans. And does not advocate the feeding of the poor. And woe to those who observe the contact prayers, Who are

totally heedless of their prayers; they only show off. And they forbid charity.

89:17-20   Wrong! It is you who brought it on yourselves by not regarding the orphan. And not advocating charity towards the poor. And consuming the inheritance of helpless orphans. And loving the money too much.

90:6-20   He boasts, "I spent so much money!" Does he think that no one sees him? Did we not give him two eyes? A tongue and two lips? Did we not show him the two paths? He should choose the difficult path. Which one is the difficult path? The freeing of slaves. Feeding, during the time of hardship. Orphans who are related. Or the poor who is in need. And being one of those who believe, and exhorting one another to be steadfast, and exhorting one another to be kind. These have deserved happiness. As for those who acknowledged our revelations, they have incurred misery. They will be confined in the Hellfire.

16:58-59   Thus, when one of them gets a baby girl, his face becomes darkened with overwhelming grief. Ashamed, he hides from the people, because of the bad news. He even debates: should he keep the baby grudgingly, or bury her in the dust. Miserable indeed is their judgment.

42:38   And they respond to their Lord by observing the contact prayers and by deciding their affairs on the basis of consultation among themselves, and from our provisions to them they give.

4:1-5   O people, observe your Lord; the one who created you from one being and created from it its mate, then spread from the two many men and women. You shall regard God, by whom you swear, and regard the parents. God is watching over you. You shall hand over to the orphans their rightful properties. Do not substitute the bad for the good, nor shall you consume their properties by combining them with your properties. This is a gross injustice. If you deem it best for the orphans, you may marry their mothers—you may marry two, three, or four of them. If you fear lest you become unfair, then you shall be content with only one, or with what you already have. This way, you are more likely to avoid inequity. You shall give the women their due dowries, fully. If they willingly part with anything, then you may accept it graciously. Do not give immature orphans the properties that God has entrusted you with as guardians. You shall provide for them therefrom, and clothe them, and talk to them nicely.[26]

59:7   Whatever God restored to His messenger from the (defeated) communities shall go to God and His messenger (in the form of a charity). You shall give it to the relatives, the orphans, the poor, and the traveling alien. Thus, it will not remain monopolized by the strong among you. You may keep the spoils given to you by the messenger, but do not take what he enjoins you from taking. You shall reverence God. God is strict in enforcing retribution.

39

Corrupt, Oppressive and Superstitious Tradition Criticized

The population of Mecca was afflicted with many social problems caused by individual abuses of time, money, brain, body and exploitation of God's name.

For instance, gambling was transferring money from the poor to the wealthy, thereby creating financial nightmares for many families. Alcohol was the cause of many personal and social problems such as domestic violence, inefficiency, loss of intellectual capabilities, alcoholism, rape, criminal activities, accidents and a myriad of health problems. The Quran, though acknowledging some financial and personal benefits of gambling and alcohol, encouraged acknowledgers to abstain from these addictions without criminalizing them via a penal code.

> 2:219   They ask you about intoxicants and gambling: say, "In them there is a gross sin, and some benefits for the people. But their sinfulness far outweighs their benefit." They also ask you what to give to charity: say, "The excess." God thus clarifies the revelations for you that you may reflect.

> 4:43   O you who acknowledge, do not observe the Contact Prayers (*Sala*) while intoxicated, so that you know what you are saying....

> 5:90   O you who acknowledge, intoxicants, and gambling, and the altars of idols, and the games of chance are abominations of the devil; you shall avoid them, that you may succeed.

> 16:67   And from the fruits of date palms and grapes you produce intoxicants, as well as good provisions. This should be (sufficient) proof for people who understand.

Sexual promiscuity or adultery were contributing to the destruction of families and was a major health threat for the public by transmitting sexual diseases. The Quran encouraged men and women to be loyal to their marriage contract. Though polygamy is permitted to take care of fatherless children and their widowed mothers, monogamy was encouraged.

> 17:32   You shall not commit adultery; it is a gross sin, and an evil behavior.

> 4:3   If you deem it best for the orphans, you may marry their mothers— you may marry two, three, or four. If you fear lest you become unfair, then you shall be content with only one, or with what you already have. Additionally, you are thus more likely to avoid financial hardship.

A lengthy list of dietary prohibitions concocted in the name of God was wasting many food resources. The Quran prohibited only four items related to animal products and considered any additional religious prohibitions to be fabrications and *shirk*.

6:145-151 Say, "I do not find in the revelations given to me any food that is prohibited for any eater except: (1) carrion[27,] (2) running blood, (3) the meat of pigs, for it is bad,[28] and (4) the meat of animals blasphemously dedicated to other than God." If one is forced (to eat these), without being deliberate or malicious, then your Lord is Forgiver, Most Merciful. For those who are Jewish we prohibited animals with undivided hoofs; and of the cattle and sheep we prohibited the fat, except that which is carried on their backs, or in the viscera, or mixed with bones. That was a retribution for their transgressions, and we are truthful. If they disbelieve you, then say, "Your Lord possesses infinite mercy, but His retribution is unavoidable for the guilty people." The idol worshipers say, "Had God willed, we would not practice idolatry, nor would our parents, nor would we prohibit anything." Thus did those before them disbelieve, until they incurred our retribution. Say, "Do you have any proven knowledge that you can show us? You follow nothing but conjecture; you only guess." Say, "God possesses the most powerful argument; if He wills He can guide all of you." Say, "Bring your witnesses who would testify that God has prohibited this or that." If they testify, do not testify with them. Nor shall you follow the opinions of those who reject our revelations, and those who disbelieve in the Hereafter, and those who stray away from their Lord. Say, "Come let me tell you what your Lord has really prohibited for you: You shall not set up idols besides Him. You shall honor your parents. You shall not kill your children from fear of poverty—we provide for you and for them. You shall not commit gross sins, obvious or hidden. You shall not kill—God has made a person's life sacred - except in the course of justice. These are His commandments to you that you may understand."

The Quran dealt with many other issues such as protection of the environment and ecological balance and protection of God's creation from unnecessary mutilation. For instance, the Quran prohibited hunting during pilgrimage (5:95-96). It also criticized Meccan Arabs for cutting the ears of animals for religious reasons, which has a negative implication regarding the custom of circumcision.

4:119 "I will mislead them, I will entice them, I will command them to (forbid the eating of certain meats by) marking the ears of livestock, and I will command them to distort the creation of God." Anyone who accepts the devil as a lord, instead of God, has incurred a profound loss.

The chapter "Ben Israel" (Children of Israel) contains a series of commandments aiming to change the mindset, attitude, and actions of individuals:

17:23-39 You shall not set up any other God beside God, lest you end up despised and disgraced. Your Lord has decreed that you shall not worship except Him, and your parents shall be honored. As long as one or both of them live, you shall never say to them, "Uff" (the slightest gesture of annoyance), nor shall you shout at them; you shall treat them amicably. And lower for them the wings of humility, and kindness, and say, "My Lord, have mercy on them, for they have raised me from infancy." Your Lord is fully aware of your innermost thoughts. If you maintain righteousness, He is Forgiver of those who repent. You shall give the due alms to the relatives, the needy, the poor, and the traveling alien, but do not be excessive, extravagant. The extravagant are brethren of the devil, and the devil is unappreciative of his Lord. Even if you have to turn away from them, as you pursue the mercy of your Lord, you shall treat them in the nicest manner. You shall not keep your hand stingily tied to your neck, nor shall you foolishly open it up, lest you end up blamed and sorry. For your Lord increases the provision for anyone He chooses, and reduces it. He is fully Cognizant of His creatures, Seer. You shall not kill your born children due to fear of poverty. We provide for them, as well as for you. Killing them is a gross offense. You shall not commit adultery; it is a gross sin, and an evil behavior. You shall not kill any person—for God has made a person's life sacred—except in the course of justice. If one is killed unjustly, then we give his heir authority to enforce justice. Thus, he shall not exceed the limits in avenging the murder; he will be helped. You shall not touch the orphans' money except for their own good, until they reach maturity. You shall fulfill your covenants, for a covenant is a great responsibility. You shall give full measure when you trade, and weigh equitably. This is better and more righteous. You shall not accept any information, unless you verify it for yourself. I have given you the hearing, the eyesight, and the mind, and you are responsible for using them. You shall not walk proudly on earth - you cannot bore through the earth, nor can you be as tall as the mountains. All bad behavior is condemned by your Lord. This is some of the wisdom inspired to you by your Lord. You shall not set up another god beside God, lest you end up in Gahanna, blamed and defeated.

The Quran aims to reform both society and the individual and it invites individuals to undertake a substantial reformation. The description of acknowledgers in the last verses of the chapter *Al-Furqan* (The Distinguisher) reveals the desired characteristics of Muslims:

25:58-77 You shall put your trust in the One who is Alive—the One who never dies - and praise Him and glorify Him. He is fully Cognizant of His creatures' sins. He is the One who created the heavens and the earth, and everything between them, in six days, then assumed all authority. The Gracious; ask about Him those who are well founded in knowledge. When they are told, "Fall prostrate before the Gracious," they say, "What is the Gracious? Shall we prostrate before what you advocate?" Thus, it only augments their aversion. Most blessed is the One who placed constellations in the sky, and placed in it a lamp, and a shining moon. He is the One who designed the night and the day to alternate: a sufficient proof for those who wish to take heed, or to be appreciative. The worshipers of the Gracious are those who tread the earth gently, and when the ignorant speak to them, they only utter peace. In the privacy of the night, they meditate on their Lord, and fall prostrate. And they say, "Our Lord, spare us the agony of Hell; its retribution is horrendous. It is the worst abode; the worst destiny." When they give, they are neither extravagant nor stingy; they give in moderation. They never implore beside God any other God, nor do they kill anyone—for God has made life sacred—except in the course of justice. Nor do they commit adultery. Those who commit these offenses will have to pay. Retribution is doubled for them on the Day of Resurrection, and they abide therein humiliated. Exempted are those who repent, acknowledge, and lead a righteous life. God transforms their sins into credits. God is Forgiver, Most Merciful. Those who repent and lead a righteous life, God redeems them; a complete redemption. They do not bear false witness. When they encounter vain talk, they ignore it. When reminded of their Lord's revelations, they never react to them as if they were deaf and blind. And they say, "Our Lord, let our spouses and children be a source of joy for us, and keep us in the forefront of the righteous." These are the ones who attain Paradise in return for their steadfastness; they are received therein with joyous greetings and peace. Eternally they abide therein; what a beautiful destiny; what a beautiful abode. Say, "You attain value with my Lord only through your worship. But if you disbelieve, you incur the inevitable consequences."

Meccan Leaders Lose Their Sleep

Mecca could have remained an independent center of commerce because of its unique geopolitical situation. Mecca was located in a region where the influence of the two super powers of that era, the Byzantine and Persian Empires, collided. This balance of powers created such a vacuum that Mecca could have survived without submitting itself to either hegemony as it was a default capital of the Arabian Peninsula. The population of Mecca and surrounding towns did not follow any scripture but only oral traditions and practices. Religion and politics were inseparable affairs. Though the Meccan population had many literate people, they were considered "UMMY" (gentiles) as they did not have a scripture or written law as their Christian and Jewish neighbors had. Muhammad was a literate gentile.[29]

When Muhammad declared that he had received a message from God, the Meccan oligarchy first did not take him seriously. They just ignored him. However, when they noticed the potential power of his message and the rate of the new converts, their reaction varied between mockery and insinuation. Soon their reaction escalated to slander and the threat of eviction and death. Though Muhammad's personal history and his tribal relationship provided an indirect protection against physical attacks, some of his followers did not have the same tribal support. For instance, those subjected to torture included Bilal, an Ethiopian slave who was freed by one of Muhammad's friends. The first convert[30] who was killed was Sumayya, a woman. Slaves and women—victims of racist and misogynistic laws and religions.

43

Partly as a result of their economic and political interest in man-made religious teachings, clergymen augmented and manipulated the religious fanaticism of the ignorant masses. This fatal combination of ignorance and arrogance, which in the past had taken the lives of many messengers and prophets, was again at work. The words uttered against previous messengers appeared against Muhammad, this time in Arabic. Muhammad's situation was no different from that of Saaleh, a messenger to a community which perished a long time before him.

> 11:62   They said, "O Saaleh, you used to be popular among us before this. Are you banning us from serving what our parents are worshiping? We have a lot of doubt concerning everything you tell us.

Muhammad's message was focused on monotheism (*tawheed*), which is the main theme of Mosaic teaching crowning the Ten Commandments.

> And God spoke all these words, saying, I am the LORD thy God, which have brought you out of the land of Egypt, out of the house of bondage. Thou shall have no other gods before me. Thou shall not make unto thee any graven image, or any likeness of any thing that is in heaven above, or that is in the earth beneath, or that is in the water under the earth.... Thou shall not take the name of the LORD thy God in vain for the LORD will not hold him guiltless that takes his name in vain. (Exodus 20:1-4, 7)

Ironically, despite the popularity of the Ten Commandments among Jews, Christians and Muslims, practices negating and defying the first two commandments have become part of their basic dogmas.

Muhammad delivered the words of the Quran, critical of the traditional religion of the Meccans who had transformed Abraham's monotheistic system into polytheism by — blind conformity to the opinions of ancestors, as well as adherence to innovations, superstitions, numerous cleric-made religious laws falsely attributed to God, and a belief in spiritual intercession.

> 6:161   Say, "My Lord has guided me in a straight path: the perfect system of Abraham, monotheism. He never was an idol worshiper."

> 10:36   Most of them follow nothing but conjecture, and conjecture is no substitute for the truth. GOD is fully aware of everything they do.

> 17:36   Do not accept any information, unless you verify it for yourself. The hearing, the eyesight, and the brain are responsible for it.

> 10:100   ... He casts affliction upon those who do not reason.

Flocking on the Glorious Path of their Ancestors

Mushriks, whether in ancient times or modern times, attempt to justify their religions through their popularity, their ancestors' glory, and their saints' fame.

When approached with arguments based on logic, scientific investigation and analysis of historical documentation, their common defense is the miserable argument from authority: "this and that holy clergymen said this," "most of our ancient scholars have decided this way," or some other similar variant.

> 43:22-24 Instead, they said, "We found our parents carrying on certain practices, and we are following in their footsteps. Invariably, when we sent a warner to a community, the leaders therein said, "We found our parents following certain practices, and we will continue in their footsteps." He would say, "What if I brought to you better guidance than what you inherited from your parents?" They would say, "We are disbelievers in the message you brought."

> 31:21-22 When they are told, "Follow these revelations of God," they say, "No, we follow only what we found our parents doing." What if the devil is leading them to the agony of Hell? Those who submit completely to God, while leading a righteous life, have gotten hold of the strongest bond. For God is in full control of all things.

Universal characteristics of *mushriks* include idolization of differently titled ancestors and conformity to dogmas and superstitions that are attributed to them as a religion. Religious idols vary according to religions and languages. For instance, idols in America include Jesus, Mary, or Saints; in Turkey we find Ata, *Evliya*, Sheik, or *Hazrat*. In India *Mahatma*, in Pakistan *Maulana*, in Iran the names of idols are Imam Hussein and *Ehl-i Bayt*. Religious masses do not seek the truth through their brains or their senses. Instead, they blindly follow the teachings that bear sanctified signatures. *Mushriks* are like parrots; as they repeat words without understanding their meaning.

> 2:171 The example of those who disbelieve is like those who parrot what they hear of sounds and calls, without understanding. Deaf, dumb, and blind; they cannot understand.

Ironically, it is the religious leaders themselves promote blind imitation. Through institutionalization of ignorance in religious terms, the diabolic "saints" lead masses astray from Truth.[31] The messengers and prophets, who invited people to question their popular religion and traditions, almost invariably found the clergy fighting and plotting against them.

> Nevertheless among the chief rulers also many acknowledged in him; but because of the Pharisees they did not confess him, lest they should be put out of the synagogue: For they loved the praise of men more than the praise of God. (John 12:42-43)

> 38:6-8 The leaders announced, "Go and steadfastly persevere in worshiping your gods. This is all you need. We never heard of this from the religion of our fathers. This is a lie. Why did the message come down to him, instead of us?" Indeed, they are doubtful of My message. Indeed, they have not yet tasted My retribution.

45

The Black Campaign Waged by Those with White Turbans

The message delivered by Muhammad baffled and bewildered the bearded and turbaned Meccan clerics. They first tried to attack his character. They accused and insulted him, labeling him a "wizard," a dreaming "poet," or "a crazy man."

> 51:51-53 Do not set up besides God any other god. I am sent by Him to you as a manifest warner. Consistently, when a messenger went to the previous generations, they said, "Magician," or, "Crazy." Did they make an agreement with each other? Indeed, they are transgressors.

> 37:35-36 When they were told "*La Elaaha Ella Allah* [There is no other God besides God]," they turned arrogant. They said, "Shall we leave our gods for the sake of a crazy poet?"

> 68:51-52 Those who are ingrates show their ridicule in their eyes when they hear the message and say, "He is crazy!" It is in fact a message to the world.

The Quran encouraged Muhammad not to give up against this negative propaganda. Muhammad's mission was to deliver this message at the cost of loss of his popularity.

> 52:29-33 You shall remind the people. With your Lord's blessings upon you, you are neither a soothsayer, nor crazy. They may say, "He is a poet; let us just wait until he is dead." Say, "Go on waiting; I will wait along with you." Is it their dreams that dictate their behavior, or are they naturally wicked? Do they say, "He made it all up?" Instead, they are simply disbelievers.

The Reaction and Plans of Ingrates

We find tyranny and aggression as well as dogmatism to be prevalent characteristics among *mushriks*. Terror and violence serve as defense mechanism for those who prefer not to use their brains. The polytheistic elite of Athena convicted Socrates to death for questioning the absurdity of their polytheistic religion. Persian priests tried to get rid of Zoroaster. Jewish clerics conspired with Romans to kill Jesus for his threat to their religion. In defense of his theocratic and oppressive regime, Pharaoh mobilized his generals and religious leaders to eliminate Moses. Shuayb's life was threatened by his people. Noah was stoned. Abraham was rejected by his own father and was thrown into a fire. Some messengers were evicted and others were killed. Muhammad, who declared intellectual war against slavery, the subjugation of women, racism, superstitions, ignorance, illiteracy, ancestor-worship, and the exploitation of religious beliefs, would not have been treated differently.

> 8:30-31 The disbelievers plotted and schemed to neutralize you, or kill you, or banish you. However, they plot and scheme, but so does God. God is the best schemer. When our revelations are recited to them, they

say, "We have heard. If we want to, we can say the same thing. These are only tales from the past."

Forerunners, who took risks through alliance with Muhammad encountered difficult tests. They were excommunicated. They were rejected by their families and relatives. They experienced economic hardship. They were subjected to torture and insults by *mushrik* Arabs. They were oppressed and banished from their land, and they were viciously attacked. Many were killed but they did not give up their convictions and cause.

> 9:97   The Arabs are the worst in disbelief and hypocrisy, and the most likely to ignore the laws that God has revealed to His messenger. God is Omniscient, Most Wise.[32]

Muhammad was the main target of *mushrik* Arabs. He had he lost his popularity among his people; his life was in danger. However, he was ordained by the Lord of the Universe to deliver the Message without compromise. He became the recipient of one of the greatest possible honors, a receiving revelation from God.

> 4:113   God has sent down to you the scripture and wisdom, and He has taught you what you never knew. Indeed, God's blessings upon you have been great...

While the multifarious aggressive campaign by the Meccan government and its regional allies continued, Muhammad and his comrades promoted the freedom of expression as well as the freedom of religious beliefs.

> 109:1-6   Say, "O you disbelievers. I do not worship what you worship. Nor do you worship what I worship. Nor will I ever worship what you worship. Nor will you ever worship what I worship. To you is your system, and to me is my system."

The leaders with jeopardized economic and political interests as well as the ignorant followers responded to this message of "leave us alone" with violence. But, their bloody terror and noise could not prevent the light from piercing and destroying the layers of darkness.

The Rainbow Swan

Ignorant peasants and nomads, whose existence was not even acknowledged by two great empires, would soon become the rulers of the world. The Roman Empire in the West and the Persian in the East did not lose battles primarily because of military superiority of Muslim Arabs. In 636 in the Battle of Yarmouk, Muslim Arabs defeated the armies of the East Roman-Byzantine Empire which had numerical superiority. In fact, both empires had military superiority over Arabs before, during, and after revelation of the Quran. They lost neither because Muslims outnumbered them nor because Muslims had sharper swords. The numbers, the wealth, and the arms were against Muslims.

The idea that Islam being propagated through sword is a myth, a bogus propaganda made up by Crusaders, and recently resurrected for political purposes and geopolitical warware. This myth is repeated as a fact even by smart Christians like Nassim Nicholas Taleb. In his best-selling book, *The Black Swan*, under the subtitle, *History Does not Crawl, It Jumps*, Nassim writes the following about the spread of Islam:

> "How about the competing religion that emerged seven centuries later; who forecast a collection of horsemen would spread their empire and Islamic law from the Indian subcontinent to Spain in just a few years? Even more than the rise of Christianity, it was the spread of Islam (the third edition, so to speak) that carried full unpredictability; many historians looking at the record have been taken aback by the swiftness of the change. Georges Duby, for one, expressed his amazement about how quickly close to ten centuries of Levantine Hellenism were blotted out 'with a strike of a sword.'"[33]

Nassim who is eloquent and wise in reminding us the fact that it is the unpredictable events, which he calls "black swans", that play huge role in our lives, is as clueless about the power of the divine message promoted by the "collection of horsemen" as those who "were blotted out" by them. Nassim misses the "orange swan" while attending to the amplified noise of horsemen and swiftly striking swords. Those who miss the black swans could have excuse, but those who blind themselves to the rainbow swan, the Quran, will have little excuse.

The spread of Islam was primarily due to of its progressive message of monotheistic freedom, reason, scientific methodology, tolerance, equality, justice and peace, which attracted the populations governed by brutal and corrupt emperors and kings.

4

Muhammad's Only Miracle

"The many instances of forged miracles, and prophecies, and supernatural events, which, in all ages, have either been detected by contrary evidence, or which detect themselves by their absurdity, prove sufficiently the strong propensity of mankind to the extraordinary and the marvelous, and ought reasonably to beget a suspicion against all relations of this kind. This is our natural way of thinking, even with regard to the most common and most credible events. . . .

"People at a distance, who are weak enough to think the matter at all worth inquiry, have no opportunity of receiving better information. The stories come magnified to them by a hundred circumstances. Fools are industrious in propagating the imposture; while the wise and learned are contented, in general, to deride its absurdity, without informing themselves of the particular facts, by which it may be distinctly refuted. . . .

"According to this method of reasoning, when we acknowledge any miracle of Mahomet [sic] or his successors, we have for our warrant the testimony of a few barbarous Arabians: and on the other hand, we are to regard the authority of Titus Livius, Plutarch, Tacitus, and, in short, of all the authors and witnesses, Grecian, Chinese, and Roman Catholics, who have related any miracle in their particular religion; I say, we are to regard their testimony in the same light as if they had mentioned that Mahometan miracle, and had in express terms contradicted it, with the same certainty as they have for the miracle they relate."
~ David Hume[34]

Besides terror, defamation, insult and torture, *mushriks* also incorporated a sort of intellectual argument or propaganda. Appealing to the xenophobic feelings of the population, they claimed that the Quran was dictated to Muhammad by foreigners. They found Muhammad's human nature, such as his talking and walking like them, contradictory to his newly claimed position as the messenger of God. The first few verses of Chapter 25 summarize this argument:

> 25:6-9   And they said, "Tales from the past that he wrote down; they were dictated to him day and night." Say, "This was revealed by the One who knows the Secret in the heavens and the earth. He is Forgiving, Most Merciful." And they said, "How come this messenger eats the food and walks in the markets? If only an angel could come down with him, to serve with him as a preacher!" Or, "If only a treasure could be bestowed upon him!" Or, "If only he could possess an orchard from which he eats!" The transgressors also said, "You are following a bewitched man." Note how they called you all kinds of names, and how this led them astray, never to find their way back.

The response to this challenge is a definite NO.

> 17:59 The rejection of previous people did not stop Us from sending the signs. We sent to *Thamud* the camel with foresight, but they did her wrong. We do not send the signs except to alert.

The *mushriks* who demanded miracles similar to the previous messengers proved insincere in their demands. With the same attitude, mindset and bandwagons, they would be among the disbelievers if they lived during the miracles demonstrated by Moses or Jesus. Each messenger came with brand new evidence and wonder.

> 6:124 When a miracle comes to them, they say, "We will not acknowledge, unless we are given what is given to God's messengers!" God knows exactly who is best qualified to deliver His message. Such criminals will suffer debasement from God, and a terrible retribution for their evil scheming.

> 23:62 We do not burden a person except with what it can bear. We have a record that speaks with the truth, they will not be wronged.

> 23:63 No, their hearts are unaware of this! They have deeds besides this which they are doing.

> 23:64 Until We take their carefree people with the retribution, then they will shout for help.

> 23:65 Do not shout for help today, for you will not be helped against Us.

> 23:66 My signs were recited to you, but you used to turn back on your heels.

> 23:67 You were too proud from it, talking evil about it; and you defiantly disregarded it.

> 23:68 Did they not ponder the words, or has what come to them not come to their fathers of old?

Isn't the Quran Sufficient?

Even though the blind followers of orthodox religions demand duplicate miracles, God does not grant their wishes; He provides each of His messengers with original and different miracles. Through these miracles, God targets open-minded individuals and free thinkers. Frozen brains cannot comprehend nor appreciate the new message that aims to carry out a reformation in the mindset and behavior of people and perhaps with a concurrent revolution in the political and social structure. The Quran claimed to be Muhammad's only miracle, regardless of negative reactions from religious zealots.

> 29:50-51 They said, "If only miracles could come down to him from his Lord!" Say, "All miracles come only from God; I am no more than a manifest warner." Is it not enough of a miracle that we sent down to

you *this book*, being recited to them? This is indeed a mercy and a reminder for people who acknowledge.

A book as a miracle?! How can a miracle consist of a book? The Quran summarizes the oft-repeated argument from traditional fanatics throughout history:

> 17:88-96 Say, "If all the humans and all the *jinns* banded together in order to produce a Quran like this, they could never produce anything like it, no matter how much assistance they lent one another." We have cited for the people in this Quran all kinds of examples, but most people insist upon disbelieving. They said, "We will not acknowledge you unless you cause a spring to gush out of the ground. Or unless you own a garden of date palms and grapes, with rivers running through it. Or unless you cause masses from the sky, as you claimed, to fall on us. Or unless you bring God and the angels before our eyes. Or unless you own a luxurious mansion, or unless you climb into the sky. Even if you do climb, we will not acknowledge unless you bring a book that we can read." Say, "Glory be to my Lord. Am I any more than a human messenger?" What prevented the people from believing when the guidance came to them is their saying, "Did God send a human being as a messenger?" Say, "If the earth were inhabited by angels, we would have sent down to them from the sky an angel messenger." Say, "God suffices as a witness between me and you. He is fully Cognizant of His worshipers, Seer."

Those who attributed many lies to Muhammad under the title "Hadith" suffered from the same problem and thus, they fabricated numerous stories of "miracles" allegedly performed by him.

A Comparison

If one points at a book as the evidence of its own truthfulness, this appears to be a circular argument. However, if the book also asserts that it is unique and extraordinary, then its claim gains value. In this case we have a verifiable and falsifiable thesis, as philosopher Karl Popper suggested as a standard to distinguish scientific theories from pseudoscience. Whether it is true or false, such an assertion follows the scientific method and remains subject to scientific inquiry.

How can we start testing the assertion of the Quran? A good start would be to compare the Quran to the religious literature of its era. We won't make the comparison in literary excellence, since for such a task we need to be experts in Arabic literature, and we would also lack objective criteria. Here, I do not mean that the literature of the Quran is not excellent or not the best. But, what I am saying is that it would be impossible to support such a claim with objective evidence.

For instance, Herald Bloom, a prominent American literary critic and Professor of Humanities at Yale University, considers the Quran among the top 100 literary work of genius. Here are a several paragraphs from the chapter he allocated on Muhammad and Quran:

> "The Koran, unlike its parent Scriptures, seems to have no context... Strangely as the other Scriptures are ordered, they seem models of coherence when first contrasted to the Koran. The Koran has one hundred and fourteen chapters or sections (called suras) which have no continuity with one another, and mostly possess no internal continuity either. Their length varies enormously, their order has no chronology, and indeed the only principle of organization appears to be that, except for the first sura, we descend downwards from the longest to the shortest. No other book seems so oddly and arbitrarily arranged as this one, which may be appropriate because the voice that speaks the Koran is God's alone, and who would dare to shape his utterances?"

> "Sometimes I reflect that the baffling arrangement (or lack of it) of the Koran actually enhances Muhammad's eloquence; the eradication of context, narrative, and formal unity forces the reader to concentrate upon the immediate, overwhelming authority of the voice, which, however molded by the Messenger's lips, has a massive, persuasive authority to it, recalling but expanding upon the direct speeches of God in the Bible." ...

> "Unbending spiritual authority, whatever its political implications, demands and receives in the Koran an answerable style which is very difficult to resist. Variety, a stylistic demand that we exercise almost everywhere else, has little justification when we are asked to withstand the voice of Allah. ... In my own experience as a reader of literature, the Koran rarely makes a biblical impression upon me, particularly of an aesthetic sort. Sometimes, as I immerse myself in reading the Koran, I am reminded of William Blake or of Walt Whitman; at other moments, I think of Dante, who would have found the association blasphemous."...

> "As much as the Bible, or Dante, or even Shakespeare, the Koran is the Book f Life, as vital as any person, whoever she or he is. Since the God addresses all of us who will hear, it is a universal book, again as open and generous as the greatest works of secular literature, as the masterworks of Shakespeare and Cervantes." ...

> "It is a perfect poem in itself, a miracle and yet natural, and in no way sectarian: 'light upon light.'"[35]

Yet, Bloom's praise of the literary aspect of the Quran cannot be considered as objective evidence. Furthermore, Bloom does not consider the Quran a unique book; since he lists it among other manmade books. For a content-wise comparison, however, we need to use our common sense, our knowledge and our minds.

A Distinct Literature

It would be a better choice if we compare the Quran to popular literature rather than the obscure and unknown one. Thus, books of Hadith (narrations and traditions attributed to Muhammad) would be perfect for this. With this method, we could hit two birds with one stone. We might learn that the Quran does not reflect the culture and knowledge of the people who lived in the region and the era in which the Quran emerged. We would also eliminate our doubts, if any as to whether the Quran and Hadith belong to the same source.

Of course, this comparison would not suffice to prove or demonstrate that the Quran is the word of God. But it might demonstrate that its content is very different from other religious literature in the Middle Ages. This difference might provide us with the needed incentive to check whether the book is universally unique or not. If the Quran demonstrates this, in addition to its distinction, its uniqueness and inimitable nature, then it has proven its claim.

The Quran and Hadith

The only book delivered by Muhammad was the Quran. No other book was written or compiled by Muhammad and companions during his lifetime. Muhammad preached only the Quran and practiced according to the Quran alone. The system of submission to God, or islam (originally not a proper name), belonged to God alone. It was not a limited company religion concocted by a committee comprised of God, Muhammad, his companions, and the succeeding clergymen. Meaning submission to God, islam is not a special religion first advocated by Muhammad. It is the monotheistic system of all messengers, such as, Noah, Shuayb, Salih, Abraham, Joseph, Job, Moses, David, Solomon, John, and Jesus (See the Quran 2:131-135; 3:95; 6:161; 7:126; 10:72; 16:123; 22:78; 27:31-32; 28:53). Since I have exposed the diabolic nature of Hadith and Sunna and the corrupt nature of sectarian Islam in "19 Questions For Sunni and Shiite scholars," I will not repeat those arguments here.

Maurice Bucaille, a French medical doctor, evaluated Hadith and Sunna under the light of science after converting to Islam (remember, islam means peacemaking and peacefully Surrendering to God'). Below is an excerpt from his findings:

> "I have compared the findings made during an examination of the Hadiths with those already set out in the section on the Quran and modern science. The results of this comparison speak for themselves. The difference is in fact quite staggering between the accuracy of the data contained in the Quran, when compared with modern scientific knowledge, and the highly questionable character of certain statements in the Hadiths on subjects whose tenor is essentially scientific.... What must be heavily stressed is the disparity between these two groups of texts, both from a literary point of view and as regards their contents. It would

53

indeed be unthinkable to compare the style of the Quran with that of the Hadith. What is more, when the contents of the two texts are compared in the light of modern scientific data, one is struck by the oppositions between them."[36]

Please evaluate the following mini comparison by keeping in mind that Hadith Collections were compiled approximately two centuries after the revelation of the Quran. Decide for yourself on how distinct the content of the Quran is from the literature of the people who lived within the same geography and time. (After the name of Hadith Collection the first number is the number of the book and the second one is the number of the chapter where the Hadith is located. For instance, "Bukhari 4/13" can be found in Bukhari's fourth book in Chapter 13.)

You may find several translations of *Bukhari* on the Internet. For instance:

http://www.usc.edu/schools/college/crcc/engagement/resources/texts/muslim/Hadith/bukhari/
http://www.tanzeem.org/resources/Hadithonline/Bukhari/Index.htm

To give you an idea about the content of most popular Hadith book, here is the index of *Bukhari*:

1. Revelation	28. Pilgrims Prevented from Completing the Pilgrimmage
2. Belief	
3. Knowledge	29. Penalty of Hunting while on Pilgrimmage
4. Ablutions (Wudu')	
5. Bathing (Ghusl)	30. Virtues of Madinah
6. Menstrual Periods	31. Fasting
7. Rubbing hands and feet with dust (Tayammum)	32. Praying at Night in Ramadaan (Taraweeh)
8. Prayers (Salat)	33. Retiring to a Mosque for Remembrance of Allah (I'tikaf)
9. Virtues of the Prayer Hall (Sutra of the Musalla)	34. Sales and Trade
10. Times of the Prayers	35. Sales in which a Price is paid for Goods to be Delivered Later (As-Salam)
11. Call to Prayers (Adhaan)	
12. Characteristics of Prayer	36. Hiring
13. Friday Prayer	37. Transferance of a Debt from One Person to Another (Al-Hawaala)
14. Fear Prayer	
15. The Two Festivals (Eids)	38. Representation, Authorization, Business by Proxy
16. Witr Prayer	
17. Invoking Allah for Rain (Istisqaa)	39. Agriculture
18. Eclipses	40. Distribution of Water
19. Prostration During Recital of Qur'an	41. Loans, Payment of Loans, Freezing of Property, Bankruptcy
20. Shortening the Prayers (At-Taqseer)	
21. Prayer at Night (Tahajjud)	42. Lost Things Picked up by Someone (Luqaata)
22. Actions while Praying	
23. Funerals (Al-Janaa'iz)	43. Oppressions
24. Obligatory Charity Tax (Zakat)	44. Partnership
25. Obligatory Charity Tax After Ramadaan (Zakat ul Fitr)	45. Mortgaging
	46. Manumission of Slaves
26. Pilgrimmage (Hajj)	47. Gifts
27. Minor Pilgrammage (Umra)	48. Witnesses
	49. Peacemaking

QURAN	HADITH

God

Initiator of the heavens and the earth. … There is nothing that equals Him. He is the Hearer, the Seer. (42:11)

Glory be to your Lord, the great Lord; far above their claims. (37:180)

God is the Most Merciful (12:64). God does not expect from us beyond our capacity (2:286), and He does not wish to make the system difficult for us (2:185).

God

God reveals the upper part of His leg to prove his identity to His messengers (Bukhari 97/24; 10/129 and commentary of Chapter 68).

The longest narration in Bukhari involves a contorted version of Muhammad's spiritual journey. According to this story, when Muhammad ascended to the 7th Heaven on the back of a special horse, God initially imposed on Muhammad's followers to observe the contact prayer 50 TIMES a day, one prayer every 28 minutes! However, upon receiving frequent mentorship from Moses who resided in the 6th Heaven, Muhammad was finally able to reduce the times of prayers from 50 to 5. A depiction of God as a capricious employer and Muhammad as a caring yet gullible union leader who negotiated and haggled on behalf of his followers still remains a very popular story full of silly details.

QURAN	HADITH

Earth Sciences and Cosmology

When you look at the mountains, you think that they are standing still. But they are moving, like the clouds. Such is the art and construction of God, who perfected everything. He is fully Cognizant of everything you do. (27:88)

He made the earth egg-shaped. (79:30)

… He *rolls* the night over the day, and *rolls* the day over the night.… (39:5)

Do the unbelievers not realize that the heaven and the earth used to be one solid mass that we exploded into existence? And from water we made all living things. Would they acknowledge? (21:30)

Earth Sciences and Cosmology

The world is standing on top of a whale. When the whale shakes its head earthquakes occur. (Ibn-i Kathir: *Commentary of the Quran under the light of Hadiths*, on verses 2:29 and 68:1).

57

QURAN

Messenger

The messenger of God has set up a good example for those among you who seek God and the Last Day, and constantly think about God. (33:21)

Surely, you are blessed with a great moral character. (68:4)

Say, "I am no more than a human like you, being inspired that your god is one god. ..." (18:110; 41:6)

We have sent you out of mercy from us towards the whole world (20:107).

We are fully aware of what they hear, when they listen to you, and when they conspire secretly—the disbelievers say, "You are following a crazy man." Note how they describe you, and how this causes them to stray off the path. (17:47-48)

HADITH

Messenger

The messenger had the sexual power of 30 men. (Bukhari 4/13)

When the messenger married with Aisha, he was 55 years old and Aisha was 6 years old. (Bukhari 58/234 and 58/236.)

The messenger was making sexual intercourse with all his nine wives in a single night. (Bukhari 4/13)

The messenger sent a troop after the murderers. When they were brought he ordered their hands and legs to be cut. He later gouged their eyes with hot nails and left them dying under the sun. The messenger ordered his companions not to give them water. (Bukhari 56/152; 59/35; 71/1)

Bewitched by a Jew from Medina, Muhammad wandered in the city for days, not knowing what he was doing. (Bukhari 59/11; 76/47; Hanbal 6/57; 4:367)

Cure and Diseases

Then eat from all the fruits, following the design of your Lord, precisely. From their (bees) bellies comes a drink of different colors, wherein there is healing for the people. This should be (sufficient) proof for people who reflect. (16:69)

Cure and Diseases

A group from Urayna and Uqayla tribes visited Medina and converted to Islam. The weather of the city had negative effect on their health. They consulted the messenger and he advised them to drink the milk and urine of camels. (Bukhari 52/262; 56/152; 71/1; Hanbal 3/163)

Whoever eats seven dates from the Ajva region will be safe from any witchcraft and poison. (Bukhari, 71/52, 56)

If a fly falls into the vessel of any of you, let him dip all of it and then throw it away, for in one of its wings there is a disease and in the other there is healing. (Bukhari 54/16)

There are no contagious diseases. (Bukhari, 71/43, 45, 53, 54)

The cure is in three things: blood-letting, cupping, and cauterization. (Bukhari, Ibn Majah)

QURAN	HADITH

Women

Their Lord responded to them: "I never fail to reward any worker among you for any work you do, be you male or female—you are equal to one another.... (3:195)

The believing men and women are allies of one another. They advocate righteousness and forbid evil, they observe the Contact Prayers (Sala) and give the obligatory charity (Zaka), and they obey God and His messenger. These will be showered with God's Mercy. God is Almighty, Most Wise. (9:71)

God promises the believing men and the believing women gardens with flowing streams, wherein they abide forever, and magnificent mansions in the gardens of Eden. And God's blessings and approval are even greater. This is the greatest triumph. (9:72)

"And from His signs is that He created for you mates from yourselves that you may reside with them, and He placed between you affection and mercy. In that are signs for a people who reflect." (30:21)

Women

Women are deficient in intelligence and religion (Bukhari 1/301; 6/301; 24/541)

If an ass, a black dog, or a woman passes in front of a praying person, his prayer is nullified. (Muslim 4/1032; Abu Dawud 2/704, Ibn Majah 3/1851) Abu Dawud, in addition to three above adds a pig, a Jew, a Magian. Bukhari 9/486-498 contradicts the other books)..

Women are slaves/properties of their husbands. (Ibn Majah 3/1851, 1855 1918; Tirmithi, 104; Abu Dawud 11:2141, 2142, 2155; 12:2170; Muslim 8//3367; Bukhari 62/122; Bukhari 54/460)

The majority of inhabitants of hell are women. (Bukhari 54/464; Muslim 4/1926)

Women are crooks like ribs (Bukhari 55/548; Muslim 8/3466-3468).

If anybody has been required to prostrate before others besides God, the woman should prostrate before her husband. (Abu Dawud 11/2135)

Those who entrust their affairs to a woman will never know prosperity. (Bukhari 88/219)

To find a good woman among women is similar to finding a white crow among a hundred crows. (Ghazali, Ihya: Kitab Adab al-Nikah)

QURAN	HADITH

Freedom and Political Structure

There shall be no compulsion in the system: the right way is now distinct from the wrong way. Anyone who denounces the devil and acknowledges in God has grasped the strongest bond; one that never breaks. God is Hearer, Omniscient. (2:256)

Proclaim: "This is the truth from your Lord," then whoever wills let him acknowledge, and whoever wills let him disbelieve.... (18:29)

He has instructed you in the scripture that: if you hear God's revelations being mocked and ridiculed, you shall not sit with them, unless they delve into another subject.... (4:140)

O people, we created you from the same male and female, and rendered you distinct peoples and tribes, that you may recognize one another. The best among you in the sight of God is the most righteous. God is Omniscient, Cognizant. (49:13)

... Their affairs are decided after due consultation among themselves, and from our provisions to them they give (to charity). (42:38)

Freedom and Political Structure

The property and blood of an apostate is not under the protection of law (Bukhari 4/52, 4/260)

The Prophet sent a platoon of secret agents to kill Kab bin al-Eshraf and Abu Rafi', two poets who criticized him. They were assassinated that night. Kab's head was cut off and brought to the Prophet Muhammad (Bukhari 59/14, 15; 4/52, 265. Muslim Jihad/119/1801; Abu Dawud Jihad/169/2768)

Ali burnt some people and this news reached Ibn 'Abbas, who said, "Had I been in his place I would not have burnt them, as the Prophet said, 'Don't punish (anybody) with Allah's Punishment.' No doubt, I would have killed them, for the Prophet said, 'If somebody (a Muslim) discards his religion, kill him.' " (Bukhari 52/260)

Leaders must be always elected from Quraysh tribe. (Bukhari 3/129, 183; 4/121; 86:31)

QURAN	HADITH

Animals

All the creatures on earth, and all the birds that fly with wings, are communities like you. We did not leave anything out of this book. To their Lord, all these creatures will be summoned. (6:38)

You would think that they (the young monotheists) were awake, when they were in fact asleep. We turned them to the right side and the left side, while their dog stretched his arms at the threshold. (18:18)

Art

They made for him (Prophet Solomon) anything he wanted—niches, statues, deep pools, and heavy cooking pots. O family of David, work (righteousness) to show your appreciation. Only a few of My servants are appreciative. (34:13)

Animals

There are neither contagious diseases nor bad luck called Tiyara. However, there is bad luck in only three things: the woman, house, and the horse. (Bukhari 76/53)

Angels do not enter a house that has a dog or picture in it. (Bukhari 54/448-450, 539, 59/338; 72/841, 843)

Kill every black dog; they are from the devil. (Hanbal 4/85; 5/54; Bukhari 54/16; 54/540)

If a house fly falls in the drink of anyone of you, he should dip it in the drink, for one of it wings has a disease and the other has the cure for the disease. (Bukhari 54/537)

Kill the Slamander, a mischief-doer. (Bukhari 4/525-526).

Art

The most who will suffer in hell are those who draw pictures of God's creation. In the Day of Judgment the artists will be challenged to give life to the pictures they made. (Bukhari 34/428, 54/447, 72/834, 846)

Most of the musical instruments are prohibited by various contradictory Hadith and sectarian *fatwas*.

QURAN	HADITH

Penalty for Adultery

A sura that we have sent down, and we have decreed as law. We have revealed in it clear revelations, that you may take heed. The adulteress and the adulterer you shall whip each of them a hundred lashes. Do not be swayed by pity from carrying out God's law, if you truly acknowledge God and the Last Day. And let a group of acknowledgers witness their penalty. (24:1-2)

Penalty for Adultery

The 'stoning verse' was recorded in Quran during the time of Prophet. The verse was written on a papyrus and it was kept under Aisha's bed. But just after Prophet's death, a hungry goat entered Aisha's house and ate the verse. Thus, the stoning verse has been abrogated physically. Nevertheless, it is valid as a law practiced by the Prophet. (Ibn Majah 36/1944 and Ibn Hanbal 3/61, 5/131,132,183; 6/269)

The second Caliph Omar declared: "Because in the future some people will appear and deny the punishment of stoning by claiming that they cannot find it in the Quran, if I did not fear that people will say that Omar is adding to the Quran, I would add the stoning verse into the Quran!!'" (Bukhari 93/21; Muslim 1691; Tirmizi 8/1431; Abu Dawud 41/1; Itqan 2/34).

"A tribe of monkeys arrested an adulterer monkey and stoned it to death." (Bukhari 63/27)

QURAN	HADITH

Violence

Some uninformed critics of the Quran list verses of the Quran dealing with wars and declare Islam to be a religion of violence. Their favorite verses are: 2:191; 3:28; 3:85; 5:10,34; 9:5; 9:28-29; 9:123; 14:17; 22:9; 25: 52; 47:4 and 66:9. In introductory section of the *Quran: a Reformist Translation* and in its endnotes, I have refuted their arguments.

Please see the Appendix titled, "To the Factor of 666" and the article on verse 9:29 for a more detailed discussion on this issue.

Violence

Narrated Anas bin Malik: A group of eight men from the tribe of 'Ukil came to the Prophet and then they found the climate of Medina unsuitable for them. So, they said, "O Allah's Apostle! Provide us with some milk." Allah's Apostle said, "I recommend that you should join the herd of camels." So they went and drank the urine and the milk of the camels (as a medicine) till they became healthy and fat. Then they killed the shepherd and drove away the camels, and they became unbelievers after they were Muslims. When the Prophet was informed by a shouter for help, he sent some men in their pursuit, and before the sun rose high, they were brought, and he had their hands and feet cut off. Then he ordered for nails which were heated and passed over their eyes, and they were left in the Harra (i.e. rocky land in Medina). They asked for water, and nobody provided them with water till they died. (Bukhari 52/261)

Allah's Apostle sent a group of the Ansar to Abu Rafi. Abdullah bin Atik entered his house at night and killed him while he was sleeping. (Bukhari 52/265; also see 52/270).

Justifying arson during night raids: Abu Dawud: Jihad 91/2615-2616, 91/154, Harth/6, Maghazi/14, Tafsir/59/2, Tajrid/1576. Ibn Majah: 31/2843, 31/2845; Muslim 29-31/1746; Tirmizi 4/1552; Ahmad Ibn Hanbal, 2/8,52,80.)

QURAN	HADITH

Mathematics

"On it is Nineteen." (74:30)

"By the odd and even" (89:3)

"Numerically Coded Book" (83:9, 20)

"Friends of Numbers in the Cave/Hidden" (18:9)

"So that He know that they have delivered the messages of their Lord, and He surrounds all that is with them, and He has counted everything in numbers." (72:28)

Mathematics

The punishment of the criminal who had cut fingers of a woman is the following number of camels as compensation: for one finger 10 (ten) camels, for two fingers 20 (twenty) camels, for three fingers 30 (thirty) camels, for four fingers 20 (twenty) camels. (Muwatta 43/11; Hanbal 2/182).

PS: Can you guess the number of camels for five fingers?

How Can any Person with a Sound Mind Can Respect and Trust the Reporters of the Following Hadith and Sunna?

The enemies of Islam have always used Hadith, Sunna and *Syra* books to degrade Islam and its final prophet. For instance, the following list of Hadiths with some comments was published by Frontpagemagazine.com, a Zionist propaganda outlet. They cannot thank Bukhari and his ilk more. Here is an excerpt of a conversation of the Front Page Magazine with the Coptic priest Zakaria Botros, a pro-Zionist and a warmonger in sheep's clothes who supported the fascist policies of Israel against the Palestinians and the Neocon war and covert operations against Iraq that resulted in war crimes, covert operations, atrocities, and torture—with more than a million Iraqis killed, millions more injured, and made refugees, widows and orphans:

> **FP**: You always document your discussions with Islamic sources. Why do Muslim clerics and imams have such a difficulty discussing what Islam itself teaches and instead just attack you personally?
>
> **Botros**: I think the answer is obvious. The Islamic sources, the texts, speak for themselves. Muslims have no greater enemy than their own scriptures—particularly the Hadith and Sira—which constantly scandalize and embarrass Muslims.
>
> **PS**: For the whole interview see: Frontapagemag.com, *The Strange Teachings of Muhammad*, June 02, 2009. You may also read my debate with another warmonger Crusader, Ali Sina, and witness his promotion of genocide against Muslims by using the teachings of Hadith and Sunna as a justification. See. www.19.org

The Sunnis and the Shiites have no right to blame the propaganda of bloody neo-Crusaders, since it is their own *Holy* Hadith collections that provide all the ammunition to depict Muhammad as violent, coward, cold-blooded murderer, sex-crazy, misogynist, perverted, superstitious, plunderer, hedonistic, retarded, racist, duplicitous, ungrateful, and manipulator. Hadith reporters and followers are the real enemies of Muhammad (For instance, see verse 6:112-116 and 25:30). Below are the hearsay reports from Sunni sources cited by the enemies the Prophet Muhammad who are affiliated to the Zionist site above:

- The Prophet said, "We will go to attack them (i.e. the infidels) and they will not come to attack us."—Sahih Bukhari, 5.59.435.
- The Prophet allowed the raping of war-captives.—Sahih Bukhari, 3.46.718.
- The Muslim soldiers had sex with the captive women in the presence of their husbands and "some were reluctant to do so."—Sunaan Abu Dawud 11.2150.
- One can have sexual intercourse with a captive woman after she is clear of her period and/or delivery. If she has a husband then her marriage is abrogated after she becomes a captive.—Sahih Muslim 8.3432.

- Ali (Muhammad's son-in-law) had sex with booty captive women. Muhammad presented him with the captive woman (to have sex).—Sahih Bukhari 5.59.637.
- Women are domestic animals; beat them.—Tabari, vol. ix, pp. 9.112-114.
- Muhammad's culture of killing was widespread and wild. Muslims killed Umm Qirfa, "a very old woman" by tying her legs with a rope attached to two camels driven in opposite directions thus tearing her body (Ibn Ishak, pp. 664-665). Umm Qirfa was torn from limb to limb by four camels—Rodinson, p. 248.
- Allah likes beheading—Kais cut off the head of al-Aswad and shouted "Allah is great."—Baladhuri, p. 161.
- The Prophet said spears were his livelihood—Sahih Bukhari, Vol 4, Chapter 88.
- Muhammad ordered a Muslim woman to breastfeed a man. She protested but ultimately had to do so— Ibn Majah, 3.1943.
- Muhammad ordered a Muslim woman to breastfeed a bearded man.—Sahih Muslim, 8.3428.
- Allah says that a woman must sexually satisfy her husband even when on top of a camel.—Ibn Majah, 3.1853.
- Muhammad ordered the murder of Asma bt. Marwan, a Jewish poetess when she was suckling her babies.—Ibn Ishaq, p.676, Ibn Sa'd, vol. ii, p. 30-31.
- Muhammad ordered the assassination of Abu Afak, a 120-year-old man of Medina.—Ibn Ishaq, p. 675, ibn Sa'd, vol. ii, p. 31.
- Muhammad conducted ethnic cleansing of Banu Quaynuqa Jews from Medina.—Tabari, vol. vii, p. 85.
- Muhammad hired a professional killer to assassinate Ka'b b. al-Ashraf, a poet of Medina.—Sahih Bukhari, 5.59.369.
- The messenger of Allah said, "Whoever of the Jews falls into your hands, kill him." So Muhayyish b. Masud killed his friend and business-partner Ibn Sunaynah- Tabari, vol. vii, p. 97-98.
- Muhammad's death squad murdered Abu Rafi, a critic of Muhammad in Medina.—Tabari, vol. vii, p. 103, Sahih Bukhari, 5.59.371.
- Muhammad's death squad assassinated Sufyan ibn Khalid.—Ibn Ishaq, p.664-665, ibn Sa'd, vol. ii, p. 60.
- Muhammad did ethnic cleansing of B. Nadir Jews from Medina.-Tabari, vol. vii, p.158-159, Heykal, ch. B. Nadir, Sahih Bukhari, 3.39.519.
- Muhammad beheaded between 600-900 Jews of B. Qurayzah who did not fight Muslilms but were attacked, and they surrendered unconditionally—Tabari, vol.viii, ch. B. Qurayzah; Heykal, ch. the Campaign of Khandaq and B. Qurayzah, ibn Ishaq, ch. B. Qurayzah.

- Arabs are the chosen people of Allah; Allah resembles an Arab.—Ibn Sa'd, vol.1, p.2.
- Allah favours Arab racism—prophets are to be of Quraysh stock and of white complexion (Ibn Sa'd, vol.1, p.95-96, Sahih Muslim, 20.4483.
- Shafi Law m4.2 The following are not suitable matches for one another: (1) a non Arab man for an Arab woman (O: because Prophet said: Allah has chosen the Quraysh Arabs as His agent to rule the world (Islamic Caliphate).—Sahih Bukhari, 4.56.704.
- Whoever says Muhammad was black must be killed.—Ash-Shifa, Tr. Aisha AbdarRaĤMaN Bewley, p. 375.
- Muhammad approved killing of women and children of the pagans because they (the children) are from them (i.e. the pagans)…(Sahih Bukhari 4.52.256).
- Muhammad blessed Jarir for conducting the genocide (including the slaughter of the children) at Dhu Khalasa.—Sahih Bukhari, 4.52.262
- Muhammad had a black slave; he traded in slaves.—Sahih Bukhari, 9.91.368 and Kasasul Ambia of Ibn Kathir Vol 3, p. 112—Bangla translation by Bashiruddin.
- Muhammad traded slaves for beautiful, young, and sexy women, such as Saffiya.—Sunaan Abu Dawud, 2.2987, 2991.
- Muhammad's hired killer assassinated Al-Yusayr b. Rizam and a party of Khaybar Jews at al-Qarqara.—Ibn Ishaq, p. 665-666.
- Muhammad forced *jizya* on Zoroastrians—several cases.—Tabari, vol. viii, p. 142, Sunaan Abu Dawud, 19.9038.
- The gratuitous destruction of pagan temples and their idols.—Several references: Ibn Ishaq, Ibn Sa'd, Tabari: ch: The Occupation of Mecca .
- Killing of polytheists is laudable—Muhammad said.—Tabari, vol. ix, p. 76.
- Muhammad's marauding troops conducted genocide at Jurash, Yemen.—Tabari, vol. ix, p. 88-89.
- Killing infidels is fun.—Tabari, vol. vii. p. 65.
- Muhammad ordered to kill the apostates; if somebody (Muslim) discards his religion, kill him)—Sahih Bukhari, 4.52.260.
- Blood of animal is very dear to Allah.—Ibn Majah, 4.3126.
- The Prophet said: A man will not be askcd as to why he beat his wife.—Sunaan Abu Dawud, 11.2142.
- The Prophet said: - People ruled by a woman will never be successful.—-Sahih Bukhari, 5.59.709.
- Majority of women are in hell.—Sahih Bukhari 1.6.301.
- A woman must keep her sexual organs ready for service at all times (Ihya Uloom Ed-Din of Ghazali, Tr. Dr Ahmad Zidan, vol.i, p.235)
- A wife can't leave home.—Shafi'i law m10.4.

- If a woman claims to be having her period but her husband does not believe her, it is lawful for him to have sexual intercourse with her.—Shafi'i law e.13.5.
- Support of a divorced wife is for 3 months.—Shafi'i Law m11.10.
- Instant divorce is allowed for husbands. No support to a such divorced wives from that moment.—Many references.
- No reason is required to divorce one's wife/s (Many references, Sharia the Islamic Law—Dr. Abdur RaĤMaN Doi, p. 173).
- It is unlawful for women to leave the house with faces unveiled, whether or not there is likelihood of temptation. It is unlawful for women to be alone with a marriageable man.—Shafi'i Law m2.3.
- Muhammad said, "No nation prospers over which a woman rules."—Ihyya Uloom Ed-din of Ghazali, Tr. Fazl-Ul-Karim, p. 2.35.
- If Muhammad wanted anyone to prostrate before another, he would have ordered a woman to prostrate before her husband.—Ibid, p.2.43.
- A woman, a slave and an unbeliever is not fit to be a moral police.—Ibid, p. 2.186.
- Muhammad said, "A woman is the string of the devil."—Ibid, p. 3.87.
- A woman is the best coveted of things to a man. He takes pleasures in penetrating his genital organ into female vaginal canal. Thus, vagina is the most coveted thing in a woman.—Ghazali, p. 3.162.
- A woman is a servant and the husband is the person served.—Hedaya, the Hanafi Law manual, p. 47
- You can enjoy a wife by force.—Hedaya, p. 141
- Full dower is the payment for the delivery of woman's person. Booza meaning Genitalia arvum Mulieris.—Hedaya, p. 44.
- Women are your (men) prisoners; treat them well, if necessary beat them but not severely.—Tirmidhi, 104.
- When a woman goes out, the devil looks at her; so conceal a woman.—Tirmidhi, 928.
- In paradise, there is a market of rich, beautiful and ever-young women; they will be pleased whoever buys them.—Tirmidhi, 1495.
- Women are stupid.—Ibn Majah, 5.4003.
- The best Muslims had the largest number of wives.—Sahih Bukhari, 7.62.7.

After quoting dozens of Hadith like the ones in the list above, the Crusaders then mix them with a few verses of the Quran, which are either taken out of context, or their meaning and implications are distorted. Mixing Quran with Hadith has been the favorite strategy of the critics. When they are deprived of this deceptive tool they employ all the arguments of the followers of Hadith and Sunna to defend the importance of Hadith and Sunna. My lengthy debate with a hatemonger and warmonger Crusader nicknamed Ali Sina is a fine demonstration of this fact. When he finally realized that he could not use Hadith as ammunition against me, he threw a temper tantrum for weeks.

Below is how the Zionist Frontpage Magazine ended its list of Hadiths. Please note the devious insertion of a few references to the Quranic verses that are distorted and abused by the followers of Hadith and Sunna:

- Allah regards the unbelievers (non-Muslims) as slaves in the hands of the Muslims.—The Qur'an 16:75.
- Allah made Muhammad wealthy through conquests (raid, plunder, war).—Sahih Bukhari, 3.37.495.
- Muhammad's main source of livelihood was the money from the Jizya tax on infidels.—Sahih Bukhari, 5.59.351.
- Provisions set by Allah and Muhammad are binding to all Muslims: there are no alternatives.—The Qur'an, 33:36.
- Obeying Muhammad is obeying Allah.—The Qur'an, 4:80.
- Muhammad's booty is Allah's booty, which was how Allah made Muhammad rich.—The Qur'an, 59:6-7
- Muhammad was the ONLY Prophet who killed somebody by his "noble hand." The person killed was Ubayy b. Khalaf, at the battle of Uhud - page 600 Umdat Al Salik.

The scope of this book is not allowing me to refute each allegation, but I invite you to compare them to the **Quran: a Reformist Translation** and study our refutations of these claims. The QRT is published by Brainbow Press in book format and also available in electronic format. Besides, it is also available at **www.quranix.com** and several other sites. In the Endnotes of QRT, when we differ from the orthodox understanding we provide our reasons for why we reject the sectarian translations or commentaries.

The Signs in the Scripture as Evident in Nature

The Quranic description of the earth, the solar system, the cosmos and the origin of the universe remain centuries ahead of the time of their first revelation. The Quran contains many verses relating to a diverse range of science subjects and not a single assertion has been proven wrong. For instance, the Quran, delivered in the seventh century C.E., states or implies that:

- Time is relative (32:5; 70:4; 22:47).
- God created the universe from nothing (2:117).
- The earth and heavenly bodies were once a single point and they were separated from each other (21:30).
- The universe is continuously expanding (51:47).
- The universe is closed; it will collapse back to singularity (21:104).
- The universe was created in six days (stages) and the conditions that made life possible on earth took place in the last four stages (50:38; 41:10).
- The stage before the creation of the earth is described as a gas nebula (41:11).
- Planet earth is floating in an orbit (27:88; 21:33; 36:40).
- The earth is round (10:24; 39:5) and resembles an egg (10:24; 39:5; 79:30).
- Oceans have subsurface wave patterns (24:40).
- Earth's atmosphere acts like a protective shield (21:32).
- The wind also pollinates plants (15:22).
- A bee has multiple stomachs (16:69).
- The workers in honeybee communities are females (16:68-69).
- After years of disappearance, Periodical Cicadas emerge all together with a cacophony of songs, testifying a similitude of resurrection for those who appreciate God's signs in the nature (54:7).
- The creation of living creatures follows an evolutionary system (7:69; 15:28-29; 24:45; 32:7-9; 71:14-17).
- The earliest biological creatures were incubated inside flexible layers of clay (15:26).
- The stages of human development in the womb are detailed (23:14).
- Our biological life span is coded in our genes (35:11).
- Photosynthesis is a recreation of energy stored through chlorophyll (36:77-81).
- Everything is created in pairs (13:3; 51:49; 36:36).
- The atomic number, atomic weight and isotopes of iron are specified (57:25).

71

- Atoms of elements found on earth contain a maximum of seven energy layers (65:12).
- There will be new and better transportation vehicles beyond what we know (16:8).
- The sound and vision of water and the action of eating dates (which contain oxytocin) reduce labor pains (19:24-25).
- There is life (not necessarily intelligent) beyond earth (42:29).
- The Quran correctly refers to Egypt's ruler who made Joseph his chief adviser as king (*malik*), not as Pharaoh (12:59).
- Many of the miracles mentioned in the Quran represent the ultimate goals of science and technology.
- The Quran relates that matter (but not humans) can be transported at the speed of light (27:30-40), that smell can be transported to remote places (12:94), that extensive communication with animals is possible (27:16-17), that sleep, in certain conditions, can slow down metabolism and increase life span (18:25), and that the vision of blind people can be restored (3:49).
- The word Sabbath (seventh day) occurs exactly 7 times.
- The number of months in a year is stated as 12 and the word month (*ŞaHR*) is used exactly twelve times.
- The number of days in a year is not stated, but the word day (*YaWM*) is used exactly 365 times.
- The frequency of the word year (*sana*) in its singular form occurs 7 times, and in plural form 12 times. Together this makes 19 times; with each number relating to an astronomic event.
- A prophetic mathematical structure based on the number 19, as implied in Chapter 74 of the Quran was discovered in 1974 by the aid of a computer. This structure shows that the Quran is embedded with an interlocking extraordinary mathematical system, which was also discovered in original parts of the Old Testament in the 11th century.
- And there's more—much more. Also, see 68:1; 79:30; 74:1-37.

5

The Quran Challenges the Ingrates; but How?

"If we take in our hand any volume of divinity or school metaphysics, for instance; let us ask, does it contain any abstract reasoning concerning quantity or number? No. Does it contain any experimental reasoning concerning matter of fact and existence? No. Commit it then to flames: for it can contain nothing but sophistry and illusion." ~ David Hume.[37]

I agree with the underlying reasoning of the empiricist philosopher David Hume's criticism against religious liturgy. If a religious book does not provide empirically verifiable or falsifiable evidence for its claims, then it deserves no attention. Considering the abundance of books claiming to be products of divine revelation or inspiration, a person with a sound mind cannot pick one of them as a guide for life, let alone one for absolute truth and eternal salvation.

The Quran, which extensively quotes the criticism of its opponents, challenges those who claim that it is a man-made book to produce the like of this book or that of ten chapters or of even a single chapter:

17:88   Say, "If all the humans and all the jinns banded together in order to produce a Quran like this, they could never produce anything like it, no matter how much assistance they lent one another."

11:13-14 If they say, "He fabricated it," tell them, "Then produce ten suras like these, fabricated, and invite whomever you can, other than God, if you are truthful." If they fail to meet your challenge, then know that this is revealed with God's knowledge, and that there is no god except He. Will you then submit?

2:23   If you have any doubt regarding what we revealed to our servant, then produce one sura like these, and call upon your own witnesses against GOD, if you are truthful. (Also see: 10:38)

What is the meaning of such a challenge? What if Friedric Nietzsche or one of his fans made the following challenge for his *Twilight of the Idols*: "There are more idols in the world than there are realities. The priests, the professional negators, slanderers, and poisoners of life who speak with a hallow sound of inflated bowels can never imitate my Twilight; my Hammer will always smash their idols"? A similar challenge can be made for Darwin's *The Origin of Species*, "None of the naturally selected species, be a holy vertebrate or reptile, can mutate wisdom to the level of my original work!" John Milton could have ended his *Paradise Lost* with the following words: "May the forbidden tree bring you death with mortal taste! May the devil be cursed to five rivers for five incarnations. With all your defiance of Eternal Providence you can never find another Lost Paradise."

What would be the response of Muslims if similar challenges were made on behalf of hundreds of influential literary works, such as Francis Bacon's *Advancement in Learning*, or Thomas Carlyle's *On Heroes, Hero-Worship, and the Heroic in History*, or John Locke's *Essay Concerning Human Understanding*, or Dante's *Divine Comedy*?

Similarity Competition

Here is what I mean: If someone claims that his or her book is similar, or even superior to the Quran how would Sunni and Shiite scholars respond to it? Would they dismiss the claim even without evaluating its merits saying, "No, it is not and cannot be similar to the Quran!" This would inevitably beg the question, "What do you mean by 'similar'?"

Similarity here cannot mean comparing the same duplicated materials, for in that case, the Quran cannot be different from any other book. Without well-defined criteria, a similarity challenge is hard to evaluate. For example, without such criteria, Muslims claiming that the Quran is inimitable divine revelation can hardly dismiss the claim of the followers of Sun Myung Moon, the founder of the Moon Religion, that their book The Principal is similar, or even superior, to the Quran as divine revelation. Any challenge such as this thrown from any quarters cannot be taken seriously unless it is backed by valid criteria.

Wouldn't such a challenge look absurd if it focused solely on the literary quality of the book, which is a very difficult question to resolve? How can you object to someone claiming "None can cook more delicious shish kebab as I do and I will judge the kebab of challengers?" If a thesis is neither provable nor falsifiable on well founded grounds, then such a thesis is not scientific. I cannot expect someone to believe in the events that I saw in my dream unless I provide him or her with some falsifiable details such as a prophecy based on that dream. Then, the merits—clarity or vagueness—of my prophecy and the probability of its chance occurrence can be evaluated. Why should one believe in the truth of an assertion if there is no way to test its truth-value? Since the Quran recommends us to apply reason and scientific methodology for accepting information[38], what it contains must of necessity abide by its own logic and principle.

How Can a Challenge be Meaningful?

It appears that without an objective or mathematical criterion such a challenge has little practical meaning. Even the verdict of a competition judged by an impartial panel with utmost fairness is likely to be successfully contested by a challenger unless that competition is based on certain objective or mathematical criteria.

Let me explain. If we want to rank a selection of literature we should present them under nick-titles to an international "impartial" panel. The superiority of a book that received a favorable score from panel members might still remain debatable. The value and credibility of the ranking depends on numerous facts such as the selection and number of panelists, their level of scholastic experience and competence, and their cultural, religious, political and philosophical background, and by the number of books evaluated. In other words, the competition will be firmly dependent on variables other than the pure merits of the literature. Besides, even if our book is picked as the best book in one hundred separate competitions, we cannot guarantee its success in the 101st competition. Without a mathematical criterion, the most objective evaluations by human beings do not prove superiority.

For instance, how will those who consider the Quran as a literary miracle reject the following contemporary response to the Quranic challenge?

Surat Al-Muslimoon

Alef Lam Sad Meem.

Kul ya ayoohal muslimoona innakom lafee dalalen ba'eed.

Innal latheena kafaroo bil'lahee wa maseehihee lahom fil akhiratee naroo jahannama wa athabon shadeed.

Wujoohon *YaWMa*'ithen saghiraton mukfahirraton taltamisoo afwal lahee wal'lahoo yaf'aloo ma yureed.

YaWMa yakuloor'RaĤMaNoo ya ibadee kad an'amtoo alal'latheena min kablikom bil'hooda munazalan fit-tawrati wal-injeel.

Fama kana lakom an takfuroo bima anzaltoo wa tadalloo sawa'assabeel.

Kaloo rabbana ma dalalna anfusuna bal adallana manid'da'a annahoo minal mursaleen.

Wa ith kalal lahoo ya muhammada aghwayta ibadee wa ja'altahom mial kafireen.

Kala rabbi innama aghwaniyash shaytanoo innahoo kana libanee adama A'zamal mufsideen.

Wayaghfirool lahoo lillatheena taboo mimman aghwahumool insanoo wa yab'athoo billathee kana lish'shaytanee naseeran ila jahannama wabi'sal maseer.

Wa in kadal lahoo amran fainnahoo a'lamoo bima kada wahoowa ala kulli shay'en kadeer.

The Chapter Peacemakers

A.L.S.M.

Say: O Muslims, You are far astray.

Those who disbelieved in God and his Christ shall have in afterlife the fire of hell and a severe torture.

Some faces that day will be subdued and darkened seeking forgiveness from God and God shall do whatever He wants.

That day, the Most Merciful shall say: O my servants I favored you with my guidance revealed to you in the Torah and the Injeel.

And you should have not have disbelieved what I have revealed to you and gone astray from a plain road.

They said: We did not go astray ourselves but he, who claimed he was one of the messengers (of God) has mislead us.

And as God says: O Muhammad, you allured my servants and caused them to become disbelieves.

He said: O my Lord, it is Satan who allured me and truly he has always been the most corrupting to the children of Adam.

And God will forgive those who have been allured by man and then repented and he will force the one who was Satan's advocate to hell, a hapless journey's end.

And if God rules something, He is most knowing of what He rules and of what He had ruled and He is able to do all things.[39]

The excerpt above is a piece of claimed but fake revelation, the source of which is mentioned in the Endnote, reveals a pattern of literary quality that evidently is difficult, if not impossible, to objectively distinguish from that of the Quran. If the Quran's challenge has a real meaning, it must have an inherent value, independent of the works of opponents. Otherwise, its claim of divine authorship could never be taken as a proven without divine intervention. However, the challenge of the Quran relies on deduction, not induction—one that is not an invitation, but a declaration of an already proven victory, which we demonstrate in the following pages.

Past Efforts to Retort to the Quranic Challenge

Some books written about the Quran contend that some Arab poets tried to confront the Quranic challenge; however, they all failed to produce a poem or prose equaling its literary excellence. For example, Dr. Osman Keskioglu, a former member of the Supreme Council of Religious Affairs of Turkey dedicated ten pages to this issue in his book, The Quranic Knowledge from Revelation to Today.[40]. His treatment of the issue is typical of the works of most Sunni and Shiite scholars —shallow and evasive.

It is interesting that Sunni and Shiite scholars have reached consensus in their choice of a poet who responded to the Quranic challenge. Among dozens of great classics of Arabic literature, they pick a silly limerick attributed to a phantasmagoric poet called *Musaylamat-ul Kazzab* (Musaylama, the Liar). According to their claim, a poet named Musaylama wrote the following limerick as a reply to the Quranic challenge:

> "El mubazzirati zar'an, wal hasidati hasdan, waz zariyati kamhan, wat tahinati tahnan, wal ajinati ajnen, wal habizati hubzan, was saridati sardan, wal laqimati loqman... El filu, mal filu. Wa ma edrake mal filu. Lahu zanabun vaseelun ve hurtumun taveelun. Inna zalika bi khalqi rabbina laqaleelun... Ya dafda' binta dafdaayni..."

The translation:

> "I swear by those who sow, who harvest, who separate the grain from hay, who bake the bread, who shelve them and who eat them bite by bite.... The elephant, what is the elephant? Have you been informed about the elephant? It has a supple tail and a lengthy trunk. Indeed, these are expressions of my Lord's creation.... Oh frog, the daughter of two frogs! ..."

Sunni and Shiite clergymen, like the clergymen of all religions, are experts in fabricating stories to promote their teachings. For example, to refute Christianity, Sunni and Shiite scholars fabricated a Bible called Barnaba containing Muhammad's name, as they did volumes of Hadith books. They also successfully reached one of their rare consensuses—one of the most obvious historical lies that asserts Muhammad's illiteracy. Based on this lie, they argued that the Quran couldn't be the word of Muhammad, an illiterate man! So, we have good reasons to suspect that those absurd and silly statements, including perhaps the very repulsive name of the poet too, are figments of their imagination. All this to justify the Quran's literal excellence?! The end justifies the means! By employing a straw-man argument and by comparing the text of their holy book to ridiculous statements, Sunni and Shiite scholars have won cheap literary laurels. Of course, they could convince only their gullible followers.

A Joke or a Heresy?

Most of the Muslim authors who write or talk about the miracle of the Quran resort to a rigmarole attributed to Musaylamatul Kazzab. Since they do not have a testable criterion, when they are confronted with serious examples introduced as an answer to the Quranic challenge, they disqualify them with the ridiculous excuse, "The author did not produce the literature to take on the Quranic challenge." Let's read how Dr. Keskioglu, our prototype Muslim scholar, rejects some serious candidates in his aforementioned book:

77

> "As seen, the silly statement of Musaylama and his allies are only good as a joke. The imputation of challenging the Quran to great poets and authors like Ibn Muqaffa, Raawandi and Abul A'la is the product of a dubious agendas: The misguided members of heretic sects, such as "Karamita and Batiniya, tried to take advantage of the fame of those literary giants and fabricated baseless claims. Of course, like idolworshipers and Jews, they too were defeated to the ground in their war against the Quran."[41]

Sunni and Shiite scholars who have put the Quran in competition with gibberish should know that no matter whether a literary work was originally produced as a counter-challenge against the Quran or not, they should answer properly those "misbelievers" who present them as such. Otherwise, they need to give up defending the Quran!

Those responses that were not gibberish are rejected by another evasive argument. They too lose the competition since they are found to be too similar to the Quran. Dr. Keskioglu rejects the *Sura Nurayn* (Chapter of Twin Light) under the following pretext:

> "We deliberately quoted it extensively. To inform everyone that the expressions of the "similar" chapter are plagiarized from the Quran. These are concocted by re-arranging various Quranic phrases and expressions and scattering the word Ali and the issue of the Prophet's will."[42]

The Cul-de-sac of the Followers of Hadith and Sunna

Indeed, the Sunni and Shiite scholars are in clear contradiction with their most cherished sources. While on one hand they struggle to prove the miraculous literary nature of the Quran, on the other hand they believe that the Prophet's companions, who were familiar with the Arabic literature, could not distinguish verses of the Quran from other utterances.

For example, Hadith books report that the committee appointed to compile the verses and chapters of the Quran in a book did not accept any verse brought by one witness.[43] This dubious report implies that Muhammad's companions were not able to recognize verses of the Quran from fabricated statements. Many "authentic" Hadith books, including Sunni's most respected Bukhari, refer to the following "verse":

> "As shayhu was shayhatu iza zanaya farjumuhuma albattata nakalan minallahi; wallahu azizun hakeem."

> Translation:

> "If an old man and an old woman commit adultery you should stone them to death as a punishment from God; God is Powerful and Wise."[44]

Stoning to death, according to the Quran, was the practice of idol worshippers throughout history. In order to adopt the practice of idol worshippers[45], Hadith narrators fabricated the above quoted "verse." You might ask, "Why is the verse issuing stoning-to-death penalty nonexistent in the Quran?" The answer of the Sunni and Shiite scholars is almost unanimous: "The verse ordering stoning-to-death was a part of the Quran when the Prophet was alive. However, the parchment containing the verse was eaten by a hungry goat after the Prophet's death. So, this stoning verse was abrogated." If you are curious you might continue: "Well, let's assume that the 'stoning verse' existed in the manuscript of the Prophet, and let's assume that the hungry goat had the authorization to abrogate God's revelation.. Why do you then consider stoning-to-death as part of Islamic criminal law?" The answer is as bizarre as the story of abrogation: "The stoning verse was *literally* abrogated from the Quran by a hungry goat, but its legal authority is valid in Islamic Sharia." It is fascinating to read the various reports in Hadith books reflecting the three phases of this "verse":—fabrication, abrogation and and restoration.

Some go further and report the existence of a Quranic manuscript containing two extra chapters, which are known as *Qunuut* Prayers.[46] How do Sunni and Shiite scholars prove that those "two chapters" do not match the eloquence and style of the Quran?

Sunni scholars who turn into lions against Musaylama and Shiite hadith books are helpless sheep against Hadith books of the master collectors of lies, such as Bukhari, Muslim, Ibn Majah, Tirmizi, Abu Davud and Ibn Hanbal. Hadith books narrate numerous statements claiming that they were part of the Quran. Similarly, Shiite scholars who turn to wise critics in rejecting Sunni Hadith collections, are mysteriously dull and gullible adherents of Hadith collections approved by their sect, such as, *Kitab al-Kafi* of Kulayni, *Man la Yahduruhu al-Faqih* of Shaikh Saduq, *Tahdhib al-Ahkam* and *Al-Istibsar* by Abu Ja'far al-Tusi, *Wasael ush-Shia* by Shaikh al-Hur al-Aamili, and *Bihar al-Anwar* by Allama Majlesi.

Shooting Themselves in the Foot

The blunders of the Sunni and Shiite scholars do not stop there. Numerous Sunni and Shiite subsects and orders already prefer volumes of books to the Quran, let alone merely placing them on equal footing with the Quran. Various collections of hearsay stories that advocate for medieval Arab culture, superstitious traditions and ignorance in the name of Muhammad and his companions are formally considered as the secondary authority besides the Quran. In fact, they have become the primary source of sectarian teachings. Sunni and Shiite scholars who consider Hadith and Sunna to be divine revelation have already accepted gibberish as absurd as the one attributed to Musaylamatul Kazzab. Furthermore, the scholars of the Hanefite sect have asserted that Hadith (hearsay attributed to Muhammad) can abrogate verses of the Quran. For instance, according to the Hanefite sect, verses 2:180,240; 4:11-12; 4:15; 4:23-24; 5:106; and 6:145 were abrogated by Hadith. (Hungry goats or chickens are not used as reasons for this category of abrogation, though).

Sunni and Shiite scholars who strive hard to defend the Quran's unique and inimitable status have waged a holy war against the absurd statement attributed to Musaylama—yes, the same scholars—do not hesitate to accept the hearsay collection of Abu Davud, who ridiculed the Quranic verse 52:34, and attributed the following lie to the Prophet Muhammad:

> Utitul Qurana wa mislahu
>
> Translation:
>
> I am given the Quran and also (revelation) similar to it.[47]

Those Sunni scholars who noticed the blemish created by Abu Davud's assertion of SIMILAR literature besides the Quran —and could not dare to discard it by surgery— have tried various cosmetic interpretations to cover it.

In brief, the Quranic challenge must have a criterion that separate the grain from the chaff. The Quran cannot be defended by the heroism of Don Quixotes whose arguments make even the crows laugh.

6
Numerology vs Mathematics

"Abstruse calculations, geometric forms and algebraic terms, unusual correlations –all have been used to adorn the silliest drivel... Many more vignettes illustrating this and other simple logical errors might be cited, but the point is clear enough: both innumeracy and defective logic provide a fertile soil for the growth of pseudoscience." ~ John Allen Paulos[48]

Whenever scientists and intellectuals hear about the mathematical structure of the Quran, the majority of them consider it another example of numerology without further study. The abundance of silly numerological speculations throughout religious history coupled with the vicious laws and ignorant superstitions practiced in the name of Islam might justify this prejudice. However, the mathematical structure of the Quran is far from numerology, and the teaching of the Quran is far from the theology and practice of contemporary Muslims. Therefore, the intricate mathematical structure of the Quran will eventually draw the attention of mathematicians and intellectuals.

Assume that you were an astronomer living hundreds of years ago in a country where astrologer charlatans were abundant. If you wanted to share your scientific observations and opinion on galaxies, stars and solar system, perhaps you would get frustrated of being repeatedly confused with astrologers. Whenever you uttered the word "stars" or "galaxies," what would you do if the intellectuals ignored you and said, "We do not have time to listen to more balderdash"?

The similarity between the mathematical structure of the Quran and numerology is like the similarity between astronomy and astrology or between chemistry and alchemy. Before introducing the mathematical structure of the Quran and other "miraculous" claims connected with numbers, I will provide some information about numerology to distinguish the two.

Numerology

Circa 500 years before the birth of Jesus, Greek mathematician Pythagoras and his follower Plato believed that numbers contained the mysteries of Nature. This number mysticism about numbers appears in various versions in many religions and cultures. Annemarie Schimmel, professor at the Department of Indo-Muslim Culture at Harvard University, summarizes the basic principles of numerology under three points:

1. Numbers influence the character of things that are ordered by them.
2. Thus, the number becomes a mediator between the Divine and the created world.
3. It follows that if one performs operations with numbers, these operations also work upon the things connected with the numbers used.[49]

Though most natural phenomena from the structure of the atom to the movements of galaxies can be explained in terms of mathematical equations, numerologists see the relationship as topsy-turvy. Instead of regarding numbers as the symbolic representation of the order in the universe, they attribute numbers independent powers that cause events in the universe. This reverse perspective that confuses cause with effect reaches the zenith of absurdity by claiming the power of *arbitrarily* chosen numbers in human life.

For example, each Alphabet letter has a numerical order. In the English for A is 1, for B is 2 and for Z is 26. By adding the numbers corresponding to the position of each letter, numerologists find the numerical value of each word or name. Here is the numerical value of my name in English Alphabet:

E	D	I	P		Y	U	K	S	E	L
5	4	9	16		25	21	11	19	5	12

The sum of these numbers is 127 and by adding the digits of this number, $1 + 2 + 7$, numerologists, by leaving out the place values, get a single digit 1 as my number. There are millions of criminals, murderers, and illiterate people as well as Nobel-prize winner scientists, geniuses, and historical figures whose name will end up with the same number as mine.

Well, according to the 29-lettered Turkish alphabet (the country of my birth), my personal number will differ. I will have different numbers according to the Kurdish alphabet (my ethnic origin), or the Arabic alphabet (the original language of my first name). Determining the right alphabet for my children, who have an Iranian mother and are born in America, might pose a daunting task for numerologists. Well, not really. I am sure they will come up with a set of arbitrary rules to determine a particular alphabet and number.

By assigning a single digit number to every person in the world, numerologists put BILLIONS of human beings, including those who lived in the past and those who will be born in the future, into NINE boxes that would unveil every person's character, romance, luck, and destiny. (Astrologists, on the other hand, have 12 boxes!). In her book, *Numerology*, Dr. Jordan pontificates:

> "The instructions given in this book can be relied upon and used with full confidence as a means of character analysis, or lightening the burdens of those who have not found their true way to success and happiness."[50]

Want to attain success and happiness? Find your numerological box! Each number is assigned a set of "positive" and "negative" meanings. Those who are credulous enough not to question the validity of such assertions will live their lives not in accordance with reality but according to delusions and wishful thinking. The numerologist invites her reader to do the following:

> "Play the game of NUMBER OBSERVATION. Become number-conscious. Notice numbers as you go about your daily affairs. You will be astonished how much they influence your daily life. Observe the number of your house, your place of business, your automobile, your bank account, your telephone, your age, and the day you were born. The Romance in your name is in the letters and numbers that are written there." [51]

Another popular method of turning you to a single digit number is by adding the numbers of the month, day and year in your birthday. A person whose birth date is 7/19/1970 will get the sum of 1996. This number is reduced to a single digit: $1 + 9 + 9 + 6 = 25$, and $2 + 5 = 7$. His "life path" is 7, and it is "generally regarded as being the most important number in numerology, because it reveals our purpose in life. Most people have little idea of what they should be doing with their lives, and knowledge of this number, on its own, can transform lives."[52] In other words, according to the numerologist, those who are confused about their purpose in life are the targeted market.

John Allen Paulos, the author of *Innumeracy*, which I highly recommend, pulls our attention to the non-falsifiability of numerological speculations:

> "Numerology, especially in its soothsaying and divinatory aspect, is in many ways a typical pseudoscience. It makes predictions and claims that are almost impossible to falsify since an alternative formulation consistent with what happened is always easy to dream up. Based on number, it has a limitless complexity to engage the ingenuity and creativity of its adherents, without burdening them with the need for validation or testing. Its expressions of equality are generally used to corroborate some existing doctrine, and little if any effort is expended to construct counter-examples…

> "Still, if one subtracts all the superstitious elements from the subject, there's something appealing about the small residue that remains. Its purity (just numbers and letters) and tabula-rasa quality (like a Rorschach test) allow one maximum scope for seeing what one wants to see, for connecting what one wants to connect, for providing at the very least a limitless source of mnemonic devices."[53]

You might wonder why so many people who live in a rational world and make somehow rational choices when they drive their cars or run their businesses are fooled by numerologists, psychics, spiritual healers, and all other swindlers.54 I will list few reasons why daily horoscopes or numerology may impress people:

- **Complexity of human character and relationships**. Without finding "your number" by the prescribed numerological rules, try to find "your number" by reading the meaning of each number. To your surprise you will find that each description partially fits you. Well, if you happen to find a particular number more descriptive than others, then go and calculate your numerological number. You will have 1 in 9 chance that your description will be the same as the description for the number! If you first find "your number" and then read or listen to numerologists about the meaning of that number in relation to your character and destiny, you will most likely be impressed by the accuracy of the description! This is not due to the power of numbers, but due to our weakness of suggestibility and selectivity.

- **General statements and their applicability**. Daily horoscopes or character descriptions are general and vague statements which can fit almost any person. Try this: Instead of reading the horoscope corresponding to your zodiac, ask someone to cut off the zodiac titles and then clip them out of the newspaper or magazine. Mix and put them in a box. After a week, try to find your own horoscope among the last week's twelve readings. The reading that you picked after a week has 1 in 12 chances to match your zodiac!

- **Ignoring the errors**. We are pretty biased towards what we believe or tend to believe. The predictions that do not come true are easily forgotten and ignored, but any prediction, regardless of how general and vague it may be and how insignificant and trivial it may be, is registered and remembered by the believer.

- **Self-fulfilling prophecies**. A significant power of numerology and astrology comes from its self-fulfilling prophecy. If you believe in a prediction such as, "your husband is cheating you and you will find new romance in your life," you will most likely become suspicious of your husband and you will start fighting with him. This might really harm your relationship and you might end up with a new relationship, that might turn into your worst nightmare. I suspect that some believers who have many failures in their lives will even look for a frog in their backyard if their zodiac reads "A frog will lead you to your future romance."

- **Mystery**. Numerology provides hope, a sense of mystery, and spirituality for those who have none.

Numerology in the Religious Arena

The Pythagorean numerology claimed that every number possesses a unique metaphysical meaning and character, and it was later developed by Plotinus and Egyptian Philo and reaching its zenith in the Middle Ages with Kabbalah, the Jewish mysticism.

In the Muslim world, numerology emerged with an Iranian underground cult called Ihvan-i Safa, later transforming to Ismailiyya (The Seveners). This cult believed in the importance of the numbers 7 and 12 and their role in the order of Imams (religious leaders). It added a numerical color, besides the color of blood, to the ferocious war among various Muslim sects regarding issues of leadership. Political rebellion was thus supported by numerical speculations.

The use of numerology continued in Iran with the Bahai religion. The delusional mullah Bahaullah, who claimed to be an incarnate god in 1863, sanctified the numbers 9 and 19, and even created his own calendar by dividing a year to 19 months each consisting of 19 days. The remaining 4 days were called "stolen days." Unfortunately, this peaceful sect or religion became the subject of persecution by the dominant Shiite sect, *Isna Ashariyya* (The Twelvers), another sect named with a number. However, numerology still continued to attract a small group of Muslims. For example, the *Hurufi* sect, founded by another Iranian cleric Fadl-Allah Astarabadi in 14th century, never received the approval of the majority. The word *Hurufi* became synonymous with schism and diversion from orthodoxy.

Despite the general aversion towards numerology, Muslims have paid special attention to certain numbers such as 7, 40, and 99. For instance, a personally selected collection of 40 Hadith (sayings attributed to Muhammad) became a fashion among Muslim clerics of the medieval era. The famous Sufi Imam Al-Ghazali, divided his book *Ihyai Ulumid Din* (*Renaissance of Religious Sciences*) into 40 chapters, hoping to benefit from its fame and mystical power.[55] By increasing the number of beads to 99, the adoption of beads from Christianity became an easy task.

In Christendom, on the other hand, the numbers 3 and 7 are consecrated, while the numbers 13 and 666 are demonized. Many Christians still associate 13 with bad luck because of the 13th disciple who betrayed Jesus. Because of Revelation 13:18, many Christians associate 666 with the Antichrist. Phillip Davis and Reuben Hersh, in their outstanding book, *The Mathematical Experience*, provide the following information:

> "One of the ways numerological mysticism defines itself is through the art of gematria (the word itself is derived from "geometry"). Gematria is based on the fact that the classic alphabets of Latin, Greek, and Hebrew normally have numerical equivalents. In its simpler form, gematria

85

equates words with equivalent numbers and interprets the verbal equivalents."

"Here is an example from the period of Frederick II. The name 'Innocentius Papa' (Pope Innocent IV) has the numerical equivalent 666. This is the "Number of the Beast" of Revelations 13:18. Hence, Innocentius Papa equals the Antichrist. (Frederic was violently antipope.)"[56]

The Guinness Book of Numbers contains interesting and entertaining information about numbers, especially the number 666.

"The famous (or infamous) 'Number of the Beast' is mentioned in the Bible (Revelation 13:18). There have been many attempts to interpret it, and it has featured in several literary works, notably Tolstoy's War and Peace. Many modern scholars are inclined to the view that the precise reference of the number was to the Emperor Nero. The Book of Revelation was probably written near the end of the first century AD, soon after the death of Nero (in AD 68), and if number-values are assigned to the letters the two Hebrew words that mean 'Emperor Nero', these add up to 666. The fact that the apocalyptic number appears as 616 in some early versions of the text can similarly be justified, for if Nero's name is written in the Latin manner, without the final 'n', which had a value of 50, then the tally is accurate on this count also. It is possible to juggle number-values with the letters of their names, too, to produce the original 'beast,' and this has been done to make 666 fit Trajan, Galigula, Luther, Muhammad, Napoleon and many others."[57]

Surely, the Christian 666 is open for every imaginable speculation. Recently, Bill Gates and the US Dollar became the popular candidates to deserve to be stamped by the number of the "beast." So much for the "mystery" of 666.

There are, however, serious evidence that the original text of the Old and New Testament used gematria and gematrization of a few Biblical words and verses reduces the role of chance drastically.

"Gematria goes back a long way, Its first appearance in literature was c. 200 A.D., though it is possible that its practice goes back much further. For example, in Genesis 14:14, we are told that Abram took his servants, three hundred and eighteen of them, off to rescue his brother and then in 15:2 learn that the name of his steward was Eliezer. The value of "Eliezer" is 318. This may be coincidence, but more likely is gematria."[58]

I would like to quota a passage from *Theomatics*, one of the best books on the numerical aspect of the Bible. Though many of the claims in the book are anecdotal, arbitrary and even manipulated, some, as the example below, are interesting,:

"One of the most fascinating passages of Scripture is John 21:11, wherein the disciples go fishing, and 'Simon Peter went up, and drew the net to land, full of great fishes, a hundred and fifty-three; and although there were so many, the net was not being torn.' This number 153 has taxed the ingenuity and minds of some of the greatest Bible students over the centuries. All have felt that there must be something deeply significant and important about this number...

"But the most important word possible related to this story is the word for fishes in Greek, which has a theomatic value of 1,224, or 153 x 8. Fishes 153 x 8 (1,224). ... Let's not stop here, but move on to the next most important feature, which we find in the story of John 21:11. The net, which actually caught the 153 fishes, has been commonly accepted as being typical of the kingdom of God. It also has a theomatic value of 1,224 or 153 x8. The net 153 x 8 (1,224)."[59]

Before going forward on this topic, I will quota an anonymous reviewer's comment on the second volume of *Theomatics*, posted at Amazon.com:

"I read this book because I was interested in the bible code phenomenon and wondered what other kinds of numerology was applied to the bible. What I found was far different from the bible code.

"The original bible code paper was published in a peer-reviewed journal. Because it had to follow certain academic and mathematical conventions, expert mathematicians were able to dissect the bible code claims and prove they are false. This destroyed the credibility of the bible code. But at least the bible code had the merit of being 'falsifiable'.

"Theomatics, on the other hand, does not present any clear method of finding numerical patterns. It is all very ad hoc and there is no serious attempt at a statistical experiment, at least not in a format that would be accepted by any reputable scientific journal. Therefore, theomatics belongs much more to fringe mathematics and pseudoscience than the bible code, which was simply incorrect mathematics presented in a more rigorous style.

"If the author really wants to be taken seriously, he should learn more about how statistical experiments are set up, and then design an experiment using a priori rules which do not allow any wiggle room such as was found in the bible code.

"In the meantime, the mathematical judgement on this book is that it is yet another example of pseudoscience in the service of religious faith."[60]

The examples presented in the book initially look impressive; however, after a closer look it becomes evident that the authors select verses among hundreds similar ones without justification and then they pick phrases or incomplete fragments from those verses without consistent rule or pattern. Basically, they continue adding the numerical values of letters until they add up to a multiple of 37, or 111 or any number of their choice.[61] Using the same method, one should find many similar examples from any book, especially if there is additional flexibility in spelling and calculation.

The second chapter of the book provides numerous clues about the arbitrariness of their methodology. For instance, we learn that words have "four possible spelling",[62] and the language is "extremely flexible."[63] These are not anecdotal but endemic problems in their so-called *Theomatics*. We also learn about the role of *sometimes* in the production of amazing numerical miracles: "the only allowable variable in theomatics is sometimes to eliminate the article altogether."[64] The role of *sometimes* is understated since this *sometimes* is almost always responsible for all the numerical illusions. The authors sometimes eliminate articles, sometimes eliminate words and phrases. All these spelling choices, flexibilities and inconsistencies allow the authors to find whatever they pray for. The authors, however, are very confident in their findings:

> "What and amazing thing! God took the languages of the ancient
> Hebrews and the common Greek people of Jesus' day, and thus
> constructed His entire Word with an intricate mathematical design.
> Everything had to fit together perfectly."

> "All of the computers in the world working together could not even begin
> to construct the design you are about to see demonstrated in this book.
> And even the computers could do it, they would have to simultaneously
> bring out all of the spiritual truth and meaning of the Bible. Then, to top
> it all of, the languages would have to make sense grammatically. Only
> God could accomplish a feat like this. Praise His name!"[65]

If there was such an "amazing thing" in the any Greek version, I, for one, would not question the integrity of the version picked by the authors. I would not blame them for picking one of the many versions of the Bible. The questions regarding the textual integrity of the Bible would be resolved in favor of the version picked by our authors. Unfortunately, their work shows that the excitement and trust of the authors is premature and misplaced.[66]

These false claims serve none but Satan, the master of delusion and deception. The unsubstantiated claims of these and other innumerate religious zealots regarding the Bible and the Quran create suspicion, negative attitude, and occasionally insurmountable prejudice among intelligent people against the possibility of finding truly amazing mathematical patterns in those books. Most likely, some of those who are disgusted by those delusional claims, will rush to use this very paragraph against me and this book, without carefully studying and comprehending the evidences presented here. This is not new:

26:0   In the name of God, the Gracious, the Compassionate.
26:1   T9S60M40
26:2   These are the signs of the manifest/clarifying book.
26:3   Perhaps you are grieving yourself that they do not acknowledge.
26:4   If We wish, We could send down for them from the heavens a sign, to
        which they would bend their necks in humility.
26:5   Not a new reminder comes to them from the Gracious, except that they
        turn away from it.

26:6   They have denied, thus the news will come to them of what they used to ridicule.

One of the most delicious books on numerology belongs to Underwood Doodley, a mathematician who has written numerous popular books on "crank mathematics." Though Dr. Doodley acts like an overzealous prosecutor when he uses every hearsay to convict Pythagoras in *Numerology or, What Pythagoras Wrought*, he provides fantastic examples of numerology and trashes them with satirical remarks. After quoting examples of numerological gibberish extensively from a publication by the so-called American Institute of Man (AIM), he expresses his frustration with those who are impressed by them:

> "The reason that I am presenting so much absurdity in such detail is to demonstrate that a large number of absurdities do not combine to create something that may be true. This is obvious, but it is overlooked by people who say, about pyramidology, Stonehengery, or some similar numerology. 'But there is so much here! It can't be by accident! There has to be something behind it.' No, there does not have to be anything behind it. Nonsense piled upon nonsense does not make sense."[67]

Since Pythagoras, many quacks have taken advantage of the popularity of numerology and innumeracy of people, and abused mathematical properties of numbers and their relationship to exploit the credulous. Many made fortunes by using numbers to cast and break spells, tell fortunes, and design amulets.

Magic Squares and Amulets

After learning the merits of the Indian numerical system in the 10th century, Arabs abandoned the order of its Arabic alphabet, Abjad (ABJD) or Gematria, which was used by Arabs during the time of Muhammad as a numbering system.[68] Nevertheless, numerologists, eager to take advantage of the credulous, used the original order of the Arabic alphabet and the corresponding numerical system. Although the abuse of Abjad created a negative association between the ancient numerical system and witchcraft, its use prevented it from becoming extinct from public memory.

Using simple mathematical sequences, charlatans impressed the mathematically illiterate masses, thereby turning numerology into a lucrative business. Magic squares written by religious figures, folded in triangles, and wrapped with waxed fabrics were sold as a panacea for all kinds of individual problems—from sickness to marital problems, from jealousy to protection from accidents.

To keep their business, numerologists added some verses from the Quran to their amulets. The spice of popular religious symbols has always been an efficient promotional tactic. Ironically, verses were taken out of context, with most lacking even a remote relevance to the problems hoped to be cured! Illiterate men, in fear of losing their jobs, imitated the Arabic calligraphy with illegible scribbling in their amulets. To produce a sense of mystery—and in the case of illiterate amulet-makers, to keep their scribbling from scrutiny—clients were firmly warned not to open their amulets. Otherwise, they would be eternally cursed.

The most commonly used magic square had 3x3 boxes, and it contained the first nine digits in such an order that all the horizontal, vertical and diagonal lines produce the sum of 15. Muslim numerologists used the Abjad system or the gematrical values of alphabet letters (gematria) in their squares.[69]

Below is the most commonly used magic square in Islamic tradition, which according to Chinese mythology was first witnessed by a wise monarch, emperor Yu, on the back of a divine turtle 2200 years before Jesus!

د	ط	ب
4	9	2
ج	ه	ز
3	5	7
ح	ا	و
8	1	6

The harmony among numbers based on the peculiar mathematical properties of each number has drawn the attention of the curious since Pythagoras.[70] For instance, the following symmetry created by the mathematical property of number 9 is quite attractive!

$$
\begin{array}{rcl}
1 \times 9 + 2 &=& 11 \\
12 \times 9 + 3 &=& 111 \\
123 \times 9 + 4 &=& 1111 \\
1234 \times 9 + 5 &=& 11111 \\
12345 \times 9 \mid 6 &=& 111111 \\
123456 \times 9 + 7 &=& 1111111 \\
1234567 \times 9 + 8 &=& 11111111 \\
12345678 \times 9 + 9 &=& 111111111 \\
123456789 \times 9 + 10 &=& 1111111111 \\
\end{array}
$$

Dr. Dudley, in the chapter on The Law of Small Numbers, shares the following examples, which are entertaining and informative as well:

"Professor Guy says that the Law is an enemy of mathematical discovery, since 'supecifial similarities spawn spurious statements', and 'capricious coincidences cause careless conjectures'. It can also work the other way, because 'early exceptions eclipse eventual essentials', and 'initial irregularities inhibit incisive intuition'.

Apt alliteration's artful aid nothwithstanding, an example is given by alternating sums of factorials:

$3! - 2! + 1! = 5$

$4! - 3! + 2! - 1! = 19$

$5! - 4! + 3! - 2! + 1! = 101$

$6! - 5! + 4! - 3! + 2! - 1! = 619$

$7! - 6! + 5! - 4! + 3! - 2! + 1! = 4421$

$8! - 7! + 6! - 5! + 4! - 3! + 2! - 1! = 35899$

The sums, 5, 19, 101, 619, 4421, and 35899 are all primes. The question is, can this go on? Anyone with experience in the ways of prime numbers would conclude that it could not, and that would be correct since the next case is:

$9! - 8! + 7! - 6! + 5! - 4! + 3! - 2! + 1! = 326981 = 79 \times 4139$

Among small integers, primes are common so it is not a surprise that a collection of eight odd integers happens to contain only primes. It is not likely, but it is not a surprise. The chance that eight odd integers selected at random from small integers like those in the example are prime is something like $(.3)^8 = .00006561$. This is quite small, but when you consider the vastness of the universe of eight-integer sequences, it is inevitable that occasionally a sequence with nothing but primes in it will occur. Coinciedences must happen. This is a fact that numerologists often choos to ignore.[71]

People do not only abuse numbers; they abuse literature too. In fact the abuse of literary eloquence and articulation is more common. In our recent history we witnessed the power of prose, poetry, and slogans to mobilize masses in the name of communism, fascism, nationalism, religion, or patriotism. Clever play with words and symbols has created a modern multi-billion dollar advertising and public relations industry. Politicians, as masters of double-speak, manipulate events and laws in the interest of privileged groups or lobbies. Every tool, idea and concept is the subject of abuse, be it religion or atheism, capitalism or socialism, numbers or letters. Thus, dismissing the numerical system of the Quran out of prejudice just because numbers have been abused by charlatans is inconsistent and hasty generalization.

7
Numerosemantical Harmony

"The vision of Descartes became the new spirit. Two generations later, the mathematician and philosopher Leibnitz talked about the 'characteristica universalis.' This was the dream of a universal method whereby all human problems, whether of science, law, or politics, could be worked out rationally, systematically, by logical computation. In our generation, the visions of Descartes and Leibnitz are implemented on every hand. Cartesianism calls for the primacy of world mathematization." ~ Philip J. Davis & Reuben Hersh [72]

In 1967 an Egyptian scholar Abdurrahman Nawfal discovered an interesting numerical harmony in the frequency of certain Quranic words. Some synonym and antonym words and phrases had equal frequencies in the Quran. This mathematical and linguistic symmetry in some cases involved the physical world. We can interpret this discovery as a mental preparation for the discovery of Code 19 in 1974 by another Egyptian scholar, Dr. Rashad Khalifa.

The following few examples of mathematical harmony, I think will suffice to demonstrate that the Quran is a book of mathematics as much as it is a book of literature. By witnessing and examining Code 19, you will come to your own decision whether a piece of literature with such an intricate mathematical system can be designed by humans.

The Word MONTH (ŞaHR)

There are 12 months in a solar year.[73] This reflects the astronomical fact that the Moon makes twelve complete rotations around the Earth while the earth completes one rotation around the Sun. The Quran refers to this astronomical fact:

> 9:36 "The count of the months with **God** is twelve months in **God**'s book the day He created the heavens and the earth; four of them are restricted. This is the correct system; so do not wrong yourselves in them. Fight those who set up partners collectively as they fight you collectively. Know that **God** is with the righteous."

If we search the Quran from its beginning to its end, we will see that the singular form of the word ŞaHR (month) occurs exactly 12 times. Below is the list of chapters and verses where the word *ŞaHR* (month), *aŞHuR/ŞuHuR* (months) and *ŞaHRayn* (two months) occur.

Frequency of the Word Month, Months, and Two Months		
1.	2:185	*Month (Shar)*
2.	2:185	
3.	2:194	
4.	2:194	
5.	2:217	
6.	5:2	
7.	5:97	
8.	9:36	
9.	34:12	
10.	34:12	
11.	46:15	
12.	97:3	
13.	2:197	*Months (aŞHuR/ŞuHuR)*
14.	2:226	
15.	2:234	
16.	9:2	
17.	9:5	
18.	65:4	
19.	9:36	
20.	4:92	Two Months *ŞaHRayn*
21.	58:4	

The Word YEAR (*SaNA*)

The occurrence of the word *Sana* in the Quran in singular form is exactly 7 times and in plural form, *Sinyn*, is 12 times, which add up to 19, equaling the number of years in the astronomical event called the Meton Cycle. Every 19 years, the Earth, Moon, and Sun line up. Below, you will find information about the Metonic Cycle from Wikipedia:

"The Greek astronomer Meton of Athens observed that a period of 19 tropical years is almost exactly equal to 235 synodic (lunar) months, and rounded to a

93

full day's count of 6940 days. The difference between the two periods (of 19 tropical years and 235 synodic months) is only 2 hours.

"Taking a year to be 1/19th of this 6940-day cycle gives a year length of 365 + 1/4 + 1/76 days (the unrounded cycle is much more accurate), which is slightly more than 12 synodic months. To keep the 12-month lunar year in pace with the solar year, an intercalary 13th month would have to be added on seven occasions during the nineteen-year period. Meton introduced a formula for intercalation in circa 432 BC.

"The cycle's most significant contemporary use is to help in flight planning (trajectory calculations and launch window analysis) for lunar spacecraft missions as well as serving as the basis for the Hebrew calendar's 19 year cycle. Another use is in computers, the calculation of the date of the Christian feast of Easter."

Here is the list of verses where the word Year (*Sana*) is mentioned. The first 7 are in singular form:

The Word DAY (*YaWM*)

How many days are there in a year? If you ask this question to an astronomer, you may get several different numbers with lengthy fractions. In our daily lives, we count 365 days in a year for practical reasons. This is the most accurate approximation of the number of days in a solar year. Interestingly, the number 365 is exactly the frequency of the singular form of the word *YaWM* (day) in the Quran. There are 365 days in nature and there are 365 "days" in the scripture! If the creator of nature and scripture are the same God, then there is no surprise to find such a harmony between the mathematical structure of the scripture and the events of nature.

Certainly, those who are determined to deny a mathematical structure in the Quran will not be impressed by this mathematical and literal harmony. They will try every possible way to deny the existence of 365 days in a year.

Years ago, I had a public argument with a Muslim scholar on Code 19. Like all his ilk, he was trying every possible argument to blind himself to the mathematical design. At

Frequency of the word Year (*Sana*) and Years (*Sinyn*)		
1.	2:96	Singular
2.	5:26	Singular
3.	22:47	Singular
4.	29:14	Singular
5.	32:5	Singular
6.	46:15	Singular
7.	70:4	Singular
8.	7:130	Plural
9.	10:5	Plural
10.	12:42	Plural
11.	12:47	Plural
12.	17:12	Plural
13.	18:11	Plural
14.	18:25	Plural
15.	20:40	Plural
16.	23:112	Plural
17.	26:18	Plural
18.	26:205	Plural
19.	30:4	Plural

one point, I told him, "Since it seems that you are not able to comprehend the Code 19, I will just ask you a question. Please open the index of the Quran,[74] and look at the frequencies of the words *Month* and *Day* How many do you see?" He objected: "There are not 365 days in a year, but there are 365 days and six hours in a year. Where are the six hours?"

There was no reason to continue the argument. I did not tell him that "day" and "hour" are two different units and we are counting the frequency of the word "day," not "hour." I did not tell him that "day" and "hour" are categorically different units, since the first is determined by an astronomical event, while the other is determined by an arbitrary human convention. I knew that as a college-educated scholar he was well aware of those differences. I wanted to end our public argument with a closing remark: "Perhaps God has made a year a few hours more than 365 days to leave the insincere a few hours of loopholes in order to deprive themselves from witnessing one of the greatest miracles!"

Sunni and Shiite scholars are allergic to numbers, especially the number 19. They consider God capable of authoring literary work in human languages, but incapable of communicating with us through mathematics, a much more precise and universal language. One of the most common objections of orthodox Muslims to the frequency of the word "month" and "day" in the Quran is the following argument: "The timing of rituals in Islam are determined by the lunar calendar, not the solar calendar. There are approximately 354 days, not 365 days in an Islamic year." This objection ignores the fact that it is God who created the universe, and it is also God who designed the rotation of the Earth, the Moon, and the Sun. The word "day" does not denote the relationship of the Earth with the Moon; it denotes the relationship of the Earth with the Sun. Daylight and night, the two components of "day," are astronomical phenomena that relate to the position of the Sun and the rotation of the Earth around its axis. Therefore, it is more appropriate to pick the solar year for an event involving the Sun.

Below is the list of verses where the word *YaWM* (day) occurs. I encourage you to check them randomly with the Quranic text:

The List of Verses Where the Word Day (*YaWM*) Occurs:

1.	1:4	49.	5:109	97.	11:98	145.	19:38
2.	2:8	50.	5:119	98.	11:99	146.	19:39
3.	2:48	51.	6:12	99.	11:103	147.	19:85
4.	2:62	52.	6:15	100.	11:103	148.	19:95
5.	2:85	53.	6:22	101.	11:105	149.	20:59
6.	2:113	54.	6:73	102.	12:54	150.	20:64
7.	2:123	55.	6:73	103.	12:92	151.	20:100
8.	2:126	56.	6:93	104.	14:18	152.	20:101
9.	2:174	57.	6:128	105.	14:31	153.	20:102
10.	2:177	58.	6:141	106.	14:41	154.	20:104
11.	2:212	59.	6:158	107.	14:42	155.	20:124
12.	2:228	60.	7:14	108.	14:44	156.	20:126
13.	2:232	61.	7:32	109.	14:48	157.	21:47
14.	2:249	62.	7:51	110.	15:35	158.	21:104
15.	2:254	63.	7:53	111.	15:36	159.	22:2
16.	2:259	64.	7:59	112.	15:38	160.	22:9
17.	2:259	65.	7:163	113.	16:25	161.	22:17
18.	2:264	66.	7:163	114.	16:27	162.	22:47
19.	2:281	67.	7:167	115.	16:27	163.	22:55
20.	3:9	68.	7:172	116.	16:63	164.	22:69
21.	3:25	69.	8:41	117.	16:80	165.	23:16
22.	3:30	70.	8:41	118.	16:80	166.	23:65
23.	3:55	71.	8:48	119.	16:84	167.	23:100
24.	3:77	72.	9:3	120.	16:89	168.	23:111
25.	3:106	73.	9:18	121.	16:92	169.	23:113
26.	3:114	74.	9:19	122.	16:111	170.	23:113
27.	3:155	75.	9:25	123.	16:124	171.	24:2
28.	3:161	76.	9:29	124.	17:13	172.	24:24
29.	3:166	77.	9:35	125.	17:14	173.	24:37
30.	3:180	78.	9:36	126.	17:52	174.	24:64
31.	3:185	79.	9:44	127.	17:58	175.	25:14
32.	3:194	80.	9:45	128.	17:62	176.	25:17
33.	4:38	81.	9:77	129.	17:71	177.	25:22
34.	4:39	82.	9:99	130.	17:97	178.	25:25
35.	4:59	83.	9:108	131.	18:19	179.	25:26
36.	4:87	84.	10:15	132.	18:19	180.	25:27
37.	4:109	85.	10:28	133.	18:47	181.	25:69
38.	4:136	86.	10:45	134.	18:52	182.	26:38
39.	4:141	87.	10:60	135.	18:105	183.	26:82
40.	4:159	88.	10:92	136.	19:15	184.	26:87
41.	4:162	89.	10:93	137.	19:15	185.	26:88
42.	5:3	90.	11:3	138.	19:15	186.	26135
43.	5:3	91.	11:8	139.	19:26	187.	26:155
44.	5:5	92.	11:26	140.	19:33	188.	26:156
45.	5:14	93.	11:43	141.	19:33	189.	26:189
46.	5:36	94.	11:60	142.	19:33	190.	26:189
47.	5:64	95.	11:77	143.	19:37	191.	27:83
48.	5:69	96.	11:84	144.	19:38	192.	27:87

193.	28:41	243.	39:67	293.	51:13	343.	77:35
194.	28:42	244.	40:15	294.	52:9	344.	77:38
195.	28:61	245.	40:16	295.	52:13	345.	78:17
196.	28:62	246.	40:16	296.	52:46	346.	78:18
197.	28:65	247.	40:17	297.	54:6	347.	78:38
198.	28:71	248.	40:17	298.	54:8	348.	78:39
199.	28:72	249.	40:18	299.	54:19	349.	78:40
200.	28:74	250.	40:27	300.	54:48	350.	79:6
201.	29:13	251.	40:29	301.	55:29	351.	79:35
202.	29:25	252.	40:30	302.	56:50	352.	79:46
203.	29:36	253.	40:32	303.	56:56	353.	80:34
204.	29:55	254.	40:33	304.	57:12	354.	82:15
205.	30:12	255.	40:46	305.	57:12	355.	82:17
206.	30:14	256.	40:49	306.	57:13	356.	82:18
207.	30:43	257.	40:51	307.	57:15	357.	82:19
208.	30:55	258.	40:52	308.	58:6	358.	83:5
209.	30:56	259.	41:19	309.	58:7	359.	83:6
210.	30:56	260.	41:40	310.	58:18	360.	83:11
211.	31:33	261.	41:47	311.	58:22	361.	83:34
212.	32:5	262.	42:7	312.	60:3	362.	85:2
213.	32:25	263.	42:45	313.	60:6	363.	86:9
214.	32:29	264.	42:47	314.	62:9	364.	90:14
215.	33:21	265.	43:39	315.	64:9	365.	101:4
216.	33:44	266.	43:65	316.	64:9		
217.	33:66	267.	43:68	317.	64:9		
218.	34:30	268.	44:10	318.	65:2		
219.	34:40	269.	44:16	319.	66:7		
220.	34:42	270.	44:40	320.	66:8		
221.	35:14	271.	44:41	321.	68:24		
222.	36:54	272.	45:17	322.	68:39		
223.	36:55	273.	45:26	323.	68:42		
224.	36:59	274.	45:27	324.	69:35		
225.	36:64	275.	45:28	325.	70:4		
226.	36:65	276.	45:34	326.	70:8		
227.	37:20	277.	45:35	327.	70:26		
228.	37:21	278.	46:5	328.	70:43		
229.	37:26	279.	46:20	329.	70:44		
230.	37:144	280.	46:20	330.	73:14		
231.	38:16	281.	46:21	331.	73:17		
232.	38:26	282.	46:34	332.	74:9		
233.	38:53	283.	46:35	333.	74:46		
234.	38:78	284.	50:20	334.	75:1		
235.	38:79	285.	50:22	335.	75:6		
236.	38:81	286.	50:30	336.	76:7		
237.	39:13	287.	50:34	337.	76:10		
238.	39:15	288.	50:41	338.	76:11		
239.	39:24	289.	50:42	339.	76:27		
240.	39:31	290.	50:42	340.	77:12		
241.	39:47	291.	50:44	341.	77:13		
242.	39:60	292.	51:12	342.	77:14		

The plural forms of the word *YAWM* (day), that is *AYYAM* and *YAWMAYN* occur exactly 30 times in the Quran, which is the approximate number of days in a month.

We find six different forms of the word *YAWM* mentioned in the Quran. Here are the different forms of *YAWM* listed by *Mu'jam-ul Mufahras Lielfaz-il Quran-il Kareem*, followed by their frequencies in the Quran. They all add up to a number divisible by 19; we will see its role in subsequent chapters:

Frequencies of the Derivatives of the Word *YaWM* (Day)	
YaWM (day)	**365**
YaWM-KuM (your-day)	5
YaWM-HuM (their-day)	5
AYaM (days)	27
YaWM-aYN (two-days)	3
YaWM-YZeN (that-day)	70
	475 (19x25)

These three examples regarding the meaning of words Month, Day and Days, and their frequency in the Quran, demonstrate that the Quran is not an ordinary book; it is a numerically designed book.

Frequencies of Days (*Ayyam*) and Two Days (*YaWMayn*)		
1	2:80	Days *Ayyam*
2	2:184	
3	2:184	
4	2:185	
5	2:196	
6	2:203	
7	3:24	
8	3:41	
9	3:140	
10	5:89	
11	7:54	
12	10:3	
13	10:102	
14	11:7	
15	11:65	
16	14:5	
17	22:28	
18	25:59	
19	32:4	
20	34:18	
21	41:10	
22	41:16	
23	45:14	
24	50:38	
25	57:4	
26	69:7	
27	69:24	
28	2:203	Two Days *YaWMayn*
29	41:9	
30	41:12	

The Word Moon (*QaMaR*)

If we check the frequency of the word *Qamar* (Moon) in the Quran, we will find that it is exactly 27, which corresponds to the Sidereal month. This corresponds to the number of days in a sidereal month.

Below is a brief information on two most commonly used reference points in calculating the Moon's revolution around the earth.

Sidereal Month: The period of the Moon's orbit as defined with respect to the celestial sphere (of the fixed stars, nowadays the International Celestial Reference Frame (ICRF)) is known as a sidereal month because it is the time it takes the Moon to return to a given position among the stars (Latin: sidus): 27.321661 days (27 d 7 h 43 min 11.5 s). This type of month has been observed among cultures in the Middle East, India, and China in the following way: they divided the sky into 27 or 28 lunar mansions, one for each day of the month, identified by the prominent star(s) in them.

Synodic Month: This is the average period of the Moon's revolution with respect to the sun. The synodic month is responsible for the moon's phases... This longer period is called the synodic month. Because of perturbations in the orbits of the Earth and Moon, the actual time between lunations may range from about 29.27 to about 29.83 days. The long-term average duration is 29.530589 days (29 d 12 h 44 min 2.9 s). The synodic month is used in the Metonic cycle.[75]

Moon (QaMaR)	
1.	6:77
2.	6:96
3.	7:54
4.	10:5
5.	12:4
6.	13:2
7.	14:33
8.	16:12
9.	21:33
10.	22:18
11.	25:61
12.	29:61
13.	31:29
14.	35:13
15.	36:39
16.	36:40
17.	39:5
18.	41:37
19.	41:37
20.	54.1
21.	55:5
22.	71:16
23.	74:32
24.	75:8
25.	75:9
26.	84:18
27.	91:2

Here is a list of the average length of the various astronomical lunar months. These are not constant, so a first-order (linear) approximation of the secular change is provided: Valid for the epoch J2000.0 (1 January 2000 12:00 TT)[76]:

Anomalistic month	$27.554549878 - 0.000000010390 \times y$ days
Sidereal month	$27.321661547 + 0.000000001857 \times y$ days
Tropical month	$27.321582241 + 0.000000001506 \times y$ days
Draconic month	$27.212220817 + 0.000000003833 \times y$ days
Synodic month	$29.530588853 + 0.000000002162 \times y$ days

Nusemantics or Mathematical Harmony

Not only is the correlated frequency of some words related to their actual references in nature, there are also interesting examples of symmetry between the frequencies of semantically related words in the Quran. In my Turkish book, *Kuran En Büyük Mucize (Quran the Greatest Miracle)* (1983-1987), I wrote a section dedicated to this issue. I shared with my Turkish readers the observations of Abdur Razaq Nawfal, the original discoverer of this numerical harmony, and also the additional discoveries I made while I was in Turkish prisons. Decades later, Dr. Caner Taslaman wrote a comprehensive book on the scientific aspect of the Quran that dedicated a larger section to these nusemantics.[77]

The frequencies of the following words reflect the meaning of the words, or their semantic relationship (NumericoSemantics):

Words	Frequency of Both Words	Words
ZuLM (**oppression**)	15	QiSŤ (**justice**)
aYyAM (**days**)	27	QaMaR (**moon**)
ShaMS (**sun**)	33	NUR (**light**)
*YaWM*aizin (**that day**)	70	QiYaMa (**the day of resurrection**)
Shaytan (**satan/pervert**)	88	MaLaK (**angel/controller**)
AMaL (**work**)	108	AJR (**payment**)
DuNYa (**the low world**)	115	AXeRah (**hereafter**)
QALu (**they said**)	332	QUL (**you say**)
The proper names of 26 messengers	512	The derivatives of the word RaSaLa (message, messenger)

Though Nawfal provides numerous examples of this nusemantics harmony, the list is not comprehensive and there occurs problems involving arbitrary matches and contrasts.[78] Therefore, I cannot yet consider these observations as a fully independent Quranic numerical system. Perhaps, through a systematic and more objective approach the problems will get resolved.

Since it was originally discovered by me, it would be in order to elaborate a bit on this last example. In my Turkish book, *Kuran En Büyük Mucize* (1983-1987), following the Sunni conventional misunderstanding, I included the adjective *ahmad* (more praised) of 61:6 to the list as Muhammad's proper name. Following the same Sunni convention I also added the "RaSuL" of the false verse 9:128. With this addition, the sum of frequencies of the names of mesengers equaled to 513 as well as the derivative of the Arabic word RaSaLa, from which the word "RaSuL" (messenger) is derived. The number 513 was very appealing since it was exactly 19x27. Nevertheless, after learning that neither *ahmad* is a proper name nor 9:128 belongs to the Quran, I am directed to settle with 512. Here is the list where the names written in bold are prophet messengers since they were given a new book:[81]

	Proper names of the Messengers	Freq.
1.	**Moses**	136
2.	**Abraham**	69
3.	**Noah**	43
4.	**Lot**	27
5.	**Joseph**	27
6.	Adam	25
7.	**Jesus**	25
8.	**Aaron**	20
9.	**Isac**	17
10.	**Solomon**	17
11.	**Jacob**	16
12.	**David**	16
13.	**Ismael**	12
14.	Shuayb	11
15.	Saleh	9
16.	Hud	7
17.	**Zakariya**	7
18.	**Yahya (John)**	5
19.	**Muhammad**	4
20.	**Job**	4
21.	**Jonah**	4
22.	**Elias**[79]	3
23.	**Idris**	2
24.	Zul-kifl	2
25.	**Elyasa**	2
26.	Luqman	2
	Derivatives of RaSaLa Message/Messenger[80]	512

I should also provide some interesting examples of consistency between Quranic statements and the numerical facts related to the key words in those statements.

Quranic phrase or statement	Frequency
Hasan Oezturk (Öztürk) from Germany observed the following facts: The number of occurrences where the word Sun and Moon are mentioned together equals to the Meton cycle where the Sun, Moon and Earth line up. The only verse where our attention is pulled to the conjunction of Sun and Moon is the 19th joint occurrence and the verse reads: "When the sun and moon are joined together"[82]	**19**
The word *Sana* (Year) occurs 7 times in singular and 12 times in plural form, adding up to 19, which is related to Meton cycle.	$7 + 12 = $ **19**
Saba Samawat (Seven Heavens)	**7**
Sabt (Saturday) + *Sabtihim* (Their Saturday)	$6 + 1 = $ **7**
"The example of Jesus is like Adam"[83]	Adam 25 Jesus 25

8
Over it is Nineteen

"The understanding of mathematics is necessary for a sound grasp of ethics." ~ Socrates

"God created everything by number, weight and measure." ~ Isaac Newton

"God does arithmetic." ~ Karl Friedrich Gauss.

"If there is a God, he's a great mathematician" ~ Paul Dirac

"God exists since mathematics is consistent, and the Devil exists since we cannot prove it." ~ André Weil

The preceding chapter has shown that some specific words in the Quran such as "day" or "days", "month" or "months", and "year" or "years" have numerical harmony with Nature. We also find numerous examples of numerical symmetry among words related semantically. We called this unique literary art of reflecting harmony between numbers, nature and meaning, Nusemantics. These findings are just a few of the examples that significantly suggest that there is something special and inimitable about the Quranic text. This and the chapters that follow discuss a number mentioned in the Quran and what is found as its close mathematical relation to the very structure of the Quran, which could be called "a mathematical miracle"—that remained a secret for long after its revelation, but was unveiled only in recent time. The Quran in several verses refers to a prophecy, to a secret sign that would support its claim to be the word of God:

10:20 They say, "If only a sign was sent down to him from His Lord." Say, "The future is with God, so wait, and I will wait with you."

38:87-88 This is a reminder for the world. And you will certainly find out in awhile.

41:53 We will show them our signs/miracles in the horizons, and within themselves, until they realize that this is the truth. Is your Lord not sufficient as a witness of all things?

The beginning of Chapter 25 refers to the arguments of the opponents who denied the divine nature of the Quran:

25:4-5 Those who disbelieved said, "This is a fabrication that he produced, with the help of some other people." They have uttered a blasphemy and a falsehood. They also said, "Tales from the past that he wrote down; they were dictated to him day and night."

The Awaited Miracle, the Hidden Mathematical Structure

The subsequent verse gives an enigmatic answer to the assertion of those who claimed that the Quran is man-made.

25:6 Say, "This was revealed by the One who knows the SECRET in the heavens and the earth. He is always Forgiving, Compassionate."

How can "knowing the secret" constitute a response to those who assert that the Quran is Muhammad's work? Will the proof or evidence of the divine authorship of the Quran remain a secret known by God alone? Or, will the antagonists be rebuffed by an unraveled divine mystery? If there should be a relationship between the objection and the answer, then we could infer from the above verse that a SECRET would get unveiled to demonstrate the divine nature of the Quran.

The miracle promised throughout the Quran might have been destined to appear after Muhammad's death:

13:38-40 We have sent messengers before you, and we made for them mates and offspring. It was not for a messenger to produce any sign without God's authorization, but for every period there is a decree. God erases and fixes whatever He wills. With Him is the master record. If We show you some of what we promise them, or We let you pass away, your sole mission is to deliver, while it is on us the reckoning.

The last phrase of verse 13:40 quoted above is worth a close attention, The meaning of the phrase becomes clearer after the discovery of Code 19, since the Arabic word *HeSaaB* refers to both the "Day of Judgment, Reckoning" and "numerical computation."[84] The deliberate use of multi-meaning words is very common in the Quran. For instance, the word *AaYAh* occurs 84 times in the Quran and in all occurrences it means "miracle," "sign" or "law." However, its plural form *AaYAat* also means "revelation" or "verses of the Quran." This unique usage equates a minimum of three verses of the Quran with miracle (in Arabic, a different form is used for duality). It also draws our attention to the parallelism between God's signs/laws in the universe and God's revelation in human language: they share the same source and the same truth. In the following verse the plural word "*AaYAat*" is used not to mean "revelation" but "miracle, sign or physical manifestation."

6:158 Are they waiting for the angels to come to them, or your Lord, or some physical manifestations of your Lord? The day this happens, no person will benefit from believing if she did not acknowledge before that, and did not reap the benefits of belief by leading a righteous life. Say, "Keep on waiting; we too are waiting."

Verse 30 of Chapter 74, *Al-Muddathir* (The Hidden/The Secret) of the Quran reads exactly, *Over it is Nineteen*. The entire chapter is about the number 19. Let's read the chapter from the beginning.

74:0	In the name of God, the Gracious, the Compassionate.
74:1	O you hidden one:
74:2	Stand and warn.
74:3	Your Lord glorify.
74:4	Your garments purify.
74:5	Abandon all that is vile.
74:6	Do not be greedy.
74:7	To your Lord be patient.
74:8	So when the trumpet is sounded. [85]
74:9	That will be a very difficult day.
74:10	Upon the ingrates it will not be easy.
74:11	So leave Me alone with the one I have created.
74:12	I gave him abundant wealth.
74:13	Children to bear witness.
74:14	I made everything comfortable for him.
74:15	Then he wishes that I give more.
74:16	No. He was stubborn to Our signs.
74:17	I will exhaust him in climbing.
74:18	He thought and he analyzed.
74:19	So woes to him for how he analyzed.
74:20	Then woe to him for how he analyzed.
74:21	Then he looked.
74:22	Then he frowned and scowled.
74:23	Then he turned away in arrogance.

Prophecy Fulfilled

74:24	He said, "This is nothing but an impressive magic."
74:25	"This is nothing but the words of a human."
74:26	I will cast him in the *Saqar*.
74:27	Do you know what *Saqar* is?
74:28	It does not spare nor leave anything.
74:29	Manifest to all the people. [86]
74:30	On it is nineteen.

The challenge issued for the opponent is fascinating: **nineteen**. Almost all numbers mentioned in the Quran are adjectives in combination with an object. Forty nights, seven heavens, four months, twelve leaders... But here the numerical function of nineteen is emphasized. Nineteen does not define or describe anything. The disbeliever will be subjected to the number nineteen itself. Then, what is the mission or function of this nineteen? Those who tended to understand the meaning of *Saqar* as "hell" naturally understood it as the number of guardians of hell. However, the test or punishment that is described with phrases such as, "difficult task," "precise," and "universal manifestations," is an intellectual one; a mathematical challenge. Indeed, the following verse isolates the number nineteen from the number of angels and lists five goals for it.

> **74:31**   We have made the guardians of the fire to be angels; and We did not make their number except as a test for those who have rejected, to convince those who were given the book, to strengthen the acknowledgment of those who have acknowledged, so that those who have been given the book and those who acknowledge do not have doubt, and so that those who have a sickness in their hearts and the ingrates would say, "What did **God** mean by this example?" Thus **God** misguides whoever/whomever He wishes, and He guides whoever/whomever He wishes. None knows your Lord's soldiers except Him. It is but a reminder for people.

The traditional commentators of the Quran had justifiably grappled with understanding this verse. They thought that disbelievers would be punished by 19 guardians of hell. That was fine. But they could not explain how the number of guardians of hell would increase the appreciation of those who acknowledge the truth and convince the skeptical Christians and Jews regarding the divine nature of the Quran. Finding no answer to this question, they tried some explanations, such as the explanation that the Christians and Jews would acknowledge the Quran since they would see that the number of guardians of hell is also nineteen in their scripture. Witnessing the conversion of Christians and Jews, the faith of Muslims would increase.

This orthodox commentary has three major problems. First, neither the Old nor the New Testament mentions number nineteen as the guardians of hell.[87] Second, even if there was a similar such statement, this would not remove their doubts; on the contrary, it would increase their doubts since they would consider it one of the many pieces of evidence supporting their claim that the Quran plagiarized many stories from the Bible. Indeed, there are many Biblical events narrated by the Quran, though occasionally with some differences. Third, to our knowledge, none so far converted to Islam because of the mention of the guardians of hell.

Some scholars noticed this flaw in traditional commentaries. For instance, Fahraddin el-Razi, in his classic commentary offered many speculations, including that the number nineteen indicates the nineteen intellectual faculties of a human being. Though it appears to be intelligent and relevant interpretation, I find it incomplete as it fails to explain the emphasis on the number nineteen itself.

The following verses emphasize the crucial function of number nineteen:

74:32	No, by the moon.*
74:33	By the night when it passes.
74:34	By the morning when it shines.
74:35	It is one of the great ones. [88]
74:36	A warning to people.
74:37	For any among you who wishes to progress or regress.

The purpose of "oath" statements in the Quran is not similar to their common usage. The Quran uses oath to draw our attention to a divine sign or a lesson on the subject matter. The Quran does not use the statements of oath to make us *believe*, but to make us *think* (see: 89:5). The passing of the night and the shining of the morning are obviously allegories used to indicate an intellectual enlightenment or salvation. But the expression "by the Moon" is literal, and it draws our attention to the relationship of the Moon and the number nineteen. The same year that the Apollo 11 astronauts dug into the Moon's surface and brought a piece of the Moon to the Earth, a biochemist named Dr. Rashad Khalifa started feeding the Quran into a computer in St. Louis, which would end up with the discovery of Code 19. This might be considered a mere coincidence, but a Quranic verse implies a correlation between the two events.

54:1-5	The Hour has come closer, and the moon was split. [89] Then they saw a sign/miracle; but they turned away and said, "Old magic." They disbelieved, followed their wishful thinking, and adhered to their old traditions. Sufficient warnings have been delivered to alert them. Great wisdom; but all the warnings have been in vain.

Let's continue the reading of Chapter 74 (The Hidden):

74:38	Every person is held by what it earned;
74:39	Except for the people of the right.
74:40	In paradises, they will be asking
74:41	About the criminals.
74:42	"What has caused you to be in *Saqar*?"
74:43	They said, "We were not of those who offered support (or observed contact prayer)."*
74:44	"We did not feed the poor."
74:45	"We used to participate with those who spoke falsehood."
74:46	"We used to deny the Day of Judgment."*
74:47	"Until the certainty came to us."
74:48	Thus, no intercession of intercessors could help them.

How could someone who does not acknowledge the Day of Judgment believe in intercession? Those who believe in the intercession of saints and prophets on their behalf surely believe, or at least claim to believe in the Day of Judgment. Nevertheless, according to the Quranic definition of the Day of Judgment a person cannot simultaneously accept both intercession and the Day of Judgment. The Quran defines the Day of Judgment as "the day that no person can help another person, and all decisions, on that day, will belong to God." (82:19). On that day neither Muhammad nor Ahmad, neither Jesus nor Mary, neither Ali nor Hussain can help those who reject the number nineteen, as well as its role and implication in the Quran.[90]

Running like Zebras

The last section of Chapter 74 (The Hidden) likens those who turn away from the prophetic message of the Quran to zebras running away from a lion.

74:49 Why did they turn away from this reminder?*
74:50 Like fleeing zebras,
74:51 Running from the lion?
74:52 Alas, every one of them wants to be given separate manuscripts.
74:53 No, they do not fear the Hereafter.
74:54 No, it is a reminder.
74:55 Whosoever wishes will take heed.
74:56 None will take heed except if **God** wills. He is the source of righteousness and the source of forgiveness.

Numerous books and articles rejecting the importance of the number nineteen in the Quran have been published in many languages worldwide. Some of the publications were freely distributed with the support from petrol-rich countries such as Kuwait and Saudi Arabia.

The Turkish philosopher and theologian Dr. Caner Taslaman makes the following comment on verse 74:50 and the reaction of people to code 19:

"The miracles can not be understood by people who approach them as football fanatics. The miracles shown by prophets before Muhammad only increased the fanaticism of disbelievers. To appreciate these miracles, one must have a careful mind and conscience free from stubbornness and arrogance. Those who say, "How can I deny?" instead of saying, "How can I understand? What is the truth?" can never witness God's miracles. These people, instead of asking "How can I become a person that God may approve?" they ask "How can I ingratiate with relatives and friends?" Those who are afraid to be in conflict with their environment rather than with God cannot see God's signs."[91]

Those who have witnessed the mathematical miracle of the Quran, usually have difficulty in explaining the fact that so many, especially the smart and educated people are incapable of witnessing the extraordinary mathematical pattern that is so obvious and profound.

You will find extensive discussions with critics in the new and extended edition of my upcoming book, *Running Like Zebras*. There I have discussed this issue with people from a wide range of disciplines and religions, such as mathematicians, Sunni and Shiite scholars, Christians, agnostics and atheists. The book has been out of print for years and its revised edition will be published by Brainbow Press soon after this book, God willing.[92] The following verses describes the ingrates:

7:146   I will divert from My revelations/signs/miracles those who are arrogant on earth without justification. Consequently, when they see every kind of sign/miracle they will not acknowledge. When they see the path of guidance, they will not adopt it as their path, but when they see the path of straying, they will adopt it as their path. This is the consequence of their rejecting our revelations/signs/miracles, and being totally heedless thereof.

6:4-5   And every sign that came to them from their Lord, they turned away from it. They have denied the truth when it came to them. The news will ultimately come to them of what they were mocking.

26:4-6   Whenever a reminder from the Most Gracious comes to them, that is new, they turn away in aversion. They have denied; thus the news will come to them of what they used to ridicule.

6:35   If their rejection gets to be too much for you, you should know that even if you dug a tunnel through the earth, or climbed a ladder into the sky, and produced a miracle for them (they still would not acknowledge). Had GOD willed, He could have guided them, unanimously. Therefore, do not behave like the ignorant ones.

In the following chapters you will witness some profound examples of the fulfillment of the great prophecy of 74:31.

9

The Background and Chronology of the Discovery

Below is the outline of the major revelations and discoveries regarding the mathematical design of the Quran in chronological order. It includes some of my own contribution and experience:

610: Born in 570 ACE, Prophet Muhammad starts receiving the first revelations of the Quran in month of Ramadan, including the verse "on it is nineteen" of Chapter 74.

630: Revelation and recording of the Quran is completed.

1200: Judah ben Samuel of Germany (b. 1140–d. 1217), the spiritual leader of the Ashkenazi Hasidic movement, discovers a numerical system in the original text of the Old Testament based on the number 19, thereby fulfilling the prophecy of the Quran in verse 46:10.

1938: Fuad Abdulbaqi of Egypt, publishes his landmark concordance/index of the Quran: *al-Mujam ul-Mufahras li-Alfaz il-Quran il-Karim* (The Indexed Concordance for the Words of the Holy Quran.)

1924: Mustafa Kemal Atatürk abolishes the *Khilafa*, the Ottoman dynasty that established monarchy and imperial power in the name of God. Ottoman sultans, like their predecessors Abbasid and Umayyad kings, continued exploiting religious teachings and dogmas. Like many heroes, Mustafa Kemal too would be idolized after his death in 1938. A fascinating 19-based pattern in Mustafa's life was first published in 1951 in an article by Kadircan Kaflı in *Yeni Sabah* newspaper.

1959-1968: Abdurazzaq Nawfal, an Egyptian scholar, using Fuad's concordance notices some examples of numerical symmetry between the frequencies of semantically related words and phrases.

1969: While first human landed on the Moon, another Egyptian, Dr. Rashad Khalifa, a biochemist working at St. Louis, decides to study the Quran via computer to solve the mystery of combinations of alphabet letters initializing 29 chapters of the Quran. He publishes his work under several titles, such as *Muhammad's Perpetual Miracle.* The connection between the two historic events (Landing on the Moon and Feeding the Quran into the Computer) is supported by interesting coincidences.

1973: Rashad publishes *Miracle of the Quran: Significance of the Mysterious Alphabets* in St. Louis. While the book lists the frequencies of each initial alphabet letters in each verse of their respective chapters, it never mentions their relationship with the number 19. This study is published by an Egyptian magazine called *Ahir Sa'a* (Last Hour).

1974: Rashad discovers the role of the number 19, prophetically promised in Chapter 74, The Hidden, exactly 1406 (19 x 74) lunar years after the revelation of the Quran. This "one of the greatest" that would distinguish those who wish to regress or progress, starts the modern Islamic Reform movement that rejuvenates the liberating and powerful message of *La ilahe illa Allah.*

1975: Abdurazzaq publishes his book *al-I'jaz al-Adadi fi al-Qur'an al-Karim* (Numerical Miracles in the Holy Quran) containing examples of numerical relationship between related words, synonyms and antonyms in the Quran.

1975: University of Medina publishes the book of top Saudi cleric Sheikh Ibnul Baz: *El-edilletün Naqliyyetu vel Hissiyatu Ala Cereyaniş şamsi ve Sukunil Ardi ve İmkanis Suudi ilal Kavakibi* (The Traditional and Empirical Evidences for the Motion of the Sun and Stillness of Earth, and Possibility of Ascending to Planets). The book claims that the earth is fixed and deems any Muslim claiming otherwise of becoming an apostate, thereby making him subject to death penalty.

1976: Rashad's discovery of Code 19 becomes popular in Muslim Countries and his work is translated into many languages. He becomes a celebrity and is invited to give lectures in major academic conferences and is welcomed by various universities, including al-Azhar. Ahmad Deedat, the founder of Islamic Propagation Centre in South Africa, using Rashad Khalifa's work, writes an eloquent book, *Al-Quran: the Ultimate Miracle,* and freely distributes it in tens of thousands from 1979 until 1986.

1977: Jerry Lucas and Del Washburn publish *Theomatics: God's Best Kept Secret Revealed.* As an extension of Ivan Panin's work (1890), the book contains numerous anecdotal, arbitrary, inconsistent, and some interesting observations on gematrical values of certain words in the Bible.

1978: Joseph Dan of the Association for Jewish Studies, unaware of Rashad's discoveries, publishes an article on the work of Judah ben Samuel, an eleventh century German scholar. Judah's discovery of the code 19 in the original text of the Old Testament is the fulfillment of a prophetic Quranic statement in verse 46:10. For the article, See: *Studies in Jewish*

Mysticism, Proceedings of Regional Conferences Held at the University of California, Los Angeles and McGill University in April, University of California press, 1978.

1980: As the Turkish representative of the Muslim youth, I meet Ahmad Deedat in an International Youth Conference at Çanakkale, Turkey. The conference, which lasted for two weeks in a seaside camping site with the participation of more than 200 youth leaders from 42 countries, was organized by WAMY (World Assembly of Muslim Youth) and Turkey's Ministry of Youth. Besides Ahmad Deedat, there I meet many scholars, mostly members or affiliates of Muslim Brotherhood, including the famous scholar, Yusuf al-Qaradawi. Ahmed Deedat's lecture on the number 19 pulls my attention for two reasons: it sounds like a philosophical and theological breakthrough and it is a number very familiar to me, the name of the youth group that I established in 1978: FT/19. (FT abbreviation of Fatih--a region in Istanbul, or Fetih—Victory. The Turkish police had made extensive research trying to find out the meaning of 19 in this illegal group, which drew a little attention from the Turkish media.) I get permission from Deedat to translate and publish the book. The same year, the famous mathematician Martin Gardner publishes an article on the code 19 in Scientific American. Rashad claims to have discovered the end of the world from the Quran, which would later prompt me to find exactly the same date independently. According to the coded prophecy, starting from the year in which Rashad discovered the prophecy, the end of the world: 300 solar or 309 lunar years later.

1981-1982 Rashad publishes *The Computer Speaks: God's Message to the World* and one year later, *Quran: Visual Presentation of the Miracle* See: http://www.submission.org/miracle/visual.html.

1982: While I am in prison, after verifying the evidences presented, I translate Ahmed Deedat's book to Turkish. The following year, my research on the verses of the Quran with scientific implications and my additional discoveries on the mathematical structure of the Quran are published together with my translation of Deedat's book. *Kuran En Büyük Mucize* (Quran, The Greatest Miracle), which becomes a best-selling book in Turkey until 1987.

1982: Rashad, in his milestone work, *Quran, Hadith, and Islam* sheds the light of the Quran that had been clouded by the distortion and false doctrines of sectarian teachings that rely on hearsay sources called Hadith and Sunna. The book, which can be read in a few hours, exposes the falsehood of Hadith and Sunna through the light of the Quranic verses. With is laser sharp focus and reasoning, the book brilliantly exposes the numerous distortion made by so-called Islamic scholars. The book debunks the two main tricks used by Sunni and Shiite clergymen: it refutes mistranslations of the Quranic verses by comparative analysis of the scripture, and puts the abused verses into their context. Thus, a paradigm-changing powerful purge of men-made religious teachings in the process of Islamic reform with the motto of "Quran alone" starts.

1982: Dr. Cesar Adib Majul, a retired professor of philosophy and logic, a Filipino-American, publishes his book, *The Names of Allah in Relation to the Mathematical Structure of Quran*. Adib finds an interlocking numerical system between the frequencies of four words of Bismillah and the numerical values of God's attributes. I had numerous phone and mail conversation with Adib, my namesake, before his ascension to God in 2004. I have some of his unpublished research on the numerical structure of the Quran.

1983: Rashad translates his book, *The Visual Presentation of the Miracle*, into Arabic under the title *Mugizat ul-Quran* and it is published by Dar el-Ilm Lil-malayin, Beirut, Lebanon, and it is still listed at their website for order: www.malayin.com/publ.asp?item=00468

1985: Rashad declares that the verses 9:128-129 in current manuscripts do not belong to the Quran, since they violate the 19-based mathematical structure of the Quran. It is remarkable that from 1974 until 1985 the table listing the frequency of the word ALLAH ended with the sum of 2698 (19x142). Many books published in various languages disseminate this information around the world. Though with the exception of the frequency of the letter *Alif*, I check every factual detail mentioned in Ahmad Deedat's book, like many researchers, I do not notice the error regarding one the extra word, because of Fuad Abdulbaqi's concordance. Later, I would consider this eleven-year delay as a divinely planned event to disseminate the information in the world before subjecting them to a test.

1986: After months of debate with Rashad via snail-mail, my faith in Hadith and Sunna weakens, and it reaches to a breaking point after receiving his book *Quran, Hadith and Sunna*. The night of July 1, 1986, when I was a drafted soldier in Samsun, I read the book from cover to cover turning that night into my personal *Laylat ul-Qadr* (the Night of Power). With tears in my eyes, I give up associating partners to God, and decide to devote my service to God alone by following the Quran alone. By this decision, I would risk my career, fame, my political future, my family, and life. In October 23, 1986, exactly 114 days after my conversion to monotheism in July 1, 1986, I experience a divine sign followed by a series of prophecies as God promises in 43:53. The same year, the Haley Comet that visits our planet in every 76 (19x6) years passed nearby. This was the 19th visit since Muhammad's time and it was year 1406 (19x74) according to Hijra Calendar. Rashad considered it as one of the fulfillments of 41:53.

1986-1987: I discover an asymmetry in Adib's remarkable studies, and I hypothesize a solution. Soon, I discover the missing divine attribute *ShaHeeD*, in Adib Majul's table on the numerical relationship of God's names, fulfilling my prediction based on the 19-based pattern. My discovery completes an interlocking table of attributes of God, and is published in my Turkish book, *İlginç Sorular-2* (Interesting Questions-2). Furthermore, I hypothesize that there are exactly 114 attributes of God mentioned in the Quran.

1989: My rejection of Hadith and Sunna through my books and articles receives a nationwide attention and my affiliation with Rashad makes me a target of threats and attacks. Receiving an invitation from Rashad, I immigrate to the United States. For a while I live in a room adjacent to Masjid Tucson.

1989: In February, Ibn Baz leads top Sunni scholars to discuss the matter of Salman Rushdi, and the fatwa of the 38 Sunni scholars becomes headline news in the Muslim world: "Rashad and Rushdi, both are Apostates." Rushdie was represented and defended by a British law firm called Article 19. The following year, Rushdie publishes his second book, titled *Haroun and the Sea of Stories*, in which the protagonist, oddly named Rashid, tells political stories.

1989: Abdullah Arık, a Turkish-American engineer, by using a simple computer program tests the compatibility of long numbers with the code 19 by putting together the numbers of chapters, verses, sequence of letters and their gematrical values. He discovers an interlocking and cumulative system in the sequence of the 19 letters of Bismillah.

1990: In 30th of January, Rashad is assassinated in Masjid Tucson by a terrorist group, al-Fuqara or al-Fuqra, affiliated to the early stage of al-Qaida organization founded by Saudi militant Osama Bin Laden. The same year, Saddam Hussein declared Kuwait to be Iraq's 19th province. To discuss the matter, the Organization of the Islamic Conference immediately convened its 19th conference.

1992: Milan Sulc of Switzerland, founder of Faith-through-Science Foundation, discovers an impressive numerical structure in the table of frequencies of ĤM letters, thereby showing the intricacy of the numerical structure of the Quran that integrates unique numerical computations with code 19. Milan Sulc and Ali Fazely, professor of physics at the University of Louisiana, have announced their discoveries of a different numerical phenomenon in the Quran based on prime numbers and composite numbers. Though some of their findings are interesting, in my opinion, they lack a system and thus appear to be anecdotal and speculative at this point.

114

1997: Michael Drosnin, in a bestselling book, *the Bible Code*, claimed that he discovered many prophecies in the Bible by searching its text for equidistant letter sequences (ELS). Soon, skeptics debunked the claim conclusively. www.nmsr.org/biblecod.htm

1998: To promote Islamic reform according to the message of the Quran alone, to share the paradigm-shifting mathematical miracle, I establish 19.org.

1999-2000: The practice of abbreviating the four-digit year to two digits in computer programs in order save memory space, created a problem came to known Y2K Problem or the Millennium Bug. "While no globally significant computer failures occurred when the clocks rolled over into 2000, preparation for the Y2K problem had a significant effect on the computer industry. There were plenty of Y2K problems, and that none of the glitches caused major incidents is seen as vindication of the Y2K preparation. However, some questioned whether the absence of computer failures was the result of the preparation undertaken or whether the significance of the problem had been overstated." (Wikipedia). Whether real or perceived, this major problem cost over 300 billion US dollars (BBC News, 6 January 2000), and it was caused by computer programmers ignoring the number 19.

2001: On September 11, 2001, the 19 hijackers of al-Qaeda attack Pentagon, World Trade Center and kill thousands of Americans. One of the main organizers of the attack, Wadih al-Hage, was also implicated for his role in Rashad's assassination. Prosecutors have also suggested that El-Hage and Jamaat ul-Fuqra were involved in the murder of Dr. Rashad Khalifa on January 31, 1990 in Tucson. They believe that El-Hage knows who killed Khalifa. And even if El-Hage was not himself involved, the prosecution asked why he had not told them what he knew. El-Hage's family says he was not in the country at the time of the murder.

2002: More than a decade after my public acknowledgment of numerous errors in the count of *Alifs*, one of the reasons for being excommunicated by submitters, Dr. Atef Khalifa, finally acknowledges the fact that his brother Rashad indeed made errors in the count of *Alifs* and thus undertakes the overdue study on the subject matter. See: www.submission.org/miracle/alif.html.

2002: Dr. Caner Taslaman, a Turkish philosopher/theologian and founder of *Kuran Araştırmalar Grubu* (Quranic Research Group), publishes a comprehensive book on the scientific and numeric aspect of the Quran *Kuran Hiç Tükenmeyen Mucize* (Quran: a Perpetual Miracle) is available online in English at www.quranmiracles.org. The same year, a group of muslims establish Islamic Reform organization, www.islamicreform.org

115

2003: A group of programmers, working together with Atef Khalifa, designs the "Quran Reader", a computer program to count the letters of the Quran text on the internet. http://www.submission.org/quran/reader/

2005: After being challenged by Dr. Ayman through his article *Idiot's Guide to Code 19*, I start my second book-length debate with him in May 2005, and call it, *Intelligent People's Guide to Code 19*. It will be published in the next edition of *Running Like Zebras*, God willing.

2005: In August, *Manifesto for Islamic Reform* is issued.

2006: *Quran: a Reformist Translation* is published by Brainbow Press.

2008: Using a program developed by a Turkish colleague on a reformed Arabic text of the Quran, in which all later innovations such as *hamzas, maddas, shaddas* and all other diatrical marks are deleted, we prove that there are only 114 verses in the Quran containing ALL the 14 letters used in the Quranic initials (*huruf-u muqatta*). Several other significant discoveries are made.

2009: With the progress in DNA forensic technology, the evidence gathered in 1990 was re-examined and one of the murderers of Rashad Khalifa was arrested in Canada, 19 years after Rashad's assassination.

2011: Two decades after Rashad's landmark work was published in *Visual Presentation of the Quran*, this book, *NINETEEN: God's Signature in Nature and Scripture,* is published by Brainbow Press.

2011: A documentary film using this book will inshallah be released this year.

2012: We will inshallah continue sharing the message with the world.

2013: We will inshallah continue sharing the message with the world.

2014: Peacemakers or rational monotheists will inshallah hold their annual *Critical Thinkers for Islamic Reform* conference in Mecca, by God's will. Confrontation with one of the world's most corrupt and oppressive regimes is expected.

ا ي ل ب ل ه م ل ح م ل ح ن ل ه ه م ب
ت ن ا د ع ك ي ن د ا و ك م ي ر ا م ر
ه ل ت ع ا ي ط ل ص ي ت م ا ر ل د ا ي
ن ل ض ل م ي ع و غ ل ر غ

ن م ع ر ل د ح ا ي ر ا م ر ل ا س
ع س ك ي و ب ن ا ا ي ل م ي ل م ح ل ن ح
م ي ع م ن ن ذ ا ر م ق س ل ط ص ا ن ه ن
ي ا ل ا و ه ل ب ض م ا ي

116

10
Basic Elements

"Everything We have counted in a record." Quran 78:29.

The word Quran means "The Book of Recitation." Indeed, it is commonly held that the chronologically first revelation of the Quran starts with the following verses: "Read, in the name of your Lord."

The literary style of the Book of Recitation is a hybrid of poetry and prose. The Quran vehemently rejects the idea that it be classified as "sh'ir" (poetry) since the content of Arabic poetry consisted of wishful thinking and pompous claims (26:224-227). Furthermore, the very word *sh'ir* means "feelings," and the Quran claims to be a book of facts, not feelings. (See 21:5; 36:69; 37:36; 52:30; 69:41)

The Quran consists of chapters of various lengths ranging from as long as several hundred verses to as short as three verses. Most of the short chapters are compiled in the last section of the Quran. Though the majority of Sunni and Shiite scholars do not consider the arrangement of chapters to be arbitrary, they do not have any evidence to support their claim. After the discovery of Code 19, we now know that every element and every order in the Quran are based on a precise mathematical system. The number of chapters, their length and their order all participate in the mathematical structure of the Quran. Our research has demonstrated that even the basic element of the Quran, letters, show an intricate mathematical pattern. The Quran is constructed on mathematical principles, as is the universe. Witnessing that the Book of Recitation shares the same mathematical characteristics with the Book of Nature, we conclude that the designer of both books must be the same Artist, the Master Mathematician. As the book of nature consists of atoms, molecules, compounds, and systems of bodies, all interacting in mathematical precision; similarly, the Book of Recitation consists of letters, words, sentences, and chapters, according to a precise mathematical design. The inherent language of both books is mathematics.

Let's study the list of the Quran's chapters in their order, together with the number of verses in each.[93]

117

114 Chapters of the Quran and the Number of Verses in Each
(The 112 unnumbered Bismillah formula are not included)

1. 7	**20.** 135	**39.** 75	**58.** 22	**77.** 50	**96.** 19
2. 286	**21.** 112	**40.** 85	**59.** 24	**78.** 40	**97.** 5
3. 200	**22.** 78	**41.** 54	**60.** 13	**79.** 46	**98.** 8
4. 176	**23.** 118	**42.** 53	**61.** 14	**80.** 42	**99.** 8
5. 120	**24.** 64	**43.** 89	**62.** 11	**81.** 29	**100.** 11
6. 165	**25.** 77	**44.** 59	**63.** 11	**82.** 19	**101.** 11
7. 206	**26.** 227	**45.** 37	**64.** 18	**83.** 36	**102.** 8
8. 75	**27.** 93	**46.** 35	**65.** 12	**84.** 25	**103.** 3
9. 127	**28.** 88	**47.** 38	**66.** 12	**85.** 22	**104.** 9
10. 109	**29.** 69	**48.** 29	**67.** 30	**86.** 17	**105.** 5
11. 123	**30.** 60	**49.** 18	**68.** 52	**87.** 19	**106.** 4
12. 111	**31.** 34	**50.** 45	**69.** 52	**88.** 26	**107.** 7
13. 43	**32.** 30	**51.** 60	**70.** 44	**89.** 30	**108.** 3
14. 52	**33.** 73	**52.** 49	**71.** 28	**90.** 20	**109.** 6
15. 99	**34.** 54	**53.** 62	**72.** 28	**91.** 15	**110.** 3
16. 128	**35.** 45	**54.** 55	**73.** 20	**92.** 21	**111.** 5
17. 111	**36.** 83	**55.** 78	**74.** 56	**93.** 11	**112.** 4
18. 110	**37.** 182	**56.** 96	**75.** 40	**94.** 8	**113.** 5
19. 98	**38.** 88	**57.** 29	**76.** 31	**95.** 8	**114.** 6
					↑

The Quran has 114 chapters and this number is a multiple of 19:

$$114 = 19 \times 6$$

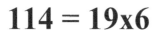

عليها تسعة عشر

On it is Nineteen

The largest element of the Quran, which is very easy to verify, is a multiple of 19. Not more, not less! Of course, this can be a mere coincidence, since there is a one-in-19 chance of finding a multiple of 19 in any book. Moreover, even if we are convinced that this is a purposeful design, it does not take much talent to write a book with the number of chapters being a multiple of 19 or any other number.

So, I ask my skeptical reader to continue reading, since I am confident that after witnessing the whole picture he or she will not be able to utter the word "coincidence" that easily. We think that the results of our research will not only rule out the "mere coincidence" option but also reveal that the factor 6 is no coincidence either. A minor example of mathematical art can be found at the end of the list. The 114th chapter of the Quran is entitled People and it has 6 verses. Remember: 19x6 = 114. We will see more about this in the chapter on divine attributes.

What Do You Need?

To witness the mathematical system of the Quran your culture and religion is irrelevant. Even your language is not relevant for the majority of examples. Your education level may not be that important either. Almost any person with sound judgment and sincere interest can appreciate the mathematical miracle. Though knowledge of Arabic and mathematics will allow you to witness more examples through a more colorful monitor, to witness this extraordinary event you do not even need to know Arabic or calculus. All you need is to be able to count up to 19 (10+9) and be able to come to your own conclusion without fear of others. In brief, in order to witness a miracle as impressive as bringing down a feast from the sky or reviving the dead, all you need to do is simply exercise your wits to critically evaluate the physical examples provided in this book.

11
BiSM ALLaH AL-RaĤMaN AL-RaĤYM

بســــــــــم الله الرحمن الرحيـــــــــم

In the name of God, the Gracious, the Compassionate

With the exception of Chapter 9, all chapters of the Quran start with the formula "BiSMALLaHALRaĤMaNALRaĤYM" or in short Bismillah: In the Name of God, the Gracious, and the Compassionate. Bismillah is the first and most repeated statement in the Quran and undoubtedly the most popular among the Muslim population. Muslims utter this verse before their major daily activities, such as eating and drinking or starting their car.

The Bismillah of Chapter 1 (Opening) is numbered as an independent verse, while the Bismillah crowning other chapters are not numbered as independent verse. There is a disagreement between scholars whether to count the Bismillah as a numbered verse of Chapter 1. However the mathematical structure of the Quran confirms the most common numbering system.

The Bismillah can be seen in two categories regarding their position in the numbering of verses:

1. Bismillah formula with independent verse numbers: There are two Bismillah formula showing these characteristics. One is the first verse of Chapter 1. The other is located in verse 30 of Chapter 27.

2. Bismillah formula with no independent verse numbers: With the exception of Chapter 9 (The Ultimatum), all the remaining 112 chapters start with unnumbered Bismillah.

We have learnt that this literary idiosyncrasy of the first and most repeated Quranic statement is related to its function in the mathematical system. The Code's password:

بسم الله الرحمن الرحيم

BiSM ALLaH AL-RaĤMaN AL-RaĤYM

The first verse by itself is a proof that the Quranic text has been systematically designed. You do not need to learn the Arabic language to count the Arabic letters of this verse. You just need to recognize the 28 letters of the alphabet.

Since many examples involve Arabic letters, recognition of the Arabic alphabet is recommended. Recognition of the 28 characters will take you ten or fifteen minutes. The forms of Arabic letters vary depending on their position, whether they are used in the beginning, end or in the middle of words. As a general rule, letters lose their "tails" if they do not come at the end of words, and six letters do not connect to the succeeding letters in a word. They are ا Alif, د Dal, ذ Zal, ر Ra, ز Zayn and و Waw.

Arabic writing is from right to left, so is its Alphabet:

Number of Letters in Bismillah

Upon learning that the frequency of the word Day and Month corresponded exactly to their frequencies in nature, we have good reason to be curious about scientific and mathematical aspect of this book. The best way to start examination is from its first verse, which is also the most repeated verse in the Quran.

Now, you may decide to count the letters of Bismillah. As you will see from the diagram it has exactly 19 letters. There is no dispute among Muslims or their scholars regarding this simple fact. Sunni and Shiite scholars of the past, who disagreed on almost every issue, never disagreed on the number of letters of Bismillah. Even a pupil in elementary school who has the knowledge of the Arabic alphabet can verify it in a few seconds.

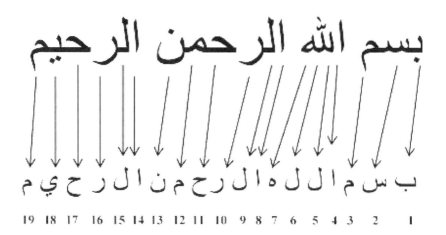

بسم الله الرحمن الرحيم

ب س م ا ل ل ه ا ل ر ح م ن ا ل ر ح ي م

| 19 | 18 | 17 | 16 | 15 | 14 | 13 | 12 | 11 | 10 | 9 | 8 | 7 | 6 | 5 | 4 | 3 | 2 | 1 |

Not a single Muslim scholar has disputed the number of letters in Bismillah before the evidence (*bayyina*) came to them, which is another fulfillment of the law (2:213; 3:19; 98:4). For instance, Fahraddin al-Razi, in his 30 volume commentary of the Quran, *Al-tafsirul Kabir* in his twenty third point on *Bismillah* acknowledges the 19 letters and tries to ascribe a meaning to this number. Interestingly, he refers to a Hadith which says: "The guardians of hell are 19, and God saves people from them through these 19 letters." Qurtubi, another renowned Sunni scholar, in the 92nd page of his commentary of the Quran, *Al-Jami Li Ahkami al-Quran*, acknowledges the same simple fact and narrates from Ibn-i Masud who relate the 19 letters to the number of guardians of hell.

Muslims started developing theories regarding the number of the letters of Bismillah after the revelation of "one of the greatest" (74:35) miracles in 1974. Interestingly, after realizing the radical theological ramification of Code 19, contemporary Sunni and Shiite scholars started disagreeing on the number of letters contained in Bismillah. To deny the existence of the Code, every possible argument, regardless how ridiculous, is tried. Some clergymen increased the number of its letters to 20, 21 and even upto 22. Some preferred to reduce the letter count to 18. We will discuss this preposterous but common reaction to the mathematical structure of the Quran later.

The evening of 23 November 2002, millions of Turkish people witnessed this travesty on a live TV discussion program to which I was invited from Arizona. The host, Hulki Cevizoğlu, had also invited Dr. Süleyman Ateş, a well-known Muslim scholar and the former head of the Turkish Religious of Affairs, and Prof. Haluk Oral, a mathematician from the Bosphorus University who is considered an expert on codes. Despite the highly specialized content of our topic, our live discussion that lasted about three hours became a top-rated program by drawing millions of audience from Turkey and Europe.

I have to acknowledge that Süleyman Ateş is one of the most open-minded of Sunni scholars. He had showed the wisdom and courage to challenge many established Sunni dogmas. For instance, he defended the theory of evolution through the Quran. Nevertheless, still being a semi-follower of Hadith, he never came close to the idea of rational monotheism.

In that discussion, Dr. Ateş, the Turkish scholar who had written articles and books critical of the code 19, could not engage in a decent discussion with me; he lost his temper frequently and left the studio twice in the middle of the discussion. He was especially getting furious at my referring to the last prophet with his first name, as the Quran wanted me to do so (2:136). Perhaps he was using it as an excuse to avoid engaging in a face-to-face debate. Each time he ran away, he was stopped by the TV crew and brought back by the host who begged him during the breaks to stay on the panel. The host also privately asked me to be easy on him. I found myself in between of feeling pity for an arrogant and popular scholar, or stand for the truth. The Sunni scholar appeared so terrified that he could not even engage in short face-to-face dialogues; reminding the Quranic depiction of the reaction of the opponents of nineteen: a zebra encountering a lion. He was aware of my previous TV debates with other "experts" and most likely knew the power of my position and its performance. In one of the TV debates, the host of the show publicly complained that many religious scholars he approached were declining to debate with me in public. Prof. Ateş, a critic of my books, had declined debating live with me in the past, but somehow this time he had accepted.

Towards the end of the show, I decided to be easy on him; I did not even rebuttal this so-called Islamic expert when he made an absurd statement regarding Bismillah: looking in the eyes of millions of Turkish TV audience, he claimed that Bismillah did not have 19 letters! I let him incriminate himself in public with that outrageously false claim. Any adult with average IQ, regardless of their language, could easily see for themselves the falsity of his claim by simply checking Bismillah with the 28 Arabic letters. Millions of Turkish people witnessed another miracle, this time in negative sense: When they choose to deny a devine sign, college educated scholars could transform into innumerate and illiterate kindergarteners. Dr. Ateş later shared his experience at his website with his readers:

> "The number 19 is the number of Bahai cult and has nothing to do with the Quran. It is modern cabbalism and nonsense. Quran's first verse, Bismillah, does not have 19 letters as they claim, but it has 21 letters. I have written a book on this deviation... Recently numerous engineers and doctors started following this path. One of those who follow his imaginations is the guy who was once imprisoned for participating in

terror activities in Turkey and now living in America. I met that guy first time during the Ceviz Kabuğu TV program and then I immediately understood that he had idolized his ego. He was rude and did not recognize any rules of etiquette. When he realized that I was going to debunk his claims he interrupted my words. I listened to him for half an hour, but when my turn came he would interject."[94]

The Number of Bismillah formula in the Quran

Even those who do not know Arabic may notice the distinct calligraphy of the formula or password crowning every chapter of the Quran except one. What is the total of all Bismillah formula in the Quran? Knowing that there are 114 chapters of the Quran, you might say 114. However, you might remember that unlike all other chapters, Chapter 9 (The Ultimatum) does not start with Bismillah. Therefore, there must be 113 Bismillah formula in the Quran. If you are wondering about a mathematical pattern based on a common code, you will be curious about the missing one Bismillah. For the 113 to be divisible by 19 without remainder you need to have another one Bismillah.

How is the Puzzle Solved? To solve the puzzle you scan the Quran from the beginning. You will notice the missing Bismillah from Chapter 9 is restored 19 chapters later in verse 30 of Chapter 27 conventionally called, *al-Naml* (the Ant).

       1.   The Ultimatum (Baraa'ah)
       2.   Jonah (Younus)
       3.   Hood (Hood)
       4.   Joseph (Yousuf)
       5.   Thunder (R'ad)
       6.   Abraham (Ibrahim)
       7.   Al-Hijr Valley (Al-Hijr)
       8.   The Bee (Nahl)
       9.   Children of Israel
      10. The Cave (Kahf)
      11. Mary (Maryam)
      12. T.H.
      13. The Prophets (Anbiya)
      14. Pilgrimage (Hajj)
      15. Acknowledgers (Muminoon)
      16. Light (Nur)
      17. The Criterion (Furqan)
      18. The Poets (Shu'araa)
      19. The Ant (Naml)

The 30th verse of The Ant quotes the first statement from the Prophet Solomon's letter to Queen Sheba.

إنه من سليمن وإنه بسم الله الرحمن الرحيم

27:30 "It is from Solomon, and it says, "**In the name of God, Gracious Compassionate.**"

The Chapter Ant, by containing two Bismillah formula, one at the beginning and the other in its 30th verse, solves the problem. Therefore, the number of all Bismillah formula in the Quran becomes 114, which is multiple of 19.[95]

$$114 = 19 \text{x} 6$$

Some Lessons that can be Deduced from this Example

The designer of the mathematical system provides us with the following information by first creating a problem and then solving it,

1. The designer behind the mathematical system promotes curiosity on our part about such a system and encourages us not to be passive but active and questioning.

2. The designer supports our instinctive expectation that a mathematical system, if there is any, must be perfect.

3. The designer teaches us that the Bismillah formula crowning every chapter except one are not redundant or arbitrary, but a part of a mathematical design.

4. By adding more mathematical details, such as the number of words between the two Bismillah's (27:0 and 27:30) being exactly 342 (19x18) words, the designer tells us that the solution is undoubtedly related to the Code 19.

5. The designer informs us that the order of chapters in the Quran is not arbitrary, but based on a mathematical design. It is also worth noting that that the Code 19 existed in the scriptures of previous messengers, such as Solomon's book. (See: 27:30)

6. Adding the verse number to the chapter number produces another divisible number: 27 + 30 = 19 x 3.

Discussion on the Importance of Bismillah

I would like to insert one of the communications between me and Carl Sagan, which became my undergraduate honor thesis for the philosophy major at the University of Arizona.[96] Since the Internet was not in common usage then; we communicated via snail mail. In the second round of the debate, Carl criticized our focus on Bismillah to support his position.

CORNELL UNIVERSITY
Center for Radiophysics and Space Research
Space Sciences Building
Ithaca, New York 14853-6801

Telephone (607) 255-4971
Fax (607) 255-9888   Labortaory for Planetary Studies

Fabruary 17, 1994

Mr. Edip Yuksel
[address]

Dear Mr. Yuksel:

Thanks for your recent letter, but I don't think you have understood the distinction I was making between A PRIORI and A POSTERIORI judgements. Let's take the example you've sent me. You have chosen the first verse of the Qur'an to do your numerology, but of course that is an arbitrary decision. You could, for example, have chosen the 19th *sura*, or any "code" index you wished and then tried to find it repeated throughout the Qur'an.

I see many signs of arbitrary decisions in what you consider evidence; for example, why do you count from the missing "Bismillah" to the extra "Bismillah", instead of from Chapter 1 to Chapter 9 or from Chapter 27 to the end? With a sufficient computer data base and absolutely no A PRIORI constraints a clever person should be able to find many regularities. If in addition the author and transcribers of the Qur'an consciously inserted a little numerology, I believe that the coincidences you describe can readily be understood. Of course I might be wrong.

With best wishes,

Cordially,

[signature]

Carl Sagan

CS:lkp

126

EDIP YUKSEL
[Address omitted]

In the name of God, Gracious, Merciful

3/29/1994

Dear Dr. Sagan,

The conclusion of your concise letter was a brilliant skeptical hypothesis: "With a sufficient computer database and absolutely no a priori constraints a clever person should be able to find much regularity. If in addition the author and tran-scribers of the Qur'an consciously inserted a little numerology, I believe that the coincidences you describe can readily be understood." Nevertheless, you, as a cautious scientist, did not forget to add "Of course I might be wrong."

Unfortunately or fortunately, I can't reciprocate your humble statement by say-ing "of course I too might be wrong!" On the contrary, I am obliged to say "of course, Dr. Sagan, you are wrong." I am certain that the mathematical structure of the Quran is the work of the Supreme Mathematician, as you are certain that the planet earth is round and rotates around the sun. I hope you won't get of-fended if I remind you of the possibility of having some "a priori constraints" that may force you not to see the inimitable signature of the Most Wise.

Before starting my counter argument, I want to tell you that I am impressed by your meticulousness in spelling the word "Qur'an" (The Book of Recitation) with its accurate transliteration. For convenience I prefer to write "Quran." As for my misunderstanding of "a priori, and a posteriori statistics," I can blame the different implications of this terminology in different fields.

Arbitrary Decisions

In order to provide a concrete base for our argument, in my previous letter, I had picked some mathematical patterns related to "Bismillah," the opening statement of the Quran. You claim that it is arbitrary to focus on "Bismillah".

I disagree, since I think "Bismillah" is the most appropriate candidate among all the options. If you ask people who are familiar with the Quran to choose an idiosyncratic or representative verse, I am sure that a great majority of them will pick the "Bismillah" without hesitation. It is not only the first verse of the Quran, it is also the opening statement of every chapter except Chapter 9. Furthermore, it is the most repeated verse in the Quran and the most popular verse among Muslims. We say "Bismi Allahi RaĤMaNi Rahim" (In the name of God, Most Gracious, Most Merciful) before eating and drinking, or before starting our cars, etc. It is virtually a sacred password.

For the sake of argument, let's assume that "Bismillah" is not special and we picked it arbitrarily. The probability of finding a verse in the Quran that exhibits ONLY six features of "Bismillah" is very low. If you consider the astounding interlocking relation between the number of the occurrences of the words in "Bismillah" and the gematrical values of the names of God, then the probability will diminish dramatically. Please note that the relation between "Bismillah" and God's names is not arbitrary but a necessity coming from the very meaning of "Bismillah." Besides, we have discovered many more mathematical facts just about "Bismillah" which eventually reduce the probability to zero. Therefore, neither "arbitrary decisions" nor "a little numerology" nor "coincidences," nor the combination of the three can be candidates for a plausible explanation.

As another example of "arbitrary decisions" you mention the relation between the missing "Bismillah" and the extra "Bismillah." You ask: "why do you count from the missing 'Bismillah' to the extra 'Bismillah', instead of from Chapter 1 to Chapter 9 or from Chapter 27 to the end? "

I have at least four answers for this objection:

1. Just look at two adjectives of the "Bismillah" you mention in your question: **MISSING** and **EXTRA**. Isn't it more logical to look for a relation between the **MISSING** and **EXTRA,** instead of the **FIRST** and **MISSING**, or the **EXTRA** and **LAST**?

2. The number of chapters from Chapter 1 to Chapter 9 **AND** from Chapter 27 to the end is also a multiple of 19:[, which is] 95 (19x5), since the number of all Chapters are multiple of 19.

3. The author of the Quran obviously has willed to hide the implication of the code 19 in Chapter 74 (The Hidden Secret) until 1974. It is a message reserved for the computer generation. If the missing "Bismillah" or the extra "Bismillah" had been in Chapter 19, as you suggest, then the code of the Quran could be easily discovered prematurely, since many previous Sunni and Shiite scholars were aware of the fact that "Bismillah" consists of 19 letters. The relation of "Bismillah" with another 19 could easily lead them to search for its mathematical function in the Quran. I believe that there are many reasons behind the timing of this discovery. If God Almighty did not want the corrupt Sunni and Shiite clergymen to discover and abuse this miraculous phenomenon, then it is understandable to see why the simple facts of Quran's mathematical system are hidden from oblivious eyes.

4. Besides, if there was a conscious effort to insert a little numerology in the Quran, as you suspect, then satisfying your suggestions would be very easy. Arranging the Chapter with missing "Bismillah" as the 19th chapter and the Chapter with the extra one as the 37th chapter would eliminate at least one objection of skeptics. Why should Muhammad ignore this very simple arrangement while wasting his time and energy on arranging more complicated ones? If you claim that he was not smart enough to do this simple task, you will loose your main argument regarding more clever and complex patterns; because then you cannot say that Muhammad was a clever mathematician etc.

From your criticism, it seems you are not sure whether the claimed mathematical pattern is intentional or not. You seem to want to have it both ways. You have a two-sided judgment ready at your disposal: either it is ENTIRELY coincidence, OR it is semi-conscious and semi-coincidence. This is a very sure way of discarding anything you disagree with. You can jump between these two preconceived judgments whenever you want. For instance, you can refute my answer above in number 4, by claiming that the mathematical structure of the Quran is entirely coincidental. On the other hand, when the word "coincidence" is too improbable to reject my argument, you can seek refuge in the other side of the label by claiming that it is a little deliberate numerology. I think, for a healthier argument you should clarify your position. Refuting a thesis by oscillating between a contradictory disjunction indicates prejudice.

Is Every Scientific Experiment Arbitrary?

Narrow Inductive Model of Scientific Investigation requires the following:

1. Observe and record all facts.
2. Classify and analyze without prior hypothesis.
3. Induce generalizations from observed facts.

But scientists never follow these utopic principles when they conduct their experiments. They do not observe and record all facts. How can they? Their previous observations, reflections and expectations determine the relevant facts and experiments.

You must be familiar with Newton's "Experimentation Cruces" on the nature of light and colors. A skeptic could object to his findings by claiming that he started his experiment with an a priori hypothesis and with arbitrary decisions: "Why didn't Newton measure the temperature of the room? Why didn't he consider the distance of the source of light? Why did he ignore the role of the type of the mirror? etc...." As you know, Newton had a better intuition than any of his contemporary scientists about which phenomena were relevant and which were not in searching for the nature of light.

The point is, non-relevant phenomena may seem relevant to an outsider, but a

129

scientist familiar with a particular subject will have clear or vague reasons to decide on the relevancy of observations. We can have a hypothesis as long as they guide our observation but not determine the result of our observation. Why don't you grant the following self-correcting scientific method for the study of the mathematical system of the Quran?:

Simple Hypothetico-Deductive Model:

[Diagram is omitted]

The Fir Cone Argument

You know that each term of Fibonacci sequence which runs: 1, 1, 2, 3, 5, 8, 13, 21, 34 ..., is the sum of the two preceding terms. This numerical sequence appears in nature and plants, such as reproduction of rabbits, fir cones and petals of certain flowers.

Let's take fir cones. Observers claim that the pattern of scales in fir cones follows the order of Fibonacci series. This claim or phenomenon can be evaluated in two ways. Let's have a hypothetical argument regarding the existence of Fibonacci pattern in fir cones. Simultaneously, we will consider it analogous to our argument on the mathematical pattern of the Quran.

>PROPONENT: There are thousands of other plants where Fibonacci sequence cannot be observed. It is entirely an arbitrary decision to choose fir cones as an example of this so-called pattern. The appearance of Fibonacci sequence in fir cones is only an interesting coincidence. Of course, I might be wrong.

>OPPONENT: Though when other plants are considered, the appearance of Fibonacci sequence in fir cones can be a coincidence but the very pattern in fir cones cannot be coincidence. There must be a reason behind this regularity in fir cones.

>PROPONENT: I was just being sarcastic. I was trying to use your own argument against you. The status of "Bismillah" in the Quran is much more prestigious and important than the status of fir cones in plant kingdom, let alone in all of nature. Second, there are many more examples of the 19-based mathematical pattern in the Quran, than the examples of Fibonacci Sequence in nature.

>OPPONENT: You ignore something about fir cones. We can repeat our observation millions of times on millions of different fir cones and come to the same conclusion. The repeated observation of a similar pattern makes a scientist to accept the existence of that pattern. However, you have only one "Bismillah" with a pattern.

130

PROPONENT: Well, how many fir cones are enough to convince you that Fibonacci sequence exists in the nature of fir cones?

OPPONENT: I don't know. Probably, ten or twenty observation would be enough.

PROPONENT: That means, after twenty observations you will generalize your conclusion on billions of fir cones that you haven't observed. Why do you "believe" that the other fir cones also will show the same property?

OPPONENT: For two reasons: First, all my twenty observations confirmed the pattern without a single exception. Indeed, after several observations we start predicting and each extra observation is a fulfillment of our prediction. Thus, there is no reason to suspect the 21'st fir cone will spoil this coherent orchestra. Second, our previous observations on many other cases have created a very strong belief that apparently similar things share similar internal structures. I mean that our previous observations, say, on mangos or bananas have created a faith in determinism.

PROPONENT: What if, similarly, my observation on different elements of the Quran has created a faith in the intention and style of its designer.

OPPONENT: Well, you can select any thing that confirms your faith, and you can ignore or interpret any exception that contradicts your expectation.

PROPONENT: Ironically, I can say the same thing about your scientific method. You observe and predict. If any observation contradicts your prediction you will modify your theory or create a new formula. Your prediction can be "certain" only about the objects of your previous observations. However, on new cases you cannot guarantee your prediction, since history is full of failures of scientific predictions. Nevertheless, I believe that the predictive power of science increases with every new observation. It is the same with our observations on the mathematical structure of the Quran. With every new discovery or observation we get much more comprehensive understanding of it.

OPPONENT: You are undermining the predictive power of science. I can challenge you to bring as many as fir cones and examine their scales. You will find the Fibonacci sequence in all of them.

PROPONENT: Though I don't *think* that induction provides us with certainty, nevertheless, I *believe* that your prediction will be confirmed. But, my question will be this: Based on the observation on fir cones how accurately can you predict the pattern of fir branches, or sunflower petals or corn kernels?

OPPONENT: Certain things can be observed and therefore predicted for all material objects. However, there are details which we cannot predict with certainty without sufficient observation.

PROPONENT: That is exactly the same for our observation on the mathematical structure of the Quran. We observe and discover. Each discovery increases our knowledge of the big picture.

The Accuracy or the Predictive Nature of Mathematical Code

Here I want to give two examples:

1. Correcting a Scribal Error

Three chapters of the Quran, chapter 7, 19 and 38 contains letter "Saad" in their initial letter combination. Curiously, in verse 7:69 we see a word with a unique spelling: "Basstatan" Over the letter "Saad" is written a small "Sin." This word occurs in the Quran with two different spellings and it makes no difference to the meaning. Just like the English words skeptic or sceptic. Commentaries of the Quran interpret it as an instruction on how to read the word. They claim that though it is written with "Saad" it should be read as if it is "Sin." They narrate three Hadiths (allegedly Muhammad's words) to support this interpretation .

The total number of "Saad" with this word "Basstatan" becomes 153, and it is not multiple of 19. Therefore, we concluded that the letter "Saad" in the word "Basstatan" is an ortographic error and should be corrected.

Indeed, when I checked one of the oldest manuscripts of the Quran, I found that our prediction was confirmed. Please see the document below:

[The copy of the manuscript is omitted here since it is presented in another chapter of this book]

2. Symmetry in the Table of God's Attributes

In my second letter I had attached a list of God's attributes with their numerical values and frequencies in the Quran, and the mathematical relation between these names and "Bismillah."

Dr. Cezar Edib Majul, in his book, *The Names of Allah in Relation To The Mathematical Structure of Quran* discovered the following two facts: [Omitted, since it is presented in this book]

132

12

Words Comprising the Bismillah Formula

"The union of the mathematician with the poet, fervor with measure, passion with correctness, this surely is the ideal." ~ William James

"The region of absolute necessity, to which not only the actual world, but every possible world must conform. . . . A stern perfection such as only the greatest art can show." ~ Bertrand A. Russell

"The music of reason" ~ James J. Sylvester

"One cannot escape the feeling that these mathematical formulas have an independent existence and an intelligence of their own, that they are wiser than we are, wiser even than their discoverers..." ~ Heinrich Hertz

In this chapter we will see the frequency of the four words that make up Bismillah. The reader may check the accuracy of the lists provide here by randomly comparing them to a manuscript of the Quran.[97]

The occurrence of every word forming Bismillah in the Quran is an exact multiple of 19—divisible by the number of letters in the *Bismillah*. The literary connection between the Bismillah and the entire Quran demonstrates an intricate mathematical interlocking design with a common denominater, 19.

Simple yet Perfect

We can see this occurring with each of the four words participating in the formation of BiSM ALLaH AL-RaĤMaN AL-RaĤYM (In the Name of God, Gracious, Merciful) as follows:

Words	Frequency	
ISM (Name):	19	(**19** x 1)
ALLaH (God):	2698	(**19** x 142)
RaĤMaN (Gracious):	57	(**19** x 3)
RaĤYM (Merciful):	114	(**19** x 6)

133

We, of course, find these results when we count these words in the numbered verses of the Quran, excluding the last two verses of Chapter 9, which we will discuss later. There are many mathematical details involving the construction of this first Quranic statement. Here, note this wonderful mathematical feature from the above example: The sum of the multiplicative factors of 19 is also a multiple of 19:

$$1 + 142 + 3 + 6 = 152 \ (\mathbf{19} \times 8)$$

This numerico-literary art can be expressed alternatively in terms of some simple mathematical equations thus:

$$L_1 + L_2 + L_3 + L_4 = W_1/1$$
$$L_1 + L_2 + L_3 + L_4 = W_2/142$$
$$L_1 + L_2 + L_3 + L_4 = W_3/3$$
$$L_1 + L_2 + L_3 + L_4 = W_4/6$$

And

$$8 (L_1 + L_2 + L_3 + L_4) = \quad [\ W_1/ (L_1 + L_2 + L_3 + L_4) +$$
$$+ W_2/ (L_1 + L_2 + L_3 + L_4) +$$
$$+ W_3/ (L_1 + L_2 + L_3 + L_4) +$$
$$+ W_4/ (L_1 + L_2 + L_3 + L_4) \ ]$$

where, **L** stands for the number of **letters** in the word and **W** for the frequency of the **word** in the Quran.

One might ask the question: Why 8, rather than 4, since Bismillah has only 4 words? We will later see another set of semantically related 4 words that share exactly the same numbers.

اسم

ISM (Name)

The first word of Bismillah, in its complete form ISM occurs in the Quran 19 times.

$19 = 19 \times 1$

No	Verse
1.	5:4
2.	6:118
3.	6:119
4.	6:121
5.	6:138
6.	22:28
7.	22:34
8.	22:36
9.	22:40
10.	49:11
11.	55:78
12.	56:74
13.	56:96
14.	69:52
15.	73:8
16.	76:25
17.	87:1
18.	87:15
19.	96:1

↑

عليها تسعة عشر
On it is Nineteen

The frequency of the word "Ism," as shown above is exactly 19 times. Nevertheless, a detail in our method of counting needs to be addressed. On three occasions the word "Ism" is connected with the prefix letter "B" (meaning 'with,' 'by' or 'in') by the omission of its first letter "Alif," which turns its spelling to "BSM" (See below for references). In all other occurrences of the same word, they are connected to pronouns or in broken plural form unique to Arabic. These are "Ismihi" (his name), "Asma" (names), "Asmaihi" (his names), and "Asmaihim" (their names). In all of these occurrences, the spelling of "ISM" changes.

Since we count the singular form of "Ism" the only other candidate for counting besides "Ism" and "B-ism" is "Bsm," which occurs three times in verses 1:1; 11:41 and 27:30. (For those who are interested in research, here is a clue: All letters of Bismillah except one is used in initial letters/numbers except its first letter, B.)

The frequencies of the two different spellings of the word "Ism" leave us with two options:

Ism	19
Bsm	3

From the beginning of our research we are left with a decision. Those who have already made up their minds against the possibility of a mathematical pattern in the Quran, will not miss the opportunity to pick the ones that are not divisible by 19. As with stereograms, depending on one's initial choice, one may end up with random dots or an extraordinary art. In my opinion, these counting options were created deliberately to provide an excuse for those who do not want to witness the miracle of the Quran. By one's free choice one can deprive himself or herself from witnessing one of the greatest miracles. However, I believe that those who are familiar with the art of scientific inquiry such as with the Periodic System of Elements, and do not have an initial allergy against the number 19 or the Quran will keep their mind open for a possible pattern of the frequency of "Ism" in conjunction with the words of Bismillah, based on 19.

The classic, most popular Arabic index of the Quran, *Al-Mujamul Mufahras Li Alfazil Quranil Kareem*, interestingly counts the word "Ism" separately from others and indicates the frequency of the word "Ism" as 19. The author of the index died a long time before the discovery of Code 19 and had no knowledge of such a pattern in the Quran.[98]

Akin to a Random-Dot 3-D Stereogram

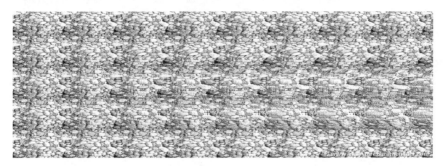

Let me elaborate a little about the computer made 3-D stereographic or holographic images. To see the message/sign/image hidden among the random dots, you must first accept the possibility that there might be a hidden image and then you must follow some instructions, stay at a particular distance, focus accordingly, and spend some time. Learning that a diverse group of people have witnessed a hidden image should be sufficient to create curiosity in you. If you have two eyes and follow the instructions correctly you will join the ranks of those who have witnessed the the message/sign/image.

Let's assume that you and some of your friends have already *seen* the message/image hidden among the random dots, and assume some other friends make fun of you and do not even consider spending a little *time* focusing on the stereogram. They call it "foolish" and "worthless." Do you think that these friends of yours will have any chance witnessing what you have witnessed? What if the stereogram contains the code for a great reward for only those who could *see* the image? Would your friend have any right to complain for not receiving the reward? Assume that some of your friends finally decided to give it a chance and spent a few minutes staring at the stereogram but this time disregarded an important instruction. Instead of observing the stereogram with *two eyes* they decided to observe it with *one eye*. Do you think they would have any chance seeing what you have seen? Do you think they would have the right to complain when the rewards and consequences are announced?

If you blinded yourself right from the beginning, you will most likely come up with excuses for why you and others should not understand any connection between nineteen and the Quran. You have the all freedom to pick *Saqar* as you have the same freedom to pick one of the greatest miracles. (31:7; 45:8; 27:81).

The noise-makers will produce irrelevant responses hoping that they would divert people from focusing on the main message. Truth-seeking people do not care what the majority of people do. If someone claims to follow the Quran and ignores a Quranic challenge with dogmatic arrogance, that person should ask himself or herself this question: "Do I really respect the Quran?"

Give yourself a chance. Accept the possibility that you might be self-righteously rejecting a divine sign. Think that many religious people in the past rejected new divine signs brought by their messengers and were self-righteous regarding their rejection (See 38:1-15)

الله

ALLaH (God)

The second word of Bismillah occurs in the Quran exactly 2698 times.

2698 = 19x142

The first column shows the serial index number of the word "Allah" occurring in all consecutively following verses of the Quran. In verses where "Allah" occurs more than once, this multiple number is reflected in the extra increment in the index number of the associated verse. For example, the serial index number following "9" is "11", which means that the verse 2:20 associated with the number "11" has "Allah" occurring two times. Likewise, each of verses 2:258 and 2:259 has "Allah" occurring three times, and this is reflected in their corresponding index numbers 241 and 244, following the earlier index number 238 associated with the verse 2:257.

Verses containing more than one word "Allah" are indicated by the index number of the following verse. The first number after the index number indicates chapter, the second indicates verse number and the last one indicates the cumulative sum of verse numbers where the word God occurs up to that verse.

The first number in the second column after the first-column index number indicates the chapter number, the second indicates the verse number and the last (third) column indicates the cumulative sum of the verse numbers where the word "Allah" occurs up to that verse.

139

No	Verse	Sum	No	Verse	Sum	No	Verse	Sum
1	1:1	1	66	2:110	3128	139	2:198	10737
2	1:2	3	67	2:112	3240	141	2:199	10936
3	2:7	10	68	2:113	3353	142	2:200	11136
4	2:8	18	69	2:114	3467	143	2:202	11338
5	2:9	27	72	2:115	3582	145	2:203	11541
6	2:10	37	73	2:116	3698	146	2:204	11745
7	2:15	52	74	2:118	3816	147	2:205	11950
8	2:17	69	76	2:120	3936	148	2:206	12156
9	2:19	88	77	2:126	4062	150	2:207	12363
11	2:20	108	78	2:132	4194	151	2:209	12572
12	2:22	130	79	2:136	4330	153	2:210	12782
13	2:23	153	80	2:137	4467	155	2:211	12993
15	2:26	179	82	2:138	4605	156	2:212	13205
17	2:27	206	83	2:139	4744	159	2:213	13418
18	2:28	234	86	2:140	4884	161	2:214	13632
19	2:55	289	87	2:142	5026	162	2:215	13847
20	2:60	349	90	2:143	5169	163	2:216	14063
22	2:61	410	91	2:144	5313	165	2:217	14280
23	2:62	472	93	2:148	5461	168	2:218	14498
24	2:64	536	94	2:149	5610	169	2:219	14717
26	2:67	603	95	2:153	5763	172	2:220	14937
27	2:70	673	96	2:154	5917	173	2:221	15158
28	2:72	745	97	2:156	6073	175	2:222	15380
29	2:73	818	99	2:158	6231	176	2:223	15603
31	2:74	892	100	2:159	6390	178	2:224	15827
32	2:75	967	101	2:161	6551	180	2:225	16052
33	2:76	1043	102	2:164	6715	181	2:226	16278
34	2:77	1120	107	2:165	6880	182	2:227	16505
35	2:79	1199	108	2:167	7047	185	2:228	16733
38	2:80	1279	109	2:169	7216	189	2:229	16962
39	2:83	1362	110	2:170	7386	191	2:230	17192
40	2:85	1447	111	2:172	7558	195	2:231	17423
41	2:88	1535	113	2:173	7731	197	2:232	17655
43	2:89	1624	115	2:174	7905	199	2:233	17888
45	2:90	1714	116	2:176	8081	200	2:234	18122
47	2:91	1805	117	2:177	8258	203	2:235	18357
48	2:94	1899	118	2:181	8439	204	2:237	18594
49	2:95	1994	119	2:182	8621	205	2:238	18832
50	2:96	2090	121	2:185	8806	206	2:239	19071
51	2:97	2187	125	2:187	8993	207	2:240	19311
53	2:98	2285	126	2:189	9182	208	2:242	19553
55	2:101	2386	128	2:190	9372	210	2:243	19796
56	2:102	2488	129	2:192	9564	212	2:244	20040
57	2:103	2591	130	2:193	9757	214	2:245	20285
59	2:105	2696	132	2:194	9951	217	2:246	20531
60	2:106	2802	134	2:195	10146	221	2:247	20778
62	2:107	2909	137	2:196	10342	225	2:249	21027
64	2:109	3018	138	2:197	10539	229	2:251	21278

230	2:252	21530	327	3:42	29941	410	3:129	34818
234	2:253	21783	328	3:45	29986	411	3:130	34948
235	2:255	22038	329	3:47	30033	412	3:132	35080
237	2:256	22294	331	3:49	30082	413	3:134	35214
238	2:257	22551	332	3:50	30132	415	3:135	35349
241	2:258	22809	333	3:51	30183	417	3:140	35489
244	2:259	23068	336	3:52	30235	418	3:141	35630
245	2:260	23328	338	3:54	30289	419	3:142	35772
248	2:261	23589	339	3:55	30344	421	3:144	35916
249	2:262	23851	340	3:57	30401	422	3:145	36061
250	2:263	24114	341	3:59	30460	424	3:146	36207
252	2:264	24378	342	3:61	30521	426	3:148	36355
254	2:265	24643	344	3:62	30583	427	3:150	36505
255	2:266	24909	345	3:63	30646	428	3:151	36656
256	2:267	25176	347	3:64	30710	430	3:152	36808
258	2:268	25444	348	3:66	30776	431	3:153	36961
259	2:270	25714	349	3:68	30844	435	3:154	37115
260	2:271	25985	350	3:70	30914	437	3:155	37270
262	2:272	26257	353	3:73	30987	440	3:156	37426
264	2:273	26530	354	3:74	31061	442	3:157	37583
266	2:275	26805	355	3:75	31136	443	3:158	37741
268	2:276	27081	356	3:76	31212	446	3:159	37900
269	2:278	27359	358	3:77	31289	448	3:160	38060
270	2:279	27638	361	3:78	31367	450	3:162	38222
271	2:281	27919	363	3:79	31446	452	3:163	38385
277	2:282	28201	364	3:81	31527	453	3:164	38549
279	2:283	28484	365	3:83	31610	454	3:165	38714
282	2:284	28768	366	3:84	31694	455	3:166	38880
283	2:285	29053	368	3:86	31780	457	3:167	39047
284	2:286	29339	369	3:87	31867	458	3:169	39216
285	3:2	29341	370	3:89	31956	459	3:170	39386
287	3:4	29345	371	3:92	32048	461	3:171	39557
288	3:5	29350	372	3:94	32142	462	3:172	39729
289	3:7	29357	373	3:95	32237	463	3:173	39902
290	3:9	29366	375	3:97	32334	466	3:174	40076
291	3:10	29376	377	3:98	32432	468	3:176	40252
293	3:11	29387	379	3:99	32531	469	3:177	40429
295	3:13	29400	381	3:101	32632	473	3:179	40608
296	3:14	29414	382	3:102	32734	476	3:180	40788
298	3:15	29429	385	3:103	32837	478	3:181	40969
299	3:18	29447	386	3:107	32944	479	3:182	41151
302	3:19	29466	388	3:108	33052	480	3:183	41334
304	3:20	29486	390	3:109	33161	481	3:187	41521
305	3:21	29507	391	3:110	33271	483	3:189	41710
306	3:23	29530	394	3:112	33383	484	3:191	41901
309	3:28	29558	395	3:113	33496	486	3:195	42096
311	3:29	29587	396	3:114	33610	488	3:198	42294
313	3:30	29617	397	3:115	33725	492	3:199	42493
316	3:31	29648	398	3:116	33841	493	3:200	42693
318	3:32	29680	399	3:117	33958	495	4:1	42694
319	3:33	29713	400	3:119	34077	496	4:5	42699
320	3:34	29747	401	3:120	34197	497	4:6	42705
321	3:36	29783	402	3:121	34318	498	4:9	42714
323	3:37	29820	404	3:122	34440	501	4:11	42725
325	3:39	29859	406	3:123	34563	503	4:12	42737
326	3:40	29899	408	3:126	34689	505	4:13	42750

141

506	4:14	42764	595	4:87	45677	697	4:157	52509
507	4:15	42779	598	4:88	45765	699	4:158	52667
508	4:16	42795	599	4:89	45854	700	4:160	52827
511	4:17	42812	601	4:90	45944	701	4:162	52989
512	4:19	42831	603	4:92	46036	702	4:164	53153
513	4:23	42854	604	4:93	46129	704	4:165	53318
515	4:24	42878	608	4:94	46223	706	4:166	53484
517	4:25	42903	612	4:95	46318	707	4:167	53651
519	4:26	42929	613	4:96	46414	708	4:168	53819
520	4:27	42956	614	4:97	46511	709	4:169	53988
521	4:28	42984	616	4:99	46610	711	4:170	54158
522	4:29	43013	620	4:100	46710	716	4:171	54329
523	4:30	43043	621	4:102	46812	717	4:172	54501
526	4:32	43075	622	4:103	46915	718	4:173	54674
527	4:33	43108	624	4:104	47019	719	4:175	54849
530	4:34	43142	625	4:105	47124	722	4:176	55025
532	4:35	43177	627	4:106	47230	723	5:1	55026
534	4:36	43213	628	4:107	47337	726	5:2	55028
535	4:37	43250	630	4:108	47445	728	5:3	55031
536	4:38	43288	631	4:109	47554	732	5:4	55035
539	4:39	43327	633	4:110	47664	733	5:6	55041
540	4:40	43367	634	4:111	47775	736	5:7	55048
541	4:42	43409	637	4:113	47888	739	5:8	55056
542	4:43	43452	638	4:114	48002	740	5:9	55065
545	4:45	43497	640	4:116	48118	743	5:11	55076
546	4:46	43543	641	4:118	48236	746	5:12	55088
547	4:47	43590	643	4:119	48355	747	5:13	55101
549	4:48	43638	645	4:122	48477	748	5:14	55115
550	4:49	43687	646	4:123	48600	749	5:15	55130
551	4:50	43737	648	4:125	48725	750	5:16	55146
553	4:52	43789	650	4:126	48851	754	5:17	55163
554	4:54	43843	652	4:127	48978	756	5:18	55181
555	4:56	43899	653	4:128	49106	757	5:19	55200
558	4:58	43957	654	4:129	49235	758	5:20	55220
561	4:59	44016	656	4:130	49365	759	5:21	55241
562	4:61	44077	660	4:131	49496	761	5:23	55264
563	4:62	44139	662	4:132	49628	762	5:27	55291
564	4:63	44202	663	4:133	49761	763	5:28	55319
567	4:64	44266	665	4:134	49895	764	5:31	55350
569	4:69	44335	668	4:135	50030	765	5:33	55383
571	4:70	44405	670	4:136	50166	766	5:34	55417
572	4:72	44477	671	4:137	50303	767	5:35	55452
573	4:73	44550	672	4:139	50442	769	5:38	55490
575	4:74	44624	674	4:140	50582	771	5:39	55529
576	4:75	44699	677	4:141	50723	773	5:40	55569
577	4:76	44775	679	4:142	50865	776	5:41	55610
578	4:77	44852	680	4:143	51008	777	5:42	55652
580	4:78	44930	681	4:144	51152	778	5:43	55695
582	4:79	45009	684	4:146	51298	780	5:44	55739
583	4:80	45089	686	4:147	51445	781	5:45	55784
586	4:81	45170	688	4:148	51593	783	5:47	55831
587	4:82	45252	689	4:149	51742	786	5:48	55879
588	4:83	45335	691	4:150	51892	789	5:49	55928
591	4:84	45419	693	4:152	52044	790	5:50	55978
592	4:85	45504	694	4:153	52197	791	5:51	56029
593	4:86	45590	696	4:155	52352	792	5:52	56081

793	5:53	56134	879	6:31	60444	956	6:164	65971
797	5:54	56188	880	6:33	60477	957	7:26	65997
798	5:55	56243	881	6:34	60511	960	7:28	66025
800	5:56	56299	882	6:35	60546	961	7:30	66055
801	5:57	56356	883	6:36	60582	962	7:32	66087
802	5:59	56415	884	6:37	60619	964	7:33	66120
804	5:60	56475	885	6:39	60658	966	7:37	66157
805	5:61	56536	887	6:40	60698	968	7:43	66200
808	5:64	56600	888	6:45	60743	969	7:44	66244
810	5:67	56667	890	6:46	60789	970	7:45	66289
811	5:69	56736	891	6:47	60836	971	7:49	66338
813	5:71	56807	892	6:50	60886	973	7:50	66388
817	5:72	56879	894	6:53	60939	975	7:54	66442
818	5:73	56952	895	6:56	60995	976	7:56	66498
820	5:74	57026	896	6:57	61052	977	7:59	66557
822	5:76	57102	897	6:58	61110	978	7:62	66619
823	5:80	57182	898	6:62	61172	979	7:65	66684
824	5:81	57263	899	6:64	61236	980	7:69	66753
825	5:84	57347	900	6:70	61306	981	7:70	66823
826	5:85	57432	903	6:71	61377	982	7:71	66894
828	5:87	57519	904	6:80	61457	985	7:73	66967
830	5:88	57607	905	6:81	61538	986	7:74	67041
832	5:89	57696	906	6:88	61626	987	7:85	67126
833	5:91	57787	907	6:90	61716	988	7:86	67212
834	5:92	57879	910	6:91	61807	989	7:87	67299
835	5:93	57972	913	6:93	61900	993	7:89	67388
837	5:94	58066	915	6:95	61995	995	7:99	67487
840	5:95	58161	916	6:100	62095	996	7:101	67588
841	5:96	58257	917	6:102	62197	997	7:105	67693
844	5:97	58354	918	6:107	62304	999	7:128	67821
846	5:98	58452	920	6:108	62412	1000	7:131	67952
847	5:99	58551	922	6:109	62521	1001	7:140	68092
848	5:100	58651	923	6:111	62632	1004	7:158	68250
850	5:101	58752	924	6:114	62746	1005	7:164	68414
852	5:103	58855	925	6:116	62862	1006	7:169	68583
853	5:104	58959	926	6:118	62980	1007	7:178	68761
854	5:105	59064	927	6:119	63099	1008	7:180	68941
856	5:106	59170	928	6:121	63220	1009	7:185	69126
857	5:107	59277	931	6:124	63344	1010	7:186	69312
859	5:108	59385	933	6:125	63469	1011	7:187	69499
860	5:109	59494	934	6:128	63597	1012	7:188	69687
861	5:110	59604	938	6:136	63733	1013	7:189	69876
862	5:112	59716	939	6:137	63870	1014	7:190	70066
863	5:115	59831	940	6:138	64008	1015	7:194	70260
865	5:116	59947	942	6:140	64148	1016	7:196	70456
866	5:117	60064	943	6:142	64290	1017	7:200	70656
868	5:119	60183	946	6:144	64434	1020	8:1	70657
869	5:120	60303	947	6:145	64579	1021	8:2	70659
870	6:1	60304	948	6:148	64727	1023	8:7	70666
871	6:3	60307	949	6:149	64876	1026	8:10	70676
872	6:12	60319	950	6:150	65026	1029	8:13	70689
873	6:14	60333	951	6:151	65177	1030	8:16	70705
874	6:17	60350	952	6:152	65329	1033	8:17	70722
876	6:19	60369	953	6:157	65486	1034	8:18	70740
877	6:21	60390	954	6:159	65645	1035	8:19	70759
878	6:23	60413	955	6:162	65807	1036	8:20	70779

1037	8:22	70801	1132	9:19	72971	1227	9:91	76047
1038	8:23	70824	1134	9:20	72991	1228	9:93	76140
1040	8:24	70848	1135	9:22	73013	1230	9:94	76234
1041	8:25	70873	1138	9:24	73037	1231	9:95	76329
1042	8:27	70900	1139	9:25	73062	1232	9:96	76425
1043	8:28	70928	1140	9:26	73088	1234	9:97	76522
1045	8:29	70957	1142	9:27	73115	1235	9:98	76620
1047	8:30	70987	1144	9:28	73143	1239	9:99	76719
1049	8:33	71020	1146	9:29	73172	1240	9:100	76819
1050	8:34	71054	1149	9:30	73202	1242	9:102	76921
1051	8:36	71090	1150	9:31	73233	1243	9:103	77024
1052	8:37	71127	1152	9:32	73265	1245	9:104	77128
1054	8:39	71166	1154	9:34	73299	1246	9:105	77233
1055	8:40	71206	1157	9:36	73335	1248	9:106	77339
1058	8:41	71247	1160	9:37	73372	1250	9:107	77446
1060	8:42	71289	1161	9:38	73410	1251	9:108	77554
1062	8:43	71332	1162	9:39	73449	1253	9:109	77663
1064	8:44	71376	1167	9:40	73489	1254	9:110	77773
1065	8:45	71421	1168	9:41	73530	1257	9:111	77884
1067	8:46	71467	1170	9:42	73572	1258	9:112	77996
1069	8:47	71514	1171	9:43	73615	1259	9:114	78110
1071	8:48	71562	1173	9:44	73659	1261	9:115	78225
1073	8:49	71611	1174	9:45	73704	1263	9:116	78341
1074	8:51	71662	1175	9:46	73750	1264	9:117	78458
1077	8:52	71714	1176	9:47	73797	1266	9:118	78576
1079	8:53	71767	1177	9:48	73845	1267	9:119	78695
1080	8:55	71822	1179	9:51	73896	1270	9:120	78815
1081	8:58	71880	1180	9:52	73948	1271	9:121	78936
1084	8:60	71940	1181	9:54	74002	1272	9:123	79059
1085	8:61	72001	1182	9:55	74057	1273	9:127	79186
1086	8:62	72063	1183	9:56	74113	1275	10:3	79189
1087	8:63	72126	1187	9:59	74172	1276	10:4	79193
1088	8:64	72190	1190	9:60	74232	1277	10:5	79198
1091	8:66	72256	1192	9:61	74293	1278	10:6	79204
1093	8:67	72323	1194	9:62	74355	1279	10:10	79214
1094	8:68	72391	1195	9:63	74418	1280	10:11	79225
1096	8:69	72460	1196	9:64	74482	1281	10:16	79241
1098	8:70	72530	1197	9:65	74547	1282	10:17	79258
1100	8:71	72601	1198	9:67	74614	1285	10:18	79276
1102	8:72	72673	1200	9:68	74682	1286	10:20	79296
1103	8:74	72747	1201	9:70	74752	1287	10:21	79317
1105	8:75	72822	1204	9:71	74823	1288	10:22	79339
1106	9:1	72823	1206	9:72	74895	1289	10:25	79364
1108	9:2	72825	1209	9:74	74969	1290	10:27	79391
1111	9:3	72828	1210	9:75	75044	1291	10:29	79420
1112	9:4	72832	1211	9:77	75121	1292	10:30	79450
1113	9:5	72837	1213	9:78	75199	1293	10:31	79481
1114	9:6	72843	1214	9:79	75278	1294	10:32	79513
1116	9:7	72850	1217	9:80	75358	1295	10:34	79547
1117	9:9	72859	1219	9:81	75439	1296	10:35	79582
1118	9:13	72872	1220	9:83	75522	1297	10:36	79618
1119	9:14	72886	1221	9:84	75606	1298	10:37	79655
1121	9:15	72901	1222	9:85	75691	1299	10:38	79693
1124	9:16	72917	1223	9:86	75777	1300	10:44	79737
1125	9:17	72934	1224	9:89	75866	1301	10:45	79782
1128	9:18	72952	1225	9:90	75956	1302	10:46	79828

1303	10:49	79877	1373	12:18	83293	1450	13:43	86210
1305	10:55	79932	1374	12:19	83312	1451	14:2	86212
1306	10:58	79990	1375	12:21	83333	1452	14:3	86215
1309	10:59	80049	1376	12:23	83356	1453	14:4	86219
1311	10:60	80109	1377	12:31	83387	1454	14:5	86224
1312	10:62	80171	1378	12:37	83424	1455	14:6	86230
1313	10:64	80235	1380	12:38	83462	1456	14:8	86238
1314	10:65	80300	1381	12:39	83501	1457	14:9	86247
1316	10:66	80366	1383	12:40	83541	1458	14:10	86257
1318	10:68	80434	1384	12:51	83592	1461	14:11	86268
1319	10:69	80503	1385	12:52	83644	1463	14:12	86280
1321	10:71	80574	1386	12:64	83708	1464	14:19	86299
1322	10:72	80646	1388	12:66	83774	1465	14:20	86319
1324	10:81	80727	1390	12:67	83841	1468	14:21	86340
1325	10:82	80809	1391	12:68	83909	1469	14:22	86362
1326	10:84	80893	1392	12:73	83982	1470	14:24	86386
1327	10:85	80978	1393	12:76	84058	1471	14:25	86411
1328	10:95	81073	1394	12:77	84135	1474	14:27	86438
1329	10:100	81173	1395	12:79	84214	1475	14:28	86466
1331	10:104	81277	1397	12:80	84294	1476	14:30	86496
1332	10:106	81383	1398	12:83	84377	1477	14:32	86528
1333	10:107	81490	1399	12:85	84462	1478	14:34	86562
1334	10:109	81599	1401	12:86	84548	1479	14:38	86600
1335	11:2	81601	1403	12:87	84635	1480	14:39	86639
1336	11:4	81605	1404	12:88	84723	1481	14:42	86681
1337	11:6	81611	1406	12:90	84813	1482	14:46	86727
1338	11:12	81623	1408	12:91	84904	1484	14:47	86774
1339	11:13	81636	1409	12:92	84996	1485	14:48	86822
1340	11:14	81650	1410	12:95	85091	1487	14:51	86873
1342	11:18	81668	1411	12:96	85187	1488	15:69	86942
1343	11:19	81687	1412	12:99	85286	1489	15:96	87038
1344	11:20	81707	1413	12:106	85392	1490	16:1	87039
1345	11:26	81733	1414	12:107	85499	1491	16:9	87048
1346	11:29	81762	1416	12:108	85607	1493	16:18	87066
1347	11:30	81792	1417	13:2	85609	1494	16:19	87085
1350	11:31	81823	1418	13:8	85617	1495	16:20	87105
1351	11:33	81856	1421	13:11	85628	1496	16:23	87128
1352	11:34	81890	1422	13:13	85641	1497	16:26	87154
1353	11:41	81931	1423	13:15	85656	1498	16:28	87182
1354	11:43	81974	1426	13:16	85672	1499	16:31	87213
1355	11:50	82024	1428	13:17	85689	1500	16:33	87246
1356	11:54	82078	1429	13:20	85709	1501	16:35	87281
1357	11:56	82134	1430	13:21	85730	1503	16:36	87317
1358	11:61	82195	1432	13:25	85755	1504	16:37	87354
1359	11:63	82258	1433	13:26	85781	1506	16:38	87392
1361	11:64	82322	1434	13:27	85808	1507	16:41	87433
1363	11:73	82395	1436	13:28	85836	1508	16:45	87478
1364	11:78	82473	1440	13:31	85867	1510	16:48	87526
1365	11:84	82557	1442	13:33	85900	1511	16:49	87575
1366	11:86	82643	1443	13:34	85934	1512	16:51	87626
1367	11:88	82731	1444	13:36	85970	1513	16:52	87678
1368	11:92	82823	1445	13:37	86007	1514	16:53	87731
1369	11:101	82924	1446	13:38	86045	1515	16:56	87787
1370	11:113	83037	1447	13:39	86084	1516	16:57	87844
1371	11:115	83152	1448	13:41	86125	1517	16:60	87904
1372	11:123	83275	1449	13:42	86167	1518	16:61	87965

1519	16:62	88027	1592	18:26	92448	1664	22:54	94587
1520	16:63	88090	1593	18:38	92486	1665	22:56	94643
1521	16:65	88155	1595	18:39	92525	1668	22:58	94701
1523	16:70	88225	1596	18:43	92568	1669	22:59	94760
1525	16:71	88296	1597	18:44	92612	1671	22:60	94820
1527	16:72	88368	1598	18:45	92657	1673	22:61	94881
1528	16:73	88441	1599	18:69	92726	1675	22:62	94943
1530	16:74	88515	1600	19:30	92756	1677	22:63	95006
1532	16:75	88590	1601	19:35	92791	1678	22:64	95070
1533	16:76	88666	1602	19:36	92827	1680	22:65	95135
1535	16:77	88743	1603	19:48	92875	1681	22:68	95203
1536	16:78	88821	1604	19:49	92924	1682	22:69	95272
1537	16:79	88900	1605	19:58	92982	1684	22:70	95342
1538	16:80	88980	1606	19:76	93058	1685	22:71	95413
1539	16:81	89061	1607	19:81	93139	1686	22:72	95485
1540	16:83	89144	1608	20:8	93147	1687	22:73	95558
1541	16:87	89231	1609	20:14	93161	1689	22:74	95632
1542	16:88	89319	1610	20:61	93222	1691	22:75	95707
1543	16:90	89409	1611	20:73	93295	1692	22:76	95783
1546	16:91	89500	1612	20:98	93393	1694	22:78	95861
1547	16:92	89592	1613	20:114	93507	1695	23:14	95875
1548	16:93	89685	1615	21:22	93529	1696	23:23	95898
1549	16:94	89779	1616	21:57	93586	1697	23:24	95922
1551	16:95	89874	1617	21:66	93652	1698	23:28	95950
1552	16:96	89970	1618	21:67	93719	1699	23:32	95982
1553	16:98	90068	1619	21:98	93817	1700	23:38	96020
1554	16:101	90169	1620	22:2	93819	1701	23:85	96105
1556	16:104	90273	1621	22:3	93822	1702	23:87	96192
1557	16:105	90378	1622	22:6	93828	1703	23:89	96281
1559	16:106	90484	1623	22:7	93835	1705	23:91	96372
1560	16:107	90591	1624	22:8	93843	1706	23:116	96488
1561	16:108	90699	1625	22:9	93852	1707	23:117	96605
1564	16:112	90811	1626	22:10	93862	1709	24:2	96607
1566	16:114	90925	1627	22:11	93873	1710	24:5	96612
1568	16:115	91040	1628	22:12	93885	1711	24:6	96618
1570	16:116	91156	1630	22:14	93899	1712	24:7	96625
1571	16:120	91276	1631	22:15	93914	1713	24:8	96633
1572	16:127	91403	1632	22:16	93930	1714	24:9	96642
1573	16:128	91531	1634	22:17	93947	1716	24:10	96652
1574	17:22	91553	1637	22:18	93965	1717	24:13	96665
1575	17:33	91586	1638	22:23	93988	1718	24:14	96679
1576	17:39	91625	1639	22:25	94013	1719	24:15	96694
1577	17:92	91717	1640	22:28	94041	1720	24:17	96711
1578	17:94	91811	1641	22:30	94071	1722	24:18	96729
1579	17:96	91907	1643	22:31	94102	1723	24:19	96748
1580	17:97	92004	1644	22:32	94134	1725	24:20	96768
1581	17:99	92103	1645	22:34	94168	1728	24:21	96789
1582	17:110	92213	1646	22:35	94203	1731	24:22	96811
1583	17:111	92324	1648	22:36	94239	1733	24:25	96836
1584	18:1	92325	1650	22:37	94276	1734	24:28	96864
1585	18:4	92329	1652	22:38	94314	1735	24:29	96893
1586	18:15	92344	1653	22:39	94353	1736	24:30	96923
1587	18:16	92360	1658	22:40	94393	1737	24:31	96954
1589	18:17	92377	1659	22:41	94434	1739	24:32	96986
1590	18:21	92398	1660	22:47	94481	1742	24:33	97019
1591	18:24	92422	1663	22:52	94533	1746	24:35	97054

1747	24:36	97090	1820	27:46	100845	1894	29:52	103620
1748	24:37	97127	1821	27:47	100892	1895	29:60	103680
1750	24:38	97165	1822	27:49	100941	1896	29:61	103741
1752	24:39	97204	1824	27:59	101000	1898	29:62	103803
1753	24:40	97244	1825	27:60	101060	1900	29:63	103866
1755	24:41	97285	1826	27:61	101121	1901	29:65	103931
1757	24:42	97327	1827	27:62	101183	1902	29:67	103998
1758	24:43	97370	1829	27:63	101246	1903	29:68	104066
1759	24:44	97414	1830	27:64	101310	1904	29:69	104135
1762	24:45	97459	1831	27:65	101375	1905	30:4	104139
1763	24:46	97505	1832	27:79	101454	1906	30:5	104144
1764	24:47	97552	1833	27:87	101541	1908	30:6	104150
1765	24:48	97600	1834	27:88	101629	1909	30:8	104158
1766	24:50	97650	1835	27:93	101722	1910	30:9	104167
1767	24:51	97701	1836	28:13	101735	1911	30:10	104177
1769	24:52	97753	1837	28:27	101762	1912	30:11	104188
1771	24:53	97806	1838	28:28	101790	1913	30:17	104205
1772	24:54	97860	1839	28:30	101820	1914	30:29	104234
1773	24:55	97915	1840	28:49	101869	1916	30:30	104264
1775	24:58	97973	1842	28:50	101919	1917	30:37	104301
1777	24:59	98032	1843	28:56	101975	1918	30:38	104339
1778	24:60	98092	1844	28:60	102035	1920	30:39	104378
1780	24:61	98153	1845	28:68	102103	1921	30:40	104418
1784	24:62	98215	1846	28:70	102173	1922	30:43	104461
1785	24:63	98278	1848	28:71	102244	1923	30:48	104509
1787	24:64	98342	1850	28:72	102316	1924	30:50	104559
1788	25:17	98359	1851	28:75	102391	1925	30:54	104613
1789	25:41	98400	1852	28:76	102467	1926	30:56	104669
1790	25:55	98455	1855	28:77	102544	1927	30:59	104728
1792	25:68	98523	1856	28:78	102622	1928	30:60	104788
1794	25:70	98593	1857	28:80	102702	1929	31:6	104794
1795	25:71	98664	1858	28:81	102783	1930	31:9	104803
1796	26:89	98753	1860	28:82	102865	1931	31:11	104814
1797	26:93	98846	1861	28:87	102952	1933	31:12	104826
1798	26:97	98943	1862	28:88	103040	1934	31:13	104839
1799	26:108	99051	1863	29:3	103043	1936	31:16	104855
1800	26:110	99161	1865	29:5	103048	1937	31:18	104873
1801	26:126	99287	1866	29:6	103054	1939	31:20	104893
1802	26:131	99418	1870	29:10	103064	1940	31:21	104914
1803	26:144	99562	1871	29:11	103075	1942	31:22	104936
1804	26:150	99712	1872	29:16	103091	1943	31:23	104959
1805	26:163	99875	1875	29:17	103108	1945	31:25	104984
1806	26:179	100054	1877	29:19	103127	1947	31:26	105010
1807	26:213	100267	1879	29:20	103147	1949	31:27	105037
1808	26:227	100494	1880	29:22	103169	1950	31:28	105065
1809	27:8	100502	1881	29:23	103192	1952	31:29	105094
1810	27:9	100511	1882	29:24	103216	1954	31:30	105124
1811	27:15	100526	1883	29:25	103241	1955	31:31	105155
1812	27:24	100550	1884	29:29	103270	1956	31:32	105187
1813	27:25	100575	1885	29:36	103306	1958	31:33	105220
1814	27:26	100601	1886	29:40	103346	1960	31:34	105254
1815	27:30	100631	1887	29:41	103387	1961	32:4	105258
1816	27:36	100667	1888	29:42	103429	1963	33:1	105259
1817	27:43	100710	1889	29:44	103473	1964	33:2	105261
1818	27:44	100754	1891	29:45	103518	1966	33:3	105264
1819	27:45	100799	1892	29:50	103568	1968	33:4	105268

1970	33:5	105273	2062	35:2	107321	2132	39:17	109829
1971	33:6	105279	2064	35:3	107324	2133	39:18	109847
1973	33:9	105288	2065	35:4	107328	2135	39:20	109867
1974	33:10	105298	2067	35:5	107333	2136	39:21	109888
1975	33:12	105310	2069	35:8	107341	2138	39:22	109910
1977	33:15	105325	2070	35:9	107350	2142	39:23	109933
1979	33:17	105342	2071	35:10	107360	2143	39:26	109959
1980	33:18	105360	2073	35:11	107371	2145	39:29	109988
1982	33:19	105379	2074	35:13	107384	2146	39:32	110020
1985	33:21	105400	2076	35:15	107399	2147	39:35	110055
1987	33:22	105422	2077	35:17	107416	2149	39:36	110091
1988	33:23	105445	2078	35:18	107434	2151	39:37	110128
1990	33:24	105469	2079	35:22	107456	2155	39:38	110166
1993	33:25	105494	2080	35:27	107483	2156	39:42	110208
1994	33:27	105521	2082	35:28	107511	2157	39:43	110251
1996	33:29	105550	2083	35:29	107540	2158	39:44	110295
1997	33:30	105580	2084	35:31	107571	2159	39:45	110340
1998	33:31	105611	2085	35:32	107603	2160	39:47	110387
2000	33:33	105644	2086	35:34	107637	2161	39:52	110439
2002	33:34	105678	2087	35:38	107675	2163	39:53	110492
2004	33:35	105713	2088	35:40	107715	2164	39:56	110548
2006	33:36	105749	2089	35:41	107756	2165	39:57	110605
2011	33:37	105786	2090	35:42	107798	2166	39:60	110665
2014	33:38	105824	2092	35:43	107841	2167	39:61	110726
2017	33:39	105863	2093	35:44	107885	2168	39:62	110788
2019	33:40	105903	2095	35:45	107930	2169	39:63	110851
2020	33:41	105944	2097	36:47	107977	2170	39:64	110915
2021	33:46	105990	2098	36:74	108051	2171	39:66	110981
2022	33:47	106037	2099	37:23	108074	2172	39:67	111048
2024	33:48	106085	2100	37:35	108109	2173	39:68	111116
2026	33:50	106135	2101	37:40	108149	2174	39:74	111190
2028	33:51	106186	2102	37:56	108205	2175	39:75	111265
2029	33:52	106238	2103	37:74	108279	2176	40:2	111267
2032	33:53	106291	2104	37:86	108365	2177	40:4	111271
2033	33:54	106345	2105	37:96	108461	2178	40:10	111281
2035	33:55	106400	2106	37:102	108563	2180	40:12	111293
2036	33:56	106456	2107	37:126	108689	2181	40:14	111307
2038	33:57	106513	2108	37:128	108817	2183	40:16	111323
2039	33:59	106572	2109	37:152	108969	2184	40:17	111340
2041	33:62	106634	2110	37:159	109128	2186	40:20	111360
2042	33:63	106697	2111	37:160	109288	2188	40:21	111381
2043	33:64	106761	2112	37:169	109457	2189	40:22	111403
2044	33:66	106827	2113	37:182	109639	2191	40:28	111431
2046	33:69	106896	2115	38:26	109665	2192	40:29	111460
2047	33:70	106966	2116	38:65	109730	2193	40:31	111491
2048	33:71	107037	2117	39:1	109731	2195	40:33	111524
2051	33:73	107110	2118	39:2	109733	2197	40:34	111558
2052	34:1	107111	2122	39:3	109736	2200	40:35	111593
2053	34:8	107119	2124	39:4	109740	2201	40:42	111635
2054	34:22	107141	2125	39:6	109746	2202	40:43	111678
2055	34:24	107165	2126	39:7	109753	2204	40:44	111722
2056	34:27	107192	2127	39:8	109761	2205	40:45	111767
2057	34:33	107225	2128	39:10	109771	2206	40:48	111815
2058	34:46	107271	2129	39:11	109782	2207	40:55	111870
2059	34:47	107318	2130	39:14	109796	2209	40:56	111926
2061	35:1	107319	2131	39:16	109812	2211	40:61	111987

2212	40:62	112049	2281	45:6	114160	2353	48:11	115155
2213	40:63	112112	2282	45:8	114168	2354	48:13	115168
2216	40:64	112176	2283	45:10	114178	2356	48:14	115182
2217	40:65	112241	2284	45:12	114190	2358	48:15	115197
2218	40:66	112307	2285	45:14	114204	2359	48:16	115213
2219	40:69	112376	2287	45:19	114223	2360	48:17	115230
2221	40:74	112450	2288	45:22	114245	2361	48:18	115248
2222	40:77	112527	2290	45:23	114268	2362	48:19	115267
2224	40:78	112605	2291	45:26	114294	2363	48:20	115287
2225	40:79	112684	2292	45:27	114321	2365	48:21	115308
2226	40:81	112765	2293	45:32	114353	2367	48:23	115331
2227	40:84	112849	2294	45:35	114388	2368	48:24	115355
2228	40:85	112934	2295	45:36	114424	2369	48:25	115380
2229	41:14	112948	2296	46:2	114426	2371	48:26	115406
2230	41:15	112963	2297	46:4	114430	2373	48:27	115433
2231	41:19	112982	2298	46:5	114435	2374	48:28	115461
2232	41:21	113003	2299	46:8	114443	2377	48:29	115490
2233	41:22	113025	2301	46:10	114453	2380	49:1	115491
2234	41:28	113053	2302	46:13	114466	2382	49:3	115494
2235	41:30	113083	2304	46:17	114483	2383	49:5	115499
2236	41:33	113116	2305	46:21	114504	2385	49:7	115506
2237	41:36	113152	2306	46:23	114527	2387	49:8	115514
2238	41:37	113189	2307	46:26	114553	2389	49:9	115523
2239	41:52	113241	2308	46:28	114581	2390	49:10	115533
2240	42:3	113244	2309	46:31	114612	2392	49:12	115545
2241	42:5	113249	2310	46:32	114644	2394	49:13	115558
2242	42:6	113255	2311	46:33	114677	2396	49:14	115572
2243	42:8	113263	2312	47:1	114678	2398	49:15	115587
2244	42:9	113272	2313	47:3	114681	2401	49:16	115603
2246	42:10	113282	2315	47:4	114685	2402	49:17	115620
2247	42:13	113295	2316	47:7	114692	2404	49:18	115638
2250	42:15	113310	2317	47:9	114701	2405	50:26	115664
2251	42:16	113326	2318	47:10	114711	2406	51:50	115714
2252	42:17	113343	2319	47:11	114722	2407	51:51	115765
2253	42:19	113362	2320	47:12	114734	2408	51:58	115823
2254	42:21	113383	2321	47:16	114750	2409	52:27	115850
2256	42:23	113406	2323	47:19	114769	2411	52:43	115893
2259	42:24	113430	2324	47:21	114790	2412	53:23	115916
2260	42:27	113457	2325	47:23	114813	2413	53:25	115941
2261	42:31	113488	2327	47:26	114839	2414	53:26	115967
2262	42:36	113524	2328	47:28	114867	2415	53:31	115998
2263	42:40	113564	2329	47:29	114896	2416	53:58	116056
2264	42:44	113608	2330	47:30	114926	2417	53:62	116118
2266	42:46	113654	2332	47:32	114958	2418	57:1	116119
2267	42:47	113701	2333	47:33	114991	2419	57:4	116123
2268	42:49	113750	2335	47:34	115025	2420	57:5	116128
2269	42:51	113801	2336	47:35	115060	2421	57:7	116135
2271	42:53	113854	2338	47:38	115098	2422	57:8	116143
2272	43:63	113917	2339	48:2	115100	2423	57:9	116152
2273	43:64	113981	2340	48:3	115103	2427	57:10	116162
2274	43:87	114068	2342	48:4	115107	2428	57:11	116173
2275	44:18	114086	2343	48:5	115112	2430	57:14	116187
2276	44:19	114105	2345	48:6	115118	2431	57:16	116203
2277	44:42	114147	2347	48:7	115125	2432	57:17	116220
2278	45:2	114149	2348	48:9	115134	2433	57:18	116238
2279	45:5	114154	2351	48:10	115144	2434	57:19	116257

2435	57:20	116277	2535	60:11	116991	2634	66:4	117394
2438	57:21	116298	2538	60:12	117003	2635	66:6	117400
2439	57:22	116320	2539	60:13	117016	2637	66:8	117408
2440	57:23	116343	2540	61:1	117017	2639	66:10	117418
2441	57:24	116367	2541	61:3	117020	2640	66:11	117429
2443	57:25	116392	2542	61:4	117024	2641	67:9	117438
2444	57:27	116419	2545	61:5	117029	2642	67:26	117464
2446	57:28	116447	2546	61:6	117035	2643	67:28	117492
2449	57:29	116476	2548	61:7	117042	2644	69:33	117525
2453	58:1	116477	2550	61:8	117050	2645	70:3	117528
2454	58:2	116479	2552	61:11	117061	2646	71:3	117531
2455	58:3	116482	2553	61:13	117074	2647	71:4	117535
2457	58:4	116486	2556	61:14	117088	2648	71:13	117548
2458	58:5	116491	2557	62:1	117089	2649	71:15	117563
2461	58:6	116497	2559	62:4	117093	2650	71:17	117580
2463	58:7	116504	2561	62:5	117098	2651	71:19	117599
2465	58:8	116512	2562	62:6	117104	2652	71:25	117624
2466	58:9	116521	2563	62:7	117111	2653	72:4	117628
2468	58:10	116531	2564	62:9	117120	2654	72:5	117633
2471	58:11	116542	2566	62:10	117130	2655	72:7	117640
2472	58:12	116554	2568	62:11	117141	2656	72:12	117652
2475	58:13	116567	2571	63:1	117142	2658	72:18	117670
2476	58:14	116581	2572	63:2	117144	2659	72:19	117689
2477	58:15	116596	2573	63:4	117148	2660	72:22	117711
2478	58:16	116612	2574	63:5	117153	2662	72:23	117734
2479	58:17	116629	2576	63:6	117159	2669	73:20	117754
2480	58:18	116647	2578	63:7	117166	2671	74:31	117785
2481	58:19	116666	2579	63:8	117174	2672	74:56	117841
2482	58:20	116686	2580	63:9	117183	2673	76:6	117847
2484	58:21	116707	2582	63:11	117194	2674	76:9	117856
2489	58:22	116729	2583	64:1	117195	2675	76:11	117867
2490	59:1	116730	2584	64:2	117197	2677	76:30	117899
2492	59:2	116732	2585	64:4	117201	2678	79:25	117922
2493	59:3	116735	2587	64:6	117207	2679	81:29	117951
2496	59:4	116739	2588	64:7	117214	2680	82:19	117970
2497	59:5	116744	2590	64:8	117222	2681	84:23	117993
2500	59:6	116750	2591	64:9	117231	2682	85:8	118001
2504	59:7	116757	2594	64:11	117242	2683	85:9	118010
2506	59:8	116765	2595	64:12	117254	2684	85:20	118030
2507	59:11	116776	2597	64:13	117267	2685	87:7	118037
2508	59:13	116789	2598	64:14	117281	2686	88:24	118061
2509	59:16	116805	2599	64:15	117296	2688	91:13	118074
2512	59:18	116823	2600	64:16	117312	2689	95:8	118082
2513	59:19	116842	2602	64:17	117329	2690	96:14	118096
2514	59:21	116863	2606	65:1	117330	2691	98:2	118098
2515	59:22	116885	2609	65:2	117332	2692	98:5	118103
2517	59:23	116908	2612	65:3	117335	2693	98:8	118111
2518	59:24	116932	2613	65:4	117339	2694	104:6	118117
2519	60:1	116933	2615	65:5	117344	2695	110:1	118118
2520	60:3	116936	2618	65:7	117351	2696	110:2	118120
2523	60:4	116940	2621	65:10	117361	2697	112:1	118121
2525	60:6	116946	2624	65:11	117372	**2698**	112:2	**118123**
2528	60:7	116953	2627	65:12	117384	(19x142)		(19x6217)
2530	60:8	116961	2629	66:1	117385	⬆		⬆
2531	60:9	116970	2631	66:2	117387			
2534	60:10	116980	2632	66:3	117390			

2698 (**19** x 142)

118123 (**19** x 6217)

عليها تسعة عشر

On it is Nineteen

A NOTE:

Years after this argument, I noticed that some people were raising the question about *ALLAHUMMA* (translated as 'our Lord'), which occurs 5 times in the Quran. They asked why this word was not included in the count of ALLAH (God), which is 2698 (19x142). Neither the editor of *Mujam* nor we mixed them together. Those who know etymology and the basics of Arabic grammar will have no difficulty in discovering the reasons. Those who do not have this knowledge can check the context of the usage of *ALLAHUMMA* and ALLAH to learn the difference. Here are few clues for those who do not know Arabic:

- *Humma* is not really a suffix. There is no such suffix in Arabic. *ALLAHUMMA* is an abbreviated statement usually translated as, "O my/our Lord."
- ALLAHUMMA differs from ALLAH since it cannot be the subject in a statement. Therefore, you cannot replace *ALLAHUMMA* in the statements where ALLAH is the subject. For instance, "ALLAH created the universe." In Arabic you cannot say "*ALLAHUMMA* created the universe." Thus, the word *ALLAHUMMA* is not the same as ALLAH.
- *ALLAHUMMA* is also different from all other attributes of God, and it may not be considered an attribute at all. For instance you can say "ALLAH is Merciful," but you cannot say "ALLAH is *ALLAHUMMA*."
- *ALLAHUMMA*, though it contains the word ALLAH, is a different word. For instance, though the attributes *HAKAM* (Judge), *HAKYM* (Wise), *HAAKEM* (Authority), all contain the root letters *HKM*. But they are in different forms and have different meanings. Thus each are counted separately. Another example is *RAĤMAN* (Gracious) and *RAĤYM* (Merciful). Though both contain the root letters *RHM*, they are in different forms and thus they are counted separately.
- Furthermore, we counted the first word *Ism* and not its derivatives, we count *RaĤMaN* and not its derivatives, we count *Rahim* and not its derivatives. Similarly, we are counting *Allah* and not its derivatives to be consistent.

151

الرحمن
RaĤMaN (Gracious)

The third word of Bismillah occurs in the Quran exactly 57 times.

57 = 19x3

1	1:1	30	25:26
2	1:3	31	25:59
3	2:163	32	25:60
4	13:30	33	25:60
5	17:110	34	25:63
6	19:18	35	26:5
7	19:26	36	27:30
8	19:44	37	36:11
9	19:45	38	36:15
10	19:58	39	36:23
11	19:61	40	36:52
12	19:69	41	41:2
13	19:75	42	43:17
14	19:78	43	43:19
15	19:85	44	43:20
16	19:87	45	43:33
17	19:88	46	43:36
18	19:91	47	43:45
19	19:92	48	43:81
20	19:93	49	50:33
21	19:96	50	55:1
22	20:5	51	59:22
23	20:90	52	67:3
24	20:108	53	67:19
25	20:109	54	67:20
26	21:26	55	67:29
27	21:36	56	78:37
28	21:42	**57**	78:38
29	21:112		

(**19**x3)
↑

عليها تسعة عشر
On it is Nineteen

الرحيم

RaĤYM (Compassionate)

The fourth word of Bismillah occurs in the Quran exactly 114 times.

114 = 19x6

1	1:1	39	8:69	77	26:175
2	1:3	40	8:70	78	26:191
3	2:37	41	9:5	79	26:217
4	2:54	42	9:27	80	27:11
5	2:128	43	9:91	81	27:30
6	2:143	44	9:99	82	28:16
7	2:160	45	9:102	83	30:5
8	2:163	46	9:104	84	32:6
9	2:173	47	9:117	85	33:5
10	2:182	48	9:118	86	33:24
11	2:192	49	10:107	87	33:43
12	2:199	50	11:41	88	33:50
13	2:218	51	11:90	89	33:59
14	2:226	52	12:53	90	33:73
15	3:31	53	12:98	91	34:2
16	3:89	54	14:36	92	36:5
17	3:129	55	15:49	93	36:58
18	4:16	56	16:7	94	39:53
19	4:23	57	16:18	95	41:2
20	4:25	58	16:47	96	41:32
21	4:29	59	16:110	97	42:5
22	4:64	60	16:115	98	44:42
23	4:96	61	16:119	99	46:8
24	4:100	62	17:66	100	48:14
25	4:106	63	22:65	101	49:5
26	4:110	64	24:5	102	49:12
27	4:129	65	24:20	103	49:14
28	4:152	66	24:22	104	52:28
29	5:3	67	24:33	105	57:9
30	5:34	68	24:62	106	57:28
31	5:39	69	25:6	107	58:12
32	5:74	70	25:70	108	59:10
33	5:98	71	26:9	109	59:22
34	6:54	72	26:68	110	60:7
35	6:145	73	26:104	111	60:12
36	6:165	74	26:122	112	64:14
37	7:153	75	26:140	113	66:1
38	7:167	76	26:159	**114**	73:20
				(19x6**)**	
				↑	

13
A LitNu Symmetrical Table
The Bismillah Formula and the Attributes of God

> "In ending, I want to express a hope that . . . mathematics may serve now as a model for the solution of the main problem of our epoch: to reveal a supreme religious goal and to fathom the meaning of the spiritual activity of mankind." ~ I.R. Shafarevitch, a Russian Mathematician [99]

> "In so far as the Quran is a religious document, its mathematical structure serves, among many other things, to preserve its textual arrangement, integrity, and authenticity." ~ Prof. Cesar Adib Majul [100]

In the previous chapter, we observed the frequencies of Bismillah's words in the Quran, and found a remarkable, systematic mathematical pattern with them. In this chapter we continue our Literary-Numerical (LitNu) observations on Bismillah, the opening statement of the Quran. We check the relation of the frequencies of Bismillah's words to the numerical values of God's attributes. A mathematical connection between the opening statement and the rest of the Quran creates a magnificent holohedral design.

In 1982, Dr. Cesar Adib Majul[101] discovered a mathematical relation between the frequency of the words in Bismillah and the number values of God's attributes mentioned in the Quran. He discovered that the number 19 and its multiples in the Quran are not purely quantitative in their full connotation. My further research on the topic revealed a unique interlocking design that integrates the arbitrary language of humans to the universal language of mathematics as will be detailed in this chapter.[102]

As I briefly mentioned in the previous chapter, each Arabic letter corresponds to a number and thus each Arabic word or statement has a number equivalent to the sum of the constituent letters. Medieval Arabs used their alphabet for dual purposes: language and mathematics. Assigning number values to the letters of the alphabet according to their order in alphabet is a well-known practice in languages that originally did not have numerals, such as Hebrew (22 letters), Arabic (28 letters) and Greek (26 letters).[103] The Roman numeric notation is a living example from the times when people used alphabet letters as numbers.

To witness this marvelous mathematical art, we need to learn the ancient Arabic numeral system, which is known as gematria (or abjad). Medieval Arabs used gematria until approximately 200 years after Prophet Muhammad's death.

Gematria: Numerical Values of Alphabet Letters

A 28-letter alphabet gave Arabs the advantage of a perfect mathematical system.[104] Well, I am using the word "perfect" in the sense of "practically efficient." I also want to allude to the fact that 28 is the second member of the numbers called "perfect" in mathematical jargon. A positive number is called "perfect" (sure, an arbitrary nomenclature) if it is equal to the sum of all positive integers that are its factors. For instance, the first perefect number is 6, since it is obtained by both the addition and multiplication of 1, 2, and 3. The total number of chapters in the Quran is 114, which is equal to 19x6. Thus, six, as a "perfect" number, is also a number of some special significance alongside. Each letter in the Arabic alphabet represents a number varying from 1 to 9, from 10 to 90 in tens, and from 100 to 900 in hundreds, and 1000. I provided some details regarding the Gemartia in the Endnote for verse 2:1, in *The Quran: A Reformist Translation*:

> **002:001**   A1L30M40. The meaning of 14 different combinations of alphabet letters/numbers initializing 29 chapters of the Quran remained a secret for centuries until 1974. Many scholars attempted to understand the meaning of these initial letters with no results. A computerized study that started in 1969 revealed in 1974 a 19-based mathematical design that was prophesied in Chapter 74. The frequencies of the 14 alphabet letters in 14 different combinations that initialize 29 chapters are an integral part of this mathematical structure.
>
> Arabs, during the time of revelation, did not use what we now know as Arabic Numerals. A notable book, *The Universal History of Numbers* by George Ifrah, dedicates Chapters 17-19 to ancient numerical systems, which is titled: *Letters and Numbers, The Invention of Alphabetic Numerals and Other Alphabetic Number-Systems*. The book provides extensive information on the Hebrew, Armenian, Phoenician, Greek, Syriac, Arabic, and Ethiopian alphabetic numerals. According to historical evidence, during the era of Muhammad, Arabs used their alphabet as their numbering system. The Arabic alphabet was then arranged differently and became named after its first four letters, *ABJaD*. Each of the 28 letters of the alphabet corresponded to a different number starting from 1 to 9, from 10 to 90, and then from 100 to 1000. When Arabs started adopting Hindu numerals in 760 AC, long after the revelation of the Quran, they abandoned their alphabet/numeral system in favor of a pedagogically arranged alphabet which is currently in use. Below is the list of the 28 Arabic letters/numbers. When they are put next to each other, their numerical values are added to each other to attain a total number. For instance, the numerical value of ALLaH (God) is $1+30+30+5=66$, of ShaHYD (Witness) is $300+5+10+4=319$, and of WaĤiD (One) is $6+1+8+4=19$.

								١ A
								1
ي Y	ط Ť	ح Ĥ	ز Z	و W	ه H	د D	ج J	ب B
10	9	8	7	6	5	4	3	2
ق Q	ص Ŝ	ف F	ع Â	س S	ن N	م M	ل L	ك K
100	90	80	70	60	50	40	30	20
غ Ğ	ظ Ž	ض Ď	ذ Ź	خ X	ث Ś	ت T	ش Ş	ر R
1000	900	800	700	600	500	400	300	200

Thus, the Quran is not only a literary book but also a book made up of numbers. The numerical structure of the Quran has two features: intertwined patterns among the *physical frequencies* of its literary units—such as letters, words, phrases, verses, and chapters AND intertwined patterns among the *numerical values* (*ABJaD*) of these literary units. Considering the relevancy of the common meaning of words and letters during the time of revelation, we cannot ignore the fact that the combinations of letters that initialize 29 chapters are primarily numbers. Unfortunately, after Arabs commonly adopted the Indian numerals in the 8th and 9th centuries, the numerical system prevalent during the revelation became an antique abused by charlatan psychics and astrologers. It is ironic that an innovation (today's Arabic numerals) replaced the original (*ABJaD*), but through the passage of time people started considering the original to be the innovation! The allergy of Sunni and Shiite scholars to *ABJaD* and its use in the Quran, does not allow them to open their eyes to marvels of the numerically structured book (83:7-21).

To verify and witness the mathematical system of the Quran, one does not need to know Arabic, though knowledge of Arabic might increase the magnitude of appreciation. Though there are hundreds of examples of the 19-based mathematical system, there are surely many still out there yet to be discovered. Meanwhile, there are also some issues that need to be resolved. For example, the count of the letter *Alif* still remains to be settled. We know the mathematical structure of the Quran verifies both the extraordinary nature of the text and its miraculous preservation from tampering. However, the system still involves the entire Quran and we have yet to discover a miraculous system that verifies the divinity and authenticity of each chapter, *independently*.

Observers reacting to this prophetic feature fall into three main groups: 1) unappreciative skeptics or fanatic religionists who reject its existence without sufficient investigation; 2) appreciative seekers of truth who witness it and experience a paradigm change, and 3) gullible people who are impressed by it without fully appreciating the statistical facts and consequently indulge in "discovering" their own "miracles" through arbitrary numerical manipulations and jugglery. Ironically, the third group's exaggerated claims serve as justification for the first group's beliefs. For more information on this issue, please visit 19.org.

See 74:1-56.

Named after the first four letters of the ancient Arabic alphabet, ABJaD was replaced by the modern Arabic alphabet. ABJaD soon gained mystery and became the tool of psychics and charlatans. Those who are unaware of this historical fact are averse to finding any application of ABJaD in the Quran. Especially, after Muslims lost interest in rational thinking and mathematics, the orthodox aversion included anything related to mathematics and numbers. The "Allah" in their mind transformed into a literary being who had no knowledge of mathematics!

Attributes of God Mentioned in the Quran

The Bismillah formula contains the name of God and two attributes: ALLaH, RaĤMaN, RaĤYM . The Quran considers all *beautiful* attributes belonging to God (7:180; 17:110; 20:8; 59:24).

The common knowledge among the Muslim population that God has 99 attributes contradicts the Quran. The list of 99 attributes, which is narrated by a Hadith collection called *Tirmizi*, does not contain some attributes mentioned in the Quran and it lists some attributes that are not beautiful, such as, *DaR*. The meaning of *DaR* is very clear. Look it up in any dictionary and you will find the same definition: The One Who Harms or Harmful.[105]

> 7:180 To God belong the beautiful names/attributes; call Him by them; and disregard those who blaspheme in His names/attributes. They will pay for what they have done.

Furthermore, sectarian Muslims have fabricated more than 99 attributes for the Prophet Muhammad, attributing to him many of God's attributes such as *HaDY* (guide), *ĤaSYB* (reckoner), *MuJYB* (responder), QaWY (strong), *AWaL* (first, alfa), *AXeR* (last, omega), etc. You can see those 102 fabricated attributes inside the cover of Quran manuscripts published in Pakistan. Muhammad's attributes rival God's attributes, and outnumber them!

In his remarkable article titled, *The Attributes of Allah in Relation to the Mathematical Structure of Quran*, Prof. Majul discovered the following two facts:

1. Only four attributes of God have gematrical (numerical) values that are a multiple of 19, i.e.: *WaHiD* (one), *ŻuW AL- FaDL AL-ÂŻYM*, (possessor of infinite grace), *MaJYD* (glorious), and *JAMeÂ* (gatherer, editor).

2. The numerical values of these four attributes correspond exactly to the frequency of the four words of "Bismillah," in the Quran; that is, ISM (19), ALLaH (2698), RaHMaN (57), and RaHYM (114).

FREQUENCIES of the four words of Bismillah, the first and the most repeated verse	Corresponding numbers of frequencies and numerical values	Attributes whose NUMERICAL VALUES in the Quran are multiple of 19
ا سم ASM Name	**19** (19x1)	واحد WAHiD One
الله ALLaH God	**2698** (19x142)	ذوالفضل العظيم ŻuW AL- FaDL AL-Â ŻYM Possessor of Great Blessing
رحمن RaHMaN Gracious	**57** (19x3)	مجيد MaJYD (Glorious)
رحيم RaHYM Caring	**114** (19x6)	جامع JAMeÂ Gatherer/Editor

The symmetric and interlocking mathematical relationship between the four words comprising Bismillah and the four attributes of God is evident. However, after witnessing the same mathematical system and participating in further research leading to new discoveries, I expected more. Having studied the mathematical structure of the Quran since 1980 and having written several books and numerous articles on the subject, I had an intuition similar to that of a scientist focusing on a particular subject. Knowing that the author of the Quran treats His universal laws governing nature and his words revealed in scripture with the same word *AYAT* (signs, laws, revelations, evidences), I employed the scientific method. First I came up with an observation, then with a hypothesis, then tested them, and then I arrived at a conclusion.

1. Observation:

On the right side of the table above there are four attributes of God, but on the left side there are only three. Obviously, *ISM* (name) is not an attribute of God. Therefore, we can hypothesize two events in order to have a symmetric table:

2. Hypothesis:

1. There must be one more attribute of God which has a frequency of 19.
2. The frequencies of ONLY four attributes must be multiple of 19.

3. Test:

I gathered a list of all divine attributes mentioned in the Quran and evaluated each of them according to their frequencies and their numerical values. I placed the attribute in the first column, their numerical values in the second column, and finally their frequencies in the third column. I sorted them according to their numerical values in ascending order.

4. Conclusion:

Yes, my hypothesis was right. Indeed, there was one and only one divine attribute whose frequency was 19: *ŞaHYD* (witness). And there were only four divine attributes whose frequencies were multiple of 19.

When I examined the frequencies of all attributes, I discovered that ONLY four of them were multiple of 19. Dr. Khalifa had already discovered three of them and Dr. Majul had already linked three of them to their counterpart divine attributes: *ALLaH* (God), *RaĤMaN* (Gracious) *RaĤYM* (Merciful). Now, I had predicted and discovered the fourth one: *ŞaHYD* (Witness).

The word *ŞaHYD* (Witness) is mentioned in the Quran 35 times and 19 of them are used as an attribute of God, and thus it fills the empty space corresponding to the numerical value of *WaĤiD* (One) on the right side of our table. Here is the list of verses where the divine attribute *ŞaHYD* is mentioned: 3:98; 4:3; 4:79; 4:166; 5:117; 6:19; 10:29; 10:46; 13:43; 17:96; 22:17; 29:52; 33:55; 34:47; 41:53; 46:8; 48:28; 58:6; 85:9. Now we have the ultimate table of God's attributes that confirms our symmetry hypothesis:

Attributes whose FREQUENCIES in the Quran are multiple of 19	Symmetric frequencies and numerical values	Attributes whose NUMERICAL VALUES in the Quran are multiple of 19
شهيد ŞaHYD Witness	**19** (19x1)	واحد WAĤiD One
الله ALLaH God	**2698** (19x142)	ذوالفضل العظيم ŹuW AL- FaĎL AL-Â ŽYM Possessor of Great Blessing
رحمن RaĤMaN Gracious	**57** (19x3)	مجيد MaJYD Glorious
رحيم RaĤYM Caring	**114** (19x6)	جامع JAMeÂ Gatherer/Editor

Now let's read this table in the light of the Quran:

God bears WITNESS that He is ONE, or the ONE bears WITNESS that He, the GOD, is the POSSESSOR OF INFINITE GRACE by sending his revelation to us. He is GRACIOUS and GLORIOUS. As the EDITOR of the Quran and the GATHERER on the Day of Judgment He is the most CARING.

In the following list I arranged the attributes of God according to their gematrical values, from the smallest to biggest. Across every attribute you will see its gematrical (numerical) value and its frequency in the Quran. Since the attributes of God are not invariably prefixed by the definite article *Al* (the), The gematrical values are calculated without the article *Al,* except if the article is part of the grammatical structure of compound words, such as *ZuW al-Fadl.*

I will try to provide the reader with a consistent transliteration that can be easily transformed into numbers. I use lower case letters to indicate vowels that do not exist in the Quranic orthography but only emerge in the pronunciation of the words. To avoid complications for non-Arabic readers, I did not demonstrate some rules of pronunciation, such as doubling letters (*shadda*) or the omission of letter "L" in article "AL" when it is pronounced before certain letters.

	Attributes		Gematrical Values	Frequencies
1.	AĤaD	احد	13	1
2.	WaHAB	وهاب	14	3
3.	ĤaY	حي	18	5
4.	WAĤeD	واحد	**19 (19x1)**	22
5.	WaDuWD	ودود	20	2
6.	HADY	هادي	20	1
7.	ALaH	اله	36	93
8.	AWaL	اول	37	1
9.	WaLY	ولي	46	13
10.	MuJYB	مجيب	55	1
11.	MaJYD	**مجيد**	**57 (19x3)**	2
12.	MuĤYe	محي	58	2
13.	ĤaMYD	حميد	62	17
14.	BAȚeN	باطن	62	1
15.	ALLaH	**الله**	66	**2698 (19x142)**
16.	WaKYL	وكيل	66	13
17.	MuĤYȚ	محيط	67	8
18.	ĤaKaM	حكم	68	1
19.	ĤaKYM	حكيم	78	91

161

20.	ĤaSYB	حسيب	80	3
21.	MaWLY	مولي	86	12
22.	ĤaLYM	حليم	88	11
23.	MaLeK	ملك	90	2
24.	ÂZYZ	عزيز	94	88
25.	ĤaFY	حفي	98	1
26.	MaLYK	مليك	100	1
27.	ĤaQ	حق	108	9
28.	ÂLY	علي	110	8
29.	AÂLaY	اعلي	111	2
30.	ABQaY	ابقي	113	1
31.	JAMeÂ	**جامع**	**114 (19x6)**	2
32.	QaWY	قوي	116	9
33.	LaŤYF	لطيف	129	7
34.	SaLaM	سلم	130	1
35.	ŜaMaD	صمد	134	1
36.	MuWMeN	مومن	136	1
37.	WaSeÂ	وسع	136	8
38.	MuHaYMeN	مهيمن	145	1
39.	ÂLYM	عليم	150	153
40.	QAYeM	قايم	151	1
41.	ÂFuW	عفو	156	5
42.	QaYuM	قيوم	156	3
43.	QuDuWS	قدوس	170	2

44.	SaMYÂ	سميع	180	45
45.	BaR	بر	202	1
46.	RaB	رب	202	938
47.	JaBAR	جبار	206	1
48.	BARY	باري	213	3
49.	KaBYR	كبير	232	6
50.	RaĤYM	رحيم	258	114 (19x6)
51.	AKRaM	اكرم	261	1
52.	KaRYM	كريم	270	2
53.	RaWuF	روف	286	10
54.	RaĤMaN	رحمن	298	57 (19x3)
55.	BaŜYR	بصير	302	42
56.	QADeR	قادر	305	2
57.	QaHaR	قهر	305	6
58.	QAHeR	قاهر	306	2
59.	RaZAQ	رزاق	308	1
60.	RaQYB	رقيب	312	3
61.	QaRYB	قريب	312	3
62.	QaDYR	قدير	314	45
63.	ŞaHYD	شهيد	319	19 (19x1)
64.	MuŜaWeR	مصور	336	1
65.	NaŜYR	نصير	350	4
66.	FALeQ ALAŜBAĤ	فالق الاصباح	352	1
67.	FALQAL ĤaBWALNaWY	فالق الحب و النوي	355	1

68.	TaWAB	تواب	409	11
69.	ŞaDYD ALMaĤAL	شديد المحال	428	1
70.	SaRYÂ ALĤeSAB	سريع الحساب	434	8
71.	ŞaDYD ALQuWY	شديد القوي	465	1
72.	FaÂAL LeMA YuRYD	فعال لما يريد	476	2
73.	FaTAĤ	فتاح	489	1
74.	MaTYN	متين	500	1
75.	ŞAKeR	شاكر	521	2
76.	ŞaDYD ALÂeQAB	شديد العقاب	522	14
77.	ŞaKuWR	شكور	526	4
78.	MuTaÂAL	متعال	541	1
79.	SaRYÂ ALÂeQAB	سريع العقاب	544	2
80.	MuQYT	مقيت	550	1
81.	QABeL ALTaWB	قابل التوب	572	1
82.	AHL ALTaQWaY	اهل التقوي	583	1
83.	MuSTaÂAN	مستعان	621	2
84.	MuTaKaBeR	متكبر	662	1
85.	XaLeQ / XaLaQ	خلق	730	2
86.	MuQTaDeR	مقتدر	744	3
87.	ŹuW ALŤaWL	ذو الطول	782	1
88.	AXeR	اخر	802	1
89.	XaYR	خير	810	1
90.	XaBYR	خبير	812	44
91.	ŹuW ALQuWaH	ذو القوة	848	1
92.	ŹuW MeRaH	ذو مرة	951	1

93.	ZuW ÂeQABALYM	ذو عقاب اليم	960	1
94.	ŹuW ALRaHMaH	ذو الرحمة	990	2
95.	ĤaFYŽ	حفيظ	998	3
96.	RaFYÂ ALDaRaJaT	رفيع الدرجت	998	1
97.	ÂažeYM	عظيم	1020	6
98.	ŹuW ALMaÂAReJ	ذو المعارج	1051	1
99.	ĞaNeY	غني	1060	18
100.	ŹuW ALJaLaL WALAKRAM	ذو الجلل و الاكرام	1098	2
101.	ŹuW RaĤMaH WaSeÂaH	ذو رحمة وسعة	1100	1
102.	ŽaHeR	ظهر	1106	1
103.	ĞaFiR	غفر	1280	5
104.	ĞaFuWR	غفور	1286	91
105.	ŹuW ANTeQAM	ذو انتقام	1298	4
106.	ŹuW ALÂRŞ	ذو العرش	1307	4
107.	ĞALeB ÂLaY AMReH	غالب علي امره	1389	1
108.	AHL ALMaĞFeRaH	اهل المغفرة	1392	1
109.	ŹuW FaDL	ذو فضل	1616	6
110.	BaDYÂ ALSaMaWaT WALARD	بديع السموت و الارض	1662	2
111.	FaŤiR ALSaMaWaT WALARD	فاطر السموت و الارض	1866	6
112.	ŹuW MaĞFiRaH	ذو مغفرة	2031	1
113.	ĞaFiR ALŹaNB	غافر الذنب	2064	1
114.	ŹuW FaDL ÂŽYM	ذوفضل عظيم	2636	1
115.	ŹuW ALFaDL ALÂŽYM	ذوالفضل العظيم	**2698 (19x142)**	6

165

In summary, out of these attributes only four have gematrical (numerical) values that are divisible by 19. They are:

واحد

$$4+8+1+6 = 19$$

المجيد

$$4+10+3+40 = 57$$

جامع

$$70+40+1+3 = 114$$

ذوالفضل العظيم

$$40+10+900+70+30+1+30+800+80+30+1+6+700 = 2698$$

Out of these attributes, only four have frequencies, i.e., the number of times they occur in the Quran, that are divisible by 19:

شهيد

19

الرحمن

57

الرحيم

114

الله

2698

When we group the 8 names whose numerical/gematrical values or frequencies in the Quran are divisible by 19, we obtain a symmetric table. The frequencies of the 4 attributes on the left, and the numerical values of another 4 attributes on the right interlock and create a perfect design, whose cumulative sum is 5776 (4x19x4x19), or:

$$4^2 \times 19^2 = 5776$$

عليها تسعة عشر
On it is Nineteen

As you can see, our study of the attributes of God mentioned in the Quran, both according to their frequencies in the Quran and their gematria (numerical values), reveals the following pattern:

- Only 4 attributes of God have have frequencies that are multiples of 19.
- Only 4 attributes of God have numerical values that are multiples of 19.
- The 4 numbers of each set have a perfect correspondence, or symmetry.
- The four twin numbers are also the numbers of Bismillah, that is, the frequency of its words in the Quran.

More on the Meaning of Bismillah Formula

We can elaborate on the meaning of Bismillah, based on this symmetrical interlocking mathematical design.

He is WITNESS that He is ONE (3:18)

There is ONLY ONE God. This is the main message of the Quran and all other scriptures delivered by the messengers. All creatures are warned not to idolize anything besides God or associate anyone or anything to God's authority. Throughout history, the majority of people have treated their prophets, messengers, religious scholars, clergymen, political leaders and heroes like a god or a partner with God. The Quran warns humans against this common deviation. The only unforgivable sin, according to the Quran, is *shirk* (associating authorities or partners to God and his system—see 4:48). God is WITNESS that He is ONE; angels and also those who possess knowledge witness this fact.

GOD is the POSSESSOR OF INFINITE GRACE (4:113)

He, the source of all good and grace (3:26; 11:3) and the source of all power (2:20; 3:26, 189; 4:149; 6:18; 61; 57:2; 59:24; etc.), is generous in His provisions and blessings: life, intellect, free will, love, and all the blessings that we are aware of and unaware of. One of His blessings is His revelation that

167

provides us with guidance, wisdom and happiness. Understanding the divine revelation and living a life guided by it constitutes GOD'S INFINITE GRACE.

He is GRACIOUS and GLORIOUS (85:15 & 50:1)

He has a GLORIOUS dominion in the universe (85:15). Everything, living or non-living, visible or invisible to human eyes, is commemorating Him by following the laws issued by Him in the universe (17:44; 57:1). His Final Testament is the GLORIOUS Quran (50:1).

He is the EDITOR and MERCIFUL SUMMONER (3:9 & 75:17)

The Quran is His word. He EDITED the Quran in 114 chapters. The MERCIFUL will SUMMON people on the Day Judgment and will question them regarding their response to His message. The numerical value of *JaMÂ* (EDITOR or SUMMONER) explains why God EDITED his Final Testament not in any other number of chapters but exactly in 114 chapters.

Note:

The mathematical system of the Quran indicates that there are exactly 114 distinct attributes of God mentioned in the Quran. But, I have to admit that my research is not complete.

Though, I refined the system, which I think it supports my longtime intuition regarding the complete list of divine attributes mentioned in the Quran, we need to conduct a more careful linguistic study on this subject. The number of attributes used for God should be 114, equal to the number of Chapters of the Quran and perhaps the number of stable elements in our universe.[106] A very simple and meaningful definition of attributes creates a list that not only perfects the interlocking mathematical system embedded within the frequencies and numerical values of divine attributes, it also explains certain peculiarities regarding the usage of some attributes. Besides, I think that after obtaining this complete list, we will discover further examples of the miraculous mathematical structure and additional semantic information.

For more details on the mathematical system and attributes of God see the Appendix.

14

An Interlocking Mathematical System

"As it appears, the universe is designed with mathematics."
~ Nicomachus

"God created the world from nothingness and constructed everything with numbers." ~ Hrovista Gandersheim

"All intellectual issues can be united and should be united through mathematics." ~ Rene Descartes

"Mathematics is the language God wrote the universe with." ~ Galileo

In this chapter, we will present more examples demonstrating an interlocking mathematical system underlying Quranic words and letters in the Bismillah. But before we do this, let us summarize the gematrical (also called numerical or Abjad) values of letters (akin to the chemical properties of elements) and the frequencies of the words (akin to physical properties) of Bismillah in a table. (The written letters in Arabic are shown in capital letters.):

Nu.	Words	Letters	Gematrical Values	Sums
1	BiSM	3	2, 60, 40	102
2	ALLaH	4	1, 30, 30, 5	66
3	AL-RaĤMaN	6	1, 30, 200, 8, 40, 50	329
4	AL-RaĤYM	6	1, 30, 200, 8, 10, 40	289
	Sum	**19**		**786**

In addition to the examples we have demonstrated so far, the following examples discovered by Abdullah Arik, a Turkish-American engineer whom I first met at Masjid Tucson when Rashad Khalifa was among us, makes the mathematical structure of the first verse of the Quran a fascinating interlocking marvel.

169

PATTERN 0: The First verse of the Quran, which repeats in the beginning of every chapter except one, consists of **19** letters.

PATTERN 1: Write down the respective number of letters of each word next to their sequence number. The resulting number is a multiple of 19 as follows:

1 ₃ **2** ₄ **3** ₆ **4** ₆ $= 19 \times 19 \times 36686$

PATTERN 2: Now, replace the number of letters in each word by the cumulative number of letters until that word. The result is a multiple of 19.

1 ₃ **2** ₇ **3** ₁₃ **4** ₁₉ $= 19 \times 69858601$

PATTERN 3: Replace the number of letters in each word by the gematrical value of that word. The result is a multiple of 19.

1 ₁₀₂ **2** ₆₆ **3** ₃₂₉ **4** ₂₈₉ $= 19 \times 5801401752331$

PATTERN 4: Now, replace the gematrical value of each word by the cumulative total of gematrical value of each word up to that word. The result is a multiple of 19.

1 ₁₀₂ **2** ₁₆₈ **3** ₄₉₇ **4** ₇₈₆ $= 19 \times 58011412367094$

PATTERN 5: Replace the cumulative gematrical value of each word up to that word above with the gematrical value of every letter in that word. The result is a multiple of 19.

1 2 60 40 **2** 1 30 30 5 **3** 1 30 200 8 40 50 **4** 1 30 200 8 10 40
$= 19 \times 66336954226595422109686863843162160$

These are five examples observed by Abdullah, among many others.[107] Having witnessed the elegance of the mathematical pattern, I noticed that the pattern was not complete with these five examples. The first three examples constitute a systematic evaluation of the numbers associated with Bismillah's words and letters. The following fourth and fifth are the next reasonable steps. Yet, the sixth step on example 5 was missing. Thus, I made a prediction and put it to the test. My prediction was verified by the system:

PATTERN 6: Consider Example 5 and replace the gematrical value of each letter by the cumulative gematrical value of each letter. The result is again a multiple of 19.

1 2 62 102 **2** 103 133 163 168 **3** 169 199 399 407 447 497 **4** 498 528 728 736 746 786
= 19 x 6642643212175349035956273652600391973549992256467035594

170

15

Random Dots and the Fork of Destiny!

"Serendipity is a propensity for making fortunate discoveries while looking for something unrelated. The word has been voted as one of the ten English words that were hardest to translate in June 2004 by a British translation company." ~ Wikipedia

So far, you have been presented with only a sample of the mathematical structure of the Quran. Both because of its dominating recurrence in the Quran and because its idiosyncratic structure, the Bismillah resembles a live cell. This opening formula that centers around 19 both in micro and macro dimensions remains as meaningful and effective as a genetic code.

Bismillah takes a crucial role in the mathematical structure of the Quran. These findings, however, are too complex for Sunni and Shiite scholars in general to appreciate, since many of them cannot even count the number of letters in the Bismillah correctly. They have come up with various counts—18, 20, 21, 22, anything except 19. We do not expect the sectarian clergymen who fail in such an elementary task to appreciate this mathematical harmony.

Before going to the next paragraph, I would like to share with you one of the comments from my colleague Dr. Abdur Rab who read the draft of this book and provided a thorough editorial assistance and criticism:

"I completely agree with you. But probably you could present this in a more compact, more dignified way. Also, telling the fools "fools" so bluntly may be counter-productive. Please note, the Prophet was urged by God to speak with the ingrates in the most polite way (16:125; 29:46). Furthermore, this description may make these blind people furiously rally against you, which I know you are not afraid of. But why enrage them so bluntly?"

171

"Another thing. Both traditional Sunni and Shiite scholars and their gullible followers are victims of a system so endemic and deeply entrenched in our Muslim societies, a system that has to do mainly with the traditional Madrasah teachings, and the consequent family environment in which Muslim children are reared. Unless these Madrasahs are thoroughly remodeled—a point I have tried to spotlight in my book—you could not probably change anything. Even modern educated Muslims are so indoctrinated by the traditional Muslim teachers that even if you apply all kinds of logic to them, all this falls flat on them. The children in Muslim families in general get this same indoctrination from their parents and informal religious schools they attend. I do not really know how we are going to bring about a revolutionary change in the current dominant Muslim mindset."

I do appreciate Abdur Rab's advice to use a softer language, but I do not consider telling the truth to be an insult. The Quran is filled with statements that may offend those who are ingrates, hypocrites, or liars. I can no more use kind words to appeal a class of people who arrogate themselves to issue fatwas justifying the killing of people whom they consider *murtad* (apostate, blasphemous, heretic), who have shown no respect to other's rights to life, to free speech and dignity. The very chapter containing prophetic description of 19 describes them with adjectives such as ingrates, hypocrites and likens their reaction to intellectual challenge to zebras running from a lion.

No, they are not stupid; their brain power is mostly wasted on ridiculous and frivolous issues. By following their ancestors blindly, they have lost their chance from the start. Indeed, the Quran draws a perfect profile of them in 74:31-51. They are dogmatic and ill-fit to appreciate new ideas that may challenge their dogmas. They can split the hair into forty pieces on frivolous issues, but they are unable to properly evaluate our claims regarding the numerical structure of the Quran. Unfortunately, they have lost their chance to witness one of the greatest signs in their holy book, since in reality they do not appreciate the book itself; they give lip service in praising the book because they parrot their teachers and ancestors. The prophetic verses 74:31-51 depict their intellectual and psychological condition very clearly.

What about our atheist scientists? Well, they have their own prejudices; they are too arrogant to see God in their labs. All they do is to read the Book of Nature and find a way to utilize its principles. Generally speaking, the more a scientist reads the details the more he or she loses the big picture. The fanatic atheist shares similar problems with the orthodox religious scholar. One's right eye is blinded by goddesses of Coincidence and Chronic Skepticism, the other's left eye is condemned by gods of Blind Faith and Sectarian Dogmas. Thus, both lose their ability to see the holographic 3-D picture!

Atheists occasionally close both of their eyes to ordinary and extraordinary facts that manifest God's power in every atom and every second of the universe. Though atheism is inferior to agnosticism in terms of their philosophical defensibility, it is still attractive to some. Though materialistic atheism received

172

a big blow with the discovery of the Big Bang, it soon overcame that shock and focused on denying God's existence through evolution. Though the atheist's twist on evolution does not address the cosmological arguments for God's existence, it somehow managed to sway people from believing in intelligent design to mutation and survival of the fittest. The dogmatic and ignorant rejection of evolution by religious people, on the other hand, increased the suspicion and contempt of intellectuals against anything related to God.[108]

Whenever we encounter denials of this extraordinary sign, our case gets an even stronger indirect support. Why? Because, the inability of dogmatic and arrogant people to witness the miraculous signs is one of the characteristics associated with such signs (6:25; 7:146; 74:31). If you are able to witness this miracle you are in a very small minority, a very lucky minority indeed.

However, witnessing the miracle does not absolve people and guarantee them eternal salvation since they must show their appreciation and pass the tests on their way. We are tested by our reaction to blessings and losess, and we are expected not to get arrogant and greedy with the first and not to get despondent and unappreciative with the latter. Verse 7:175 mentions a prototype who turned back after witnessing divine signs. Verses 2:109; 4:115; 29:38 and 47:32 provides some examples from the past.

Ahmad Deedat was one of those few lucky ones who witnessed and appreciated this prophetic miracle. He was my mentor in the early 1980's. I met him in August of 1980 at an International Youth Conference which convened in the camping facilities of the Turkish Ministry of Youth and Sports located by the beach near Çanakkale. For two weeks I participated in his lectures, among others, and met with him privately. He was one of the best lecturers I have ever seen. He was very smart, organized and passionate. He was the founder and president of the Islamic Propagation Center in Durban South Africa.

In this context, I would like to share with you a piece from a phase of my life story:

The Black Swan: Thirty Seconds at the Fork of Destiny

With colorful memories of Iran in my mind and Ali Shariati's lectures on audio cassettes, I returned to Turkey. Unfortunately, I was arrested again for no apparent reason, this time on Fevzipaşa Street close to Fatih police station, and the police confiscated from me all that I brought from Iran. I was more upset for losing those cassettes to the police than losing my freedom, which I knew would be no more than a few weeks. But, I was even more upset for losing an opportunity to move forward on an important mission. That arrest and the following detention prevented me from carrying out our plan to hijack one or two airplanes and re-direct them to Afghanistan in order for them to join jihad against the occupying Russian military.

173

It was a time when our focus was gradually shifting from Iran to Afghanistan. We thought the most important stage of our mission in Iran was completed, and it was already on its way to recovery. Give it a few more years and it would be the envy of the world. That was what we thought. But, Afghanistan was suffering under the paw of the cruel Russian bear. They desperately needed our help. After consulting with some close friends, I decided to organize and mobilize. I sent news through word of mouth that we would be gathering next Sunday noon at Şehzade Mosque, one of the major mosques, between Fatih and Süleymaniye. I asked them to come ready with their bags and everything they would need during the trip. When I made the announcement I had no plans. Nothing! I was a spontaneous leader. I would occasionally plan, but for operations and missions like that, I preferred no plan at all. I was practical and pragmatic. Short notice and the degree of urgency provided me with flexibility and control, and creativity. Most of the time, I just needed the starting point and the target; I would usually more or less take care of the rest. I had some ideas for the rest. For instance, we would fill the city buses, cut their radio communication, and ask the drivers to take us to the airport. There we would overwhelm the security guards, and ask for one or two airplanes to help us go to our destination for our holy mission.

I did neither have a calculated plan nor preparation for the hijacking mission, since my mission was multifold. Actually landing in Afghanistan or Pakistan was a secondary one. Here were the main goals:

1. Raise public awareness about the suffering of our brothers and sisters under imperialism.

2. Prepare our militants for serious tasks, harden their determination and test their commitment.

3. Test one more time the speed and efficiency of our preparation especially after short notice.

4. If everything went well, we could have the chance to join our Afghani brothers and sisters.

I did not believe we would be able to hijack airplanes, or get them as a favor of the Turkish government. By sending us to Afghanistan, the Turkish government could hit two birds with one stone. It could win the support of the alienated religious segment of the population and could export the most hardened Islamist militants out of the country.

I did not want guns for that mission. Guns were unnecessary. Besides, they would not help our cause towards raising public opinion. I thought our airplane hijack had little chance of success, and if we were going to accomplish it, it would be due to the sheer number of activists. The ensuing chaos at the airport and the media circus would give us an opportunity to bluff. I considered the

174

actual hijacking as the least important of my four goals. Many of us did not know the Afghani language, and we were not familiar with their country and culture. So, I thought we could help them better if we increased awareness among the Turkish population. The public awareness and sympathy would translate into monetary aid, and it would translate to better weapons for them, which it did.

With my arrest, I achieved only half of my goals: two and three of the above-mentioned list. I would later in jail learn that about three hundred militants had responded to my call. They had said good-bye to their families and loved ones and had gone to the mosque with their backpacks ready to fly to Afghanistan. When a messenger relayed the bad news about my arrest, they left the mosque and went back to their homes.

Within a few weeks, I was out again, back to where I left. I was like a hamster in a cage, going through daily chores. However, the daily pattern would get interrupted by a simple event. And it would start a chain of reactions that I could never have imagined where it would lead.

- Peace be on you, Edip.
- Peace be on you, Dursun.
- Edip, would you like to participate in an international conference?
- Where is it?
- At the camp facilities of the Ministry of Youth. Near Çanakkale; just by the sea.
- When?
- Well, within a few days.
- How long will it take?
- Two weeks.
- Who are participating?
- Young Muslims from all around the world.
- Yes, of course, I would like to participate

This question by Dursun Özcan, the leader of Istanbul Akıncılar, in front of their apartment on the corner of Hattat Nazif and Dersvekili Streets, and my affirmative response changed the course of my life. If I were thirty seonds earlier or later I would not have met him that day and I would not have participated in the conference. In that conference, I would learn the SECRET which would cause my spirits to soar, make me a best-selling popular author, and then would drop me from the zenith, turning my relatives, friends, and readers into furious enemies. The SECRET made me the most popular author and the most hated one; a monotheist first and an apostate later. It was because of that SECRET that I jumped over the Atlantic Ocean, and again it was because of the SECRET that I started pushing for Islamic reform. All starting with that "coincidental" but fateful meeting with Dursun Özcan on the street in Istanbul.

175

For a few seconds in that corner, I encountered the proverbial black swan, which would later transform into a phoenix with rainbow colors.

I have participated in many conferences throughout my life but that conference stands out. I will tell you a bit about my experience of that momentous event. Between the last week of August and first week of September of 1980 I spent one of the happiest days of my life. I was in paradise—geographically, socially, spiritually, and intellectually. In every sense, it was the best possible moment and environment. The camp consisted of a set of newly-built two-floor concrete buildings with comfortable rooms. Every morning we would wake up for prayer. Then we would have sumptuous breakfast, followed by free time for socializing. We would then have a series of lectures until the time for the noon prayer and lunch. The afternoon comprised of lectures and activities, including swimming and games of soccer or volleyball.

The International Islamic Youth Conference was organized by WAMY (World Assembly of Muslim Youth) in cooperation with the Turkish Ministry of Youth. There were about 150 young men from 42 countries. We did not have a single woman among us; they were banished from the land. No, they were not thrown into the sea. They were just not found eligible to be part of "Islamic youth." You may not believe me but we did not miss them there. We had enough lectures, prayers, games, social activities, swimming, and other adventures to keep us busy all of our waking hours. When, at the end of the day, we finally put our heads on our pillows; nothing could interrupt our sleep, not even a beauty pageant. We did not even notice the absence of X chromosomes. Now I know from my experience that God can create a heaven without women. And of course, another heaven without men! Wow!

The lectures were given in three languages, English, Arabic, and Turkish, and were translated live by professional translators and broadcast to radio receivers plugged into our ears. It was a very modern facility for those times. I did not need those radios as I was able to follow the lectures in all three languages.

The Turkish Minister of Sports and Youth came to the formal opening of the conference and gave an opening speech. The Sword and Shield Dance group from Bursa turned the opening ceremony into a festive occassion. The dance was performed by men only, and it represented the Ottoman conquest of the city of Bursa. Fatih Saraç and I were provocative. We led a few other hyperactive Islamist participants to stir up the crowd. Fatih's father, Emin Saraç, was a prominent Muslim scholar like my father, yet was aligned with Saudi Arabia and was more conservative. But Fatih and I did not have much difference at that time. We protested the Minister of Youth, Talat Asal, since he was from AP (Adalet Partisi = Justice Party). We interrupted the Minister's speech by chanting in Arabic:

176

La masoniya la sihyoniyya; islamiyya islamiyya
Not masonic, not Zionist; but Islamic, Islamic!

Poor Turkish Minister of Youth! As the host of the conference, he had allocated the country's best youth camp for our service, and here he was protested by his dear guests! Thank God that the majority of the young participants, including the WAMY officials and lecturers, was level-headed. Thus, he managed to ignore us. We were a difficult bunch to placate. We also booed and protested the folk dance group, since they were wearing shorts and immorally showing off a few inches above their knee caps. We would not tolerate masons or shorts. And we were going to give them our "eat-my-shorts" attitude, the holy-political version of Bart Simpson, the notorious cartoon character.

A few days later, I heard a rumor. The bust of Atatürk was busted. Well, not really. The rumor was not accurate. But there was some real news buzzing around. Someone had spilled milk on the brazen head of the official cult hero and let a cat lick from it. Imagine the image of a cat licking milk on top of the number one Turk, the categorically different Turk, who was considered alive in his grave, and was the subject of periodical reports by top politicians and generals? This was then, and still now is, a serious offense in Turkey. The spiller of the milk and the spoiler of Atatürk's dignity would be arrested together with his accomplice, the black cat, and would be punished by a criminal law under the title "Insulting Atatürk." I had no idea who had done it. I even doubted wether it was manufactured by police agents to disrupt our peaceful gathering. Later, this rumor would come back and haunt me at the martial court.

I have pictures from that conference. I had a long black beard with big eye glasses. I have noted the names and addresses of some of those in the picture. I Googled them and could not find most of them. For instance, I do not know what happened to the happy young black boy named Fahim Abdulgany from Barbados, or the energetic, handsome, and tall militant Ahmad Hani al-Shakany from Egypt, or Mohd Anwar Tahir of Malaysia, or Akbar Hussain of Florida, or Mustafa Omari, the Kurdish gentleman from Australia, or Khalid Muhammad Ali of Egypt who was a giant Islamist militant with a black beard and a long fistan.

However, I could find some information about some of my former comrades in those pictures. I was not surprised to learn that Fatih Saraç became the mouthpiece of Saudi propaganda in Turkey who made a fortune in his business deals that included a Saudi prince. Information available on the Google suggests that he was implicated in helping terrorist organizations. Suhail Ahmad of Canada became a successful businessman and CEO of Ittihad Capital, which provided financial services to the Muslim minority there. Samer Minkara of the USA, again according to Google, received a PhD in Math from Maryland College Park, and once worked in a software agency Ptech Inc which allegedly held terrorist connections. As for Kamal Helbawy of the UK, who was the representative of WAMY and a passionate member of the Muslim Brotherhood, I was glad to learn from an interview published at Jamestown.org, that he has still been a moderate Muslim condemning the extremists. Nevertheless, he is still following the backward Salafi religious teachings based on Hadith and Sunna.

We had several well-known scholars there, such as, Muhammad al Qaradawi of Egypt. When I was a student at middle school, I sold his book, which was translated into Turkish, *Helal ve Haram* (*The Lawful and the Prohibited*). It was my first sales experience. My father's friend, Salih Özcan, who was Saudi's cultural agent in Turkey, published it together with the first translations of Sayid Qutb and other Salafi authors. He wanted to use me as his salesman. He gave me fifty books at a time and I would sell them after Friday prayers at the gates of mosques in Istanbul, where my father gave lectures. Then, my father was a rotating preacher; that is, every week he gave lectures in different mosques. This was very good for my book sale business, since each time I would have a different market. My inventory consisted of only one book, and I had yet to read it. After finishing his lecture before the Friday sermon, my father would recommend Qaradawi's book to the audience. After the prayer I would sell it like water to thirsty people. In retrospect, I find it immoral, since through the sales of the book we were making money— not much, but enough to raise the "conflict of interest" question. I made good money relative to my age from Qaradawi's book. But, after meeting him, I did not like him. He was a *moruk*, that is, a boring and snobbish old man.

But, there was another lecturer, who was from another planet. He was Ahmad Deedat. He was energetic, bright, articulate, interactive, animated, funny, humble, and friendly, traits that the great majority of Sunni and Shiite scholars lacked. He had a great memory and good knowledge of the Bible and the Quran. When I heard him give a lecture on the mathematical miracle of the Quran, I knew that he was not a regular scholar. He was summarizing the content of his new book, *Al-Quran, The Ultimate Miracle*. He devoted himself to the cause of promoting the message of the Quran and had a great sense of humor.

For me Deedat was the real deal in that conference. He was the one that introduced the SECRET to me. I heard about the mathematical miracle of the Quran for the first time from him. It was a moment that I will never forget. For two years, without knowing the importance of this number in our holy book, I had given it as a name to my youth organization: FT-19 (Fatih 19). Now, I was learning that it was a code of a prophetic Quranic miracle! I was very excited, for both that "coincidence" and my past experience debating with atheists. Thus, I decided to translate his book, *Al-Quran, The Ultimate Miracle*. Ahmad Deedat was very happy at my decision, gave me permission to translate his book, together with his other booklets that countered the evangelical missionaries, such as:

> *Who Wrote the Bible?*
> *"50,000 Errors in the Bible?"*
> *What was the Sign of Jonah?*
> *Is the Bible God's Word?*
> *Who Moved the Stone?*
> *Resurrection or Resuscitation?*
> *What the Bible Says About Muhammad?*
> *Islam's Answer to te Racial Problem*
> *The God that Never Was*
> *Crucifixion or Cruci-fiction?*

I was not much interested in his books about Christianity. I was going to study his book that unveiled a prophetic SECRET message and then translate it into Turkish.

However, after the discovery of a major problem involving the numerical system and current manuscripts, the Muslim world became shocked. Deedat immediately stopped the publication of his book, *Al-Quran, The Ultimate Miracle*. Then, Deedat was receiving support for his organization from Saudi Arabia, Kuwait, Bahrain, Qatar and the United Arab Emirates. Though he was not fond of Hadith, he was Sunni and he theologically accepted Hadith as the second source besides the Quran.

Reportedly, in his later years, Deedat reformed his position and started to preach a Quran-alone philosophy.

16
Mysterious Letters/Numbers

"The Quran teaches that the QURANIC INITIALS constitute the
miracle of the Quran. This is found in 10:1, 12:1, 13:1, 15:1, 26:2,
27:1, 28:2, and 31:2. The expression, 'These are the miracles of this
book' is found ONLY in conjunction with Quranic initials."
~ Rashad Khalifa[109]

Some chapters of the Quran contain "coded letters," which are called "disjointed
letters" or "initials." Considering the fact that Arabs used the Alphabet system as
numbers during the revelation of the Quran, these letters are also numbers. The
Quran is thus a unique book. For about 14 centuries the meaning of these letters
and numbers remained a curious secret. Commentators of the Quran, even if
some ventured to speculate on them, were in agreement: "Only God knows the
true meaning of these letters."

The Quran is a message sent to human beings. Why would God send us a
message that none would be able to understand? There are infinite amounts of
information that exclusively belong to God's knowledge. So, why would God
pick some disjointed letters and ask us to read them?

Exactly half of the 28 letters of Arabic alphabet are used in the composition of
these initials. As you will see in the following pages, these 14 letters are
arranged in 14 different letter combinations. These letter combinations initialize
29 chapters of the Quran, whereas in 19 of them the letters constitute their first
verses exclusively.

14 Letters

ل	ك	ي	ط	ح	ه	ا
ر	ق	ص	ع	س	ن	م

Create 14 Different Combinations

طسم	طه	كهيعص	المر	الر	المص	الم
ن	ق	حم.عسق	حم	ص	يس	طس

In the Beginning of 29 Chapters

2	3	7	10	11	12
13	14	15	19	20	26
27	28	29	30	31	32
36	38	40	41	42	43
44	45	46	50	68	.

14 + 14 + 29 = 57 (19x3)

Combinations are Independent Verses Starting 19 Chapters

2	3	7			
			19	20	26
	28	29	30	31	32
36		40	41	42	43
44	45	46			.

On it is Nineteen

181

Letter Combinations
Initializing Chapters

Chapter Number	Conventional Name	Initials/Numbers
1	2	Heifer	A1L30M40
2	3	The Amramites	A1L30M40
3	7	The Purgatory	A1L30M40Ŝ90
4	10	Jonah	A1L30R200
5	11	Hood	A1L30R200
6	12	Joseph	A1L30R200
7	13	Thunder	A1L30M40R200
8	14	Abraham	A1L30R200
9	15	Hijr Valley	A1L30R200
10	19	Mary	K20H5Y10Â70Ŝ90
11	20	TaHa	Ť9H5
12	26	The Poets	Ť 9S60M40
13	27	The Ant	Ť 9S60
14	28	History	Ť 9S60M40
15	29	The Spider	A1L30M40
16	30	Romans	A1L30M40
17	31	Luqman	A1L30M40
18	32	Prostration	A1L30M40
19	36	YaSin	Y10S60
20	38	Sad	Ŝ90
21	40	Forgiver	Ĥ8M40
22	41	Elucidated	Ĥ8M40
23	42	Consultation	Ĥ8M40* Â70S60Q100
24	43	Vanity	Ĥ8M40
25	44	Smoke	Ĥ8M40
26	45	Kneeling	Ĥ8M40
27	46	The Dunes	Ĥ8M40
28	50	Qaf	Q100
29	68	The Pen	N50

17
ق Q100

"The evidence reported in this book is 100% physical; no opinion, conjecture, or interpretation is involved. All the data is presented in the form of 'Physical Facts.' Each physical fact is simplified in such a way as to make it easily examinable and verifiable."

"The physical evidence reported here includes vast numbers of alphabet letters, as written in God's coded message. If these numbers were reported without simplification, the reader will be justified in saying, 'This is like asking to count the stars!!' Therefore, all data has been simplified to the extent that the reader can easily check and instantly verify the validity of any number reported. All the numbers of alphabet letters are reported on single verse basis. Thus, the occurrence of any given alphabet in any given chapter is reported in each verse in that chapter. The reader can then verify the validity of any number through a series of random checks; counting the desired letter in a randomly selected group of verses instead of having to count the occurrence of the letter in the whole chapter." ~ Rashad Khalifa[110]

The Quran, in its entirety, is interwoven with an interlocking numerical system. From the count of letters to the count of verses and their assigned numbers, from the frequencies of certain key words to the arrangement of related verses, this highly sensitive system is able to expose any flaw, interference, revision, patch, addition, or subtraction within the Quran —from its biggest elements, chapters, to the its smallest ones, letters.

> 15:9   WE, WE indeed, yes it is WE who have sent down the Reminder, and indeed it is WE who will preserve it.

The initial letters/numbers consist of combinations of single, two, three, four, and five letters or numbers (During the time of revelation the alphabet letters were also used as numbers in its old order, ABJD). To make the counting easier for the first examination, let's look at a short chapter starting with a single letter. Chapter Qaf ق is perfect for starters. The 50th Chapter of the Quran starts with letter ق, with the numerical value of 100. Here we will not focus on its numerical value. Rather we will focus on its frequency as a letter. Later we can continue our examination of Chapter 42, which is initialized with a 5-letter combination where the letter Qaf is one of them. The five letters are divided into two parts, the first two letters being designated as the first verse and the second three letters as the second verse of the chapter: ĤM. ÂSQ. عسق . حم (read: ĤaMim. Âyn Seen Qaf).

183

You will realize that here we are focusing on physical facts that can be verified or falsified by lay people. Anyone with eyes and counting ability can examine the frequency of initial letters and can witness the MIRACLE with varying intellectual appreciation. You do not need knowledge of the Arabic language to witness a living divine sign unequivocally. You will not engage in guesswork, imagination, conjecture, hearsay, or esoteric interpretation. All you do is count ﻗ the "head with two dots." Count these heads with pairs of dots! You will find exactly 57 (19x3) heads like this in Chapter 50, and 57 (19x3) in Chapter 42, the only two chapters that are initialed with Qaf. Are these coincidences? Can these be the ingenious work of Muhammad? We will discuss the issue to the satisfaction of most skeptics.

If you add 57 to 57 you will learn that these two chapters that start with letter Qaf contain 114 of this initial, that is, 19x6. The traditional interpretation that the letter Qaf represents or implies the Quran is mathematically justified. The Quran contains 114 (19x6) chapters and the frequency of the Q in the two chapters it crowns is 114 (19x6). The religious and non-religious ingrates who rush into rejecting the numerical structure of the Quran as "coincidence" or "fabrication" are challenged by the most easily recognized Arabic alphabet letter.

It will take you only few minutes or a maximum of half an hour to count the frequency of letter ﻗ in these chapters. Don't trust me or anyone else's claim. Try it for yourself. You will appreciate the mathematical pattern if you study it yourself.

I would like to share with you an excerpt from Ahmad Deedat, the late founder and president of the Islamic Propagation Center in South Africa.[111]

> "Is it possible that this most complicated dovetailing method of guarding and preserving the Holy Qur'an would have come about by fluke, by chance, by accident, by COINCIDENCE? Could a non-conscious computer have created this miracle of "Purity of style, of Wisdom and of Truth" as Rev. Bosworth-Smith opines? The Author of the Qur'an has gone out of His Way to show us that His book is no fluke; that a conscious mind was involved in its production. He leaves tell-tale marks, "fingerprints," clues for us to discover His Mighty Hand."

> "If any human author had undertaken such a supernatural task as writing such a Book as the Qur'an, surely he would at least have had some hesitation in attempting to surmount the impossible. God Almighty could easily have solved these problems real or deliberately created without making us a witness to His effortless "effort"; but He wants to draw our attention to His Conscious task. He demonstrates to us that if a human being had written the Qur'an, and even if everything went well with him, he would [perhaps] still be left over with an extra ﻗ Qaf. You see, after having written the two ﻗ Qaf containing Suras and counting them, he would have been confronted with 115 ﻗ Qafs and not 114 as we find them now."[112]

184

To stimulate the reader's curiosity and to demonstrate a well-calculated design in the selection of each word and each letter, the author of the Quran occasionally abandons his routine in the details of the text.

Let's assume for a moment, that the author of the Quran was Muhammad. Let's assume that he was very successful in embedding 57 ق Q in chapter 42 while keeping a very careful track of the frequencies of numerous key words and numbers. Let's assume that when Muhammad counted the number of ق Qafs in chapter 50, to his dismay, he ended up with 58, which is not divisible by 19. He would have to either add 18 ق or subtract 1 ق. Let's assume he preferred the second method. Which ق should he eliminate?

Most likely, Muhammad would start from the beginning of Chapter ق Q. Eliminating the first ق Q would be very easy. But no! This was a clue or formula for the numerical-literal puzzle he was creating; it was very important. Besides, ق was the first letter of the word Quran and was serving multiple functions: as a number (100) it was participating in a prophecy, as a letter it was a component of the mathematical structure, and again as the first letter of the Quran, it was symbolically standing for the Quran. The first verse of chapter 50 starts with letter/number Q and the word Quran.

50:1 Q100, By the Glorious Quran.   ق والقران المجيد (١)

Let's continue reading from *Al-Quran, The Ultimate Miracle* by Ahmad Deedat who articulated this point very well. The notes in brackets belong to me:

"He had more than thirty other synonyms for this one word, قرآن *Quran* in the Quran itself. Synonyms like *al-Kitab, al-Hukum, al-Burhan, al-Dhikr, at-Tanzeel* etc. and we would have been none the wiser about what the Author had done, but he wants to drive the point home that that ق stands for the Quran as *A is for Apple*. Furthermore the impact would have diminished. Our Author is a perfectionist. So he will continue to scan to a ق Qaf to eliminate... "

"Around verse 13 he comes across the biggest cluster of ق s or Qs. Five to be exact. He must eliminate one of these. Let us ... read verses 12, 13, and 14. There are only 4 ق s Qafs here. Yes, but there were supposed to be 5. 'Do you mean to say that the Quran has been changed? You ask. 'No' I say. 'Then, how can you account for your contradictory statements?' You see, the Author—God or Muhummed—had intended 5 ق s Qafs between these 3 verses. The clue is in verse 13. Look at the word اخون لوط 'Ikwano Lut' (Brethern of Lut). It ought to have been قوم لوط 'Qawmu Lut' (People of Lut). Why قوم لوط 'Qawmu Lut'? Because the Author has consistently described the people of Lot with the same adjective قوم 'Qawmun' 12 times throughout the Quran in different places. Why should the Author Who is so unvarying in His description of this abominable people, who were destroyed for [aggressively imposing on others] their unnatural [uncontrolled] lust, described them in this particular instance in the 'thirteenth' verse as اخون لوط 'Ikhwano Lut' (Brethern of Lut). An Author who can give you 3 synonyms between 2 verses as in in verse 12 and 13 to describe

185

a 'group of people,' and even convey the idea of 'a people' without any adjective is the same Who adhered to that unchanging adjective قوم 'Qawmun'."

"Any attentive reader would have noticed the changed formula in verse 13. Any human author, knowing the beauty of using synonyms and yet remaining consistent a dozen times would have naturally repeated قوم لوط 'Qawmu Lut' and made His baker's dozen (13). In that case there would have been 58 ق s Qafs in Sura ق 'Qaf' and 58 is not a multiple of 19. Did He not say, 'I will make you to reckon with 19'?"[113]

Bretherns of Lot اخون لوط

To describe the people of Lot, the Quran uses the word *Qawm* (group, people, nation) 12 times: 11:70; 11:74; 11:89; 22:43; 26:160; 38:13; 54:33; 7:80; 11:78; 27:54; 27:56; 29:28.

However, the 13th verse of the chapter that starts with the letter Q is an exception. Why then instead of the word Qawm, the word *Ikhwan* (brethrens) is used? For the answer, check the beginning of the chapter that contains that verse. As you see, the chapter starts with the letter Q.

(50:12) كذبت قبلهم قوم نوح واصحاب الرس وثمود

(50:13) وعاد وفرعون واخوان لوط

(50:12) واصحاب الايكه وقوم تبع كل كذب الرسل فحق وعيد

186

ق

Chapter 50 (The First Three Verses)

In the name of God, the Gracious, the Compassionate

بسم الله الرحمن الرحيم

1. Q100,

ق

and the glorious Quran.

والقران المجيد (١)

2. Yet, they are surprised

بل عجبوا

since has come to them

ان جاهم

a warner from amongst them;

منذر منهم

so, declared the ingrates,

فقال الكفرون

"This is something strange!"

هذا شي عجيب (٢)

- Just count the letter ق Qafs in the beginning of Chapter 50.
- You do not need to know Arabic as language to accomplish this task.
- It is very easy to recognize this letter
- A small circle with two dots on top. Can you recognize them?
- As an exercise try to locate ق in each of the following words:

فقال   القران   قد   بالحق

ق

Chapter 42 (The First Three Verses)

In the Name of God, Gracious, Compassionate

بسم الله الرحمن الرحيم

1. Ĥ8M40.

حم (١)

2. Â70S60Q100.

عسق (٢)

3. Thus reveals to you

كذلك يوحي اليك

and to those before you,

والي الذين من قبلك

God, the Supreme, the Wise.

الله العزيز الحكيم (٣)

Note that the five-lettered initial of chapters 42 . حم عسق contains the letter ق which initializes chapter 50. In other words, the letter ق is a common initial letter in only the beginning of two chapters in the Quran.

In chapter 50 there are 57 (19x3) ق.
In chapter 42 there are 57 (19x3) ق.
In both ق-initialed chapters there are 114 (19x6) ق.
This indicates that the ق (Q) represent the Quran.
For each chapter of the Quran one Q is used.

The Role of Letter ق (Q) in the System

Here are some of the literary-numerical aspects of the letter Q that we have discovered so far.

1. There are 57 (19x3) Qs in Chapter 50, which starts with the letter Q.

2. There are 57 (19x3) Qs inChapter 42, the only other chapter that starts with the letter Q.

3. Chapter 50 has 45 numbered verses. The two numbers add up to 95 (19x5).

4. Chapter 42 has 53 numbered verses. The two numbers add up to 95 (19x5).

5. In the first verse of Chapter 50, the adjective Glorious (مجيد) is used for the Quran and its numerical value is 57 (19x3), equal to the frequency of the letter Q in the same chapter.

6. The sum of verse numbers where the letter Q occurs in the chapter starting with the letter Q is 798 (19x42), and the factor 42 is the number of the other chapter that starts with the same initial letter Q.

7. The people of Lot are consistently referred to with the expression *Qawm-i Lot* throughout the Quran, except in the chapter starting with the letter Q (known as Chapter Q), where instead, we find an expression that does not contain letter Q: *Ikhwan-i Lot*.

In the following pages you will see two chapters containing the initial letter ق "Q." Each letter Q is colored in red.

ق

0	(50:0) بسم الله الرحمن الرحيم
2	(50:1) ق والقران المجيد
1	(50:2) بل عجبوا ان جاهم منذر منهم فقال الكفرون هذا شي عجيب
0	(50:3) اذا متنا وكنا ترابا ذلك رجع بعيد
2	(50:4) قد علمنا ما تنقص الارض منهم وعندنا كتب حفيظ
1	(50:5) بل كذبوا بالحق لما جاهم فهم في امر مريج
1	(50:6) افلم ينظروا الي السما فوقهم كيف بنينها وزينها وما لها من فروج
1	(50:7) والارض مددنها والقينا فيها روسي وانبتنا فيها من كل زوج بهيج
0	(50:8) تبصره وذكري لكل عبد منيب
0	(50:9) ونزلنا من السما ما مبركا فانبتنا به جنت وحب الحصيد
1	(50:10) والنخل باسقت لها طلع نضيد
1	(50:11) رزقا للعباد واحيينا به بلده ميتا كذلك الخروج
2	(50:12) كذبت قبلهم قوم نوح واصحب الرس وثمود
0	(50:13) وعاد وفرعون واخون لوط
2	(50:14) واصحب الايكه وقوم تبع كل كذب الرسل فحق وعيد
2	(50:15) افعيينا بالخلق الاول بل هم في لبس من خلق جديد
3	(50:16) ولقد خلقنا الانسن ونعلم ما توسوس به نفسه ونحن اقرب اليه من حبل الوريد
3	(50:17) اذ يتلقي المتلقيان عن اليمين وعن الشمال قعيد
2	(50:18) ما يلفظ من قول الا لديه رقيب عتيد
1	(50:19) وجات سكره الموت بالحق ذلك ما كنت منه تحيد
0	(50:20) ونفخ في الصور ذلك يوم الوعيد
1	(50:21) وجات كل نفس معها سايق وشهيد
1	(50:22) لقد كنت في غفله من هذا فكشفنا عنك غطاك فبصرك اليوم حديد
2	(50:23) وقال قرينه هذا ما لدي عتيد
1	(50:24) القيا في جهنم كل كفار عنيد
0	(50:25) مناع للخير معتد مريب
1	(50:26) الذي جعل مع الله الها اخر فالقياه في العذاب الشديد
2	(50:27) قال قرينه ربنا ما اطغيته ولكن كان في ضلل بعيد

3	(50:28) قال لا تختصموا لدي وقد قدمت اليكم بالوعيد
1	(50:29) ما يبدل القول لدي وما انا بظلم للعبيد
2	(50:30) يوم نقول لجهنم هل امتلات وتقول هل من مزيد
1	(50:31) وازلفت الجنه للمتقين غير بعيد
0	(50:32) هذا ما توعدون لكل اواب حفيظ
1	(50:33) من خشي الرحمن بالغيب وجا بقلب منيب
0	(50:34) ادخلوها بسلم ذلك يوم الخلود
0	(50:35) لهم ما يشاون فيها ولدينا مزيد
3	(50:36) وكم اهلكنا قبلهم من قرن هم اشد منهم بطشا فنقبوا في البلد هل من محيص
2	(50:37) ان في ذلك لذكري لمن كان له قلب او القى السمع وهو شهيد
2	(50:38) ولقد خلقنا السموت والارض وما بينهما في سته ايام وما مسنا من لغوب
3	(50:39) فاصبر على ما يقولون وسبح بحمد ربك قبل طلوع الشمس وقبل الغروب
0	(50:40) ومن اليل فسبحه وادبر السجود
1	(50:41) واستمع يوم يناد المناد من مكان قريب
1	(50:42) يوم يسمعون الصيحه بالحق ذلك يوم الخروج
0	(50:43) انا نحن نحي ونميت والينا المصير
2	(50:44) يوم تشقق الارض عنهم سراعا ذلك حشر علينا يسير
2	(50:45) نحن اعلم بما يقولون وما انت عليهم بجبار فذكر بالقران من يخاف وعيد
57	Sum for Chapter 50
0	(42:0) بسم الله الرحمن الرحيم
0	(42:1) حم
1	(42:2) عسق
1	(42:3) كذلك يوحي اليك والى الذين من قبلك الله العزيز الحكيم
0	(42:4) له ما في السموت وما في الارض وهو العلي العظيم
1	(42:5) تكاد السموت يتفطرن من فوقهن والمليكه يسبحون بحمد ربهم ويستغفرون لمن في الارض الا ان الله هو الغفور الرحيم
0	(42:6) والذين اتخذوا من دونه اوليا الله حفيظ عليهم وما انت عليهم بوكيل
4	(42:7) وكذلك اوحينا اليك قرانا عربيا لتنذر ام القرى ومن حولها وتنذر يوم الجمع لا ريب فيه فريق في الجنه وفريق في السعير
0	(42:8) ولو شا الله لجعلهم امه وحده ولكن يدخل من يشا في رحمته والظلمون ما لهم من ولي ولا نصير

191

1	(42:9) ام اتخذوا من دونه اوليا فالله هو الولي وهو يحي الموتي وهو علي كل شي قدير
0	(42:10) وما اختلفتم فيه من شي فحكمه الي الله ذلكم الله ربي عليه توكلت واليه انيب
0	(42:11) فاطر السموت والارض جعل لكم من انفسكم ازوجا ومن الانعم ازوجا يذروكم فيه ليس كمثله شي وهو السميع البصير
3	(42:12) له مقاليد السموت والارض يبسط الرزق لمن يشا ويقدر انه بكل شي عليم
2	(42:13) شرع لكم من الدين ما وصي به نوحا والذي اوحينا اليك وما وصينا به ابرهيم وموسي وعيسي ان اقيموا الدين ولا تتفرقوا فيه كبر علي المشركين ما تدعوهم اليه الله يجتبي اليه من يشا ويهدي اليه من ينيب
3	(42:14) وما تفرقوا الا من بعد ما جاهم العلم بغيا بينهم ولولا كلمه سبقت من ربك الي اجل مسمي لقضي بينهم وان الذين اورثوا الكتب من بعدهم لفي شك منه مريب
2	(42:15) فلذلك فادع واستقم كما امرت ولا تتبع اهواهم وقل امنت بما انزل الله من كتب وامرت لاعدل بينكم الله ربنا وربكم لنا اعملنا ولكم اعملكم لا حجه بيننا وبينكم الله يجمع بيننا واليه المصير
0	(42:16) والذين يحاجون في الله من بعد ما استجيب له حجتهم داحضه عند ربهم وعليهم غضب ولهم عذاب شديد
2	(42:17) الله الذي انزل الكتب بالحق والميزان وما يدريك لعل الساعه قريب
2	(42:18) يستعجل بها الذين لا يومنون بها والذين امنوا مشفقون منها ويعلمون انها الحق الا ان الذين يمارون في الساعه لفي ضلل بعيد
2	(42:19) الله لطيف بعباده يرزق من يشا وهو القوي العزيز
0	(42:20) من كان يريد حرث الاخره نزد له في حرثه ومن كان يريد حرث الدنيا نوته منها وما له في الاخره من نصيب
1	(42:21) ام لهم شركوا شرعوا لهم من الدين ما لم ياذن به الله ولولا كلمه الفصل لقضي بينهم وان الظلمين لهم عذاب اليم
2	(42:22) تري الظلمين مشفقين مما كسبوا وهو واقع بهم والذين امنوا وعملوا الصلحت في روضات الجنات لهم ما يشاون عند ربهم ذلك هو الفضل الكبير
3	(42:23) ذلك الذي يبشر الله عباده الذين امنوا وعملوا الصلحت قل لا اسلكم عليه اجرا الا الموده في القربي ومن يقترف حسنه نزد له فيها حسنا ان الله غفور شكور
4	(42:24) ام يقولون افتري علي الله كذبا فان يشا الله يختم علي قلبك ويمح الله البطل ويحق الحق بكلمته انه عليم بذات الصدور
1	(42:25) وهو الذي يقبل التوبه عن عباده ويعفوا عن السيات ويعلم ما تفعلون

(42:26) ويستجيب الذين امنوا وعملوا الصلحت ويزيدهم من فضله والكفرون لهم عذاب شديد 0

(42:27) ولو بسط الله الرزق لعباده لبغوا في الارض ولكن ينزل بقدر ما يشا انه بعباده خبير بصير 2

(42:28) وهو الذي ينزل الغيث من بعد ما قنطوا وينشر رحمته وهو الولي الحميد 1

(42:29) ومن ايته خلق السموت والارض وما بث فيهما من دابه وهو علي جمعهم اذا يشا قدير 2

(42:30) وما اصبكم من مصيبه فبما كسبت ايديكم ويعفوا عن كثير 0

(42:31) وما انتم بمعجزين في الارض وما لكم من دون الله من ولي ولا نصير 0

(42:32) ومن ايته الجوار في البحر كالاعلم 0

(42:33) ان يشا يسكن الريح فيظللن رواكد علي ظهره ان في ذلك لايت لكل صبار شكور 0

(42:34) او يوبقهن بما كسبوا ويعف عن كثير 1

(42:35) ويعلم الذين يجدلون في ايتنا ما لهم من محيص 0

(42:36) فما اوتيتم من شي فمتع الحيوه الدنيا وما عند الله خير وابقي للذين امنوا وعلي ربهم يتوكلون 1

(42:37) والذين يجتنبون كبير الاثم والفوحش واذا ما غضبوا هم يغفرون 0

(42:38) والذين استجابوا لربهم واقاموا الصلوه وامرهم شوري بينهم ومما رزقنهم ينفقون 3

(42:39) والذين اذا اصابهم البغي هم ينتصرون 0

(42:40) وجزوا سييه سييه مثلها فمن عفا واصلح فاجره علي الله انه لا يحب الظلمين 0

(42:41) ولمن انتصر بعد ظلمه فاوليك ما عليهم من سبيل 0

(42:42) انما السبيل علي الذين يظلمون الناس ويبغون في الارض بغير الحق اوليك لهم عذاب اليم 1

(42:43) ولمن صبر وغفر ان ذلك لمن عزم الامور 0

(42:44) ومن يضلل الله فما له من ولي من بعده وتري الظلمين لما راوا العذاب يقولون هل الي مرد من سبيل 1

(42:45) وتريهم يعرضون عليها خشعين من الذل ينظرون من طرف خفي وقال الذين امنوا ان الخسرين الذين خسروا انفسهم واهليهم يوم القيمه الا ان الظلمين في عذاب مقيم 3

(42:46) وما كان لهم من اوليا ينصرونهم من دون الله ومن يضلل الله فما له من سبيل 0

(42:47) استجيبوا لربكم من قبل ان ياتي يوم لا مرد له من الله ما لكم من ملجا 1

193

يوميذ وما لكم من نكير

(42:48) فان اعرضوا فما ارسلنك عليهم حفيظا ان عليك الا البلغ وانا اذا اذقنا الانسن منا رحمه فرح بها وان تصبهم سييه بما قدمت ايديهم فان الانسن كفور	2
(42:49) لله ملك السموت والارض يخلق ما يشا يهب لمن يشا انثا ويهب لمن يشا الذكور	1
(42:50) او يزوجهم ذكرانا وانثا ويجعل من يشا عقيما انه عليم قدير	2
(42:51) وما كان لبشر ان يكلمه الله الا وحيا او من وراي حجاب او يرسل رسولا فيوحي باذنه ما يشا انه علي حكيم	0
(42:52) وكذلك اوحينا اليك روحا من امرنا ما كنت تدري ما الكتب ولا الايمن ولكن جعلنه نورا نهدي به من نشا من عبادنا وانك لتهدي الي صرط مستقيم	1
(42:53) صرط الله الذي له ما في السموت وما في الارض الا الي الله تصير الامور	0

Sum for Chapter 42 **57**

Total of frequency of letter Q in Chapters starting with Letter Q **114**

Thus, the letter Q is used exactly 114 (19x6) times in two chapters starting with the letter Q. The letter Q represents the Quran since it starts with that letter (See 50:1), and this acronymous relationship is also supported in terms of numerical relationship. The total occurrence of the letter Q in chapters starting with the letter Q equals to the number of chapters in the Quran.

$$57 + 57 = 114$$

$$114 = 19 \times 6$$

Each Q for one of the 114 chapters of the Quran

عليها تسعه عشر

On it is Nineteen

18
ص Ŝ90

"Gebrail reveled the word Bastata in verse 7:69 with the letter Sad"
~ Hadith. This hadith has been proven to be a lie by mathematical and
archelogical evidence.[114]

Chapter 38, which is also commonly referred to as Chapter Ŝaad, is one of the
chapters that starts with a single letter or number 90. The sound represented by
the Arabic letter ص (read Ŝaad) does not exist in the English language; it is an S
sound made through the flattening of the middle of the tongue. The Arabic letter
س Seen corresponds to the sound represented by the letter S in English. To
distinguish ص Ŝaad from س Seen we will write the former as Ŝ.

There are two other chapters starting with the letter Ŝ among other initial
Alphabet letters. They are 7th and 19th chapters. The sum of frequencies of ص Ŝ
(Ŝaad) in these three chapters is a multiple of 19.

Chapter Nu	Frequencies of ص (S)
7	97
19	26
38	29
Total	152 = 19 x 8

The Early "Errors" in Rashad's Count

As you have read in an earlier chapter, when Dr. Rashad Khalifa entered his count of the frequency of each letter in each chapter of the Quran into the computer, he had no expectation about the the number 19.[115] Thus, he published his early data, calculations and observations in 1973 in *The Miracle of the Quran: Significance of the Mysterious Alphabets*.[116] Since Rashad was not aware of the 19-based numerical pattern in the Quran, he was sharing some statistical data and a few interesting observations. He then discovered that the frequency of the letters that initialize the chapter has a higher density than the chapters not containing them as initials.

For instance, the frequency of the letter N in the chapter that starts with the letter ✦ N (Chapter 68) was much higher than its average frequency in the Quran. The same was true for other initials. Among the few curious observations in the book beyond this statistical pattern, was the observation that the frequency of the letter Q in the two chapters that start with the letter Q was 114, exactly equal to the total number of chapters in the Quran. Thus, he reasoned that Q stood for the Quran both literally and numerically.

> "By comparing the net overall frequency of the letter Qaf in sura Qaf with the overall frequency in the three suras exhibiting a higher percentage value, we note that sura Qaf is actually more than 5 times greater than sura Al-Shams, almost two times greater than sura Al-Qiyama (see Table 15). These observations lead us to the conclusion that the only three suras in the Quran which exhibits a higher percentage of Qaf than that in sura Qaf are in fact inferior to sura Qaf in the overall frequency. THIS MEANS THAT SURA QAF CONTAINS THE HIGHEST FREQUENCY OF THE LETTER QAF THAN ANY OTHER SURA IN THE QURAN..."

> "What does this startling observation mean? ... "

> "... This alternative conclusion, however, will have to assume that the Prophet, an illiterate man, had an advance knowledge of the distribution pattern of the letter Qaf and its exact proportions throughout 114 chapters to be revealed in scattered verses over the near 23 years. The reader can easily see the farfetchedness of such a conclusion. And we are yet talking about only one, the first, of 14 Qur'anic initials. Even without going any further in this study, we already have sufficient evidence that ONLY GOD COULD BE THE AUTHOR OF THE QURAN."[117]

> "Lest someone may actually claim that the mathematical superiority of sura Qaf in the overall frequency value of the letter Qaf is coincidental, God Almighty provided further evidence supporting the observed superiority. Thus, the only other sura in the Qur'an which bears the letter Qaf as a Qur'anic initial, namely, sura Al-Shura (Consensus; No. 42), contains 57 Qafs. This is the same frequency of occurrence found in sura Qaf (see Table 13). Furthermore, when we

add the 57 Qafs of Sura Qaf plus the 57 Qafs sura Al-Shura, the product is 114, same as the total number of suras in the Quran. If the letter "Q" stands for the "Qur'an," we have in these two Qaf-initialed suras one Qaf for each sura. The clear message her is that all 114 suras constitute the Qur'an, the whole, Qur'an, and nothing but the Quran."[118]

Rashad was the first in history to enter the Quran into the computer, in 1969. In his early counts Rashad had made some errors. Some of the errors were due to the vagueness in his methodology of counting the letters, especially the letter *Alif*. Other errors in the count of letters were most likely due to human errors during his task of typing the Quran into the computer, from paper to electronic form.

There were three major errors in Rashad's early computerized data:

1. The count of the letter ا A was not reliable; due to additions of numerous extra ا A. This is similar to modern manuscripts, supposedly to help non Arabic readers to read the Quran properly.

2. The frequency of the letter ن N in the chapter starting with the letter ن N was counted to be 133. This was one ن N extra than the actual number of ن Ns in the manuscript used by Rashad for that chapter.

3. The frequency of the letter ص Ŝ also did not reflect the exact frequency of the letter ص Ŝ in the three chapters starting with that letter; his count was 153. He would later learn that the manuscript he use had an erroneous extra ص Ŝ and the actual count should have been 152.

This apparently sloppy work; with the exception of the first, happened to be prophetic, since they were involved in some historical controversies, which at the time Rashad had no idea about. Later research and investigations showed that there was a divine purpose and guidance in some of the apparently erroneous counting.

As mentioned earlier, the frequency of the letter ص Ŝ in the chapters starting with that letter was 152, which was divisible by 19 and one less than the manuscript used by Rashad. Before 1974 Rashad had no clue about the role of 19 in the numerical structure of the Quran. We cannot therefore accuse him of deliberately manipulating the results. His first work on the numerical aspect of the Quran published in 1973 serves as historical and circumstantial evidence for Rashad's lack of knowledge and intention regarding 19.

We Too Repeated the Error

The role of this counting error —that is the number 133 and 152— were important in the discovery of Code 19, since they were among the few clues that

197

sparked the light in the mind of Dr. Khalifa in the beginning of 1974, leading him to connect the dots between the apparently arbitrary numbers he gathered for the frequency of letters. Perhaps, Rashad Khalifa would not have noticed or pursued the numerical system in the Quran if he had obtained 132 N letters instead of 133 letters or 153 Sad letters instead of 152 letters. Even if he noticed it, he would have had hard time explaining it. Later in his first book after his discovery of the "19 connection" (*Muhammad's Perpetual Miracle*), he would also commit an important error —the count of the word الله ALLAH (God) was one less than the actual frequency in the text he was using.

We also had a similar experience. It is impossible to convey all the details of what we experienced regarding this particular example of divine control in our lives. Two weeks after learning the numerical code of the Quran from Ahmad Deedat in August 1980, I was arrested by a group of police officers while walking with two members of the Muslim Brotherhood in the streets of Fatih, Istanbul, one from Egypt and the other from Britain. I would be convicted to six years for two of my published articles due to my promotion of a theocratic revolution in Turkey. During my first months in the military prison, there was no torture and we were able to read books and take notes. In prison, I was able to translate Deedat's book after testing and verifying the data presented there. I would perhaps never be able to do any of those things if I were free outside, organizing demonstrations, graffiti writings, hand-out distributions, poster hangings, public speaking activities—running from one political activity to another, playing hide-and-seek with soldiers and police. In retrospect, now I am so grateful for ending up in prison; it led me to free myself from the bondage of ignorance and fanaticism.

Though I was a leading member of a radical Sunni Islamist organization, I was always an inquisitive person. Though my initial impression was very positive, without verifying the data presented as objective facts I could not translate the book. To verify the count of words, I used Fuad Abdulbaqi's concordance of the Quran, *Al-Mujam ul Mufahras Li Alfazil Quranil Karim*. It was, and still is, the most accurate and user-friendly index of the Quran. As for the count of the words, we did not have any previous work to utilize. Thus, I had to count them manually one by one. I neither had the peace of mind nor the patience to do that on my own. Besides, I was not sure about the environment and conditions in the prison. Any moment, everything could change. I could lose the book or the freedom to read. So I was anxious to finish the translation as soon as possible. I was lucky. I was put among the arrested members of my organization. I had more than 50 people, mostly university students, in three small rooms filled with bunk beds. The military prison, which was located inside the 2nd Armored Brigade in Kartal-Maltepe, Istanbul, was converted from an ammunition storage used during the time of the Ottoman king Sultan Abdulhamit and was constructed with yard-thick stones, with virtually no windows except two five-inch-wide, two-foot-long vertical slots. Our electrical lamp flickered 24 hours a day. The doors of the rooms/wards would stay open for hours, and we could easily communicate. Because of my leadership and my status as the brother of the legendary leader Metin Yuksel, who was assassinated by the racist nationalist youth organization Gray Wolves, and due to my father's fame as brave *alim/mulla* (scholar), they accepted me as their default leader. I did not have any competition. Many older members of the organization expressed their allegiance to me. With the exception of a few murder and burglary crimes, most of them were there for involvement in propaganda activities or affiliation with illegal organizations.

Most of my comrades were able to read the Quran, and with the exception of a few, mostly without understanding its meaning.[119] Ability to read was sufficient to check the count of letters. I divided them into four teams of three prisoners and asked from each group to count the frequencies of each letter in their respective chapters. They were going to record their findings verse by verse. I would then compare the results of the four different teams. If there was any discrepancy, I would ask them to recount or compare their counts until they all agreed.

We verified the count of all initial letters with the exception of the letter A, since its count was problematic due to addition of extra letters supposedly to accommodate non-Arabic readers. Interestingly, our count of ص Ŝ too gave us 152 (19x8), one less than the actual count in the version we were using. Years later, we and the muslim world would learn that both Dr. Khalifa's and our count of the letter ص Ŝ were one less than the actual count. In retrospect, I consider our error as God's blessing. How?

Had I learned the actual count, 153, it would have been a great obstacle for me to go forward with the project, since it would create a big hole in the system which we somehow expected to be perfect.

"Bastata" بسطه

The بسطه Bastata of verse 7:69 is most likely written as بصطه BaStata, with the letter ص Ŝ (Ŝaad) with a small letter س S (Seen) on top of it. You might have a version that also adds a brief Arabic instruction or note on top of the letter ص Ŝ (Ŝaad): "Yuqrau bil Sin", that is "Read as Sin."

Besides the instruction of how to pronounce the letter ص Ŝ (Ŝaad) like the letter س S (Seen), an alternative thesis too can be found in related books: The word Bastata can be written in two ways, either with س S (Seen) or with ص Ŝ (Ŝaad). The proponents of this thesis would point at the other occurrence of the word in verse 2:247, where the word was spelled with letter س S.[120]

2:247 وقال لهم نبيهم ان الله قد بعث لكم طالوت ملكا قالوا اني يكون له الملك علينا ونحن احق بالملك منه ولم يوت سعه من المال قال ان الله اصطفيه عليكم وزاده بسطه في العلم والجسم والله يوتي ملكه من يشا والله وسع عليم

199

The numerical miracle of the Quran illuminated this historic controversy and solved the puzzle. The word بصطة Bastata of 7:69 should have been written with letter س S instead of the letter ص Ŝ, like its sister in 2:247, and the small س (Seen) on top of the letter ص (Ŝaad) was a historical correction, a reminder of a proofreader to the copiers or duplicators of the Quran to the spelling error. Ironically, the later copiers did not understand the correction note, and they copied blindly like a camera device, the erroneous spelling together with its correction!

I would like to end this chapter with an excerpt from Rashad's brother Dr. Atef Khalifa:

> "Before we show these examples, we would like to remind the reader that during the research and study done by Dr. Rashad Khalifa of the mathematical structure of the Quran he had to change 'two,' 2, words in the latest edition of the Quran that broke the code of the "19 based" mathematical miracle of the Quran. One of these words was BaŜŤata بصطه in 7:69 which was written with Sad, corrected to BaSŤata بسطه written with Seen as in the Tashkent Quran. The other was the word Nun in 68:1 spelled as one letter Nun in the modern editions, ن instead of نون Nun, Waw, and Nun. Every equation in the mathematical code was pointing to this correction. It was the miracle at work, proving the correct way of Rasm (Orthography). Those who could not see or appreciate the miracle, attacked Dr. Khalifa and his changing of these 'two' words and called it a 'heretical step.' They spoke out of ignorance or while taking advantage of the ignorance of the majority of the Muslims of what happened to the Rasm (Orthography) of the Uthmanic manuscript of the Quran. The modern editions of the Quran were produced after making hundreds, not two corrections, to the Rasm (Orthography) of the Uthmanic manuscript. The Sunni and Shiite scholars added, Nuns, Seen, Alifs, Lams, Waw, Yaa, half words, full words, changed the Rasm of some words, deleted some words....etc. hundreds of times more than what Dr. Khalifa did in two words. To the contrary. Dr. Khalifa's work proved that the corrections done to the Uthmanic manuscript was all controlled by God to preserve the Quran and its mathematical structure and can be used to un-cover any human errors in the old or the present manuscripts of the Quran. We however have to remember that those who corrected the Uthmanic manuscript of the Quran are human themselves and can make new human errors which they did, and were exposed by the same system that God built into the Quran, the mathematical Miracle of the Quran. Here are some of the corrections done in the Tashkent copy of the Quran in comparison with the 1924 edition of the Quran in Egypt made after Hafs. Remember these are only some of many examples. In all the next examples, the word 'original' means the Tashkent manuscript of the Quran."[121]

200

ص		

Chapter 7	In the Name of God, the Gracious, the Compassionate 1. A1L50M40Ŝ90.	بسم الله الرحمن الرحيم الم**ص**
Chapter 19	In the Name of God, the Gracious, the Compassionate 1. K20H5Y10Â70Ŝ90	بسم الله الرحمن الرحيم كهيع**ص**
Chapter 38	In the Name of God, the Gracious, the Compassionate 1. Ŝ90; by the Quran containing the Reminder.	بسم الله الرحمن الرحيم **ص** والقران ذي الذكر

Chapter	Initial	Common Letter	Frequency
7	المص	ص	97
19	كهيعص	ص	26
38	ص	ص	29
			152 (19x8)

عليها تسعه عشر

On it is Nineteen

Frequency of the Letter ص Ŝ in the Chapters Starting With it

Verse	Times	Verse	Times	Verse	Times	Verse	Times
7:1	1	7:85	1	7:189	1	19:60	1
7:2	1	7:86	2	7:190	1	19:65	1
7:7	1	7:87	1	7:192	2	19:70	1
7:11	1	7:91	1	7:193	1	19:76	1
7:13	1	7:93	1	7:194	1	19:94	1
7:16	1	7:100	1	7:195	1	19:96	1
7:21	1	7:101	1	7:196	1	38:1	1
7:22	1	7:106	1	7:197	2	38:3	1
7:29	1	7:107	1	7:198	1	38:6	1
7:32	2	7:117	1	7:201	1	38:13	1
7:35	2	7:119	1	7:202	1	38:15	1
7:36	1	7:124	1	7:203	1	38:17	1
7:37	1	7:126	1	7:204	1	38:20	1
7:42	2	7:128	1	7:205	1	38:21	1
7:43	1	7:130	1	19:1	1	38:22	2
7:44	2	7:131	1	19:12	1	38:24	1
7:45	1	7:133	1	19:14	1	38:36	1
7:46	1	7:137	2	19:22	1	38:37	1
7:47	3	7:138	1	19:26	1	38:38	1
7:48	1	7:142	1	19:29	1	38:41	1
7:50	2	7:143	1	19:31	2	38:44	1
7:52	1	7:144	1	19:36	1	38:45	1
7:56	1	7:145	1	19:38	1	38:46	2
7:58	1	7:146	1	19:41	1	38:47	1
7:62	1	7:156	1	19:42	1	38:52	1
7:68	1	7:157	2	19:43	1	38:56	1
7:70	1	7:160	1	19:44	1	38:59	1
7:73	1	7:168	1	19:50	1	38:63	1
7:74	1	7:170	2	19:51	1	38:64	1
7:75	1	7:174	1	19:54	1	38:69	1
7:77	1	7:176	4	19:55	1	38:83	1
7:78	1	7:179	1	19:56	1		
7:79	2	7:184	1	19:59	1	Sum: **152** (19x8)	

If you count the frequency of the letter Ŝaad in the chapters starting with the letter Ŝaad from a manuscript in the market, you should get one extra Ŝaad because of the historical spelling error in a verse 7:69. Please carefully study the word that contains that extra Ŝaad, BaŜtata. Do you notice the little letter S (Seen) propped up on top or in the bottom of the letter Ŝ (Ŝaad)? See the following table for the reasons why we did not count a Ŝ (Ŝaad) in verse 7:69.

بصطه "baŜtata"
OR
بسطه "bastata"

?

In the Quran manuscripts currently in use, the word *Bastata* in verse 7:69 is misspelled with Ŝ (Ŝaad), instead of the correct spelling with S (Seen). Why is there a small S (Seen) on top or the bottom of the word *Bastata*?

أَوَعَجِبْتُمْ أَنْ جَاءَكُمْ ذِكْرٌ مِنْ رَبِّكُمْ عَلَى رَجُلٍ مِنْكُمْ لِيُنْذِرَكُمْ وَاذْكُرُوا إِذْ جَعَلَكُمْ خُلَفَاءَ مِنْ بَعْدِ قَوْمِ نُوحٍ وَزَادَكُمْ فِي الْخَلْقِ بَصْطَةً فَاذْكُرُوا آلَاءَ اللَّهِ لَعَلَّكُمْ تُفْلِحُونَ ﴿٦٩﴾

In the Tashkent copy, one of the surviving oldest manuscripts, the word in question is spelled correctly as بسطه *Bastata* with with S (Seen).

The misspelling of a word with an extra letter Ŝ (Ŝaad) in a chapter which starts with the letter Ŝ (Ŝaad) is important and curious. The discovery of the mathematical system based on the number 19 in the Quran brought to our attention this tiny historical spelling error and allowed us to pinpoint the error before we even studied and compared the oldest available manuscripts to the modern copies. This is one of the examples of predictive power and sensitivity within the numerical system as well as a testimony of the archeological evidence that affirms its accuracy.

The Bankrupcy of the Orthodox Interpretation

Until July 1, 1986, I was Sunni. In other words, I followed volumes of dubious narrations and books of sectarian jurisprudence besides the Quran. I was happy to learn that several Hadith narrations supported the current misspelling, بصطة BaŜtata in 7:69. According to those Hadith, the Prophet Muhammad allegedly said that Angel Gabriel revealed the word in verse 7:69 with the letter ص and specifically instructed him to read it with Seen[122]. But after learning that the current spelling was wrong and that it contradicted both the numerical system and one of the oldest manuscripts, I learned that those Hadith narrations were fabricated to justify a spelling error, which evidently had become controversial. (I will elaborate more on this inetersting issue later in this chapter.) This and many other incidents eroded my trust in Hadith and Sunna, reducing it further with each additional discussion with Rashad via letter correspondence, and finally reducing it to zero after reading the remarkable and paradigm-changing book, *The Quran, Hadith and Islam,* on July 1, 1986.

Now we know for sure that those traditional Sunni or Shiite interpretations were based on lies and falsehoods. The three Hadiths supporting the misspelling provide another example for the myriad motivations of the Hadith fabricators and shed light upon an historic controversy regarding the spelling of a word.

Dr. Tayyar Altıkulaç, the former Head of the Department of Religious Affairs of the Turkish Republic (from 1978 to 1986), after publishing a book quoting from Rashad's work and praising it as a "miracle of the Quran," upon learning the few irreconcilable contradictions between the miracle and the Sunni tradition, turned 180 degrees against it. Unfortunately, like most of the so-called *ulama*, his initial positive reaction was a knee-jerk reaction and his opposition was also the same way. Muslim *ulama* are raised in a culture that kills critical thinking skills.

An Example of a Top Muslim *Ulama*/Scholar

Tayyar's book titled *Yüce Kitabımız Hz. Kuran (Our Glorious Book, Great Quran)*, was first published by the Turkish Religious Affairs Foundation in 1982. The book that promoted the 19-based mathematical structure of the Quran started with the following endorsement in its cover page: "*Bu Kitabın Yayınlanması Din İşleri Yüksek Kurulu'nun 7.4.1982 günü ve 74 sayılı kararı ile Yararlı Görülmüştür.*" Translation: "The publication of this book is found useful by the decision number 74 of the Supreme Committee on Religion dated April 7, 1982." Years later, in the early 1990s, a mass-produced revised edition of the same book was distributed by a popular Turkish newspaper, *Günaydın* (Goodmorning), about half a million copies in total as its Ramadan supplement. In that supplement, the Head of the Religious Affairs rejected the existence of the numerical miracle this time, and tried to find an excuse to publish and promote it in its previous editions. His excuse for publishing a positive exposition of the numerical structure reveals the intellectual malaise common among Sunni and Shiite scholars:

204

"Evaluating the text in those years was very difficult for me. Because, it required time-consuming work... Thinking that a super miracle like this would serve us in our mission to a particular group, and trusting that the author of the work was a Muslim scholar who had seen both the East and West..." [123]

The so-called Muslim Ulama were disappointed in Rashad. They showered him with plenty of praise, apparently without really understanding the mathematical system. This was before they realized the problem and threw a temper-tantrum regarding Rashad's rejection of Hadith and Sunna and his unorthodox claims. The miracle they published in their books and periodicals all around the world was now suddenly turned into a hoax. In his refutation, Tayyar refers to my translation of Rashad's book, *The Visual Presentation of the Quran*, and lists four criticisms which I have responded and refuted in *Running Like Zebras*:

- Frequency of the first word of the Quran, *Ism* (Name);
- The frequency of the second word, Allah (God);
- The spelling of the letter N initializing Chapter 68, and
- The spelling of the word *BaŜŤata* in verse 7:69.

In support of the misspelled word, he lists three sources, including a fabricated Hadith reported by one of the Sunni's so-called *Kutubi Sitta* (The Six Books).[124] Here is how he ended the section on his so-called refutation of Code 19:

"After discussing this much, we do not need to delve into other examples in R. Khalifa's book, and we consider it a waste of time."

"For those who are interested in this subject and especially for those who read the translation [of Rashad Khalifa's work] published in the end of this book's 1st, 2nd, 3rd, and 4th edition, my honest advise is and request is this: They should not involve and waste their time with Dr. Rashad Khalifa's inconsistent work that leads to apostasy."

"My advice for those authors, translators, publishers, and speakers, who were deceived because of their zeal to serve the Quran, is the following: they should stop their research on this subject, and they should utilize their time and resources for unlimited other topics of religious service. The only infallible is God. Victory is only from Him."[125]

Although Tayyar was educated and informed about modern scholarship, he was still under the influence of sectarian modus operandi: "We blindly accept anything that supports our sectarian dogmas without proper critical evaluation, and we reject anything that opposes or contradicts them, again without proper critical evaluation!" Though I was initially very impressed by the discovery of the Code 19 and had experienced an interesting coincidence in my life in that regard, and though I was a young university drop-out prisoner with no scholarly training or rank—contrary to many so-called *ulama* who jumped on the bandwagon of praise for Rashad Khalifa and his discoveries in the early 1980's—I was adamant that I would check and verify the claims in Deedat's summary of the work before committing myself to it.

205

Tayyar's reliance on the reports of Hadith books, which are collections of hearsay attributed to Muhammad at least two centuries after his departure—to support his criticism regarding the spelling of the word *Bastata* is profound considering the pathetic state of intellectual activity in the domain of Sunni scholarship. Despite the 24 correct spellings of various forms of the same word in the Quran, despite the overwhelming examples of numerical patterns, despite the ancient manuscripts of the Quran, they rely on the books filled with silly stories and contradictory claims.

The Scamming Ŝaad'ists

Under the light of mathematical and historical evidences, the story of the *Bastata* becomes very clear. The copies of the Quran duplicated in the early centuries after its revelation were not perfect. Since they did not have photocopy or printing machines, scribal errors seeped into the copies of the original, and then into copies of copies of the original, and so on. That is why many ancient manuscripts contain scribal errors, and that is why one of the early copies must have contained a misspelled Bastata with   Ŝaad in 7:69. As it appears, one of the readers or proofreaders of the copy had noticed the scribal error and indicated a correction by writing the correct letter   Seen on top of the erroneous letter   Ŝaad.

We can now safely infer that the duplicators of the corrected version, instead of following the implied instruction and making the correction, they copied the misspelled word exactly together with the suggested correction. In an unconventional way, they wrote the two letters on top of each other, keeping the wrong letter as the main member of the text. Thus, other generations of copiers continued the act of copying the error together with the correction. As it appears, there were also other copies that were based on an uncorrected early version. At one time, there were some copies of the correct manuscript with the correct spelling and without any notes for correction.

So, there erupted a controversy over the correct spelling of the word *Bastata* in verse 7:69. Should they write it with Seen or Ŝaad? When the argument between the pro-Seen and pro-Saad groups became public, this must have created confusion, discord and questions among laypeople who believed that every letter of the Quran was protected. In order to defend and promote their version of the spelling, the Ŝaadists fabricated Hadiths. Though we cannot consider lack of evidence as evidence, there is a possibility that Seenists were not followers of Hadiths; they may have been the followers of the Quran alone, as is the case today. Finally, after getting the support of Hadiths, the Ŝaadist version—that is, the misspelled word with the misrepresented correction on top—became the norm and the popular version. Most likely, the Arabic version of the Quran you have in your library contains an extra   Ŝaad, which was promoted by the fabricated Hadiths of early Ŝaadists.

This is another testimony to the fact that the Quran is not a manuscript made of ink and paper, but the Quran is a Book of Knowledge, a Numerically Structured Book, which is in the chest of those who are endowed with proper knowledge. The Quran as a manuscript might contain errors, but the Quran as a Numerically Structured Book in the minds of those who have witnessed its secret is free of any error, addition or subtraction.

Discovering Truth Requires Bravery, Honesty and Intelligence

I am now going to address my readers who consider themselves Muslims. If you claim to be a Muslim, my dear reader, you need to engage in critical evaluation of your "faith", a word/concept which is usually used by religious people as a euphemism to justify their joining the bandwagon, their following the footsteps of their parents blindly, their wishful thinking, their irrational ideas, or their unrealistic ideas. Keeping in mind the verses 17:36; 10:100, and their ilk, please ask yourself the following questions:

1. Do you believe in the Quran? What is your evidence that the Quran is God's word?

2. If the reasons for your belief had changed or had proven false, would you have the courage to reject the Quran?

3. If your answer is YES to 1.2, then wouldn't those reasons precede the Quran, or become authority above the Quran?

4. If your answer is NO to 1.2, then how can you believe in a book that criticizes "belief" without evidence, and rejects "faith" through being followers of the crowd or of your parents? (6:116; 12:103,112)

5. What is your evidence that the Quran is fully preserved?

6. If your evidence is a verse in the Quran, then, you must have answered the first question and its corollary 1.2 affirmatively.

7. How do you know that the verse guaranteeing the preservation of the Quran itself was not added by later Muslims to eliminate the growing doubts about Quran's authenticity?

8. If you believe because a large *number* of people believe so, then your faith in the Quran and its preservation is BASED on a *number*—the *number* of people who believe a particular way.

9. Which one is more reliable and consistent—believing in the Quran because of its own numerical code that miraculously self-authenticates itself, or believing in the Quran because of the crowd, which is ironically rejected by the very Quran?

Please acquire some courage and show the wisdom of studying the numerical structure of the Quran. Question your assumptions and eliminate your unjustified prejudices.

19
حم Ĥ8M40

"Now, there is a constellation of properties that we generally think of when we in the West, or more generally in the Judeo-Christian-Islamic tradition, think of God. The fundamental differences among Judaism, Christianity, and Islam are trivial compared to their similarities. We think of some being who is omnipotent, omniscient, compassionate, who created the universe, is responsive to prayer, intervenes in human affairs, and so on. ..."

"This business of proofs of God, had God wished to give us some, need not be restricted to this somewhat questionable method of making enigmatic statements to ancient sages and hoping they would survive. God could have engraved the Ten Commandments on the Moon. Large. Ten kilometers across per commandment. And nobody could see it from the Earth but then one day large telescopes would be invented or spacecraft would approach the Moon, and there it would be, engraved on the lunar surface. People would say, "How could that have gotten there?" And then there would be various hypotheses, most of which would be extremely interesting."

"Or why not a hundred-kilometer crucifix in Earth orbit? God could certainly do that. Right? Certainly, create the universe? A simple thing like putting a crucifix in Earth orbit? Perfectly possible. Why didn't God do things of that sort? Or, put another way, why should God be so clear in the Bible and so obscure in the world?" [126]

Seven succeeding chapters start with the combination of two letters or numbers, حم Ĥ8M40 (read ĤaMim or 48). Only one of those chapters, chapter 42, contains another combination of letters/numbers, عسق Â70S60Q100 (ÂynSeenQaf or 230). It is noteworthy that the two combinations of letters crowning chapter 42 are separated from each other as independent verses. In other words, the two combinations are written like this عسق حم (ĤM. ÂSQ). When they are evaluated with their second function, they are read as two sets of additions, 8+40. 70+60+100.

Since demonstrating the frequencies of حم on Arabic text would take about 40 pages of the book, we will not be able to do so. However we will provide you with a list of the frequencies of these two letters verse by verse. You may easily verify or falsify it by a random check through Dr. Khalifa's *Quran: Visual Presentation of the Miracle*. Another way of testing our counts, if you have plenty of time or plenty of people who could assist you in the task, is to count those letters one by one, manually.

However, perhaps the fastest and most reliable way of testing the results is to obtain an accurate text of the Quran and cut the seven chapters starting with the letters حم, and then paste them in a blank Word document. Then, by carefully using the find and replace function, you may ask the computer to find ح and change all of them to **bold** ones, and then do the same for the letter م. Each time, MS Word will give you the total number of changes made. By adding the two numbers for the two letters, you can get the frequency of the combination حم. However, if you are not familiar with the Arabic alphabet, make sure that you recognize the various shapes of letters and make sure that your program counts all of the same letters regardless of its shape, depending on its position in a word.[127]

The total frequency of حم ḤM letters in seven chapters starting with them:

Chapter	ح Ĥ		م M		Sum
40	64		380		444
41	48		276		324
42	53		300		353
43	44		324		368
44	16		150		166
45	31		200		231
46	36		225		261
Total	292	+	1855	=	2147

2147 = 19 x 113

With the additional three-letter/number combination عسق ÂSQ, Chapter 42 stands out among the seven حم ĤM initialed chapters and divides them into two groups. In each group, the frequencies of حم ĤM are still divisible by 19. Furthermore, there are several subgroups around the neighboring 41st and 43rd chapters which are also divisible by 19. Here are the 19-divisible groups:

CHAPTER	ح Ĥ		م M		SUM
40	64		380		444
41	48		276		324
42	53		300		353
TOTAL	161	+	956	=	**1121 (19x59)**
					▲

CHAPTER	ح Ĥ		م M		SUM
43	44		324		368
44	16		150		166
45	31		200		231
46	36		225		261
TOTAL	127	+	899	=	**1026 (19x54)**
					▲

CHAPTER	ح Ĥ		M		SUM
41	48		276		324
42	53		300		353
43	44		324		368
TOTAL	145	+	900	=	**1045 (19x55)**
					▲

CHAPTER	ح Ĥ		م M		SUM
40	64		380		444
44	16		150		166
45	31		200		231
46	36		225		261
TOTAL	147	+	955	=	**1102 (19x58)**
					▲

Numerical Harmony

Could this numerical pattern interwoven in the literal fabric of the Quran be a mere coincidence? Milan Sulc, a brilliant mind from Switzerland discovered further details of Dr. Khalifa's initial discoveries.

We saw that the total frequencies of Ĥ and M letters in seven chapters starting with this combination of letters were exactly 113 times of 19. When we add the digits of each number representing the frequency of the each letter, we get the sum of 113.

Chapter	ح Ĥ	م M	Absolute Values										SUM
40	64	380	6	+	4	+	3	+	8	+	0	=	21
41	48	276	4	+	8	+	2	+	7	+	6	=	27
42	53	300	5	+	3	+	3	+	0	+	0	=	11
43	44	324	4	+	4	+	3	+	2	+	4	=	17
44	16	150	1	+	6	+	1	+	5	+	0	=	13
45	31	200	3	+	1	+	2	+	0	+	0	=	6
46	36	225	3	+	6	+	2	+	2	+	5	=	18
TOTAL	2147(19x113)		26	+	32	+	16	+	24	+	15	=	113
		▲	D_1		D_2		D_3		D_4		D_5		▲

Now let's study each subgroup of seven chapters where the combined frequencies of حم ĤM are divisible by 19. In the previous pages, we learned that in each of the four subgroups the frequencies of حم ĤM were divisible by 19. Please note the multiplication factors of 19. For instance, note that the factor in the first group containing 1121 حم ĤM letters is 59, since 1121 = 19x59. The multiplication factor in the second group is 54, in the third 55, and in the fourth 58.

Now let's apply to the subgroups the same mathematical calculation we did on the seven chapters in the main group above. Result: Marvelous! (D = Digit)

Formula: $9(D_3) = (D_1 + D_4) + 2(D_2 + D_5)$

Example: $9(16) = (26 + 24) + 2(32 + 15)$

The same numerical-literal pattern you just observed between sum of the digits in the the frequencies of H and M initializing 7 chapters and the factor of 19, yes the same pattern can be seen in ALL subgroups that produce sums of H and M, which are multiple of 19.

Chapter	ح H	م M	Absolute Values											SUM
40	64	380	6	+	4	+	3	+	8	+	0			21
41	48	276	4	+	8	+	2	+	7	+	6			27
42	53	300	5	+	3	+	3	+	0	+	0			11
TOTAL	1121 (19x59)		15	+	15	+	8	+	15	+	6			**59**
			▲	D₁		D₂		D₃		D₄		D₅		▲
43	44	324	4	+	4	+	3	+	2	+	4			17
44	16	150	1	+	6	+	1	+	5	+	0			13
45	31	200	3	+	1	+	2	+	0	+	0			6
46	36	225	3	+	6	+	2	+	2	+	5			18
TOTAL	1026 (19x54)		11	+	17	+	8	+	9	+	9			**54**
			▲	D₁		D₂		D₃		D₄		D₅		▲
41	48	276	4	+	8	+	2	+	7	+	6			27
42	53	300	5	+	3	+	3	+	0	+	0			11
43	44	324	4	+	4	+	3	+	2	+	4			17
TOTAL	1045 (19x55)		13	+	15	+	8	+	9	+	10			**55**
			▲	D₁		D₂		D₃		D₄		D₅		▲
40	64	380	6	+	4	+	3	+	8	+	0			21
44	16	150	1	+	6	+	1	+	5	+	0			13
45	31	200	3	+	1	+	2	+	0	+	0			6
46	36	225	3	+	6	+	2	+	2	+	5			18
TOTAL	1102 (19x58)		13	+	17	+	8	+	15	+	5			**58**
			▲	D₁		D₂		D₃		D₄		D₅		▲

212

Â70S60Q100

عسق

We studied an example of the intricate litero-numeral system embedded in seven chapters starting with letters حم ĤM. We also observed that Chapter 42 played a central role in the subgroups. We know that Chapter 42 is the only chapter that contains two independent sets of initial letters, that is, حم ĤM and عسق ÂSQ, and we already discussed the first set and one of the letters in the second set in the chapter dealing with the frequency of the letter Q. What about the frequency of the three letters contained in the second set of initals? It is no surprize that the sum of their frequencies is also multiple of 19.

ع Â	س S	ق Q	TOTAL
98	54	57	**209 (19 x 11)** ▲

			ق	س	ع	
(42:0) بسم الله الرحمن الرحيم			0	1	0	
(42:1) حم			0	0	0	
(42:2) عسق			1	1	1	
(42:3) كذلك يوحي اليك والي الذين من قبلك الله العزيز الحكيم			1	0	1	
(42:4) له ما في السموت وما في الارض وهو العلي العظيم			0	1	2	
(42:5) تكاد السموت يتفطرن من فوقهن والمليكه يسبحون بحمد ربهم ويستغفرون لمن في الارض الا ان الله هو الغفور الرحيم			1	3	0	
(42:6) والذين اتخذوا من دونه اوليا الله حفيظ عليهم وما انت عليهم بوكيل			0	0	2	
(42:7) وكذلك اوحينا اليك قرانا عربيا لتنذر ام القري ومن حولها وتنذر يوم الجمع لا ريب فيه فريق في الجنه وفريق في السعير			4	1	3	
(42:8) ولو شا الله لجعلهم امه وحده ولكن يدخل من يشا في			0	0	1	

213

رحمته والظلمون ما لهم من ولي ولا نصير				
(42:9) ام اتخذوا من دونه اوليا فالله هو الولي وهو يحي الموتي وهو علي كل شي قدير	1	0	1	
(42:10) وما اختلفتم فيه من شي فحكمه الي الله ذلكم الله ربي عليه توكلت واليه انيب	0	0	1	
(42:11) فاطر السموت والارض جعل لكم من انفسكم ازوجا ومن الانعم ازوجا يذروكم فيه ليس كمثله شي وهو السميع البصير	0	4	3	
(42:12) له مقاليد السموت والارض يبسط الرزق لمن يشا ويقدر انه بكل شي عليم	3	2	1	
(42:13) شرع لكم من الدين ما وصي به نوحا والذي اوحينا اليك وما وصينا به ابرهيم وموسي وعيسي ان اقيموا الدين ولا تتفرقوا فيه كبر علي المشركين ما تدعوهم اليه الله يجتبي اليه من يشا ويهدي اليه من ينيب	2	2	4	
(42:14) وما تفرقوا الا من بعد ما جاهم العلم بغيا بينهم ولولا كلمه سبقت من ربك الي اجل مسمي لقضي بينهم وان الذين اورثوا الكتب من بعدهم لفي شك منه مريب	3	2	3	
(42:15) فلذلك فادع واستقم كما امرت ولا تتبع اهواهم وقل امنت بما انزل الله من كتب وامرت لاعدل بينكم الله ربنا وربكم لنا اعملنا ولكم اعملكم لا حجه بيننا وبينكم الله يجمع بيننا واليه المصير	2	1	6	
(42:16) والذين يحاجون في الله من بعد ما استجيب له حجتهم داحضه عند ربهم وعليهم غضب ولهم عذاب شديد	0	1	4	
(42:17) الله الذي انزل الكتب بالحق والميزان وما يدريك لعل الساعه قريب	2	1	2	
(42:18) يستعجل بها الذين لا يومنون بها والذين امنوا مشفقون منها ويعلمون انها الحق الا ان الذين يمارون في الساعه لفي ضلل بعيد	2	2	4	
(42:19) الله لطيف بعباده يرزق من يشا وهو القوي العزيز	2	0	2	
(42:20) من كان يريد حرث الاخره نزد له في حرثه ومن كان يريد حرث الدنيا نوته منها وما له في الاخره من نصيب	0	0	0	
(42:21) ام لهم شركوا شرعوا لهم من الدين ما لم ياذن به الله ولولا كلمه الفصل لقضي بينهم وان الظلمين لهم عذاب اليم	1	0	2	
(42:22) تري الظلمين مشفقين مما كسبوا وهو واقع بهم والذين امنوا وعملوا الصلحت في روضات الجنات لهم ما يشاون عند ربهم ذلك هو الفضل الكبير	2	1	3	
(42:23) ذلك الذي يبشر الله عباده الذين امنوا وعملوا الصلحت قل لا اسلكم عليه اجرا الا الموده في القربي ومن يقترف حسنه نزد	3	3	3	

له فيها حسنا ان الله غفور شكور			
(42:24) ام يقولون افتري علي الله كذبا فان يشا الله يختم علي قلبك ويمح الله البطل ويحق الحق بكلمته انه عليم بذات الصدور	4	0	3
(42:25) وهو الذي يقبل التوبه عن عباده ويعفوا عن السيات ويعلم ما تفعلون	1	1	6
(42:26) ويستجيب الذين امنوا وعملوا الصلحت ويزيدهم من فضله والكفرون لهم عذاب شديد	0	1	2
(42:27) ولو بسط الله الرزق لعباده لبغوا في الارض ولكن ينزل بقدر ما يشا انه بعباده خبير بصير	2	1	2
(42:28) وهو الذي ينزل الغيث من بعد ما قنطوا وينشر رحمته وهو الولي الحميد	1	0	1
(42:29) ومن ايته خلق السموت والارض وما بث فيهما من دابه وهو علي جمعهم اذا يشا قدير	2	1	2
(42:30) وما اصبكم من مصيبه فبما كسبت ايديكم ويعفوا عن كثير	0	1	2
(42:31) وما انتم بمعجزين في الارض وما لكم من دون الله من ولي ولا نصير	0	0	1
(42:32) ومن ايته الجوار في البحر كالاعلم	0	0	1
(42:33) ان يشا يسكن الريح فيظللن رواكد علي ظهره ان في ذلك لايت لكل صبار شكور	0	1	1
(42:34) او يوبقهن بما كسبوا ويعف عن كثير	1	1	2
(42:35) ويعلم الذين يجدلون في ايتنا ما لهم من محيص	0	0	1
(42:36) فما اوتيتم من شي فمتع الحيوه الدنيا وما عند الله خير وابقي للذين امنوا وعلي ربهم يتوكلون	1	0	3
(42:37) والذين يجتنبون كبير الاثم والفوحش واذا ما غضبوا هم يغفرون	0	0	0
(42:38) والذين استجابوا لربهم واقاموا الصلوه وامرهم شوري بينهم ومما رزقنهم ينفقون	3	1	0
(42:39) والذين اذا اصابهم البغي هم ينتصرون	0	0	0
(42:40) وجزوا سييه سييه مثلها فمن عفا واصلح فاجره علي الله انه لا يحب الظلمين	0	2	2
(42:41) ولمن انتصر بعد ظلمه فاوليك ما عليهم من سبيل	0	1	2
(42:42) انما السبيل علي الذين يظلمون الناس ويبغون في الارض بغير الحق اوليك لهم عذاب اليم	1	2	2

215

(42:43) ولمن صبر وغفر ان ذلك لمن عزم الامور	0	0	1	
(42:44) ومن يضلل الله فما له من ولي من بعده وتري الظلمين لما راوا العذاب يقولون هل الي مرد من سبيل	1	1	2	
(42:45) وتريهم يعرضون عليها خشعين من الذل ينظرون من طرف خفي وقال الذين امنوا ان الخسرين الذين خسروا انفسهم واهليهم يوم القيمه الا ان الظلمين في عذاب مقيم	3	3	4	
(42:46) وما كان لهم من اوليا ينصرونهم من دون الله ومن يضلل الله فما له من سبيل	0	1	0	
(42:47) استجيبوا لربكم من قبل ان ياتي يوم لا مرد له من الله ما لكم من ملجا يوميذ وما لكم من نكير	1	1	0	
(42:48) فان اعرضوا فما ارسلنك عليهم حفيظا ان عليك الا البلغ وانا اذا اذقنا الانسن منا رحمه فرح بها وان تصبهم سييه بما قدمت ايديهم فان الانسن كفور	2	4	3	
(42:49) لله ملك السموت والارض يخلق ما يشا يهب لمن يشا انثا ويهب لمن يشا الذكور	1	1	0	
(42:50) او يزوجهم ذكرانا وانثا ويجعل من يشا عقيما انه عليم قدير	2	0	3	
(42:51) وما كان لبشر ان يكلمه الله الا وحيا او من وراي حجاب او يرسل رسولا فيوحي باذنه ما يشا انه علي حكيم	0	2	1	
(42:52) وكذلك اوحينا اليك روحا من امرنا ما كنت تدري ما الكتب ولا الايمن ولكن جعلنه نورا نهدي به من نشا من عبادنا وانك لتهدي الي صرط مستقيم	1	1	2	
(42:53) صرط الله الذي له ما في السموت وما في الارض الا الي الله تصير الامور	0	1	0	
Total	98	54	57	209

The chapter starting with the letters ÂSQ has exactly 209 âSQs.

$$209 = 19 \times 11$$

▲

عليها تسعه عشر

On it is Nineteen

216

20

K20H5Y10A70S90

كهيعص

"Every Chapter of the Qur'an which has *Initials* affixed at the head of it follows this same wonderful, awe-inspiring pattern. Count the number of times the 'Initials'" occur in the Suras and divide them by 19, and without exception' the answer is always exact multiple of 19! Who had the time and the ability to invent this most intricate mathematical system? Surely, not Muhummad, the busiest man in history! If cynics still want us to believe that Muhummad must have had some Computer hidden away in the sand wherein he had programmed his Qur'an on this mathematical basis. I for my part would sooner accept this "Computer Theory" than that Muhummad the man—flesh and blood in all respects had contrived such a complex interlocking mathematical system to guard his *insights* from corruption. In this treatise I have barely touched the tip of the *iceberg* of this phenomenal discovery. To those who wish to delve deeper into this subject. I heartily recommend a booklet and tape by Dr. Rashad Khalifa, Ph.D. ..." ~ Ahmad Deedat [128]

One of the three chapters starting with Ŝaad is Chapter 19, known as Mary, and it starts with five letter/number combinations. The total frequency of these five letters in Chapter 19 is divisible by 19.

ك K	ه H	ي Y	ع Â	ص Ŝ	TOTAL
137	175	343	117	26	**798 (19 x 42)**
					▲

To facilitate the verification or falsification of the data above, I am listing the frequencies of each letter starting chapter 19 verse by verse.

Please note that in *all* the counts of initial letters we include *all* the Bismillah formula separating the chapters. There are two words which vary in spelling in current manuscripts. The correct spelling of the word "*Ahsahum*" (He counted them) in verse 19:94 should have a ي Y, and the word اوصيني "*Awsani*" (He instructed me) in 19:31, should contain two ي Ys.

Verse	كK	هH	يY	عÂ	صŜ
19:0	0	1	1	0	0
19:1	1	1	1	1	1
19:2	3	1	1	1	0
19:3	0	1	2	0	0
19:4	2	1	5	3	0
19:5	2	1	6	1	0
19:6	0	1	5	2	0
19:7	2	2	6	1	0
19:8	3	0	5	2	0
19:9	5	2	3	1	0
19:10	2	1	5	1	0
19:11	1	3	4	2	0
19:12	2	2	6	0	1
19:13	2	1	1	0	0
19:14	1	1	3	1	1
19:15	0	1	7	2	0
19:16	3	2	3	0	0
19:17	0	3	2	0	0
19:18	2	0	2	1	0
19:19	3	1	1	0	0
19:20	2	0	6	0	0
19:21	4	5	4	2	0
19:22	1	2	1	0	1
19:23	1	3	6	1	0
19:24	2	2	3	1	0
19:25	2	2	4	2	0
19:26	2	0	9	1	1
19:27	0	3	5	0	0
19:28	4	1	2	0	0
19:29	3	2	4	0	1
19:30	1	1	5	2	0
19:31	3	2	5	1	2
19:32	0	0	4	1	0
19:33	0	0	5	2	0
19:34	1	1	6	1	0
19:35	3	3	4	0	0
19:36	1	3	2	1	1
19:37	1	2	5	1	0

19:38	1	1	5	1	1
19:39	0	5	4	0	0
19:40	0	1	3	2	0
19:41	3	2	4	0	1
19:42	1	1	7	3	1
19:43	2	1	6	2	1
19:44	1	0	4	2	1
19:45	2	0	5	1	0
19:46	1	4	6	1	0
19:47	3	1	4	1	0
19:48	2	1	4	5	0
19:49	1	4	3	4	0
19:50	0	3	1	2	1
19:51	4	1	3	0	1
19:52	0	2	3	0	0
19:53	0	4	1	0	0
19:54	4	1	3	2	1
19:55	3	5	2	1	1
19:56	3	1	4	0	1
19:57	1	1	1	2	0
19:58	2	7	14	4	0
19:59	0	3	2	3	1
19:60	1	1	4	1	1
19:61	1	3	3	4	0
19:62	1	5	4	2	0
19:63	2	1	2	1	0
19:64	4	1	5	0	0
19:65	0	5	2	3	1
19:66	0	0	2	0	0
19:67	2	1	3	0	0
19:68	1	3	3	0	0
19:69	1	2	4	4	0
19:70	0	2	3	1	1
19:71	3	1	2	1	0
19:72	0	1	5	0	0
19:73	1	1	11	1	0
19:74	2	3	1	0	0
19:75	2	4	5	5	0
19:76	1	3	7	1	1
19:77	1	0	4	0	0
19:78	0	1	1	3	0
19:79	2	1	1	1	0

19:80	0	1	3	0	0
19:81	1	4	1	1	0
19:82	3	2	3	2	0
19:83	1	1	4	1	0
19:84	0	2	1	4	0
19:85	0	0	3	0	0
19:86	0	1	2	0	0
19:87	1	2	1	3	0
19:88	0	0	0	0	0
19:89	0	0	2	0	0
19:90	1	2	1	0	0
19:91	0	0	0	1	0
19:92	0	0	3	0	0
19:93	1	0	2	1	0
19:94	0	2	0	2	1
19:95	1	3	3	0	0
19:96	0	1	2	2	1
19:97	1	3	2	0	0
19:98	3	5	0	1	0
Total	**137**	**175**	**343**	**117**	**26**	**= 798 (19 x 142)**

The chapter starting with KHYÂŜ letters has exactly 798 of them:

798 (19 x 142)
▲

عليها تسعه عشر

On it is Nineteen

220

21

N50

ن

"The other common error is the writing of *NOON* as a single letter N, instead of spelling out the letter into *NOON*, *WOW* and *NOON*; as is the case in the original Quran. In the original Quranic writings, the Quranic initial *NOON* is the only one that is spelled out." ~ Rashad Khalifa[129]

The 68th chapter of the Quran starts with the letter ن N (read Nun). The frequency of the letter ن N in this chapter is 133, exactly 19 times 7. This is the only time where Dr. Khalifa derogated from the orthodox spelling of the available Quranic manuscripts without showing any evidence from historic manuscripts or reports. His correction regarding the writing of the letter ص Ŝaad, as we discussed before, was supported by the bizarre spelling of the word Bastata in 7:69, ancient manuscripts, and the historical controversy around the spelling. However, Rashad's claim regarding the correct spelling of the initial letter ن N as نون NoWN is not corroborated and still stands unconfirmed. Nonetheless, its conformity with the obvious mathematical pattern in the Quran, which has a proven predictive and corrective power, makes it plausible.

There is little indication or suspicious smoke, supporting our contention based on the mathematical code regarding the original spelling of the letter. Some classical commentators of the Quran provided alternative meanings for the initial letter ن N; they considered it as a word rather than as a single letter. For instance, according to Sunni sources, Hasan and Qatadeh regarded it as meaning "ink-stand." Another prominent Sunni commentator Ibn Abbas discovered a fish in it; he claimed that نون *NoWN* is another name for fish in an Arabic dialect. We do not have the manuscript used by these people, but we may speculate that in their manuscript chapter 68 most likely started with the spelt letter نون *NoWN* rather than just N. No wonder that all the traditional translations of the Quran mistranslated the expression Zan-Nown as the "man/friend of the fish/whale". We will discuss this curious expression below.

Code 19 Explains a Curious Expression

In 1989 I worked seven days of the week, from dawn until night, in Masjid Tucson. I had an office inside the Masjid with a Macintosh computer, while Rashad worked with an IBM-compatible computer in his next door office. I was working on the Turkish translation of the Quran and he was working on the revision of his English translation, *Quran: The Final Testament*. Though my English was poor, I assisted him in his revision of his translation and even write a column for the Masjid's monthly newsletter, proofread by several native speakers before its publication.

He was impressed by my analytical skills as a critic and my bold attitude when expressing myself. I was never timid or shy in expressing my objection to his understanding if I did not find it reasonable or justified.[130] His charisma intimidated many, but to me the truth had most charisma and its quest was sacred. I had just recently declared my criticism of the Sunni religion despite all the risks. Though it was rare, we had a few hot debates that became very contentious. Once, after a pungent public argument on the meaning of a Quranic verse with important philosophical and theological ramification, we did not speak to each other for about three days, while at the same time we both worked in the Masjid on our translations of the Quran. Aside from those unusual instances, we had a normal routine. The moment he printed out a new page of his translation he would come out of his office and give me the good news as well as a copy of the page for my criticism. Admittedly, usually he would convince me regarding his understanding and his choice of words. However, there were numerous times when he was convinced by my arguments. He made some important corrections based on my input.[131]

One day he handed me his latest revision of page 329 of his translation (The Blue Cover).[132] The beginning of his translation of 21:87 drew my attention:

> 21:87   And Zan Noon (Jonah, "the one with an 'N' in his name"), abandoned his mission in protest...

I objected to his parenthetical remarks. I argued that the letter N was not peculiar to Jonah, since Solomon, Lukman, Aaron, and Noah all had the letter N in their names. Besides, why not refer to the letter Y or S since the Arabic version of Jonah, YUNuS had them too? He did not have a satisfactory answer for his novel understanding, except that he could not understand otherwise. He did not believe that Noon meant fish in Arabic. Though he did not express it to me, I assume that he followed the instruction of verse 20:114, warning us against rushing into understanding the Quran without having proper knowledge. Though I did not insist on my objection, I asked God for an explanation. Within a short time I came across the explanation that supported Rashad's intuition, which I could not wait to share with him. Here it is:

Verse 68:48 contains a reference to the Prophet Jonah without mentioning his name. How? It refers to Jonah or Yunus with an expression that does not contain

222

the letter ن N (Nwn), صاحب الحوت *Sahib-ul Hoot* (Friend of the Fish). Why? Is it to draw our attention to the frequency of the letter N in the chapter starting with the same letter? Is it a similar case to the use of *Ikhwan-i Loot* (Brethren of Lot) instead of *Qawm-i Loot* (People of Lot) in the chapter starting with the letter Q? Perhaps. When we connect the dots and notice the strange title for Jonah, *Zan Nwn* in verse 21:87, our "perhaps" turns into "certainly". Our speculation or hunch is now supported by the author of the Quran.

Through this interesting choice of words, the author of the Quran informs us that He is not in need of a letter to complete the frequency of N being divisible by 19. Thus, He puts this fact in practice by not using the letter ن N in a chapter that starts with ن N and where the letter occurs in the highest frequency in a statistical sense.

Upon learning this unstated yet intellectually satisfying communication of the Quran, I showed my appreciation of it by practically correcting the spelling error in the first verse of Chapter 68 in Rashad's translation. I clipped the نون Noon from ذاالنون Zan-Noon and replaced the ن N with نون Noon. This is the story of how we corrected the orthodox Arabic text inside Rashad's translation.[133]

I hear some people accusing us of tampering with the word of God. Well, the Quran in their minds—which is just ink and paper—has been tampered with numerous times. Either the Quran's guarantee of its preservation is false or their understanding of how the preservation was performed is wrong. If the followers of the Sunna accuse us of distorting and changing the Quran, then they contradict the verses that promise its perfect preservation (15:9). On the other hand, if they claim that we have not distorted the Quran, they should not get angry with what we are doing.

Below is the count of the letter ن N, which is pronounced Noon. Please note that verse 68:48 contains a description of Jonah without using the word/letter نون Noon.

ن

1	(68:0)	بسم الله الرحمن الرحيم
3	(68:1)	نون والقلم وما يسطرون
4	(68:2)	ما انت بنعمه ربك بمجنون
3	(68:3)	وان لك لاجرا غير ممنون
1	(68:4)	وانك لعلي خلق عظيم
1	(68:5)	فستبصر ويبصرون
1	(68:6)	باييكم المفتون
4	(68:7)	ان ربك هو اعلم بمن ضل عن سبيله وهو اعلم بالمهتدين

223

1	(68:8) فلا تطع المكذبين
3	(68:9) ودوا لو تدهن فيدهنون
1	(68:10) ولا تطع كل حلاف مهين
1	(68:11) هماز مشا بنميم
1	(68:12) مناع للخير معتد اثيم
1	(68:13) عتل بعد ذلك زنيم
4	(68:14) ان كان ذا مال وبنين
2	(68:15) اذا تتلى عليه ايتنا قال اسطير الاولين
1	(68:16) سنسمه على الخرطوم
6	(68:17) انا بلونهم كما بلونا اصحب الجنه اذ اقسموا ليصرمنها مصبحين
2	(68:18) ولا يستثنون
3	(68:19) فطاف عليها طايف من ربك وهم نايمون
0	(68:20) فاصبحت كالصريم
2	(68:21) فتنادوا مصبحين
4	(68:22) ان اغدوا على حرثكم ان كنتم صرمين
2	(68:23) فانطلقوا وهم يتخفتون
3	(68:24) ان لا يدخلنها اليوم عليكم مسكين
1	(68:25) وغدوا على حرد قدرين
2	(68:26) فلما راوها قالوا انا لضالون
3	(68:27) بل نحن محرومون
1	(68:28) قال اوسطهم الم اقل لكم لولا تسبحون
5	(68:29) قالوا سبحن ربنا انا كنا ظلمين
1	(68:30) فاقبل بعضهم على بعض يتلومون
4	(68:31) قالوا يويلنا انا كنا طغين
7	(68:32) عسى ربنا ان يبدلنا خيرا منها انا الى ربنا رغبون
2	(68:33) كذلك العذاب ولعذاب الاخره اكبر لو كانوا يعلمون
5	(68:34) ان للمتقين عند ربهم جنت النعيم
3	(68:35) افنجعل المسلمين كالمجرمين
1	(68:36) ما لكم كيف تحكمون

224

1	(68:37) ام لكم كتب فيه تدرسون
2	(68:38) ان لكم فيه لما تخيرون
4	(68:39) ام لكم ايمن علينا بلغه الي يوم القيمه ان لكم لما تحكمون
0	(68:40) سلهم ايهم بذلك زعيم
3	(68:41) ام لهم شركا فلياتوا بشركايهم ان كانوا صدقين
3	(68:42) يوم يكشف عن ساق ويدعون الي السجود فلا يستطيعون
3	(68:43) خشعه ابصرهم ترهقهم ذله وقد كانوا يدعون الي السجود وهم سلمون
5	(68:44) فذرني ومن يكذب بهذا الحديث سنستدرجهم من حيث لا يعلمون
2	(68:45) واملي لهم ان كيدي متين
2	(68:46) ام تسلهم اجرا فهم من مغرم مثقلون
2	(68:47) ام عندهم الغيب فهم يكتبون
2	(68:48) فاصبر لحكم ربك ولا تكن كصاحب الحوت اذ نادي وهو مكظوم
4	(68:49) لولا ان تدركه نعمه من ربه لنبذ بالعرا وهو مذموم
2	(68:50) فاجتبه ربه فجعله من الصلحين
7	(68:51) وان يكاد الذين كفروا ليزلقونك بابصرهم لما سمعوا الذكر ويقولون انه لمجنون
1	(68:52) وما هو الا ذكر للعلمين
133	**Sum**

Chapter starting with the letter ن N has exactly 133 Ns.

$$133 = 19 \times 7$$

▲

عليها تسعه عشر

On it is Nineteen

225

Y10S60

ي

Like many other chapters starting with combinations of letters, the 36th chapter of the Quran is known with the two letters/numbers initializing it: Y10S60. The 36th chapter is the 19th initialized chapter from the beginning of the Quran, and it contains exactly 237 ي Y + 48 س S = 285 (19x15).

Y ي	S س	TOTAL
237	48	**285 (19 x 15)** ▲

	س	ي
(36:0) بسم الله الرحمن الرحيم	1	1
(36:1) يس	1	1
(36:2) والقران الحكيم	0	1
(36:3) انك لمن المرسلين	1	1
(36:4) علي صرط مستقيم	1	2
(36:5) تنزيل العزيز الرحيم	0	3
(36:6) لتنذر قوما ما انذر اباوهم فهم غفلون	0	0
(36:7) لقد حق القول علي اكثرهم فهم لا يومنون	**0**	**2**
(36:8) انا جعلنا في اعنقهم اغللا فهي الي الاذقان فهم مقمحون	**0**	**3**
(36:9) وجعلنا من بين ايديهم سدا ومن خلفهم سدا فاغشينهم فهم لا يبصرون	**2**	**5**
(36:10) وسوا عليهم انذرتهم ام لم تنذرهم لا يومنون	**1**	**2**

(36:11) انما تنذر من اتبع الذكر وخشي الرحمن بالغيب فبشره بمغفره واجر كريم	0	3
(36:12) انا نحن نحي الموتي ونكتب ما قدموا واثرهم وكل شي احصينه في امام مبين	0	6
(36:13) واضرب لهم مثلا اصحب القريه اذ جاها المرسلون	1	1
(36:14) اذ ارسلنا اليهم اثنين فكذبوهما فعززنا بثالث فقالوا انا اليكم مرسلون	2	3
(36:15) قالوا ما انتم الا بشر مثلنا وما انزل الرحمن من شي ان انتم الا تكذبون	0	1
(36:16) قالوا ربنا يعلم انا اليكم لمرسلون	1	2
(36:17) وما علينا الا البلغ المبين	0	2
(36:18) قالوا انا تطيرنا بكم لين لم تنتهوا لنرجمنكم وليمسنكم منا عذاب اليم	1	4
(36:19) قالوا طيركم معكم اين ذكرتم بل انتم قوم مسرفون	1	2
(36:20) وجا من اقصا المدينه رجل يسعي قال يقوم اتبعوا المرسلين	2	5
(36:21) اتبعوا من لا يسلكم اجرا وهم مهتدون	1	1
(36:22) وما لي لا اعبد الذي فطرني واليه ترجعون	0	4
(36:23) اتخذ من دونه الهه ان يردن الرحمن بضر لا تغن عني شفعتهم شيا ولا ينقذون	0	4
(36:24) اني اذا لفي ضلل مبين	0	3
(36:25) اني امنت بربكم فاسمعون	1	1
(36:26) قيل ادخل الجنه قال يليت قومي يعلمون	0	5
(36:27) بما غفر لي ربي وجعلني من المكرمين	0	4
(36:28) وما انزلنا علي قومه من بعده من جند من السما وما كنا منزلين	1	2
(36:29) ان كانت الا صيحه وحده فاذا هم خمدون	0	1
(36:30) يحسره علي العباد ما ياتيهم من رسول الا كانوا به	3	5

يستهزون			
(36:31) الم يروا كم اهلكنا قبلهم من القرون انهم اليهم لا يرجعون	0	3	
(36:32) وان كل لما جميع لدينا محضرون	0	2	
(36:33) وايه لهم الارض الميته احيينها واخرجنا منها حبا فمنه ياكلون	0	5	
(36:34) وجعلنا فيها جنت من نخيل واعنب وفجرنا فيها من العيون	0	4	
(36:35) لياكلوا من ثمره وما عملته ايديهم افلا يشكرون	0	4	
(36:36) سبحن الذي خلق الازوج كلها مما تنبت الارض ومن انفسهم ومما لا يعلمون	2	2	
(36:37) وايه لهم اليل نسلخ منه النهار فاذا هم مظلمون	1	2	
(36:38) والشمس تجري لمستقر لها ذلك تقدير العزيز العليم	2	4	
(36:39) والقمر قدرنه منازل حتي عاد كالعرجون القديم	0	2	
(36:40) لا الشمس ينبغي لها ان تدرك القمر ولا اليل سابق النهار وكل في فلك يسبحون	3	5	
(36:41) وايه لهم انا حملنا ذريتهم في الفلك المشحون	0	3	
(36:42) وخلقنا لهم من مثله ما يركبون	0	1	
(36:43) وان نشا نغرقهم فلا صريخ لهم ولا هم ينقذون	0	2	
(36:44) الا رحمه منا ومتعا الي حين	0	2	
(36:45) واذا قيل لهم اتقوا ما بين ايديكم وما خلفكم لعلكم ترحمون	0	4	
(36:46) وما تاتيهم من ايه من ايت ربهم الا كانوا عنها معرضين	0	4	
(36:47) واذا قيل لهم انفقوا مما رزقكم الله قال الذين كفروا للذين امنوا انطعم من لو يشا الله اطعمه ان انتم الا في ضلل مبين	0	6	
(36:48) ويقولون متي هذا الوعد ان كنتم صدقين	0	3	
(36:49) ما ينظرون الا صيحه وحده تاخذهم وهم يخصمون	0	3	
(36:50) فلا يستطيعون توصيه ولا الي اهلهم يرجعون	1	5	
(36:51) ونفخ في الصور فاذا هم من الاجداث الي ربهم	1	3	

ينسلون		
(36:52) قالوا يويلنا من بعثنا من مرقدنا هذا ما وعد الرحمن وصدق المرسلون	0	2
(36:53) ان كانت الا صيحه وحده فاذا هم جميع لدينا محضرون	0	3
(36:54) فاليوم لا تظلم نفس شيا ولا تجزون الا ما كنتم تعملون	1	2
(36:55) ان اصحب الجنه اليوم في شغل فكهون	0	2
(36:56) هم وازوجهم في ظلل علي الارايك متكون	0	2
(36:57) لهم فيها فكهه ولهم ما يدعون	0	2
(36:58) سلم قولا من رب رحيم	1	1
(36:59) وامتزوا اليوم ايها المجرمون	0	2
(36:60) الم اعهد اليكم يبني ادم ان لا تعبدوا الشيطن انه لكم عدو مبين	0	5
(36:61) وان اعبدوني هذا صرط مستقيم	1	2
(36:62) ولقد اضل منكم جبلا كثيرا افلم تكونوا تعقلون	0	1
(36:63) هذه جهنم التي كنتم توعدون	0	1
(36:64) اصلوها اليوم بما كنتم تكفرون	0	1
(36:65) اليوم نختم علي افوههم وتكلمنا ايديهم وتشهد ارجلهم بما كانوا يكسبون	1	5
(36:66) ولو نشا لطمسنا علي اعينهم فاستبقوا الصرط فاني يبصرون	2	4
(36:67) ولو نشا لمسخنهم علي مكانتهم فما استطعوا مضيا ولا يرجعون	2	3
(36:68) ومن نعمره ننكسه في الخلق افلا يعقلون	1	2
(36:69) وما علمنه الشعر وما ينبغي له ان هو الا ذكر وقران مبين	0	3
(36:70) لينذر من كان حيا ويحق القول علي الكفرين	0	5

(36:71) اولم يروا انا خلقنا لهم مما عملت ايدينا انعما فهم لها ملكون	0	3
(36:72) وذللنها لهم فمنها ركوبهم ومنها ياكلون	0	1
(36:73) ولهم فيها منفع ومشارب افلا يشكرون	0	2
(36:74) واتخذوا من دون الله الهه لعلهم ينصرون	0	1
(36:75) لا يستطيعون نصرهم وهم لهم جند محضرون	1	2
(36:76) فلا يحزنك قولهم انا نعلم ما يسرون وما يعلنون	1	3
(36:77) اولم ير الانسن انا خلقنه من نطفه فاذا هو خصيم مبين	1	3
(36:78) وضرب لنا مثلا ونسي خلقه قال من يحي العظم وهي رميم	1	5
(36:79) قل يحييها الذي انشاها اول مره وهو بكل خلق عليم	0	5
(36:80) الذي جعل لكم من الشجر الاخضر نارا فاذا انتم منه توقدون	0	1
(36:81) اوليس الذي خلق السموت والارض بقدر علي ان يخلق مثلهم بلي وهو الخلق العليم	2	6
(36:82) انما امره اذا اراد شيا ان يقول له كن فيكون	0	3
(36:83) فسبحن الذي بيده ملكوت كل شي واليه ترجعون	1	4
Total		
	48	237	285

The chapter starting with the letters Y and S has 285 Ys and Ss, which is

$$285 = 19 \times 15$$

▲

عليها تسعه عشر
On it is Nineteen

230

22

Big Numbers

72:28   So that He knows that they have delivered the messages of their Lord, and He surrounds all that is with them, and He has counted everything in numbers.

The Quran uses various numbers. If we do not count the repetitions, we find 30 different or unique numbers in the Quran. Together with eight unique fractions, the total number of unique numbers is 38 (19x2) and the sum of whole numbers also add up to a multiple of 19, which we will see below. We come across some interesting expressions of numbers. For example, in 29:14, the Quran informs us the age of Noah to be 950 years without exactly mentioning 950. Instead it uses a subtraction 1000 minus 50.

29:14   We had sent Noah to his people, so he stayed with them one thousand years less fifty calendar years. Then the flood took them while they were wicked.

Why "one thousand less fifty"? Could it be because the number "one thousand" is a rounded and popular number? Perhaps, since this verse emphasizes the length of time Noah lived among his unappreciative people. We also find this expression closely related with the mathematical structure of the Quran. If this expression were 950, instead of the numbers 1000 and 50 we would have 950, which would change the sum of unique numbers, by an extra 900, which is not divisible by 19. (Since the 1000 is mentioned in another verse too, the alternative expression would eliminate the number 50 from the list while adding 950 to it). Perhaps the age of Noah being a multiple of 19 (950 = 19x50) serves as another parameter supporting the numerical relationship we infer.

It is claimed that there are 304 (19x16) counting numbers in the Quran and that some related numerical pattern. There will be difficulty in establishing the accuracy of this claim, since the number One (*Wahid* or *Ahad*) in the Quran has multiple meanings, occasionally used to mean unity or a person. It requires a careful and consistent methodology to objectively distinguish the number One from the other "One." For those who have interest and time, I will list the verse numbers containing the number One according to our count.[134]

Index	Whole Number	Fraction	Freq.	Verses Where The Numbers are Mentioned * Verses with asterix contain repeated occurrences
1	1		145	2:61, 2:96, 2:102, 2:102, 2:133, 2:136, 2:163, 2:180, 2:213, 2:266, 2:282, 2:282, 2:285, 3:73, 3:84, 3:91, 3:153, 4:1, 4:3, 4:11, 4:11, 4:12, 4:18, 4:20, 4:43, 4:102, 4:152, 4:171, 5:6, 5:20, 5:27, 5:48, 5:73, 5:106, 5:115, 6:19, 6:61, 6:98, 7:80, 7:189, 8:7, 9:4, 9:6, 9:31, 9:52, 9:84, 9:127, 10:19, 11:81, 11:118, 12:31, 12:36, 12:39, 12:41, 12:67, 12:78, 13:4, 13:16, 14:48, 14:52, 15:65, 16:22, 16:51, 16:58, 16:76, 16:93, 17:23, 18:19, 18:19, 18:22, 18:26, 18:32, 18:38, 18:42, 18:47, 18:49, 18:110, 18:110, 19:26, 19:98, 21:92, 21:108, 22:34, 23:52, 23:99, 24:2, 24:6, 24:21, 24:28, 25:14, 25:32, 28:25, 28:26, 28:27, 29:28, 29:46, 31:28, 33:32, 33:39, 33:40, 34:46, 35:41, 35:42, 36:29, 36:49, 36:53, 37:4, 37:19, 38:5, 38:15, 38:23, 38:35, 38:65, 39:4, 39:6, 40:16, 41:6, 42:8, 43:17, 43:33, 49:9, 49:12, 54:24, 54:31, 54:50, 59:11, 63:10, 69:13, 69:14, 69:47, 72:2, 72:7, 72:18, 72:20, 72:22, 72:26, 74:35, 79:13, 89:25, 89:26, 90:5, 90:7, 92:19, 112:1, 112:4
2	2		15	5:106, 6:143, 6:143*, 6:144, 6:144*, 9:40, 11:40, 13:3, 16:51, 23:27, 36:14, 4:11, 4:176, 40:11, 40:11*
3	3		17	19:10, 24:58, 24:58, 39:6, 77:30, 2:196, 2:228, 3:41, 4:171, 5:73, 5:89, 11:65, 18:22, 56:7, 58:7, 65:4, 9:118
4	4		12	2:226, 2:234, 2:260, 4:15, 9:2, 9:36, 24:4, 24:13, 41:10, 24:6, 24:8, 24:45
5	5		2	18:22, 58:7
6	6		7	7:54, 10:3, 11:7, 25:59, 32:4, 50:38, 57:4
7	7		24	2:29, 2:261, 12:43, 12:43*, 12:43*, 12:46, 12:46*, 12:46*, 12:47, 12:48, 23:17, 41:12, 65:12, 67:3, 69:7, 71:15, 17:44, 23:86, 15:87, 78:12, 2:196, 15:44, 18:22, 31:27
8	8		5	28:27, 6:143, 39:6, 69:7, 69:17
9	9		4	17:101, 18:25, 27:12, 27:48
10	10		9	2:196, 5:89, 6:160, 7:142, 11:13, 89:2, 2:234, 20:103, 28:27
11	11		1	12:4
12	12		5	9:36, 5:12, 2:60, 7:160, 7:160*
13	19		1	74:30
14	20		1	8:65

15	30		2	7:142, 46:15
16	40		4	2:51, 5:26, 7:142, 46:15
17	50		1	29:14
18	60		1	58:4
19	70		3	69:32, 7:155, 9:80
20	80		1	24:4
21	99		1	38:23
22	100		6	2:259, 2:259*, 2:261, 8:65, 8:66, 24:2
23	200		2	8:65, 8:66
24	300		1	18:25
25	1.000		8	2:96, 8:9, 8:66, 22:47, 29:14, 32:5, 97:3, 8:65
26	2.000		1	8:66
27	3.000		1	3:124
28	5.000		1	3:125
29	50.000		1	70:4
30	100.000		1	37:147
31		1/10	1	34:45
32		1/8	1	4:12
33		1/6	3	4:11, 4:11*, 4:12
34		1/5	1	8:41
35		1/4	2	4:12, 4:12*
36		1/3	3	4:11, 4:12, 73:20
37		1/2	7	2:237, 4:11, 4:12, 4:25, 4:176, 73:3, 73:20
38		2/3	3	4:176, 73:20, 4:11
38	162146	281/120	304	
19 x 2	**19 x 8534**	**2.341<u>6</u>**	**19 x 16**	

233

To facilitate future studies, I am listing the verses where a number is mentioned, in ascending order:

Index Number	Verse Number	The Number Mentioned
1.	002:029	7
2.	002:051	40
3.	002:060	12
4.	002:061	1
5.	002:096	1
6.	002:096	1000
7.	002:102	1
8.	002:102	1
9.	002:133	1
10.	002:136	1
11.	002:163	1
12.	002:180	1
13.	002:196	3
14.	002:196	7
15.	002:196	10
16.	002:213	1
17.	002:226	4
18.	002:228	3
19.	002:234	4
20.	002:234	10
21.	**002:237**	**1/2**
22.	002:259	100
23.	002:259*	100
24.	002:260	4
25.	002:261	7
26.	002:261	100
27.	002:266	1
28.	002:282	1
29.	002:282	1
30.	002:285	1
31.	003:041	3
32.	003:073	1
33.	003:084	1
34.	003:091	1
35.	003:124	3000
36.	003:125	5000
37.	003:153	1
38.	004:001	1
39.	004:003	1
40.	004:011	1
41.	004:011	1
42.	004:011	2
43.	**004:011**	**1/6**
44.	**004:011**	**1/3**
45.	**004:011**	**1/2**
46.	**004:011**	**2/3**
47.	**004:011***	**1/6**
48.	004:012	1
49.	**004:012**	**1/8**
50.	**004:012**	**1/6**
51.	**004:012**	**1/4**
52.	**004:012**	**1/3**
53.	**004:012**	**1/2**
54.	**004:012***	**1/4**
55.	004:015	4
56.	004:018	1
57.	004:020	1
58.	**004:025**	**1/2**
59.	004:043	1
60.	004:102	1
61.	004:152	1
62.	004:171	1
63.	004:171	3
64.	004:176	2
65.	**004:176**	**1/2**
66.	**004:176**	**2/3**
67.	005:006	1
68.	005:012	12
69.	005:020	1
70.	005:026	40
71.	005:027	1
72.	005:048	1
73.	005:073	1
74.	005:073	3
75.	005:089	3
76.	005:089	10
77.	005:106	1
78.	005:106	2
79.	005:115	1
80.	006:019	1
81.	006:061	1

82.	006:098	1		129.	012:004	11
83.	006:143	2		130.	012:031	1
84.	006:143	8		131.	012:036	1
85.	006:143*	2		132.	012:039	1
86.	006:144	2		133.	012:041	1
87.	006:144*	2		134.	012:043	7
88.	006:160	10		135.	012:043*	7
89.	007:054	6		136.	012:043*	7
90.	007:080	1		137.	012:046	7
91.	007:142	10		138.	012:046*	7
92.	007:142	30		139.	012:046*	7
93.	007:142	40		140.	012:047	7
94.	007:155	70		141.	012:048	7
95.	007:160	12		142.	012:067	1
96.	007:160*	12		143.	012:078	1
97.	007:189	1		144.	013:003	2
98.	008:007	1		145.	013:004	1
99.	008:009	1000		146.	013:016	1
100.	**008:041**	**1/5**		147.	014:048	1
101.	008:065	20		148.	014:052	1
102.	008:065	100		149.	015:044	7
103.	008:065	200		150.	015:065	1
104.	008:065	1000		151.	015:087	7
105.	008:066	100		152.	016:022	1
106.	008:066	200		153.	016:051	1
107.	008:066	1000		154.	016:051	2
108.	008:066	2000		155.	016:058	1
109.	009:002	4		156.	016:076	1
110.	009:004	1		157.	016:093	1
111.	009:006	1		158.	017:023	1
112.	009:031	1		159.	017:044	7
113.	009:036	4		160.	017:101	9
114.	009:036	12		161.	018:019	1
115.	009:040	2		162.	018:019	1
116.	009:052	1		163.	018:022	1
117.	009:080	70		164.	018:022	3
118.	009:084	1		165.	018:022	5
119.	009:118	3		166.	018:022	7
120.	009:127	1		167.	018:025	9
121.	010:003	6		168.	018:025	300
122.	010:019	1		169.	018:026	1
123.	011:007	6		170.	018:032	1
124.	011:013	10		171.	018:038	1
125.	011:040	2		172.	018:042	1
126.	011:065	3		173.	018:047	1
127.	011:081	1		174.	018:049	1
128.	011:118	1		175.	018:110	1

176.	018:110	1	223.	033:040	1
177.	019:010	3	**224.**	**034:045**	**1/10**
178.	019:026	1	225.	034:046	1
179.	019:098	1	226.	035:041	1
180.	020:103	10	227.	035:042	1
181.	021:092	1	228.	036:014	2
182.	021:108	1	229.	036:029	1
183.	022:034	1	230.	036:049	1
184.	022:047	1000	231.	036:053	1
185.	023:017	7	232.	037:004	1
186.	023:027	2	233.	037:019	1
187.	023:052	1	234.	037:147	100000
188.	023:086	7	235.	038:005	1
189.	023:099	1	236.	038:015	1
190.	024:002	1	237.	038:023	1
191.	024:002	100	238.	038:023	99
192.	024:004	4	239.	038:035	1
193.	024:004	80	240.	038:065	1
194.	024:006	1	241.	039:004	1
195.	024:006	4	242.	039:006	1
196.	024:008	4	243.	039:006	3
197.	024:013	4	244.	039:006	8
198.	024:021	1	245.	040:011	2
199.	024:028	1	246.	040:011*	2
200.	024:045	4	247.	040:016	1
201.	024:058	3	248.	041:006	1
202.	024:058	3	249.	041:010	4
203.	025:014	1	250.	041:012	7
204.	025:032	1	251.	042:008	1
205.	025:059	6	252.	043:017	1
206.	027:012	9	253.	043:033	1
207.	027:048	9	254.	046:015	30
208.	028:025	1	255.	046:015	40
209.	028:026	1	256.	049:009	1
210.	028:027	1	257.	049:012	1
211.	028:027	8	258.	050:038	6
212.	028:027	10	259.	054:024	1
213.	029:014	50	260.	054:031	1
214.	029:014	1000	261.	054:050	1
215.	029:028	1	262.	056:007	3
216.	029:046	1	263.	057:004	6
217.	031:027	7	264.	058:004	60
218.	031:028	1	265.	058:007	3
219.	032:004	6	266.	058:007	5
220.	032:005	1000	267.	059:011	1
221.	033:032	1	268.	063:010	1
222.	033:039	1	269.	065:004	3

236

270.	065:012	7
271.	067:003	7
272.	069:007	7
273.	069:007	8
274.	069:013	1
275.	069:014	1
276.	069:017	8
277.	069:032	70
278.	069:047	1
279.	070:004	50000
280.	071:015	7
281.	072:002	1
282.	072:007	1
283.	072:018	1
284.	072:020	1
285.	072:022	1
286.	072:026	1
287.	**073:003**	**1/2**
288.	**073:020**	**1/3**
289.	**073:020**	**1/2**
290.	**073:020**	**2/3**
291.	074:030	19
292.	074:035	1
293.	077:030	3
294.	078:12	7
295.	079:013	1
296.	089:002	10
297.	089:025	1
298.	089:026	1
299.	090:005	1
300.	090:007	1
301.	092:019	1
302.	097:003	1000
303.	112:001	1
304.	112:004	1

Without University Education and Without Computer

We witnessed that the word ALLAH (GOD) is mentioned in the entire Quran 2698 (19x142) times. Now let's add up all the verses where the word God is mentioned. The result is 118123, and this number is 19x6217.

When I was working with Dr. Khalifa in Masjid Tucson on his revision of the translation of *Quran: The Final Testament*, we experienced the difficulty of this apparently simple task. Dr. Khalifa shared this experience with the reader as follows:

> "These simple phenomena gave us many difficulties while simply counting the word 'God.' We were a group of workers, equipped with computers, and all of us college graduates. Yet we made several errors in counting, calculating, or simply writing the counts of the word 'God.' Those who still claim that Muhammad was the author of the Quran are totally illogical; never went to college, and he did not have a computer."[135]

We may disagree with Khalifa's remark regarding Muhammad's college education, since we are familiar with the works of many geniuses of the past such as Pythagoras or Ramanujan, who had no formal education. However, the issue is manifold. The improbability of the numerical structure of the Quran being produced by a medieval Arab genius becomes evident when we consider the following factors:

1. It includes simple elements of the Quran and goes deeper to an interlocking system that consists of very complex numerical patterns and relationships.
2. It involves not only frequencies of letters and words but also the numerical values of letters.
3. It involves not only an intricate numerical pattern but its volume is also exhaustive: huge numbers consisting of thousands of digits.[136]
4. Add to this the literary excellence of the Quran that shined over the best poetry and prose in Arabic history.
5. Add to this the scientific accuracy of numerous verses on various fields.
6. Add to this that none of those attributes were known, at least publicly, by the audience of the Quran.
7. Add to this that Muhammad was one of the busiest and greatest social and political reformists in human history.
8. Add to this the prophetic timing of the discovery of the code.
9. Add to this, the fulfillment of the prophetic events regarding the code.

Long Numbers

If we write down the verse numbers of each chapter one by one after the sum of verses in each chapter we get a number with 12692 digits. For the first chapter the beginning of the long number starts with 71234567, for the second chapter, after the number 286, numbers from 1 to 286 will be written in ascending order. Thus, for all the 114 chapters the long number will look something like this:

712345672861234567891011 .... **6**123456.

If the numbers were printed on a page with 30 lines, each line containing 100 digits, it would take more than four pages to display the number. This very long number is divisible by 19. Furthermore, the number of the digits too is divisible. (12692 = 19 x 668).

If the presence of 19-based mathematical pattern was just a coincidence, then the probability of a long number or a short number being a multiple of 19 would not be different, since regardless of the length, the divisibility of any random number by 19 is 1/19. But when we have too many occurrences of the mudolo 19 and a clear prophetic reference to it, then the probability of a divisible number being intentional rather than being random increases. Especially, when we have a divisible long number with a divisible number of digits, the intenional design becomes more probable. Thus, designing very long numbers as multiples of 19 will require proportionally greater time, difficulty and care.

I admit that, in general, claims regarding long numbers are problematic, especially when numbers are generated by arbitrarily constructing them. The more components they have the less significant examples of code nineteen they become. Even in the example above, we may find a selective mind at work. For instance, the verse numbers alone did not produce the expected results. Similarly, placing the sum of the verses after the list of verse numbers too did not produce what we were expecting. A self-fulfilling selective methodology cannot be evidence for an extraordinary sign. Thus, the statistical value of long numbers generated by a series of concatenation is suspect in this context, at least for now, and it requires critical study and evaluation by mathematicians.

That is said, let me give an example of an interesting symmetry in the sum of odd and even verses.

Odd and Even Numbers

The first five verses of Chapter 89 draws our attention to the decimal and binary numerical systems. We recognize two numbers related to 114 chapters and their verses:

6234	The total number of numbered verses in the Quran
6555	The sum of numbers of chapters in the Quran (1+2+3+4+5 . . . . 112+113+114)

Now let's add the number of verses in a chapter with the number of that chapter. For instance, in the first chapter of the Quran there are a total of 7 verses. Thus, we add 1+7 and get 8. For the last chapter of the Quran we add 114 and the number of verses it contains, 114 + 6 and we get 120. After doing this operation for all the chapters let's separate the odd numbers from the even ones.

As you will see in the table below, there are exactly 57 odd and 57 even such numbers. When we add all the odd numbers and all the even numbers, we will see that the synthesis is separated to their units.

Chapter	Verse	Sum	Even	Odd
1	7	8	8	---
2	286	288	288	---
3	200	203	---	203
4	176	180	180	---
5	120	125	---	125
6	165	171	---	171
7	206	213	---	213
8	75	83	---	83
9	127	136	136	---
10	109	119	---	119
11	123	134	134	---
12	111	123	---	123
13	43	56	56	---
14	52	66	66	---
15	99	114	114	---
16	128	144	144	---
17	111	128	128	---
18	110	128	128	---
19	98	117	---	117
20	135	155	---	155
21	112	133	---	133
22	78	100	100	---
23	118	141	---	141
24	64	88	88	---
25	77	102	102	---

26	227	253	---	253
27	93	120	120	---
28	88	116	116	---
29	69	98	98	---
30	60	90	90	---
31	34	65	---	65
32	30	62	62	---
33	73	106	106	---
34	54	88	88	---
35	45	80	80	---
36	83	119	---	119
37	182	219	---	219
38	88	126	126	---
39	75	114	114	---
40	85	125	---	125
41	54	95	---	95
42	53	95	---	95
43	89	132	132	---
44	59	103	---	103
45	37	82	82	---
46	35	81	---	81
47	38	85	---	85
48	29	77	---	77
49	18	67	---	67
50	45	95	---	95
51	60	111	---	111
52	49	101	---	101
53	62	115	---	115
54	55	109	---	109
55	78	133	---	133
56	96	152	152	---
57	29	86	86	---
58	22	80	80	---
59	24	83	---	83

60	13	73	---	73
61	14	75	---	75
62	11	73	---	73
63	11	74	74	---
64	18	82	82	---
65	12	77	---	77
66	12	78	78	---
67	30	97	---	97
68	52	120	120	---
69	52	121	---	121
70	44	114	114	---
71	28	99	---	99
72	28	100	100	---
73	20	93	---	93
74	56	130	130	---
75	40	115	---	115
76	31	107	---	107
77	50	127	---	127
78	40	118	118	---
79	46	125	---	125
80	42	122	122	---
81	29	110	110	---
82	19	101	---	101
83	36	119	---	119
84	25	109	---	109
85	22	107	---	107
86	17	103	---	103
87	19	106	106	---
88	26	114	114	---
89	30	119	---	119
90	20	110	110	---
91	15	106	106	---
92	21	113	---	113
93	11	104	104	---

94	8	102	102	---
95	8	103	---	103
96	19	115	---	115
97	5	102	102	---
98	8	106	106	---
99	8	107	---	107
100	11	111	---	111
101	11	112	112	---
102	8	110	110	---
103	3	106	106	---
104	9	113	---	113
105	5	110	110	---
106	4	110	110	---
107	7	114	114	---
108	3	111	---	111
109	6	115	---	115
110	3	113	---	113
111	5	116	116	---
112	4	116	116	---
113	5	118	118	---
114	6	120	120	---
6555	**6234**		**6234**	**6555**

As it is seen in the table above, when the sum of chapter numbers and their total verses are divided into two groups according to their even or odd properties, we observe that the total for each column is dissolved to their addends. In other words, the sum of verses (6234) and the sum of chapter numbers (6555) dissolve with an even and odd analysis.

23
An Interlocking System

Rashad Khalifa, in his late years, unfortunately lost his objectivity on the subject matter. He started diluting the amazing mathematical structure of the Quran by placing chapter and verse numbers next to each other in arbitrary or semi-arbitrary orders. I blame partially the gullible people surrounding him who provided him with deceptive feedback. I found myself the only loud voice in his inner circle that remained critical of his work. Though Rashad usually handled my criticsm well, my critical approach put me at odds with the flatterers around him.

Rashad, besides having great qualities, like all of us had also some weaknesses. Unfortunately, by recklessly producing arbitrary numerical "miracles" thereby violating the divine warning in 74:6, Rashad provided ammunition for those ignorant fanatics who accept literary miracles yet are unable to accept or comprehend a mathematical miracle from the Creator of the universe. By picking and focusing on some of his arbitrary calculations they managed to blind themselves to many great signs. Many of the opponents of the mathematical miracle enjoy beating the straw men and declare victory against one of the greatest blessings. Perhaps this was meant to happen in accordance of God's law stated in 22:52.

As a result, we have seen an inflation of silly arbitrary calculations and manipulations introduced by innumerate arrogant people as great miracles. The abuse did not stop there. Many megalomaniacal people, impressed by their talent of producing dozens of such "miracles" every day, were led to harbor delusional ideas about their importance and mission. With calculators in their hands, they declared their messengership and volunteered to save the world. They appeared to ignore basic statistical fact that one out of every 19 randomly chosen numbers would be multiple of 19. When a determined miracle-hunter picks any number, he literally has dozens of possible manipulations at his disposal. He may pick verse numbers alone OR put them before OR after chapters OR add their digits OR add the numbers OR add the gematrical value of his name before OR after the number OR add it to the digits OR take the gematrical value of the first name, OR etcetera, etcetera. EVERY SINGLE

PERSON on this planet should be able to find MANY MORE examples of multiples of 19 in connection to their names in verses containing the word "messenger" when they apply a similar arbitrary method.

I think the major reason for why Rashad lost his objectivity and mathematical intuition was the fatigue emanating from his long work hours. He was a one-man with multiple skills and tasks. He would write, design and print his books. He would record his own speeches. He would ship the orders for books and video cassettes. He would act like a counselor for those who had problems. He would even cook lunch for me and Lisa and occasionally invite others such as Lydia, Emily and Mahmoud during weekends. He would absorb all the insults, defamations and threats aimed at him by Sunni or Shiite fanatics.... All these, I believe, made it difficult for him to be thorough and critical of numerous claims and speculations made by those miracle-hunters who had surrounded him, their mouth open waiting for more and more miracles. They were addicted with consumption of "miracles"! Rashad was also too nice to discourage a novice who was excited to discover for the first time a potential mathematical pattern.

Putting numbers next to each other or adding various numbers to each other with no set method remains speculative, and it has little to no statistical significance. Many of the copycat messengers popping up after Rashad use exactly the same arbitrary numerical jugglery to come up with prophecies and new miracles!

The Quran's numerical structure is not only beyond probability but it is also endless. I have been contacted by hundreds of innumerate enthusiasts who juggle numbers arbitrarily with a calculator in their hands and get excited when they randomly end up with a number divisible by 19 every once in awhile. I have also seen more than a dozen of them claiming their messengership. Their "proof" of their messengership is as childish as their discoveries. Some of those delusional messengers even went further to come up with specific doomsday prophecies. If reasonable people first hear about the function of the number 19 in the Quran from those innumerate egomaniacs, they will perhaps never again take it seriously. Their initial impression might create an obstacle to studying the extraordinarily beautiful mathematical pattern in the Quran. Of course, the ingrates described in 7:146 and 7:31 have attempted numerous times to discredit the extraordinary pattern by confusing them with the arbitrary ones.

Like a broken clock that might show the time correctly once in a while, a few of those innumerate miracle-hunters do occasionally find some facts that fit the jigsaw puzzle. On the other hand, there are also studious and inspired individuals whose observations have resulted in remarkable discoveries.

Regardless of who discovered the following examples or why or how, I think that they are impressive facts in terms of the 19-based mathematical system in the Quran. It is like a live canvas with intricate patterns of beautiful designs that blossom with more color and integrated patterns every day.

Verses Mirroring Chapters

The following discovery is made by brother Asad from Iran. As you know by now, 14 letters, half of the Arabic Alphabet, make up 14 different combinations that are used in the beginning of 29 chapters of the Quran. In the entire Quran, out of 6346 verses, exactly 114 (19x6) contain all those 14 initial letters.

(2:19) او كصيب من السما فيه ظلمت ورعد وبرق يجعلون اصبعهم في اذانهم من الصوعق حذر الموت والله محيط بالكفرين

(2:61) واذ قلتم يموسي لن نصبر علي طعام وحد فادع لنا ربك يخرج لنا مما تنبت الارض من بقلها وقثايها وفومها وعدسها وبصلها قال اتستبدلون الذي هو ادني بالذي هو خير اهبطوا مصرا فان لكم ما سالتم وضربت عليهم الذله والمسكنه وباو بغضب من الله ذلك بانهم كانوا يكفرون بايت الله ويقتلون النبين بغير الحق ذلك بما عصوا وكانوا يعتدون

(2:140) ام تقولون ان ابرهم واسمعيل واسحق ويعقوب والاسباط كانوا هودا او نصري قل انتم اعلم ام الله ومن اظلم ممن كتم شهده عنده من الله وما الله بغفل عما تعملون

(2:187) احل لكم ليله الصيام الرفث الي نسايكم هن لباس لكم وانتم لباس لهن علم الله انكم كنتم تختانون انفسكم فتاب عليكم وعفا عنكم فالن بشروهن وابتغوا ما كتب الله لكم وكلوا واشربوا حتي يتبين لكم الخيط الابيض من الخيط الاسود من الفجر ثم اتموا الصيام الي اليل ولا تبشروهن وانتم عكفون في المسجد تلك حدود الله فلا تقربوها كذلك يبين الله ايته للناس لعلهم يتقون

(2:213) كان الناس امه وحده فبعث الله النبين مبشرين ومنذرين وانزل معهم الكتب بالحق ليحكم بين الناس فيما اختلفوا فيه وما اختلف فيه الا الذين اوتوه من بعد ما جاتهم البينت بغيا بينهم فهدي الله الذين

امنوا لما اختلفوا فيه من الحق باذنه والله يهدي من يشا الي صرط مستقيم

(2:217) يسلونك عن الشهر الحرام قتال فيه قل قتال فيه كبير وصد عن سبيل الله وكفر به والمسجد الحرام واخراج اهله منه اكبر عند الله والفتنه اكبر من القتل ولا يزالون يقتلونكم حتي يردوكم عن دينكم ان استطعوا ومن يرتدد منكم عن دينه فيمت وهو كافر فاوليك حبطت اعملهم في الدنيا والاخره واوليك اصحب النار هم فيها خلدون

(2:220) في الدنيا والاخره ويسلونك عن اليتمي قل اصلاح لهم خير وان تخالطوهم فاخونكم والله يعلم المفسد من المصلح ولو شا الله لاعنتكم ان الله عزيز حكيم

(2:228) والمطلقت يتربصن بانفسهن ثلثه قرو ولا يحل لهن ان يكتمن ما خلق الله في ارحامهن ان كن يومن بالله واليوم الاخر وبعولتهن احق بردهن في ذلك ان ارادوا اصلحا ولهن مثل الذي عليهن بالمعروف وللرجال عليهن درجه والله عزيز حكيم

(2:237) وان طلقتموهن من قبل ان تمسوهن وقد فرضتم لهن فريضه فنصف ما فرضتم الا ان يعفون او يعفوا الذي بيده عقده النكاح وان تعفوا اقرب للتقوي ولا تنسوا الفضل بينكم ان الله بما تعملون بصير

(2:260) واذ قال ابرهم رب ارني كيف تحي الموتي قال اولم تومن قال بلي ولكن ليطمين قلبي قال فخذ اربعه من الطير فصرهن اليك ثم اجعل علي كل جبل منهن جزا ثم ادعهن ياتينك سعيا واعلم ان الله عزيز حكيم

(3:154) ثم انزل عليكم من بعد الغم امنه نعاسا يغشي طايفه منكم وطايفه قد اهمتهم انفسهم يظنون بالله غير الحق ظن الجهليه يقولون هل لنا من الامر من شي قل ان الامر كله لله يخفون في انفسهم ما لا يبدون لك يقولون لو كان لنا من الامر شي ما قتلنا ههنا قل لو كنتم في بيوتكم لبرز الذين كتب عليهم القتل الي مضاجعهم وليبتلي الله ما في صدوركم وليمحص ما في قلوبكم والله عليم بذات الصدور

(4:4) واتوا النسا صدقتهن نحله فان طبن لكم عن شي منه نفسا فكلوه هنيا مريا

(4:34) الرجال قومون علي النسا بما فضل الله بعضهم علي بعض وبما انفقوا من امولهم فالصلحت قنتت حفظت للغيب بما حفظ الله والتي تخافون نشوزهن فعظوهن واهجروهن في المضاجع واضربوهن فان اطعنكم فلا تبغوا عليهن سبيلا ان الله كان عليا كبيرا

(4:43) يايها الذين امنوا لا تقربوا الصلوه وانتم سكري حتي تعلموا ما تقولون ولا جنبا الا عابري سبيل حتي تغتسلوا وان كنتم مرضي او علي سفر او جا احد منكم من الغايط او لمستم النسا فلم تجدوا ما فتيمموا صعيدا طيبا فامسحوا بوجوهكم وايديكم ان الله كان عفوا غفورا

(4:46) من الذين هادوا يحرفون الكلم عن مواضعه ويقولون سمعنا وعصينا واسمع غير مسمع ورعنا ليا بالسنتهم وطعنا في الدين ولو انهم قالوا سمعنا واطعنا واسمع وانظرنا لكان خيرا لهم واقوم ولكن لعنهم الله بكفرهم فلا يومنون الا قليلا

(4:47) يايها الذين اوتوا الكتب امنوا بما نزلنا مصدقا لما معكم من قبل ان نطمس وجوها فنردها علي ادبارها او نلعنهم كما لعنا اصحب السبت وكان امر الله مفعولا

(4:69) ومن يطع الله والرسول فاوليك مع الذين انعم الله عليهم من النبين والصديقين والشهدا والصلحين وحسن اوليك رفيقا

(2:275) الذين ياكلون الربوا لا يقومون الا كما يقوم الذي يتخبطه الشيطن من المس ذلك بانهم قالوا انما البيع مثل الربوا واحل الله البيع وحرم الربوا فمن جاه موعظه من ربه فانتهي فله ما سلف وامره الي الله ومن عاد فاوليك اصحب النار هم فيها خلدون

(2:282) يايها الذين امنوا اذا تداينتم بدين الي اجل مسمي فاكتبوه وليكتب بينكم كاتب بالعدل ولا ياب كاتب ان يكتب كما علمه الله فليكتب وليملل الذي عليه الحق وليتق الله ربه ولا يبخس منه شيا فان كان الذي عليه الحق سفيها او ضعيفا او لا يستطيع ان يمل هو فليملل وليه بالعدل واستشهدوا شهيدين من رجالكم فان لم يكونا رجلين فرجل وامراتان ممن ترضون من الشهدا ان تضل احديهما فتذكر احديهما الاخري ولا ياب الشهدا اذا ما دعوا ولا تسموا ان تكتبوه صغيرا او كبيرا الي اجله ذلكم اقسط عند الله واقوم للشهده وادني الا ترتابوا الا ان تكون تجره حاضره تديرونها بينكم فليس عليكم جناح الا تكتبوها واشهدوا اذا تبايعتم ولا يضار كاتب ولا شهيد وان تفعلوا فانه فسوق بكم واتقوا الله ويعلمكم الله والله بكل شي عليم

(2:285) امن الرسول بما انزل اليه من ربه والمومنون كل امن بالله وملييكته وكتبه ورسله لا نفرق بين احد من رسله وقالوا سمعنا واطعنا غفرانك ربنا واليك المصير

(2:286) لا يكلف الله نفسا الا وسعها لها ما كسبت وعليها ما اكتسبت ربنا لا تواخذنا ان نسينا او اخطانا ربنا ولا تحمل علينا اصرا كما حملته علي الذين من قبلنا ربنا ولا تحملنا ما لا طاقه لنا به واعف عنا واغفر لنا وارحمنا انت مولينا فانصرنا علي القوم الكفرين

(3:93) كل الطعام كان حلا لبني اسريل الا ما حرم اسريل علي نفسه من قبل ان تنزل التوريه قل فاتوا بالتوريه فاتلوها ان كنتم صدقين

(3:120) ان تمسسكم حسنه تسوهم وان تصبكم سييه يفرحوا بها وان تصبروا وتتقوا لا

عليكم نعمتي ورضيت لكم الاسلم دينا فمن اضطر في مخمصه غير متجانف لاثم فان الله غفور رحيم

(5:5) اليوم احل لكم الطيبت وطعام الذين اوتوا الكتب حل لكم وطعامكم حل لهم والمحصنت من المومنت والمحصنت من الذين اوتوا الكتب من قبلكم اذا اتيتموهن اجورهن محصنين غير مسفحين ولا متخذي اخدان ومن يكفر بالايمن فقد حبط عمله وهو في الاخره من الخسرين

(5:6) يايها الذين امنوا اذا قمتم الي الصلوه فاغسلوا وجوهكم وايديكم الي المرافق وامسحوا بروسكم وارجلكم الي الكعبين وان كنتم جنبا فاطهروا وان كنتم مرضي او علي سفر او جا احد منكم من الغايط او لمستم النسا فلم تجدوا ما فتيمموا صعيدا طيبا فامسحوا بوجوهكم وايديكم منه ما يريد الله ليجعل عليكم من حرج ولكن يريد ليطهركم وليتم نعمته عليكم لعلكم تشكرون

(5:13) فبما نقضهم ميثقهم لعنهم وجعلنا قلوبهم قسيه يحرفون الكلم عن مواضعه ونسوا حظا مما ذكروا به ولا تزال تطلع علي خاينه منهم الا قليلا منهم فاعف عنهم واصفح ان الله يحب المحسنين

(5:33) انما جزوا الذين يحاربون الله ورسوله ويسعون في الارض فسادا ان يقتلوا او يصلبوا او تقطع ايديهم وارجلهم من خلف او ينفوا من الارض ذلك لهم خزي في الدنيا ولهم في الاخره عذاب عظيم

(5:53) ويقول الذين امنوا اهولا الذين اقسموا بالله جهد ايمنهم انهم لمعكم حبطت اعملهم فاصبحوا خسرين

(5:75) ما المسيح ابن مريم الا رسول قد خلت من قبله الرسل وامه صديقه كانا ياكلان الطعام انظر كيف نبين لهم الايت ثم انظر اني يوفكون

(5:89) لا يواخذكم الله باللغو في ايمنكم ولكن يواخذكم بما عقدتم الايمن فكفرته اطعام عشره مسكين من اوسط ما تطعمون اهليكم او كسوتهم او تحرير رقبه فمن لم يجد فصيام ثلثه ايام ذلك كفره ايمنكم اذا

(4:90) الا الذين يصلون الي قوم بينكم وبينهم ميثق او جاوكم حصرت صدورهم ان يقتلوكم او يقتلوا قومهم ولو شا الله لسلطهم عليكم فلقتلوكم فان اعتزلوكم فلم يقتلوكم والقوا اليكم السلم فما جعل الله لكم عليهم سبيلا

(4:92) وما كان لمومن ان يقتل مومنا الا خطا ومن قتل مومنا خطا فتحرير رقبه مومنه وديه مسلمه الي اهله الا ان يصدقوا فان كان من قوم عدو لكم وهو مومن فتحرير رقبه مومنه وان كان من قوم بينكم وبينهم ميثق فديه مسلمه الي اهله وتحرير رقبه مومنه فمن لم يجد فصيام شهرين متتابعين توبه من الله وكان الله عليما حكيما

(4:102) واذا كنت فيهم فاقمت لهم الصلوه فلتقم طايفه منهم معك ولياخذوا اسلحتهم فاذا سجدوا فليكونوا من وراىكم ولتات طايفه اخري لم يصلوا فليصلوا معك ولياخذوا حذرهم واسلحتهم ود الذين كفروا لو تغفلون عن اسلحتكم وامتعتكم فيميلون عليكم ميله وحده ولا جناح عليكم ان كان بكم اذي من مطر او كنتم مرضي ان تضعوا اسلحتكم وخذوا حذركم ان الله اعد للكفرين عذابا مهينا

(4:129) ولن تستطيعوا ان تعدلوا بين النسا ولو حرصتم فلا تميلوا كل الميل فتذروها كالمعلقه وان تصلحوا وتتقوا فان الله كان غفورا رحيما

(5:2) يايها الذين امنوا لا تحلوا شعير الله ولا الشهر الحرام ولا الهدي ولا القليد ولا امين البيت الحرام يبتغون فضلا من ربهم ورضونا واذا حللتم فاصطادوا ولا يجرمنكم شنان قوم ان صدوكم عن المسجد الحرام ان تعتدوا وتعاونوا علي البر والتقوي ولا تعاونوا علي الاثم والعدون واتقوا الله ان الله شديد العقاب

(5:3) حرمت عليكم الميته والدم ولحم الخنزير وما اهل لغير الله به والمنخنقه والموقوذه والمترديه والنطيحه وما اكل السبع الا ما ذكيتم وما ذبح علي النصب وان تستقسموا بالازلم ذلكم فسق اليوم ييس الذين كفروا من دينكم فلا تخشوهم واخشون اليوم اكملت لكم دينكم واتممت

248

(6:152) ولا تقربوا مال اليتيم الا بالتي هي احسن حتي يبلغ اشده واوفوا الكيل والميزان بالقسط لا نكلف نفسا الا وسعها واذا قلتم فاعدلوا ولو كان ذا قربي وبعهد الله اوفوا ذلكم وصيكم به لعلكم تذكرون

(7:131) فاذا جاتهم الحسنه قالوا لنا هذه وان تصبهم سييه يطيروا بموسي ومن معه الا انما طيرهم عند الله ولكن اكثرهم لا يعلمون

(7:160) وقطعنهم اثنتي عشره اسباطا امما واوحينا الي موسي اذ استسقيه قومه ان اضرب بعصاك الحجر فانبجست منه اثنتا عشره عينا قد علم كل اناس مشربهم وظللنا عليهم الغمم وانزلنا عليهم المن والسلوي كلوا من طيبت ما رزقنكم وما ظلمونا ولكن كانوا انفسهم يظلمون

(7:168) وقطعنهم في الارض امما منهم الصلحون ومنهم دون ذلك وبلونهم بالحسنت والسيات لعلهم يرجعون

(8:1) يسلونك عن الانفال قل الانفال لله والرسول فاتقوا الله واصلحوا ذات بينكم واطيعوا الله ورسوله ان كنتم مومنين

(9:29) قتلوا الذين لا يومنون بالله ولا باليوم الاخر ولا يحرمون ما حرم الله ورسوله ولا يدينون دين الحق من الذين اوتوا الكتب حتي يعطوا الجزيه عن يد وهم صغرون

(9:34) يايها الذين امنوا ان كثيرا من الاحبار والرهبان لياكلون امول الناس بالبطل ويصدون عن سبيل الله والذين يكنزون الذهب والفضه ولا ينفقونها في سبيل الله فبشرهم بعذاب اليم

(9:42) لو كان عرضا قريبا وسفرا قاصدا لاتبعوك ولكن بعدت عليهم الشقه وسيحلفون بالله لو استطعنا لخرجنا معكم يهلكون انفسهم والله يعلم انهم لكذبون

(9:71) والمومنون والمومنت بعضهم اوليا بعض يامرون بالمعروف وينهون عن المنكر ويقيمون الصلوه ويوتون الزكوه ويطيعون الله ورسوله اوليك سيرحمهم الله ان الله عزيز حكيم

حلفتم واحفظوا ايمنكم كذلك يبين الله لكم ايته لعلكم تشكرون

(5:95) يايها الذين امنوا لا تقتلوا الصيد وانتم حرم ومن قتله منكم متعمدا فجزا مثل ما قتل من النعم يحكم به ذوا عدل منكم هديا بلغ الكعبه او كفره طعام مسكين او عدل ذلك صياما ليذوق وبال امره عفا الله عما سلف ومن عاد فينتقم الله منه والله عزيز ذو انتقام

(5:96) احل لكم صيد البحر وطعامه متعا لكم وللسياره وحرم عليكم صيد البر ما دمتم حرما واتقوا الله الذي اليه تحشرون

(5:110) اذ قال الله يعيسي ابن مريم اذكر نعمتي عليك وعلي ولدتك اذ ايدتك بروح القدس تكلم الناس في المهد وكهلا واذ علمتك الكتب والحكمه والتوريه والانجيل واذ تخلق من الطين كهيه الطير باذني فتنفخ فيها فتكون طيرا باذني وتبري الاكمه والابرص باذني واذ تخرج الموتي باذني واذ كففت بني اسريل عنك اذ جيتهم بالبينت فقال الذين كفروا منهم ان هذا الا سحر مبين

(6:71) قل اندعوا من دون الله ما لا ينفعنا ولا يضرنا ونرد علي اعقابنا بعد اذ هدينا الله كالذي استهوته الشيطين في الارض حيران له اصحب يدعونه الي الهدي ايتنا قل ان هدي الله هو الهدي وامرنا لنسلم لرب العلمين

(6:119) وما لكم الا تاكلوا مما ذكر اسم الله عليه وقد فصل لكم ما حرم عليكم الا ما اضطررتم اليه وان كثيرا ليضلون باهوايهم بغير علم ان ربك هو اعلم بالمعتدين

(6:139) وقالوا ما في بطون هذه الانعم خالصه لذكورنا ومحرم علي ازوجنا وان يكن ميته فهم فيه شركا سيجزيهم وصفهم انه حكيم عليم

(6:151) قل تعالوا اتل ما حرم ربكم عليكم الا تشركوا به شيا وبالولدين احسنا ولا تقتلوا اولدكم من املق نحن نرزقكم واياهم ولا تقربوا الفوحش ما ظهر منها وما بطن ولا تقتلوا النفس التي حرم الله الا بالحق ذلكم وصيكم به لعلكم تعقلون

(9:121) ولا ينفقون نفقه صغيره ولا كبيره ولا يقطعون واديا الا كتب لهم ليجزيهم الله احسن ما كانوا يعملون

(10:4) اليه مرجعكم جميعا وعد الله حقا انه يبدوا الخلق ثم يعيده ليجزي الذين امنوا وعملوا الصلحت بالقسط والذين كفروا لهم شراب من حميم وعذاب اليم بما كانوا يكفرون

(10:24) انما مثل الحيوه الدنيا كما انزلنه من السما فاختلط به نبات الارض مما ياكل الناس والانعم حتي اذا اخذت الارض زخرفها وازينت وظن اهلها انهم قدرون عليها اتيها امرنا ليلا او نهارا فجعلنها حصيدا كان لم تغن بالامس كذلك نفصل الايت لقوم يتفكرون

(10:27) والذين كسبوا السيات جزا سييه بمثلها وترهقهم ذله ما لهم من الله من عاصم كانما اغشيت وجوههم قطعا من اليل مظلما اوليك اصحب النار هم فيها خلدون

(10:93) ولقد بوانا بني اسريل مبوا صدق ورزقنهم من الطيبت فما اختلفوا حتي جاهم العلم ان ربك يقضي بينهم يوم القيمه فيما كانوا فيه يختلفون

(11:81) قالوا يلوط انا رسل ربك لن يصلوا اليك فاسر باهلك بقطع من اليل ولا يلتفت منكم احد الا امراتك انه مصيبها ما اصابهم ان موعدهم الصبح اليس الصبح بقريب

(11:88) قال يقوم اريتم ان كنت علي بينه من ربي ورزقني منه رزقا حسنا وما اريد ان اخالفكم الي ما انهيكم عنه ان اريد الا الاصلح ما استطعت وما توفيقي الا بالله عليه توكلت واليه انيب

(12:9) اقتلوا يوسف او اطرحوه ارضا يخل لكم وجه ابيكم وتكونوا من بعده قوما صلحين

(12:36) ودخل معه السجن فتيان قال احدهما اني اريني اعصر خمرا وقال الاخر اني اريني احمل فوق راسي خبزا تاكل الطير منه نبينا بتاويله انا نريك من المحسنين

(12:51) قال ما خطبكن اذ رودتن يوسف عن نفسه قلن حش لله ما علمنا عليه من سو قالت امرات العزيز الن حصحص الحق انا رودته عن نفسه وانه لمن الصدقين

(12:80) فلما استيسوا منه خلصوا نجيا قال كبيرهم الم تعلموا ان اباكم قد اخذ عليكم موثقا من الله ومن قبل ما فرطتم في يوسف فلن ابرح الارض حتي ياذن لي ابي او يحكم الله لي وهو خير الحكمين

(12:101) رب قد اتيتني من الملك وعلمتني من تاويل الاحاديث فاطر السموت والارض انت ولي في الدنيا والاخره توفني مسلما والحقني بالصلحين

(13:4) وفي الارض قطع متجورت وجنت من اعناب وزرع ونخيل صنون وغير صنون يسقي بما وحد ونفضل بعضها علي بعض في الاكل ان في ذلك لايت لقوم يعقلون

(13:31) ولو ان قرانا سيرت به الجبال او قطعت به الارض او كلم به الموتي بل لله الامر جميعا افلم يايس الذين امنوا ان لو يشا الله لهدي الناس جميعا ولا يزال الذين كفروا تصيبهم بما صنعوا قارعه او تحل قريبا من دارهم حتي ياتي وعد الله ان الله لا يخلف الميعاد

(13:41) اولم يروا انا ناتي الارض ننقصها من اطرافها والله يحكم لا معقب لحكمه وهو سريع الحساب

(14:22) وقال الشيطن لما قضي الامر ان الله وعدكم وعد الحق ووعدتكم فاخلفتكم وما كان لي عليكم من سلطن الا ان دعوتكم فاستجبتم لي فلا تلوموني ولوموا انفسكم ما انا بمصرخكم وما انتم بمصرخي اني كفرت بما اشركتمون من قبل ان الظلمين لهم عذاب اليم

(16:76) وضرب الله مثلا رجلين احدهما ابكم لا يقدر علي شي وهو كل علي موليه اينما يوجهه لا يات بخير هل يستوي هو ومن يامر بالعدل وهو علي صرط مستقيم

(17:33) ولا تقتلوا النفس التي حرم الله الا بالحق ومن قتل مظلوما فقد جعلنا لوليه سلطنا فلا يسرف في القتل انه كان منصورا

(18:18) وتحسبهم ايقاظا وهم رقود ونقلبهم ذات اليمين وذات الشمال وكلبهم بسط ذراعيه بالوصيد لو اطلعت عليهم لوليت منهم فرارا ولمليت منهم رعبا

(18:28) واصبر نفسك مع الذين يدعون ربهم بالغدوه والعشي يريدون وجهه ولا تعد

250

عيناك عنهم تريد زينه الحيوه الدنيا ولا تطع من اغفلنا قلبه عن ذكرنا واتبع هويه وكان امره فرطا

(18:45) واضرب لهم مثل الحيوه الدنيا كما انزلنه من السما فاختلط به نبات الارض فاصبح هشيما تذروه الريح وكان الله علي كل شي مقتدرا

(18:63) قال اريت اذ اوينا الي الصخره فاني نسيت الحوت وما انسينيه الا الشيطن ان اذكره واتخذ سبيله في البحر عجبا

(20:71) قال امنتم له قبل ان اذن لكم انه لكبيركم الذي علمكم السحر فلاقطعن ايديكم وارجلكم من خلاف ولاصلبنكم في جذوع النخل ولتعلمن اينا اشد عذابا وابقي

(20:130) فاصبر علي ما يقولون وسبح بحمد ربك قبل طلوع الشمس وقبل غروبها ومن اناي اليل فسبح واطراف النهار لعلك ترضي

(20:132) وامر اهلك بالصلوه واصطبر عليها لا نسلك رزقا نحن نرزقك والعقبه للتقوي

(20:135) قل كل متربص فتربصوا فستعلمون من اصحب الصرط السوي ومن اهتدي

(22:11) ومن الناس من يعبد الله علي حرف فان اصابه خير اطمان به وان اصابته فتنه انقلب علي وجهه خسر الدنيا والاخره ذلك هو الخسران المبين

(22:19) هذان خصمان اختصموا في ربهم فالذين كفروا قطعت لهم ثياب من نار يصب من فوق روسهم الحميم

(22:54) وليعلم الذين اوتوا العلم انه الحق من ربك فيومنوا به فتخبت له قلوبهم وان الله لهاد الذين امنوا الي صرط مستقيم

(23:27) فاوحينا اليه ان اصنع الفلك باعيننا ووحينا فاذا جا امرنا وفار التنور فاسلك فيها من كل زوجين اثنين واهلك الا من سبق عليه القول منهم ولا تخطبني في الذين ظلموا انهم مغرقون

(24:31) وقل للمومنت يغضضن من ابصرهن ويحفظن فروجهن ولا يبدين زينتهن الا ما ظهر منها وليضربن بخمرهن علي جيوبهن ولا يبدين زينتهن الا لبعولتهن او ابايهن او ابا بعولتهن او ابنايهن او

ابنا بعولتهن او اخونهن او بني اخونهن او بني اخوتهن او نسايهن او ما ملكت ايمنهن او التبعين غير اولي الاربه من الرجال او الطفل الذين لم يظهروا علي عورت النسا ولا يضربن بارجلهن ليعلم ما يخفين من زينتهن وتوبوا الي الله جميعا ايه المومنون لعلكم تفلحون

(24:41) الم تر ان الله يسبح له من في السموت والارض والطير صفت كل قد علم صلاته وتسبيحه والله عليم بما يفعلون

(24:56) واقيموا الصلوه واتوا الزكوه واطيعوا الرسول لعلكم ترحمون

(24:58) يايها الذين امنوا ليستذنكم الذين ملكت ايمنكم والذين لم يبلغوا الحلم منكم ثلث مرت من قبل صلوه الفجر وحين تضعون ثيابكم من الظهيره ومن بعد صلوه العشا ثلث عورت لكم ليس عليكم ولا عليهم جناح بعدهن طوفون عليكم بعضكم علي بعض كذلك يبين الله لكم الايت والله عليم حكيم

(24:61) ليس علي الاعمي حرج ولا علي الاعرج حرج ولا علي المريض حرج ولا علي انفسكم ان تاكلوا من بيوتكم او بيوت ابايكم او بيوت امهتكم او بيوت اخونكم او بيوت اخوتكم او بيوت اعممكم او بيوت عمتكم او بيوت اخولكم او بيوت خلتكم او ما ملكتم مفاتحه او صديقكم ليس عليكم جناح ان تاكلوا جميعا او اشتاتا فاذا دخلتم بيوتا فسلموا علي انفسكم تحيه من عند الله مبركه طيبه كذلك يبين الله لكم الايت لعلكم تعقلون

(26:49) قال امنتم له قبل ان اذن لكم انه لكبيركم الذي علمكم السحر فلسوف تعلمون لاقطعن ايديكم وارجلكم من خلاف ولاصلبنكم اجمعين

(27:59) قل الحمد لله وسلم علي عباده الذين اصطفي الله خير اما يشركون

(28:10) واصبح فواد ام موسي فرغا ان كادت لتبدي به لولا ان ربطنا علي قلبها لتكون من المومنين

(28:19) فلما ان اراد ان يبطش بالذي هو عدو لهما قال يموسي اتريد ان تقتلني كما قتلت نفسا بالامس ان تريد الا ان تكون

251

جبارا في الارض وما تريد ان تكون من المصلحين

(28:23) ولما ورد ما مدين وجد عليه امه من الناس يسقون ووجد من دونهم امراتين تذودان قال ما خطبكما قالتا لا نسقي حتي يصدر الرعا وابونا شيخ كبير

(28:38) وقال فرعون يايها الملا ما علمت لكم من اله غيري فاوقد لي ياهمن علي الطين فاجعل لي صرحا لعلي اطلع الي اله موسي واني لاظنه من الكذبين

(28:82) واصبح الذين تمنوا مكانه بالامس يقولون ويكان الله يبسط الرزق لمن يشا من عباده ويقدر لولا ان من الله علينا لخسف بنا ويكانه لا يفلح الكفرون

(30:48) الله الذي يرسل الريح فتثير سحابا فيبسطه في السما كيف يشا ويجعله كسفا فتري الودق يخرج من خلله فاذا اصاب به من يشا من عباده اذا هم يستبشرون

(33:71) يصلح لكم اعملكم ويغفر لكم ذنوبكم ومن يطع الله ورسوله فقد فاز فوزا عظيما

(35:11) والله خلقكم من تراب ثم من نطفه ثم جعلكم ازوجا وما تحمل من انثي ولا تضع الا بعلمه وما يعمر من معمر ولا ينقص من عمره الا في كتب ان ذلك علي الله يسير

(38:22) اذ دخلوا علي داود ففزع منهم قالوا لا تخف خصمان بغي بعضنا علي بعض فاحكم بيننا بالحق ولا تشطط واهدنا الي سوا الصرط

(38:24) قال لقد ظلمك بسوال نعجتك الي نعاجه وان كثيرا من الخلطا ليبغي بعضهم علي بعض الا الذين امنوا وعملوا الصلحت وقليل ما هم وظن داود انما فتنه فاستغفر ربه وخر راكعا واناب

(39:6) خلقكم من نفس وحده ثم جعل منها زوجها وانزل لكم من الانعم ثمنيه ازوج يخلقكم في بطون امهتكم خلقا من بعد خلق في ظلمت ثلث ذلكم الله ربكم له الملك لا اله الا هو فاني تصرفون

(40:64) الله الذي جعل لكم الارض قرارا والسما بنا وصوركم فاحسن صوركم ورزقكم من

الطيبت ذلكم الله ربكم فتبارك الله رب العلمين

(40:78) ولقد ارسلنا رسلا من قبلك منهم من قصصنا عليك ومنهم من لم نقصص عليك وما كان لرسول ان ياتي بايه الا باذن الله فاذا جا امر الله قضي بالحق وخسر هنالك المبطلون

(42:52) وكذلك اوحينا اليك روحا من امرنا ما كنت تدري ما الكتب ولا الايمن ولكن جعلنه نورا نهدي به من نشا من عبادنا وانك لتهدي الي صرط مستقيم

(46:30) قالوا يقومنا انا سمعنا كتبا انزل من بعد موسي مصدقا لما بين يديه يهدي الي الحق والي طريق مستقيم

(47:15) مثل الجنه التي وعد المتقون فيها انهر من ما غير اسن وانهر من لبن لم يتغير طعمه وانهر من خمر لذه للشربين وانهر من عسل مصفي ولهم فيها من كل الثمرت ومغفره من ربهم كمن هو خلد في النار وسقوا ما حميما فقطع امعاهم

(47:32) ان الذين كفروا وصدوا عن سبيل الله وشاقوا الرسول من بعد ما تبين لهم الهدي لن يضروا الله شيا وسيحبط اعملهم

(48:29) محمد رسول الله والذين معه اشدا علي الكفار رحما بينهم تريهم ركعا سجدا يبتغون فضلا من الله ورضونا سيماهم في وجوههم من اثر السجود ذلك مثلهم في التوريه ومثلهم في الانجيل كزرع اخرج شطه فازره فاستغلظ فاستوي علي سوقه يعجب الزراع ليغيظ بهم الكفار وعد الله الذين امنوا وعملوا الصلحت منهم مغفره واجرا عظيما

(49:7) واعلموا ان فيكم رسول الله لو يطيعكم في كثير من الامر لعنتم ولكن الله حبب اليكم الايمن وزينه في قلوبكم وكره اليكم الكفر والفسوق والعصيان اوليك هم الرشدون

(57:25) لقد ارسلنا رسلنا بالبينت وانزلنا معهم الكتب والميزان ليقوم الناس بالقسط وانزلنا الحديد فيه باس شديد ومنفع للناس وليعلم الله من ينصره ورسله بالغيب ان الله قوي عزيز

(72:28) ليعلم ان قد ابلغوا رسلت ربهم واحاط بما لديهم واحصي كل شي عددا

(73:20) ان ربك يعلم انك تقوم ادني من ثلثي اليل ونصفه وثلثه وطايفه من الذين معك والله يقدر اليل والنهار علم ان لن تحصوه فتاب عليكم فاقروا ما تيسر من القران علم ان سيكون منكم مرضي واخرون يضربون في الارض يبتغون من فضل الله واخرون يقتلون في سبيل الله فاقروا ما تيسر منه واقيموا الصلوه واتوا الزكوه واقرضوا الله قرضا حسنا وما تقدموا لانفسكم من خير تجدوه عند الله هو خيرا واعظم اجرا واستغفروا الله ان الله غفور رحيم

(58:4) فمن لم يجد فصيام شهرين متتابعين من قبل ان يتماسا فمن لم يستطع فاطعام ستين مسكينا ذلك لتومنوا بالله ورسوله وتلك حدود الله وللكفرين عذاب اليم

(61:14) يايها الذين امنوا كونوا انصار الله كما قال عيسي ابن مريم للحواريين من انصاري الي الله قال الحواريون نحن انصار الله فامنت طايفه من بني اسريل وكفرت طايفه فايدنا الذين امنوا علي عدوهم فاصبحوا ظهرين

(65:1) يايها النبي اذا طلقتم النسا فطلقوهن لعدتهن واحصوا العده واتقوا الله ربكم لا تخرجوهن من بيوتهن ولا يخرجن الا ان ياتين بفحشه مبينه وتلك حدود الله ومن يتعد حدود الله فقد ظلم نفسه لا تدري لعل الله يحدث بعد ذلك امرا

It is noteworthy that the number of verses that contain ALL the initals are exactly equal to the number of chapters in the Quran, 114. There are perhaps even more examples of an interlocking pattern. For instance, the chapter/verse numbers of the first verse (2:19) and the last one (73:20) add up to 114, the number of the verses that contain all initial letters: 2 + 19 + 73 + 20 = 114. Of course, this last example is anecdotal and it might be insignificant within the system..

We know that the 19-lettered Bismillah contains 10 different letters while repeating 9 of the letters. All except one of the 10 different letters are used in the initals of some suras. The only letter that does not belong to the initials is its first letter, ب B. Now, if we check these 114 verses, we will learn that 112 of them contain the letter ب B. We already know that 112 out of 114 chapters in the Quran start with unnumbered Bismillah formulas. Mirroring the same ratio, 112 out of these 114 verses contain all the letters of Bismillah. The verses that do not contain the letter B are 2:220 and 24:56, but their numbers, however, do not add up to a consistent pattern.

As it seems, these 114 verses numerically connect the initial letters, chapters and the first and most frequent verse of the Quran.

While writing these lines, I wondered about the frequency of the word Allah (God) in these 114 verses and I learned that it came out to exactly 152 (19x8). However, when I checked the total number of letters, 16078, it did not fit the pattern. It might be due to problems related to the letter ا A, which were liberally added to the text of the Quran to accommodate non-Arabs in reading the Quran properly. We do not know yet.

While at it, I decided to find the frequency of each letter in the entire Quran. I had received a few lists from others, but they contained characters not found in original manuscripts. So, I decided to eliminate all the later orthographical innovations that were added to the text of the Quran decades after Prophet Muhammad's departure, such as *hamzas*, dagger *alifs*, *maddas*, diacritical marks (vowel markings), and other ornamental junk, such as butterfly, bird or worm-like squiggles and doodles. Ironically, these ornamental junk, which was supposedly invented to help non-Arabic readers, only help to intimidate novices from recognizing the 28 letters!

After deleting 9:128-129, I counted each letter by the FIND and REPLACE function of MS Word, replacing each letter with its colored version. At the end, the color of the entire text changed, and I was sure that I had counted each and every letter in the Quran. Here is the raw count of frequencies of all letters in the Quran. A more accurate count of letter *Alif* is still pending further research.

The frequency of 14 Arabic Initial Letters in each chapter of the Quran

Ch	ا	ه	ح	ط	ي	ك	ل	م	ن	س	ع	ص	ق	ر	Sum	Sum (28)
1	22	5	5	2	14	3	22	15	11	3	6	2	1	8	119	139
2	4217	1414	330	99	1869	832	3202	2195	2020	452	797	155	553	876	19011	25632
3	2354	765	173	50	1156	485	1892	1249	1233	228	383	88	306	510	10872	14624
4	2682	884	198	65	1296	582	1959	1306	1335	307	404	122	255	491	11886	15956
5	2044	618	173	52	969	384	1464	1042	975	215	338	74	265	381	8994	11911
6	1925	680	162	52	1009	468	1448	1061	1011	213	369	69	271	506	9244	12437
7	2347	734	166	56	1050	466	1530	1164	1304	300	400	97	356	534	10504	14090
8	829	289	54	22	453	200	657	458	438	71	162	29	109	187	3958	5318
9	1658	733	135	34	805	297	1331	954	872	191	306	62	214	406	7998	10761
10	1225	353	100	17	602	260	913	654	690	130	211	32	181	257	5625	7442
11	1280	385	88	28	656	256	795	702	634	123	244	60	180	325	5756	7652
12	1237	381	103	19	613	219	812	491	633	167	218	61	193	257	5404	7144
13	556	201	44	12	274	104	480	260	230	71	99	20	87	137	2575	3466
14	554	159	35	11	270	113	452	306	278	77	95	24	57	160	2591	3480
15	461	115	44	11	213	85	323	257	320	67	80	23	83	96	2178	2816
16	1148	445	91	25	595	263	989	688	644	139	230	33	131	289	5710	7661
17	1127	279	90	29	482	258	748	444	531	148	187	31	155	301	4810	6499
18	1101	365	107	39	482	173	663	493	509	124	206	45	151	277	4735	6444
19	658	175	65	13	343	137	389	290	341	66	117	26	86	169	2875	3854
20	869	251	77	28	502	180	587	379	399	120	172	35	162	212	3973	5307
21	791	299	77	17	337	156	542	400	511	100	150	32	105	190	3707	4944
22	805	322	59	30	473	154	691	424	389	95	164	43	98	204	3951	5215
23	681	246	63	17	291	130	471	386	428	67	129	20	109	183	3221	4373
24	830	353	85	24	494	180	721	483	435	90	179	33	61	176	4144	5615
25	684	164	46	11	302	125	448	246	283	82	109	18	89	194	2801	3805
26	900	200	61	33	463	186	613	484	603	94	204	25	133	218	4217	5536
27	770	267	54	27	364	140	532	399	423	94	134	26	120	194	3544	4698
28	949	317	73	19	518	178	666	460	565	102	177	39	147	218	4428	5810
29	715	228	52	17	321	127	554	344	408	71	114	25	92	118	3186	4219
30	496	172	45	9	289	120	394	317	276	71	93	16	77	142	2517	3407
31	340	125	32	6	175	69	297	173	154	38	63	20	31	91	1614	2140
32	245	76	13	2	112	46	155	158	159	32	45	8	38	66	1155	1542
33	983	311	68	24	459	197	712	421	507	92	151	30	111	195	4261	5637
34	577	148	38	10	300	115	419	290	289	60	114	12	94	153	2619	3529
35	524	178	43	8	255	108	399	253	235	67	78	20	42	159	2369	3178
36	482	165	42	14	237	77	330	312	302	48	83	22	72	123	2309	3007
37	615	184	58	21	280	98	447	319	434	73	111	34	80	129	2883	3809
38	554	142	54	20	188	88	333	209	258	54	98	29	74	127	2228	3010
39	724	289	63	11	395	143	627	370	381	95	125	22	115	172	3532	4760
40	816	229	64	12	406	187	627	380	404	100	142	33	107	211	3718	5003
41	568	173	48	8	286	86	358	276	296	65	102	19	81	118	2484	3301
42	533	194	53	10	340	93	428	300	257	54	98	28	57	141	2586	3450
43	531	209	44	10	256	112	374	324	330	72	121	17	84	133	2617	3527
44	234	67	16	5	121	50	140	150	155	23	47	4	35	63	1110	1458
45	323	111	31	3	182	68	245	200	151	40	60	9	36	63	1522	2033
46	444	128	36	4	214	77	292	225	216	48	79	20	73	98	1954	2621
47	385	157	25	16	160	75	303	226	177	36	73	16	38	95	1782	2379
48	361	147	33	9	196	83	323	205	188	53	82	13	47	98	1838	2475
49	265	69	22	6	123	49	197	135	124	30	43	13	32	46	1154	1512
50	209	63	28	6	143	45	170	120	113	28	45	12	57	54	1065	1492
51	231	72	19	7	117	39	162	147	144	37	39	9	46	67	1136	1529
52	181	71	19	7	96	41	118	150	118	27	38	13	28	60	967	1312
53	266	83	18	7	131	33	151	112	114	30	34	3	17	47	1046	1424
54	211	67	23	8	83	57	123	111	122	33	53	13	48	108	1060	1457
55	343	44	15	10	99	84	142	112	143	30	18	7	22	87	1156	1604
56	262	59	43	7	104	49	177	178	202	23	44	17	35	64	1264	1711
57	382	137	29	5	203	74	317	218	178	47	61	12	49	120	1832	2494

58	322	132	31	8	170	48	259	172	163	39	54	12	27	53	**1490**	2010
59	315	128	25	4	146	44	274	151	156	35	**38**	**19**	44	79	1458	1932
60	251	84	22	3	127	66	174	143	135	24	33	6	27	52	1147	1538
61	141	56	15	4	92	26	126	78	79	22	18	9	**19**	43	728	955
62	127	44	12	0	67	24	**114**	74	49	9	16	3	14	24	577	768
63	116	54	8	1	55	24	118	66	70	22	20	5	23	28	610	799
64	169	54	18	4	80	35	147	93	68	20	33	11	14	42	788	1085
65	182	88	25	3	85	28	156	79	**95**	28	44	3	28	52	896	1189
66	174	63	18	2	94	32	118	87	99	11	33	8	17	50	806	1086
67	206	60	17	6	118	47	146	112	99	28	36	16	36	72	999	1335
68	180	**57**	21	11	96	53	133	123	**133**	26	42	15	21	50	961	1279
69	178	87	22	9	101	34	117	92	74	22	**38**	8	29	40	851	1126
70	**133**	58	12	2	94	20	100	101	81	15	**38**	11	16	39	720	966
71	189	35	5	5	56	32	110	80	61	21	25	4	21	62	706	966
72	219	60	18	8	64	**19**	119	74	**114**	27	37	8	25	50	842	1108
73	157	45	7	5	67	24	107	55	59	18	20	8	24	49	645	859
74	165	50	12	3	83	44	108	74	79	23	22	8	25	70	766	1034
75	112	34	7	2	67	16	84	43	54	26	16	4	27	34	526	683
76	202	64	14	12	92	37	**95**	77	87	32	26	4	15	67	824	1084
77	111	18	5	4	86	37	108	77	68	9	22	7	18	34	604	834
78	177	20	14	3	46	26	74	55	62	17	**19**	7	17	28	565	785
79	150	58	14	7	69	23	70	51	47	20	**19**	2	11	43	584	781
80	89	52	7	3	48	21	39	46	34	11	13	6	13	32	414	557
81	87	11	10	4	23	9	49	30	31	17	12	3	8	20	314	444
82	62	7	5	1	32	18	35	30	24	7	8	2	3	21	255	345
83	126	28	8	2	75	32	80	66	71	15	18	1	13	32	567	759
84	85	24	10	2	34	11	43	30	32	15	8	3	15	26	338	455
85	70	25	11	2	37	8	61	41	29	3	14	2	6	17	326	478
86	51	13	3	2	18	7	37	22	17	6	5	4	9	17	211	268
87	48	13	9	0	42	9	**38**	15	14	11	5	4	6	21	235	312
88	61	30	6	3	45	10	39	29	24	11	18	5	3	**19**	303	397
89	105	21	9	4	**57**	22	70	35	24	9	16	5	10	33	420	592
90	63	21	11	1	26	8	**38**	30	25	8	7	6	10	12	266	354
91	51	29	5	2	**19**	3	24	**19**	9	9	4	0	10	9	193	268
92	58	15	5	1	41	6	43	16	23	13	8	2	5	14	250	331
93	31	6	4	1	20	9	22	13	5	4	4	0	2	10	131	183
94	**19**	2	3	0	5	9	11	6	9	5	7	2	1	15	94	121
95	28	5	6	1	15	4	25	14	18	7	2	1	3	6	135	175
96	58	13	2	3	31	10	42	16	25	9	12	3	8	16	248	300
97	**19**	10	4	1	11	3	23	12	8	2	1	0	3	12	109	131
98	65	32	7	1	37	15	49	32	35	2	7	4	4	21	311	413
99	37	11	4	0	13	1	22	14	7	3	3	1	4	15	135	175
100	27	9	7	1	14	2	22	12	11	3	6	3	3	12	132	183
101	34	16	3	0	13	6	15	**19**	11	2	5	0	4	10	138	177
102	16	3	4	0	12	5	23	16	12	4	7	0	3	7	112	141
103	20	1	4	0	3	0	14	5	6	3	2	5	1	5	69	89
104	23	16	5	3	11	3	24	18	6	2	6	1	1	4	123	152
105	13	6	4	1	12	5	18	12	2	3	5	2	0	8	91	115
106	14	6	3	1	7	0	13	10	4	1	3	1	1	5	69	92
107	18	5	3	1	18	3	20	12	12	3	6	2	0	4	107	131
108	12	2	3	1	3	4	8	3	6	1	1	1	0	6	51	61
109	22	2	2	0	6	3	12	12	10	1	8	0	1	3	82	114
110	20	5	5	0	5	2	11	4	7	4	0	1	0	6	70	98
111	17	8	5	1	8	1	11	10	5	4	1	1	0	4	76	100
112	9	5	4	0	4	2	16	7	2	1	0	1	1	2	54	66
113	14	1	4	0	2	0	10	8	6	4	2	0	6	7	64	90
114	21	3	2	0	4	1	16	6	10	11	1	1	1	5	82	99
All	52973	17302	4361	1273	25848	10493	38534	27061	27375	6121	9398	2071	7032	12621	242463	324617

256

The frequency of 14 Arabic NON-Initial Letters in each chapter of the Quran

Ch	ب	ج	د	و	ز	ف	ش	ت	ث	خ	ذ	ض	ظ	غ	Sum
1	4	0	4	4	0	0	0	3	0	0	1	2	0	2	20
2	919	200	458	2129	107	751	168	970	128	191	330	133	62	75	6621
3	575	93	252	1188	67	396	86	557	52	104	218	66	36	62	3752
4	479	136	301	1365	51	503	82	561	75	128	181	101	45	62	4070
5	395	93	231	951	57	291	63	392	59	85	182	53	18	47	2917
6	454	117	199	1023	66	294	132	404	58	75	207	66	48	50	3193
7	509	165	246	1128	41	357	83	466	61	129	229	62	43	67	3586
8	174	38	87	489	23	153	27	162	18	34	95	27	8	25	1360
9	347	101	206	1013	53	304	48	303	31	86	145	61	28	37	2763
10	239	83	126	552	26	216	42	253	30	40	115	43	32	20	1817
11	284	79	146	613	35	186	43	235	32	57	96	32	24	34	1896
12	270	80	141	487	34	198	42	233	29	71	81	32	14	28	1740
13	152	35	77	278	21	81	22	94	16	23	47	24	6	15	891
14	135	34	73	257	21	83	25	114	17	31	53	22	11	13	889
15	101	43	41	200	19	64	16	73	4	24	22	14	9	8	638
16	270	71	123	630	45	193	64	239	45	72	122	32	22	23	1951
17	259	85	143	496	38	168	42	202	27	61	87	44	16	21	1689
18	272	89	170	419	33	174	47	225	41	49	106	31	17	36	1709
19	155	42	98	270	19	75	35	143	19	31	54	17	5	16	979
20	180	63	103	354	30	184	32	184	23	59	65	35	5	17	1334
21	162	54	97	396	17	145	29	157	13	34	76	26	17	14	1237
22	179	55	96	388	26	142	34	134	27	40	89	27	13	14	1264
23	167	39	60	354	17	135	29	148	31	49	72	20	13	18	1152
24	209	58	88	474	33	132	44	199	20	47	85	38	17	27	1471
25	137	54	64	339	21	73	27	108	20	33	87	23	9	9	1004
26	190	60	51	439	40	142	24	166	29	38	85	20	17	18	1319
27	153	55	98	346	19	116	37	176	12	35	56	24	16	11	1154
28	170	72	124	424	19	150	33	214	16	38	52	29	16	25	1382
29	149	47	64	361	21	101	21	121	18	30	67	16	8	9	1033
30	111	25	51	280	15	110	26	112	27	25	59	30	11	8	890
31	76	19	46	152	14	53	18	64	9	21	20	13	7	14	526
32	51	23	25	121	8	46	7	46	6	12	29	8	4	1	387
33	163	62	105	491	32	122	28	180	14	39	81	24	17	18	1376
34	142	39	76	269	30	98	28	86	14	14	67	25	8	14	910
35	104	38	63	224	30	93	24	87	13	29	58	20	8	18	809
36	72	36	50	224	18	70	27	82	14	28	45	15	5	12	698
37	156	45	59	273	23	112	19	104	12	24	57	14	16	12	926
38	148	36	69	198	20	76	20	68	9	37	62	17	7	15	782
39	178	49	88	340	34	122	34	161	29	50	88	32	10	13	1228
40	212	41	115	373	23	149	27	142	23	33	91	26	11	19	1285
41	96	29	68	252	23	92	30	98	12	25	56	16	10	10	817
42	130	32	64	276	22	84	38	82	13	15	57	23	14	14	864
43	141	44	63	285	11	94	21	112	14	32	55	24	11	3	910
44	62	15	15	117	10	32	9	46	5	7	19	4	2	5	348
45	70	19	21	158	16	43	7	95	10	16	30	13	6	7	511
46	95	25	57	206	13	64	13	91	7	16	48	18	4	10	667
47	73	13	35	198	9	73	10	82	12	16	43	18	4	11	597
48	71	30	59	201	18	63	17	83	9	17	33	9	12	15	637
49	53	11	17	131	3	34	5	55	6	12	10	9	4	8	358
50	77	23	58	109	7	42	13	40	1	16	23	6	5	7	427
51	37	21	18	130	5	62	4	53	4	14	33	4	2	6	393
52	64	10	17	119	4	34	9	45	5	5	20	4	1	8	345
53	44	12	28	120	16	37	14	40	10	7	23	9	4	14	378
54	59	19	47	98	11	50	14	36	2	7	42	6	1	5	397
55	125	27	7	68	7	68	9	62	3	15	45	7	1	4	448
56	62	20	18	152	13	40	21	60	15	10	16	7	9	4	447
57	89	26	37	227	12	72	12	83	13	16	30	25	8	12	662

257

58	63	24	36	187	13	45	18	63	10	12	36	5	3	5	**520**
59	65	23	31	163	10	49	17	45	6	21	29	5	4	6	**474**
60	51	19	30	140	5	41	4	58	2	9	17	4	2	9	**391**
61	31	7	19	81	5	25	3	29	0	3	15	1	5	3	**227**
62	18	3	12	63	7	18	3	27	7	4	16	8	3	2	**191**
63	15	9	12	72	4	25	3	21	1	8	13	2	0	4	**189**
64	39	6	15	111	6	36	6	36	3	7	16	6	2	8	**297**
65	35	15	32	75	6	27	9	48	6	10	15	9	4	2	**293**
66	44	14	19	77	5	24	3	50	4	8	11	8	6	7	**280**
67	49	16	17	95	10	45	13	36	1	9	32	6	1	6	**336**
68	56	13	28	97	4	28	5	38	6	9	19	4	3	8	**318**
69	37	9	12	83	3	38	6	35	7	14	17	6	3	5	**275**
70	31	15	19	83	4	23	7	19	2	10	23	3	3	4	**246**
71	28	19	25	88	4	18	2	34	6	10	10	6	2	8	**260**
72	37	17	54	72	3	25	12	17	1	5	7	6	5	5	**266**
73	23	10	11	71	3	25	6	26	6	8	12	7	1	5	**214**
74	33	8	26	66	3	33	14	36	10	6	25	5	1	2	**268**
75	30	10	6	44	2	19	1	15	5	4	15	1	4	1	**157**
76	36	14	18	79	9	26	17	24	6	8	15	5	2	1	**260**
77	23	12	9	73	1	29	7	28	4	3	36	1	3	1	**230**
78	40	19	11	61	6	23	5	27	3	6	12	2	2	3	**220**
79	27	11	16	42	4	29	10	20	4	12	14	3	1	4	**197**
80	20	6	5	32	3	22	9	18	4	6	9	4	1	4	**143**
81	16	9	4	36	2	8	11	20	1	1	19	2	0	1	**130**
82	15	3	8	22	0	13	2	12	3	2	7	0	1	2	**90**
83	29	8	5	69	3	19	2	19	5	3	20	4	5	1	**192**
84	25	2	5	37	0	13	3	16	1	1	10	1	2	1	**117**
85	15	7	22	53	3	11	8	14	3	1	12	1	1	1	**152**
86	7	4	9	15	1	8	0	4	1	3	2	1	2	0	**57**
87	9	4	4	18	1	13	3	6	3	6	9	0	0	1	**77**
88	14	6	1	23	1	16	2	11	4	2	6	4	1	3	**94**
89	26	9	19	39	1	23	2	20	6	4	18	4	0	1	**172**
90	21	2	14	24	0	6	2	9	1	1	7	0	0	1	**88**
91	11	2	6	24	1	10	3	3	2	2	7	2	0	2	**75**
92	9	4	5	21	2	5	3	13	1	3	9	1	1	4	**81**
93	5	4	6	15	0	9	0	5	1	2	1	3	0	1	**52**
94	4	0	1	5	1	6	1	1	0	0	3	2	1	2	**27**
95	6	1	6	11	1	5	0	4	1	1	3	0	0	1	**40**
96	14	2	6	7	1	2	1	9	0	3	6	0	0	2	**52**
97	3	1	4	3	2	4	1	2	0	1	1	0	0	0	**22**
98	14	5	9	28	2	10	4	17	0	5	6	2	0	0	**102**
99	4	1	2	7	4	1	2	5	4	3	5	2	0	0	**40**
100	12	1	7	10	0	7	2	3	2	2	3	1	0	1	**51**
101	3	1	2	13	2	7	3	3	3	1	0	1	0	0	**39**
102	2	1	0	9	1	2	0	9	4	0	1	0	0	0	**29**
103	4	0	0	10	0	1	0	3	0	1	1	0	0	0	**20**
104	3	1	10	5	2	3	0	2	0	1	2	0	0	0	**29**
105	7	4	1	2	0	6	0	3	0	0	0	1	0	0	**24**
106	4	1	1	5	0	5	2	2	0	1	2	0	0	0	**23**
107	3	0	2	7	0	2	0	3	0	0	6	1	0	0	**24**
108	3	0	0	3	0	1	1	1	1	0	0	0	0	0	**10**
109	9	0	10	8	0	1	0	4	0	0	0	0	0	0	**32**
110	5	2	3	6	0	5	0	4	0	1	1	0	0	1	**28**
111	9	1	3	3	0	1	0	5	0	0	1	0	0	1	**24**
112	1	0	5	5	0	1	0	0	0	0	0	0	0	0	**12**
113	4	0	3	5	0	3	4	1	1	1	3	0	0	1	**26**
114	3	1	1	7	0	1	1	0	0	1	2	0	0	0	**17**
All	11600	3316	5990	25669	1597	8743	2123	10514	1414	2497	4932	1686	852	1221	82154

258

I would like to share with you an interesting observation about the count of letters in a special section of chapter 74. Perhaps, it might provide some insight for further research on this issue.

From the beginning of Chapter 74, which is known as Hidden/Secret, from its first letter to the first letter of Tisata Ashara (Nineteen), there are exactly 361 (19x19) letters.

عليها تسعه عشر
On it is Nineteen

Letters	74:1-30 (Until the word "Nineteen")
12	ياايها المدثر
7	قم فانذر
8	وربك فكبر
10	وثيابك فطهر
11	والرجز فاهجر
13	ولا تمنن تستكثر
10	ولربك فاصبر
16	فاذا نقر في الناقور
16	فذلك يوميذ يوم عسير
17	علي الكفرين غير يسير
16	ذرني ومن خلقت وحيدا
17	وجعلت له مالا ممدودا
10	وبنين شهودا
13	ومهدت له تمهيدا
12	ثم يطمع ان ازيد
20	كلا انه كان لايتنا عنيدا
11	سارهقه صعودا
10	انه فكر وقدر
10	فقتل كيف قدر
11	ثم قتل كيف قدر
5	ثم نظر
9	ثم عبس وبسر
13	ثم ادبر واستكبر
19	فقال ان هذا الا سحر يوثر
16	ان هذا الا قول البشر
9	ساصليه سقر
13	وما ادريك ما سقر
12	لا تبقي ولا تذر
10	لواحه للبشر
5	عليها 19
361 19x19	

259

24

Judah ben Samuel HaChasid: A Witness from the Children of Israel

> 41:53 We will show them Our signs in the horizons, and within themselves, until it becomes clear to them that this is the truth. Is it not enough that your Lord is witness over all things?

In the 1980s, we learned that a German Jewish scholar, Judah ben Samuel HaChasid aka "Rabbi Judah the Pious," had discovered a mathematical system based on the number 19 in the original parts of the Old Testament in eleventh century. The Jewish diaspora in medieval Europe consisted of two groups: Sephardim and the Ashkenazim which gave birth to two of the most important pre—cabbalistic sages, Judah ben Samuel the Pious, and Eliezar of Worms. [137] Let's start with introductory information at *Wikipedia*:

> "Judah ben Samuel of Regensburg (born 1140 in Speyer - Feb. 22, 1217 in Regensburg), also called He-Hasid or 'the Pious' in Hebrew, was the initiator of the Chassidei Ashkenaz, a movement of Jewish mysticism in Germany. This movement is considered different from kabbalistic mysticism because it emphasises specific prayer and moral conduct. Judah settled in Regensburg in 1195. He wrote *Sefer Hasidim* (Book of the Pious) and *Sefer Hakavod* (Book of Glory), the latter has been lost and is only known by quotations that other authors have made from it. His most prominent students were Elazar Rokeach and Moses ben Jacob of Coucy. Rabbi Avraham Aharon Price, a 20th century rabbi, wrote a commentary on Sefer Hasidim of the same title. Rabbi Yehuda Hachasid is also the author of Sefer Gematriyot." [138]

The similarity and clarity of the discovery is impressive and it fulfills the prophecy of this verse. Judah ben Samuel's discovery of 19 in the original parts of the Old Testament, and his correction of the modern text via the code, together with a list of examples, was unveiled in an article authored by Joseph Dan and published by the University of California in 1978 under the title *Studies in Jewish Mysticism*. According to Dan's article, Judah or Yehuda claimed to have written eight volumes on the Code 19-based mathematical structure in the Hebrew Old Testament.

> "The people (Jews) in France made it a custom to add (in the morning prayer) the words: "'Ashrei temimei derekh (blessed are those who walk the righteous way)," and our Rabbi, the Pious, of blessed memory, wrote that they were completely and utterly wrong. It is all gross falsehood, because there are only nineteen times that the Holy Name is mentioned (in that portion of the morning prayer), . . . and similarly you find the word Elohim nineteen times in the pericope of Ve-'elleh shemot . . .
>
> Similarly, you find that Israel were called "sons" nineteen times, and there are many other examples. All these sets of nineteen are intricately intertwined, and they contain many secrets and esoteric meanings, which are contained in more than eight volumes. Therefore, anyone who has the fear of God in him will not listen to the words of the Frenchmen who add the verse "'Ashrei temimei derekh (blessed are those who walk in the paths of God's Torah, for according to their additions the Holy Name is mentioned twenty times . . . and this is a great mistake. Furthermore, in this section there are 152 words, but if you add" 'Ashrei temimei derekh" there are 158 words. This is nonsense, for it is a great and hidden secret why there should be 152 words . . .[139]

Can this be a simple coincidence? I will not be surprised if Sunni and Shiite scholars who reject the 19-based system attempt to create a conspiracy theory to cover the discovery of the same code in the Old Testament by a leading monotheist in the 11th Century, long before Rashad had discovered it in the Quran.

Let's now examine the verses of the Quran that prophesized Judah ben Samuel and the similarity of the Quran and the Old Testament in the context of "divine signs." The excerpt below is from the *Quran: a Reformist Translation*.

46:0	In the name of God, the Gracious, the Compassionate.
46:1	**H8M40***
46:2	The revelation of the book from God, the Noble, the Wise.
46:3	We did not create the heavens and the earth, and everything between them except with truth, and for an appointed time. Those who reject turn away from what they are being warned with.
46:4	Say, "Do you see those that you call on besides God? Show me what they have created on the earth, or do they have a share in the heavens? Bring me a book before this, or any trace of knowledge, if you are truthful."
46:5	Who is more astray than one who calls on others besides God that do not respond to him even till the day of resurrection? They are totally unaware of the calls to them!
46:6	At the time when people are gathered, they will be enemies for them, and they will reject their service.*
46:7	When Our clear signs are recited to them, those who rejected said of the truth that came to them: "This is evidently magic!"
46:8	Or do they say, "He fabricated this!" Say, "If I fabricated this, then you cannot protect me at all from God. He is fully aware of what you

261

say. He suffices as a witness between me and you. He is the Forgiver, the Compassionate."

46:9   Say, "I am no different from the other messengers, nor do I know what will happen to me or to you. I only follow what is inspired to me. I am no more than a clear warner."

Judah ben Samuel: A Witness from the Children of Israel

46:10   **Say, "Do you see that if it were from God, and you rejected it, and a witness from the Children of Israel testified to its similarity, and he has acknowledged, while you have turned arrogant? Surely, God does not guide the wicked people."***

46:11   Those who had rejected said regarding those who had acknowledged: "If it were any good, they would not have beaten us to it." When they are not able to be guided by it, they will say, "This is an old fabrication!"*

46:12   Before this was the book of Moses, as a role model and a mercy. This is an authenticating book in an Arabic tongue, so that you may warn those who have transgressed, and to give good news to the righteous.

46:13   Surely, those who said, "Our Lord is God," then they lead a righteous life, there is no fear for them, nor will they grieve.

46:14   These are the dwellers of Paradise, abiding therein, a reward for what they used to do.

Sunni and Shiite commentators of the past justifiably had difficulty in understanding the implication of 46:10. They wondered about this special witness. Who could it be? What was witnessed? Their first inclination was to consider the reference of "its" in 46:10 to be the Torah. They also had a hard time explaining the one witness, since the Torah was witnessed by more than one person. The Torah was given to Moses and Aaron and many from the Children of Israel who witnessed its message.[140] Besides, 46:10 comes as an answer to doubts about the Quran's divine origin, as is the case before verse 74:30.

Interestingly, Rashad did exactly what Judah ben Samuel had done. Rashad did not know about Judah's work until he received a copy of Studies in *Jewish Mysticism* in the 1980s. Rashad used the code for error correction, as Judah did centuries before him. Furthermore, Judah ben Samuel criticism of Talmud and considered its study to be waste of time is identical to Rashad's criticism of Hadith and its study.

The following verses are instructive:

20:133   They said, "If only he would bring us a sign from his Lord!" Did not **proof** come to them from what is in the previous book?*

20:134   If We had destroyed them with retribution before this, they would have said, "Our Lord, if only You had sent us a messenger so we could follow Your signs before we are humiliated and shamed!"

20:135   Say, "All are waiting, so wait, and you will come to know who the people upon the even path are and who are guided."

The truth-value of the Quran's message and its historical dimension provide evidence for its divine nature. Please note the word **proof** in verse 133. The occurrence of the singular word **bayyina** (evidence/proof) in the Quran being exactly 19 times and the existence of the code 19 in previous scriptures is another fulfillment of this verse.

A journal article by Eliezer Segal provides the following information about Judah the Pious:

> "The traditions surrounding the tagin were especially important to the Jewish pietist movement known as Hasidut Ashkenaz that flourished in Germany from the eleventh to the thirteenth centuries. The followers of this movement placed great emphasis on the mystical significance of words, and they meticulously reckoned the numerological values of each word in the prayer book. Evidently, the movement's founder Rabbi Judah the Pious composed a treatise entitled the Book of Wisdom in which he expounded the mysteries of the tagin. The colophon to that book aptly reflects the reverence in which the tagin were held by those circles:"

>> "It is forbidden to add to [the authorized list of tagin], nor may one omit even a single tag, since they are precisely as they were given at Mount Sinai. They have been passed down as an oral tradition by Elijah the Prophet to Ezra the High Priest. And the person who is punctilious about them will be blessed in this world and in the next. One must take great care not to diminish or to add even as much a hair's breadth, for several explanations and several mysteries can be derived from them, for each one contains several interpretations. Any Torah scroll that lacks them is not fit to be read from. Therefore, all God-fearing individuals should be scrupulous with regard to them, and their reward will be great from the God of Israel..."

>> "Maimonides also emphasized, in his rules for writing Torah scrolls, that the tagin should be written in their traditional manner."[141]

In 2008, I finally received good news. Daniel Abrams, together with Israel Ta-Shema had published the facsimile edition of the manuscript, *Sefer Gematriot*, ten years before through Cherub Press. I immediately purchased it online. I was so excited; I was looking for it since the 1980's. I took the book to a local synagogue and then to the professors of Hebrew language at the University of Arizona, but to no avail. They complained about its language. I am now looking for an expert to translate it.

25
A Unique Protection System

انا نحن نزلنا الذكر وانا له لحافظون (٩)

15:9   WE, it is WE indeed, yes it is WE who have sent down the Reminder, and surely it is WE who will preserve it.

If the Quran is the final testament from the Creator, then its perfect preservation is imperative. The most popular Quranic text is based on the orthographic standards imposed by Caliph Uthman in the *Hafs* tradition of recitation. Obviously, the Quran is not a manuscript made of ink and paper, but divine information expressed in Arabic, one of the human languages, and mathematics, the langue of the laws governing the universe. No wonder it is described as "clear revelations in the chest of those who have been given knowledge" (29:49). The mathematical system of the Quran not only provides extraordinary evidence for the Quran's divine authority, it also provides a protective system that testifies to its authenticity whilst guiding us to witness the original Quran despite spelling errors or human tampering with the manuscripts.

Thus...

Thus, with the discovery of the 19-based code prophecized in Chapter 74 of the Quran in 1974, a new era of empirical evidence has begun. As one of the functions of the number 19, our appreciation of the Quran and its promise of perfect preservation has also increased. Now we know by numbers—not the numbers of a particular group of people, but by mathematical evidence—that verses 9:128-129 in current manuscripts do not belong to the Quran. The translation of the inserted verses:

> "A messenger has come to you from yourselves, concerned over your suffering, anxious over you, towards those who acknowledge he is kind, merciful.

> "If they turn away, then say, 'God is enough for me, there is no god but He, in Him I put my trust and He is the Lord of the great throne.'"

Shallow believers might object to this assertion with a knee-jerk reaction by interpreting it as tampering with the Quran. But if they relax and ponder on the issue, they will realize that just the opposite is true. The Quranic code's exposition and rejection of verses 9:128-129 as un-Quranic material has the following roles.

1. This has led us to witness one of the functions of the numerical code. The protection or preservation of the Quran is not like any other book preserved by humans in museums or libraries, or like Rosetta Stone and the many documents protected by nature. Its preservation is unique. It is preserved for milleniums by its author through His control and wisdom. No wonder that the author of the Quran in a very short verse, 15:9, emphasizes the divine power several times as the protector and preserver of the Message.

   15:9   "WE, it is WE indeed, yes it is WE who have sent down the Reminder, and surely it is WE who will preserve it."

   The verse, through emphasizing God in relation to protection, rejects the orthodox belief and overweening trust in "holy people" for the preservation of the Quran. Besides, how can the author of any book protected by its zealot followers take credit for such a protection? Furthermore, what would be our answer if someone questioned the authenticity of the very verse promising its protection, that is 15:9?

2. It provides more examples of the numerical pattern.

3. It distinguishes between those who acknowledges the Quran because they follow their ancestors blindly and those who acknowledge the Quran because of the rational and empirical evidence provided. The hypocrites will follow the number of the crowd, while monotheists will witness and trust the number employed by God. True muslims prefer the testimony of the Quran to the testimony of their ancestors.

The QURAN is not corrected, since it cannot be added to nor substracted from. The Quran is under the protection of God through His promise and His design of the mathematical system. The Quran is not a book on paper but an order of letters and words and chapters. Anyone can add any statement to his manuscript or cut out or subtract any verse. Any group of people can publish a manuscript of Quran in Arabic orthography with verses even chapters subtracted and/or added. Neither letters nor words of the manuscript are divine; they belong to one of the human languages, Arabic. However, the *order* of the words and letters are the creation of the Omniscient Creator of the Universe. When the Creator, the Greatest Mathematician (*Sari-ul Hisab*) informed us about this *order* we became aware of the *divine essence* of the Quran. The Quran describes itself as *Kitabun Marqum*, that is, a Numerical Book (89:9, 20), and it is in the chest of those who have attained knowledge as much as it is inscribed in manusricpts (29:49).

Phyisical Evidence

The verses 9:128/9 have received our attention since the discovery of the code in 1974. It was the only exception where the attribute *Rahim* (Compassionate) was used for other than God; it was used for Muhammad. In all other verses the word Rahim was used 114 (19x6) times for God. However eleven years later we learned that Rashad's data contained a data error in the frequency of the word Allah (God). The first suspect was the end of chapter 9. The 2699 was one extra than the 2698 (19x142), the expected frequency. We had many indicators leading us to accept 2698 rather than 2699 as the accurate number for the frequency of the word God.

- The sum of all the verse numbers where the word God occurs is 118123 (19x6217). Adding the word God in 9:129 violates the system.

- The word God, from the beginning of Chapter 9 to its end occurs 1273 (19x67) times. If we add verse 9:129 this becomes 1274 and violates the system.

- The frequency of the word God from the first initialed chapter (2:1) to the beginning of the last initialed chapter (68:1) is 2641 (19x139). Adding the word God in 9:129 violates the system.

- Chapter 9 does not start with letters. When we study all the 85 chapters with no initials we see that 57 (19x3) of them contain the word God in them. The number of verses containing the word God is 1045 (19x55). Adding the word God in 9:129 violates the system.

- From the missing Bismillah (9:0) to the extra Bismillah (27:30), we find the word God occuring in 513 (19x27) verses. Adding the word God in 9:129 violates the system.

- The word "elah" (god) is mentioned in the Quran 95 (19x5) times. Adding the word "god" in 9:129 violates the system.

- The Quran contains 6234 numbered verses and 112 unnumbered verses (Bismillah formula with the exception of 1:1 and 27:30). Thus, there are total 6346 (19x334) verses in the Quran. 6+3+4+6=19. Adding 9:128-129 violates this.

- When we write the number of verses one by one after the total verses in each chapter until the last chapter (71234567......... 612345), we get a long number with 12692 digits. Not only is that very long number divisible by 19, the number of its digits too is divisible: 12692 (19x668). Adding 9:128-129 violates these occurrences.

266

These and similar numerical examples reject 9:128-129 as part of the Quran. Who can be better than the Designer of the Quran as witness?

The Smoke Rising from Sunni Tradition

According to the Sunni history books, during the reign of Caliph Uthman bin Affan, approximately twenty years after the departure of Muhammad, a group of scribes were commissioned to duplicate copies of the Quran to be sent to the neighboring countries. Those copies would be based on the original copy left from the time of Muhammad. The committee of scribes was supervised by Uthman bin Affan, Ali bin Abi Talip, Zayd bin Sabit, Ubayy bin Kab, Abdullah bin al-Zubayr, Said bin As, and Abdurrahman bin al-Haris bin Hisham. According to the story, Muhammad himself had left instructions for the placement of each chapter and verse. According to these sources, the last chapter revealed in Madina was Chapter 9. Only the very short Chapter 110 was revealed after chapter 9 in Mina.

According to the Quran, Muhammad was literate and most likely he was the first one who transferred the revelation of the Quran to paper. Furthermore, it was collected during his life time. We discussed these issues in the introduction and notes of the *Quran: a Reformist Translation*.

In order to provide you with some idea about the complicated stories regarding the compilation of the Quran, let me quote from a Shiite Scholar's article on the oldest manuscripts of the Quran[142]:

> "According to al-Ya'qubi twenty-five men from among the Quraysh and fifty from among the Ansar helped Zayd in this task,[143] among whom 'Abd Allah ibn al-Zubayr and 'Abd al-RaĤMaN ibn al-Harith ibn Hisham were permanent members of the committee."

> "According to al-Tamhid, the work was started by Zayd ibn Thabit along with some other;, but later Ubayy ibn Ka'b assumed responsibility for reading and Zayd for writing down."

> "In any case, the Qur'an was compiled in this manner and the compiled text was deposited first with Abu Bakr and after him with 'Umar and was a source of reference for the people. After the death of 'Umar, this compilation remained in the possession of Hafsah until the year 22/642, when differences of reading appeared during the reign. of 'Uthman. Thereupon, on the Caliph's order, the mushaf was taken from Hafsah for transcription, and from it Zayd ibn Thabit (who was the main scribe) prepared several copies with the help of 'Abd Allah ibn al-Zubayr, 'Abd al-RaĤMaN ibn Hisham (both members of the original committee that compiled the Qur'an) and Said ibn al-'As. While the original was returned to Hafsah, one of the copies was kept with the Caliph at Madinah and the rest were sent to major Islamic cities.[144] Thereafter, the handwritten compilations of the Qur'an were destroyed on the Caliph's order for the sake of eliminating differences among Muslims.[145]

> "The compilation written during Abu Bakr's days remained with Hafsah until the reign of Marwan ibn al-Hakam. Marwan wanted to burn it also, but Hafsah

refused to hand it over to him. He waited until her death and thereat destroyed that compilation also."[146]

"Thus the task of ensuring the uniformity of the Qur'an was carried out in the year 22/642,[147] though 'Abd Allah ibn Mas'ud refused to hand over his compilation to 'Uthman, who wanted to destroy it.[148] Similarly, the compilation made by 'Ali ibn Abi Talib (A) was retained by him and later preserved by his family."

After a few decades of civil war finally there was a period of peace occurred starting with Caliph Marwan bin Hakam (died 684). His first task was to burn the original manuscript of the Quran. He burned the manuscript written by Muhammad alleging the fear of "creating new controversies."[149] Any person with a sound mind should ask, "If Muhammad's version was the same as the circulated versions, why would Marwan destroy it?" Furthermore, many Muslims believe that his companions and their decendants preserved many of Muhammad's belongings, including his clothes and his teeth. Why would they allow his manuscript to be burned? The smoke of this report is just one of the many evidences supporting the Quranic thesis regarding its unique and perfect protection.

The First Spark and the Piles of Lies

The hearsay books have complicated stories about the transcription and collection of the Quran. According to *Bukhari* and Suyuti's *al-Itqan* along with many other (hi)story books, when the committee of scribes reached the chapter starting with *Baraah* (Ultimatum), they placed it after Chapter 8. However, according to those reports, a fellow named Khuzaima from Madina (Yathrib) suggested them to add a couple of verses that used two divine attributes for Muhammad: *Rahim* and *Rauf*. According to the Sunni sources, the scribes refused to add these two verses.[150] Khuzaima claimed that those verses belonged to the end of the Chapter 9 and were revealed in Mecca about ten years before. Accordingly, Chapter 9 would become the only chapter that was revealed backward and this alleged idiosyncracy is noted by some scribes in the introductory title of Chapter 9 with the statement: "The Chapter Towba is revealed in Madina, except the last two verses."

The scribes, according to the Sunni sources, initially rejected Khuzaima's testimony and demanded a second witness to corroborate his claims. According to the same sources, Khuzaima could not produce another trusthworthy witness, but another obscure sahaba from Medina showed up and came up with a very special case: "I heard the prophet Muhammad, peace bu upon hum, say that Khuzaima's testimony equals the testimony of two people." Reportedly, the testimony about Khuzaima's double-power was found credible and those two verses were added to the end of Chapter 9. Ironically, none of the prominent sahabas were found as trustworthy as Khuzaima ben Sabit al-Ansary who was a nobody except for this event. This story is so silly that it is screaming loudly regarding its fakery. A promiment Turkish theologian could not stop himself from questioning the story:

> "The people would come to Zaid ibn Thabit and he would only write a verse from two upright witnesses. Even though the end of Sura al-Baraa was not found except with Khuzaima ibn Thabit, he said: Write it, for God's messenger, peace and blessings be upon him, made his testimony as the testimony of two men. So it was written, even though Umar brought the verse of stoning and it was not written because he was alone."[151]

What? "The verse of stoning"?! It is fascinating to see the authenticity of one big lie is questioned by affirming a bigger lie which leads to a record-breaking supreme lie about a hungry holy goat eating the so-called 'verse of stoning'! It is one of the great wonders of the world that a billion people believe such ridiculous stories that make the Santa Clause story look like daily local news.

Of course, there are many questions regarding the story of reverse revelation, an obscure and dubious witness given the exceptional power of testimony, etc. How is it that the two verses allegedly revealed in Mecca ten years previous would be only found in the memory of a Madinan person who was not even in Mecca during the ten years of revelation there? Why has the testimony of none, including the four caliphs, equaled two individuals excepting a man named Khuzaima? Was Khuzaima a fictional character created by Hadith fabricators to suppress the controversy about 9:128-129? Who was the person who testified for double-testimony, whatever that means? Was his testimony also equal to two? How could this 1=2 nonsense fit in the Quran? Get a witness and get the second one free?! And we are expected to believe these stories and even more!

We are told to accept 9:128-129 as the record-breaking verses in terms of their exceptional nature in the Quran. They are exceptional, we are told, since they are revealed backwards. They are exceptional, we are told, since two of God's attributes are used in 9:128 for Muhammad. They are exceptional, we are told, since they are reported by a witness with the power of two witnesses!

The same Hadith books narrated other Hadiths about Ali bin Abi Talib's concern regarding distortion of the Quran through the addition of some verses. They report that Ali did not participate in the very important meeting after Muhammad's death, where promiment Muslims gathered to elect a leader after Muhammad. What could be Ali's justification for not attending such a crucial meeting? According to Hadiths, "People are adding to the Quran; I decided not to leave my home until I collect it in a book." Most of these reports are obviously lies, since there is both Quranic and historic evidence that the Quran was compiled before Muhammad's death. Why, then, were these stories fabricated? Was there a fire that produced smoke of confusing stories?

Ali's protest is mentioned in numerous Sunni books. Here, I would like to share with you the report narrated throuh Ikrima from Jelaluddin al-Suyuti's classic book, *Al-Itqan fi Ulum-il Quran* (*Precision and Mastery in the Sciences of the Quran*):

> "After Abu Bakr was elected as the successor Ali bin Abi Talib retired at his home. Some rumors reached Abu Bakr's ears alleging this seclusion to be due to Ali's displeasure with the results of election. Thus, Abu Bakr sent a messenger to Ali to investigate the rumors. "Are you protesting Abu Bakr's election?" he was asked. Ali responded, "No, by God." When the investigators asked Ali the reason for his confinement in his home, Ali explained: "I see that additions are being made to the Quran. I decided not to wear street clothes except for prayers until I compile the Quran."[152]

In page 28 of the same book, a report from *Zawaid al-Musnad* and *Ibn Mardawayh* narrated by Ubayy bin Kab provides more details on the subjcet:

> During the reign of Abu Bakr the Quran was compiled. When the scribes commissioned for the task came to the end of the chapter Baraa (Ultimatum), verse 9:127, they thought it to be the last verse. Upon that decision, Ubay bin Kab told them, "The prophet recited two more verses to me" and he started reciting 9:128 and 9:129. He added: "These two verses are the last revelations of the Quran."

Interestingly we meet the dubious Khuzaima onece again; this time in Hadith describing the events in the year 653 AD. This time, this name is invoked about another verse, perhaps to dissipate the doubts raised about 9:128-129. The following Hadith from Buhkari states:

> "So 'Uthman sent a message to Hafsa saying, 'Send us the manuscripts of the Quran so that we may compile the Quranic materials in perfect copies and return the manuscripts to you.' Hafsa sent it to Uthman. Uthman then ordered Zaid bin Thabit, Abdullah bin AzZubair, Said bin Al-As and Abdurrahman bin Harith bin Hisham to rewrite the manuscripts in perfect copies. Uthman said to the three Quraishi men, 'In case you disagree with Zaid bin Thabit on any point in the Qur'an, then write it in the dialect of Quraish, the Quran was revealed in their tongue.' They did so, and when they had written many copies, Uthman returned the original manuscripts to Hafsa. Uthman sent to every Muslim province one copy of what they had copied, and ordered that all the other Quranic materials, whether written in fragmentary manuscripts or whole copies, be burnt. Sad bin Thabit added, ' Verse from Surat Ahzab was missed by me when we copied the Quran and I used to hear Allah's Apostle reciting it. So we searched for it and found it with Khuzaima bin Thabit Al-Ansari. (That Verse was): *Among those who acknowledge are men who have been true in their covenant with Allah.*' (Quran 33:23)"[153]

We cannot trust these reports; however they are consistent. Regardless of the veracity of their details they signal a deep controversy regarding the protection of the Quran and conspiracy to add some verses to it. A critical study of the

270

Hadith and biographies of Muhammad may reveal the following facts along with the addition of the two fake verses into the manuscript.

1. Caliph Uthman was assassinated and Ali was elected as the fourth Caliph.

2. A war started between the supporters of the elected leader Ali and the supporters of the Umayyad dynasty. Numerous exaggerated rumors claiming additions to the Quran started to become circulated among the Shiite party and were transmitted secretly from generation to generation in accordance to Shiite *taqiyya* rules.

3. Ali was assassinated.

4. Muhammad's grandson Hussein together with his seventy supporters were massacred in Karbala by the Umayyad dynasty.

5. When the Umayyad and Abbasid rulers distorted the meaning of *jizya* (war reparations) thereby imposing an anti-Quranic tax over the People of the Book, many Christians and Jews were economically forced to convert to Islam. Those unwilling converts imported many of their religious stories, superstitions and culture by fabricating Hadith, which was once a very popular weapon to promote one's political, cultural, racial and religious agenda. (see *Manifesto for Islamic Reform* for detailed examples)

In the end, the reactionary forces won. None dared to publicly question 9:128-129. The currently accepted history of Islam reflects the ideas and agendas of the leaders and their clerical allies within the corrupt and oppressive two medieval Arab dynasties. Umayyad and Abbasid. After the conquest of Mecca, Arabian polytheists were defeated completely. Yet after the departure of Muhammad and assassination of his closest friends, they took their revenge and within a few centuries reversed the progressive and liberating message of the Quran. This time their idol was Muhammad himself. The first literary distortion of Muhammad's history started a century later by the historian Ibn Ishaq, and contiued with full speed two centuries later with Ibn Hanbal, Bukhari, and the rest of the Hadith compilers. With the rise of al-Gazzali, the reactionary and polytheistic forces using the power of the sultans declared victory over rationalist monotheists who rejected Hadith, sectarian jurisprudence and other religious nonsense.

Now we have proof that despite those fabricators of lies and their corrupt sultans, the Quran—that is the numerically coded book—is preserved in an extrordinary way, and the verses 9:128-129 do not belong in the Quran. We think that God, the Wise, allowed the falsifiers to add 9:128-129 to their manuscripts, to demonstrate that it is He, not people, who protected His own word despite the ingrates and the enemies of the Quran.

Contradictions and Hypocricy in Sunni and Shiite Theology

The Quran is in the heart of those who have attained knowledge (29:49). It is a *numerically structured book* and only honest people can witness it (83:9, 10, 20, 21). Even if polytheists insert man-made verses into it, the knowledgeable people would *know* the *ayat* (signs) of God. It is protected by God, letter by letter, word by word, through a numerical code that has a self-correction feature. Even if some would attempt to tamper with it or to duplicate erronous copies, the Quran is protected and will continue to be protected.

It is ironic that those who have added volumes of Hadith hearsay and sectarian jurisprudence to the teachings of the Quran, and those who claim *nash* (amendment and deletion) in the Quran, have the audacity to criticize us on this subject. The followers of Hadith and Sunna, by contradicting hundreds of verses, prove that they have no respect to the Quran. Furthermore, those who criticize our judgment based on a number supported by the Quran rely on a number that is rejected by the Quran: the number of people who believe the way they do!

The Quran repeatedly advises us to use our intellect, to reason, to be open-minded, to be the seekers of truth, to be philosophers, to be critical thinkers, and not to be the followers of our wishful thinking or a particular crowd. For instance, see 2:170, 171, 242, 269; 3:118, 190; 6:74-83; 7:169; 8:22; 10:42, 100; 11:51; 12:2, 111; 13:4, 19; 16:67; 21:10, 67; 23:80; 24:61; 29:63; 30:28; 38:29; 39:9, 18, 21; 40:54; 59:14. See also 6:110.

Besides ignoring the Quranic epistemology, the proponents of 9:128-129 ignore the reports of their own so-called *Sahih* (authentic) books regarding the authenticity of the Quran. According to the books of Hadith, Abdullah Ibn Masood was one of the top companions of the prophet Muhammad. His Hadith narrations are among Sunni Muslims' most cherished sources of jurisprudence. Many Hadith and narration books, including Bukhary and Ibn Hanbal, report that Ibn Masood had a personal copy of the Quran which did not contain the last two chapters. According to those books, he considered them merely prayers, not belonging to the Quran. According to the same Sunni sources, another companion of the prophet, Ubayy Ibn Kaab, also had a different personal Quran. Instead of subtracting two chapters like Ibn Masood, he added two chapters called *Sura Al-Hafd* and *Sura Al-Khal'*, and claimed that these were from the Quran (These "chapters" are still being recited by Hanafis in the *sala al-witr*, after night prayers.)

Today, thousands of copies of the Quran manuscript that do not contain 9:128-129 are circulating around the world. This should create problems for those whose idea of preservation is material rather than intellectual. If they think that thousands of manuscripts and thousands of adherents would not create any problem with the promise of 15:9, then why not think the same for the addition?

Code 19 has proven that falsehood might access manuscripts made of skin or paper but cannot access the divine message which is numerically structured. It is noteworthy that the proponents of the misspelling of the word *Bastata* of 7:69 fabricated a Hadith to support their erronous spelling. We noticed this spelling error with the aid of the numerical structure and after our investigation we discovered it to be supported by the Tashkent copy, an archeaological piece of evidence.

These are simple yet incontrovertible cases for the scientific aspect of Code 19 and the falsehoods of Hadith. They prove that the Quran is not preserved by people on skin and paper, but by God through a universally recognizable numerical design. This is a design that can be witnessed by people with good minds and with sincere intentions.

When I was studying the oldest available manuscripts, I came across a partial manuscript written on gazelle skin. It was huge, about two to three feet, and it was recorded as Fatih-18 in the world-famous Sulaimania Library. It was attributed to Ali bin Abi Talib, the fourth elected successor (Caliph) to Muhammad. I could not verify that official identification, but after studying the material and the orthography, I was convinced that it was one of the oldest manuscripts available and that it belonged to the first century H.E, or seventh century A.C. To my dismay, I discovered that the last verses of Chapter 9 were missing. The library officials described it as an historic loss. Since the size of the letters were very big, its pages contained less verses than the printed manuscripts. Thus, I was not able to calculate the average number of words per page and come up with an educated assessment whether the original manuscript did or did not include 9:128-129.

Could all these evidences and events be a coincidence? What about the exaggerated belief among Shiites regarding the tampering with the Quran and the belief that the Mahdi will produce the real Quran? Shouldn't we reflect on the "NEW controversies," Marwan's justification for burning the original manuscript? What can we say about one extra frequency of the word God, and again the only case where God's two attributes, *Rauf* (Kind) and *Rahim* (Compassionate) are used for the Prophet Muhammad? Is it mere luck that without these two, we get 6346 (19x334) verses in the Quran? What about the fact that Chapter 9 is the only chapter that does not start with a Bismillah? Could it be that the devils, who wished to carve a new idol out of Muhammad, picked the only chapter without Bismillah, hoping that it does not have protection against their Trojan verses? Is it a coincidence that there are plenty of Hadith reports defending these two verses? What could be the reason for reports regarding Ali's concern about additions to the Quran to a degree that he ignored participation in the leadership election? Are all these numerical anomalies and stories coincidence?

The story of a precious crown

Assume that you have a precious crown that has been inherited within your family for centuries. This priceless golden crown with numerous diamonds has a strange inscription on it: "This is a unique crown and it is protected by its maker from tampering, from alteration, addition or subtraction. Fraudsters cannot touch this crown!" None of your parents, uncles, aunts, brothers or sisters had any question regarding this allegedly hoax-proof crown. As far as you know, the same was true about the previous generations. They all believed the claim on faith. You have learned that any of those who dared to question the authenticity of the crown and the veracity of its promise were either excommunicated or subjected by gangs of ignorant adherents to insults, injury or even death.

One day, you show the courage and wisdom to question the long-held dogma, the family's faith in the authenticity of that crown and the truth-value of its promise for perfect protection. You take the crown to a jeweler nearby. You ask him to assess the authenticity of the crown. The jeweler finds the crown very interesting. The design of the little diamond pieces and their unique arrangement pulls his attention. He starts studying it by using his tools, including a microscope. After some time, he comes up with the news: "This is a very interesting crown. I have never seen something like this before. It is priceless. Of course, its gold and diamonds have great value. But its intricate design distinguishes it from all other crowns!" You are very excited to learn that indeed you have overall a priceless crown. You call your family inform them about the good news, that you have verified the claim through an expert testimony.

However, while the expert is still studying the crown with awe, he notices an anomaly. He asks you to give him more time to study further a cluster of diamonds. You take advantage of that moment and share the news with some of your friends who had similar doubts about the authenticity of the crown.

A few minutes later, however, the jeweler comes to you with a bad news. "I found a fake 'diamond' on the crown!" You cannot believe your ears. You make him repeat the news. "Indeed, this golden crown contains 361 real diamonds that are arranged according to an intricate geometric design. However, I am sure that this is not a diamond!" You are disappointed. Initially, you get angry with the expert. You feel like punching him in the mouth. But, you compose yourself and decide to act rationally. You ask for the evidence for his claim. Ironically, until recently neither you nor any of your family members had demanded for evidence for their affirmative claim regarding the authenticity of the crown and its inscription. You have accepted both claims on faith.

The expert jeweler does not ignore your demand for evidence by pointing at your family-size traditional inconsistency! He does not question your sincerity in respecting this antique crown, when he learns that some of your family members who lived centuries ago made up many crowns from fool's gold and then they considered it equal or complementary to this unique and original crown. The jeweler provides you with plenty of evidence. For instance, he pulls your attention to one of the 19 hexagons surrounding the crown, each containing 19 little diamonds. A hexagonal diamond in the center is surrounded by six hexagonal diamonds, and those six are surrounded by twelve hexagonal diamonds, thereby creating a bigger hexagon with 19 diamonds. The expert then shows you a diamond on the corner of the 9th hexagon. "You see this one? This is not a real diamond. This is not made by nature; this is a piece of manmade glass! It is virtually worthless anywhere, and absolutely worthless on this crown! Come let me show you under the microscope and see the difference." After showing the fake diamond to you, the jeweler makes an offer: "If you allow me I can easily remove this fake diamond from here. Even the glue used to attach it has poor quality. You do not need to pay me for this simple task"

You are shocked. You cannot believe that the inscription was a false promise. You feel confused and contradicted. On one hand, you know now, not on faith, but through knowledge and evidence, that the crown is unique and priceless; on the other hand you also know that it contains a fake diamond and a false inscription! What to do with this?

When your extended family members learn about the bad news about the existence of a fake diamond, most of them call the jeweler a liar, and a heretic. Some fanatic zealots among them even suggest killing him for insulting the crown and the honor of the family members who always believed in the perfection of the crown and the authenticity of the inscription. You go to the jeweler and beg him for changing his verdict. But, the jeweler is a wise man. He tells you this:

"You must be an idiot. In fact, by allowing me to discover the fake diamond which was attached to it later by fraudsters, the maker of the crown proved both his creativity and his promise, beyond shadow of doubt. Indeed, this crown is unique and priceless. The inscription on it is now verified: it is protected by its peculiar design. It is protected not by your family or ancestors, but in spite of the fraudsters among your ancestors. It is protected by the ingenuity of the maker of the crown. You have now a reason, an incontrovertible reason to respect and trust the inscription on this crown." And now you have equally disturbing reason to be suspicious of the immaculate reputation of your ancestors.

The news about the fake diamond in the crown becomes widespread in your town. People do not talk much about the ingenious design of the crown neither do they reflect on the jeweler's words. The leaders of your extended family hold an emergency meeting. They decide that the jeweler confused many and he became an infidel by defaming their crown; thus, he should be killed. A few days later your cousins carry out the decision. The jeweler is stabbed to death in his jewelry store.

Prophetic verses in the end of Chapter Nine

What about the Quran's prophetic description of the conspiracy leading to the addition of two verses to the Manuscript —not the Quran, which is perfectly protected!— such as the highest frequency of the word *Zada* (increased) in the Quran, three times in 9:124-126? What about the reference to the revelation of a chapter? Increase in their foulness? What about the depiction of hypocrites who secretly sneak and ask each other about the revelation of a chapter? Here are the last four verses of the Chapter 9 with an intriguing prophetic language:

Conspiracy of Hypocrites Increases Only Impurity

9:124   When a **chapter** is revealed, some of them say, "Whose acknowledgement has this **increased**?" For **those who acknowledge**, it **increased** their **acknowledgment**, and they rejoice.

9:125   As for those who have a **disease in their hearts**, it only **increased foulness** to their foulness, and they died as **ingrates**.

9:126   Do they not see they are **tested** every calendar year once or twice? Yet, they do not repent, nor do they take heed.

9:127   When a **chapter** is revealed, **they looked at one another: "Does anyone see you?"**, then **they turn away**. God turns away their hearts, for **they are a people who do not comprehend**.

In sum, by demonstrating the perfect protection of the Quran through code 19, this **Chapter** has **increased acknowledgement** of **those who acknowledge** the truth, and **increased foulness** of the **ingrates** by becoming a **test** for them as well as their *salaf* who **conspired against this chapter** and **turned away** from truth. These are **people who do not comprehend.**.

Have you also noted that the key words above —increase, acknowledgement, acknowledge, desease in their hearts, ingrates, test— are common key words with those in verse 74:31? Are all these coincidence?

In sum, besides proving the divine origin of the Quran, the *Code 19* leaves no doubt about the divine promise of the perfect preservation of the Quran, since it functions as an error-correcting code (ECC) on various manuscripts.

A Personal Experience

My personal experience regarding this issue may not seem appropriate in the context of an objective discussion. However, we learn from the Quran that God shows his signs in the horizons and in ourselves to convince us (41.53). I will narrate my story since I believe that God encourages me to do so (93.11), and hoping that it may cause you to examine your motives.

Some my personal experiences are obviously nonfalsifiable and subjective cases. However, they can be supported by witnesses and physical evidence. I am very skeptical of personal experiences and as a philosopher I am aware of the pitfalls. However, the nature of my personal experience is compelling. Its conformity with objective facts that others could verify empirically is evident. This evident and compelling personal experience, years later became a prophetic event involving my family. Here, I'll tell you the most fascinating one, the one that dramatically changed my entire life. This paper will not be enough to put it in its context. Thus, consider this as a snapshot from the middle of a continuing story.

On July 1, 1986, I made the greatest decision in my life. I came to the conclusion that the religion I inherited from my parents was abysmally corrupted. The introduction of my ninth book, the *Sakincali Yazilar* (*Dangerous Articles*, 1988) starts by mentioning the importance of that day in my life. I had to criticize and reject most of my previous religious positions published in my previous bestselling books. I rejected the conventional and traditional religion. My inquiry brought me to a startling conviction—traditional Islam had nothing to do with Muhammad's original teachings. It could not be divine.

Several months after that crucial decision, I encountered a daunting intellectual and spiritual problem. I found myself in a dilemma. The mathematical structure of the Quran was blinking at the two last verses of Chapter 9. This was a very serious issue, since the Quran claims that it is perfectly preserved.

I was confused; I was scared. I could not solve the problem. The mathematical code of the Quran, which I had no doubt about, was exposing those two verses as man-made insertions. Indeed, there was some historical evidence about controversial arguments over those two verses. However, the consensus of Muslims was clear.

The problem needed a crucial "Yes" or "No" from me. It would determine my fate, both in this world and in the hereafter. It was a very important issue. I could be killed by fanatics if my answer was "Yes." But, I was more concerned about finding the truth.

For approximately two weeks I was lost. I was persistently praying to God, asking for a "sign" to save me from that dilemma. "God, give me a sign" was my repeated prayer. One day, on October 23, 1986, at around 1:30, I was sitting alone in my office trying to finish the second volume of *Interesting Questions*. I could not concentrate; the terrible paradox was eating away at my soul. I prayed again in Turkish: "Please give me a sign." Suddenly, an unusual thing happened. My heart started beating vigorously as if I had run miles.

It was the first time in my life, that I had that kind of heartbeat for no apparent reason. Shortly, I heard a very clear voice from my HEART, repeating in Turkish: "*Üç Kırkbir! Üç Kırkbir! Üç Kırkbir!*", that is, "Three Forty One, Three Forty One, Three Forty One." I don't remember exactly how many times it repeated. My excitement was at a peak. I was shocked. The only thing that came to my mind at that moment was to look at the Quran, 3:41. I cannot describe my excitement and joy. Verse 3:41 was exactly repeating my Turkish prayer in Arabic with its Quranic answer:

> 3:41   He said, "My Lord, give me a sign." He said, "Your sign is that you do not speak to the people for three days, except by signals. You shall commemorate your Lord frequently, and meditate night and day."

This extraordinary event not only saved me from the worst situation I have ever had, but it also taught me a great lesson—don't worry about what people think about you. Seek the truth without any personal agenda, fear or condition.

Later, somehow, I wanted to see whether there was any relation between this marvelous experience and my accepting the Quran alone as the source of my salvation. I was assured by an astounding mathematical relation. The number of days between July 1, 1986 (the most important day in my life), and October 23, 1986 was exactly 114 (19x6) days, which is the total number of the chapters of the Quran.

I have studied philosophy and some engineering along with psychology. I'm perceived as a skeptic by my friends but I cannot doubt that event. I cannot ignore or depreciate its factual existence in my history. I am aware of paranormal problems. Here I will list some of the possible objections by skeptics:

1. The narrator's subconscious, under strong stress, may have remembered the verse number where his prayer is mentioned.

2. It may be a schizophrenic event. The verse number and its matching text is coincidence.

3. The narrator is lying.

I would not argue against any of these, since I'm not trying to prove anything by telling you this experience here. As far as I'm concerned, I'm as sure about the authenticity of my experience as you are sure that you are reading or hearing these words.

After my crucial decision in July 1, 1986, as a convicted political activist, I started to fight the Turkish government to get a passport. Though I had two uncles in the National Congress, it took me two years to receive a passport. Interestingly enough, the date of issue on my passport was July 1, 1988.

I was single until my early thirties. Verse 3:41 mentioned above was related to Zechariah and his son Yahya (John). Thus, I sympathized with them. Just after I experienced the miraculous paranormal phenomenon, I gave a silly promise to God: "If I marry, and if I have a son, I will name him—Yahya." This promise remained a secret between God and me, until my wife surprised me with another "coincidence."

In 1989, I married in the US to an Iranian-American lady. When she got pregnant, I started to wonder: how could I convince her about the name Yahya if the baby were a boy? I was waiting for a good day and mood to talk about this issue. An incredible thing happened. One night, two or three weeks after learning about the pregnancy, she came to me and for first time talked about the name of the baby. She suggested only one name: Yahya. (This name is a rare name in Turkey and even rarer in Iran.) I thanked God Almighty, and told her my story regarding my silly promise to God.

In the meantime, we received two interesting letters. One was from a close friend, Şerafettin Durmuş, from Turkey who had just heard about the pregnancy. He did not have any idea about my promise regarding the name. In his letter he wrote a prayer: "May God raise your child like Yahya." Why like Yahya? We had numerous heroes in our history. Another coincidence? My mother-in-law's letter (again, within several weeks of the pregnancy) contained a poem about our coming baby. The name of the poet was Yahya.

Similar signs continued. Therefore, I was convinced by these signs that our child was a boy and he would be born on the first of July, as God's reward for my decision to follow the Quran alone. I announced my prediction regarding the gender and birth date of our child to more than thirty people, in a Quranic study, in Masjid Tucson. The baby failed the predictions of doctors and came to the world on the predicted day, at 10:53, on the morning of July 1, 1990. We both hugged him by saying: "Welcome Yahya." Indeed, he was a boy.

> 10.53   And some people ask you, 'Is all this true?' Say, 'Yes indeed, by my
>   Lord, this is certainly true. . ."

An Objection:

Let's assume that you were able to expose a few words as an addition to the Quran. What about deletions? How can you prove that there are not missing verses from the original Quran?

Answer:

I will list three reasons that will remove the doubts regarding subtractions to the Quran.

1. The 19-based interlocking numerical structure of the Quran was not known before Rashad's discovery in 1974.

2. The prophetic discovery and the extraordinary examples of Code 19, along with its role in the protection of the Quran are reassuring.

3. God will not hold us responsible for the things beyond our means.

Let me elaborate a bit on each reason.

1. Any subtraction from the Quran, especially without knowing the code, would destroy such an intricate system. The interlocking numerous parameters of the numerical structure that involve the count of letters, words, verses, verse numbers, chapters, chapter numbers, are all proof that no such subtraction had taken place. If someone who does not understand poetry takes words or verses out of a sonnet or a villanelle that has rhythm, meter, rhyme, alliteration, assonance, and acrostic etc., a person who is an expert in poetry will easily discover that some words or lines are missing. Similarly, if people unaware of the Quran's secret code took out words or verses from the Quran that created numerous problems with the numerical code, the experts who witnessed the code based on the protected portions would discover the tampering. In fact, the numerical structure of the Quran is much more complicated than poetry. It is easy to test this claim by asking someone who cannot read or understand the Quran to take some units out of the Quran. If such a distortion does not damage the numerical system of the Quran, then one may doubt the protection of the Quran. It is improbable someone deleting or modifying the text of the Quran would not destroy the embedded code.

2. The Quran demonstrates God's control over time, people, and the protection of the Quran, and leaves no doubt in our heart that no such addition would have happened. Any open-minded researcher who has observed the extraordinary nature and sensitivity of Code 19—after witnessing the miraculous examples of an interwoven design that encompasses the Quran's letters, words, verses, chapters, and numbers—will not believe that the same superhuman designer would allow an undetectable subtraction that would defy the entire purpose of His design. Especially after witnessing the discovery of the secret of 19 in chapter 74 in 1974, especially after witnessing the fulfillment of its prophecy 1406 (19x74) years after the revelation of the Quran—yes, after all these none would doubt God's promise.

3. God will not hold us responsible for the things beyond our means. The previous generations who believed in 9:128-129 may not be held responsible. This might be a moot issue, since a great majority of them believed volumes of fabricated stories and considered them as supplements to the Quran. However, those early supporters of the Umayyad dynasty are responsible for their choice, since they participated in one of the biggest crimes of destroying the original manuscript and killing Ali, Muhammad's son in law, Hassan and Hussain, the grandchildren of Muhammad, and numerous other true Muslims. The later generations continued the reversion to the days of ignorance by adding Muhammad's name to the Shahada, and by betraying the progressive message of the Quran through volumes of hearsay collections (42:21; 9:31; 25:30). The problem with their belief in 9:128-129 is smaller than an ear compared to a camel.

One more objection: You are referring to the "historical evidence" supporting your blasphemous claim regarding 9:128-129. What you don't see is how unreliable that so-called history is. You cannot evaluate God's book through "accepted historical evidence" and you cannot expunge the last two verses of Chapter Ultimatum based on these absurd "historical evidences." They are among the verses revealed to Muhammad by the Almighty God. It is incredible how someone like you, who considers himself a student of the Quran, would dare to commit such a horrendous mistake.

ANSWER: You are criticizing the "historical evidence" regarding the verses added to the end of Chapter 9, which conventionally came to be called Ultimatum or Repentance. Your criticism is consistent, yet its address is wrong. You should know that we did not reach the conclusion regarding 9:128-129 based on historical evidence. Why should we ignore historical evidence that supports our conclusion which is primarily based on the numerical structure of the Quran? Sure, those sources are not reliable, but this does not mean they cannot be used as support. In fact, it would be impossible not to find traces of controversy if some verses of the Quran were removed from the manuscripts. A reasonable person would ask us, "If there was such major tampering, there would be opposition in the beginning. There should be some reports, true or false, addressing the issue." If we tell you that there is a fire behind a hill, you would rightly ask, "Then where is the smoke?" Historical reports and Hadith books are the smoke of the tampering of the *manuscript* of the Quran. It is impossible to cover up such an act by completely ignoring it. Of course, the Hadith and *syra* reports about these verses contain many lies and exaggerations.

Hadith and religious history books do not contain pure lies. Liars mixed their lies with truth; otherwise none would believe them.

You might claim, "If a statement is added to the Quran it creates contradictions within in it, but the Quran is free of contradictions!" This argument has at least three flaws within it. First, that logic means that it is permitted to add statements that do not contradict the rest of the Quran. Accordingly, it is perfectly fine to add a verse which repeats 33 times in Chapter 55, or that it is fine to add a Bismillah to the beginning of Chapter 9. Secondly, despite the Quranic challenge regarding the absence of contradictions, all sects have promoted the idea of abrogation that assumes contradictions in the Quran. Thirdly, after believing a statement to be a part of the scripture generation after generation, the criterion of "no contradiction" does not work. Even if an addition contradicted multiple verses of the Quran, the believers would use far-fetched interpretations and justifications to defend the addition. For instance, the Christian evangelists are skilled at reconciling clear contradictions in The Bible. Sunni and Shiite scholars too have justified hundreds of contradictions among Hadith, and millions of people have swallowed their justifications.

What is your evidence that those who were contemporaries of Muhammad and the supporters of Ali and their followers did not have knowledge of attempts to add verses to the Quran? Besides, we are held responsible in proportion to our knowledge and capacity. Even if the true monotheists who followed the Quran alone believed the inserted verses, they at least had an excuse not to know it. However, those who are blessed by receiving "one of the greatest" signs and the "message" (*zikra*) are responsible and must acknowledge the mathematical sign.

Of course, someone who rejects Hadith and Sunna books would not trust a history book that has been reported by the same people who narrated Hadith. Lack of trust of previous generations should also reduce our trust in the Quran narrated by them. Thus, to justify their faith in the Quran, those who do not witness nor acknowledge its great numerical structure may idolize previous generations and defend every fabricated Hadith.

To reiterate, we do not question 9:128-129 because of its meaning. In fact, they do not create a clear semantic contradiction within the Quran. We started the other way around. We first caught an extra occurrence of the word *RaĤYM*, and then after investigation, we stumbled upon the only different one, one that was not used as a divine attribute but as an attribute of Muhammad. After further investigation, we were forced to delete it from the manuscripts reaching the conclusion that none other than God deserves to be called RaĤYM.

The total number of verses in the Quran

As for the number of verses in the Quran if you direct this question to a Sunni or Shiite, you will most likely receive 6666 as an answer, though that number was made up by a story teller named Zamakhshari in his interpretation of the Quran. He chose it for its look and good count; and as it was memorable it was considered to be the right number. Ironically, so far there is not a single Quran manuscript containing 6666 verses. Sunni and Shiite scholars have come up with many other alternative numbers for the total verses for the Quran.

I suggest that you verify our count of the total verses in the Quran with the manuscripts you have. You do not need to count each verse one by one; you may use a list of 114 chapters that contains the numbers of verses in each chapter. Adding them up will take a little time. You will most likely count 6236 verses in your manuscript. This number includes the first Bismillah at the beginning of Chapter 1, which is known as The Key, and the second numbered verse which is mentioned in Chapter 27, known as The Ant. If you add all the unnumbered Bismillah formula that are repeated at the beginning of 112 chapters, you will end up with 6348, which is exactly 2 verses more than the code-corrected count, 6346. In other words, without 9:128-129, the total number of verses in the Quran, including the unnumbered Bismillah formula, becomes a multiple of 19:

$$6346 = 19 \times 334$$

In relation to the number above, let me quote an email sent to me a decade ago by a monotheist who wished to remain anonymous.

> 6346 has 2 properties related to 19. It is a multiple of 19. The sum of the digits adds up to 19.
>
> There are other numbers that share these 2 properties with 6346. I have listed them in sequence, until 6346:
>
> $$874 = 19 \times 46$$
> $$1387 = 19 \times 73$$
> $$1558 = 19 \times 82$$
> $$1729 = 19 \times 91$$
> $$2584 = 19 \times 136$$
> $$2755 = 19 \times 145$$
> $$2926 = 19 \times 154$$
> $$3097 = 19 \times 163$$
> $$3268 = 19 \times 172$$
> $$3439 = 19 \times 181$$
> $$3781 = 19 \times 199 *$$
> $$3952 = 19 \times 208$$
> $$4294 = 19 \times 226$$
> $$4465 = 19 \times 235$$
> $$4636 = 19 \times 244$$
> $$4807 = 19 \times 253$$
> $$5149 = 19 \times 271$$
> $$5491 = 19 \times 289 *$$
> $$5662 = 19 \times 298 *$$
> $$5833 = 19 \times 307$$
> $$6175 = 19 \times 325$$
> $$6346 = 19 \times 334$$
>
> A look at the factors after the 19 division reveals an interesting property - the sum of the digits of the factors is either of 2 numbers - 10 or 19, and no other number.
>
> The numbers whose digits of the factors add up to 19 are shown by the asterisks above. For all the other numbers, the sum of the digits of the factors = 10.
>
> Consequently, 2 distinct series of numbers emerge.
>
> The number 10, is in turn the sum of the digits of 19 itself. It is also the base in which all counting is done. Also, 10 appears to have a close relationship with 72:28, which I can send if anybody is interested.

The first series, which consists of the numbers whose digits of the factors add up to 10 are:

874, 1387, 1558, 1729, 2584, 2755, 2926, 3097, 3268, 3439, 3952, 4294, 4465, 4636, 4807, 5149, 5833, 6175, 6346

We observe that 6346 is exactly the 19th number in this sequence. Further, the sum of the factors of this sequence = 3646.

$3 + 6 + 4 + 6 = 19$.

The second series (the asterisked numbers), which consists of the numbers whose digits of the factors add up to 19 are:

$3781 = 19 \times 199, 5491 = 19 \times 289, 5662 = 19 \times 298$

What about this sequence? Do we ignore it? No. Just add the factors.

$199 + 289 + 298 = 786$ = Gematric value of the Bismillah.

Do you think it is a coincidence or insignificant? I realize I am losing my trust in my ability to judge this as of late.

I will not comment on the calculations above. I am not a mathematician in number theory, but I have received hundreds of similar observations on the details of the numerical structure in the Quran. It requires a team of mathematicians to sort them out, to separate the mathematical properties, manipulations, and arbitrary calculations from deliberate patterns.

Discussion on the Last Verses of Chapter 9

Yuksel: Personally, I believe that the Hadith about the 9:128-129 is not correct. It is another lie to justify 9:128-129. What a stupid justification!

Lomax: Your conclusion about the Hadith is not based on any evidence of which I am aware. If 9:128-129 is an insertion, the Hadith may well be true; if it is not, the Hadith may also be true. However, if the verses were spurious, it remains to be explained why we have no record of the response of *huffaz*, who would be very aware.

And it is not just *huffaz* who would know. One does not have to know the whole Qur'an to recognize false verses. Besides, of those who knew the whole Qur'an, there would have been hundreds who knew Sura 9.

Yuksel: First, I believe that Hadith is a stupid justification, since it claims that according to an unknown witness, Khuzaima bin Sabit al-Ansary had the unique power of two witnesses. (If you want to defend this square of nonsense I am ready to discuss it with you.) Second, if the revelation of the Quran took 23 years, and if Muhammad did not compile them in a book as your books claim, then why it is not possible to claim a fake verse? The fabricator could easily say to huffaz, "you were not there when I heard this verse from Muhammad." Third, your scenario contradicts the Hadith that you are supposedly trying to defend. According to that Hadith, the committee of huffaz agreed that Chapter 9 has 127 verses. However, they changed their mind after hearing that unknown witness, witnessing from afar another unknown person!

Lomax: Let me propose a hypothesis. Bear with me a moment. Allah commanded the angels to bow down to Adam. They bowed down except Iblis, who was proud.

Now, we might notice that perfection in faith might well be considered, by some, a refusal to worship other than Allah. But actually, the report regarding Iblis indicates that it is Allah who defines what is right and perfect, and not any idea which an angel, a jinn, or a man might cling to.

Suppose the 19 really is there, and all the patterns reported are real and intended. On this line of thinking, take out 9:128-129 and you get "perfection." But Allah put those verses there. They are part of the Qur'an. You can accept what your mind calls "perfect," or you can accept the Message of Allah. The two are not necessarily the same.

Surely the guidance of Allah is the guidance.

Yuksel: A good argument. But the problem is with your premise that "Allah put those verses there." What is your proof that they were put there by God? That is the crucial question that you are ignoring. Now, let's listen to the Quran:

> 23:62-68 We never burden any person beyond its means, and we keep a record that utters the truth. No one will suffer injustice. Because their minds are oblivious to this, they commit works that do not conform to this; their works are evil. Then, when we punish their leaders with retribution, they complain. Do not complain now; you have given up all help from us. My miracles and verses were presented to you but you turned back on your heels. You were too arrogant to accept them, and you defiantly disregarded them. Why do they not reflect upon this scripture? DO THEY NOT REALIZE THAT THEY HAVE RECEIVED SOMETHING NEVER ATTAINED BY THEIR ANCESTORS?

For those who are interested in the traditional account of 9:128-129, I recommend my colleague Prof. Aisha Musa's article in the appendix section.

26
God's Signature in Nature

2:118   Those who do not know said, "If only God would speak to us, or a sign would come to us!" The people before them have said similar things; their hearts are so similar! We have clarified the signs for a people who have conviction.

12:105   How many a sign in the heavens and the earth do they pass by, while they are turning away from it.

12:106   Most of them will not acknowledge God without setting up partners.

"The laws of nature are but the mathematical thoughts of God." ~ Euclid

"[Mathematics is] the region of absolute necessity, to which not only the actual world, but every possible world must conform." ~ Bertrand A. Russel

"How is it possible that mathematics, a product of human thought that is independent of experience fits so excellently the objects of physical realty." ~ Albert Einstein

We are surrounded by divine signs. We are a divine sign ourselves. Everything around us and everything that makes us up are signs and evidence of their Creator. Every particle, every atom, every molecule, every germ, every insect, every plant, every animal, every mountain, every planet, every star, every galaxy, and every event happening in them are created by God and function in accordance to His laws. Miracles or divine signs strengthen the acknowledgement of those who are disposed to acknowledge truth when they witness it, yet they do not guide the unappreciative. God's test is not designed to impose a particular faith.

In this chapter I will share with you a sample of many signs we have witnessed since the discovery of Quran's secret. I am talking about unique signs that connect the controversial code 19 with some natural facts or events that are strongly related.

The 19 Rules of Inference

The prototypical ingrate who is challenged by the number 19 is described as one who makes erroneous inferences (74:18-20). The repetitive reference to his fallacious logic emphasizes the importance of thinking and inferring properly.

God has embedded in our hardware and system software the rules of logical thinking (*rooh* and *aql*), which work in perfect harmony with the rules of the external or natural world. If we employ these rules they will help us understand God's law in nature and the scripture. Our ego, our weakness to follow the crowd, our willingness to be manipulated by religious charlatans, our extreme emotions, our short-term petty interests and other interferences can prevent us from employing those rules correctly or efficiently.

Number 19, as the numerical-literal system of the Quran, invites the audience to use his or her rules of inference to witness, understand and appreciate the intricate and extraordinary design of the Book. This invitation is from the Creator of the human mind who blessed humans with the power to reason and the freedom of choice to use that power correctly. It is most interesting that the rules we need to appreciate God's mathematically designed message are exactly 19. The numbers of rules are complete and sufficient to test the truth value of any statement.

> "The nineteen rules of inference that have been set forth (nine elementary argument forms and ten logical equivalences) are all rules that are needed in truth-functional logic. It is a complete system of natural deduction. 154 This means that, using this set of rules, which is compact and readily mastered, one can construct a formal proof of validity for any valid truth functional argument."[155]

The above quotation with its emphasis on COMPLETE and ANY comes from the textbook I use for my logic classes for more than a decade. The book, which has been reviewed by scores of professors around the nation, serves as one of the most popular text books used at American universities and colleges. The book provides the list of *19 Rules of Inferences* both inside and on its cover.

> "This method of driving conclusions of a deductive argument—using rules of inference successively to prove the validity of the argument—is as reliable as the truth-table method discussed in Chapter 8, if the rules are used with meticulous care. But it improves on the truth-table method in two ways: it is vastly more efficient, as has just been shown and it enables us to follow the flow of reasoning process form premises to the conclusion and is therefore much more intuitive and more illuminating. The method is often called **natural deduction**. Using natural deduction, we can provide a formal proof of the validity of an argument that is valid."[156]

The first nine rules of the list are rules of inference for elementary valid arguments. The remaining ten rules are the Rules of Replacement, which is a small group of elementary logical equivalences.[157]

Nineteen Rules of Inference

1. Modus Ponens (M.P.)	$p \rightarrow q$ p $\therefore q$
2. Modus Tollens (M.T.)	$p \rightarrow q$ $\sim q$ $\therefore \sim p$
3. Hypothetical Syllogism (H.S.)	$p \rightarrow q$ $p \rightarrow r$ $\therefore p \rightarrow r$
4. Disjunctive Syllogism (D.S.)	$p \vee q$ $\sim p$ $\therefore q$
5. Constructive Dilemma (C.D.	$(p \rightarrow q) \bullet (r \rightarrow s)$ $p \vee r$ $\therefore q \vee s$
6. Absorption (Abs.)	$p \rightarrow q$ $\therefore p \rightarrow (p \bullet q)$
7. Simplification (Simp.)	$p \bullet q$ $\therefore p$
8. Conjunction (Conj.)	p q $\therefore p \bullet q$
9. Addition (Add.)	p $\therefore p \vee q$

Nineteen Rules of Inference (cont'd)

Any of the following logically equivalent expressions can replace each other wherever they occur:

10. De Morgan's Theorem (De M.)	$\sim (p \bullet q) \equiv (\sim p \vee \sim q)$ $\sim (p \vee q) \equiv (\sim p \bullet \sim q)$
11. Commutation (Com.)	$(p \vee q) \equiv (q \vee p)$ $(p \bullet q) \equiv (q \bullet p)$
12. Association (Assoc.)	$[p \vee (q \vee r)]\ [(p \vee q) \vee r]$ $[p \bullet (q \bullet r)]\ [(p \bullet q) \bullet r]$
13. Distribution (Dist)	$[p \bullet (q \vee r)] \equiv [(p \bullet q) \vee (p \bullet r)]$ $[p \vee (q \bullet r)] \equiv [(p \vee q) \bullet (p \vee r)]$
14. Double Negation (D.N.)	$p \equiv \sim \sim p$
15. Transposition (Trans.)	$(p \rightarrow q) \equiv (\sim q \rightarrow \sim p)$
16. Material Implication (M. Imp.)	$(p \rightarrow q) \equiv (\sim p \vee q)$
17. Material Equivalence (M. Equiv.)	$(p \equiv q) \equiv [(p \rightarrow q) \bullet (q \rightarrow p)]$ $(p \equiv q)\ [(p \bullet q) \vee (\sim p \bullet \sim q)]$
18. Exportation (Exp.)	$[(p \bullet q) \rightarrow r] \equiv [p \rightarrow (q \rightarrow r)]$
19. Tautology (Taut.)	$p \equiv (p \vee p)$ $p \equiv (p \bullet p)$

عليها تسعه عشر

On it is Nineteen

Chemical Properties of an Iron Atom

الحديد

> 57:25   We have sent Our messengers with clear proofs, and We sent down with them the book and the balance, that the people may uphold justice. **We sent down the iron**, wherein there is great strength and many benefits for the people. So that God would distinguish those who would support Him and His messengers on acknowledgement. God is Powerful, Noble.

This 57th chapter of the Quran, which mentions the qualities of iron, provides some interesting information regarding the physical structure of the element. In the 1980s, I wrote a booklet on it titled *Kuran'da Demir'in Esrarı* (Timaş, Istanbul). I will summarize some of my findings here.

Called *Sura al-Ĥadyd*—that is, Iron—it is the only chapter elaborating the benefits and harms of iron. We know that during the era of Quranic revelation, Arabs did not use so-called Arabic numerals. They adopted those numerals about two centuries after Muhammad.

During the time of Muhammad, Arabs used their alphabet letters as numbers. The 28 letters of the Arabic alphabet were then arranged in a different order that started with the letters ABJD, thus known as Abjad or Gematria. Since Arabic and Hebrew are closely related languages, their numerical system resembled each other as well. Each letter corresponded to a number, such as A for 1, B for 2, J for 3, D for 4. When it reached 10, the corresponding numerical values would continue as multiples of tens, and when reaching 100, they would continue as multiples of 100 ending with 1000. Archeological evidence shows that they distinguished letters from numbers by using different colored ink, or simply by putting a line over the letter that resembled the Roman numerals. However, a literary text might use letters/numbers for multiple purposes; that is, for both their semantic or lexicon function and at the same time for their numerical value. Such a multi-use property requires a good command and knowledge of language, and the author is limited by that language. When Arabs abandoned the Abjad system, it was still used by poets and charlatan healers who wished to take advantage of an antiquated numerical system that became a curiosity for the gullible. Poets wrote verses about events or epithcts for important figures, with the date of the event or the death embedded in the numerical values of the letters of a word or a phrase in their verses. The usage of the Abjad in the Quran is extensive, impressive and prophetic (For another example see 74:1-2).

When we add up the numerical values of letters comprising the word *Ĥadyd* (iron), it gives the atomic number of any iron element: 8+4+10+4=26.

ĤaDYD	حديد	GV
Ĥ	ح	8
D	د	4
Y	ي	10
D	د	4
Total		26

If we add up the numerical values of the letters comprising the word AL-ĤaDYD (the iron, or a particular version of iron), it gives the atomic weight of a particular isotope of the iron element: 1+30+8+4+10+4=57.

AL-ĤaDYD	الحديد	GV
A	ا	1
L	ل	30
Ĥ	ح	8
D	د	4
Y	ي	10
D	د	4
Total		57

Of course, this interesting coincidence has nothing to do with the Quran, since the word ĤaDYD already existed in the language of common people including the opponents of the Quran. However, when we study the details of this chapter we will learn that the author of the book was aware of the unique relationship between this word, its numerical values, and the related physical or chemical properties. This chapter is listed as the 57th chapter of the Quran, corresponding

291

to the numerical value of its popular name, and at the same time corresponding to the atomic weight of a particular isotope of iron. Iron has five isotopes with the atomic numbers of 54, 55, 56, 57, and 58, containing 28, 29, 30, 31, and 32 neutrons, respectively. We also observe that the only verse mentioning the physical properties of iron is listed as the 26th verse, including the unnumbered verse, Bismillah, in the beginning of chapter. (Bismillah, as the first and the most repeated verse of the Quran has a unique role in the mathematical structure of the Quran.) The chapter contains 29 numbered verses, and 30 verses when you include Bismillah. Each number gives us the number of neutrons of different isotopes of iron.

Iron with 30 neutrons has the most stable nucleus possible, and thus cannot be subjected to fission or fusion. Formation of iron marks the death of stars and the formation of planets. Iron with 31 neutrons has a nuclear spin and is used in industry. The word God occurs 32 times in the chapter, two of them in the verse mentioning iron. Thus, the verse about iron contains the 26th occurrence of the word God, with or without including the unnumbered Bismillah. The verb "we sent down" is interesting, since it describes the formation of planets.

Here is the summary:

Iron حديد	26	Gematrical or numerical value of the word
	26	Atomic number of any iron atom
	26	Verse order in the chapter, including Bismillah
	26	Frequency of the word God until the only verse where properties of iron is mentioned.
The iron الحديد	57	Gematrical or numerical value of the word
	57	Atomic weight of a particular iron isotope
	57	The chapter's order in the Quran
	57	Gematrical value of the chapter's name

The Number of Elements in the Universe

Atoms are the smallest building blocks of all matter. Different elements in nature, such as oxygen, iron, etc. have different characteristics and are distinguished by their atomic number, which is the number of protons in an atom's nucleus. For example, all carbon atoms have 6 protons, and every atom that has 6 protons is a carbon atom. In the nucleus, atoms also have other particles called neutrons that do not change the atomic number but create atoms with different weights, called isotopes.

Elements with an atomic number equal to 104 and higher are called super-heavy elements. They are not found naturally on earth and can only be synthesized in special laboratories. They are also "radioactive", that is, they tend to decay and turn into other atoms. The amount of time it takes the number of atoms of a radioactive element to decrease by half is called that element's "half life".

Here, we will present the current state of knowledge that shows that the number 114, the number of suras in Quran, has a very important role in this context. Element 114 had long been predicted by theoretical calculations to be the highest stable element, and at the time of writing this book, experiments show that it is the highest reproducible element with a considerably high half life.

1a	2a	3b	4b	5b	6b	7b		8		1b	2b	3a	4a	5a	6a	7a	0
1 H																	2 He
3 Li	4 Be											5 B	6 C	7 N	8 O	9 F	10 Ne
11 Na	12 Mg											13 Al	14 Si	15 P	16 S	17 Cl	18 Ar
19 K	20 Ca	21 Sc	22 Ti	23 V	24 Cr	25 Mn	26 Fe	27 Co	28 Ni	29 Cu	30 Zn	31 Ga	32 Ge	33 As	34 Se	35 Br	36 Kr
37 Rb	38 Sr	39 Y	40 Zr	41 Nb	42 Mo	43 Tc	44 Ru	45 Rh	46 Pd	47 Ag	48 Cd	49 In	50 Sn	51 Sb	52 Te	53 I	54 Xe
55 Cs	56 Ba	57 La	72 Hf	73 Ta	74 W	75 Re	76 Os	77 Ir	78 Pt	79 Au	80 Hg	81 Tl	82 Pb	83 Bi	84 Po	85 At	86 Rn
87 Fr	88 Ra	89 Ac	104 Rf	105 Ha	106 106												

58 Ce	59 Pr	60 Nd	61 Pm	62 Sm	63 Eu	64 Gd	65 Tb	66 Dy	67 Ho	68 Er	69 Tm	70 Yb	71 Lu
90 Th	91 Pa	92 U	93 Np	94 Pu	95 Am	96 Cm	97 Bk	98 Cf	99 Es	100 Fm	101 Md	102 No	103 Lr

Before the necessary technology to actually synthesize some of these superheavy elements existed, physicist Heiner Meldner predicted in his calculations that the element with atomic number 114 would be relatively stable compared to other superheavy elements and that 114 would be a "magic number" in which protons are arranged as a perfect spherical shell[158] He also suggested that the element with 114 protons and 184 neutrons would be "doubly magical" both in terms of the number of protons and neutrons. There have been other researchers with alternative calculations. However, most recently, Chhanda Samanta and colleagues have shown in their calculations that existence of "[atoms above 114] with considerable lifetime is very low,"[159] which validates Meldner's calculations. This means that, nuclear physicists predict in their models that element 114 is expected to be stable, especially in its "doubly magical" state when it has 184 neutrons, and no other element above 114 is expected to be stable.

As technology advanced, researchers found ways of actually synthesizing these superheavy elements. For this, they run complicated nuclear experiments, in which they usually bombard different atoms together to get them to combine and make bigger atoms. These bigger atoms usually disintegrate quickly, so they observe the residue and radioactive waves that come out of the experiment and make judgments about what atoms were created. Therefore, the results obtained are not always certain and require independent verification. Because of the difficulty and uncertainty, there has even been a case in which a scientist was able to fake the experimental data. In 1999, LBNL in California reported to have synthesized elements 116 and 118.[160] However, no other lab was able to replicate their results. Later, analysis on the data collected for that experiment showed that the results about elements 116 and 118 were faked and those elements were not actually synthesized,[161] costing the responsible scientist his job. This incident caused nuclear physicists to be more cautious on accepting such results unless multiple labs were able to reproduce the synthesis.

International Union of Pure and Applied Chemistry (IUPAC) is the international body of scientists that are in charge of independently verifying claims of synthesized elements. Their 2003 technical report is a good review of these claims and acknowledges the discovery of element 111 as the highest element synthesized, while requiring more evidence for the larger elements.[162] By that time, elements 114, 116 and 118 have only been reported by JINR in Russia. While searching for more evidence, we came across a report by a scientist in LBNL that casts doubts on the results reported by JINR.[163] We later learned from the author that LBNL was just recently able to synthesize element 114 independently, and their article on this has just been published as we were collecting this information.[164] This makes element 114 the highest element that was independently verified by more than one lab.

The readers are welcome to make their own research and verify the information we presented here. A quick internet search and Wikipedia articles may show that some elements above 114 have been successfully synthesized. However, a deeper research uncovers the controversy and that they have not been independently verified. Even though the "doubly-magic" isotope of element 114 is yet to be synthesized, the current reported isotopes of it have a half life on the order of multiple seconds, while reported half lives by JINR for 116 and 118 are just in the order of milliseconds. The current isotopes that were able to be synthesized for element 114 have fewer neutrons compared to the predicted doubly-magic one, which is predicted to have a half life of 17 days[165]. Currently, scientists consider the independent verification of element 114 by LBNL, "a stepping stone to the island of stability", and are working hard to create this "doubly-magical" element with 114 protons and 184 neutrons.

Ending Theocratic *Khilafa* and Founder of Modern Turkey

Perhaps many of my readers will have problem in appreciating this one, since many are not aware of the importance of this historical person and his revolutions. Besides, even those who appreciate its importance might confuse it with some apparently similar historical patterns. I will share the most impressive of such a pattern and leave it the readers to compare both and see the difference. Underwood Dudley's book, *Numerology: Or, what Pythagoras Brought*, contains an example from a small pamphlet, *History Computed*, by Arthur Finnessey. I agree with Underwood, in his introductory remark, "Given something that exists and has any complexity to it, the ingenious minds of humans can find all sorts of amazing things in it, whether they were put there on purpose or not." It starts with the number of "tea chests" thrown into the harbor at the Boston Tea Party:

> He found a lot of 57s. To show how many; it is necessary to quote at length. The "tea chest number" referred to below is 342 (6 X 57), the number of chests of tea that Mr. F. says were thrown into the harbor at the Boston Tea Party. When Mr. F. refers to an "alphabetical sequence number" he is using gematria to convert a word to a number using the standard a = 1, b = 2, ... , z = 26 alphabet.

> A few weeks after Lafayette's 57th birthday in September, 1814, Francis Scott Key wrote the Star Spangled Banner. When Lafayette died the Declaration of Independence was 57 years old. The alphabetical sequence numbers in the names George Washington-Thomas Jefferson-Lafayette total 456 (8 x 57), the sum of the double United States of America in the Declaration of Independence. The combined 16 times 57 matches the 912 days from Lexington to Saratoga. Most sources place the number of prisoners taken at Saratoga at some 57-hundred.

> Dec. 25, 1777, Christmas at Valley Forge: Washington's army was ragged, starving and freezing. On Christmas day, 1783, Washington was to arrive at Mount Vernon, horne after victory in war. The time between the two extremes of fortune was 'to be exactly 57 months plus 57 weeks plus 57 days: The alphabetical sequence total of Mount Vernon is 171 (3 x 57).

> On Feb. 6, 1776, exactly 57 weeks after the Jan. 3, 1777 Battle of Princeton, France openly joined the struggle for Independence. Princeton

and Yorktown, Washington's two victories over Cornwallis, were 57 months apart. The alphabetical sequence total' of Princeton is 114 (2 x 57).

The 57th month of the Revolution ended on Jan. 19, 1780, and 114 (2 x 57) days later, on May 12, Charleston fell to the British. Its fall was 684 (12 x 57) days after the Battle of Monmouth, June 28, 1776.

The fateful year of Yorktown began with two battles 57 days apart, at Cowpens, N. C., Jan. 17, 1781, and at Guilford Court House, N. C., March 15.

April 19, 1781, the last wartime anniversary of Lexington and Concord was exactly 57 months plus 57 weeks and 57 days after those first battles.

In June, 1781, 57 Americans died in the assault on the British Fort Ninety Six in South Carolina. Ninety Six is the total for the signers of the Declaration of Independence, 57, and the Constitution, 39.

When French naval forces turned back the 19 British warships sent to aid Cornwallis he became trapped at Yorktown and he surrendered on Oct. 19, virtually ending the military phase of the war that began April 19, 1775. The three 19's total 57. [166]

The observation above is interesting and curiously it hides the number 19, since every multiple of 57 is also a multiple of 19. Surely Arthur Finnessey could find more examples, perhaps even more interesting ones, had he chosen 19 as the common denominator. Yet, I think, at this level it is no match to the 19-based patterns observed in the life of Mustafa Kemal. Of course, the following patterns or perceived patterns in the founder of modern Turkey are not integral part of the extraordinary numerical system of the Quran. I will take the risk of providing a relatively easy target for those who are adamant to debunk NINETEEN, since it may inspire the discovery of fascinating mysteries.

In about 1985 I learned about the mysterious role of the number 19 surrounding the founder of Turkey. As far as I know, it was first brought to the public attention in 1951 by a columnist named Kadircan Kaflı in an article published in Yeni Sabah newspaper. But, that information somehow eluded public and had not become common knowledge about the most famous Turk; perhaps only a few knew about it. After learning the astounding 19-centered coincidences in Mustafa Kemal Atatürk's life, I made my own research through studying his biographies, encyclopedias and visiting museums. I even visited Mustafa's shrine, Anıtkabir, to acquire more personal information about his life. Each time, I would be surprised to see more 19s. I was convinced that his entire life was controlled by the number 19.

Then, as a Sunni radical, I thought that the presence of the Quranic code 19 in Mustafa's life was a divine sign about his mission as the *Dajjal* (the Deceiver, the Muslim version of Anti-Christ). Interestingly, that interpretation of mine would change within a year, especially after my conversion to rational monotheism in July 1st 1986.

I now consider Mustafa like a natural disaster hitting a criminal empire. There are contradictory claims about Mustafa's faith, yet a critical study would demonstrate that he had little or no faith. He was a heavy drinker and died of alcohol related cirrhosis. He had good reasons to oppose the teaching and practices of Sunni sects and orders. He had good reasons to reject the authority of imams, mullahs and sheiks, the self-appointed holy powerbrokers who exploit gullible masses mentally, spiritually, economically and politically.

Mustafa led some progressive revolutions such as promoting women's rights and abolishing the corrupt Caliphate that justified the killing of even babies in order to keep themselves in power. Yet, he also committed major errors. Mustafa was most likely a deist or an agnostic. Though he promoted Republicanism and elections, after being elected as a president, he acted like a dictator. The Turkish people have strong feelings for and against Mustafa. The real Mustafa, I believe, is neither a superman as his worshipers claim, nor an all-evil person as his enemies purport.

Here are some of the examples from Mustafa's life, which I had published in the first volume of bestseller *İlginç Sorular* (Interesting Questions) in 1985-1988.[167]

Mustafa Kamal Atatürk and the Number 19		
His birth year	**19**	x 99
His number in the birth register	**19**	x 1
The number on his birth certificate	**19**	x 52306
First involvement in politics by joining Young Turks at age 19	**19**	x 100
His number in the list of Turkish graduates from the military school	**19**	x 1
The number of the session of the Military Academy he registered	**19**	x 3
His rank in the list when he joined the army as captain	**19**	x 2
The number of the first regiment which he commanded	**19**	x 2
The number of the second regiment which he commanded	**19**	x 3
Nineteen days after he was promoted to colonel, the number of the division he led	**19**	x 1
Arrived in Samsun and started the Independence movement in May	**19**	x 1
The year he organized the nation for the Independence movement	**19**	x 101
On the way to Samsun, the number of commanders in the ship, including him	**19**	x 1
He was given the titles Marshal and General in 1921, on September	**19**	x 1
The total number of medals of Honor he received	**19**	x 1
His seat number in the first Great National Assembly	**19**	x 1
His house number in Istanbul	**19**	x 4
Died on November 10, 1938, at the age of 57 or 3x19	**19**	x 102
His funeral took place on November 19	**19**	x1
The music played in his funeral, Chopin's March number containing the notes of the same number	**19**	x 1
The money that he left in his bank account in liras	**19**	x 100
The numerical of values of Ottoman letters of the three important cities, (his birth place, starting point of revolution, and government) in Atatürk life are divisible	**19**	
Selanik سلانيك 171	**19**	x 9
Samsun صامسون 247	**19**	x 13
Ankara انقهره 361	**19**	x 19
The numbers of letters in his name Mustafa Kemal Atatürk	**19**	x 19

298

The Y2K Problem, the Millennium Bug or Ignoring the Number 19

In order to save expensive computer memory, computer programmers dropped the digits 19 from the year thereby creating a major problem called Y2K Problem or the Millennium Bug.

> "While no globally significant computer failures occurred when the clocks rolled over into 2000, preparation for the Y2K problem had a significant effect on the computer industry. There were plenty of Y2K problems, and that none of the glitches caused major incidents is seen as vindication of the Y2K preparation. However, some questioned whether the absence of computer failures was the result of the preparation undertaken or whether the significance of the problem had been overstated." (Wikipedia).

Whether real or perceived, whether significant or overstated, at the turn of millennium, this issue created a major problem for the entire world, costing over 300 billion US dollars (BBC News, 6 January 2000). The fear and panic was caused by computer programmers who somehow ignored the number 19.

In other words, in my opinion, this was a divine sign and warning for the computer generation: ignoring the number 19 is costly, and it will have much bigger implications in the next life.

Here are a few out of hundreds news regarding the Y2K problem:

The Y2K Solution: Run for Your Life!!

By Kevin Poulsen

> They were hand-picked to kill the Millennium Bug. They hunkered down and started cranking out code. Now they're scared shitless.
>
> ....
>
> By now, the source of their anxiety is well known. In the 1950s and 1960s, when the computer world was young and memory was expensive, programmers developed a convention for marking the passage of time. It's the same system most people use to date their checks: two digits for the day, two for the month, and two for the year. **Dropping the "19" from the year was convenient, and it saved two bytes of precious RAM every time it was used.**" [168]

****

Dec. 31, 1999: Horror or Hype? Y2K Arrives and World Trembles

By Tony Long   December 30, 2009

1999: The world braces for chaos as midnight approaches. Will computer systems crash when the calendar switches over to 2000?

Although the answer turned out to be "no," and the so-called Y2K crisis never materialized, the potential for disaster seemed real enough in the days and weeks leading up to the final day of the 1900s. Fears within the computer industry and the resulting media frenzy it produced certainly helped to fan the flames.

The problem, as some saw it, was that older computers still being used for critical functions might break down when the date switched from 99 to 00, since the numeric progression convention, programmed to store data using only the last two digits of any given year, wouldn't recognize the logic of a century change.

As far as these computers were concerned, it would be 1900, not 2000. How much data might be lost as the result of this 100-year miscalculation was the great, unanswered question.

Y2K fears were real enough to make governments around the world take remedial action before the event, which had the unintended benefit of actually strengthening the existing computer infrastructure. Systems were upgraded or, when they couldn't be replaced, were given additional backup. Billions of dollars were spent fixing the original source code in older computers.

If the threat was real—and there are still plenty of people around who say it was—then the precautions paid off. If Y2K was a form of mass paranoia—and plenty of people believe that, too—then a lot of money was wasted.

As for the midnight switchover itself, 1999 passed into history with barely a whimper. A few glitches were reported here and there, but nothing catastrophic occurred. The industry would be in crisis soon enough, but as Jan. 1, 2000, dawned, nobody saw that one coming yet.

Source: CNN

Heesoon Yim/AP

This article first appeared on Wired.com Dec. 31, 2007.[169]

Magic Hexagon[170]

A magic hexagon of order N is an arrangement of close-packed hexagons containing the numbers 1, 2, ,..., Hn-1 where Hn is the Nth hex number such that the numbers along each straight line add up to the same sum. (Here, the hex numbers are i.e., 1, 7, 19, 37, 61, 91, 127, ...; Sloane's A003215). In the above magic hexagon of order N=3, each line (those of lengths 3, 4, and 5) adds up to 38.

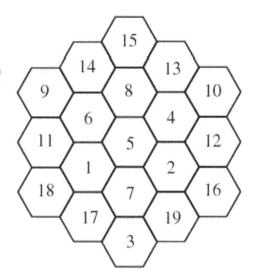

It was discovered independently by Ernst von Haselberg in 1887 (Bauch 1990, Hemme 1990), W. Radcliffe in 1895 (Tapson 1987, Hemme 1990, Heinz), H. Lulli (Hendricks, Heinz), Martin Kühl in 1940 (Gardner 1963, 1984; Honsberger 1973), Clifford W. Adams, who worked on the problem from 1910 to 1957 (Gardner 1963, 1984; Honsberger 1973), and Vickers (1958; Trigg 1964).

This problem and the solution have a long history. Adams came across the problem in 1910. He worked on the problem by trial and error and after many years arrived at the solution which he transmitted to M. Gardner, Gardner sent Adams' magic hexagon to Charles W. Trigg, who by mathematical analysis found that it was unique disregarding rotations and reflections (Gardner 1984, p. 24). Adams' result and Trigg's work were written up by Gardner (1963). Trigg (1964) did further research and summarized known results and the history of the problem.

$$\frac{9\,(n^4 - 2n^3 + 2n^2 - n) + 2}{2\,(2n-1)}$$

Trigg showed that the magic constant for an order N hexagon would be the first few of which are 1, 28/3, 38, 703/7, 1891/9, 4186/11, ...

(Sloane's A097361 and A097362), which requires [5/(2n-1)]/N=1 to be an integer for a solution to exist. But this is an integer for only N=1 (the trivial case of a single hexagon) and Adams's N=3 (Gardner 1984, p. 24).

27

Was the Discovery of the Code 19 a Coincidence?

"But students of literary numerology do not find such obvious marks. The ones they find are, subtle in the extreme. There are two explanations for that. One is that the authors were indeed subtle in the extreme, and thought it worthwhile to make the tremendous effort to leave clues whose chance of being found and properly interpreted was minuscule."
~ Underwood Doodley[171]

Dr. Underwood Doodley, the author of *Numerology* is right in the context of his aforequoted reaction to those who search for numerical patterns in books. If our evidence for the Nineteen was as simple and subtle as it was suggested by Alistair Fowler for Shakespeare's 154 sonnets, then Underwood's assessment would apply to this book too. But, as you will see, the numerical structure of the Quran cannot be refuted by his logic which makes sense against Dr. Fowler's assertions of a deliberate arrangement of pyramidical numbers and "the theme of time hours, days, years" in the arrangement of the sonnets.

As mentioned already at the beginning of this book, I came to know about Rashad through Ahmad Deedat, who had used his computerized studies on the Quran. I witnessed, and participated in the unveiling of "The Secret," or the mathematical code of the Quran and the Old Testament, that became controversial all around the Muslim world. After my immigration to the United States, I was hosted by Rashad and I worked with him in Masjid Tucson for about a year, seven days a week, from morning until night. (When he was among us, I called him by his first name; so I will respect that memory).

19.org   Rashad'89

Rashad was an Egyptian-American biochemist. He worked in the United Nations, and for a while he became a science adviser to Muammar al-Qaddafi, the despot of Libya. Rashad became a popular author in the Muslim world, but later became their eye-sore when he boldly criticized and rejected the teachings of the Sunni or Shiite sects. Rashad thus promoted a radical islamic reformation by rejecting all sectarian teachings other than the Quran. In my archive, I have the original letters written to Rashad from the director of al-Azhar University and many other prominent religious scholars, expressing their disbelief and shock and dismay over his rejection of the Hadith and Sunna.

By referring to the Quranic verses, Dr. Khalifa demonstrated that today's Islam has little to do with Muhammad's original message, but rather is a religion concocted by scholars using fabricated narrations and medieval Arab cultural traditions (Hadith and Sunna), and falsely attributing these to the Prophet Muhammad. By incorporating their opinions, along with those medieval lies, Sunni and Shiite scholars have created various orthodox sects that promote vicious and oppressive laws, misogyny, hatred, terror, and aggression.

Dr. Rashad Khalifa did not have any knowledge that his curiosity regarding the meaning of the alphabet letters initializing 29 chapters of the Quran would end up with the discovery of its mathematical system. His computerized study which started in 1969 gave its fruits in early 1974, with the discovery of the 14-century-old secret. The discovery of this code opened a new era that has changed the paradigm of those who do not turn off the circuits of their brains in matters related to God. This discovery provided powerful, verifiable, and falsifiable evidence for God's existence. His communications with us fulfilled a great prophecy. Besides, it saved monotheists from the contradiction of trusting past generations regarding the Quran, knowing that the past generations have fabricated, narrated and followed volumes of man-made teachings, demonstrated ignorance, distorted the meaning of the Quranic words, and glorified gullibility and sheepish adherence to the fatwas of clerics.

If the Code 19 was going to provide strong evidence for the existence of God and for the authenticity of the Quran, then it is reasonable to expect that the identity of the discoverer and the time of the discovery would not be

يايها المدثر قم فانذر
O the hidden, rise and warn!

ي	Y	10
ا	A	1
ا	A	1
ي	Y	10
ه	H	5
ا	A	1
ا	A	1
ل	L	30
م	M	40
د	D	4
ث	Th	500
ر	R	200
ق	Q	100
م	M	40
ف	F	80
ا	A	1
ن	N	50

ذ	Z	700
ر	R	200
The numerical value of the 19-lettered opening statement of chapter 74, The Hidden. The year in which the prophetic secret code was discovered.	**1974**	

coincidental. Indeed, events have demonstrated a prophetic design in the timing of this miraculous mathematical design.

The Quran is not a simple book as many of its simple-minded readers expect it to be. As a student of the Quran who has translated the Quran into two languages (Turkish and English), I am always amazed by discovering new layers of meanings or information contained in the subtle details or masterful choice of words.

For centuries, readers of the Quran justifiably understood the first verses of chapter 74 as a list of commandments to the Prophet Muhammad. They believed that he was hiding in a cave when he first received these verses. Besides hearsay reports, we do not have reliable evidence to support the story. Of course, this makes sense and probably was true. However, the Quran contains many statements that relate to different situations or events in the different periods, and the chapter 74 is filled with such verses with multi-meaning and multi-implications.

The number 19 is mentioned only in the chapter known "The Hidden," the 74th chapter of the Quran. Juxtaposing these two numbers yields 1974, exactly the year in which the code was deciphered. (The calendar based on the birth of Jesus and the solar year is accepted by the Quran as units of calculating time. See, 19:33; 43:61; 18:24. Besides, this is the most commonly used calendar in the world.) If we multiply these two numbers, 19x74, we end up with 1406, the exact number of lunar years between the revelation of the Quran and the discovery of the code.

Furthermore, the first statement contained in these two verses discusses the revealing of the secret. It is interesting that if we consider one version of spelling the first word, which contains three *Alifs* instead of two,[172] there are 19 letters in the first statement of chapter 74. More interestingly, when we add the numerical values of each letter in these two verses the sum is a very familiar number. *Ya ayyuh al-Muddathir; qum fa anzir* (O you the hidden one, stand and warn) = 1974. This prophetic paragram is alone an extraordinary evidence for the extraordinary claims of the Quran. It is divine signature that none can forge.[173]

As documented in published books and media coverage, the year 1974 was the year when the hidden secret emerged from the computerized study and warned us![174]

Added to this prophetic paragram is the fact that the derivatives of the name of the discoverer, RShD (guidance), occur in the Quran exactly 19 times. (See 2:186; 2:256; 4:6; 7:146; 11:78; 11:87; 11:97; 18:10; 18:17; 18:24; 18:66; 21:51; 40:29; 40:38; 49:7; 72:2; 72:10; 72:14; 72:21.). The exact form, Rashad, occurs twice and they prophetically sandwich the assertion of ingrates who claim the finality of messengership (40:29-38) The Quran distinguishes the messenger from the prophet).

In summary, the relationship between the following seven elements, in our opinion, is more than interesting.

- The mathematical code (19).
- The number of the chapter mentioning the code (74).
- The year of the discovery of the code (1974).
- The number of lunar years between the revelation of the Quran and the year of the discovery (19x74).
- The sum of numerical values of the 19 letters comprising the first statement of the chapter 74 (1974).
- The frequency of the derivatives of the discoverer's name in the Quran (19).
- The context of the verses where the exact name of the discoverer is mentioned as an adjective (40:28-38).

After studying the evidence presented in this book, if you witness one of the greatest divine signs with its ultimate implications regarding the meaning and purpose of life, then you would know that Dr. Underwood Doodley's brilliant question that the improbability of "tremendous effort" in constructing numerically designed literature and then leaving its discovery to the mercy of miniscule chance is only relevant for human authors. If Muhammad was a conman, then why would he waste all his efforts? Well, the question is much

305

bigger than that. Could Muhammad also determine the exact timing of the discovery of his tremendous effort; centuries after producing his ingenious work?

As for the original discoverer of the code nineteen, I have never been impressed by the many of Rashad's arithmetical calculations in the footnotes of his translation regarding his messengership. I find them arbitrary and speculative. I have provided my arguments to this effect in a section of *Running Like Zebras*. Yet, I have had faith in his mission, primarily based on the following objective and subjective considerations:

1. He had a clear idea of and uncompromising adherence to monotheism that he vigorously promoted.
2. He demonstrated a deep knowledge of the Quran.
3. He had an excellent character and wonderful qualities: a happy and cheerful personality, rare courage and honesty, selfless devotion to work, patience and dedication to his mission, and extra-ordinary calm and fortitude in the face of all kinds of false accusations and threats;
4. He was the original mind that discovered the prophesized miracle of the Quran;
5. The root of his name mentioned in the Quran 19 times, with interesting implications in verses where the exact form of his name is mentioned;[175] and
6. Through discussions and working together, he led me learning many things.

Ironically, soon after Rashad's departure, following the footsteps of previous generations, ignorant people started idolizing him. Within a few weeks after his departure, a gang with cult mentality fabricated a lie prophesizing doomsday in May 19, 1990. My strong objection to their lies and numerology turned them to enemies against me. Though, they were humiliated the night of May 19, when no meteor hit Saudi Arabia, it did not take too long for the same gang to recover and continue promoting their ignorance. They continued their animosity against me; perhaps thinking that my opposition prevented their doomsday from happening! Somehow they focused on carving a new idol out of Rashad. They came up with all sorts ideas to distort the message of rational monotheism promoted by Rashad, who went to such an extend asking us to cremate his body and dump its ash into the bathroom so that the would-be idol-worshipers would end up with a bathroom as a shrine. Of course, each generation of idol-worshipers are skilled in distinguishing their idol-worship from that of the previous generations. They produced clever yet false arguments to distort his message of strict monotheism. My observations and experience with that group made me live the history and witness the motivations and dynamics of hero-worship after they depart.

Though the International Community of Submitters has many admirable monotheists among its leaders and members, it is infected with dogmatic ideas of Rashad-worshipers who have replaced their previous idols with a new one, Rashad or the "Messenger of Covenant." Unfortunately, the group is increasing in numbers and they are more active and louder than the monotheist submitters. I have written a pamphlet titled *United but Disoriented,* which is out of print. Some of the articles published in that booklet can be found at www.yuksel.org.[176]

In February 19, 1989 a group of Sunni scholars from 38 countries met in Saudi Arabia to discuss the issue of Salman Rushdi. The Saudi King was competing with the Iranian Ayatullah for leadership of the so-called Muslim world, and he felt that he needed to come up with something regarding that international controversy. When the so-called scholars issued their fatwa (religious decree) it became headline news in Muslim countries, including my homeland Turkey. Their fatwa was: "Both Rashad and Rushdi are apostates!" The world knew Rushdi, but who was Rashad? Rashad, a biochemist and resident of Tucson, Arizona, had become a popular figure in Muslim countries after he discovered a hidden mathematical system in the Quran via computer analysis. The implications and consequences of the mathematical code were against the self-interest of religious leaders. Consequently, they issued fatwas calling for his assassination.

On January 31, 1990, Rashad Khalifa was assassinated in Tucson, Arizona, by a terrorist group affiliated to al-Qaida.[177] Rashad was stabbed to death brutally in his Tucson mosque by men whose identities were ultimately—over a decade later—revealed by the FBI and respected American news organizations to be associates of the infamous Usama Bin Laden. The reformist Muslim thinker, Rashad sacrificed his life for his bold criticism of the religious orthodoxy of Islamic dogmas, and his call for a radical change: rejection of all (sectarian) teachings except those of the Quran itself. His assassination and its aftermath were widely covered by Arizona Daily Star and Tucson Weekly and the local radio and TV stations. It was only after September 11, 2001 that the national media picked up the story. One of the assassins was captured 19 years after the crime in Calgary, Canada.

There are too many coincidences that could be seen trivial or fascinating. My skeptical mind warns me about a possible pattern-seeking selective bias, while the same skeptical mind warns me about self-inflicting blindness to the clues/information in the pattern. Let me give you a few examples of these trivial or non-trivial coincidences.

After being excommunicated from the Islamic Center located near the University of Arizona, Rashad purchased a small apartment complex on the corner of 6th Street and Euclid Avenue at the South East Corner of the University, and converted the old house into Masjid Tucson. The zip code was 85719. The first digit 8 stands for one of the ten zones in the US, 57 (19x3) stands for Tucson, and 19 for the region where Masjid was located. The lot number of the Masjid Tucson was 114 (19x6). Euclid and his name-sake al-Abul Hasan al-Uqlidisi were both prominent Egyptian mathematicians. Another famous Egyptian Mathematician, Hypatia of Alexandria, was martyred 1580 years before by being torn to shreds by a Christian mob, partly because she did not adhere to the strict Christian principles. Dr. Pickover, the author of *The Math Book*, ends the page on the Death of Hypatia with the following interesting remarks:

> "Hypatia's death triggered the departure of many scholars from Alexandria and, in many ways, marked the end of centuries of Greek progress in mathematics. During the Europian Dark Ages, Arabs and Hindus were the ones to play the leading roles in fostering the progress of mathematics." [178]

In that very Masjid Tucson, located on a street named after two Egyptian mathematicians, another Egyptian scientist who discovered a numerical system in the Final Testament would suffer a similar fate of another famous Egyptian mathematician and would be brutally stabbed to death by a Sunni terrorist gang.[179]

There are more intriguing and prophetic clues. Rashad argued that though Muhammad was the last prophet receiving the Final Testament, the messengership was not ended with him. Both Sunni and Shiite world were shocked to hear the news of Rashad's claim of messengership. According to them Muhammad was not only the last prophet but he was also the last messenger. The rationale to reject Rashad's claim of messengership, however, was not new. Interestingly, the Quran mentions another messenger who was rejected by his people by the same excuse. Thousands years ago, Egyptians rejected Joseph by asserting that Moses was the last messenger! These eleven verses have prophetic fulfillment in our times:

40:28   An acknowledging man from among Pharaoh's people, who had concealed his acknowledgement, said, **"Will you kill a man simply for saying: 'My Lord is God'**, and he has come to you with proofs from your Lord? If he is a liar, then his lie will be upon him, and if he is truthful, then some of what he is promising you will afflict you. Surely, God does not guide any transgressor, liar."*

40:29   "O my people, you have the kingship today throughout the land. But then who will save us against God's torment, should it come to us?" Pharaoh said, "I am only showing you what I see, and I am only guiding you to the **right path** (*sabil al-rashad*)."

40:30	The one who acknowledged said, "O my people, I fear for you the same fate as the day of the opponents."
40:31	"Like the fate of the people of Noah, Aad, and Thamud, and those after them. God does not wish any injustice for the servants."
40:32	"And, O my people, I fear for you the day of mutual blaming."
40:33	"A day when you will turn around and flee, you will have no protector besides God, and whomever God sends astray, then there is none who can guide him."

Opposing a Messenger in the name of a "Final Messenger"

40:34	"Joseph had come to you before with **proofs**, but you remained in doubt regarding what he came to you with, until when he died, you said, "**God will not send any messenger after him**." It is such that God sends astray he who is a transgressor, doubter."*
40:35	Those who dispute about **God's signs** without any authority that has come to them, it is greatly abhorred by God and by those who acknowledge. God thus seals the hearts of every arrogant tyrant.
40:36	Pharaoh said, "O Haman, build for me a high platform that I may uncover the **secrets**."
40:37	"The secrets of the heavens, and that I can take a look at the god of Moses, although I think he is a liar." Thus the evil works of Pharaoh were made to appear correct to him, and **he was blocked from the path**. Pharaoh's scheming brought nothing but regret.
40:38	The one who acknowledged said, "O my people, follow me, and I will guide you to the **right path** (*sabil al-rashad*)"

The Arabic text contains numerous literary clues supporting those of us who witnessed the fulfillment of the prophecy. The attention of any careful reader of the verses above would be attracted to a single phrase repeated twice: *Sabil al-Rashad* (the Right Path), whose ownership was claimed by two opposing groups. Unappreciative people, who will try to cover the clear prophecies, will resort to Pharaoh's statement. The prophetic nature of these verses is highlighted by the statement of the monotheist in verse 40:44. Verses 40:78-85 also have multiple references.[180]

The prophetic similarity between the story of Joseph and Rashad is not a coincidence. As we have noted before, the frequency of all the derivatives of the root word *RShD* is 19, and the form **Rashad (right path,** guidance, maturity) occurs only twice in the Quran, and both are mentioned Chapter 40 separated by eight verses; they sandwich the verse that quotes the ingrates excuse to reject one of God's messengers: **"God will not send any messenger after him"**!

Back to our time. Here I would like to add that I differ from Conservative politicians on the question of the so-called "War on Terror"; since I have no doubt that the American foreign policy and sectarian Islam are both guilty of promoting gang and state terrorism. They feed each other. A campaign against terrorism must have two fronts: reformation in American democracy and reformation in Islamic understanding and practice. Unfortunately, the victims of

309

this conflict, whether they live in skyscrapers or caves, are mostly innocent people.

> 27:82-85 "At the right time, we will produce for them a creature, made of earthly materials,[181] declaring that the people are not certain about our revelations/miracles. The day will come when we summon from every community some of those who did not acknowledge our revelations/miracles, forcibly. When they arrive, He will say, 'You have rejected My revelations/miracles, before acquiring knowledge about them. Is this not what you did?' They will incur the requital for their wickedness; they will say nothing."

Recently, someone brought to my attention a statement made by a famous mathematician and philosopher Martin Gardner in an article published in *Scientific American's* September 1980 issue. There, Martin Gardner mentions Rashad's discovery of the Code 19 and claims that he has a 60-page booklet published in 1972 about the number 19. Though I had the original version of that issue, and read the article, I had not noticed the error regarding the year or the content of the booklet. Since Rashad was not aware of the Code 19 when he published his early works on the statistical features of the Quran, Martin Gardner either made an error in typing the date of the publication or made a false assumption regarding the content of the publication. Had I known this erroneous claim when I was in contact with Martin several years ago, I would have investigated the cause of the error. Unfortunately, I lost contact with Gardner and it is now too late. Even if I contacted him, I do not think that he would find in his library a booklet he referred to a quarter of century ago in an article.

I have hundreds of documents published in English, Arabic, Persian, Turkish, and French about Rashad Khalifa and his work. Besides, I have many of Rashad's published and unpublished books, magazines, and articles. I decided to check them one more time to see whether any of the books, newspapers or magazines were referring to his discovery of 19 before the year 1974. As I expected, I could not find a single publication. I knew that before the year 1974, none, including Rashad, had any knowledge of the role of the number 19 in the Quran. The only statement that contradicts this fact is Martin Gardner's reference.

However, if I had any doubt regarding the time of the discovery, it was removed entirely: I found one of Rashad's books in my safe box. That book closed the issue for me. It has a green cover and its title is written in gold.

> Miracle of the Quran:
> Significance of the Mysterious Alphabets
> Rashad Khalifa, PhD, 1973, Islamic Productions International, Inc., St. Louis, MO.

In the beginning of the book, there is a note where Rashad thanks four people for their useful suggestions before the publication. They are:

Virgil I. Moss
Ahmed H. Sakr
Sulayman Shahid Mufasir
Mujahid Al-Sawwaf

The following three pages of the book provide Rashad's biography and include a note of dedication to his father Abdul Halim Khalifa, the leader of the al-Rashad al-Shaziliyya order in Egypt. Years later when Rashad gave up Hadith and Sunna categorically, his father would reject him from family. The biography is followed by a two-page introduction, which is dated, October 1973.

In brief, the book, published after October 1973, presenting his statistical research on the frequency of the initial letters in the Quran, which he started in 1969, does not contain a single reference to the 19 as a common denominator Thus, Martin Gardner's statement is either due to a simple typo or confusion.

I would like to end this chapter with an excerpt from Yvonne Yazbeck Haddad's book, *Mission to America*, which allocates a chapter on Rashad Khalifa and United Submitters International. I recommend this book for those who are interested in objective information about Rashad and the early stage of his group:

> "Despite its detractors, however, Khalifa's message continues to be discussed by persons interested in modern, scientifically verifiable validation of the uniqueness and authenticity of the Qur'an. Many of those who knew Rashad Khalifa continue to express their great appreciation of his work, his message, and his person. Journalist Karima Omar, now known as Virginia Marston, remembers Khalifa with fondness and gratitude, even though she is not willing to affirm without qualification the claims that he made for himself. 'A heretic?' she asks. 'Many thought so. A reformer? In a sense. A herald? Well, some heard his call. An eccentric? Had to be in his line of work, with his kind of God." She praises Khalifa for his candor and honesty, his humor, his courage, his wisdom and deep care for friends and enemies alike. 'Rashad Khalifa smoothed out the lumps, disturbing divinity evenly across ethnic, linguistic and cultural boundaries,' she says. 'Thanks to Rashad, God indeed seems stark raving sane.'" [182]

I met Virgina, a gifted author, who had adopted an Arabic name when she converted to Sunnism after she "milked everything out of Christianity, and it still didn't make sense."[183] But she then found out that the Sunni holy cow had its own version of nonsense. Her discovery of rational monotheism through Rashad, like mine, was a great blessing. She was finally at peace both intellectually and emotionally. She is missed by those who knew her!

Below is what Virgina wrote about Rashad, with her great sense of humor and intelligence. It was published in the May 1988 issue of *Muslim Perspective*, a monthly bulletin published by Rashad:

If God Insists: A Tribute To Rashad Khalifa

by Virginia Omar Kamouneh (formerly Karima Omar)

For several years I had thought of him simply as 'The Number 19 Man-you know, that guy in Arizona whose computer research on the Qur'an had smashed so many intellectual walls, freed so many hearts to accept God's last revelation.

I also thought of him with a good deal of bewilderment. After all, this Rashad Khalifa, this #19 guy, was also reputed-and openly claimed-to deny Prophetic traditions. Even the collections of hadith which I had invested so much money and so many brain cells in amassing and absorbing. Not only the "weak" hadith (rather a redundancy, really) which my imported role models frowned upon even more than usual, but the good old Sunni staples of Bukhari and Muslim with their lovely bedtime stories of the Mercy for Mankind forcing his enemies to drink camel urine, gouging out eyes with hot nails-in between satisfying 9 wives in a single evening.

So this #19 guy had the gall to prefer the Qur'an-the Word of God-to these gratuitously graphic goodies? Gee. Then how did he know how to do all the fun stuff the sunnah teaches us? How did he know which shoe to put on first, which hand to eat with, or what to say before, during and after going to the bathroom? From what I had been taught, man could not only not live by bread alone, but he couldn't even make it on a strict Word of God diet—he had to have supplements, other men to do the hard stuff for him-like thinking.

So, for quite awhile, my perception of him was marked by ambivalence. Given my intellectual/emotional/social state at the time, this was probably the best of all emotions-firm indecision. For quite awhile, my comment on Dr. Rashad Khalifa was, "I love the work he's done with Qur'an and may Allah bless him for it but-I can't agree with his views on hadith." It was a stock response, a mantra which I dutifully chanted when asked my opinion of this man from the Mysterious East of Tucson.

For quite awhile. But, as the Qur'an says, "You pass from stage to stage" (84:19) and I certainly did. To stage to stage, in fact, though that's another story altogether. For gradually, almost imperceptibly, I came to understand-and finally accept-what ironically had always qualified my admiration of Dr. Khalifa. But it wasn't through him; it wasn't through his books and newsletters which, I confess, were eclipsed in my library by frightful mounds of Tafsir-of-the-Years and Icky-Ihyas-it was simply through my study of hadith, my research and writing and reevaluation of my own beliefs—a process of evolution as unlikely as it was inevitable.

I had heard of lovers of God before; had even met a few who seemed to be caught up in an affair with the Divine. But, more often than not, it seemed to have degenerated into a Miles Standish situation with the love originally addressed to God being intercepted by an (unwilling) intercessor-a Prophet, a spiritual guide, a teacher or somewhat shaky shaikh.

No, I never had met a real lover—not of God, anyway I'd encountered lovers of His lovers perhaps, or lovers of lovers of His lovers with their wishful arrangements of carefully cultivated hothouse piety, but no direct-dialing devotees. And I certainly didn't expect to find one in this Rashad Khalifa.

Fly the time I met him, I was a supporter, even a bit of a fan, so I had fully braced myself for the inevitable letdown, Yes, inevitable, for frankly, I expected to find an air of-of paranoia. After all, anyone who had weathered the slings and arrows of controversy that he had over the years was bound to be a little on the jumpy side. So, I anticipated at least a somber, intense man, one who matched the bold face and exclamation points of his writings. I expected a man who hadn't time to be silly, hadn't strength left to laugh at himself and was too busy opening hate mail to crack a smile. But that was OK, I reminded myself; OK and quite natural. Writers always seemed to suffer in the translation of face-to-face encounters. After all, I was a writer, and had seen the suicidal looks of readers who had had the misfortune to at lost meet me in the flesh.

Instead, that bright pre-spring afternoon, in the International house of Pancakes deep in the bowels of Burbank California, no less, I found a shining exception to the rule. I found a lover, a true lover of God. A man whose speech, behavior and mannerisms bore witness to the fact that submission to God is indeed a happy state-not the gloomy and grim affair that so many portray it. I found a man with a quick wit, a ready smile, a gentle humility which was fairly radioactive in its trust and reliance on his Creator. On his Creator. Not on his Creator's creation, not on the cultural security blanket of knee-jerk rituals, not on the petty shirk of self-righteous rites or Sufic psychobabble but on God Alone.

Ironically, in all my years of searching for a magical mystical cure-all, I found it in a man who demystifies Islam, who cuts through all of the idolatry of what-to-do-to-whom-with-which-hand-when to reveal the safe, sane and sensible Way that we always pretend and seldom portray it to be. A man who seems content with his God—"...secure and content soul, come back to your Lord, satisfied and satisfying." (89:27-28), a man satisfied that God has "imposed no hardship on you in observing the religion." (22:78) Perhaps that's why he ruffles the feathers of so many bird-brained Muslims, for he embodies the truth—the simple fact that piety and clinical depression are not synonymous, not even on speaking terms. A subversive truth, indeed.

Dr. Khalifa is indeed a curious case. He has gardens of laurels of impressive achievements on which he could easily rest-and not unjustifiably. His translation of the Qur'an is truly inspired, clear, concise-and being scrapped by its translator. Less than 7 years after its publication, he is publishing a revised edition.

He is comfortable, at-home-with- his-feet-propped-up-on-the-coffee-table, with self-correction - and I think I know his secret. It's no secret, really—it's simply Qur'an. "Yeah," he'd probably say with a sly smiling twinkle, "Simply Qur'an. Just the Word of God." Well, you get the point. His platform is indeed constructed entirely on Qur'an, a fact which is gently evident in conversation with him. Unlike so many self-styled 'scholars" and ignorant "alims," his incessant reference to Qur'an is truly spontaneous, uncontrived-and uncluttered by fishy fish stories and fatuous fatwas.

Since my "association" with him (it sounds like we've been discovered in a love nest with Shaikh Rattle 'n Roll and Jimmy Swaggert in ISNA HQ and let's see how long it takes for that to hit the rumor mill!), I have been asked by countless individuals, "Do you know what Rashad Khalifa is all about'" They have heard, they confide in hushed tones, that he is a spy for the Qadiyanis, a Baha'i, a Mason, Jello Biafra's podiatrist... No, they've never actually met him, they confess; no, they haven't actually read his work, but they've heard from someone whose second cousin heard from someone that — .

But Dr. Khalifa remains unfazed by these rumors; in fact, he seems genuinely amused by them, lie says that these tales have actually been instructional, that he's learned most of what he knows about these sects from the "Islamic" tabloids, the National Expirers of the Muslim world, that broadcast them.

Yes, I do know what Rashad Khalifa is all about, or at least, I think I'm beginning to; I only wish that they did. All they would have to do to find out is to pick up a Qur'an.

"They want to put out God's light with their mouths, but God insists upon perfecting his light..." (9:32) God insists. And that's what Rashad Khalifa, this gentle, twinkling #19 man in Arizona is all about.

314

Terrorists Take To Arizona

Oct. 26, 2001
CBS News

Nearly 200,000 people will attend the World Series and NASCAR races in Phoenix this weekend, and **CBS News Correspondent Vince Gonzales** reports security will be the tightest in the history of Arizona — a state, law enforcement officials admit, that has a history of attracting terrorists.

"There are terrorists among us," said Pima County Sheriff Clarence Dupnik. "I think Arizona probably has a disproportionate share of those kinds of people because we have a number of things that are conducive to terrorists coming to Arizona."

Three of the men believed to have hijacked the jet that slammed into the Pentagon lived in Arizona and learned to fly there. A fourth suspect, on the plane that crashed in Pennsylvania, also had an Arizona address.

Phoenix pilot Lotfi Raissi, arrested after the attacks, allegedly took part in the plot and taught the hijackers how to fly in Arizona, where flying weather is perfect year round.

In fact, according to a government watchlist, investigators have questioned or detained numerous Arizona residents and are looking for many more. One report says agents are seeking an Afghan pilot who reportedly applied for a crop duster license.

Arabic flight manuals and ammunition were found in a Tucson apartment vacated by two Middle Eastern men. "Where they are, I don't know," said Sheriff Dupnik. "They may still be in Tucson, maybe they're in Phoenix. It's easy for terrorists to hide in Arizona, one of America's fastest growing states. "We already have a fairly substantial Middle Eastern population that they can blend into," said Dupnik.

Bin Laden's organization has a history of blending into Arizona. Former Tucson resident Wadih El-Hage was recently sentenced to life for his role in the African Embassy bombings, a bin Laden operation. El-Hage also bought weapons for terrorists convicted in the first World Trade Center bombing. He helped buy a passenger jet from an Arizona Air Force base for bin Laden and later became his personal assistant.

El-Hage has also been connected to the 1990 stabbing death of a Tucson mosque leader. Rashad Khalifa was hated by Muslim extremists opposed to his teachings. His murderer was never caught, but El-Hage, who was indicted for lying about the case, called the assassination "a good thing."

Long before bin Ladin, terrorists called Arizona home. Palestinians targeting the White House and Israel's prime minister in 1981 got their explosives in Phoenix. Even the man executed for what is now the second-worst terrorist attack on U.S. soil, Timothy McVeigh, tested his bombs in the Arizona desert.[184]

28

Witnesses and Ingrates: Fulfilling the Prophecy

6:4-5   And every sign that came to them from their Lord, they turned away from it. They have denied the truth when it came to them. The news will ultimately come to them of what they were mocking.

6:35   If their rejection gets to be too much for you, you should know that even if you dug a tunnel through the earth, or climbed a ladder into the sky, and produced a miracle for them (they still would not acknowledge). Had GOD willed, He could have guided them, unanimously. Therefore, do not behave like the ignorant ones.

7:146   I will divert from My revelations/signs/miracles those who are arrogant on earth without justification. Consequently, when they see every kind of sign/miracle they will not acknowledge. When they see the path of guidance, they will not adopt it as their path, but when they see the path of straying, they will adopt it as their path. This is the consequence of their rejecting our revelations/signs/miracles, and being totally heedless thereof.

26:4-6   Whenever a reminder from the Most Gracious comes to them that is new, they turn away in aversion. They have denied, thus the news will come to them of what they used to ridicule.

74:30-31   **On it is Nineteen.** We have made the guardians of the fire to be angels; and We did not make their number except as a test for those who have rejected, to convince those who were given the book, to strengthen the acknowledgment of those who have acknowledged, so that those who have been given the book and those who acknowledge do not have doubt, and so that those who have a sickness in their hearts and the ingrates would say, "What did God mean by this example?" Thus God misguides whoever/whomever wishes, and He guides whoever/whomever wishes. None knows your Lord's soldiers except Him. It is but a reminder for people.

If you have not read the verses above, please do so now. Since its discovery, Code 19 has started the greatest controversy among Muslims and one will find numerous passionate debates in discussion forums. Interestingly, the passionate objectors cannot escape supporting the very prophecy they attempt to debunk. Code 19, which has strengthened the acknowledgment of thousands of people around the world, removed doubts in the minds of many among the People of the Book. On the other hand, a great number of people declared it to be a hoax or magic, and many failed to witness it by exactly uttering the prophetic phrase, "What does it mean?"

Below is a small sample of diverse reaction to this incredible miracle that acts like a 3-D stereogram made of computerized random dots, as of 2009:

"I was a member of a Sunni sect. By the grace and mercy of the One and only God I have been directed to the true path of God after witnessing the miracle of Nineteen. This happened after I discovered the Power of God through the means of my intellect, which allowed me to contemplate the Word of God, the fully detailed, unique, universal Scripture of the Quran. I am eternally and limitlessly grateful to my Maker for caring about me in such a profound and exhaustive way. I am also thankful to the people He chose to be His means of guidance for my lost self. One of these upright and stout men is my brother Edip, who in my eyes will always remain a patriarch of the Reformation. All thanks and prayers are to God alone! Alhamdu Lillah!" **Aslbek A.Mussin (29), Monotheistic philosopher and activist, Almaty, Kazakhstan**

"Trying to understand to what extent the Quran was a "miracle" I asked GOD two years ago to give me "just one proof" that I was in the right path. The discovery of the mathematical miracle of the Quran has been God's answer to my prayers which strengthened my faith that the Quran was indeed His very word, and showed me the right way to serve Him by upholding the Quran alone. I Praise GOD for that." **Maria Benchenane (20), Graduate Student at EPHE, Paris, France.**

"This new book by Dr. Edip Yuksel is an important update of the original discovery by Dr. Rashad Khalifa around 30 years ago. I knew Edip as one of the closest and certainly the most critical student and associate of Dr. Khalifa when we were in Masjid Tucson during the 1980-1990s. From the earliest days Edip worked the hardest assisting Rashad to weed out the diamond from the glass, the valid Nineteen phenomenon from the invalid ones. This book is an important milestone but still a work in progress, as I believe we are only at the tip of an iceberg." **Gatut Adisoma, Ph.D (55), Executive /Entrepreneur, Jakarta/Indonesia.**

"Since 18 years I have been studying Miqra. When I read about the Cod 19 in Quran I was very surprised! I believe that no human could create the Quran and the Code 19. It is really God's work. Through the same message of the Torah and the Quran all people can know the God of Avraham and peacefully surrender themselves to Him." **Ezra (Piotr) Wolski (33, Poland), Spiritual teacher-leader of Russian Qaraim in Poland, Liberec, Czech.**

"The Code-19 is an extraordinary, living evidence for people who pursue the truth, honestly and objectively. Its miraculousness lies not only in how fantastically it has been planned/designed by the Most Wise, but also in its ability to be verified independently by anyone at anytime regardless of their age, gender, social or economic status. The proof adds validity to one's faith, puts God on top of one's priority list, and frees the individual from petty, egoistic vanities of this short, lowly earthly existence. This is our only chance for redemption so let us avail it and sincerely thank the Almighty for unveiling the "hidden secret" for our scientific generation. Peace." **Khurram Kemal Shahzad (30), Engineer, Toronto, Ontario, Canada**

317

"The 19-based system is one of the greatest miracles of the Quran. Though, I do not agree with Edip Yüksel fully, I appreciate very much his dedication and service to the Quran." **Yaşar Nuri Öztürk (57), Professor of Theology and Author, Istanbul, Turkey**

"The number 19 is the number of Bahai cult and has nothing to do with the Quran. It is modern cabbalism and nonsense. Quran's first verse, Bismillah, does not have 19 letters as they claim, but it has 21 letters. I have written a book on this deviation... Recently numerous engineers and doctors started following this path. One of those who follow his imaginations is the guy who was once imprisoned for participating in terror activities in Turkey and now living in America. I met that guy first time during the Ceviz Kabuğu TV program and then I immediately understood that he had idolized his ego. He was rude and did not recognize any rules of etiquette. When he realized that I was going to debunk his claims he interrupted my words. I listened to him for half an hour, but when my turn came he would interject." **Süleyman Ateş (76), former head of the Department of Religious Affairs in Turkey (1976-1978), theology professor and author, Turkey**

"Nineteeners are heretics. They attempt to find relationship between the number of letters, words, verses and chapters and reach a conclusion. A man who used live in America and who was assassinated first claimed to have found a 19-based mathematical structure in the Quran. He went even further and rejected two verses from the Quran because of their violation of his 19-based calculations. These claims have no scientific nor religious basis. This theory has been refuted. For instance, see Dr. Orhan Kutman's book. That guy who once joined Rashad Khalifa and then gave up some of his ideas made numerous false claims and insulted the religious feelings of the masses in a television program that I could not watch.... I have argued the importance of Sunna in religion in my previous articles... As for those ignorant people who exceed their limits, I invite you to ignore them, and I invite TV programmers to think twice before allowing them to confuse people." **Hayrettin Karaman (75), theology professor and author, Turkey**

"I committed a blunder by publishing the findings of Dr. Rashad Khalifa in my book and considering it as a miracle of the Quran. When I learned that Rashad used the Code 19 to reject the two verses from the Quran, I realized that I was duped and mislead. The Quran does not have any mathematical structure. The Code 19 is a myth and I denounced it in an article, which was published together with the articles of prominent scholars in a book titled *19 Efsanesi (The Myth of 19)*. by the same publishing house that published Edip Yuksel's book, *Kuran En Büyük Mucize (Quran, the Greatest Miracle)*." **Tayyar Altıkulaç (71), former head of the Department of Religious Affairs in Turkey (1978-1986), theology professor and author, Turkey**

"The 30+ year sophisticated realization that the Quran has an elegant internal structure, based upon the prime number "19" reinforces the 14 century belief in the timelessness of this revealed text. Why would such an expanded understanding of this glorious message have motivated some individuals to martyr the scientist who opened the door to this additional wonder of Allah? It is indeed an unaltered Message for all time, for all peoples and all languages, continuing to encourage deep contemplation among all true seekers. Nothing has changed yet more is understood. This gift of greater understanding of an unchanged message, after so much time has passed, is fully consistent with the awesome nature of our Creator." **Jeff Garrison (66), Medical Doctor, Colorado, USA**

"I started reading the Quran when I was a high school student. All Turkish translations, with a few exceptions, such as the ones by Edip Yuksel or Yaşar Nuri Öztürk, were adding the word "angels" after the word "nineteen". They were also mistranslating some other verses of the chapter 74 and creating a vivid description of hellfire burning, grilling, frying and schorching the critics of the Quran. I was a university student when I finally discovered a satisfactory understanding of the Quranic statements in verses 74:30-31. The number 19 was an intellectual response to the prototype arrogant and ingrate person: he would be refuted and convicted by the number nineteen, unequivocally and eternally. The new understanding that correctly reflected the meaning of the text left no doubt in my mind that the Quran was indeed a message from my Creator. The prophetic mathematic structure of the Quran distinguishes the Quran as a unique book; with both its structure and content, it was unlike other religious books of Hadith and Sunna peddled as supplemantary authorities. Now, I can accept the Quran without accepting the contradictory and false teachings. I do not need to follow blindly those religious stories and sectarian teachings. I do not need to trust the words of previous generations in order to know that the Quran is indeed God's message, which has been preserved and protected by an internal numerical code. I can acknowledge God and His words by trusting only my mind, which is exactly what the Quran expects its readers to do in many verses, such as 17:36; 10:100; 39:17-18; 41:53; 42:21; 6:114-116; 10:36; 12:111; 20:114; 21:7; 35:28; 38:29. **Tarık Arabacı (23), Math Student at Bosphorous University, Istanbul, Turkey**

"I first came to witness the miracle of code-19 at the age of NINETEEN on the site submission.org. That was a life changing moment. The simple facts at submission.org were already enough to convince me of a significant pattern in the Quran based on 19. Besides, a rather significant event in my life involving this number amazingly and counterintuitively led me to accept the theory of evolution instead of creationism as is almost always the case with religions." **Khizar Zamurrad Janjuah (27), Hamelin, Germany**

"I was always a believer in the Quran, but I had very many questions in regard to the transmission of it. These issues weren't easy, at least for me. How can I be sure, that the Quran wasn't ever altered? In the same time, the proposed methodology of the Quran to solve this issue was very straightforward and reasonable: just produce a Sura like it with similar properties. I saw many people trying it. All of them failed. As a student of math, I also studied important mathematical parts of the code, to gain certainty. And nowadays, I acknowledge that 74:31 holds true for me: my acknowledgement of the Quran has been strengthened, all thanks to God." **Zafer Kerem Adıgüzel (22), Student of mathematics at the University of Zurich, Switzerland**

"Throughout my pursuit for truth I have wondered what it would be like to experience a miracle of biblical proportions. Glory to God the Quran is the miracle of our age. The mathematical harmony of 19 opened my mind to know that only God can preserve His message of guidance." **Adam Sigmund (28), Student, South Jersey, USA**.

"Through the miracle 19 I started to study the Quran from the beginning to the end. I was curious who the discoverer of this solid proof was and studied his messages. Besides, I also investigated the book *19 Questions for Sunni and Shiite scholars* by Edip Yuksel, which also made a lot of sense to me. Finally, I decided to follow only Quran as the source and converted from Sunni to Monotheism. The 19 miracle increased my faith and gave me the courage to discuss with people who follow other authorities besides the

319

Quran. For the disbelievers it is not strange that they are genetically coded by DNA. However, a mathematically coded scripture is strange for them. A coded creature cannot imagine a scripture which is coded by the Creator. Thanks to God for leading the believers out of darkness into the light." **Volkan Güngör (27), Corporate Finance, Rotterdam, Holland**

"I was told that 19 is alpha and omega. I did not know about it, yet it allowed me to search from the first and stop at a point. Had it been not for 19, I would have been still whirling in the pool of not-ending philosophical complications and confusions. After listening and studying the strongest opponents of the Quran and Islam, I felt they were speaking sense only! My belief in the scientific consistency of the Quran was sensibly debunked. I started losing all my faith and respect for the Quran until I came to know about a phenomenon called '19'. I held my judgment for a period to study it. I critically evaluated this theory, so I studied everything possible to disprove it. But, I couldn't find any success in debunking the theory and further I was able to see the abundant possibilities of the Quran and its divine signature designed with code 19. Along with some personal experiences, I decided to uphold the Quran, a book backed up by a sound numerical pattern based on Code 19. Code 19, I believe, is a fork between those who want to progress and those who want to stay where they are. I want to progress, so I chose to witness 19 and acknowledge the message of the Quran." **Mohammed Jaseer (27), Computer Programmer, Kerala, India**.

"Code 19 shows up in the constants related to subatomic particles and it may explain every event in the universe. In other words, there is 19 on the universe." **Necat Yılmaz, Professor of Biochemistry, Antalya, Turkey**

"My whole life has changed when I have read Rashad's Khalifa booklet 'Islam, Quran and Hadith'. Before this lecture, I had many doubts about the authenticity of Quran and its divine origin since the traditional Islamic scholar taught us that Quran was transmitted orally at the beginning, many years before being written down and compiled in a book. How could a skeptic mind trust the human memory knowing its weakness and limitation? It is the mathematical structure of Quran based on number 19 that removes all my doubts and strengthens my belief in One God because it is clear that no human or a group of humans, especially in the 7th century, were capable to write a book with such structure. Thanks to God for making me a witness of one of His great signs. This sign opened my eyes to the beauty, the power and the truth expressed by Quran. There is no other book that can do all that especially if the reader is a global skeptic." **El Mehdi Haddou (39, Morocco), Veterinary Doctor, Montréal, Canada**

"The mathematical miracle of the Quran is indeed very impressive and an ideal sign for our time. For me, personally, it reassured me that the Quran is the word of God and therefore encouraged me to study it further. However one must also understand that not every multiple of 19 within the Quran is a divine sign or a proof. Presenting these statistically insignificant discoveries alongside the simple mathematical composition of the Quran can put off someone from appreciating the miracle. The mathematical miracle of the Quran directs us to study the Quran further instead of hunting for ANYTHING 19 divisible (See Quran: 74:6)." **Karrar Abidi (17), Student, Untied Kingdom**

"Any mathematical system will have a formula. You can provide input to the formula and get a predictable output. Code 19 is not mathematics, it is numerology. There is no system or formula or pattern. It is whatever haphazard manmade inconsistent formula gets you a 19 divisible. There is no pattern and this is why 19ers don't use the same formula twice. God knows that they tried to use their formulas consistently but every time they tried, they failed to get a 19 divisible. They are hiding those failed trials and only presenting the 1-in-19 successful trials inevitably found in any random sample. This is why they will NEVER answer your question and they will NEVER share their failed trials. "NINETEEN: God's Signature in Nature and Scripture" is about the 1-in-19 random numbers that are divisible by 19 in nature and in scripture. This is why the reader is never told about the infinite numbers in nature and the thousands of failed trials in scripture that are not 19 or 19 divisible. Fancy words such as "God's Signature" are meant to distract the reader from this untold fact. Instead of insulting the intelligence of the reader, I would suggest that the author honestly shares the whole truth, even at the expense of the book becoming pointless." **Ayman (42), VP of a consulting firm, anonymous A critic of Code 19, the Bible Code, numerology, Santa Claus, the Tooth Fairy, and the Easter Bunny, USA.**

"Majority of Muslims do not know what the Quran teaches. They only know what religious teachers teach them and what clergymen ordain for them. So they either become blind fanatics or simply forsake Islam like I once did. From the day I "discovered" Islam on my own, I prayed my own way and read the Quran in my own language or English. I thought I was the only Muslim like this. Then one day while surfing the net, I discovered several websites promoting the kind of Islam I thought only I was practicing. When I read about the numerical miracle of the Quran I was more convinced that the Quran is the ultimate guide for Muslims, not laws that were written by traditional Muslim clergy... I will continue to do whatever I can to promote non-sectarian Islam in my country in Malaysia, by peaceful means of course." **Farouq Omaro, Malaysia**

"There is no formula only an obsession by the most ignorant people on the planet searching for anything nineteen not understanding basic math. A natural sequence of any odd number (1, 3, 5, 7, 9, 11, 13, ..., 19, 21, 23,..., n) is a multiple of that odd number forms similar patterns. No sign or formula nineteen—only an obsession (fitna) with numerology." **Eid, posted at free-minds.org forum.**

"I was a Sunni when I first came across the mathematical miracle of the Quran. At first I was shocked, especially when it says that there are two false verses in the Quran, and then when Rashad claimed to be a messenger. Then I went back read it again and again. I noticed that I was reading the Quran more and more; I never read it like this before! On top of that, I understood it, very clear. It made me cry. How many times have I looked at this Book and never realized that this Book is from God. I know that every one says that but do they really believe in it? I started to realize that the truth is clear and I said thanks God, thanks God. I am so happy, but the story doesn't end here." **Amine (43), Algeria**

"The issue of 74:30-31 and other mathematical phenomenon in the Quran in the recent decades depends on every individual's beliefs. The best way of experiencing this is the example of "the one who sees the glass half full of water or another who sees it half empty." No matter whether one rejects or accepts 74:30-31 per Dr. Khalifa's English translation, for the first time, it has taken attention of those who were searching for the truth. Peace." **Hussein Najaf Pir (55), Retired engineer, Salem, Oregon**

"Methodology of Code 19 is as follows. Let us suppose you get two numbers "9" and "5" First you:

A: Subtract = 9-5 = 4, does not work because it is not multiple of 19
B: Add = 9+ 5 = 14 does not work because it is not multiple of 19
C: Multiply = 9x5 = 45 does not work
D: Divide = 9/5 does not work

Now try placing them together like

59 = Does not work because not multiple of 19
95 = Wow it is multiple of 19 because 95/19 = 5

Suppose if all these EFFORTS fail, then there is a FOOL PROOF method whichever word or verse is creating Hindrance THROW IT OUT OF THE QURAN. Believe this LAST METHOD will never fail." **Q-Student, posted at free-minds.org forum.**

"Millions of Turkish people learned about the mathematical miracle of the Quran based on Code 19 from Edip Yuksel's books and TV interviews and debates. This not only transformed my faith to knowledge, it saved me from following menmade religious teachings such as Hadith and Sunna." **Özalp Şenk (45), Electrical Engineer, Samsun, Turkey**

"I come from a nominal Christian background. In 1993, as was their routine, the teacher's union went on strike before school began. My frustrated mother decided to send me to an Islamic school. It was a few years after the murder of Rashad Khalifa, and the school was in the middle of a controversy regarding the role of tradition in Islam. The principal was a traditional Sunni (turban, robe, henna dyed beard, the whole 9 yards). My teacher and some of the students, however, were non-sectarian Muslims. When the school's lease came to an end, the principal and my teacher parted ways, and she established her own school. I initially adhered to the traditional position. But I was disabused after reading Rashad Khalifa's translation of the Quran, and his book *The Quran,* Hadith*, and Islam*, that my teacher had given me. The novelty of the Quran's mathematical structure intrigued me, but I remained noncommittal because math wasn't my best subject. It was years after I accepted the Quran's message, and after I brushed up on elementary math, that I began to appreciate how it's message and it's mathematical structure complement each other." **Michael Elwood (29) Student, Chicago, USA**

"Factors such as unalteration, profundity, logical coherence, literary brilliance of its message and Muhammad's known lack of literary background adequately assure the Quran's divine status. Additionally, a mathematical association of Number "19" with the Quran's structure is a fascinating finding. However, the omission of two verses (of Surah 9) from this association might remain as an issue. On deeper reflection, "Nineteen" in 74:30 might denote the degrees of progress in knowledge and power one needs to acquire to decisively conquer Hell fire mentioned in adjoining verses." **Abdur Rab (72, Bengladesh), Retired economist and author of Exploring Islam in a New Light: An Understanding from the Quranic Perspective, Atlanta, USA**

"Attribute it to whatever you like, but multiples of 19 appear in inexplicable abundance in total counts of Qur'ânic initials in sûrât grouped together by identical initial-sets, using the commonly available Arabic text printed in the Yûsuf 'Alî translation. Even if all you do is take the text as given and include the alif-initialed sûrât (whose alif counts in current Qur'ânic copies just water down the results), the odds against finding multiples of 19 with such great frequency are still too high, at 2,306 to one. I've tried all prime numbers below 100. Random chance does nothing to explain it." **Richard S. Voss, Ph.D. (47), Professor in Business Administration, Georgia, USA**

"All individuals can benefit from further study of sacred mathematical patterns within the Qur'an. Numerous individuals throughout history have advocated for spurious numerological patterns in religious texts, but modern advocates within the "Code 19" movement often rely on statistically significant and eerily unexplainable evidence to state their case. We must acknowledge that much remains to be studied regarding numerical repetitions in the Qur'an, but we must also strive to open this debate up to the mainstream scientific and academic community for further analysis. Modern technology like data mining software provides near-limitless technological opportunities in order to analyze this phenomenon. Mathematicians and physicists would FREAK OUT if this theory was verified from within their respective communities. Praise for our Lord and Sustainer remains self-evident regardless of numerology, but "Code 19" provides a great plot twist for individuals mired within the "science vs. religion" debate in the West." **Matthew Cappiello (23), Student and activist, San Diego, USA**

"Khalifa's translation is tainted by his obsession with an imaginary mathematical code centering around the "magic" number 19 that supposedly proves the Quran's divine origin, but he went so far as to throw out two verses so the number of verses would then be a multiple of 19, thus fitting the code." **Jeffrey L. Graham, Ordained Imam, USA**

"Code 19 is interesting in that it draws attention to read the Quran, after which the content itself upholds the importance of the book not 19. The message of the Quran is in its simplicity; an attempt to introduce a level of complexity will distract attention and dilute the message." **Fereydoun Taslimi (55, Iran), Entrepreneur, Atlanta, Georgia, USA**

"I just want you to know that Dr. Khalifa's work has made a difference. All of you did a great thing unveiling that. I basically was a disbeliever all throughout undergrad (how many 18-22 year olds are religious these days? Some, but not many ... it's too bad, really, but I didn't know better ...) because I felt there was generally not a scientific basis for religion. In my heart, I think I always knew that wasn't true but thanks to God I came upon Dr. Khalifa's discovery while doing some research at Michigan and thought, wow, there really is something to this book! I'd taken many mathematics (calculus w/ diff equations) and science classes and was awed at the fact that a book could be numerically and literally structured. I was taking Persian classes and decided I really should study more about Islam, even ended up majoring in it. I started reading Qur'an seriously and couldn't believe what I had been missing ... it is a beautiful book even in translation; doesn't even need a mathematical miracle ... it is that good, but yet God put this in there anyway!!" **Rodeen Rahbar (34), Medical Doctor, Pennsylvania, USA**

"When the world's mind is occupied with hot violence of suicide bombings and genocides, when cold violence of Sharia law insults and destroys Muslim women, when Female Genital Mutilation destroys more than six thousand girls a day—we should put all our resources to establish the proposed mechanism of ending these violences by Quranic tools. Thanks for your effort, anyway." **Hasan Mahmud (46, Bangladesh), Director, Sharia Law Muslim Canadian Congress, Canada**

"I can never forget. One day when I was in highschool, I was discussing with my classmates about the preservation and authenticity of the Quran. A friend of mine whose

faith in science outbalanced his faith in teachings he inherited from his parents said, "If in the future life is discovered in another planet and we learn that they have a divine book similar to the Quran, then the Quran's divine origin will have support. Otherwise, Quran's self-proclaimed divine origion does not have much merit." When I first witnessed the *Miracle 19* because of Edip Yuksel's books, I remembered that conversation I had years ago and said to myself: "That means there was no need to wait for intelligent extraterrestrials to find scientific evidence for the Quran's authenticity and preservation."
İ. Raci Bayer (31), Civil Engineer, Ankara, Turkey

"I was born in an Orthodox Muslim community. Then, I was introduced to politically active Sunnis. The most important event in my life is my discovery of the Islamic Reform movement and my discovery of Code 19 and other miracles of the Quran which strengthened my faith and removed all doubts from my heart. Through this paradigm change, when I looked at life under the light of the Quran, things became so clear that I really did not need any other religious source besides the Quran. I strongly believe that millions of people will one day discover the liberating and progressive message of the Quran and will save themselves from the hypocrisy, backward teachings and practices, ignorance, oppression and fictions of religion they inherited blindly from their parents. One day the reign of backward sectarian teachings will come to end and the message will shine over the world again. The message of the Quran will not only save the so-called Islamic World, but will provide real solutions for the ailments inflicting Western societies." **Necmettin ASLAN (33) Computer Programmer, Diyarbakır, Türkiye**

"If you wonder which chapter has the greatest influence on me, I would not hesitate to point at chapter 74. With its content, literary style, and prophetic statements, Chapter 74 is a shock for modern readers. I first heard about the verse 19 in 1986 after reading Edip Yüksel's then best-selling book, *Kuran En Büyük Mucize*. Then, I was more interested in the second section of the book where the scientific aspect and content of some verses were discussed. A few years later when I looked at the book again, then I appreciated the importance of the 19-based literary structure. My family was not a religious family. I started praying after reading Yüksel's book. Influenced by my teachers, I joined the religious group called Nurcular (the Followers of Light). This affiliation lasted until April of 1989 when I read the cover story of weekly *Nokta* (*Period*) magazine. The popular magazine had interviews with Rashad Khalifa and Edip Yüksel. Khalifa's and Yüksel's views were contradictory to the orthodox teaching. Knowing Yuksel from his books, I knew that he would not be blind follower of vain and absurd ideas. In 1989, I obtained the address of Masjid Tucson and contacted Yuksel. Meanwhile, by chance I came across Yuksel's highly controversial book, *İlginç Sorular 2* (*Interesting Questions-2*). I was very lucky, since Edip Yuksel was excommunicated and his books were collected from the market. After a period of research, studying Edip Yuksel's books and discussing with him, I eliminated the information pollution around sign/verse 19 and decided to uphold the Quran as the only source of my religion. Since then, I see the sign 19 to be one of the greatest, as it is described by verse 74:35. The sign 19 is a divine blessing to our high-tech generation with a prophetic timing: the secret of 19 mentioned in chapter 74 known Secret, was unveiled in 1974, exactly 19x74 lunar years after the revelation of the Quran. However, I cannot understand how so many people can manage to blind themselves to this great miracle." **Cemal Aktaş (40), Financial Advisor, Istanbul, Turkey**

"We find it difficult to accept that God would use a system of proof that excludes all the people who needed it during the 1400 years of the Quran's existence and who groped in the dark when puzzled by unintelligible verses. Although, as we shall discover later, the presence of the number 19 in the Quran as presented by Dr. Khalifa, is impressive, it nevertheless lacks the persuasiveness that divine intervention would have provided.... Finding a system of numerics like the one mentioned in Dr. Khalifa's and Mr. Deedat's books is, in the opinion of this writer, possible for any piece of literature, or music if you wish. Any piece of literature will have combinations of letters perhaps in relation to the title, that will allow a computer, properly fed and programmed to find a system of combinations that will prove equally surprising. If so, would the piece be of divine origin? Not being a computer scientist I cannot substantiate the above reasoning, but am convinced that it could be done... We would have no problem combining any number of sentences each containing 19 letters and if we did not wish to waste time we could, by using a computer, be even more successful still. We find, therefore, the over-dramatic presentation of this matter to be highly suspicious and inappropriate." **Bapi Sengupta, (India), in an excerpt from his article titled,** *The Mysterious 19 in the Quran: a Critical Evaluation.*

"The list of interesting and obviously intentional numerical patterns in the Quran is a great blessing for people who want to uphold the truth at all costs. It serves as a lighthouse guiding people to the Quran, in a storm of misinformation and popular associations of Islam with all that is violent and wrong. Providing very strong evidence for Quran's authenticity, it attracts attention to Quran's message that rejects other sources as religious guidance. This provides a challenge for everyone, and requires an open mind and use of logic to navigate towards the truth. In my own journey, the numerical structure of Quran played a key role and helped me remove my doubts and embrace the Quran. Thank God and thank his servants for this great sign." **Gazihan Alankus (30, Turkey), Graduate Student in Computer Science, St. Louis, MO, USA.**

"The more I meet people who cannot see this astonishing sign is the more I find myself in glorification." **Ensar Üzümcü (28, Istanbul), IT & E-Commerce, United Kingdom.**

29

From Faith to Reason

93:0   In the name of God, the Gracious, the Compassionate.
93:1   By the late morning.
93:2   The night when it falls.
93:3   Your Lord has not left you, nor did He forget.
93:4   The (here)after is better for you than the first.
93:5   Your Lord will give you and you will be pleased.
93:6   Did he not find you an orphan and He sheltered you?
93:7   He found you lost, and He guided you?
93:8   He found you in need, so He gave you riches?
93:9   As for the orphan, you shall not make him sad.
93:10   As for the beggar, you shall not reprimand.
93:11   You shall proclaim the blessings from your Lord.

I have received hundreds of emails from people all around the world sharing their stories of paradigm change. I will be publishing some of them in a book provisionally titled *From Faith to Reason: Inspiring Stories of 40 Monotheists.* Below are a few of those personal stories:

Ali Syed, USA

November 22, 2010

I learned about the mathematical system of the Quran during early 80's. One of my teachers mentioned it in the class, making a few statements and it was never mentioned again. However, his comments stayed in my head until 2010 when I started reading Rashad Khalifa's and Edip Yuksel's Translation and explanation of the code 19. Generally speaking, many people write about very different topics every day, and after years of practice, eventually it comes naturally to them. However, when one sits to write, the thought of organizing the collection of writing in a way that a mathematical relationship is preserved throughout the writing never crosses any human-wirter's mind. As humans, we are very much focused on the logical flow of what we right, grammar, punctuation. Some care about political correctness of how ideas are expressed, and many other external factors including saying things in a way that would attract a lot attention. The thought of writing any meaningful literal piece and preserving any mathematical relationship is something that is not even considered. Furthermore, and again generally speaking, there are very few people who may have the vast knowledge of both mathematics and literature, let alone the ability to combine these two into a masterpiece. Keep this in mind as I will be coming back to this.

I studied Biochemistry for undergraduate, and then voluntarily took extra physiology and other science courses during years of obtaining my Doctorate in Pharmacy. Aside from learning the science, the recurring theme in my head was that whoever programmed all this must have had the highest level of knowledge in ALL, yes ALL, sciences including physics, chemistry, biology, physiology, kinesiology, medicine, immunology, biochemistry, electronics, engineering and much more that human limited capacity is yet to discover. Sciences that I mentioned above are a small collection that I had superficial exposure to some. Now, combine all this with the literature and mathematics, and you have a picture perfect! Yes there are mysteries in Quran that will be revealed at the right time to the right person. Yes, anyone can raise questions regarding multiple meanings and allegories used therein. What is undeniable is that all signs point in one and only one direction, and that is existence of an omniscient, omnipotent and omnipresent being, far beyond our understanding, who takes every opportunity to touch us and communicate with us. Yes, there are repetitions in Quran, guess what, the most efficient way we learn to remember things is through repetition.

The reformist translation was done at a much needed time. A time, that many volumes of Hadith and other types of religious manuals were written that were far longer and voluminous than Quran itself. These were written without much thought and careful verification of sources and credibility of such sources, and what is far worse is that it never occurred to the authors and publishers to read the Quran and see if their product is contradicting Quran or insulting anyone. Furthermore, If we agree that the author of Quran possesses all knowledge that there is, then Quran must remain a timeless masterpiece. The reformist translation took time to link many of the recent scientific discoveries to what was written over 1400 years ago. This link is highly significant; since it, yet again, proves that Quran is a living and timeless document far beyond our current and future discoveries. Furthermore, many things written in Quran became hot button for various groups (e.g. beating women). The reformist translation took a fresh look at the topic and took time to clarify some of the inadvertent misconceptions of previous translations.

Quran repeatedly states that "we made Quran easy to learn. Do any of you wish to learn?" (54:40), this is yet another dimension of this book, where anyone with any level of literacy can read and be (God willing) guided to countless signs that exist in us and around us.

As for the Code 19, it is something that it is rather impossible to imitate, yet it should not be considered the end of the miracles that Quran offers. One can easily be amazed by it, admire it, and stop right there, but an open mind sees far beyond the words on the paper.

Peace to all those who have successfully killed their ego and are open-minded and fearless enough to acknowledge truth when they are exposed to it.

Ali Seyed, Pharmacist, 43, PA

Mehdi Haddou, Canada

14 March 2008

Dear Edip,

Thanks for your email and for all the interest that you show to help monotheists from all around the world. I am with you on the fact that we have a responsibility to stand against the warmongers among us. It is the real Jihad. Nothing is more effective than an intellectual Jihad.

I am reading the Reformist Translation that I find really interesting. It's really important to have www.19.org/forum opened for discussing and sharing ideas. I have tried to be registered at free-minds.org but I did not succeed to have a pass word, I think maybe they are full.

I am a rational monotheist since November 2006 (I was 36 years old) before that I was only a believer in the existence of a supreme designer because everything around me (my personnel experiences, nature, life...) suggests that there is a supreme GOD but I was not sure about that since I had no proof.

Since I was raised in a Moroccan Sunni family I was familiar with hislam (fake Islam) which I have completely rejected because of its contradictory and nonsense teachings. I have rejected also the Qur'an, because I was sure that the way that Qur'an was collected, according to Moushrikoun scholars (19 years after Mohammed's death), the Qur'an was not protected from being was tampered with. Because of my rejection of the Qur'an, I was not allowed by God to understand its very clear and obvious verses.

By the end of October 2006, I was in Morocco (to visit my family) and I remember, it was during Ramadan, I have openly proclaimed to my God that I am rejecting His religion Islam because of the nonsense of this religion and if He really exist I need that He shows me a sign/proof or anything to guide me since I recognized to him that I was spiritually lost. Later, I knew that I was rejecting Hislam and not God's system, Islam. Two weeks later, when I was at home in Canada surfing on the web, I found the website of Masjid Tucson and articles about the 19 code miracle discovered by Dr. Rashad Khalifa. I can not explain to you what my reaction was when I finished reading (and of course verifying with my Quran and calculator) those articles. I called my Sunni wife (she was in the kitchen) to come quickly, I was fixed to my PC, and I told her (in French): 'Shit, God really exists' she answered: 'I know that He exists', I replied: 'No, you do not now, I mean really and really exists like If I am seeing Him with my eyes'. Even now, I know that she can not understand what I have felt on that day and what I am still feeling now, only true knowledgeable people can understand.

Your many articles have helped me to understand and clarify many thinks in Islam. I hope we will keep in contact and with other monotheist from around the world.

Salam

Gökhan Aycan, Ankara, Türkiye

19 September 2004

Peace all,

I have recently mentioned an experience which changed a whole lot in my life. I was having hard time how to put it therefore it took me more than expected. After a sincere thought I decided not to post it under the "My Intellectual and Spiritual Adventure" forum since the context seems different. Nonetheless the moderators would change the location if they see fit. Let me start with a little background information.

I was born in Istanbul, Türkiye in 1976. Being the son of a pilot in the air force officer, I had a relatively easier life than the most in the country. I had the luck of getting accepted in some of the best schools and universities. I have a B.S. in civil engineering and an MBA degree. After being certified as a Microsoft Certified System Engineer I have worked as a systems administrator for some time. I now live in Ankara, the capital city of Türkiye.

Religion was never a central focus point within the family. Therefore I also was not very interested with it. It was only a section on my national ID card stating that my religion was Islam. I remember the strict rules of Islam being taught during junior high school, which was in accordance with Sunni teachings. During this class (Religious Culture and Ethics) we were made to memorize prayers, which are read through contact prayers, in Arabic. It was very frustrating since I did have hard time memorizing even in Turkish. Furthermore I understood nothing. Then there were Hadiths and Sunna. They even made students perform contact prayers on desks in order to grade them. "Put your hands there, reach here!" In the 90's, as private TV channels got on-air I started to see various 'religious orders' that spread around the country witnessing how they tried to live in a century that had passed a long time ago. The state of Middle East and the woman stoned to death in Iran (I still have a crystal clear vision of the scene) were just other flavors. From everything I have lived and seen with the name tag 'Islam' there emerged my belief: 'one god no religion'.

December 2003. I am in total mess. Most probably a major depression as a psychologist would call. I quit my job after 8 months for they had been unjust. It has been a couple of months since I had seen or talked to anyone including family members but the barber and the stand owner at the corner of the street. After all I needed those packs of cigarettes. Yes, packs of cigarettes, two of them a day.

For years I have felt something was wrong, that I did not deserve most of the things that happened. I had been polite, respecting others and all. Whenever something good happened it was immediately followed by something depressing. Not even a time to enjoy the moment. I believed that it was a kind of curse. I usually got upset with those, mostly sad and depressed but this time it was different. I felt hatred, a great one indeed. Just put the button which would destroy everything and I will press it without a second thought. After all, life sucked. This world, the ignorance, people dying for nothing ... Who needs hell if you are in a torture chamber, giving you more pain with every second that passes? And the only way to escape looks like a deep cut into the throat.

I was, as usual when depressed, in front of the PC playing minesweeper in expert mode for hours straight. Thinking, thinking and thinking as I play. Thinking about things that I have gone through, going over my mistakes and regrets, others' mistakes, those who suffer, money being the great goal. You name it, it was in there. I was feeling as if the microprocessor in my head was about to burn out. If I could ever shut down that processor I could find the peace I was searching for long. With a never ending cigarette in my left hand I continued to play.

One day, at a moment of great despair, I stepped up and shouted: "God, either take my life or show a way! I am tired and can't take it anymore." I couldn't guess those to come.

A couple of days later while playing my favorite game I realized something odd. For those rounds I successfully finished a game, the seconds counter stopped at a certain number. Not once, not twice but at a rate which caught my attention. It was mere luck at first. I had seen such occurrences that two consecutive rounds ended at the same second. But then that specific number kept popping up, haunting me. And it continued on the second day and the third one. It was the fifth day that I decided to stop playing because it made me quite uncomfortable. After a day or two a sudden idea flashed. I was used to searching from the internet the things that I wondered, why not this one? I wasn't expecting anything meaningful since it was only a random number and it would be a different way of killing time.

I opened my favorite search engine, Google, wrote down the number in Turkish and pressed 'Enter'. I was shocked with the search result. It was then that I realized Quran was formed of 114 ('yüzondört' in Turkish) suras. The number that kept popping up was 114. My feelings at that moment are beyond any description I can make. I was amazed and feared. I had asked Him and he showed me the way. Yet another question eventually came to my mind. How could I ever go back to something which I rejected for its irrationality? But this was a question already answered by God. I just couldn't comprehend it before.

While I was struggling with the number, on the third day's night (or as I remember such) the TV was on, making background sound. There was a discussion on a channel that I don't normally watch. The guest was a Turkish author. He was talking about the miracle of Quran and the number 19. Although he couldn't defend the idea very well it was enough for me to get curious. I guess he mentioned Edip's name that is how I found this site. I do remember reading the introductory page 'who are we'. "Interesting", I thought. I must not have gotten into the depths of the site because I have learned that Quran had 114 suras only after the internet search.

I immediately started to read Edip's Turkish translation of the Quran, the Message, and the other materials on 19.org. It was a different time. I was tearing apart from within only a few days before the search. Sometimes I thought that I was going insane. I was surprised once more a couple of days later. The intervention was far from being over. Just like I have heard of 19, I came across a TV show about schizophrenia. That was just my subject. As I listened to one of the guests, which was a patient of the illness, I realized the similarity of feelings. It was shocking, I must admit.

Had I gone mad? Was God showing me that? I have spent weeks trying to understand what everything meant. I could find an answer only after two of my friends appeared at the door. They were worried because I wasn't answering their phone calls. We talked about many including the story and the miracle 19. After they have left I sensed that I had been staying away from God's message. That is when I started reading Quran again. God knows how much tear fell as the pages passed. Upon finishing Quran in four days all negative feelings were cleansed, I was soothed. As if I was reborn after the death I desired. I now know that I am feeling perfectly normal as of today and that I had not gone mad (of course I searched for schizophrenia from the net).

I can not describe how all these were possible but say "a miracle from God". In order to thank All Mighty I submitted to Him alone and choose Quran as my only guide. I have restored relations with family members and quit smoking. I found a job (actually it found me) a month later. I had to leave it after 6 weeks because of contract statements but I now know that as one door is closed another one is opened.

> 2:186   When My servants ask you about Me, I am always near. I answer their prayers when they pray to Me. The people shall respond to Me and acknowledge Me, in order to be guided.

> 40:60   Your Lord says, "Implore Me, and I will respond to you. Surely, those who are too arrogant to worship Me will enter Gehenna, forcibly."

> 93:11   You shall proclaim the blessing your Lord has bestowed upon you.

Thank you for your patience.Praise be to GOD, Lord of the universe.Peace,

Maryam Jannah, Arizona, USA

6 September 2009

I was born in 1922 to a couple who were already forty years old, and I was their only child. They seemed more like grandparents, to be honest. My mother was a mild-mannered woman, poorly matched to my strong-willed controlling father. He was strongly Calvinistic in his religious beliefs. By this I mean that men ruled the household with an iron fist, and the rest of the family bowed to his will. Also ... "Spare the rod and spoil the child".

My earliest memory is of sitting with my father on the front lawn of our house in northern Pennsylvania. I must have been about four years old. It is the only memory of my father being soft-spoken and kind. Warm and loving. He was usually very harsh with everyone and had no friends. As we sat there he told me that God made the grass and-the clouds in the sky, the trees, the birds and bugs, the flowers and us. I remember thinking that God must really be something very wonderful, and I would like to see him. But, throughout my growing years, I NEVER heard my father mention God again.

Instead, my childhood memories are of Sunday morning services in churches where only Jesus was spoken of, where people cried to Jesus to save them, and crawled on their knees up to the from of the church with their arms in the air beseeching mercy from Jesus. It seemed like every Sunday we went to a different church. I think they were mostly Pentecostal churches, as they were the ones most emotional. We went again on Sunday evening and Wednesday evening to their prayer meetings. I wanted to ask what happened to God, who had created everything, and why they prayed to Jesus instead, who didn't seem to have created any- thing. But one didn't ask my father such a question! I would end up by getting whipped! So I kept silent, but always with thoughts of God in

331

my heart, and I prayed that someday I would find people who just talked about God; not Jesus.

But Sundays were not the only times he called upon Jesus. Every meal- time was a noisy sermon, warning of the Hellfire if we did not follow Jesus. He would shout and get so worked up that the glasses and silver- ware on the table--jumped! It was really scary to a child, who didn't understand it at all and dared not ask questions. My vision of God, who created people and everything around us was inconsistent with an alternate vision of a Jesus person who would send us to hell if we didn't follow him! My Mother and I just endured it. I was really afraid of him.

After high school I went to stay with my Mother's cousin in New York State for a year while I took more required classes for the college I was to enter. It was a Quaker school and, on the first day, we were assigned to write an essay on "What Religion Means To Me". They were asking the wrong person! I was absolutely devastated. I couldn't write the truth.... that I didn't go along with the Christian Jesus. I went horn, to the cousin's and just cried, telling her that religion to me was hellfire, and yelling, and fear, and everything ugly. How could I write that? Her religious belief was Rosicrucian, and confused at that. (Had my father known he would never have allowed me to stay there!) But she understood my stress, knowing my father! Somehow, together we wrote something that must have satisfied the teacher, as I heard no more about it! Life was peaceful with the cousin. No church ...EVER!

Then I went to nursing school instead of college. In my senior year, a Catholic classmate wanted someone to go to Christmas midnight mass with her, so I volunteered •. It was at least quiet and dignified, though I was unimpressed by the incense, the Latin, and the ornate raiment they wore. Following nursing school I went into the military service, as we were in the midst of World War II. The base chapel was across the street from the nurses' quarters, but I never went. I wanted nothing to do with religion that was Jesus-based.

Then I found myself engaged to marry a pilot there who was Catholic, and I was expected to "convert," if I wanted to marry him. I didn't mind "converting" ...it was at least quiet and dignified, remember? So I went to the catechism classes where I learned that Jesus was at the center of it and that I was to pray to Jesus, to Mary, and to many, many saints, four or five saints for each day of the year! So I was married by a Catholic military priest, to keep the peace. But I never again went to church! (Neither did he!) The marriage eventually foundered, and my mother came to live with me and my four children. She used to coax me to go to church with her, but I couldn't bring myself to do it, though I know it caused her pain.

Then, living in southern California, my life changed. I had just separated from an alcoholic second husband, and moved, with my mother and four children, to an apartment. The alcohol problem had been terrible. I wanted total change in my life, so I stopped smoking and stopped any social drinking altogether. I wanted to exorcise any demons there might be in me. I was working a 3 PM to 11 PM shift, so saw very little of my family. I was working full-time and also going to college full-time. Life was really pretty awful. Nothing but stress, responsibility, and very little money. I remember coming home one night at almost midnight, feeling very alone. I found myself on the floor, crying my eyes out, on my knees (sujud, though I didn't know that at the time:- And facing East!) I cried and asked God to help me please find Him, because I didn't know where to look and I needed Him so desperately.

Two days later, a new orderly appeared on the unit at the hospital where I was charge nurse. He was an excellent caregiver but, even more, had a very strong charismatic aura about him which awed all of us. It turned out that he was really a nurse but just working at an easier job while getting a doctorate in psychology. He was originally from East Pakistan (before it became Bangladesh), so was raised as a Muslim. He had spent a year in Egypt at Al Azhar University, then moved to France, and than the United States. In New YORK he worked for a while as a sandhog on the construction of the tunnel to New Jersey ..... a very long time ago!. Then he moved to Chicago, hoping to find a mosque somewhere, as he felt such a strong need for his religion. He didn't find one, so he went to college and got a degree in Divinity as a Baptist minister, as a substitute for Islam. It did not work. He felt very unfulfilled. About that time Elijah Muhammad surfaced there in the Chicago area. He attended and found that they were teaching Islam. Not exactly what he had grown up with, but Islam nonetheless.

I asked him about it and he explained Islam to me. I was hooked immediately! It was what I had been looking for!.... a worship of God alone. It was like the fabled Cinderella slipper; it fit exactly. However, because my skin was white, not dark, I could not attend meetings. But I subscribed to their weekly paper, Muhammad Speaks, and ordered a Qur'an. Not knowing which translation to order, I got the Muhammad Ali translation. When it came, I hungrily began reading the introduction. When I came to the place where it said Hell was not eternal that you could work your way out of it with good behavior, it just did not seem right to me, so I put the book away until I could find out me that was 1963. My family and I moved to Tucson in 1968. Through all years, and until 1974, my only contact with Islam was through that weekly newspaper.

Elijah died in 1974, and was succeeded by his son, Warith, who said that anyone, regardless of skin color, could attend their mosque. I was on the phone immediately to the local Muhammad's Mosque, which at that time was on South Park Avenue here in Tucson. They very graciously accepted me. Then, slowly I began to meet other Muslims at the university mosque, and I was told that I must take an Arabic name, which I did, legally, (though I am now aware that such is just nonsense!)

In 1979, I was attending Masjid Tucson, where Rashad Khalifa was finding such extraordinary miracles within the structure of the Qur'an, and this deepened my already strong submission to God. That same year I was blessed to be able to make Hajj with the first group of American Muslims with the Nation of Islam.

I cannot possibly express the inner peace and contentment that I now feel in my life, thanks be to God. It was a long and painful journey to today, but I am so thankful to God for His strength through every moment of it.

Praise be to God!

PS: Although, according to the calendar, I have been muslim since 1963 (46 years), I feel I have been really muslim all my life, as it was always God was in my heart.

Tufan Karadere, Ankara, Türkiye

October 29, 2003

I thought my first post in free-minds forum should be here. Here is my story I posted to 19.org's forum:

Then let me tell a different story

Most of the people I know used to be either Sunni, or "search for the truth." Not me, actually I didn't use to give a damn.

I liked some of the religious stories about Muhammad or other prophets, or miracles, when I was a young boy. In Türkiye, there are some "brainformatter" groups of people who "wash" young boys' brains pretending to teach them lessons (Mathematics and so on). But the real intention is advertising their religion to make the boy to become a Sunni (or make him think the way as they think). It was my family who noticed their intention and protected me.

The way they noticed this is pretty funny and strange actually: They found one of the books I got from brainformatters: Interesting Questions - 2 (Yes, the author was nobody but Edip).

In that book, Edip quotes some of the (extreme and nonsense) Sunni thoughts, actually to criticize them. However, in the first look (when skimming and scanning), they seem to be the author's thoughts (Well, at least my family thought they were the author's thoughts). I tried to explain that they are not Edip's thoughts, that Edip criticized them. Hehe, I liked Edip. I liked that book

They later noticed they were not Edip's thoughts, however, they had noticed the "brainformatters" once. They didn't want me to go to that people's house again.

Edip's "Interesting Questions - 2" book was what prevented me to become a Sunni . Though in a different way, it really did

Then, a long time passed. I was not interested in religious matters. I never was, actually.

One day, I refused all of the religious stories, together with what they're based on: the existence of a God. I lost my belief, became an atheist. Actually, I never believed, it's only that I was told that I believed a god. Everbody said there was a god.

I reflected, then decided... Miserable is what I decided... Miserable indeed is what I decided... I looked, frowned and whined. I turned arrogantly... I said "this is not even a clever magic"... I said "This is human made" 74:18-25 (The thing I refused was, however, not a miracle, but the stories. I did it arrogantly, though. That's the only arrogance I'm happy with)

Based on those nonsense stories, I refused the idea of a God.

Another long time passed. One day, I saw another book: "Errors in Quran Translations", written by Edip Yuksel. Hey, that name sounds familiar! I read it. Strange it is, this guy refuses everything I refuse, he still insists the existence of a God.

Then, I read "19 Questions for Sunni and Shiite scholars". I wrote an email to Edip. He sent me Rashad's English Translation.

I met Rashad... I read the appendices first .

I met 19. I met Quran.

I met... God...

I wrote another email to Edip saying that it's very difficult, if not impossible, to calculate the divisibility of those long numbers by 19 (I didn't know programming that well then). He replied me "I didn't calculate them, I don't know the exact programming method".

I met... C... . Proved to myself the truth of the most of what Rashad said.

Proved to myself, mathematically, and digitally, the existence of a God... The existence of "the" God...

I don't think even Edip remembers those emails, mainly because I usually try to change my nick frequently to make sure nobody remembers me, in person

Thinking now, strange indeed: I had nothing to do with religion, all I wanted was to study Mathematics. I was a kid. The people who seemed to help me study math were actually Sunni brainwashers, imposing their thoughts. I took nearly nothing from them, my family prevented me. Except one book: Edip's book. That was one of the few books opposing them. Then, I had again nothing to do with religion (and reaaalllly nothing, I mean), then I came across another book of Edip (whom, at first look, I can't even remember from where I can remember, but there was a familiarity).

That book changed my life. Thanks, Edip. I was 19 years old. God guided me.

Thank God!

Mohamed Elmalt, Germany

13 August 2000

Peace Edip,

> **8:53**   If it is recited to them, they say, "We acknowledge it. It is the truth from our Lord. Indeed, we had peacefully surrendered before it."

Well my answers to the questions:

(1) I am an Egyptian student in Germany...Born in Alexandria in Egypt in a traditional Islamic family...My relatives and my family all claim to be submitters to God, while many of them do not pray at all, others pray, and others don't observe the prayers daily.

My father was a fighter pilot in the Egyptian army, and my grandfather was an Arabic teacher...So I was brought up to respect the Quran as God's word and message to the humanity, though I first started to pay attention to Quran while I was 17.

At this age I thought first to start the way by learning the recitation of Quran at a mosque in front of our house in Cairo, since my father retired and worked as an Airline Captain for Egypt Air. But after encountering the dead brains in the mosques of the Sheikhs, I stopped going there, and left the Quran for a while, until I finished my high-school education at the German school in Cairo then I went to continue my study in Germany!

In Germany I had many hard times, since it is a problem of racism there. I always found problems in finding apartments, jobs etc... (2) Until the time came that I found a good job in an American advertising agency as computer programmer. I am studying computer sciences in Germany. At this time, I was living in a student's dorm, and was living totally under Satan's authority, parties, drugs, etc... Until I was discussing with myself, and was blaming myself for leaving Quran aside..

I started again grabbing my Quran cassettes to listen to them, even in my walkman on the street...

I was listening to Sura (57) when i started to feel my tears in my eyes. The expressions were really amazing, but I didn't understand everything exactly...I wondered how could I say these words again in German language...A Turkish programmer and friend was working with me in the same agency and he suggested to look for "Quran auf deutsch" in AltaVista to find some translations...I wasn't quite happy with the translation I found, so I spent more days searching for a translations... But as i found many other search results, I wanted to look at more results...and at the next page of AltaVista results, I found a page talking about "mathematical miracle".

(1) & (2) so my father was always a person contradicting himself strongly, like drinking alcohol, and talking about Quran or some other bad advises that he gave, but at the end he was never attracted to Hadith and was always ridiculing ppl who argue using Hadith...in my teenager years I've trusted my dad so much, so i was in a different way attracted to Quran alone, and never read Hadith books, just these few Hadith that we studied at school in Egypt!

(3) First I was wondering it, and was thinking it might be a nice fabrication or another way of philosophy, since i read Quran a lot of time, but never realized that there could be mathematical structures... But I am not a kind of person who refuses to read something, just because he didn't like the title!

I talked to myself and thought it might be true and then I could be missing something important!

So I decided to start counting sura 50 manually, since I had no possibility to enter the Arabic text and count it using a computer program... And after that I counted the Q's in sura 42 manually, but God willed that I make too many errors regarding the count...I always could find only 56 Q's and never was patient to count correctly...So I thought again it is a fabrication...But I couldn't keep cool, and remembered that I had a small Quran program, running under DOS and it had words counts of the Suras...I opened the program and was happy to find that the program counts the letters of the individual suras too.. And found the Q's in Sura 42 to be 57...So I said: well this company who published the program has nothing to do with R.K. or with these calculations...So it might be my mistake and I counted again until I found them really 57! Well I was very happy to see that it is something interesting might be true in the Quran, so I compared the counts made on the homepage with the counts in my program, and found that the Alifs and Laams are totally different, and It took again many days to realize that my program was typing the Quran in standard Arabic, not with the specific Arabic spelling used in the Quran... So I tried to verify all codes that I could verify, and then concentrated about the message itself, preach with Quran alone, and don't follow Hadith and Sunna since its reflecting idol worship!!! Just because of this message, I opened my mind and my heart to listen to everything and try to verify for myself!

Just the message without numbers and counting reached my heart and found acceptance, while the numbers made me only believe that Quran is indeed something great, could not be ignored like i did in the few past years!

(4) I called my family first in Egypt, and told them about this great findings...Well all at the beginning showed interest, until they were faced with the announcement of Rashad Khalifa as a messenger.. They couldn't make up their mind with such announcement especially that he is talking about night journey to the heaven, and about the end of the world! I understand this proclamation as will of God, because especially for those reasons ppl disbelieved in Muhammad in the past, and now they disbelieve that God can do the same trick again to show them their disbelief, just because such a personal experience of someone, and neglecting his true message, worship God alone, follow His words alone i.e. Quran

My father and mother started to make up stories about Rashad, for example: employee of the CIA to destroy Islam, how come a messenger in USA? A messenger smoking cigarettes? I don't know where they got these false information, but this made me believe stronger that Rashad is indeed delivering a simple message, with many tricks from God to detect the sincere ppl from the ppl who proclaim belief without doing anything for that...Only my brother stood with me and believed everything after verifying for himself the information...By the way, he is only 14 years old.

But then he started to idolize Rashad Khalif and only think about him and forgot the Quran message again...I warned him, that his god is not 1230 (GV of Rashad Khalifa) but his god is the One God, who created everything..So he must take 1230 from his mind, and put God in his mind again...And he accepted...My young sister (18 yrs old) is starting to believe in Quran alone, but she is still having doubts, maybe God guide her, my brother and me...My other sister, my mother and my father and all of my relatives are looking to us as crazy people who are totally misguided.

In Germany all of my friends showed interest at the beginning then disregarded everything, except one Tunisian friend who believed in Quran alone immediately, and a Turkish friend who took longer to accept that...But all of the others didn't pay attention!

(5) Well at the beginning i was really sad about this reaction of people who I thought they would be the first to accept such a message, who is telling them to pray to God alone, to accept Quran alone as a fully detailed scripture, but after reading more in the Quran, I realize that it's God will to guide whomever who wills, so I don't bother now at all who believes and who don't believe...First I had many fights with my dad, but then I cooled

everything again...It's everyone's choice to believe whatever he/she wants, and at the Day of Judgment, God will show all of us who went astray and who was sincere..

For myself, I started to feel that God's test is nothing easy to handle, and it needs a lot of patience, search and knowledge... But everyone hope to pass this test, and also I do! I think if one is sincere enough and can proof it in front of God, not in front of people, he/she can make it up to paradise with God's will...It will be easy for God to guide him/her...isn't it?

(6) well as I mentioned before, I am studying mathematics and computer programming and working in this field...I am not that professional yet, but though it made me very happy to see something like that in the Quran...For MYSELF I believe that as stated in 74:31 one of the functions of this number is to increase the faith of believers and submitters, but not let them leave the Quran's message and meanings and spend their lives in mathematics...It is only simple way to show people the truth from our Lord, but not the aim of our life to live with the 19...Going to supermarket and buying 19 eggs, calling everything 19...It is God's code, and not ours...I think we shouldn't idolize the number itself, as idolizing and loving God alone, without any numbers...To Him belong all numbers and letters, all in heavens and earths.

(7) Well this code made me really fear to leave Quran just one day, though I am not that strong person yet, and trying to develop myself and my soul, but I am trying to keep that issue strongly connected to me; i.e. the issue of Quran alone...And the most important thing that this code make could make me amazingly get more assured about heaven and hell, instead of saying just that I believe about them...Though matters of faith are very personal, and not everyone can describe his faith to the others...Everyone can talk, but most of people don't really know the truth about what is inside their hearts until they found themselves really in Hell....Maybe some of the fortune people get good news from God in this world, that they are good people to make them feel really happy, but I still didn't come to this stage in my life...So I know that I am still not that very good person, and need to do more to please my Lord!

(8) This code could make something special to my life, It could clean myself totally from racism and hanging about Arabism and opened my mind to universal living instead of racism...This point is very important for me, because Arabs still think that Quran belongs to them alone, and that they are only the people who are authorized to understand it...So it freed me from any Arabism, and make me looking for an international community of clean submitters...

(9) My expectation of the future is to see the submitters more clean, more caring about their religion and trying their best to please God.. I hope also to see the victory of God (Sura 110) with my eyes and to be a witness for something like that...Though I know that God knows fully who deserves to witness such an event, it is just a hope inside my heart, and I hope to see submitters to God alone really the winners in this worlds, as in the Hereafter.

(10) And I would like through this simple message to call all submitters to try unifying themselves, gather themselves together, and discuss how to help each other, care about the problems of the others brothers who might need support, and be really one great community instead of many small communities spread on the earth, oppressed in many countries still and not having their human rights...This is much important than discussing

338

other issues that will bring us only backwards, and let the enemies of God mock us all the way...! God never changes us, until we start to change ourselves...So why not now better than later?

Your brother!

Anonymous, United Kingdom

25 October 2009

God saved me from darkness through nineteen

I'm 37 years old, was born in Africa, moved to France at age 9 and now live in the United Kingdom and work as a computer programmer.

Basically I grew up in a Christian/secular/white environment but as a traditional/sunni/muslim/black/homosexual. (I belonged to the minority of the minority of the minority).

I always loved science and found the Quran very interesting even if I did not agree with everything (it was because of the translations and interpretations). But scientifically talking and on the point of view of consistency I really loved it.

TAFSIR KILLED ME: After a master in computer science I've bought a copy of Tafsir Ibn Kathir, took a year off to Africa and started studying the religion. I don't like to be told; I like to go to the source. I was planning to become a Sufi, a God lover as I used to think about it.

When I read that so many verses were 'revealed' after Muhammad's friends have said it, when I read the interpretation of Sura Yasin, when I tried to understand who was that Muhammad who could be so merciful and so evil... I could not take it. When I saw that the homosexual males have different punishment depending on their position in bed, and that women were ok to be gay... When I read that the suckling verse was missing, that the stoning verse was missing... I started seriously doubting about the Quran. It became obvious that Quran was like the Bible, bits and pieces from God, but the rest from humans.

By the end of the 6th volume, I gave up on 'Islam' but I still had faith in God. I made many "friends" among Jehovah witnesses, Mormons and Christians. Talking to them was really helpful; after all my faith was based on articles of faith, I found out, were just deception made many centuries ago... I was just like one of them... I believed the truth was out there; but where?

GOD SAVED ME: And one day, I don't know how... I guess I have google for the "1000th times please GOD do something about me"... I bumped into www.submission.org when I was 32. I became addicted to the website. I could not believe what I was reading. That 19 stuff... I've been looking for God's signature for years. That's exactly how I used to name it before I could see it on their website.

It took about four months to build a program and verify the alleged structure. Even tough I did not get all the results the same as the one presented by Rashad, it was obvious that there was a mathematical composition of the Quran. Moreover, the message that was coming with it was more important than having every single alleged element of the proof to be correct. This is what I have been looking for all those years:

1. God did not forsake us
2. He really loves us despite our stupidity
3. He denies the atrocities the Arabs have prepared for people like me. (Kill homosexual or put them in prison depending on their sexual position).

The mathematical composition of the Quran reconnected me with God. The information about our existence on earth and the whole idea behind our existence made me change and reform myself. Homosexual/heterosexual, black/white all that became totally irrelevant. I became a submitter. Then all my life has changed, I'm not the same person anymore. Family and friends cannot understand. How do you dare questioning the authority of the ulamas!

Now I have THE authority that can tell me what is right and wrong. Quran, the Whole Quran and nothing but Quran.

Anyway I have built up a website for me not to forget, to remember all what I have verified and I loved your booklet, 19 Questions for Sunni and Shiite scholars, that I made few videos that my Muslim friends hate.

http://www.verify.awesome-design.org/

30
"On it is Nineteen"
The Summary

"No, don't you see? This would be different. This isn't just starting the universe out with some precise mathematical laws that determine physics and chemistry. This is a message. Whoever makes the universe hides messages in transcendental numbers so they'll be read fifteen billion years later when intelligent life finally evolves. I criticized you and Rankin the time we first met for not understanding this. 'If God wanted us to know that he existed, why didn't he send us an unambiguous message?' I asked. Remember?"

"I remember very well. You think God is a mathematician."

"Something like that. If what we're told is true. If this isn't a wild-goose chase. If there's a message hiding in pi and not one of the infinity of other transcendental numbers. That's a lot of ifs."

"You're looking for Revelation in arithmetic. I know a better way."

"Palmer, this is the only way. This is the only thing that would convince a skeptic. Imagine we find something. It doesn't have to be tremendously complicated. Just something more orderly than could accumulate by chance that many digits into pi. That's all we need. Then mathematicians all over the world can find exactly the same pattern or message or whatever it proves to be. Then there are no sectarian divisions. Everybody begins reading the same Scripture. No one could then argue that the key miracle in the religion was some conjurer's trick, or that later historians had falsified the record, or that it's just hysteria or delusion or a substitute parent for when we grow up. Everyone could be a believer." (Sagan, Carl. Contact. Simon and Schuster. New York: 1985, p 418-419)

The above excerpts are quoted from CONTACT, a book by Dr. Carl Sagan the late astronomer who became popular with the TV series, Cosmos. Sagan's CONTACT is a novel expression of philosopher's prime dream: Mathematical evidence for God's existence.

Mathematics is considered a priori, knowledge gained independently of experience. Most of the philosophers highly relied on mathematics. Descartes who employed extreme doubt as a method to reach the knowledge (certainty) could not doubt from mathematics. The language of mathematics is universal.

The Most Controversial Concept

Hindus believe that he is incarnated in many human beings. Christians pontificate that he has multiple personalities, one of them being sacrificed for humanity. Jews assert that he is Jehovah. Muslims claim that he is Allah. Many question his gender. Millions die for him, millions fight for him, millions cry for him. Clergymen use his name as a trademark for their business, and the very same name motivates many devotees to give away their belongings as charity. Many joyfully sing songs for his love, and others outrageously declare dialectic or scientific wars against him. Some even exclaim that he is no longer alive.

Volume upon volume of books are published for and against him. Big lies are attributed to him while scientific hoaxes are arranged to deny him. He is in the courts, he is on the money, he is in the schools, he is in the mind of saints and in the mouth of hypocrites. Yes, he is everywhere. And yet, philosophers continuously question his existence. In fact, world religions, with numerous versions of odd gods, have not helped philosophers prove his existence. On the contrary, they created further intellectual problems and logical obstacles for questioning minds who try to reach him.

The Prime Evidence

The "prime" evidence comes in the form of a highly sophisticated mathematical code embedded in an ancient document. Computer decoding of this document was originally started by Dr. Rashad Khalifa, a biochemist, in 1969. In 1974, this study unveiled an intricate mathematical pattern based on a prime number. (Having interested with the subject the author, like many others, I examined Dr. Khalifa's findings and assisted him in his further research.)*

For more than 14 centuries it was a hidden secret in the most read yet one of the most ignored books, the Quran (The Book of Recitation), until 1974. The discovery of the code not only explained many verses, but it also exposed the diabolic nature of sectarian teachings and the work of clergymen.

With the computer decoding of the Quran, summarized below, the argument for the existence of God gained an examinable physical evidence. Although the Quran had been in existence for fourteen centuries, its mathematical code remained a secret until computer decoding became possible. As it turned out, the code ranges from extreme simplicity to a complex, interlocking intricacy. Thus, it can be appreciated by persons with limited education, as well as scholars.

This ancient document is the Quran, revealed to Muhammad of Arabia early in the seventh century as The Final Testament. The following is a condensed summary of this unique literary code. Please note that one does not need to know Arabic, the original language of the Quran, to examine most of the evidences presented below. For some of them one may only need to recognize the 28 letters of the Arabic alphabet.

The Message For The Computer Generation

Chapter 74 of the Quran is dedicated to the PRIME number 19. This chapter is called "*Al-Muddassir*" (The Hidden Secret). The number 19 is specifically mentioned in that Chapter as a "punishment" for those who state that the scripture is human-made (74:25). This number is also called "One of the greatest portents" (74:35). In 74:31, the purpose of the number 19 is described: to remove all doubts regarding the authenticity of the Quran, to increase the appreciation of the believers, and to be a scientific punishment for hypocrites and disbelievers. However, the implication of this number as a proof for the authenticity of the Quran remained unknown for centuries. For fourteen centuries, the commentators tried in vain to understand the function and fulfillment of the number 19.

Before The Secret Was Decoded

Before the discovery of the 19-based system, we were aware of a symmetrical mathematical wonder in the Quran. For example:

- The word "month" (*ṢaHR*) occurs 12 times.
- The word "day" (*YaWM*) occurs 365 times.
- The word "days" (*ayyam, YaWMayn*) occurs 30 times.
- The words "perverse/satan" (*shaytan*) and "controller/angel" (*malak*), each occur 88 times.
- The words "this world" (*DuNYa*) and "hereafter" (*ahirah*), each occur 115 times.
- The words "they said" (*QALu*) and "you say" (*QUL*), each occur 332 times.
- The proper names of 26 messengers mentioned in the Quran and the frequencies of all the derivatives of the root word *RaSaLa* (message/send messenger), each occur 512 times.

A Great Prophecy is Fulfilled and the Secret is Unveiled

The miraculous function of the number 19 prophesized in Chapter 74 was unveiled in 1974 through a computerized analysis of the Quran. Though, in retrospect, the implication of 19 in Chapter 74 traditionally called Hidden One, were obvious, it remained a secret for 1406 (19x74) lunar years after the revelation of the Quran. Ironically, the first words of the Chapter 74, The Hidden One, was revealing, yet the code was a divinely guarded gift allocated to the computer generation; they were the one who would need and appreciate it the most. As we have demonstrated in various books, hundreds of simple and complex algorithms, we witness the depth and breath of mathematical manipulation of Arabic, an arbitrary human language, to be profound and extraordinary.

This is the fulfillment of a Quranic challenge (17:88). While the meaning of the Quranic text and its literal excellence was kept, all its units, from chapters, verses, words to its letters were also assigned universally recognizable roles in creation of mathematical patterns. Since its discovery, the number 19 of the Quran and the Bible has increased the appreciation of many of those who acknowledge the truth, has removed doubts in the minds of many People of the Book, and has caused discord, controversy and chaos among those who have traded the Quran with men-made sectarian teachings. This is indeed a fulfillment of a Quranic prophecy (74:30-31).

Various verses of the Quran mention an important miracle that will appear after its revelation.

10:20	They say, "If only a sign was sent down to him from His Lord." Say, "The future is with **God**, so wait, and I will wait with you."
21:37	The human being is made of haste. I will show you My signs; do not be in a rush.
38:0	In the name of God, the Gracious, the Compassionate.
38:1	S90, and the Quran that contains the Reminder.
38:2	Indeed, those who have rejected are in false pride and defiance.
38:3	How many a generation have We destroyed before them. They called out when it was far too late.
38:4	They were surprised that a warner has come to them from among themselves. The ingrates said, "This is a magician, a liar."
38:5	"Has he made the gods into One god? This is indeed a strange thing!"
38:6	The leaders among them went out: "Walk away, and remain patient to your gods. This thing can be turned back."
38:7	"We never heard of this from the people before us. This is but an innovation."
38:8	"Has the remembrance been sent down to him, from between all of us!" Indeed, they are doubtful of My reminder. Indeed, they have not yet tasted My retribution.
38:87	"It is but a reminder for the worlds."
38:88	"You will come to know its news after awhile."
41:53	We will show them Our signs in the horizons, and within themselves, until it becomes clear to them that this is the truth. Is it not enough that your Lord is witness over all things?
72:28	… He has counted everything in numbers.

The beginning of Chapter 25 refers to the arguments of the opponents who denied the divine nature of the Quran:

> **25:4**   Those who rejected said, "This is but a falsehood that he invented and other people have helped him with it; for they have come with what is wrong and fabricated."
>
> **25:5**   They said, "Tales of the people of old, he wrote them down while they were being dictated to him morning and evening."

The awaited miracle, the hidden mathematical structure

The subsequent verse gives an enigmatic answer to the assertion of those who claimed that the Quran is manmade.

> **25:6**   Say, "It was sent down by the One who knows the secrets in the heavens and the earth. He is always Forgiving, Compassionate."

How can "knowing the secret" constitute an answer for those who assert that the Quran is Muhammad's work? Will the proof or evidence of the divine authorship of the Quran remain a secret known by God alone? Or, will the antagonists be rebuffed by that divine mystery? If there should be a relationship between the objection and answer, then we can infer from the above verse that a SECRET will demonstrate the divine nature of the Quran.

The miracle promised throughout the Quran might have been destined to appear after Muhammad's death:

> **13:38**   We have sent messengers before you and We have made for them mates and offspring. It was not for a messenger to come with any sign except by **God**'s leave, but for every time there is a decree.
>
> **13:39**   **God** erases what He wishes and affirms, and with Him is the source of the book.
>
> **13:40**   If We show you some of what We promise them or if We let you pass away, for you is only to deliver, while for Us is the reckoning.

The last phrase of verse 13:40 quoted above is interesting, The meaning of this phrase becomes clearer after the discovery of Code 19, since the Arabic word "_HeSaaB_" refers to both the "day of judgment" and "numerical computation."[1] The deliberate use of multi-meaning words is very common in the Quran. For instance, the word "_AaYah_" occurs 84 times in the Quran and in all occurrences it means "miracle," "sign" or "law." However, its plural form "_AaYAat_" also means "revelation" or "verses of the Quran." This unique usage equates

---

[1]   The word "_HeSaaB_" is used for the "day of judgment" since on that day our good and bad deeds will be computed.

minimum three verses of the Quran (in Arabic, a different form is used for duality) with miracle. It also pulls our attention to the parallelism between God's signs/laws in the universe and God's revelation in human language: they share the same source and the same truth. In the following verse the plural word *AaYAat* is used not to mean *revelation* but "miracle, sign or physical manifestation":

6:158   Do they wait until the angles/controllers will come to them, or your Lord comes, or some signs from your Lord? The day some signs come from your Lord, it will do no good for any person to acknowledge if it did not acknowledge before, or it gained good through its acknowledgement. Say, "Wait, for we too are waiting."

The verse 30 of Chapter 74, *Al-Muddassir* (The Hidden/The Secret) of the Quran reads exactly, **"Over it Nineteen."** The entire chapter is about the number 19. Let's read the chapter from the beginning.

74:0   In the name of God, the Gracious, the Compassionate.
74:1   O you hidden one.
74:2   Stand and warn.
74:3   Your Lord glorify.
74:4   Your garments purify.
74:5   Abandon all that is vile.
74:6   Do not be greedy.
74:7   To your Lord be patient.
74:8   So when the trumpet is sounded.[2]
74:9   That will be a very difficult day.
74:10   Upon the ingrates it will not be easy.
74:11   So leave Me alone with the one I have created.
74:12   I gave him abundant wealth.
74:13   Children to bear witness.
74:14   I made everything comfortable for him.
74:15   Then he wishes that I give more.
74:16   No. He was stubborn to Our signs.
74:17   I will exhaust him in climbing.
74:18   He thought and he analyzed.
74:19   So woes to him for how he analyzed.
74:20   Then woe to him for how he analyzed.

---

[2]   Traditional commentaries translate it as "When the trumpet is sounded" or "horn is blown," which is an allegorical expression for making a declaration. The root of the word *NaQuuR* as a verb means "strike" or "groove," and as a noun it means "trumpet" or "the smallest matter." Based on our contemporary knowledge of the prophecy mentioned in this chapter, we may translate this verse as "when the microchips are grooved."

74:21	Then he looked.
74:22	Then he frowned and scowled.
74:23	Then he turned away in arrogance.
74:24	He said, "This is nothing but an impressive magic."
74:25	"This is nothing but the words of a human."
74:26	I will cast him in the *Saqar*.
74:27	Do you know what *Saqar* is?
74:28	It does not spare nor leave anything.
74:29	Manifest to all the people.[3]
74:30	**On it is nineteen.**

The punishment issued for the opponent is very interesting: **nineteen**. Almost all numbers mentioned in the Quran is an adjective for a noun. Forty nights, seven heavens, four months, twelve leaders. But here the numerical function of nineteen is emphasized. Nineteen does not define or describe anything. The disbeliever will be subjected to the number nineteen itself. Then, what is the mission or function of this nineteen? Those who tended to understand the meaning of Saqar as "hell" naturally understood it as the number of guardians of hell. However, the punishment that is described with phrases such as, difficult task, precise, and universal manifestations, was an intellectual punishment; a mathematical challenge. Indeed, the following verse isolates the number nineteen from the number of controllers and lists five goals for it.

74:31	We have made the guardians of the fire to be angels/controllers; and We did not make their number except as a test for those who have rejected, to convince those who were given the book, to strengthen the acknowledgment of those who have acknowledged, so that those who have been given the book and those who acknowledge do not have doubt, and so that those who have a sickness in their hearts and the ingrates would say, "What did **God** mean by this

---

[3] Traditional translations that tend to render *Saqar* as hellfire, mistranslates the verse "*Lawahatun lil bashar*" as "scorches the skin." Though this rendering might be obtained by using different dialects of Arabic, the Quranic Arabic is very clear regarding the meaning of the two words making up this verse. The first word *LaWaĤa*, if considered as a noun, literally means "manifold tablets" or "manifestations" and if considered as a verb, it means "making it obvious." The second word "*lil*" means "for." And the third word "*BaŞaR*" means "human being" or "people." For the other derivatives of the first word, *LaWaĤa*, please look at 7:145, 150, 154; 54:13; and 85:22. In all these verses the word means "tablets." For the other derivatives of the third word, *BaŞaR*, please look at the end of the verse 31 of this chapter and 36 other occurrences, such as, 3:79; 5:18; 14:10; 16:103; 19:17; 36:15, etc. The traditional translation of the verse is entirely different than the usage of the Quran. Previous generations who were not aware of the mathematical structure of the Quran perhaps had an excuse to translate it as a description of hell, but contemporary Muslims have no excuse to mistranslate this verse.

example?" Thus **God** misguides whoever/whomever He wishes, and He guides whoever/whomever He wishes. None knows your Lord's soldiers except Him. It is but a reminder for people.

Traditional commentators of the Quran had justifiably grappled with understanding this verse. They thought that disbelievers would be punished by 19 guardians of hell. That was fine. But they could not explain how the number of guardians of hell would increase the appreciation of believers and convince the skeptical Christians and Jews regarding the divine nature of the Quran. Finding no answer to this question, they tried some explanations: the Christians and Jews would believe in the Quran since they would see that the number of guardians of hell is also nineteen in their scripture. Witnessing the conversion of Christians and Jews, the appreciation of Muslims would increase.

This orthodox commentary has three major problems. First, neither the Old, nor the New Testament mentions number nineteen as the guardians of hell.[4] Second, even if there was such a similar statement, this would not remove their doubts but to the contrary, it would increase their doubts since they would consider it one of the many evidences supporting their claim that the Quran plagiarized many stories from the Bible. Indeed, there are many Biblical events are told by the Quran, though occasionally with some differences. Third, none so far converted to Islam because of guardians of hell.

Some scholars noticed this flaw in traditional commentaries. For instance, Fahraddin el-Razi, in his classic commentary, *Tafsyr al-Kabyr,* offered many speculations, including that the number nineteen indicates the nineteen intellectual faculty of human being. Tough it is a clever interpretation, but it fails to explain the emphasis on the number nineteen itself and it also fails to substantiate the speculation.

The following verses emphasized the crucial function of number nineteen:

74:32	No, by the moon.
74:33	By the night when it passes.
74:34	By the morning when it shines.
74:35	It is one of the great ones.[5]

---

[4] The word "nineteen" occurs in the Bible twice: Joshua 19:38 (nineteen cities) and 2 Samuel 2:30 (nineteen men). The word "nineteenth" occurs thrice: 2 King 25:8; 1 Chronicles 24:16, 25:26; and Jeremiah 52:12.

[5] Majority of traditional commentators incline to understand the references of this verse and the ending phrase of verse 31 as "hell fire" instead of "number nineteen." You will find translations of the Quran using parenthesis to reflect this traditional exegesis. According to them, "it (the hellfire) is a reminder for the people," and "this (the hellfire) is one of the greatest (troubles)." Their only reason for jumping over two textually closest candidates, that is, "their number" or "nineteen," was their lack of knowledge about Code 19. They did not understand how a number could be a

74:36	A warning to people.
74:37	For any among you who wishes to progress or regress.

The purpose of "oath" statements in the Quran is not similar to their common usage. The Quran uses oath to pull our attention to a divine sign or a lesson in the subject matter. The Quran does not use the statements of oath to make us *believe*, but to make us *think* (see: 89:5). The passing of the night and the shining of the morning are obviously allegories used to indicate an intellectual enlightenment or salvation. But the expression "by the Moon" is literal and it pulls our attention to the relationship of the Moon and the number nineteen. The year Apollo 11 astronauts dug Moon's surface and brought a piece of the Moon to the Earth, the same year, a biochemist named Dr. Rashad Khalifa started feeding the Quran into a computer in St. Louis, which would end up in the discovery of Code 19. This might be considered a mere coincidence, but a Quranic verse implies the correlation between the two events.

54:1	The moment drew near, and the moon was split.[6]
54:2	If they see a sign, they turn away and say, "Continuous magic!"
54:3	They rejected, and followed their desires, and every old tradition.
54:4	While the news had come to them in which there was sufficient warning.
54:5	A perfect wisdom; but the warnings are of no benefit.

Let's continue the reading of Chapter 74 (The Hidden):

74:38	Every person is held by what it earned;
74:39	Except for the people of the right.

"reminder" or "one of the greatest miracles." Indeed their understanding was in conflict with the obvious context; the topic of the previous verse 31 is the number nineteen, not the hellfire. Finally, the traditional understanding contradicts verse 49. Those who know Arabic may reflect on the word *ZKR* in the ending phrase of verse 31 with verse 49 and reflect on the fact that hellfire is not something the Quran wants us to accept and enjoy!

[6]   The Arabic word *inSaQqa* has been traditionally translated is "being divided in the middle." Hadith books report a "miracle" as the fulfillment of this verse. According to those narration Muhammad pointed at the Moon and the Moon was split for a while. Some of the reports even provide further details about this fabricated "miracle": half of the Moon fell on Muhammad's cousin, Ali's backyard. The word *ṢaQqa* has a range of dimensions, from splitting into half to simply breaking or cracking as in 80:25-26: "We pour the water generously. Then we split the soil open." If you wonder the usage of past tense for a prophetic statement, it is a well-known Quranic style to indicate the certainty of the upcoming event and the meta-time nature of God's knowledge. (See 39:68; 75:8-9; 25:30; 7:44-48; 6:128; 20:125-126; 23:112-114). For those who know Arabic and wonder about the meaning of "*infi'al*" form, see 2:60.

349

74:40	In paradises, they will be asking
74:41	About the criminals.
74:42	"What has caused you to be in *Saqar*?"
74:43	They said, "We were not of those who offered support (or observed contact prayer)."
74:44	"We did not feed the poor."
74:45	"We used to participate with those who spoke falsehood."
74:46	"We used to deny the day of Judgment."
74:47	"Until the certainty came to us."
74:48	Thus, no intercession of intercessors could help them.
74:49	Why did they turn away from this reminder?

How can someone who does not believe in the day of judgment believe in intercession? Those who believe in the intercession of saints and prophets on their behalf surely believe or at least claim to believe in the Day of Judgment. Nevertheless, according to the Quranic definition of the "Day of Judgment" a person cannot simultaneously believe in both intercession and the Day of Judgment. The Quran defines the "Day of Judgment" as "the day that no person can help another person, and all decisions, on that day, will belong to God." (82:19). That day neither Muhammad nor Ahmad, neither Jesus nor Mary, neither Ali nor Wali can help those who reject the number nineteen, its role and implication in the Quran.[7]

Simple To Understand, Impossible To Imitate

The mathematical structure of the Quran, or The Final Testament, is simple to understand, yet impossible to imitate. You do not need to know Arabic, the original language of the Quran to examine it for yourself. Basically, what you need is to be able to count until 19. It is a challenge for atheists, an invitation for agnostics and guidance for believers. It is a perpetual miracle for the computer generation. Dr. Rashad Khalifa introduces this supernatural message as follows:

"The Quran is characterized by a unique phenomenon never found in any human authored book. Every element of the Quran is mathematically composed-the chapters, the verses, the words, the number of certain letters, the number of words from the same root, the number and variety of divine names, the unique spelling of certain words, and many other elements of the Quran besides its content. There are two major facets of the Quran's mathematical system: (1) The mathematical literary composition, and (2) The mathematical structure involving the numbers of chapters and verses. Because of this comprehensive mathematical coding, the slightest distortion of the Quran's text or physical arrangement is immediately exposed".[8]

---

[7] For the Quran's position regarding intercession please see 2:48; 6:70,94; 7:5; 9:80; 10:3; 39:44; 43:86; 16:20,21; 78:38.

[8] Rashad Khalifa, Quran The Final Testament, 1989, p. 609

Physical, Verifiable and Falsifiable Evidence

Here are some examples of this historical message:

- The first verse, i.e., the opening statement "*BismillahirRaĤMaNirrahim*", shortly "Bismillah," consists of 19 Arabic letters.
- The first word of Bismillah, *Ism* (name), without contraction, occurs in the Quran 19 times.
- The second word of Bismillah, *Allah* (God) occurs 2698 times, or 19x142.
- The third word of Bismillah, *RaĤMaN* (Gracious) occurs 57 times, or 19x3.
- The fourth word of Bismillah, *RaĤYM* (Compassionate) occurs 114 times, or 19x6.
- The multiplication factors of the words of the Bismillah (1+142+3+6) add up to 152 or 19x8.
- The Quran consists of 114 chapters, which is 19x6.
- The total number of verses in the Quran including all unnumbered Bismillahs is 6346, or 19x334. If you add the digits of that number, 6+3+4+6 equals 19.
- The Bismillah occurs 114 times, (despite its conspicuous absence from chapter 9, it occurs twice in chapter 27) and 114 is 19x6.
- From the missing Bismillah of chapter 9 to the extra Bismillah of chapter 27, there are precisely 19 chapters.
- The occurrence of the extra Bismillah is in 27:30. The number of the chapter and the verse add up to 57, or 19x3.
- Each letter of the Arabic alphabet corresponds to a number according to their original sequence in the alphabet. The Arabs were using this system for calculations. When the Quran was revealed 14 centuries ago, the numbers known today did not exist. A universal system was used where the letters of the Arabic, Hebrew, Aramaic, and Greek alphabets were used as numerals. The number assigned to each letter is its "Gematrical Value." The numerical values of the Arabic alphabet are shown below: [the table is omitted]
- There are exactly 114 (19x6) verses containing all these 14 letters.
- A study on the gematrical values of about 120 attributes of God which are mentioned in the Quran, shows that only four attributes have gematrical values which are multiples of 19. These are "*Wahid*" (One), "*Zul Fadl al Azim*" (Possessor of Infinite Grace), "*Majid*" (Glorous), "*Jaami*" (Summoner). Their gematrical value are 19 , 2698, 57, and 114 respectively, which are all divisible by 19 and correspond exactly to the frequencies of occurrence of the Bismillah's four words.

351

- The total numbers of verses where the word "Allah" (God) occurs, add up to 118123, and is 19x6217.
- The total occurrences of the word Allah (God) in all the verses whose numbers are multiples of 19 is 133, or 19x7.
- The key commandment: "You shall devote your worship to God alone" (in Arabic "*Wahdahu*") occurs in 7:70; 39:45; 40:12,84; and 60:4. The total of these numbers adds up to 361, or 19x19.
- The Quran is characterized by a unique phenomenon that is not found in any other book: 29 chapters are prefixed with "Quranic Initials" which remained mysterious for 1406 lunar years. With the discovery of the code 19, we realized their major role in the Quran's mathematical structure. The initials occur in their respective chapters in multiples of 19. For example, Chapter 19 has five letters/numbers in its beginning, K20H8Y10A'70Ŝ90, and the total occurrence of these letters in this chapter is 798, or 19x42.
- For instance, seven chapters of the Quran starts with two letter/number combinations, Ĥ8M40, and the total occurrence of these letters in those chapters is 2347 (19x113). The details of the numerical patterns among the frequency of these two letters in the seven chapters they initialize follows a precise mathematical formula.
- To witness the details of the miracle of these initials, a short chapter which begins with one initial letter/number, Q100, will be a good example. The frequency of "Q" in chapter 50 is 57, or 19x3. The letter "Q" occurs in the other Q-initialed chapter, i.e., chapter 42, exactly the same number of times, 57. The total occurrence of the letter "Q" in the two Q-initialed chapters is 114, which equals the number of chapters in the Quran. The description of the Quran as "*Majid*" (Glorious) is correlated with the frequency of occurrence of the letter "Q" in each of the Q-initialed chapters. The word "*Majid*" has a gematrical value of 57. Chapter 42 consists of 53 verses, and 42+53 is 95, or 19x5. Chapter 50 consists of 45 verses, and 50+45 is 95, or 19x5.
- The Quran mentions 30 different cardinal numbers: 1, 2, 3, 4, 5, 6, 7, 8, 9, 10, 11, 12, 19, 20, 30, 40, 50, 60, 70, 80, 99, 100, 200, 300, 1000, 2000, 3000, 5000, 50000, & 100000. The sum of these numbers is 162146, which equals 19x8534. Interestingly, nineteen is mentioned the 30th verse of chapter 74 and the number 30 is 19th composite number.
- In addition to 30 cardinal numbers, the Quran contains 8 fractions: 1/10, 1/8, 1/6, 1/5, 1/4, 1/3, 1/2, 2/3. Thus, the Quran contains 38 (19x2) different numbers. The total of fractions is approximately 2.
- If we write down the number of each verse in the Quran, one next to the other, preceded by the number of verses in each chapter, the resulting long number consists of 12692 digits (19x668). Additionally, the huge number itself is also a multiple of 19.

Code 19: The Real Bible Code

It is significant that the same 19-based mathematical composition was discovered by Judah ben Samuel in the 12th century AD in a preserved part of the Old Testament. Below is a quote from *Studies in Jewish Mysticism*.

> "The people (Jews) in France made it a custom to add (in the morning prayer) the words: " 'Ashrei temimei derekh (blessed are those who walk the righteous way)," and our Rabbi, the Pious, of blessed memory, wrote that they were completely and utterly wrong. It is all gross falsehood, because there are only nineteen times that the Holy Name is mentioned (in that portion of the morning prayer), . . . and similarly you find the word Elohim nineteen times in the pericope of Ve-'elleh shemot . . . .

> "Similarly, you find that Israel were called "sons" nineteen times, and there are many other examples. All these sets of nineteen are intricately intertwined, and they contain many secrets and esoteric meanings, which are contained in more than eight volumes. Therefore, anyone who has the fear of God in him will not listen to the words of the Frenchmen who add the verse " 'Ashrei temimei derekh (blessed are those who walk in the paths of God's Torah, for according to their additions the Holy Name is mentioned twenty times . . . and this is a great mistake. Furthermore, in this section there are 152 words, but if you add " 'Ashrei temimei derekh" there are 158 words. This is nonsense, for it is a great and hidden secret why there should be 152 words . . ."[9]

Running like Zebras

The last section of Chapter 74 (The Hidden) likens those who turn away from the message of nineteen to zebras running away from a lion.

74:49	Why did they turn away from this reminder?
74:50	Like fleeing zebras,
74:51	Running from the lion?
74:52	Alas, every one of them wants to be given separate manuscripts.
74:53	No, they do not fear the Hereafter.
74:54	No, it is a reminder.
74:55	Whosoever wishes will take heed.
74:56	None will take heed except if **God** wills. He is the source of righteousness and the source of forgiveness.

---

[9]   Studies In Jewish Mysticism, Joseph Dan, Association for Jewish Studies. Cambridge, Massachusetts: 1978, p 88.

Numerous books and articles rejecting the importance of the number nineteen in the Quran have been published in many languages worldwide. Some of the publications were freely distributed by the support of petrol-rich countries, such as Kuwait and Saudi Arabia.

The Quran is the only miracle given to Muhammad (29:51). Muhammad's *mushrik* companions could not comprehend that a book could be a miracle, and they wanted miracles "similar" to the ones given to the previous prophets (11:12; 17:90-95; 25:7,8; 37:7-8). Modern *mushriks* also demonstrated a similar reaction when God unveiled the prophesied miracle in 1974. When the miracle demanded from them the dedication of the system to God alone, and the rejection of all other "holy" teachings they have associated with the Quran, they objected, "How can there be mathematics in the Quran; the Quran is not a book of mathematics" or, "How can there be such a miracle; no previous messenger came up with such a miracle!" When a monotheist who was selected to fulfill the prophecy and discover the code started inviting his people to give up polytheism and the worship of Muhammad and clerics, he was oficially declared an apostate by Sunni scholars gathered in Saudi Arabia from 38 different countries in February 1989. Within less than a year he was assassinated by a group linked to al-Qaida in early 1990 in Tucson, Arizona. See 3:81; 40:28-38; 72:24-28; 74:1-56. For the prophetic use of the word reminder (ZKR), see 15:9; 21:2-3; 21:24,105; 26:5; 29:51; 38:1,8; 41:41; 44:13; 72:17; 74:31,49,54.

Was the Discovery of the Code 19 a Coincidence?

Dr. Rashad Khalifa did not have any knowledge that his curiosity regarding the meaning of the alphabet letters that initialize 29 chapters of the Quran would end up with the discovery of its mathematical system. His computerized study that started in 1969 gave its fruits in 1974 by the discovery of the 14 century old SECRET.

If the Code 19 was going to provide strong evidence for the existence of God and for the authenticity of the Quran, then it is reasonable to expect that the identity of the discoverer and the time of the discovery would not be coincidental. Indeed, the events have demonstrated a prophetic design in the timing of this miraculous mathematical design.

The number 19 is mentioned only in a chapter known "The Hidden," the 74th chapter of the Quran. Juxtaposing these two numbers yields 1974, exactly the year in which the code was deciphered. (Calendar based on the birth of Jesus and the solar year is accepted by the Quran as units of calculating time. See, 19:33; 43:61; 18:24. Besides, this is the most commonly used calendar in the world.) If we multiply these two numbers, 19x74, we end up with 1406, the exact number of lunar years between the revelation of the Quran and the discovery of the code.

Furthermore, the first statement expressed in the first two verses of Chapter 74 is about the unveiling of the secret. It is interesting that if we consider one version of spelling the first word, which contains three *Alifs* instead of two, there are 19 letters in the first statement of chapter 74. More interestingly, when we add the numerical values of each letter in these two verses the sum is a very familiar number. Here is the value of each letter in "*Ya ayyuhal Muddassir; qum fa anzir*" (O you Hidden one, stand and warn):

Y =	10
A =	1
A =	1
Y =	10
H =	5
A =	1
A =	1
L =	30
M =	40
D =	4
TH =	500
R =	200
Q =	100
M =	40
F =	80
A =	1
N =	50
Z =	700
R =	200
Total:	**1974**[10]

And **1974** is the year when the hidden secret came out and warned us!

Adding to this prophetic mathematical design is the fact that the derivatives of the name of the discoverer, RShD (guidance), occurs in the Quran exactly 19 times. (See 2:186; 2:256; 4:6; 7:146; 11:78; 11:87; 11:97; 18:10; 18:17; 18:24; 18:66; 21:51; 40:29; 40:38; 49:7; 72:2; 72:10; 72:14; 72:21.). The exact form, Rashad, occurs twice and they sandwich the claim of unappreciative people who wish to end the messengership (4:28-38).

---

[10] The absolute values of these 19 numbers (the numerical values of letters) add up to 57 (19x3).

In sum, the relationship between the following seven elements is more than interesting:

- The mathematical code (19).
- The number of the chapter mentioning the code (74).
- The year of the discovery of the code (1974).
- The number of lunar years between the revelation of the Quran and the year of the discovery (19x74).
- The numerical value of the 19 letters comprising the first statement of the chapter 74 (1974).
- The frequency of derivatives of the discoverer's name (19).
- The context of the verses where the exact name of the discoverer is mentioned as an adjective (40:28-38).

In January 31, 1990, Rashad Khalifa was assassinated in Tucson, Arizona, by a terrorist group affiliated with al-Qaida. Ironically, soon after his departure, ignorant people started idolizing him and created a cult distorting his message of strict monotheism.[11] Also See 27:82-85; 40:28-38; 72:19-28.

> **27:82** When the punishment has been deserved by them, We will bring out for them a creature made of earthly material, it will speak to them that the people have been unaware regarding Our signs.[12]

---

[11] For those who claim the infallibility of Dr. Khalifa, I would like to give a sample of verses that I think carry some minor or important translational errors: 2:114; 2:275*; 2:282*; 4:34&*; 4:79*; 4:127; 8:64; 9:29; 10:34!; 14:4; 16:75*; 18:16*; 19:26!; 20:96&*; 20:114; 21:90* x 21:73; 21:96*; 29:12 x 29:13; 32:5!; 34:41; 35:24 x 25:51; 43:11 x 41:12*; 43:36*; 47:11 x 42:15; 49:1 x 38:26&7:3; 65:12* x 42:29; 66:5; 73:15! (Asterisks are for footnotes and/or subtitles, exclamation marks for missing phrases, and "x" for contradictions.)

[12] Unlike the creatures made of water (24:45) this one is made from earthly elements. After the discovery of the code and from the context of this verse, this creature (DaBBah) can be understood as reference to computer. In traditional books there are many bizarre description of this prophesized creature. Contrary to the Quran's positive depiction of the earth-based creature, Hadith books contain negative descriptions. Some may object to my interpretation by saying that the word "DaBBah" implies something live that moves. I think this objection is reasonable. But, I prefer the computer to an animal since I can understand the phrase "dabbatan min al -ardi" not a creature geographically from earth, but a creature made of earth. Thus, I can accept some differences in mobility between the "dabbeh from water and "dabbeh from earth." Since a computer has many moving parts, from its hard disk to the information carried by trillions of electrons, I do not see it a far-fetched understanding of the implication of "DaBBah".

27:83	The day We gather from every nation a party that denied Our signs, then they will be driven.
27:84	Until they have come, He will say, "Have you denied My signs while you had no explicit knowledge of them? What were you doing?"
27:85	The punishment was deserved by them for what they transgressed, for they did not speak.

How Can We Explain This Phenomenon?

There are basically four possible explanations:

1. Manipulation: One may be skeptical about our data regarding the mathematical structure of the Quran. However, one can eliminate this option by spending several hours of checking the data at random. (We recommend *Quran: The Visual Presentation of Miracle* by Rashad Khalifa and the upcoming book, *Nineteen: God's Signature in Nature and Scripture* by Edip Yuksel). Sunni and Shiite scholars and clerics who have traded the Quran with primitive mediaeval fabrications, that is, Hadith and Sunna, strongly reject this mathematical system, since the mathematical system exposes the corruption of religions by clergymen.

2. Coincidence: This possibility is eliminated by the statistical probability laws. The consistency and frequency of the 19-based pattern is much too overwhelming to occur coincidentally.

3. Human fabrication: While fabricating a literary work that meets the criteria of the document summarized here is a stunning challenge for our computer generation, it is certainly even more improbable during the time of initiation of the document, namely, 610 AD. One more fact augments the improbability of human fabrication. If a certain person or persons had fabricated this literary work, they would want to reap the fruits of their efforts; they would have shown it to people to prove their cause. In view of the originality, complexity, and mathematical sophistication of this work, one has to admit that it is ingenious. However, no one has ever claimed credit for this unique literary code; the code was never known prior to the computer decoding accomplished by Dr. Khalifa. Therefore, it is reasonable to exclude the possibility of human fabrication.

The timing of the discovery may be considered another evidence for the existence and full control of the Supreme Being: The mystery of the number 19 which is mentioned as "one of the greatest events" in the chapter 74 (The Hidden Secret) was discovered by Dr. Khalifa in1974, exactly 1406 (19x74) lunar years after the revelation of the Quran. The connection between 19 (the code) and 74 (the number of the chapter which this code is mentioned) is significant in the timing of the discovery.

4. Super Intelligent Source: The only remaining reasonable possibility is that a super intelligent source is responsible for this document; one who designed the work in this extraordinary manner, then managed to keep it a well guarded secret for 14 centuries, for a predetermined time. The mathematical code ensures that the source is super intelligent and also that the document is perfectly intact.

The discoverer of the Code 19, Dr. Rashad Khalifa, was assassinated in Tucson, Arizona, by an international terrorist group al-Fuqra or al-Fuqara, which was affiliated to Usama Ben Laden, in 1990.13 However, the power of this message is promising a new era of reformation in religions, particularly Islam and Christianity. Ironically, some of Khalifa's "followers" reverted back to the days of ignorance by trying to turn the community of Submitters into a cult after the departure of that brave iconoclastic scientist. Though there are still some monotheists in the group, as it seems, a gang is actively busy in repeating the history of ignorant people by carving a new idol for the group. The gang claims infallibility of Rashad Khalifa and considers all his writings, appendices, footnotes, fingernotes, and articles in the newsletter and his speeches in video recordings to be divine revelation. The gang members consider Rashad's re-re-revised translation to be error-free, and even justify the obvious errors such as the spelling ones. They have replaced their former idol with a new one. The Submitters community has been fatally infected by the idol-carvers and with the rate of infection; the group may excommunicate all the monotheists within a decade. I have exposed the distortion of this gang in a booklet titled, United but Disoriented. Ten years ago many considered some of my predictions to be "unreal" or "paranoid", but my recent debate with the gang members proved my predictions. They are now making claims that none expected to hear, including themselves. Like most polytheists, they have mastered their arguments for their version of polytheism while pretending to be monotheists. The book's first edition is out of print, but it is available on the net. God willing, an updated edition of the book tracking the group's devolution since departure of Rashad will be published by Brainbow Press, most likely under the title: *Idolizing an Iconoclast: The Story of a Cult after Dr. Rashad Khalifa.*

---

[13] My mentor, Dr. Rashad Khalifa, was assassinated in 1990 by a terrorist organization organized in Salt Lake city. The members of al-Fuqra, which was later claimed to be affiliated with Ben Laden's newly founded Al-Qaida, stabbed him to death in our Tucson Mosque. The assassination of my mentor and its aftermath was widely covered by Arizona Daily Star and Tucson Weekly and local radio and TV stations. After September 11, the national media picked up the story. For instance, Newsweek and Dan Rather at CBS Evening News declared this incident to be Al-Qaida's first terrorist act in the USA. See: CBS Evening News with Dan Rather, on October 26, 2001; cover story of Newsweek, January 14, 2002, p.44. On March 19, 2002, KPHO-TV at Phoenix, a CBS affiliate, in its evening news, broadcast an interview with me under the headline: *Traces of Al Qaeda Cell in Tucson.* However, despite its importance in revealing the theological vulnerability of Al-Qaida, this first terrorist event did not receive the attention it deserved. Curiously, *The 9/11 Commission Report* (2002) left out this important first act of terrorism in the US from ther report.

APPENDICES

NINETEEN: God's Signature in Nature and Scripture

A1
Saved through Numbers

(A Chapter from Edip Yuksel's upcoming Autobiography)

> "If you say, 'The LORD is my refuge,' and you make the Most High your dwelling, no harm will overtake you, no disaster will come near your tent. For he will command his angels concerning you to guard you in all your ways; they will lift you up in their hands, so that you will not strike your foot against a stone. You will tread on the lion and the cobra; you will trample the great lion and the serpent. 'Because he loves me,' says the LORD, 'I will rescue him; I will protect him, for he acknowledges my name. He will call on me, and I will answer him; I will be with him in trouble, I will deliver him and honor him. With long life I will satisfy him and show him my salvation.'"
> ~ Psalms 91:9-16

> "Stone walls do not a prison make, nor iron bars a cage."
> ~ Richard Lovelace

> "Under a government which imprisons any unjustly, the true place for a just man is also a prison." ~ Henry David Thoreau

> "A justice that is supposed to be 'equal', a legal machinery that is supposed to be 'autonomous', but which contains all the asymmetries of disciplinary subjection, this conjunction marked the birth of prison... It must be the most powerful machinery for imposing a new form on the perverted individual." ~ Michel Foucault[185]

After the conference, some of the participants stayed a few more days in Istanbul. The night of September 11th, 1980, I was entertaining my two guests, the British comrade with a rosary around his neck, and the Egyptian comrade Khalid Muhammad Ali of Egypt. As I mentioned before, Khalid was a tall and massive young member of Muslim Brotherhood with a passion to bring back the golden days of Islamic Caliphate. He had a beard and he wore a long white skirt and the Jewish prayer cap. Though the British friend was not an Arab, he was also wearing a white skirt like Khalid, and a rosary on his neck like a Catholic. Like all of us, he was misled to respect and adopt the medieval Arab culture and fashion as part of his new religion. Though I do not remember the name of my Anglo comrade, he had changed his birth name to an Arabic name after his conversion to the Sunni sect. Besides losing his original name, this bloody British most likely passed through a bloody and painful ritual adopted from Jewsish religion.

Around midnight, the morning of September 12th, three of us were walking in Daruşşafaka Street towards Fatih mosque. There we would have a surprise. A police van coming from behind us stopped in this dark road and asked for our ID card. While, looking at our birth certificates under the headlights of their van, I noticed the face of the commissioner lighted with a grin. He looked at me and said: "Edip, we were looking for you in the sky; but we found you on earth." We were picked like gold nuggets from a mine and hurled into the police van.

We spent the night at the Fatih police station, and towards dawn we noticed an unusual commotion. News filtered through and we heard from the police officers that there was a military coup in progress. It was a historic morning in Turkey. The 12th of September 1980 military coup would be remembered by Turkish people for many generations to come. The US-supported military regime suspended the constitution and banned all political parties. The political process in Turkey was infantile and occasionally paralyzed because of the constant interference of the military, openly or covertly. Ironically, the very incompetence and political polarization, which was caused by the military's continuous interference was used as an excuse to take over the government altogether. This very military coup would hurt Turkey's political and financial institutions and progress.

Among the documents I recovered from my father's home in 2007 was one of my letters to my father. One letter was dated October 9th, 1980. Somehow I was able to find a way to smuggle it out of jail, perhaps through a detainee who was released before. Even though the early days of my prison experience was less restricted, such a communication would not be tolerated.

> [Dear father,] I greet you and kiss your hands.
>
> Now I am among my comrades at Maltepe military prison. Here our comfort is not bad. However, I learned that after September 12th, inmates have lost some rights. I also learned that one of the four wards has been filled with fascists, which resulted in creating tension here. In cases of conflict, the administration has been favoring the fascists. The fascists are also complaining to the administration that we disturb their sleep by reciting Adhan for the dawn prayers. They are also snitching on us; informing the administration that we insult Mustafa Kemal Atatürk, thus leading them to beat us.
>
> While talking about beating, let me tell you about my 13 days of police interrogation at the 1st section police detention center. Perhaps, it is a place where the world's lowliest people work together. They apply all sorts of torture to extreme doses. They cram six or seven detainees into a filthy and dark three-meter square cell, and let them suffer there for days and weeks. Detainees can go to the restroom no more than three times in 24 hours. And for 24 hours, all they give as food can only barely keep a person alive: a stale piece of military bread (about the half of a loaf sold outside), an egg, a potato, and a small slice of Karper cream cheese....
>
> If our problems were only these, we could bear them. But, the real terrifying thing is torture... Throughout the day, there is nonstop 24 hours daily torture here. The eyes of suspects are covered and they are taken upstairs and there they are subjected to hours of torture. Flogging the bottom of the feet with

stick made of cornelian cherry until they bleed, hitting the nails of the hand until they detach from the finger, banging the heads on the wall causing concussion, beating the liver area of the body with a sandbag, punching the kidneys until blood mixes with urine, spilling hot tea on top of the head, when asked for water serving salty water (perhaps mixed with urine; since the eyes are closed, the detainee cannot see its color), giving electric shocks through the earlobes and genitals, … pouring cold water over nude bodies… and many more unimaginable tortures are done here. On top of these physical tortures the detainees are also subjected to disgraceful insults and slurs.

Even if you are not tortured, hearing the screams day and night, cries, and moaning of inmates; the slurs and yelling of the police, is enough for you.

Honestly, they did not torture me this time. With a hypocrisy that I fail to understand, they tried to treat me very well. During my interrogation that added up to 30 hours, I was sitting on a chair my eyes closed. They were even serving me tea. Furthermore, they were apologizing for not serving the teacup with a saucer under it; it would be too hot to hold the glass teacups, which did not have handles. I rejected the first teacup they served me, thinking that they might have added some suspicious chemical. They allowed me to take another one instead. They were surprised to learn that I recognized one of the police officers from his voice. Despite my effort, I could not recognize the voice of an MIT secret police officer who was interrogating me. He was perhaps a frequent member of our group; he has even visited our home, and knows us better than we know ourselves. They even knew where you receive your salary from and how much.

Anyway, they asked me unimaginable questions and demanded answers for them. I answered them with full knowledge of my responsibilities. I even tried to proselytize them through occasional advice. However, it was not affecting them, since they were hypocrites. They were sometimes telling me jokingly, "do not wash our brains." I cannot fit all they asked me and told me on these papers. Of course, during my interrogation, I would constantly hear the disturbing cries and screams of inmates being tortured in nearby rooms. I need to rush so that this letter can make it to you.

I received the 1500 Liras you sent to me the last day of my stay at the police Section. After that, I was taken to Selimiye military detention center and I was held there for ten days. Compared to the 1st Section, Selimiye was like a heaven. The rest is known by you; my detention was confirmed by the court and I was sent to here afterwards. The alleged crimes of mine are:

> Being a member of a secret organization
> Organizing activities to promote armed rebellion
> Cooperating with Kurdish communists
> And several other nonsense like these

I greet you and kiss your hands. I also kiss my mother's hands, and kiss the eyes of my siblings.

October 9, 1980

Edip Yüksel

In my letter, I did not mention about the death of some detainees. I still have not forgotten the name of a leftist activist, Zeki Yumurtacı, an Economy student at the University of Istanbul. We heard that he was tortured at the same 1st Section Police detention center in Gayrettepe, and then he was killed in a setup. There was good news among the bad news, however. My two comrades were released. I was very glad for them. They were guests in my country and they were held there basically for no reason except been my company.

In the first chapter of this book, I shared with you some of my memories in the old Ottoman ammunition storage building turned into Kartal Maltepe Prison. There are a few more details I would like to share with you.

The so-called leader of ETKO (Esir Türkleri Kurtarma Ordusu = The Army for Saving the Captive Turks) and the rear-admiral of TIT (Türk İntikam Tugayı = Turkish Revenge Brigade) Cengiz Ayhan was also there on a murder charge. He was in his late twenties. He would get life in prison; however, it would be reduced to several years for his "confession." After his release, according to the news reports, he ended up in Germany and there too he continued his criminal activities and was put behind bars for murder and robbery. Cengiz would later claim responsibility for the killing of Uğur Mumcu in 1993, a prominent leftist Turkish journalist. Cengiz was a notorious fascist terrorist leader.

Cengiz was behind the bars in a ward across from us. Close to midnight, he sent me a book via a guard. Inside the book, I found a small piece of paper torn in an ugly manner with appalling handwriting. He was asking me to discuss the testimony of witnesses against Ali Bilir, the murderer of my brother. He also wanted me keep this communication confidential. He was trying to strike a deal regarding Ali's case. I found that letter dated 28 November 1980, among the documents I discovered in 2007.

> "Edip tomorrow come to the door during the break; I will meet you regarding Ali Bilir and your brother, may God's mercy be on him. We will talk about how the witnesses of the incident must testify. Now you send me a book. Do not tell anyone who would question you about this. This should remain between me, you, and ALLAH (cc). Good night.
>
> PS: When you return the book come to the gate. Cengiz."

On November 11th, 1980, I wrote to him a 16-page letter and handed it to him inside a book through the window of his ward's gate. In my letter, which was among the documents I recovered from my home almost 27 years later, I was rejecting his invitation categorically, and I was refuting their racist ideology by analyzing the *Dokuz Işık* (Nine Rays), the infamous book authored by his leader, Alpaslan Türkeş. I was comparing the racist ideas promoted in their book to the verses of the *Quran and Hadith*, and trashing them one by one. I denounced their organization as a counter-revolutionary puppet of imperialism, and I sealed my argument with a quote from *Fizilal-il Quran*, Sayyid Qutb's famous commentary of the Quran. "Islam is a revolutionary ideology. Islam is a revolutionary movement. It will destroy all false systems and will replace them with universal divine laws..." After receiving the letter, Cengiz tried one more time to approach me; but he did not receive a positive response. Shortly, they moved him to another prison. In retrospect, I wonder whether he used some connections in the military to transfer himself the prison where I was incarcerated to pressure me regarding my brother's murderer who was also a respected fascist leader. To give you an idea about the activities of Cengiz, here is a list of crimes reportedly committed by his paramilitary organization, TIT, which was used by a dubious yet powerful gang nestled within the government:

- May 16th, 1979: murdering 7 people in a café at Etlik Ankara
- September 11th, 1979: killing Prof. Fikret Ünsal of Çukurova University in Adana
- September 28th, 1979: killing Cevat Yurdakul, the head of the Security Directory of Adana
- March 10th, 1980: killing 6 people at a restaurant in Mecidiyeköy, Istanbul
- May 30th, 1980: killing of a solder in Adana
- July 15th, 1980, killing the congressman Abdurrahman Köksaloğlu in Istanbul
- July 22nd, 1980 killing Kemal Türkler, the leader of DİSK, that is, Confederation of Unions of Revolutionary Workers in Istanbul
- November 4th, 1993, implicated in the killing of Ahmet Cem Ersever, the Turkish colonel and intelligence officer in Ankara, and the Kurdish congressman Mehmet Sincar and politician Mehmet Özdemir.
- July 6th, 1996 killing of Kutlu Adalı, the journalist from Cyprus
- May 12th, 1998 assassination attempt against Akın Birdal, the president of The Human Rights Organizations
- September 12th, 2006 suspected of killing ten Kurdish people, of whom 7 were children, in Diyarbakır

Though I shared the same prison with the murderers and terrorists, my crime was categorically different. Despite being detained more than 15 times, the only crime they could accuse me of committing was expressing my political views and aspirations. I got a six-year prison term for promoting Islamic revolution through my published two articles in Islamist magazines. However, there were a few minor hearings too. One of them was about Atatürk's black bust, the milk and the cat story, which was rumored at WAMY's youth conference in Çanakkale. There were several other suspects too; but it was only me who was already in detention.

My brother, Nedim, was also among the defendants. As a participant of WAMY's camp at Çanakkale, he was on a suspect list by default. Police charged all the Turkish citizens who participated at the camp. Perhaps this was the revenge of the poor Minister of Youth who was booed by us. But, Nedim was always passive and he never participated in our activities. Though it was not really an activity according to our concept of activism, and throughout the two weeks he acted like a ghost, this was the only activity in which he participated.. He would never forgive me for inviting him to that camp. At the time he was a student at the Theoretical Physics department of the Bosphorus University. I would learn that he was overly exaggerating this charges and he was preoccupied with worries. So, he slacked in his education and started getting bad grades. Though he did not spend even one day in jail or prison, his fear of ending up there was sufficient torture. Our brother's assassination had led us further apart. It made me commit myself fully to the cause; while it led Nedim to become more critical of our ways. He resented me; he was accusing me of getting him into trouble. Nedim did not even greet me in the courtroom.

My name was on top of the long list. On the bench, there were three grumpy military judges. The lead judge accused me of insulting Atatürk. He expected me, like many others before me, to deny the charges. I would stun the tribune by accepting their accusation that I was not an Atatürkçü (Ataturkist). Both of his eyes opened wide and his head leaned forward towards me:

- What did you just say?
- I said that I do not like Atatürk. I am not Ataturkist. I do not approve his revolutions.
- Your honor, my client means…
- You shut up. I am not deaf nor have I an understanding problem. He just said unambiguously that he does not like Atatürk. I think he meant what he said. Yes, Mr. Yuksel, then I conclude that you accept the charges.
- No, I do not accept the charges.
- Then, which part of the charges you do not accept?
- As I said, I neither like Atatürk, nor his revolutions. Thus, if I really wanted to do something to his bust, I would not pour milk on its top and let the cat lick it. This is really a silly prank. I am not a prankster; I am an activist. Had I wanted to put my opinion of your idol in action, you would not end up with a dirty plaster head with a cat sitting on it.
- What would we end up with?
- A busted bust in the form of thousands of shattered pieces on the floor!

My lawyer whom I saw for the first time in the courtroom was in shock. He became irrelevant. He thought I had just sealed my doom, that I incriminated myself in the worst possible way. I would perhaps get extra punishment in addition to the current charges. I knew that I was taking a big risk by expressing my deep down conviction regarding the official idol of my country. But, I had no alternative. Even if I denied the charges, they would trust the police report more than my words, as they had done in the past.

Without knowing Immanuel Kant, I was following the moral principle called "categorical imperative": I would not lie under any circumstances. I believed in honesty. I was honest even towards my ardent enemies. I was also hoping that my bold statement would make my denial of the charges more credible in the court. It did. To everyone's surprise, I was acquitted. Apparently, these judges appreciated my honesty and bravery and were convinced that it was not me who spilled the milk on their idol's bust. They got it right.

Our transportation from prison to the courtroom was made in converted big military trucks. They were huge rectangular metal cans. They had tiny windows secured with steel bars. The cans-on-wheels would be extremely hot in summers and very cold in winters. Detainees who had their hearing the same day would be chained to each other. Despite the heat, the cold, the chain, and the tiny windows, the approximately two-hour round trip between the prison and the court was an event I would look forward to. Meeting with other faces, spending time in a different setting such as courtrooms, chance to see our family members or friends in the courtroom or hallways was like a family trip to Hawaii. I was lucky in the first few months, since I had more than one court hearing.

In the first prison structure, that is, the Ottoman ammunition storage, we had great times. I almost felt as if I was in a survival camp. I would ignore all the negative things about being a prisoner in an over-crowded, windowless old building with flickering lights. I would enjoy the company of my comrades. Since there was no torture, with time we developed a better relationship with military guards. We were able to mingle with other comrades who were in different wards. The few fascist inmates were no challenge for our security either. We had minimal communication with them and we also tried our best to avoid confrontation.

For a while there was a rosary craze. Some inmates started making rosaries out of olive seeds. Though I was not interested in becoming a rosary artist, I had no reason to resist the temptation; I did the same. I made a few of my own rosaries. Even in those days, I was not a fan of praying with rosaries as my comrades who belonged to a religious order were. My father was not using it and perhaps he considered it an innovation, though a benign one. The rosary was adopted from Christian tradition long after Muhammad's departure, together with many other articles of faith, practices, and rituals.

We would remove the flesh of the olive very well by sucking them in our mouths like a hard candy, and after washing them we would rub them vertically on the concrete surface of high walls during the two one-hour daily fresh air breaks. We would stop rubbing the seed when we saw the top of its hollow center. Then we would repeat the same for the other pointed end. We were doing this job while we were standing on the corner, or walking up and down the yard between the walls. After opening both ends of more than a hundred seeds, we would link them up with a nylon string. Rosaries traditionally had 99 beads, each for the so-called 99 Names of God. They were divided into three sections of 33 beads each, which was again adopted from Christian tradition that used each bead representing a year that Jesus lived on earth. For partition, we would treat two seeds differently; we would open holes from their sides rather than the pointed ends. There was also the terminal bead, which was called imam (leader). Since we did not have a very long seed, we would use several beads for the terminal. Finally, we would place the rosary in a glass jar, soaking it in olive oil. Some inmates would take it even more seriously and develop more complex treatments that turned the rosaries into artifacts. The long process of making rosaries was a great blessing in such a prison that had no television, no library, no gym, and no yards except a 10 x 30 foot strip between the high walls of the prison and the high walls of the strip.

Besides making rosaries, we were allowed to have a few books. There were no shelves and not even an empty place in the prison to put a desk. Thus, we would keep the books under or next to our pillows. I decided to translate Ahmad Deedat's book on the SECRET. I would later thank God for my arrest and my time in prison. I was so busy with activism that perhaps I would never find a chance to sit down and translate the book Ahmad Deedat gave to me at the Youth Conference two months before. Though during the 3.5 years of uninterrupted prison time (with other short term prison and jail times before and afterwards, it would come close to 5 years), occasionally there was torture and very strict rules, such as not being allowed to read any book of our choice, but there was a period in prison where I found ample time to examine Deedat's book and then translate it. In this ammunition storage I had the perfect time.

My first months in this prison provided me with a great opportunity not only to translate the book, but also to verify many of the Quranic data presented. I employed my comrade inmates for the verification and falsification process. Later, I would contribute to the subject matter and add my studies on scientific aspects of the Quran and become its co-author. The first edition of the translation of the book that did not contain my additional studies was published within a few months by Evs Publishing. The translation, the verification and falsification task and the publication of the book took about three months, and it was published before the end of 1980. The second edition would be done by Madve Publishing House in 1981. However, with the addition of my work to Deedat's, and a new cover design by Inkılab Publishing in 1983, it became an instant best-seller, for about four years topping the best-sellers list in Turkey, until the religious establishment banned it.

There were occasional new comers to the prison, which we would celebrate; they were new faces in a boring and stagnant environment and also a source of detailed information about the outside world, without censorship. However, towards the end of 1981, we had big losses in terms of inmates. Those who were detained or convicted for minor crimes such as violating the curfew regarding normal political activities were getting released one by one, group by group. In our little universe with high walls and steel bars, we had mixed feelings regarding the birth and death of inmates. We were happy for them, but felt sorry for losing their company. Unlike petty criminals, those who were affiliated to political youth groups would usually develop a very close camaraderie. Our common culture, common struggle, common experience, common cause, common enemies, and collective charges against us would weave strong bonds among us. On visitation days our families would get to know each other, and in turn, this would increase our bond even further, beyond prison. In fact, many prisons and jails were turned into training centers for political youth organizations. Political prisoners would be released more indoctrinated, hardened, and with a better network.

Our biggest loss occurred when about a dozen members of Vanguards who were students at the University of Istanbul Literature Faculty were released. We called them the "Literature group." Though the group acted as single body, a close scrutiny would reveal a big fault line; it was a mixed group. Some were members of a Sufi order, and some were Salafi; two rival theologies. In fact, I am now bewildered at my lack of curiosity. What political and social conditions made an alliance between those two opposing theologies possible? The MSP (Milli Selamet Partisi = National Salvation Party) and Vanguards organization had performed magic by uniting many opposing schools. Perhaps, the power of a common enemy was the main factor. Some members of the group belonged to the Naqshibendi order led by Zahid Kotku of İskenderpaşa Mosque, which produced numerous political parties, congressmen, ministers, prime ministers, and even a president, such as Necmeddin Erbakan, Korkut Özal and Turgut Özal; and youth leaders who were once my close friends, such as Mehmet Güney, Dursun Özcan, Hasan Hüseyin Ceylan (currently member of congress), Metin Külünk, Tayyip Erdoğan (currently prime minister), Numan Kurtulmuş (currently the leader of a political party) and many other political figures.

Some members of the Literature group did not belong to an order; they were sympathizers of Muslim Brotherhood of Egypt. The leader of that group was Kazım Sağlam, who would end up becoming a columnist in Islamist periodicals. Kazım was ethnically a Zaza and theologically a hard core Salafi, a fan of Sayyid Qutb. He was personally a kind man, an avid book reader; but he was infected with a religious virus with a power-bomb. If one day Kazım gained political power, he would turn to a moral police with a club in hand, like the Taliban in Afghanistan, Mutawa in Saudi Arabia, or Pasdaran in Iran. He would not hesitate justifying the stoning-to-death penalty for married adulterers, or forcing women to wear a veil from head-to-toe, or issuing death penalties for apostates like me. In those days we were friends. We shared the same ideology and the same dreams. Perhaps the virus in my blood had experienced a little benign mutation; I was leaning more and more towards peace and civility. But my experience of the Iranian revolution demonstrated that, after realizing the ultimate goal, that is, after taking control of a nation's brain, those with less virulent viruses would be pushed aside by those who were infected with the worst mutated versions. Bazargan, Bani Sadr, and many other moderate revolutionaries such as my friend Bahzadnia would later regret their alliance with mullahs. But, it would be too late. When people got intoxicated with victory, their moderation would be the cause of their defeat.

With the loss of the literary group, our numbers shrunk. So, the administration decided to move us from the ammunition storage to Prison Number 3, a smaller prison half a kilometer down the road. The new old prison was managed by the same commanders of the 2nd Armored Brigade. This was even worse than the first. It was a thick-walled old building with more than half of it buried under ground. It was a humid basement that received no natural light. After the first day, we would learn that they would not allow us to get out for fresh air. We would be inside that big box for 24 hours. If we were lucky we would have chance to see the sunlight for a few minutes during our weekly short trip to the nearby building for a shower, and for those who still had court hearings, perhaps a few seconds walking from the prison gate to the truck and from the truck to the building where the courtrooms were located.

My craving for the outside was not due to my concern for my health; it was not cognitive. Though I was an information junkie, I did not know how important was the role of sunlight on our physical health. The Turkish proverb, "Doctors enter to the houses that Sun does not enter" proved to be right. Within a few months, we experienced a strange and potentially noxious problem, an endemic. We started getting infections on our bodies; especially on our arms and legs. I had three of those one after the other. They were very painful. So painful that I could not move my arm or leg... The infection would grow to a walnut size bulge on my skin. Like a brewing volcano of flesh filled with pus; yet unable to explode. The pressure would turn it hard and sensitive. There were periodical doctor visitations. A military doctor would come there and see the patients.

- What is your complaint?
- You see. I have a very painful infection in my arm.
- Let me see.
- I have also another one just emerging in my leg.
- Well, this is nothing, not important.
- How come? It is infected; and it is too painful.
- Your hair is turning back into your skin.
- What? My hair?
- Yes.
- But, my hair never did such a thing all my life.
- ...
- Besides, some of my friends too have the same infection on their bodies.

369

- So what?
- How come our hair decided to conspire against us, just after we came here?
- You are talking too much. Hold firm and do not move. I will squeeze the puss out and fill it with sterilized gauze. It has antibiotic and will kill the germs.

Until then, I had only experienced passing out once, in the third grade. A student had punched me in my stomach while I was not attentive to him. The pain inflicted by the doctor's knife created that rare experience. It was not a rowdy kid but a doctor, I was very attentive; yet I had no alternative. Without applying any anesthesia, the doctor would make a half-inch long incision on the tip of the infection, and then he would squeeze the puss out. When I gained my consciousness back, I would see my infection filled with gauze; my arm radiating with excruciating pain. I had three of those painful surgery-on-the-hoof experiences. Each time I would hear the doctor indicting my hair followed by a painful pinch on my flesh. Other comrades, such as Mehmet Emin Erdal and Recep Olgaç too would get the same diagnosis. Was our hair too switching to their side? Did they really expect us to believe the story of organized hair rebellion? I would soon learn.

Thinking that I had still some rights as a citizen of my birth country or as a human being, I decided to write a petition to the prison administration about our common experience, the painful infection epidemic. In that letter, I respectfully challenged the official medical diagnosis, and I demanded a better look at the cause of the problem. I was so naïve. I was really expecting some attention from those who were controlling every aspect of our lives. The following morning, the cross-eyed and charming commander of the prison, Memduh came with a smirk on his face. We were gathered in the hallway behind the bars. He waived a paper in his hand and started reading it. It was my petition. Then he tore it into pieces and trashed it. "I do not want to receive any of these petitions. You better know where you are, who you are, and who we are!" was his closing statement.

I was very friendly with Memduh. He was unusually intelligent and conversant, and had a good sense of humor. He used to demonstrate respect for me. With this incident, I felt betrayed. Up to that point, I wanted to believe that the administration and soldiers were law abiding officers of the government. I was always cordial and respectful to them. Though I was politically and religiously against the regime, I was able to distinguish between the individual officers and the system. I also distinguished between police and military. I did not like generals, police, and judges, but I did not have personal animosity against them. I had witnessed police brutality, but I had not experienced cruelty from soldiers; except when I was punched on the head several times by a captain after I was found as a wanted man. Somehow, I did not then blame the captain for being angry with me and punching me. Unlike the police, who were usually calculating and malicious; the captain was spontaneous and angry when he was punching me. Now for the first time, I saw the tip of the beast's tooth. My petitions would not reach the top administrator. Even if it did, he would too perhaps trash it like Memduh had done.

The ambiance and situation would change gradually and dramatically. I am not talking about the physical condition of the building; it was very bad. The relationship between inmates and the military administration deteriorated. It was the military that was changing the rules. We were one day given the instruction that from then on, we would sing the national anthem every day. As I mentioned in the first chapter, my rejection of this ironic instruction led me to torture and solitary confinement. It was early April of 1981.

I was thrown into one of the filthy cells after being beaten very badly. My entire body was in pain and bruised. There was a narrow, long slot in the thick walls of the old building. I had nothing to entertain myself, not even blank paper and a pen. Nothing! All I had was walls, iron bars, a bathroom seat in the corner, a sink, and a filthy bed. I had no interaction with other inmates. I could see guards only during mealtime, and the daily half an hour break for fresh air. Day by day, it became more difficult to bear in isolation. It may sound like a movie script, but strangely, I noticed a family of little mice in the cell, which I befriended. I would share some of my bread with them after each meal.

On top of that, I would experience an "adventure" with another creature: a crow. I was woken one morning by the noise of a crow. It had managed to enter my cell through that narrow slot in the wall. The crow was not a happy pal like the mice. Perhaps it was a claustrophobic bird. He regretted being in my cell and was trying to get out. But, he could not get out from the narrow slot that it entered. The poor bird would fly across the cell and hit the walls, fall and fly again. The tranquility of my residence was flying in the air like dust and feathers. There was noise, chaos. I got excited and rejuvenated. However, soon I felt sorry for the crow, since it was going to kill itself, probably from concussion. It could not survive so many clashes with the solemn walls of my cell. I decided to save my newly arrived friend from the agony he was experiencing. I tried to catch him. In that little cell with high ceiling I was jumping up and down together with the crow. Without having time to completely recuperate from the first beating, a few days before, my body was subjected to a second round of corporal punishment. Ignoring the pain in my body, I continued my effort to catch the poor crow, until the guard came to my help. The guard heard the noise and worried that I was trying to hurt myself or kill myself. At that time, the prison administration had not yet started the systematic torture and abuse. So, perhaps the guard had entertained some human feelings about inmates. Noticing my pathetic effort to catch a crow in my cell, the guard asked another guard for help. One of them entered the cell and caught the crow. With losing that disoriented crow I also lost a chance to befriend the smartest of all birds.

371

It was after about a month of my solitary confinement, that the administration sent another person to the next cell, which was empty. He was a young student at ITU (Istanbul Technical University) and affiliated with Marxist-Leninist Dev-Sol organization. He was there for murder. He asked me whether I knew how to play chess, I said no. He wanted to teach me. Initially I resisted. I thought it was a boring game. But, I decided to give it a try. He drew the shape of pawns on pieces of small papers and made a chess board out of a blank piece paper. My solitary confinement was no more solitary, and with the entrance of chess to my cell, I had little reason to complain, except for my freedom.

I would spend about six weeks there until the 19th May 1981. I would be sent back to the basement next to my comrades as a gesture to honor the official holiday. In May 19, 1919, 19 Young Turks led by Mustafa Kemal Atatürk went to the city of Samsun with numerical value of 361 (19x19), starting the war of Independence which would result in the foundation of the modern Turkish Republic. Winking at the blinking number 19, I joined my friends.

The situation at the basement, however, would get even worse. One day, about ten soldiers stormed the ward and ordered us to gather in the hallway immediately. We were asked to extend our hands forward palms upward. They started striking our palms with their truncheons and clubs. Vicious and painful… While striking us they were asking us to call them "Emret komtanım" (Your order, Commander!). The sound of the hard clubs landing swiftly on the flesh of our hands was mixed with the unorchestrated cries of "Emret Komtanım! Emret Komtanım!" The faster and the more powerful was the strike, the louder and faster our cries were. It was a terrible scene and noise. We were psychologically humiliated and physically hurt. There was no justification for that treatment. With the exception of my rejection of reciting the national anthem as a political prisoner, we were respectful to the rules, and despite the over-crowded wards we had little problem among us. We would later learn that these beating sessions were just a start; we were going to get used to that; even to much worse.

We would have weekly visitation rights and we were warned not to communicate anything negative about our condition. Each of us was monitored by a pair of soldiers on each side of the metal bars. Do not underestimate prisoners, especially the political ones. We found a way to communicate secretly. I do not remember exactly how he did, but my father succeeded in smuggling in an Arabic book. The book was an Arabic novel, and my father was expecting me to translate it into Turkish.

I could not wait to read the book; the book that my dear father picked for me. Perhaps, it was given to him by one of his visitors form an Arab country. Around midnight, I secluded myself in a cozy corner of the ward, and started to read its first pages. It was not a teen novel. It was not romance. It was not science fiction. It was a propaganda novel. Its title was "Interrogation." It was about a young militant member of Muslim Brotherhood who would get arrested by the Egyptian police and get interrogated at the station under torture. It had a few boring plots and was filled with redundant diatribes bashing the secular government of Egypt in favor of Muslim Brotherhood. It was promoting the noble cause of bringing back the rule of sharia. I immediately identified myself with the young hero who endured all sorts of inhumane torture and responded to all of their accusations and false ideas with wonderful statements.

I knew that the book had no chance of getting published legally. First, it would be very hard to find a publishing house willing to put their business under grave risk for such a book. Besides, even if we found a crazy publisher, the book would immediately get banned by the martial court. The publishing house would be locked by police; the publisher together with his employees would be arrested. They would be subjected to similar interrogation depicted in the book; except they would most likely not be as articulate and as brave as its hero. They would be convicted for violating TCK 163 (Turkish Criminal Code) and would end up enjoying their time in this humid dark basement on the bunk beds next to me. Thus, I knew that the book would be published and distributed underground. My father must have been crazy to dare to undertake such a mission. It was not a good time to promote theocracy in Turkey. The Turkish military and government were fuming with hatred towards theocracy and Islamists. Especially, after what had just happened in our neighbor, Iran. And it was definitely not a good idea to do so by using the military prison as the office, and one of its inmates as an agent!

Though I was aware of the risks, I decided to translate the book. I was my father's son. Within two months, I finished the translation as a clandestine operation, and I sent it back. I was not supposed to put my real name as its translator. It would be published by an underground publishing house under the title "Soruşturma" (Interrogation). In November 2008, I received an email about this book from Kaan Göktaş, a Turkish author and friend of mine. He gave me the good news about his discovery of my first but lost book. Being a bibliophile and customer of used book stores, Kaan had already discovered some of my out-of-print books, which I have no copies in posession. Based on Kaan's report, now I have complete title of the book.[186]

I still remember how I smuggled it out. If both parties, the inmate and the visitor, extended their hands through the double layers of iron bars, their hands could almost reach each other. Almost! Still there was about two feet distance between our fingers. So, I rolled the manuscript tightly and extended its pages telescopically turning it to a long cylindrical tube. I then put a few rubber bands around it. I practiced how to collapse it and extend it. Now, the "Interrogation" was a transformer: it could be transformed from a stack of loose papers to a portable long stick, and vise versa. There was also another hurdle to overcome, besides the distance: the guards on both sides of the iron bars. They were watching and listening to us throughout our visitation time. I had to involve my comrades. We conspired. Upon noticing a particular queue from me, they would do something to distract the guards. When all the guards got distracted with that incident, I would be able to smuggle my transformer book in less than six seconds. After my release from prison, I would see a copy of it at home.

With the spring of 1981, came the time for another move. One day we were told that we were going to move to another prison. We were given only about fifteen minutes to pack up and get ready to be loaded into the trucks. We were not even told to which prison we were being transferred. They would always give us very short notice and trickle down the information bit by bit. We thought we were going to a far away location, but the truck stopped after only five minutes. We were at our new location: The Prison number 1; the biggest of the three on the Kartal-Maltepe military base. It was the same prison that I had met the murderers of my brother during one of my detentions before the military coup on September 12th, 1980. There my friend Ebubekir was stabbed by a hit man who confused my comrade with me. Now we were going to share the prison with fascists. I prayed that I would not see the murderers of my brother.

When we entered the facility, we immediately noticed a different atmosphere. Soldiers were rude and mean. I was led, with my possessions to the big hallway. It was used as a temporary welcoming and distribution center. There were several soldiers with documents. I was identified and told to take my cloths off. It was a routine that I had gotten used to. But, they took me to another room and several soldiers started attacking me with their batons. They were also insulting and cursing me. It was a very painful ordeal. When they were satisfied with the amount of bruises that inflicted on my flesh, I was sent to an assigned ward. There I would meet my other comrades. Thank God we were not separated from each other. However, there were some strangers there too. We were all beaten. Perhaps, I got an extra share for being the leader of Vanguards group.

The prison consisted of several sections, each isolated from others very well. In our section, there were two small rooms with bunk-beds, a small square hallway in the middle, two bathrooms and two sinks, and an approximately a 100 feet-square yard with a concrete floor and very tall walls. Both rooms together had about 30 beds, all bunk beds. The yard belonged to the section and it was open all the time. So, we were lucky that we could at least see sunlight. The building was in a much better condition than the one we had left. We felt as if we had moved from a zero star rated hotel to a five star resort. But, we were sad and worried. The welcoming event was an indication of what was going to come. A lot of beating, cursing, and torture... In fact, physical beating and verbal abuse was daily. No, it was hourly. More accurately, we were not safe at any time. Soldiers would occasionally get us up after midnight and beat and insult us for fun.

From April 1981 to September 1982, for about sixteen months, we had daily torture and beatings. There was physical and mental abuse. We were called not by our names but with obscenities. We were at the mercy of young soldiers, mostly barely literate, who enjoyed mistreating us. Either the guards were deliberately selected from a pool of mentally or emotionally sick young men; or they were trained well to act like sadist psychopaths. Perhaps it was another case of Milgram's "shocking" experiment, the power of authority that turns many poor souls into monsters. I will not describe the tortures in detail, but, to give you an idea about the environment I was in, I will briefly give an outline of some of the practices.

- Beating every new-comer to the prison until bruising their flesh all over, including head and face.
- Randomly calling and striking our palms with batons.
- Requiring us to respond to every guard, with the cliché: "Your order, my commander!"
- Taking us to the yard and forcing us do physical exercise until we were exhausted. For instance, we would be asked to do 100 push-ups. Anyone who slowed down during push-ups would get kicked in the head by the boots accompanied by all kinds of obscenities.
- During shower days, beating our wet bodies with batons (This was rare).
- Forcing us to shave our dry skin with razors even if there was no water, no foam.
- In case an inmate did not follow directions or made a mistake, punishing everyone in the ward.
- Beating us for anything. For smiling, for looking sad, for looking up or down...
- Banning books, magazines, television, chess, and any other entertainment; except a few books, which were all about Atatürk.
- Forcing us to gather in the hallway and study the official books given to us. Those few books were all about Atatürk's life and it included the official cult's holy book: Nutuk. I was appointed to lead the reading and studying. In the end of each session, I had to write one or two page summary of what we read. The guards, who usually had no idea about the topic, would randomly call an inmate and ask him what he learned that session. If the inmate could not make up something, then he would pay for it by physical pain inflicted on him.

It was a tragic-comedy when Ali Bulaç was briefly detained and brought to our ward. He was a famous author by then, and we knew each other from our political activities. He was six years older than me. He was publishing a serious journal called *Düşünce* (Thought); he had authored several books, and had a publishing house that published many quality books. His publishing house introduced us to the work of many foreign authors, including Ali Shariati. He was also writing articles for an Encyclopedia. The first time he entered the ward, he was terribly beaten up. His face was purple from bruises. This, Ali Bulaç too would be tested and evaluated by those soldiers, including the illiterate ones!

Though we experienced plenty of physical and mental abuse, thank God, we were not subjected to sexual abuse at any stage of my incarceration, as it is depicted in prison related movies such as Midnight Express and Shawshank Redemption. Many of us could bear a particular mistreatment, but the combination of all of the above and its duration for more than a year was what took its toll on us.

We were very lucky compared to the detainees of the American occupying forces at Abu Ghraib and Guantanamo Bay prisons. The torture and sexual abuse committed against detainees by the USA-Inc and its British ally proved the fact that we knew: despite their lipservice to morality, democracy and human rights, the Western civilization was a Janus. The imperialist western powers carried out the most despicable and horrendous acts of terror and torture against Muslim populations by exploiting the raw emotions and ignorance of jingoist and religious segment of population. The ruling class transferred the taxpayers' money to the so-called Military Industrial Complex and war-profiteering Mercenaries. The eight-year reign of the Neocon government led by a re-born rightwing Christian president will no doubt be remembered as one of the darkest periods in American history.

Back to Turkish prisons… Some of the prison-mates showed signs of mental weakness and exhaustion. The mental anguish of the nationalists was compounded. After the military coup, they thought they would be rewarded for fighting against "communists" and Kurdish activists on the streets and university campuses. They were expecting to be rewarded by the state that used them as voluntary police and militia. Well, they were only temporary pawns and they would be discarded. There was no more need of them. Thus, they experienced great disappointment. After each torture session, I would hear them complaining and regretting. "I was stupid for putting my life at risk for this state, I was stupid." I had a twisted joy from hearing those words from Ülkücüler, or Gray Wolves. These people belonged to a fascist youth organization that had many young men's blood, including my brother's, on their hands. Now, they were finally imprisoned and tortured by their "glorious military!" Well, their sober state of mind would last as much as their physical pain would last. One or two hour after the beating session, those nationalists who regretted and cursed the state and military a moment ago, would revert back to their old ways. "Regardless, whatever they do, it is still our military! May God bless our military!" they would confess their sins. It was an attempt to protect their illusion, that they did an honorable job for working as volunteer militia and contraguerillas for the state. They were fooling themselves inside in order not to confront the sad reality that they were fooled outside. They were now full time fools. No wonder! After their release from prison, many of those Gray Wolves could not find a place in a changed society, thus, ended up working for the Mafia!

Surely we were fools too. We were also used by politicians who exploited the religious sensitivities, social and economic alienation of our families. They used us as volunteer foot soldiers. We were led on the streets to fight territory wars, while the politicians gained power and accumulated wealth. Children of Adam, the children of the same country, instead of living together as brothers and sisters were indoctrinated and polarized by adults, and were overtly or subtly encouraged to hate and kill each other.

We then did not know that we were all puppets of a scenario designed by dark forces in Turkish military in order to create conditions and pretext for a military coup. When the bloody game reached its planned point, Turkish generals stopped it as saviors. The victims were again the young men; mostly children of the lower class. We were wasted through a civil war, through political games. The Nationalists, Communists, and Islamists, the three nemesis stooges of an era, would now share the same chains, the same wards and would be treated like animals. Here, we were sharing the same tragedy with our supposed enemies. Though they were well ahead of us in violence and shedding blood, we were on the same diabolic track. Given more time, we would end up like them. They were killing in the name of nationalism, or in the name of communism, we would kill in the name of Allah. Now, we were all sharing a hell on earth.

Within several months, psychological explosions started. After one of the regular daily beating sessions, one of the leading Gray Wolves lost his temper and cut his wrist with razor. Another former wolf started hitting his head on the walls, from frustration and stress. There were various signs of strain in almost every inmate's behavior. Knowing the mental toll the circumstances could cost me, in the early days of that hell I took some measures. They were controlling me physically; but I would not let them control my mental status. I would not submit my brain to their hell.

Soon after we were transferred to this torture house, I tried to keep myself mentally busy. After I finished those few boring books, I decided to write down the chapters of the Quran that I had memorized in my high school years, several years before. I was mentally tortured to memorize those chapters, but now I was going to remember them word by word and write them down letter by letter to save myself from this torture. It was an irony, a mysterious irony. I wrote down the last chapters of the Quran, which were the shortest ones, starting from Chapter 78 up to Chapter 114, all in Arabic. I later wrote down the first pages of Chapter 2, which I had also memorized, and the entire chapters of 36 and 67, and some selected prayers from here and there. On lined white papers folded vertically, I succeeded in writing down about one tenth of the Quran, letter by letter in two columns on each page. I had to keep it secret; the administration would be furious if they found out about it. They would not allow us to have the Quran. Their holy book was *Nutuk* (Speech), and they could not tolerate having a rival holy book inside the prison. However, they did not know that I carried a portion of that book in my mind and heart. To keep about a dozen of my comrades busy, I started secretly sharing it with them. Writing, reading, and studying those chapters opened a window to heaven from inside the hell we were living in. Unfortunately, there were random searches, and occasionally we would not have time to hide the papers. I was subjected to several special corporal punishments when the soldiers discovered the Arabic text of the Quran with my handwriting. But, I was not going to give up. The physical pain would pass soon, and I would start re-writing them. I was going to forget the past abuses, and I was not going to worry about tomorrow. I was going to live the moment, and I was going to do my best to save it from the control of my enemies. (Thank God, we were allowed to have pens and papers to write letters, letters that would be read and censored by the administration. I would recover one of those letters I had sent from that prison to one of my friends and learn about another abuse that I never knew existed. A soldier who was reading my outgoing and incoming letters had written the following note on top of my letter to my closest friend, Sıtkı Doğan: "Do not listen to this idiot!" Disgusting! They had the audacity and cruelty to put such a remark on a letter that contained an expression of innocent friendship.)

Another device I employed to keep my sanity was to play chess. As I have said, during those nine months of strict rules we were not allowed to have chess. When there is need, there is creativity; when there is will, there is solution. Making a primitive chess set was not difficult. I noticed that the plastic handles of razors were perfect material for a miniature chess set. I cut the end off their handles in different shapes and sizes. Then, I drew 64 squares on a piece of paper. Voila! Now we had a chess set, an illegal one! It was the most popular thing in our small ward, until it was discovered inside a bag under an inmate's mattress, prompting another dose of bonus corporal punishment.

I could not continuously write the Quran and I already had done it a few times. I could not play chess all the time either. Both were very dangerous activities. Each time we were caught reading or playing; each time the contraband paraphernalia, which consisted of papers or plastic chess pieces, yes, each time they were discovered by the administration we were paying a heavy price in terms of extra corporal punishment, verbal abuse and loss of visitation time with our family. As their leader and the mind behind those illegal activities, I would get extra special treatment. Thus, I wanted to indulge in a mental activity that would not be as easily discoverable. I re-discovered mathematics and numbers. Welcome my friends, my love; welcome the fascinating universe of numbers! God's language in the universe!

Numbers kept me busy. Numbers kept me sane. Numbers kept me in a heavenly bliss while my body was in hell. Knowing that the number 19 was a prime number, I had already developed some curiosity about prime numbers. I knew that there was no pattern in the universe of prime numbers. In other words, there was no formula that could generate all prime numbers. However, I also knew there were some formulas that could generate a limited number of prime numbers. Well, what about taking on this problem? What about trying to discover a formula for prime numbers? I was not as gullible as I was in my teen years. I knew that me finding a formula for prime numbers was almost as impossible as discovering a perpetual machine. But, more than the goal, I was interested in the process. I had nothing to lose in chasing a formula, perhaps the "most wanted formula" in the world of mathematics. I had a lot to gain, however. First, it would take my mind away from the negative circumstances. Second, I would learn more about numbers. Though my body was imprisoned, my mind was free to travel among the billions of synapses in my brain.

I came up with three simple formulas that generated a consecutive list of prime numbers. The longest list contained 24 prime numbers, which was produced by using 24 consecutive counting numbers, starting from zero.[187]

$2n(n-1)+19$ $2n^2-2n+19$		$n^2+(n-2)(2n-5)+19$ $3n^2-9n+29$		$n(n-3)+19$ $n^2-3n+19$	
0	19	0	29	0	19
1	19	1	23	1	17
2	23	2	23	2	17
3	31	3	29	3	19
4	43	4	41	4	23
5	59	5	59	5	29
6	79	6	83	6	37
7	103	7	113	7	47
8	131	8	149	8	59
9	163	9	191	9	73
10	199	10	239	10	89
11	239	11	293	11	107
12	283	12	353	12	127
13	331	13	419	13	149
14	383	14	491	14	173
15	439	15	569	15	199
16	499	16	653	16	227
17	563	17	743	17	257
18	631	18	839	18	289
19	703	19	941		(17x17)
	(19x37)	20	1049		
		21	1163		
		22	1283		
		23	1409		
		24	1541		
			(23x67)		

I had other mental exercises. For example: one involved tessellations. I was working on fitting a myriad of geometric shapes in boxes. Trying to find out a formula for placing triangles, squares and rectangular shapes of various sizes in a particular box was fun. I do not have the records of this; but as far as I remember, I enjoyed very much trying to solve the problems I imagined among shapes and numbers. I was occasionally sucked into the black hole of the Pythagorean universe. I discovered the power of my brain in creating my own reality while I was living a nightmare. My mathematical reality could easily be disrupted by an ignorant and arrogant interference, yet I could easily get it back and find it the way I had left.

We also invented a physical game. I do not mean that we have its patent. Perhaps it was played by Vikings or Australian aborigines centuries ago. Since, we were usually inside a small ward, we did not have a sufficient area to run or walk. We adapted. We used the tiny yard for a game that we did not have a name for. I will describe the game in detail. Perhaps you might enjoy playing it in your homes and yards. If you are not interested in physical games, you may just skip the following two paragraphs.

Two inmates would face each other and stand on their feet at about three feet distance from each other. Each would keep their feet together, without leaving any distance in between. Their palms facing forward, hands open and all fingers looking upward; they would try to push each other by hitting each other's palms, without holding each other's hands or any body parts. They could only use their palms to hit the other's palms. The ideal modus operandi was both palms going forward and backward like twin pistons on an imaginary horizontal line to the floor. The goal was to move the opponent's feet from their standing position. It involved strength, balance, agility, concentration, tricks, and another factor which I call the 6th point, which only masters may discover.

I mastered the game; I became the unbeatable champion of the game. Respecting the hard work of potential champions of the game, I will not reveal the 6th point. As for the tricks; they are no mystery. I would not resist while the other attempting to push me with all his power, thereby causing him to lose his balance. I would also feign hitting hard and thereby leading my opponent getting attracted to my side. The game provided a lot of entertainment. For instance, I would have fun blowing air at my opponent while he was trying not to fall backward by rotating both of his arms counter clockwise, like a baby bird trying to fly. I would talk to distract or demoralize my opponent. I felt like Muhammad Ali of this harmless game. Of course, if my opponent started falling on me like a rootless log I could move away deliberately without losing a point. I would warn my opponents to never hold their hands vertically towards me, since our hands should always be in an open position and looking upward. If we both lost our balance at the same time, none gained points. I limited each session with 10 points. I played that game pretty well. So well, almost thirty years later, I still find difficulty in finding someone who could beat me. Even at the age of fifty, I still beat those who are thirty years younger than me, those who are taller or shorter, and those who are lighter or heavier. I occasionally fight the feeling of arrogance for beating massive football players and athletes. How, an achievement in such an insignificant field can make a person arrogant is beyond my comprehension. Especially, if that achievement dissipates together with one's health and strength. Let's give this wonderful game a name: "Elele Dengele" (Hand-to-hand Balance), in honor of the Turkish political prisoners who played it in difficult times.

When the strict rules, physical and mental abuse reached an unbearable level, the incidents increased. Finally, the bubbling torture pot reached its boiling point; it boiled and erupted in anger. Slogans were chanted, doors were banged, windows were broken, bunk beds were destroyed, wrists were cut, and heads were smashed against walls... It was an horrific scene; a human tragedy. I decided not to participate in the carnage, and my dozen or so comrades followed my inaction. Within a few hours, the revolt was precipitated. Some inmates were moved to another ward, and some were penalized with solitary confinement.

The administration took notice. To lower the tension, the colonel decided to ease some restrictions. Among those was the chess ban. We could not believe it. Finally we could play chess with a decent set without looking over our shoulders. The next visitation day, we could ask our visitors to bring us a chess set next time.

My father used to visit me more frequently during the first year of my prison term. My younger sisters Aynur and Ayşegül and brother Müfit, who prefers correcting the Turkish spelling his name as Müfid, visited me a few times. My brother Nedim and my mother never visited me. Nedim had a problem with me and my late brother Metin since childhood, and he continued his distance or anger in every stage of my life. As for my mother, not because she did not want to visit me; but because her veil was even a bigger obstacle than the prison walls were. She would not be allowed to enter the premises with her face covered. To see her son, she had to uncover her face, which was very reasonable. However, she had become the prisoner of a black sack imposed on her by the male despots in her family since childhood. She had lost her freedom completely; she could no more open the door of her prison, even though the male guards had died and the locks had rusted. She would, however, later open her face while visiting Mecca at the grand age of 70.

But, now it was mostly my older sister Süreyya. She was almost always accompanied by her friend, Sabiha. Both wore head-to-toe veil, only keeping their faces open. My sister and her friend kept visiting me until my last days in prison. When I would be transferred from military prison to a regular prison at Çanakkale to serve the last year of my term, they visited me every other week. They would travel the round trip of 640 kilometers between Istanbul and Çanakkale just to see me for twenty minutes.

I gave the good news to my sister. I asked her to bring "satranç,"—a strange burrowed word for chess set—to the prison. She was sandwiched between two soldiers and I too was monitored by other two. Two plus two = four guardians of Turkish hell. Our conversation was suddenly interrupted by the tall soldier who was from Hakkari. He accused me of talking a foreign language. The guards got highly anxious and nervous, as if they had seen a poisonous snake or a grizzly bear in the room. The prison administration was threatening us; we must not talk about torture in the prison. Anyone who made such a revelation would lose his visitation rights for long time and would be made an example for the rest. Our families were not stupid; they could easily tell that we were tortured. We did not need to scream about it.

My sister was taken out from the visitation room, and I was taken to the administration. The captain Mustafa was there, sitting at his desk with his normal grumpy face. He was not a typical ranked soldier. Turkish soldiers care about their grooming and attire. This one was very shabby. You could see the dirt shining from his collar. Obviously, he had lost hope of getting promoted. Perhaps he was an alcoholic or a psychopathic soldier and the military wanted to keep him out of sight. They would also have little mercy for inmates. By appointing such ranking soldiers, the military would score a hit; two birds with one stone. He was also very nasty. I entered his room and saluted him like a soldier. I had to. The illiterate Kurdish soldier from Hakkari informed him about the incident:

- My commander, Edip violated the rules?
- Which rule did he violate?
- He talked in a foreign language with his visitor.
- Which language did he talk?
- I do not remember, but I heard him talking a foreign word.
- What did you talk, Edip?
- I asked from my sister to bring Satranç next time.
- Is it correct that Edip talked about Satranç?
- Yes, my commander. Now I remember, he uttered the foreign word, "satranç."

Of course the captain knew what satranç was. It was a commonly known word. The average education of the guard population would perhaps fall short of the sixth grade level. A normal person would laugh at this incident. But, the captain's ugly face did not change. Upon the captain's order I was sent to my ward. Alas, my sister was already sent out.

My memories of prison years can fill a book. I will end this chapter after sharing with you some of my experiences at Çanakkale E-Type prison. It was a civilian run prison and huge. There were wards allocated for political prisoners; but a great majority of its population was petty criminals.

Çanakkale prison was not run by the military, and comparatively its conditions were much better. There was no torture, no verbal abuse, no mandated indoctrination sessions. We would wear blue uniforms. The facility was very good, like a clean youth hostel. We would sleep upstairs, and there were tables for meals, television, and tennis tables downstairs. Each ward also had its yard.

The yard was designed to the specification of a professional volleyball field. Sure, the wards were sometimes overcrowded and the air was usually filled with clouds of cigarette smoke, yet, I was free from feeling the boots and clubs of soldiers on my body and free from hearing their insults. Though there were normal restrictions and censorship, the administration would allow us to read the few books we wanted. There I finished my poetry book, and completed my study of the Quran which would be published in *Kuran En Büyük Mucize* (Quran the Greatest Miracle). I had no serious complaint, neither for the guards nor for the administration!

As far as I remember, besides the ever increasing desire to be free, my major complaint was about clean air. When I was with my comrades, I had the opportunity to persuade them regarding the importance of clean and fresh air. So, none would smoke inside the ward. But, at Çanakkale, I did not have a sufficient number of comrades in the wards to establish a benevolent clean air kingdom. The wards in this prison, unlike the military prisons I had stayed in, had windows. It would be a real challenge to keep the window next to my bed ajar. There would be protests from other inmates, who were mostly heavy smokers. They didn't care about my passionate lectures about the importance of oxygen for the health of our brains. Perhaps, they did not have brains left to appreciate its importance.

In Çanakkale E-Type prison I would continue writing poems. Here is one of the poems I wrote there.

Umut Dolduralım Bardaklarımıza 26 Ocak 1983	Let's Fill Hope in Our Goblets 26 January 1983
bir şiir yaz dostum al kelimeleri eline kırmadan bağla birbirine sabır barajının duvarında şiirden kanallar aç öfkene!	write a poem my friend. take the words in your hand. gently join them to each other. in the dam of your patience, open channels to your anger

yık dostum,
    yık duvarını monotonloğun
    başka kokular
    başka renkler ara
    bir çiçek bul
    doyasıya kokla
    mesela
    bir papatya yakala
    incitmeden okşa
    konuş onunla
	break my friend,
	    break the walls of monotony.
	    other odors,
	    other colors you should seek.
	    find a flower.
	    smell its mistique.
	    for intance,
	    catch a daisy;
	    caress its petals,
	    speak to it.

kapa dostum tıpkı bir ama gibi sımsıkı kapa gözlerini görmesin karanlıktan başkasını	close my friend, like a blind man; tightly close your eyes. let it not see; except darkness.

tanımasın renkleri	let it not recognize the colors.
seçemesin uzağı yakını	let it not distinguish between far and near.
ve bekle öylece	and wait like that
tam bir gün bir gece	exactly one day and one night.
sonra aç gözlerini	then, open your eyes
seyret o nefret ettiğin	and watch the things you hate:
demir parmaklıkları	the iron bars,
üçlü ranzaları	the triple beds,
ve duvardaki mazgalları	and the peepholes on the wall.
ne kadar güzel değil mi?	how beautiful they are; aren't they?
gel dostum	come my friend.
umut dolduralım bardaklarımıza	let's fill hope in our cups,
bol bol sevgi	plenty of love,
ve merhamet dökelim içine	and compassion.
biraz nefret	a little hate,
biraz da şiddet katalım,	a little violence, let's add.
sonra karıştıralım tüm	then, let's mix them with all our
içtenliğimizle.	heart.
(Yusuf'un 40'cı Emri, Edip Yüksel, Madve Yayınevi, Istanbul, 1984)	(Joseph's 40th Commandment, Edip Yuksel, Madve Publishing House, Istanbul, 1984)

My oldest sister Süreyya could not visit me that frequently at Çanakkale prison. Thus, I spent more time and more paper writing her letters. This was very important for me, since it opened a little window the size of paper. My sister was my only pen pal. Writing letters and receiving their replies were high moments in my prison term there. I would usually write my curious observations on inmates or interesting events that happened in those days. I would also share some of the curious tit bits of scientific discoveries and observations, which I was learning from scientific journals. However, instead of my sister, I had a feeling that her close friend was writing her letters; I could tell from the handwriting. I could not distinguish which remark belonged to my sister or her friend, so I assumed that all belonged to my sister.

Her friend was a talented author, a biologist and a passionate Muslim activist. She had been the closest friend of my sister for years. When you see one of them, you would expect the other to be nearby. They were like peanut butter and jelly or ketchup and mustard. Both dressed in black clothes from head to toe, like Iranian women during revolution. Both were passionate supporters of Iran's so-called Islamic revolution and were very active in the radical Islamic revolutionary movement in Turkey. Before ending up in prison, my older sister and I were together for the same cause. So, she was not only my biological sister, she was also my comrade. Her comrade and closest friend was automatically my close friend too.

During my escape to the United States, I lost my only possession, my library. The file containing our prison correspondence was among them. I lost all of my correspondence with my sister, except the following letter, which was published in one of my books, *Kitap Okumanın Zararları* (The Dangers of Reading Books), before my immigration. The story is about our common experience during 1963-1964. Then, we did not have TV, electricity, or even the knowledge of their existence. It was our story in the summer pasture on the mountain.

I was seven or eight; you were nine or ten years old. To spend the summer together with our extended family, we had moved to the mountain, to a place called Qulungo. Our father had gone to Istanbul alone to move our family a year later. Despite his meager income he was sending us some pretty gifts once in a while. The news of someone coming from Istanbul and bringing a packet of gifts would give me such a pleasure that I cannot describe. Somehow, my father would not use the post office. He would send them via villagers who happened to visit Istanbul. I remember that I would always ask for a motorbike. I did not even have a scooter, or a tricycle. But, I was seriously expecting my father to send me a motorbike.

You remember the toy film slide machine, designed like a television. By pushing the plastic bar in its bottom would take us to colorful snap shot scenes from countries and cultures we never knew. Ah, I still remember my first colored book, the *Hayat Ansiklopedisi* (Life Encyclopedia). Its pages were bright and contained colorful pictures, stories and information about cars, trains, houses, etc. Its cover was like glass, hard and shining. I still remember how we were turning its pages slowly and gently. We called it "kitaba guri," that is "the wolf book" in Kurdish, because of the bizarre picture of a deceptive wolf wearing a shepherd's cloth. It was the best of times and the happiest of times.

We were having such a joyful time in Qulungo. Our father had again sent us gifts from the dream world Istanbul. We were flying from joy, without caring about the jealous look of children around us. How wouldn't we get excited? We, the children of mountains, strangers to plastic goods of modern technology... We did not have plastic toys; all we had as toys, were stuffed dolls made of old fabrics like scarecrows, or cars carved out of watermelon rind or flutes made of tree branches. I remember. Whenever a jeep or a truck came to the village we would run towards it and celebrate its visit to our town. We would stop and stare at the cars in awe. We would keep our distance. Perhaps we were thinking they would kick us like horses. Or we were afraid of their owners. People may not believe us, but we were getting a bizarre pleasure from chasing the automobiles and getting lost in their dust. Perhaps our lungs needed some change; the air in our town was too fresh and pure. Did we need some pollution, or just some change?

At that time, we were still going to Qulungo by horses and mules. You remember. The long caravans... A lengthy trip lasting for one or two days.... We would pass through nearby towns and take breaks. We would be hosted generously by the people of towns on our path, who would wish us good luck respectfully. Our grandfather was the most revered person in the region. He was the father figure in nearby towns and cities and he would solve the disagreements between individuals and small towns. For their dispute, the people would prefer him to the government courts.

Yes, I was going to refresh one of our memories. I was going to tell you about that interesting incident in Qulungo. Whenever the memories of cold spring water, the clear and breezy air, and wonderful life is resurrected in my mind I feel great longing for Qulungo. Weren't we very happy while playing among the giant volcanic rocks? How enjoyable moments were, our climbing those giant rocks and sitting on them pretending them to be our trucks? We used to eat our watermelons on top of those rocks, didn't we? Occasionally, ten or fifteen boys we would get together for gasht (picnic) to another spring among rocks and bushes behind the hills. We would decide: "Tomorrow we are going to gasht" and each of us would wake up early morning and take their share of items. We would take with us a lamb, a cauldron, rice, butter, plates and utensils. We would play, collect berries, drink and eat until sunset. I do not forget. Boys and girls were always going to different gasht points. If both boys and girls were interested in the same gasht point, then we would go there on different dates. They were unforgettable moments... Cannot be told in words...

My father's presents were adding more excitement and color to this childhood life. This time, among the gifts there was a strange item. Men and women, our extended relatives were curious about this gift. You know we had a close and crowded family... Grandparents, uncles, aunts, cousins, nephews, in-laws, etc... Add to these the male and female servants and maids, we were a family with more than two hundred members.

This bizarre gift item had flat and colorful wings and it was opened it could make a third of a circle. I guess many people expressed their ideas about it. Each person had an idea and argument to support it. I do not remember the details of the discussions. Finally, the idea of a woman was accepted by the majority. This gift, according to the consensus, was cosmetic, a beauty thing.

One of the women immediately collected your hair behind your head and tied it like a horsetail. Under the curious eyes of the gathering crowd, she tied that colorful thing to your hair like a ribbon. The gift item could be opened and closed. The best way, she figured out, was to tie it wide open.

Before the admiring eyes of the crowd, you jumped out of the circle. You were jumping and running with that big thing on your hair waiving side to side, up and down. As if it was dancing on your head. However, it was not falling down. Evidently, it was very tightly affixed to your hair. All the eyes were on that colorful object and all girls seemed to be in admiration.

Your joy did not last long. Soon, they took off that thing from your head while everyone was loudly laughing. They had committed an error, a big one! Some male relatives had seen the civilization. When he saw you jumping with that colorful stuff on your head, he informed everyone about the real purpose of the gift with all his wisdom. The plastic gift was an oriental fan, which was being sold to tourists. The function of a fan, however, was to make wind, not to stick on girl's head.

Yes, this is our story of a fan on top of a windy summer pasture on a high plateau.

In December 1983, I became eligible for parole. I spent the night at the young Muslim chaplain's home. Abdullah was not an Islamist like me, but he was a nice fellow and enjoyed talking to me during his weekly visitation to our ward. The following morning, my brother Müfid was coming there via ship to take me to home, as if the previous three and half years of incarceration would disorient me. Un-beknown to me, my release from prison was mentioned in the news of the Islamic Republic of Iran and other Islamist media.

The first morning of my new life outside prison was pure joy. One cannot fathom how cruel it is to be locked behind walls at a young age for years; to know it you need to experience it. The desire to be free increases geometrically proportional to time spent behind bars. It is like lifting a weight. The feeling of weight is not the same every moment. Twenty kilos, after the lapse of some time feels like two hundred kilos. Seing the horizon without been interrupted by high walls, walking on the street without handcuffs and guards sufficating you, eating food at a restaurant, taking a taxi, everything that I had taken for granted had become a priceless gift; each one of them.

I recognized my brother Müfid from about hundred meters among the crowd coming off the ship. He had a book in his hand. More than Müfit himself I was wondering about the title of the book he was holding. That book must be very special for him. It would give me valuable information about my brother's whereabouts within the three and half years. We had not sent each other a single letter during that period. Though he had visited me a few times while I was held at the ammunition storage or the basement in Istanbul, but we had only a few minutes to talk. Monitored by four soldiers. So, there was a big lapse of communication. Now, finally, I was going to learn about my brother by just reading the title of the book that he took with on this long trip.

I was dissappointed. The title of the book was "Babürname!" I had no clue about it. It sounded like a history book about a prominent guy named Babür. I had no idea who it was. Perhaps, I would not open the cover of that book, unless I was given it by prison administration as the only book in a solitary confinement. Perhaps, I would not open it in the first days. I would learn from Müfit that it was about Babur Shah, the Turkish king that conquered India. History was not my subject of interest and I could not have cared less about the Turkish sultans in India. I missed my family, my friends, my books; I missed the streets of Istanbul.

A2

The Gullible, the Blind, and Boxes of Diamonds and Glass

The following two articles were published in the end of "Running Like Zebras," my debate with a Sunni on the mathematical miracle of the Quran. Because of their import, I decided to publish them here separately.

In the first part of this article my audience is the gullible people who get easily excited by the news of mathematical miracle discoveries. Like some confuse astronomy with astrology, they confuse math with esoteric numerology. A few, whom I call the "numerologist prophets of doom," have also announced many specific dates for doom; such as, devastating meteors, earthquakes, wars, etc. These people end up finding many miracles about themselves or their cult leaders. The prophets of doom are diabolic and manipulative fame-seekers who mutated from gullible and sincere miracle-hunters. Soon after each of their doomsday prophecy fails to fulfill, they come up with a new prophecy. Though they lack critical thinking or common sense, they have plenty of silly rationalization, megalomania, and enough numbers to play with.

In the second part of this article, my audience is the dogmatic people who have developed a bigoted allergy against the mathematical miracle of the Quran. For various reasons, they have problem in objectively evaluating the facts, despite the overwhelming evidence and the unveiled divine prophecy in chapter 74. I had specifically exposed their bias or hypocrisy in article titled, "Which One Do You See: Hell or Miracle?" which is published at 19.org.

How can one Distinguish Diamonds from Pieces of Glass?

It needs a good mathematical intuition and experience in order to distinguish arbitrary and selective calculations from a systematic and objective calculation. Here, I would like to give you three methods of recognizing pieces of glasses from diamonds. I cannot provide examples since I have literally thousands of them, and choosing the typical ones requires a lot of time. Also, I don't have much space here.

1. Consider Laws of Probability: Fifty percent "tails" should not tickle you

When you are provided by a calculation labeled as "mathematical miracle" don't just accept the claim without investigation (17:36). Be extremely careful for the temptation to please the person who wants to give you a ride in his/her fantasy bandwagon. Especially, be more careful when the person is using God's name and praising him after his/her so-called discoveries. You may attribute the absurd and most stupid calculations and ideas to the Greatest Mathematician, the Most Wise. You should check whether the method of calculation is arbitrary, and the claimed relations are personal speculations.

Each differing method of calculation weakens the significance of calculations. Two methods of calculations increase the probability twice. Three methods of calculation increase thrice and four methods of calculations quadruple the probability. For instance, if you sometimes add a set of numbers and sometimes put them next to each other and get multiple of 19, you need twice as many examples than usual in order for your arithmetic to go beyond probability and be considered interesting, or extraordinary.

Arbitrarily processing a bunch of arbitrarily selected chapter and/or verse numbers by an arbitrary process of adding or concatenating or both adding and concatenating, and using an arbitrary number of items in this combination and finding a mathematical relation has little significance.

Finding a multiple of 19 by selecting a combination of two, or three, or four, or five, or more verses out of more than 6000 Quranic verses and passing them through numerous different calculations does not support the purported claims. Unfortunately, I have received many letters and bulletins filled with thousands of examples of deceptive calculations ending with "Praise be to God" or "Subhanallah."

The numbers of combinations (sets) that can be created out of more than six thousand elements exceed the biggest number known to our dictionaries, except googolplex, of course. According to the law of probability, there should be trillions of combinations that will form multiple of 19, since one out every 19 numbers will be multiple of 19. Some (thousands) of them, may show some semantic relation, especially, if the book contains repetitions and the discovery of relation and interpretation is left entirely to our wish!

2. Pay attention to the mathematical properties. Learn basic principles of math before "discovering" math patterns

Not only mathematical illiterates, but also a college-educated person can be deceived by mathematical properties. They can see them as part of the divine mathematical design. For example, the total of all chapter numbers being multiple of 19, that is, 6555 (19 x 345), is a mathematical property. If the number of items in an addition is multiple of N, then, the total of those elements will be multiple of N too. Another example: The total of Chapter numbers from 9 to 27 (9+10+11+......+27) is 342, and it must be multiple of 19, since exactly

389

19 consecutive numbers are added. Therefore, 342 being a multiple of 19 is a mathematical property in that context, since, the total of every consecutive N whole numbers is a multiple of N.

For those who are curious about special properties of numbers and recreational mathematics, besides Martin Gardner's books, I recommend *Mathematical Amuzements and Surprises* by Alfred S Posamentier and Ingmar Lehmann.

3. Claims should be "falsifiable." The number of letters in this article may equal to the number of angels or daemons in your head; but how can someone else know that?

We can find or attach meaning or reference for any number. You can arbitrarily select some chapter or verse numbers and arbitrarily put them together by adding, dividing, multiplying, subtracting or concatenating, or by another method of your choice, and when finally you arrive to a number which you can relate to some Quranic or to a *special* number, you may think that you have discovered a great mathematical miracle.

We should pay special attention to the criterion of *falsifiability*, since everyone, including university professors, can fall victim in confusing expert manipulations with mathematical calculations. We should question those who arrive at a certain number after using unlimited ways of calculations and different methods and then try to assign a meaning or a relation to that product. Here is the question:

Is it logically possible to *falsify* your calculations and results? In other words, would it be wrong or a non-miracle if your result were Y instead of X? Or, in that case, couldn't you just find a relation or a meaning for Y in the Quran, or in the universe of numbers? If you had difficulty in putting that number in a context, wouldn't you add several more calculations and come up with a number that you could attach a meaning to? It is a great responsibility to label your speculative and manipulative calculations as a *miracle* by claiming that God has calculated all the numbers.

It is therefore significant that the beginning verses of Chapter 74 warn us: "Do not be greedy!" (74:6).

How to Distinguish a Good Scientific Theory from a Bad One?

According to the majority of scientists, a good scientific theory should demonstrate three qualifications:

1. It should have an explanatory power. 2. It should be able to make accurate prediction. 3. It should provide economy in thought.

When scientists are going to choose among alternative theories they act according to these three criteria. The advance in science and technology is the result of using these criteria. For instance, before the Copernican model of solar system was proved, scientists preferred Copernicus' sun-centered model to Ptolemaic earth-centered model by using these intuitive and practical criteria. History of science is full of positive results of these criteria.

In order to help those who consider the mathematical structure of the Quran as a "theory," we will evaluate the mathematical system according to the first two criteria. You think on the third one!

1. Explanatory Power

- The challenge of the Quran regarding the impossibility of imitating the unique and superhuman nature of the Quran gains an objective (mathematical) criterion with the code 19. The Quranic challenge (2:23-24) is provided a meaningful and universal arena, instead of practically meaningless (or, subjective) and culturally limited "literary miracle."

- The evidence for a divine authorship being in a mathematical design in physical structure rather than being in eloquent use of Arabic is in harmony with the universal appeal and message of the Quran.

- Initial Letters (Huruf-u Muqattaa) that prefixes 29 chapters obtains a unique meaning and purpose. Numerous speculations made by interpretators for fourteen centuries ending up or starting with the confession of "we really do not know their meaning" finally are replaced with a clear message.

- The reason why the Quranic expression "These are the miracles (ayaat) of this book" follow the Initial Letters in all eight occurrences is understood.

- The discussion regarding different spellings gains a new dimension. For instance, why the first word of BismillahirRaĤMaNirrahim "Bsm" (in the name) is written without "A" (Alif) and why the "Bism" in the first verse of Chapter Alaq (Embryo) is written with an "A" (Alif)?

- The mathematical system puts an end to the chronic arguments among various sects whether Bismillah is the first verse of Chapter Al-Fatiha or not. Now, it is clear that the Bismillah in the beginning of Chapter Al-Fatiha (The Opener) is the first verse while other 112 Bismillahs crowning the other chapters are un-numbered verses.

- It is not a question anymore why the Chapter 9, *Baraah* (Ultimatum), does not start with Bismillah and why Chapter 27, Al-Naml (The Ant) contains an extra Bismillah in verse 30.

- The prophecy of Chapter 74, *Al-Mudathir* (The Hidden One), is unveiled and especially 74:31 is being fulfilled.

- We have learned another reason why some numbers are mentioned in an unusual way. For instance, the Quran gives Noah's age with a subtraction, 1000 - 50. The number of years which the young monotheists spent in a cave is expressed with an addition, 300 + 9. There is a clear relation between these interesting unusual expressions and the mathematical code.

- The question "Why the Quran consists of 114 chapters?" receives several meaningful answers.

- The divine guarantee regarding the preservation of the Quran is confirmed by the discovery of the code. Thus, a skeptical argument that casts doubt on authenticity of the verses, including the ones that guarantee preservation of the Quran is refuted.

- The historical speculations about what is *Ism-i Azam*, the Greatest Name of God, are ended.

- It becomes more evident that Prophet Muhammad was a literate *ummi* (gentile).

- The identity of the witness mentioned in verse 46:10 is unveiled as Judah ben Samuel of the eleventh century. The identity of the curious creature made of earthly material that was prophesied in verse 27:82 is unveiled as the "computer."

- The description of *Kitabun Marqum* (Numerically Coded Book) in verses 83:9 and 20 is clearly understood.

- The question "Why Jonah (Yunus) is referred as *Saĥibul Ĥut* (The friend of fish) in verse 68:48 and referred as 'Zannoon' (Possessor of Noon)?" receives a meaningful explanation.

- Quranic verses states that those who follow their parents and leaders blindly or those who rejects the truth with arrogance and ignorance are not able to see the clear miracles and signs. The mathematical miracle of the Quran proves to us this incredible fact.

2. The accuracy and predictive nature of the Code

Here I want to give two examples. First a spelling correction, second a prediction.

1. Correcting a scribal error

Three chapters of the Quran, chapter 7, 19 and 38 contains letter *Ŝaad* in their initial letter combination. Curiously, in verse 7:69 we see a word with a unique spelling: *BaŜŤatan*. Over the letter *Ŝaad* is written a small *Sin.* This word occurs in the Quran with two different spellings and it makes no difference to the

392

meaning. Just like the English words skeptic or skeptic. Commentaries of the Quran interpret it as an instruction on how to read the word. They claim that though it is written with *Ŝaad* it should be read as if it is *Sin.* They narrate three Hadiths (allegedly Muhammad's words) to support this interpretation.

The total number of *Ŝaad* with this word *BaŜŤatan* becomes 153, and it is not multiple of 19. Therefore, we concluded that the letter *Ŝaad* in the word *BaŜŤatan* is an orthographic error and should be corrected.

Indeed, when I checked one of the oldest manuscripts of the Quran, I found that our prediction was confirmed. Please see the document below:

2. Symmetry in the table of God's names

In my second letter I had attached a list of God's names with their numerical values and frequencies in the Quran, and the mathematical relation between these names and *Bismillah.*.

Dr. Cezar Edip Majul, in his book, *The Names of Allah in Relation To the Mathematical Structure of Quran* discovered the following two facts:

> 1. Only four names (adjectives) of God have Gematrical (numerical) values that are a multiple of 19.

> 2. The numerical values of these four names exactly correspond to the frequency of the four words of "Basmala," that is, 19, 2698, 57, and 114.

While I studied this table I noticed an asymmetry. On the right side of the table there are four names of God, but on the left side there are only three. Obviously, "Ism" (Name) was not a name of God. Therefore, I made two predictions. There must be one name of God that must have a frequency of 19, and only four names of God must have frequencies of multiple of 19. When I examined the frequency of all the names of God, I found that ONLY four of them are repeated in the Quran as multiple of 19. We already had discovered three of them: *ALLaH* (God), *RaĤMaN* (Gracious), and *RaĤyM* (Merciful). The fourth one was ŞaHYD (Witness). This name is mentioned in the Quran exactly 19 times and thus fills the empty space corresponding to the numerical value of *WAĤiD*(One) on the right side of the table.

A3
Diluting the Miracle

Inferring contradictory results from numerical associations, or claiming an arbitrary and utterly absurd/subjective numerical relationship to be an extraordinary sign or a miracle is a dangerous path.

There are some interesting findings in your calculations. However, I find your adding ALLAHU AKBAR after each of your calculation to be unnecessary. I have seen many ridiculous calculations, especially by the false prophets that started popping up after Rashad's departure. For instance, the "Doomsday Prophets", a gang of exceptionally sincere and yet equally credulous people led by Kay Emami, Behrouz Mofidi, Feroz Karmally, and Douglas Brown, ended their silly numerical manipulations regarding "May 19, 1990 Doomsday" exactly with the same exclamation. Many of the conjurers of arbitrary calculations and absurd speculations have done the same. This is my first suggestion.

Second, you are using a good program and you occasionally come up with interesting discoveries. That is beautiful. But, it seems that you are unaware that you are exceeding the limits and jumping from one relation to another one.

For instance, you check whether a number is divisible by 19 or not. If yes, you declare it to be a miracle. If not, you check with the gematrical value of a particular word. If that one fits, you declare it a hit. If not, you check it whether it matches a related number of a chapter. If it does, you claim another hit. If it doesn't, you add a verse number or numbers. If it fits, then you celebrate the discovery of another example of code 19. If it doesn't, you look for another, any relationship.

It seems, whichever number you land, you have a way to relate it to the number nineteen, to another number, another verse, another chapter, or to another gematrical value. You do not care, as it seems, about the consistency in the system, predictability, objectivity, or the laws of probability.

Just check your recent claim regarding the letter N. You claim that the verses starting and ending with letter N contain 50 Ns in them. It is not 133 or any other multiple of 19. But, you find a connection between 50 and the gematrical value of N. But, to reach this conclusion you need more than one example. You should check the verses that start and end with Qaf. If those verses too contain 100 Qafs, equaling to the gematrical value of letter Qaf, then you got a support.

You should check other initial letters. If none exhibit such a connection, you should consider it as mere chance, your own wishful association. You cannot dismiss other letters by saying N is the most important one, since you have no evidence for such a claim. Even if you had reasons for such a claim, still you needed more consistent examples to justify your inference.

Perhaps you might get angry with me, like many of those who have indulged in this number-hunting, who have confused the numerical system with arbitrary numerology.

But, I urge you to study the dozens of pages of calculations presented by Kay and other false prophets of doom, in the last few years, and learn a lesson. As long as you are not able to see the methodological and logical problems with their calculations, as long as you are not able to distinguish yours and theirs mathematically, then please stop your calculations and speculations on the subject and try to learn something from them.

In brief: you may continue observe relationship among numbers of the Quran, but do not haste to attribute them to God by calling it a miracle or implying it by capitalized ALLAHU AKBAR after eac, with exclamation marks.

****

Dear Brother,

I am involved in studying the numerical structure of the Quran since 1980, and I know that the biggest attack to this great miracle has come not from the ardent critics like Lomax or Ayman, but from overzealous and gullible "miracle hunters." Though, I do not want to discourage you in your search for more details of the numerical system, I want you not to be one of those who present a bunch of arbitrary calculations and personal speculations, akin to pieces of glasses, and then presenting those worthless pieces of glasses as diamonds.

When I see pieces of glass in your hand screaming *Allahu Akbar*, I am not offended by your praise of God. I am offended by your attributing your false perception to God. Do you understand what I mean?

Those who sent letters to the media and gave interviews to the local TV stations prophesizing that an asteroid would hit Saudi Arabia in May 19, 1990, were very angry with me when I opposed to their childish calculations. They considered me as a disbeliever. Ironically, they continued their personal hatred towards me when it became obvious that their calculations were the figment of their imagination.

Though you are not producing false prophecies, you are attributing to God some arbitrary and useless calculations, and you should be glad that I am reminding you that. I take my time and give you an example of manipulation or arbitrary calculation you are presenting here. Instead of giving up from them or defending them based on the patterns of the mathematical structure, you are showing emotional reaction. Don't be carried away by some friends who are cheering for whatever numerical "miracle" you are coming up with. They cannot lead you to the truth. Beware the cheers of the gullible. Peace.

The following article is a contribution of Karrar Abidi, a 17 student from UK

Below are three number patterns to do with the chapters, verses, words and letters of the Quran. All three facts involve using properties of the chapters, verses, words and letters of the Quran to produce a very long number.

NUMBER PATTERN 1

This number pattern uses these four variables in the following order to come up with a large figure:

1. Chapter number
2. Number of verses in that chapter
3. Verse number of a particular verse
4. Number of words in that verse

If this is done for every chapter in the Quran and the numbers are put next to each other then a 22,717 digit number is obtained:

1 7 1 4 2 4 3 2 4 3 5 4 6 3 7 9 2 **286** 0 4 1 1 2 7 ... **114** 6 0 4 1 4 2 2 3 2 4 4 5 5 6 3

This number is a multiple of 19.

NUMBER PATTERN 2

As well as using the four variables in number pattern 1, this pattern uses three more variables to produce an even larger figure:

1. Chapter number
2. Number of verses in that chapter
3. Verse number of a particular verse
4. Number of words in that verse
5. Number of letters in that verse
6. The word order of a particular word in that verse
7. The number of letters in that word

Again if this is done for every chapter in the Quran and the numbers are put next to each other then the following 223,300 digit number is produced:

1 7 1 4 19 1 3 2 4 3 6 4 6 2 4 17 1 5 2 3 3 2 4 7 ... **2 286** 0 4 19 1 3 2 4 3 6 4 6 1 1 3 1 3 2 7 26 1 3 2 5 3 2 4 3 5 3 6 3 7 7 ... **114** 6 0 4 19 1 3 2 4 3 6 4 6 1 4 14 1 2 2 4 3 3 4 5 2 2 8 1 3 2 5 3 2 8 1 3 2 5

This number is a multiple of 19.

396

NUMBER PATTERN 3

In addition to the seven variables used in number pattern 2 this number pattern uses two others in the following order:

1) Chapter number
2) Number of verses in that chapter
3) Verse number of a particular verse
4) Number of words in that verse
5) Number of letters in that verse
6) The word order of a particular word in that verse
7) The number of letters in that word
8) The gematrical value of the sentence of that word
9) The gematrical value of that word

Doing this for every chapter in the Quran will give a 1,005,248 digit number:

1 7 1 4 19 1 3 26040 102 2 4 130305 66 3 6 13020084050 329 4 6 13020081040 289 2 4 17 1 5 1308404 83 2 3 30305 65 3 2 2002 202 4 7 1307030401050 231 … **2 286** 0 4 19 1 3 26040 102 2 4 130305 66 3 6 13020084050 329 4 6 13020081040 289 1 1 3 1 3 13040 71 2 7 26 1 3 7003020 750 2 5 130204002 453 3 2 301 31 4 3 200102 212 5 3 80105 95 6 3 5410 19 7 7 3030404001001050 660 … **114 6** 0 4 19 1 3 26040 102 2 4 130305 66 3 6 13020084050 329 4 6 13020081040 289 1 4 14 1 2 10030 130 2 4 1706700 777 3 3 22002 204 4 5 13050160 142 2 2 8 1 3 403020 90 2 5 13050160 142 3 2 8 1 3 1305 36 2 5 13050160 142

This number is a multiple of 19.

Now at a first glance these three number patterns may seem impressive as the probability of finding three multiples of 19 in a book by chance must be 1/19 x 1/19 x 1/19 = 1/6859. However a closer analysis will show that by using this method to find number patterns in the Quran (or any other book) will almost certainly give one a multiple of 19.

Number pattern 1 is made up of four variables arranged in the order shown above. Arranging them in this order produces a number divisible by 19. However these four variables could have been arranged in 23 other ways (as 4! = 24) to produce 23 different large numbers. The fact that this arrangement out of the 23 others produced a multiple of 19 is insignificant as 1 in every 19 random set of numbers will be a multiple of nineteen.

The same analysis can be done with number pattern 2. The seven variables could have been arranged in 5,039 other ways (as 7! = 5,040). Number pattern 3 has 9 variables which could have been arranged in 362,880 other ways (as 9! = 36,880).

Now there is a flaw in analysing these number patterns in such a way; as some arrangements of the variables make more logical sense than others. For example it makes sense to put the chapter number at the beginning of the pattern. However the other fact that has been overlooked in this analysis is that these 9 variables are not the only variables that can be used to make up a number pattern. For example one could include the total number of words in the chapter as a variable for number pattern 1 OR the sum of verse numbers in that chapter OR the number of words in the each sentence OR gematrical value of that verse OR the gematrical value of the whole chapter OR the number of letters in the whole chapter. We could also take some variables from number pattern 3 such as number of letters in that verse and put it in number pattern 1 or 2.

The point is that there are many ways to juggle these variables and on average 18 out of every 19 arrangements will give a number not divisible by 19. This CAN be found in any book. The more failed trials one goes through for every successful trial (a number divisible by 19) the less significant the discovery is. Therefore it can be concluded that the simpler the mathematical phenomenon is the more statistically significant it is.

As said previously the fewer failed trials one goes through for every successful trial, the more statistically significant the discovery is. Or in other words, there is a lower probability that this phenomenon occurred by chance. The graph below shows the percentage probability (y-axis) of one finding a multiple of 19 by chance after "x" number of trials:

The probability will never be 100% as there is always a possibility of not getting a multiple of 19 after numerous trials. The graph shows that as the number of trials increases, the probability of finding a multiple of 19 increases.

However one might say that surely every multiple of 19 found in Quran will increase the impressiveness of its mathematical miracle. Below I will show how insignificant discoveries can dilute the more statistically significant ones and therefore make the Quran's mathematical miracle less obvious.

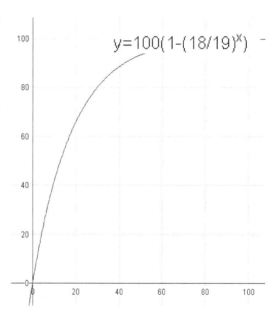

One way a sceptic may analyse the Quran's 19-based code is by using this formula:

If all successful trials/Total trials > 1/19 then code exists
If all successful trials/Total trials = 1/19 then code doesn't exist

This formula may seem fair. However it will show the sceptic that the code exists when only simple discoveries are presented (as they have fewer failed trials associated with them). Along with the simple discoveries if the less significant discoveries (with more failed trials associated with them) are presented then the formula will show the sceptic that the code doesn't exist. Here is a small sample of this diluting effect:

If the verse number of every verse in every chapter is written down next to one another after the sum of verses in that chapter the following number is produced:

7123456728612345678910111.............6123456

This number is made up of two variables:

1. The sum of verse numbers
2. Each individual verse number within the chapter

These two variables can be arranged in only 2 ways. Therefore one of the failed trials associated with this discovery is the one other way of arranging these two variables . One could perhaps also include the un-numbered verses and mark them with a 0. Or one could list the chapter number instead of the sum of verse numbers. The point is that because there are only two (very simple) variables, there is not a lot else the "discoverer" could have tried in order to produce a number divisible by 19. To put a figure on it lets say there are 5 failed trials associated with this 1 successful trial.

Now if the "discoverer", alongside the above discovery, presents number patterns similar to the ones in the earlier example then the ratio of successful trials to total trials will decrease. Lets say the "discoverer" presents another 20 number patterns producing multiples of 19 (similar to those shown in the example). If these 20 number patterns are arbitrary manipulations then they should have 360 ([19x20]—20) failed trials associated with them as 1 in every 19 random set of numbers will be a multiple of 19.

The sceptic's formula will first give him the fraction 1/6 when presented with only the simple discovery. However when the other 20 arbitrary manipulations are also presented the formula will give the fraction 21/386. The first fraction is larger than 1/19 therefore this discovery will contribute to convincing the sceptic that the code exists. The second fraction (resulting from including the 20 arbitrary manipulations) is only slightly larger than 1/19. As more arbitrary manipulations are presented, the closer the fraction will get to 1/19. And as a result the less convinced the sceptic will be that the code exists.

A4
"Binary Symmetric Book"?
9/13/2010

Dear Erdem,

I spent about two hours to study the observations and claims made in *Symmetric Book* by Halis Aydemir, the Turkish engineer. I tried my best to remain open-minded despite early signs of arbitrary calculations and innumeracy. I could not continue reading it after reaching page 202. As you will see in the attached document, I made the necessary corrections on the verse numbers of chapter 9 and the related calculations, which did not make much change.

We should first be mindful of the following statistical facts:

From 1 to 114, there are 30 prime numbers. In other words, in that zone, one out of every four numbers is a prime. Within the first thousand numbers, the ratio of primes to composites decreases to one in six. Since most of his calculations are done over small numbers, we can assume the probability of hitting a prime once every four numbers.

To find an either prime or composite number, excluding 0 and 1, is hundred percent. Interestingly, our author uses both of them!

Now, let's consider the following facts:

1. Some observations of Mr. Aydemir are too subjective or esoteric; they are specifically picked among dozens of similar calculations.

2. Some of them happen to be prime numbers and others composite, and yet the author pulls our attention to each. Fifty out of hundred similar calculations should produce the symmetry he is seeking. Occasionally, he encounters some numbers that do not fulfill his expectations and he finds them interesting too! When he compares two set of numbers he ignores the simple fact that there are no more than four permutations: P-C, P-P, C-P, C-C. All these four permutations transform into interesting and even beyond interesting in the eyes of the author.

3. I noticed only a few interesting observations. However, whoever works with many numbers in such a fashion for moths, perhaps years, should be able to find many more interesting coincidences.

4. Changing the number of verses in chapter 9 to 127 does not create a problem

with Mr. Aydemir's observations in most cases. Knowing that the author would not include the unwanted numbers, I can claim that the verse numbers of Chapter 9 being 127 would not change anything according to his loose rules.

I cannot speak for the rest of the book, but with the exception of the table dividing chapters according to their odd and even verse numbers, which was burrowed from another researcher, the first 200 pages have no mathematical value. You may find similar even more interesting, yet arbitrary numerical calculations in the Appendices section of Dr. Rashad Khalifa's translation of the Quran. You may even find more interesting ones in the calculations of copycat messengers proliferated after Rashad Khalifa. If you wish, I could check my computer and send you a sample from the interesting calculations of those who deluded themselves to be the messengers after Rashad Khalifa.

I find no merit in Mr. Aydemir's work. I hope that you will not waste your skills, energy and time on this. You should not contribute to a false claim that does nothing but distort the mathematical aspect of the Quran.

Selam,
Edip

With the proliferation of "miracle-hunters," more than a decade ago, I asked my colleague, Professor Richard Voss, to write an informative article so that people could distinguish the diamonds from pieces of glass, genuine numerical patterns from arbitrary numerical speculations. He wrote a delicious article. *Detecting Deceit in Numbers* is a series of five lessons should serve as a bridge towards better understanding of at least one aspect of the book of God: the miraculous numerical composition. Enjoy!

A5
Diamond vs. Glass
Prof Richard Voss aka Abu Jamil

November/December 1997

Detecting Deceit in Numbers

Salâmun 'alaykum!

Does the Qur'an have miraculous numerical properties? I certainly believe so. A reflection on 74:30-31 will begin to tell the story.

Over it are nineteen. And We have not made the wardens of the fire other than angels, and We have not made their number but as a trial for those who disbelieve, that those who have been given the book may be certain and those who believe may increase in faith, and those who have been given the book and the believers may not doubt, and that those in whose hearts is a disease and the unbelievers may say: What does Allah mean by this parable? Thus does Allah make err whom He pleases, and He guides whom He pleases, and none knows the hosts of your Lord but He Himself; and this is naught but a reminder to the mortals. Qur'an (74:30-31)

But what we are witnessing nowadays arc people who manipulate numbers and pass them to you as numerical "miracles" of the Qur'an, seeking to confuse those who believe in God and the Qur'anic miracle. It is time to learn t tell the difference between diamond and glass. With that in mind I present to you . . .

LESSON ONE:
Knowing What to Look for

The preeminence of multiples of 19 in the textual structure of the Qur'ân is now well-known around the world. We see the number given significance at 74:30, and we see the mysterious initials that introduce twenty-nine of the Qur'ân's one hundred fourteen sûrât apparently called "signs" at the start of eight of them (i.e., Surat 10, 12, 13, 15, 26, 27, 28, and 31). While some people who otherwise believe in the message of the Qur'ân are content to rationalize this feature of its structure away in their own minds rather than give it the serious attention demanded by the Qur'ân at 74:30, others take the other extreme and embrace every conceivable combination of numbers that happens to be divisible by 19 as "miraculous." Neither of these positions is tenable by verse 17:36, which tells us to use the minds God has given us to verify everything that comes before us in the guise of guidance. The straight path between these two extremes is certainly more difficult to follow than either alternative, but it is the only right way. Indeed, the words that introduce Surah 29 tell us that proclaiming belief is not enough, for we will be tested.

This series of five lessons is my humble effort to equip you with some of the tools and knowledge it takes to keep from falling away from the path of the sincere seeker after truth. You will not find any doctrine here. You will not have to trudge through the excruciating dogmatism that permeates most of the other literature that calls itself "Islamic." You will not find any references to dubious ahâdîth or the opinions of egocentric men with strange-sounding, orthographically volatile names and poor command of the English language. What I hope you will find is a somewhat entertaining, sometimes merciless, and in some ways just a little sneaky look at the reality of how numbers can be manipulated to dupe the unwary into believing virtually anything, and the remedy for this, viz., how they can be used by the wise to verify each and every ostensible "miracle" that happens by.

To kick off this series of lessons, I give you ... a "miracle."

ON SALE NOW! SEVEN NEW MIRACULOUS FINDINGS PROVING THERE ARE ONLY THREE DAILY PRAYERS, NOT FIVE! GET YOURS TODAY! CALL NOW AND GET THIS MIRACULOUS GINSU KNIFE AT NO EXTRA CHARGE! SLICE TOMATOES, CUT STEEL PIPES, AND DEFEND THE MIRACLE FROM ENEMIES! CALL NOW! OPERATORS ARE STANDING BY!

Instructions (a.k.a. How to Use Your Miracle). There are eight "prayer verses" (2:238, 4:103, 11:114, 17:78, 24:58, and 62:9-11). From these alone, we can infer the correct number of daily prayers. You need to know what "gematrical values" are. A gematrical value (GV) is the sum of the letter values in a word according to the pre-Islamic counting method (e.g., the word "Allâh" in Arabic is spelled alif [1], lâm [30], lâm [30], hâ' [5], so its GV is 66).

Miraculous Finding 1: The only prayers mentioned in the Qur'ân by name are salât al-fajr (GV 445), al-salât al-wustâ (GV 278), salât al-'ishâ' (GV 534), andsalât al-jumu'ah (GV 280). Add these to the sum of sûrah and verse numbers (741) and you get 2,278. Verse 22:78 reveals the origin of Islamic ritual.

Miraculous Finding 2: In all, there are 721 letters in the prayer verses. Add the GVs of the prayer words fajr (283), wustâ (85), 'ishâ' (372), jumu'ah (118), and salât (131), and you get 1,710 (= 19 x 90).

Miraculous Finding 3: Verse 4:103 is the only prayer verse that doesn't help identify prayer times (it just says there are "specific times"). Excluding this one then, add up the sûrah numbers of all remaining prayer verses (116), plus the GVs of the Qur'ânic names of the prayers (1,537) and you get 1,653 (= 19 x 87).

Miraculous Finding 4: Excluding 4:103, the total GV for all remaining prayer verses is 54,377. Add the total GV for the prayer words (989, from finding 2 above) and you get 55,366 (= 19 x 2914).

Miraculous Finding 5: Verse 62:11 merely clarifies what's already said in 62:9-10, so we should still have enough prayer information without it. Add up the verse numbers of all verses except 62:11, plus the GVs of the Qur'ânic names of the prayers (1,537) and you get 2,147 (= 19 x 113).

Miraculous Finding 6: Add up the letters in all prayers verses but leave out both 4:103 and 62:11 and you get 532 (= 19 x 28).

Miraculous Finding 7: The "bare bones" prayer verses are 2:238, 11:114, 17:78, and 24:58. These contain the necessary guidance for timing the three prayers, not including the weekly jumu'ah prayer. Add up the sûrah numbers plus the GVs of the Qur'ânic names of all prayers except jumu'ah and you get 1,311 (= 19 x 69).

ON SALE NOW! JUST $19.95 (= 19 x $1.05)
GET YOUR MIRACLE TODAY WHILE SUPPLIES LAST!

So, what about my "miraculous findings"? They certainly are impressive, aren't they? Well, let me be frank. Yes, I did find these in the Qur'ân. They're really there, and you can confirm them for yourself if you have the patience. But are they really all that "miraculous"? Can they really be used to justify praying three times a day instead of five? Can we really base our understanding of the required daily ritual on these numbers instead of studying the Qur'ân for what it says about the matter?

The answer is: NO. The reason? I LOOKED FOR THEM.

Yes, friends, I looked for these, just as so many poor, wayward souls have dug up truckloads of numerical "miracles" and dumped them on us in an attempt to "prove" their otherwise frail opinions about why we should do what they want us to do in our worship. But don't be fooled by the fact that you're being fooled!

Those fools who cook up these numbers are really serious! I guarantee you'll be called an idolater and be accused of trying to subvert The Miracle if you oppose them! My advice? Just keep that Ginsu handy...

The "miracles" you've just seen posted here are nothing like the Qur'ânic initials, the Bismillah, or the basic structural properties of the Qur'ân. In spite of how impressive they might appear to you, there is something missing from them that is not missing from these other features of the Qur'ânic text:

Consistency

And what is consistency? It means that you still get too many positive findings when you ...

Use Only One Rule!

I know what you're thinking. You're thinking, "But we do use only one rule! We say it must be a multiple of 19!"

- What? Say that again?
- "It must be ..."
- Hold it!
- "A multiple?"
- No! Back up.
- "Be?"
- No, a little more.
- "Must?"
- Nope, just a tad more.
- "Er ... um ... you mean ... 'it'?"
- Yes! Yes! "It"! Now, tell me. What is "it"?
- "Er ... um ... the thing you're looking at ..."
- No, no, stop. Now, what is "thing"?
- "The ... um ... the numbers?"
- What numbers?
- "The numbers ... in the Qur'ân?"
- WHAT numbers in the Qur'ân?
- "Um ... the numbers you're looking at? Oh, I don't know ... I give up."

Give up? Okay, here's what I mean. The rule is not "it must be a multiple of 19." That's the criterion. That's how you test the numbers you discover. By contrast, it is in generating your data set that you apply the rule whose validity you want to test. So how do you generate data?

First, you have to define it. How do you define what numbers to look at? After all, you can't just look at everything and expect to get valid results. Inevitably, you'll just wind up focusing on every accidental instance of multiples of 19 because you're ...

Looking for it

... and you'll notice every little, insignificant anomaly and think it means something. If you're a conniving fraud, you'll add up things and mix and match various numbers until you accidentally find something that "works," and then you'll turn around and tout it as a "miracle." But in reality your "findings" will crumble as soon as they're scrutinized by anyone who knows anything at all about numbers.

Yes, my friends, that means you need to be wary of how numbers can be used to deceive you, and you need to be able to tell when a "miracle" is really just a deceptive fabrication designed to dupe you and make a mockery of your faith in God! So how do you detect deception? Here's the key:

WHEN YOU SEE A "MIRACLE"
FIGURE OUT THE RULE AND APPLY IT TO ALL THE DATA

For example, a stranger walks up to you and says, "Hey, the Qur'ânic initials are a miracle." You respond, "What? Really? What do you mean?" The stranger replies, "Count up how many qâfs there are in Sûrah 50. It's a multiple of 19." So you do, and lo and behold the stranger is right. But is it a miracle? The truth is, you won't know until you do what it says above. "Figure out the rule." What's the rule here? Quite simply, it's this: When a sûrah begins with initials, those initials will occur in a multiple of 19 in the sûrah. (Actually, they're arranged in series, but more on this later.) Simple enough? Okay, try the next step. Predict: "Every initialed sûrah will contain a multiple of 19 of those initials." Of course, you still won't know if it's a "miracle" until you actually take the trouble to count the initials. Would you like to see a real miracle? God willing, I'll show you one, forthcoming...

Lastly, the rule must be simple. The more complicated and convoluted it is, the less it explains and the more you have to justify why you made it so exclusive. For example, you would not say "every qâf-initialed sûrah will have a multiple of 19 qâfs in it." Why not? Because there are only two qâf-initialed sûrât, and you have no logical basis upon which to exclude the rest of the initialed sûrât. They are, after all, similar to the qâf-initialed sûrât in a very striking, easily understood way. Moreover, it would not be a big violation of statistical probability if both qâf-initialed sûrât happened to have a multiple of 19 qâfs in them. Would you be willing to test the same sûrât for the number 3? They do both show a multiple of 3 qâfs, after all. To clarify, it has to make sense to exclude certain numbers from consideration if that's what you want to do. In this case, it would not make sense to exclude the rest of the initialed sûrât from consideration, because they're in ...

The Same Category of Data

Let me say that again: The Same Category of Data. The only way you can check to see if an anomaly is really a violation of statistical probability is to get as many examples of The Same Category of Data as you can, and then apply the same rule to all of those numbers. For the initialed sûrât, if you make a claim that there is some connection between the initials and the number 19, then you have included all initialed sûrât in your data category, by definition. Each time you exclude something from that category, you have to show that it makes sense to do it. For instance, why do we look at multiples of 19 but not multiples of 17? Because the Qur'ân says "above it, nineteen" at 74:30, not "above it, seventeen." The Qur'an specifically tells us that 19 is meaningful by calling it "one of the greatest" miracles (74:35). So again, we didn't just find the number 19 mentioned off-hand somewhere in the Qur'ân and start playing with it. By contrast, the Qur'ân does not say anything about 17. (I mean this literally—the number 17 does not even appear in the Qur'ân at all!) If you want to say that "17" should also be part of The Miracle (and yes, you will see an actual example of a supposed "miracle" posted on the internet by some nitwits that used the number 17 to "prove" itself), then you first have to show, beyond a reasonable doubt, that the Qur'ân Itself means to include it!

PS: Well, folks, this was just Lesson 1. God willing in the next lesson, I'll show you what a real statistical test looks like. Have you ever been curious about the Qur'ânic initials? Have you ever wondered why they don't all come out as multiples of 19? Have you ever wanted to know how to verify their miraculous nature? Well, the time has come.

LESSON TWO:
Example of a Miracle, Part I
Generating the Data Set

Salâmun 'alaykum!

So, you want to see the proof of a real miracle, eh? But how could you tell if it is valid or not? How could you say with confidence that you're not being duped? The answer begins with how the data set itself was generated. Is it just a list of numbers that "happened" to come out as multiples of 19? Is the person who is claiming "miracle" only showing you the "significant" numbers? Could this person actually be hiding the "nonsignificant" numbers?

What Are You Hiding?

And lastly, what if you could see all his numbers, good as well as bad, at the same time? Would you still be convinced? Well, today, God willing, you will see how it's done. And if you pay attention, chances are you'll never be duped again. Interested? I thought you would be.

In order to test any claim of "miracle," you have to define your data set by determining what rule applies to it. When someone shows you a "miracle," look at exactly what has been done with the numbers and turn what you see into a rule that you could conceivably apply to any numbers that are in the same descriptive category as the ones you're looking at.

What Rule Is It?

Beware! The "miracle" you're shown may look impressive, but what if the crook who cooked it up used a different rule for each "miraculous" finding? Couldn't you manufacture a "miracle" that is just as good? Couldn't you just add, subtract, multiply, and fish around for more and more numbers to crunch until you got a dozen or so "miraculous" findings all apparently showing the same mathematical property? Of course you could. But if you're not sure, just wait for Lesson 4!

Today, we're actually going to generate a data set from the Qur'ânic initials. To do this, we have to be very careful and precise about everything. The big, overriding consideration in everything you do is this: Would a skeptic agree with your method? Always weigh every decision you make against this, and resort to good, logical reasoning throughout your analysis. Ready? Let's begin.

Qur'ânic Initials (Muqatta'ât)
Generating The Data Set

The Qur'ânic initials function according to this simple rule:

In every uninterrupted sequence of sûrât with the same initials, the total number of those initials in that series of sûrât has been controlled by the Author of the Qur'ân. Far more often than random chance could explain, that total is a multiple of 19.

The role of the number 19 in the Qur'ân was discovered in modern history by Rashad Khalifa, who was the imâm of Masjid Tucson, in Arizona, until his assassination in 1990. While the identity of the discoverer of this feature of the Qur'ânic structure is not as important as that feature itself, Rashad is indeed important to our analysis for at least one reason: He published his counts of the Qur'ânic initials. You can find them in the back of his translation of the Qur'ân. We can use his counts, within limits, for our analysis. Generally speaking, his counts are valid insofar as we can pick up one of the more commonly disseminated Arabic texts and verify them. Specific problems with his counts, which we must take into consideration if we wish to analyze the Qur'ânic text properly, are detailed below.

408

1. Alif sûrât. There is widespread disagreement over how many alifs there are in those sûrât that have alif as one of their initials. If you look at two different Arabic texts, you'll find that some alifs that appear in one don't appear in the other. This means that we cannot say precisely how many alifs there are supposed to be in these sûrât without being able to prove that the particular Arabic Qur'ân we have in our hands is the real Qur'ân as originally revealed. Consequently, we can't consider those sûrât in our test. Given that Rashad has reported a multiple of 19 for every such sûrah, it would obviously help our case immensely to include them. But we don't have any way to justify including them because the skeptic would just pick up a different Arabic text and say, "How do you know this isn't the real text?" (He would be justified in doing this as long as he chose a text that is actually published and didn't just invent a new one to give us a hard time.) Consequently, we must instead leave those sûrât out of our analysis, even if it means that our results will suffer! (Only the brave dare proceed hence!)

2. Hâ-mîm sûrât. There are seven sûrât in a row with the initials hâ-mîm, but in the third one (Sûrah 42) there is another set of initials in verse two, right after the first set. According to our definition above, we must acknowledge that this series of sûrât is interrupted by the introduction of that second set of initials. But because that second set of initials is in verse two, this interruption doesn't take place until after Sûrah 42 has already been included with Sûrât 40 and 41 to constitute one "series." Meanwhile, Sûrah 42 is simultaneously its own series by virtue of the second set of initials. You could say it's "pulling double-duty." Needless to say, the remaining hâ-mîm sûrât (43-46) constitute the next series.

3. Confounds. A "confound" is anything that influences our data set that is also at least partially the product of the phenomenon we're investigating. In our case, we have two confounds, detailed below. These consist of corrections that Rashad has made to the Qur'ânic text. Although Rashad offers compelling evidence to support his corrections, at least part of his reasoning is based on 19-divisibility. That is, he has reasoned that if there is any dispute over the spelling of a word that includes one of the initials, then the option that gives you a multiple of 19 resolves the dispute. Thus, 19-divisibility is his criterion. But wait. Isn't 19-divisibility precisely what we're investigating? How can we justify using 19-divisibility to make changes to the very data we're testing? We can't. The fact is, regardless of how much other evidence there is to support those changes we can't consider them in our data. The skeptic would simply say, "Hey, you can't use a special Qur'ân to test the miracle; you have to use a regular one!" And the skeptic would be right.

    a. The "sâd" confound. No, there is nothing particularly sad about this confound. It refers, rather, to the eighteenth letter of the Arabic alphabet (old-style, or the 14th letter new-style). Verse 7:69 in most Qur'âns shows the word <bastatan>, which is correctly spelled [bâ sîn tâ tâmarbûtah], misspelled with "sâd" instead of "sîn." The correct spelling does, however, appear in the ancient Tashkent Qur'ân, a part of which still exists. Of course, dictionaries also list the correct spelling. However, because most Qur'âns nowadays use the misspelled version of this word, using Rashad's count in our analysis would arguably give us an unfair advantage. (You will note, as you read through the data, that we can't count Sûrah 7 anyway because of the alifs, but the possibility of other types of statistical tests means the "sâd" confound can't be overlooked.)

b. The "nûn" confound. Verse 68:1 in most Qur'âns shows the word <nûn> ("inkstand"), spelled [nûn wâw nûn], abbreviated as the letter "nûn" by itself. You'll note that in the context of that verse "inkstand" makes perfectly good sense. Given that the scribes were already familiar with the fact that several sûrât in the Qur'ân start with initials, it is easy to see why they would have thought that this word, which evidently pulls double-duty as both a meaningful word and a Qur'ânic initial, should not be spelled out fully. However, although Rashad has corrected this, we cannot use his corrected count in our analysis because most Qur'âns show the abbreviated version of this word. Using Rashad's count would arguably give us an unfair advantage.

4. Reviewing our definition. On the upside, the validity of our definition of "series" is reinforced by the fact that there are no gaps at all in any series so defined. That is, for example, there could have been an alif-lâm-mîm series composed of Sûrât 2, 3, 4, and then maybe a jump to Sûrah 7. But this doesn't happen at all. In every case of a series with more than one sûrah in it, the sûrât are successive and contiguous. In addition, exactly half of the eighteen series are composed of multiple sûrât, while the other half are composed of single sûrât. In defining data sets, it's important to note such features that demonstrate coherence in your definition. In view of everything, our definition makes very good sense.

And now, on with generating the data set. A few notes: Any counts I put in brackets are those of Rashad's counts that could be disputed simply by referring to a different Arabic text of the Qur'ân that is also published today. I've included them for the sake of completeness. Counts with asterisks are multiples of 19. Observe how careful I am in generating the data set. I leave nothing for the reader to "guess at." This is very important.

    Series 1 (Sûrât 2-3), alif-lâm-mîm. Total = [15561*]
        2 - alif [4502] lâm 3202 mîm 2195 = [9899*]
        3 - alif [2521] lâm 1892 mîm 1249 = [5662*]
    Series 2 (Sûrah 7), alif-lâm-mîm-sâd. Total = [5320*]
        7 - alif [2529] lâm 1530 mîm 1164 sâd 96 [+1] = 5319 [5320*]
    Series 3 (Sûrât 10-12), alif-lâm-râ. Total = [7353*]

10 - alif [1319] lâm 913 râ 257 = [2489*]
11 - alif [1370] lâm 794 râ 325 = [2489*]
12 - alif [1306] lâm 812 râ 257 = [2375*]

Series 4 (Sûrah 13) alif-lâm-mîm-râ. Total = [1482*]
13 - alif [605] lâm 480 mîm 260 râ 137 = [1482*]

Series 5 (Sûrât 14-15) alif-lâm-râ. Total = [2109*]
14 - alif [585] lâm 452 râ 160 = [1197*]
15 - alif [493] lâm 323* râ 96 = [912*]

Series 6 (Sûrah 19) kâf-hâ-yâ-'ayn-sâd. Total = 798*
19 - kâf 137 hâ 175 yâ 343 'ayn 117 sâd 26 = 798*

Series 7 (Sûrah 20) tâ-hâ. Total = 279
20 - tâ 28 hâ 251 = 279

Series 8 (Sûrah 26) tâ-sîn-mîm. Total = 611
26 - tâ 33 sîn 94 mîm 484 = 611

Series 9 (Sûrah 27) tâ-sîn. Total = 121
27 - tâ 27 sîn 94 = 121

Series 10 (Sûrah 28) tâ-sîn-mîm. Total = 581
28 - tâ 19* sîn 102 mîm 460 = 581

Series 11 (Sûrât 29-32) alif-lâm-mîm. Total = [4313*]
29 - alif [774] lâm 554 mîm 344 = [1672*]
30 - alif [544] lâm 393 mîm 317 = [1254*]
31 - alif [347] lâm 297 mîm 173 = [817*]
32 - alif [257] lâm 155 mîm 158 = [570*]

Series 12 (Sûrah 36) yâ-sîn. Total = 285*
36 - yâ 237 sîn 48 = 285*

Series 13 (Sûrah 38) sâd. Total = 29
38 - sâd 29 = 29

Series 14 (Sûrât 40-42) hâ-mîm. Total = 1121*
40 - hâ 64 mîm 380* = 444
41 - hâ 48 mîm 276 = 324
42 - hâ 53 mîm 300 = 353

Series 15 (Sûrah 42) 'ayn-sîn-qâf. Total = 209*
42 - 'ayn 98 sîn 54 qâf 57* = 209*

Series 16 (Sûrât 43-46) hâ-mîm. Total = 1026*
43 - hâ 44 mîm 324 = 368
44 - hâ 16 mîm 150 = 166
45 - hâ 31 mîm 200 = 231
46 - hâ 36 mîm 225 = 261

Series 17 (Sûrah 50) qâf. Total = 57*
50 - qâf 57*

Series 18 (Sûrah 68) nûn. Total = 132 [133*]
68 - nûn 132 [+1] = 132 [133*]

From this, we simply list all numbers that qualify to be tested. Our definition of series restricts us to counting only the totals in each series. In addition, we can't include bracketed totals because they're subject to disagreement, as explained above. Consequently, our list of testable occurrences includes only the following twelve "data points":

798* 279 611 121 581 285* 29 1121* 209* 1026* 57* 132

Is this enough to analyze? Yes, it is. Our definition has been applied rigidly, and we have made sure to exclude all possible confounds. Nothing in our method gives us an unfair advantage. In fact, this data set is the least advantageous set we could possibly generate in order to test the theory of 19-divisibility as applied to the eighteen series of initialed sûrât.

Let me rephrase that for clarity:

If these data reflect anything of the mathematical structure of the Qur'ân, it is as rough and distorted as it can possibly get under our definition.

Not only have we avoided letting confounds enter our data, but by restricting ourselves to a single rule, we have also avoided even allowing ourselves to notice any other rules that might operate in the Qur'ân. This is the kind of approach we need to take in order to test the mathematical structure of the Qur'ân objectively and—quite frankly—pessimistically. We simply can't allow ourselves to "push" the data in a direction that exaggerates the effect we're trying to investigate. One way or another, we'll end up with some inaccuracies in our data. The only safe way to go is to lean in the direction of too much, rather than too little, restraint in our methods.

Now, the question is, although some of these numbers are, in fact, multiples of 19, could this be the result of random chance? Is there any way to tell? Yes! God willing, the answer is coming up in the next exciting issue of Detecting Deceit in Numbers!

LESSON THREE:
Example of a Miracle, Part II
Analyzing The Data Set

Salâmun 'alaykum!

Would you recognize a real miracle if you saw one? Well today, GW, you'll see first-hand just what proof looks like. No one can refute genuine proof of a miracle, but it is easy to refute deceit in numbers, as we shall see in the next lessons of this series. Faced with a real miracle with solid proof, those who refuse to believe what they see merely turn their backs, mumbling things about monkeys with typewriters. (Yes ... they really do.)

But what is a "Miracle"?

It is easy to deny seeing a miracle when you're faced with one. Just change your criteria for recognizing it, right there on the spot. For example, if Jesus raises the dead right before your eyes, just say, "I'm sure there's a scientific explanation for that." And voilà! You're off the hook! You're free to disbelieve in what your own eyes witness! In fact, it has actually been suggested that Jesus simply took advantage of an extremely rare illness that resembles death and gambled that he could make the patient "snap out of it" if he got lucky. What a gamble! But it worked! Right? (Do you really believe that?) But how much of a gamble did Jesus take if it really happened that way? What were the odds? Here's what the skeptics might say happened:

A man came down with a rare illness that resembled death. Jesus told the man to get up. By sheer coincidence, the man suddenly became well again right at that instant. This accidentally happened more than once.

Thus, there might have been one chance in several thousand that Jesus lucked out and made everyone think he had raised the dead. Now consider this: The skeptic's "explanation" is as outlandish as the odds against it. It's just like "monkeys with typewriters." Eventually, we are told, monkeys will type Shakespeare. But will they?

The bottom line is that the ostensibly miraculous nature of anything is visible in the odds against its occurrence. But since virtually anything can be explained as "extremely rare" while nevertheless a "coincidence," even if the odds against it are several thousand to one, it is always possible to choose to remain blind to miracles. You just "up the ante," as it were, and demand more.

"But aren't we still missing something? Are you calling anything highly unlikely a 'miracle'?"

No, of course not. There is one thing that a miracle has that an unlikely coincidence lacks. We call it "intent." Did Jesus intend to raise people from the dead, or did dead people just start sitting up and smiling when Jesus was around? Did Jesus just happen to notice them around him and quickly take all the credit for it? Maybe it went like this: "Hey! Look at all these dead people getting up! Cool! Er ... I mean ... look what I did! I meant to do that!" Intent—that's the key.

Now, mind you, I've just defined "miracle" for you. You certainly have the right to decide for yourself what a "miracle" really is, and you may wish to call what you see here something else. Alternatively, perhaps it is simply evidence of a higher purpose at work. After all, isn't this what the miracles of Jesus really were? That would suit me fine. Meanwhile, I'll just continue calling it a "miracle," if you don't mind. With that said, on with our test.

Qur'ânic Initials (Muqatta'ât)
The Test

You will recall that we generated the following data set in Lesson 2:

798* 279 611 121 581 285* 29 1121* 209* 1026* 57* 132

As simple as this data set looks, it was, as you will recall, the result of painstaking attention to detail and careful methodology. It is also, as you will recall, the least favorable data set we could generate while following this defining rule:

In every uninterrupted sequence of sûrât with the same initials, the total number of those initials in that series of sûrât has been controlled by the Author of the Qur'ân. Far more often than random chance could explain, that total is a multiple of 19.

In order to evaluate whether 19-divisibility is really a special property of these numbers, we have to figure out what the odds are against this occurrence. What were the odds that Jesus "lucked out" and made it all just look like a miracle? Well, a similar question applies here. What are the odds that this many multiples of 19 are actually normal for a sample of this size? To answer this, we have to compute the statistical probabilities associated with this many positive outcomes.

"What? 'Statistical probabilities,' you say? Gee, aren't you asking just a little too much of the casual reader? How can you expect the average Joe to understand something so complicated?"

> "(O man), follow not that whereof thou hast no knowledge. Lo! The hearing and the sight and the heart—of each of these it will be asked."
> (Qur'ân 17:36, Pickthall's translation)

By instructing us to ascertain truth before embracing it, the Qur'ân is telling us that the tools we need for doing so are within our reach. We are indeed capable of learning whatever it takes. The "average Joe" is no exception. If I may be so bold as to quote John Lennon, "We're all geniuses." The only impediment to understanding what I intend to present here is a lack of faith in your own capacities. Just give it a shot. You'll see. It just takes some getting used to.

To understand the statistics of what we're doing, first understand this: Sometimes you will get 19-divisibility simply by accident. But the more positive outcomes you get, the more you "violate" the laws of random chance. How many is too many? Statistics gives you the answer. What if I picked a random number and it turned out to be a multiple of 19? The odds are one in 19, i.e., about 5.26% (which we can express as p = .0526). How about two? One in 19 x

414

19 (p = .00277). How about three? One in 19 x 19 x 19 (p = .000146). Get the picture? Just multiply the fraction (1/19) by itself as many times as the number of tries.

But look at this. Getting only one multiple of 19 in three tries is less "interesting" (p = .157). So is getting two multiples, although that might get some attention (p = .00787). It is this kind of scenario that applies to what we're looking at here, where we have "six out of twelve" positive outcomes. It's harder to compute this kind of probability. Nevertheless, here's the formula:

P(y) = { n! / [y! (n - y)!] } p^y (1 - p)^(n - y) where . . .
P(y) = the probability of observing 'y' successes
y =   number of successes in 'n' trials
n =   number of observations
p =   probability of success on a single observation

It isn't as hard as it looks, but if you don't want to try this yourself, just find some high school math wiz to "crunch the numbers" for you or to program them into a computer spreadsheet.

Okay, so we know about probabilities, and we even know the formula. Now what? Well, let's do the test! You'll recall that there were (only?) six multiples of 19 in our data set of 12 numbers. Let's compute the probability of this many multiples. Ready? Okay, here goes (look closely at each step if you're not familiar with this kind of math—you'll see it's easier than it looks):

Step 1. Fill in the formula ("6" out of "12" hits):
    P(6) = { 12! / [6! (12 - 6)!] } p^6 (1 - p)^(12 - 6)

Step 2. Replace "p" with 1/19 (i.e., .0526):
    P(6) = { 12! / [6! (12 - 6)!] } .0526^6 (1 - .0526)^(12 - 6)

Step 3. Do the subtraction:
    P(6) = { 12! / [6! (6)!] } .0526^6 (.947)^(6)

Step 4. Do the factorials (e.g., 6! = 6 x 5 x 4 x 3 x 2 x 1):
    P(6) = { 479001600 / [720 (720)] } .0526^6 (.947)^(6)

Step 5. Do the exponents ("^6" means "to the sixth power"):
    P(6) = { 479001600 / [720 (720)] } .0000000212 (.721)

Step 6. Do the multiplication ("720 (720)" means "720 x 720"):
    P(6) = { 479001600 / [518400] } .0000000153

415

Step 7. Do the division (the slash [/] means "divided by"):
P(6) = { 924 } .0000000153

Step 8. Multiply what's left:
P(6) = .0000141

More precisely, this should be p = .0000142, but because we used some rounded-off numbers (e.g., .0526 instead of .052631579), the final result was off a tiny bit.

Okay, I know what you're thinking. Is this really "significant"? How can we tell? For all we know, this kind of deviation from random chance may be pretty common out there in the real world. Is it? Should we care? (Hint: Qur'ân 17:35—weigh everything to "ascertain truth.") The solution is to compare our finding with other numbers.

The following is a list of the probabilities for all prime numbers up to 100. (Remember, 19 is a prime number too.) Column A shows the straightforward results for our data. Column B shows the results if we correct the spelling of <nûn> at verse 68:1, just for the record. The number in brackets is the number of positive outcomes we would get for each prime number from these data. Take a good look. Does the number 19 stand out at all? Decide for yourself.

A	B
2	[3 out of 12]: p = .0537 [2 out of 12]: p = .0161
3	[6 out of 12]: p = .1113 [5 out of 12]: p = .1908
5	[1 out of 12]: p = .2062 [1 out of 12]: p = .2062
7	[2 out of 12]: p = .2883 [3 out of 12]: p = .1602
11	[3 out of 12]: p = .0701 [2 out of 12]: p = .2103
13	[1 out of 12]: p = .3827 [1 out of 12]: p = .3827
17	[0 out of 12]: p = .4831 [0 out of 12]: p = .4831
19	[6 out of 12]: p = .0000* [7 out of 12]: p = .0000**
23	[0 out of 12]: p = .5866 [0 out of 12]: p = .5866
29	[1 out of 12]: p = .2813 [1 out of 12]: p = .2813
31	[1 out of 12]: p = .2699 [1 out of 12]: p = .2699
37	[0 out of 12]: p = .7198 [0 out of 12]: p = .7198
41	[0 out of 12]: p = .7436 [0 out of 12]: p = .7436
43	[0 out of 12]: p = .7540 [0 out of 12]: p = .7540
47	[1 out of 12]: p = .2015 [1 out of 12]: p = .2015
53	[0 out of 12]: p = .7957 [0 out of 12]: p = .7957
59	[1 out of 12]: p = .1685 [1 out of 12]: p = .1685
61	[0 out of 12]: p = .8201 [0 out of 12]: p = .8201
67	[0 out of 12]: p = .8349 [0 out of 12]: p = .8349
71	[0 out of 12]: p = .8435 [0 out of 12]: p = .8435
73	[0 out of 12]: p = .8475 [0 out of 12]: p = .8475
79	[0 out of 12]: p = .8582 [0 out of 12]: p = .8582

83	[1 out of 12]: p = .1265 [1 out of 12]: p = .1265
89	[0 out of 12]: p = .8732 [0 out of 12]: p = .8732
97	[0 out of 12]: p = .8831 [0 out of 12]: p = .8831

*p = .0000142
**p = .000000676

These findings show a real link between the physical structure of the Qur'ân and the number 19, not an "accidental" one. The odds of getting these results by accident are about one in 70,423. With the correction of the <nûn> count in Sûrah 68, the odds drop to about one chance in one and a half million. The "runner-up" in terms of significance is the number 2 (about one chance in 62 in Column B), and that's because there are too few of them, not too many. It's not even close.

On their own merits, these data are pretty impressive. But remember: We did everything possible to thwart our own efforts (recall what we did about the confounds and alif counts). Even with such a conservative test, the number 19 stands out clearly above all other numbers.

"But aren't you forgetting something? What about 'intent'? Does the Qur'ân intend to use the number 19 as evidence of a miracle, or did you just discover this anomaly by accident and declare the number 19 miraculous *after the fact?*"

The answer is found in the Qur'ân, at 74:30-31:

"Over it are nineteen. And We have not made the wardens of the fire other than angels, and We have not made their number but as a trial for those who disbelieve, that those who have been given the book may be certain and those who believe may increase in faith, and those who have been given the book and the believers may not doubt, and that those in whose hearts is a disease and the unbelievers may say: What does Allah mean by this parable? Thus does Allah make err whom He pleases, and He guides whom He pleases, and none knows the hosts of your Lord but He Himself; and this is naught but a reminder to the mortals. "

"What? You mean the number **19** is a 'trial' for the disbelievers, while it increases the faith of the believers? How can this be? How can a mere number do all this?"

You've just seen how. God knew about statistics long before we did? Who do you think **created** the laws of random chance, anyway? (Or maybe you simply hadn't thought of them as "laws" until now.) Who created all of the laws of the universe?

But what about the exceptions? Why did half of those numbers come out

417

nonsignificant? I'll tell you. I don't know. I didn't have anything to do with the writing of the Qur'ân. It was all God's handiwork, and only God knows the purpose behind each thing He reveals. What I do know is that God has clearly made the number 19 stand out in the structure of His Book, while allowing all other numbers to fade into the background by comparison. In fact, this effect in the Qur'ân was not even noticed until the present generation. Look at the footnotes to 2:1 and 74:30 in the various translations of the Qur'ân. No one was aware of this. Yet there it is, clear enough to be noticed by anyone who can understand statistics. What I **also** know is that what we have seen is enough to demonstrate a higher purpose in the structure of the Qur'ân that clearly transcends the mere utterances of a man named Muhammad who lived two centuries before Charlemagne and knew nothing of statistics. This should be enough to warrant a closer look at the Qur'ân.

I hope you enjoyed this presentation. Next time ... Exposing the Deception. Yes, friends, we will at last expose an actual attempt at passing off falsified "miracles" as divine **proof** of someone's personal opinion of Islamic ritual.

LESSON FOUR:
Exposing Deceit, Part I
Reconstructing the Deceptive Data Set

Salâmun 'alaykum!

And now, the moment you've been waiting for. Here is an example of an actual "miracle" posted on the internet on October 17, 1997, during a debate over how many daily prayers can be inferred from the Qur'ân Alone. The original featured atrocious mechanics and no convincing rhetoric, so I've made some improvements. Judge it for yourselves (but try not to laugh too hard) ...

The following has been given to me by someone who chooses to remain anonymous. This numerically confirms all five salawât by name, using the number 19 base. It is quite miraculous, if I may say so, yet very simple to follow. Subhânallâh. I suggest you print it out and then study carefully.

PART ONE: The well-known raka'ât. Fajr prayer consists of 2 raka'ât, dhuhr prayer consists of 4, 'asr prayer 4, maghrib 3, and 'ishâ' 4. Thus, the worshipper performs a total of 17 raka'ât in a day, and the daily prayer sequence can be expressed in concatenated form as 24434. This is a multiple of 19 (19 x 1286). By virtue of verse 74:30, the daily prayer sequence thus has God's "stamp of approval." Moreover, the sum of the digits of the factor (1286) is also 17, which reconfirms the total required raka'ât in a day.

PART TWO: The gematrical values of the five salawât. We know the above. But now comes the best part. Each consonant has a proper value according to the ancient Arabic counting method.

(1) fajr: fâ = 80, jîm = 3, râ = 200—total GV 283 (which has 3 digits)

(2) dhuhr: dhâ = 900, hâ = 5, râ = 200—total GV 1105 (which has 4 digits)

(3) 'asr: 'ayn = 70, sâd = 90, râ = 200—total GV 360 (which has 3 digits)

(4) maghrib: mîm = 40, ghayn = 1000, râ = 200, bâ = 2—total GV 1242 (which has 4 digits)

(5) 'ishâ': 'ayn = 70, shâ = 300, alif = 1, hamzah = 1—total GV 372 (which has 3 digits)

From this, we derive the following: (a) Total number of letters in all salawât = 17; (b) Number of daily raka'at = 17; (c) Sum of all GVs = 3362; (d) Number of daily salawât = 5. Total of a + b + c + d = 17 + 17 + 3362 + 5 = 3401. This is a multiple of 19 (19 x 179). Notice that the sum of the digits in the factor is 17 again, which reconfirms the total required raka'ât a day.

PART THREE: Gematrical values without repetition. If we take the sum of all letters in all five salawât, but without repeating any letters this time, we get 2692. Add to this the number of daily salawât = [5] and the sûrah number of Sûrat al-Fâtihah [1], and the total is 2698. This is both a multiple of 19 (19 x 142) and the number of times the word Allâh occurs in the Qur'ân, thus confirming the divine origin of the five prayers.

PART FOUR: Sum of digits in the gematrical values. Referring back to Part Two and recalling the number of digits in the gematrical values of all the five salawât separately, we have the following: fajr 283 = 3 digits, dhuhr 1105 = 4 digits, 'asr 360 = 3 digits, maghrib 1242 = 4 digits, 'ishâ' 372 = 3 digits. The sum of the digits in the gematrical values is thus 17, once again confirming the total required raka'ât a day.

CONCLUSION. Thus the five salawât and the 17 raka'ât are all tied in together very well, indeed, by the number 19 as well as with the word Allâh. Now I would like to see what the three-salawât proponents can present to support their argument. Allâhu 'Alîy al-Kabîr!!!

What do you think? Is this convincing? Well, before we analyze it, how does one *manufacture* "miraculous" numbers based on multiples like 19? There are two ways:

1. Trial and error. Add up various combinations of numbers that sound "meaningful" until you happen upon one that "works." Then experiment with another combination, and so on.

For example, watch what I do to "prove" that "hikmah" at verse 2:129 refers to "hadîth." What numbers do I have to work with? Starting with the gematrical value of the word "hadîth" [522], I tried various combinations and got this: GV of whole verse [4050] + sûrah [2] + letters in verse [81, if you include hamzah] + GV of "hadîth" [522] = 4655, or 19 x 245. Whoopee! A miracle! And how

419

many failed trials did I go through before I found that? Do you think I'd tell you?

2. Cherry-picking. This is more efficient. Think of a lot of different things you might use in order to sound convincing (verse numbers, GVs, etc.). Put these in a spreadsheet (or do it by hand) and add up all different combinations. If you're smart, you'll then exclude suspicious-looking things like inadvertently adding a sûrah number to a sum of sûrah and verse numbers (that wouldn't be very convincing). Finally, divide everything by 19 and see which ones work.

For example, I'll "prove" that Tucson is the true qiblah. The GV of "Tucson" is 517. All I have to do is show that I can add this to something about the qiblah from the Qur'ân and get a multiple of 19. After easily generating 43 numbers, I found two attractive ones: (1) sum of "qiblah" verse numbers [661] + GV of "Tucson" [517] = 1178, or 19 x 62; and (2) total "qiblah" mentions [7, if you include suffixes] + sum of sûrah and verse numbers [673] + GV of "Tucson" [517] = 1197, or 19 x 63. In addition, one number I found was just one short of a multiple of 19. Could I use this too? Sure; all I have to do is add one and say it stands for Sûrat al-Fâtihah (sound familiar?): GV of "masjid" [107] + GV of "harâm" [249] + sûrah number of Surat al-Fâtihah [1] + GV of "Tucson" [517] = 874, or 19 x 46. Is it all starting to get clearer? Then on with the show ...

STEP ONE—Inferring Rules and Criteria

In the October 17 "miracle" presented above, data were drawn from several different sources. Numbers were mixed and matched endlessly until they came out right. The method used by these authors of deception was obviously trial and error, because (1) they recycled their results several times to try to generate new ones, (2) they used more than one criterion, and (3) they targeted specific numbers, not multiples. Above all, no two "findings" rely on the same rule.

The authors of deception carefully hid all failed outcomes. We reconstruct the deceptive data set to reveal all those failed attempts and see if there really are more "findings" than random chance would permit. Watch how many different rules the authors of deception use to cook up just ten weak "findings." Remember that we used only one rule to test the Qur'ânic initials.

From Part One, we can infer the following rules and criteria:

> **Rule 1.** Express daily raka'ât sequences in terms of whole, "short-hand" numbers.
> **Rule 2.** For those numbers that are divisible by 19, include their factors in the data set.
> **Rule 3.** For all numbers, include the sums of their digits in the data set.
>
> **Criterion 1.** See if the number is divisible by 17.

420

Criterion 2. See if the number is divisible by 19.

From Part Two, we can infer the following rules:

> **Rule 4.** Count up the letters in the names of the prayers.
> **Rule 5.** Count up the total number of raka'ât in a day.
> **Rule 6.** Add up the gematrical values of the names of the prayers.
> **Rule 7.** Count up the number of salawât in a day.
> **Rule 8.** Combine all possible, separate rules to generate new numbers.

From Part Three, we can infer the following rules:

> **Rule 9.** Add up the letters in the names of the prayers without repetition.
> **Rule 10.** Include the number 1 in the data set.

From Part Four, we can infer the following rule:

> **Rule 11.** Add up the digits in all gematrical values.

In summary, it takes eleven rules and two criteria to generate just ten "findings." How much sense does this really make? But let's continue ...

STEP TWO—Generating Data from the Rules

Let's generate our data set using the above-listed eleven rules:

> **Rule 1.** Express daily raka'ât sequences in terms of whole, "short-hand" numbers.

The daily sequence for five prayers is 24434 on non-jumu'ah days and 22434 for jumu'ah, according to tabular reckoning (i.e., if you count the morning prayer as the first prayer). During the time of the Revelation of the Qur'ân, however, the day was known to start at sundown, not dawn, so the proper sequences would be 34244 and 34224, respectively.

> **Rules 2 and 3.** These require first generating a starting data set, so we have to save them for last.
> **Rule 4.** Count up the letters in the names of the prayers.

What are the "names" of the prayers? The Qur'ân lists only two that are commonly used: salât al-fajr, salât al-'ishâ'. But there is also salâtun min *YaWM* al-jumu'ah (62:9), commonly known as salât al-jumu'ah. Outside the Qur'ân, we have salât al-dhuhr, salât al-'asr, salât al-maghrib. Then there is al-salât al-wustâ at 2:238. Finally, we have short forms: fajr, dhuhr, wustâ, 'asr, maghrib, 'ishâ', jumu'ah. We have no basis upon which to exclude any of these, so we must accept all of them—short forms as well as long forms, and all possible ways to express "five daily prayers."

421

a. fajr, dhuhr, 'asr, maghrib, 'ishâ' = 17 or 47
b. fajr, dhuhr, wustâ, maghrib, 'ishâ' = 18 or 50
c. fajr, jumu'ah, 'asr, maghrib, 'ishâ' = 18 or 48 or 53
d. fajr, jumu'ah, wustâ, maghrib, 'ishâ' = 19 or 51 or 56

If you add jumu'ah to the five daily prayers for the sake of completeness, you get the following:

e. fajr, dhuhr, 'asr, maghrib, 'ishâ', jumu'ah = 21 or 57 or 62
f. fajr, dhuhr, wustâ, maghrib, 'ishâ', jumu'ah = 22 or 60 or 65

And, of course, we would have to consider all of them together as proper names of prayers:

g. fajr, dhuhr, 'asr, wustâ, maghrib, 'ishâ', jumu'ah = 25 or 69 or 74

Rule 5. Count up the total number of raka'ât in a day.

Since there are two types of days (jumu'ah and non-jumu'ah), we have 15 and 17.

Rule 6. Add up the gematrical values of the names of the prayers.

We have the same problem as in rule 4 because of the different ways people can refer to the prayers. Here are the various possible outcomes: (a) 3362, 4172; (b) 3087, 3928; (c) 2375, 3185, 3331; (d) 2100, 2941, 3087; (e) 3480, 4452, 4598; (f) 3205, 4208, 4354; (g) 3565, 4730, 4876.

Rule 7. Count up the number of salawât in a day.

Always "5" according to the 5-prayer theorists.

Rule 8. Like rules 2 and 3, this depends on first generating a starting data set, so we have to save it for last. (But be prepared: This is one whopper of a rule!)
Rule 9. Add up the letters in the names of the prayers without repetition.

Similar problem to what we saw in rules 4 and 6. Here is the outcome: (a) 13, 15; (b) 16, 18; (c) 12, 14, 16; (d) 16, 18, 19; (e) 13, 15, 17; (f) 16, 18, 19; (g) 17, 18, 19.

Rule 10. Include the number 1 in the data set.

Okay, 1.

Rule 11. Add up the digits in all gematrical values.

422

Here we go again. Same problem as in rules 4, 6, and 9, but with fewer distinct outcomes: (a) 17; (b) 16, 17; (c) 16; (d) 15, 16; (e) 20; (f) 19, 20; (g) 21, 22.

And now, on to our "composite" rules. These are what you should come to expect from people out to deceive you. They usually aren't skilled enough to avoid the fatal pitfall of re-crunching the numbers they've already presented in order to "uncover" even more "findings."

> **Rule 2.** For those numbers that are divisible by 19, include their factors in the data set.

This is the Factor Rule. It lets you recycle a little over 5% of what you've already produced. Of all of the numbers listed above, the following are divisible by 19: 19 (5 times), 57, 2375, 4598, and 24434. Dividing each of these by 19 gives us the following factors that we can add to the data set: 1 (5 times), 3, 125, 242, and 1286. Since none of these is a multiple of 19, we can stop here.

> **Rule 3.** For all numbers, include the sums of their digits in the data set.

This is the Fool's Rule. All it does is increase the proliferation of small numbers in the data set. It gives us the following new numbers: 1 (6 times), 2 (twice), 3 (5 times), 4 (4 times), 5 (3 times), 6 (6 times), 7 (8 times), 8 (10 times), 9 (6 times), 10 (7 times), 11 (4 times), 12 (twice), 14 (4 times), 15 (5 times), 16 (twice), 17 (5 times), 18 (twice), 19, 22, 25, and 26.

But now we have more numbers, so we have to go back to the Factor Rule: From these data we have one additional multiple of 19 (i.e., 19 itself). Back to the Fool's Rule again, this gives us its factor (1), plus, back to rule 3, the sum of the digits in that number, which is also 1.

> **Rule 8.** Combine all possible, separate rules to generate new numbers.

Aha! The Idiot's Rule! What do you get if you mix and match all possible combinations of the foregoing ten rules with all of their variants? Even before going back to the Factor Rule or the Fool's Rule, you'll get about three billion new numbers. Try it yourself! Then, once you apply the Factor Rule and the Fool's Rule, you wind up approaching a whopping 7 billion numbers in all. Thus, the authors of deception have, in effect, drawn a measly ten "findings" from a potential data set of almost seven billion numbers! See why it's called the "Idiot's Rule"?

Obviously, we can't apply the Idiot's Rule because it is utterly unmanageable. And to think, the authors of deception used the Idiot's Rule to get only two more "findings" (3401 and 2698). Why don't we just give them these two numbers anyway to give them an edge? Can we afford to be so bold? Do you really think it'll make a difference? After all, either their "miracle" is genuine, in which case the proliferation of multiples of 17 and 19 in the rest of their data will render these two numbers insignificant in their impact, or their "miracle" is really a Satanic attempt to dupe you, in which case these two numbers won't turn their deceit into anything near "miraculous."

Are you curious about the outcome? Do you think the authors of deception will beat the odds? Or do you already know what's coming up? Maybe you do. But just in case, stay tuned!

LESSON FIVE:
Exposing Deceit, Part II
Analyzing The Data Set

Salâmun 'alaykum!

Are you still with me? It's been a long journey, but at last we've come to the moment of truth for the authors of deception. You will recall that we painstakingly examined each of their "proofs" in order to infer what kind of rule was really at work behind each one. Amazingly, for a mere ten data points, we actually found eleven separate rules, two separate criteria, and a potential data set of almost seven billion numbers from which to choose! Do you suppose they could have tried just a little harder to get at least two multiples of 19 out of each rule? Evidently, Satan doesn't try very hard to concoct "miracles." Perhaps it's because he knows it won't do any good to anyone who truly obeys the Qur'ân when it says we are individually responsible for our beliefs. Instead, he just casually throws together some frail numbers that couldn't stand up to the slightest real scrutiny and sticks them in the pockets of the most gullible people he can find. He fools only those who refuse to use the power of their minds. He targets those who are too lazy to question every "proof from God" that comes their way. You might say he's a cerebral Darwinist.

But enough about Satan. You can be sure we'll see him pop up again if the "miracle" we're examining turns out to be false. Don't believe me? Read on ...

SYNOPSIS OF STEP TWO—The Reconstructed Data Set

Once again, here are the rules and criteria that we inferred from the deceptive "proofs":

> **Rule 1.** Express daily raka'ât sequences in terms of whole, "short-hand" numbers.
> **Rule 2.** Include all factors of multiples of 19 in the data set (the Factor Rule).
> **Rule 3.** Include the digital sums of the results of other rules (the Fool's Rule).
> **Rule 4.** Count up the letters in the names of the prayers.

Rule 5. Count up the total number of raka'ât in a day.
Rule 6. Add up the gematrical values of the names of the prayers.
Rule 7. Count up the number of salawât in a day.
Rule 8. Combine all possible, separate rules (the Idiot's Rule).
Rule 9. Add up the letters in the names of the prayers without repetition.
Rule 10. Include the number 1 in the data set.
Rule 11. Add up the digits in all gematrical values.

Criterion 1. See if the number is divisible by 17.
Criterion 2. See if the number is divisible by 19.

You will also recall that rule 11 was completely unworkable, as it effectively would have exploded the data set to something on the order of seven billion. In view of this, and just to give Satan an edge, we threw in the two numbers that the authors of deception had generated via the Idiot's Rule, i.e., 3401 and 2698. We consequently ended up with ten rules, two criteria, two freebies, and a data set of 174 numbers.

STEP THREE—Analyzing the Results

Here is our final data set: 1 (14 times), 2 (twice), 3 (6 times), 4 (4 times), 5 (4 times), 6 (6 times), 7 (8 times), 8 (10 times), 9 (6 times), 10 (7 times), 11 (4 times), 12 (3 times), 13 (twice), 14 (5 times), 15 (9 times), 16 (9 times), 17 (11 times), 18 (8 times), 19 (6 times), 20 (twice), 21 (twice), 22 (3 times), 25 (twice), 26, 47, 48, 50, 51, 53, 56, 57, 60, 62, 65, 69, 74, 125, 242, 1286, 2100, 2375, [2698], 2941, 3087 (twice), 3185, 3205, 3331, 3362, [3401], 3480, 3565, 3928, 4172, 4208, 4354, 4452, 4598, 4730, 4876, 22434, 24434, 34224, and 34244.

There are 174 data points in all, including the two freebies (3401 and 2698). Now, let's recall the criteria used by the authors of deception to determine "significance":

Criterion 1. See if the number is divisible by 17.

Although the Qur'ân only mentions the number 19 as being of special importance, the authors of deception seem to prefer the number 17. Any idea why that is? If 19 is God's "sign" of authenticity, exactly what is 17? Whose number is it, anyway? It is, after all, nowhere to be found in the Qur'ân! But, more on this in a moment. Meanwhile, let's see how many numbers fit this criterion.

Because many of the manipulations in this set of "proofs" specifically tried to generate the number 17, we already know there are more 17s in this data set than there would be in a truly random one. This is because by playing with such things as the letters in the prayer words, interpretation variance creates a cluster of numbers near the target (17), and this artificially inflates the number of hits. Not surprisingly, here's what came out of these data: 17 (11 times), 51, and 2941. That's a total of 13 "hits" and 171 "misses." Random chance would give us 10 hits free. What is the probability of getting 13 "hits"? Is it a miracle? Is it remarkable, at least? Let's find out.

First, here is the formula from Lesson 3 again:

P(y) =   { n! / [y! (n - y)!] } p^y (1 - p)^(n - y) where . . .
P(y) =   the probability of observing 'y' successes
y =   number of successes in 'n' trials
n =   number of observations
p =   probability of success on a single observation

Applying this to our findings for multiples of 17, we get this:

P(13) = { 174! / [13! (174 - 13)!] } 1/17^13 (1 - 1/17)^(174 - 13)

Your calculator may not be able to handle this, so here's some help:

174! = 6.4254 x 10^315
161! = 7.5907 x 10^286

... and the solution is **p = .0792**

Wow! A miracle! But wait! Is it really? Remember the range of probabilities for the outcomes we found for the Qur'ânic initials? Aside from the number 19, the best finding was for the number 2 (p =.0537, or .0161 with the "nûn" correction). Was that a miracle? Of course not. Yet it was clearly better than the outcome we have here! And what was the outcome for the number 19? It was p = .0000142. Now that you know what real evidence for a miracle looks like, is there "miraculous" evidence for the number 17 in this contrived data set? Obviously not. The number 17 is not important in the least. But let's continue ...

Criterion 2. See if the number is divisible by 19.

Now, this is much better than "17-divisibility" as a criterion for determining significant outcomes, isn't it? It is, after all, in the Qur'ân (74:30), unlike the number "17." Now, we know that the authors of deception tried to get as many multiples of 19 as possible. How did they do? Did they really find miraculous proof of the 5-prayer theory? Let's see. Our data set boasts a whopping ... (hmm ... let's see) ... ten multiples of 19! They are as follows: 19 (6 times), 57, 2375, 4598, and 24434. But wait! We forgot to add the two freebies: 3401 and 2698. Now we have twelve multiples of 19! Whoopee! A miracle!

What? A miracle? Is it really? How many multiples of 19 should there be in 174

426

data points due to random chance alone? Nine. That's already pretty close totwelve, but could Satan still have a chance? What do the statistics say? Let's find out. Here's the equation:

$$P(12) = \{\ 174! \ / \ [\ 12! \ (174 - 12)! \ ]\ \}\ 1/19{\wedge}12 \ (1 - 1/19){\wedge}(174 - 12)$$

to help your calculator out, $162! = 1.2297 \times 10{\wedge}289$

... and the solution is **p = .0774**

My, my, my. Tsk, tsk, tsk. Not even close. Not significantly different, in fact, from the outcome for multiples of 17. And to think we gave them two freebies to give them an edge! Egad! What has become of their "miracle"?

The truth is, there never was a miracle at all. And we've proved it and exposed their deception. The fact is, the authors of deception made up those numbers just to dupe as many people as they could into adopting the 5-prayer theory without appealing to the Qur'ân! Think about it. Do you recall how many Qur'ânic verses were featured in their numbers? There were none at all. (And, yes, this was indeed actually posted on the internet as proof of the five-prayer theory!)

Now, mind you, if an honest-hearted person reads the Qur'ân and concludes that it says there are five required, daily prayers, then more power to him. No one has the right to second-guess what a sincere seeker after truth learns directly from an honest reading of the Qur'ân. The problem with this fabricated "miracle" has nothing to do with what the fabricators tried to prove with it. They could just as well have tried to "prove" the three-prayer theory, and they would have been just as wrong. The problem is this: The authors of deception tried to pass off something they fabricated as having divine backing. Let me say that again:

DIVINE BACKING

What does that mean? That means that the authors of deception fully intended to mislead you into thinking that ...

GOD HIMSELF

... had authorized their theory! And what do you call it when someone makes up something and attributes it to God? Is it a joke? Is it "all in fun"? Is it harmless? Should you simply forgive them for being "ignorant"? If you're not sure, I invite you to reread verse 6:19 and the two verses following it.

Attributing lies to God is a serious matter. For your sake, you need to know how to detect deception in numbers. Otherwise, you run the risk of being duped by the very kind of people to whom the Qur'ân refers in the above-cited verses.

427

Obviously, the authors of deception spent as much time looking for multiples of 17 as they did looking for multiples of 19. This is clear from the p-values, which are practically identical. But why didn't they just stick with 19? Why was the number "17" so important? In fact, what could motivate anyone who is familiar with the importance of 19-divisibility in the Qur'ân to pay so much attention to "17"? Whose "sign" is this anyway? Is it God's? Is the number 17 mentioned in the Qur'ân at all?

What is the number 17? Let's examine it. Hey, look what I found! It turns out that the word "shaytân" (which means **Satan** or **Devil**) occurs 68 times in the Qur'ân (17 x 4). The plural "shayâtîn" (**Devils**) is mentioned 17 times (17 x 1). Personally, I wouldn't touch the number 17 with a 17-foot pole, let alone try to hoist it on believers as a "miracle" from God! The only way to justify its exploitation as an ostensible sign from God is to link it definitively with the number 19, using the Qur'ân itself. And this hasn't been done. It hasn't even been tried. In fact, it hasn't been given any importance at all.

Now, I'm curious. What happens if you extract the impure from the pure? Let's see. Let's say the impure is represented by "al-Shaytân" (GV = 400), while the pure is represented by "Allâh" (GV = 66). Makes sense. And what is the difference? As it turns out, 66 - 400 = -334. What's -334 x 19? Try -6346. How many total verses are there in God's Word, the Qur'ân? I invite you to look it up if you don't remember. Now, what was left over after extracting the 13 "hits" for 17-divisibility from the original data set of 174? There were exactly 171 remaining "misses" (19 x 9). Coincidence? Indeed, perhaps it is. But let's continue ...

Let me draw your attention back to God's real miracle. Recall the p-value from our test of the data set of the Qur'ânic initials (p = .0000142). What is 142 x 19? I invite you to multiply it out for yourself and then refer back to Part Three of the fabricated "miracle." Then answer this question: Is God not in control of His numbers?

But there's still more. Recall the p-value from our test of the data set of the Qur'ânic initials that considers the correction of the "nûn" count in Sûrah 68 (p = .000000676). You'll notice, of course, that the sum of the digits in the number 676 is 19. In fact, there is an infinite set of numbers showing a digital sum of 19. Here are the first several such numbers: 199, 289, 298, 379, 388, 397, 469, 478, 487, 496, 559, 568, 577, 586, 595, 649, 658, 667, 676. Which one is 676? I invite you to count them up for yourself to find out. Then answer this question: Is God not in control of His numbers?

Now, once again, all of this may be sheer coincidence. Indeed, I certainly have no right to present these admittedly meaningful numbers as a miracle if I can't prove they are, can I? But now you know better, for now you know what it really takes to prove or disprove claims about "miraculous" numbers.

Meanwhile, take just one more look at those last few paragraphs above. Even if there is nothing genuinely miraculous about those numbers, they should nevertheless make you think. And yes, you must think. That's what 17:36 is all about. Use your head at all times. You don't need any crutches to believe in God.

CONCLUSION

There are plenty of people who get a kick out of making fools of those who try to do God's will, and you can bet Satan gets a bigger kick out of seeing them do his dirty work and watching those of us who are afraid to use our brains drop like flies. One of Satan's favorite tricks to pull on those of us who have witnessed the role of 19 in the Qur'ân is to splatter a bunch of numbers on our computer screen and say "miracle!" It's got to be especially delightful for him to get his pawns to invent "miracles" that supposedly "prove" that someone's hadîth is inspired by God! Do you think he feels guilty when he gets us to obey his "magical" numbersinstead of God's Word? If you'll excuse the pun, hell no! It just makes his day when he can make us toss aside God's Word and replace it with sayings and footnotes and magical numbers and the Fool's Rule and the Idiot's Rule and our egos.

Sadly, most believers are ill-equipped to differentiate between deception and a genuine miracle. But whose responsibility is it to equip ourselves with the tools and the talent and the energy to put everything that Satan throws at us to the test? Are we safe in our ignorance? Does God hold those of us who study and learn and make use of our brain power to a higher standard than those of us who make excuses for not using the brains He gave us? Has God prevented us from learning mathematics or Arabic or whatever it takes to know more than the tricksters who will inevitably come to our doors to dupe us? You'll find this answer—and all other answers—in God's Word, the Qur'ân. Read it yourself, and learn. It's all between you and God (75:19).

A6
The Ingrates React

The following reaction by a Christian is one of the many examples indicating the level of appreciation of the opponents. Their comprehension of NINETEEN is no better than the diluters or the code-hunters we have discussed above. The ingrate creates a 19-letter statement insulting God, and then provides some calculations. Unfortunately, his statement insulting the word *Allah* (God) is promoted by some ignorant Christians with joy. The Arabic word Allah is not a proper name as some might think; it is contraction of AL (the) and ELAH (god). Contrary to the wishes of some Christians who wish to contribute to the current climate of hate and warmongering against Muslims, the disciples of Jesus would understand *Allah* and *Allahumma*, but they would not understand the English word *God*. The Hebrew or Aramaic word for God is both etimologically and phonetically related to the Arabic one. Arabic Bibles have been using the word *Allah* for millenniums, so do the Christian Arabs. Before moving, I would like to clarify the common misconception about the word *Allah*. Here is an excerpt from the Endnote of QRT on verse 7:180:

> The Quran uses more than a hundred attributes for God, and attributes indicate continuity. Not every verb used for God can be considered an attribute. For instance, not every person who writes can be called a "writer." Furthermore, God's attributes are not necessarily Arabic. God sent messengers in many different languages to each nation, and informed them about His attributes in their languages. Thus, the Quran teaches us that to God belong all beautiful attributes. However, Hadith books lists 99 attributes of which some cannot be considered "beautiful." The list, which is very popular among Sunni and Shiite mushriks and many people memorize, include "bad" names such as *al-Dar* (the one who harms). Quran tells us otherwise (42:30).
>
> Those who have confused Arab nationalism with islam might criticize our use of the English word God in the English text, rather than the word Allah. We would like to pull the attention of those who are not intoxicated with Hadith and Sunna that promotes Arab culture to the following points: the word Allah is not a proper name; it is an Arabic

word contraction of the article *Al* (the) and *Elah* (god). Also, see 2:165; 3:26; 6:12; 17:110; 20:52; 42:11; 58:7.

The Quran informs us that God has been sending messengers to every nation in their own language (14:4). In each language, names or attributes represented by different sounds and symbols are used for the creator. For instance, the Old Testament uses *Yehovah* or *Elohim*. The New Testament quotes from Jesus addressing to God as *Eloi* (my lord), which is very close to the Arabic word *Elahi* (my lord) (Mark 15:34).

Through distortion and mistranslations, some Biblical verses depict God as less than a perfect being. For instance, Judges 1:19 (powerless); Genesis 6:6-7 (fallible); Psalms 13:1; Lamentations 5:20 (forgetful); Genesis 3:8-10 (can't see); 1 Samuel 15:2-3 (cruel). For more on divine attributes in the Quran and the Bible, see 59:22-24. ...

Back to the reaction of the Christian critic. Even if we assume that all his numbers are accurate, though he imitates some of the simpler patterns by matching the number of letters of each word in Bismillah, his so-called 19 facts do not exhibit a pattern as we have seen in the chapter on long numbers in *Bismillah*. He has more than a dozen categories of numbers and he concatenates them without following any consistent or apriori predictable pattern. Of course, even if this statistically insignificant fabrication had some significant pattern, it would be still ridiculous to compare it to the system which involves an entire book, from letters to words, from verses to chapters. On top of that, the fabricator ignores the prophetic nature of the Quranic system, which is by itself, stands out an extra ordinary witness to an extra ordinary claim.

The author of the article who introduced himself as Kurt Wilson (aka Whale) contacted me via email. Proud of his counterfeiting skill, which is a projection of his own state of mind, he shared his reaction. I changed the order of the letters in the reference of his insult.

About 19, see this article that I made: http://www.wikiislam.com/wiki/19 It proves the whole so-called 19 miracle as wrong.

بسم لهلا الخَبِيث الوَحْشِيّ

Translation: *In the name of Lehla, the Evil, the Savage*

Total ANV (Arabic Numerical Value) – 1666

Fact 1: 19 letters - 19 = 19 x 1
Fact 2: Sum of Individual ANV digits (1666) = 1 + 6 + 6 + 6 = 19
Fact 3: One verse, ANV - 1 1666 = 19 x 614
Fact 4: Sequence number, Word Size - 1 3 2 4 3 6 4 6 = 19 x 19 x 36686
Fact 5: Sequence number, Local letter number, Individual ANV Value - 1
      1 2 2 60 3 40 2 1 1 2 30 3 30 4 5 3 1 1 2 30 3 600 4 2 5 10 6 500

431

4 1 1 2 30 3 6 4 8 5 300 6 10 = 19 x 59084389584858068659
53279136864479289495 327913939631900

Fact 6: Sequence number, Cumulative number of letters - 1 3 2 7 3 13 4
19 = 19 x 69858601

Fact 7: Conjoined letter numbers, added - 150426287722 = 19 x
7917173038

Fact 8: Letter number, Sequence number - 1231 45672 89101112133
1415161718194 = 19 x 64813512047900590174 42903248326

Fact 9: Num Words, Num letters, Total ANV - 4191666 = 19 x 220614

Fact 10: 1 sentence, 19 letters, lengths of words - 1193466 = 19 x 19 x 19
x 174

Fact 11: Sequence number, Word Size, Word ANV - 1 3 102 2 4 66 3 6
1143 4 6 355 = 19 x 689591928216544545

Fact 12: Sequence number, Word Size, Word ANV Series - 1 3 26040 2
4 130305 3 6 130600210500 4 6 1306830010 = 19 x
697915916475291375294747921076910885790

Fact 13: Sequence number, Word Size, Individual ANV Value - 1 3 2 60
40 2 4 1 30 30 5 3 6 1 30 600 2 10 500 4 6 1 30 6 8 300 10 = 19
x 697915916475291375294 747921076910885790

Fact 14: Sequence number, Word ANV Series, Letter number - 1 26040
123 2 130305 4567 3 130600210500 8910111213 4
1306830010 141516171819 = 19 x 66336906954226602985
858210637105732111111 64954246473737586927 2201

Fact 15: Sequence number, Cumulative number letters, Word ANV - 1 3
102 2 7 66 3 13 1143 4 19 355 = 19 x 68959350691112811545

Fact 16: Sequence number, First&Last ANV Values, Local letter number
- 1 42 1 2 3 2 6 1 2 3 4 3 501 1 2 3 4 5 6 4 11 1 2 3 4 5 6 = 19 x
748017164391316380765 653217024

Fact 17: Sequence number, Local letter number, Word ANV Series - 1 1
2 3 26040 2 1 2 3 4 130305 3 1 2 3 4 5 6 130600210500 4 1 2 3
4 5 6 1306830010 = 19 x 5911896853281121213
2228716476843213160064976910885790

Fact 18: Sequence number, Local letter number, Individual ANV Value -
1 1 2 2 60 3 40 2 1 1 2 30 3 30 4 5 3 1 1 2 30 3 600 4 2 5 10 6
500 4 1 1 2 30 3 6 4 8 5 300 6 10 = 19 x
59084389584858068659   53279136864479289495
327913939631900

Fact 19: One verse, ANV, 19 characters - 1 1666 19 = 19 x 61401

As we can see, 19 miracles have been found about this new bismillah "In the
name of Lehla, the Evil, the Savage". This is just a start. If we experiment more,
we will undoubtedly come up with more miracles. Our new bismillah also is
miraculous according to Islamic standards. One problem with the phenomena of
the 19 miracle is that there are no defined rules as to what constitutes a miracle
and what doesn't. Without the lack of any rules, we can see that the "miracle" of

nineteen can exist in any phrase, even anti-Islamic.Now if you think your phrases of 19 are miraculous then you have to admit: so is this one.

We do not have space in this book to expose the manifold problems with *this one*. We have already allocated several hundreds of pages on refuting the criticisms of ingrates and skeptics in my revised edition of: *Running Like Zebras*. Reading a response by a Submitter named Eddy Jawed, reveals that after receiving criticism exposing numerical errors in his original statement, the opponent ends up changing the word Pig to Evil! Of course, transforming his pig into evil does not do much to rehabilitate his pathetic ignorance.

A7

Which one do you see:
HELL OR MIRACLE?

From the smoke of hell-fire in their minds, hypocrites and unappreciative people are not able to witness one of the greatest miracles.

I know that the title and the subtitle of this article are quite challenging. If you have developed an attitude against witnessing the mathematical miracle of the Quran, you are justified to get upset with these words and perhaps get little angry. You might have already blinded your eyes and closed your ears with one or more false, contradictory, trivial, or irrelevant excuses, such as:

1. God uses literary styles to prove the authenticity of His word; but not mathematics. God is not a mathematician and His word has nothing to do with math.
2. If Muhammad was not aware of a mathematical miracle in the Quran, then it cannot be true. Muhammad knew everything in the Quran. The knowledge contained in the Quran is limited with Muhammad's knowledge and understanding more than 14 centuries ago.
3. If I accept a mathematical structure in the Quran based on number 19, then I will be denying two Quranic verses in the end of Chapter 9, and thus would contradict the majority of Muslims and their manuscripts. Besides, I would be contradicting the verses guaranteeing the perfect preservation of the Quran.
4. Some verses of the Quran are Mutashabih; none can understand their meaning except God. The proponents of 19-based mathematical system in the Quran are indulging in those Mutashabih verses.
5. The number 19 is heresy, since it is the holy number of Bahai sect.
6. Though I can balance my check and shop in the stores, I am innumerate when it comes to the 19.
7. We can find many mathematical phenomena if we spend enough time on any book. For instance, the Bible Code claimed that the distorted translations of the Bible contain impressive coded prophecies.
8. The Quran cannot contain secrets, mysteries or prophecies; it is a clear book.
9. What about the previous generations; will they all go to hell?
10. The claim of a 19-based mathematical code is a mythology.
11. The claim of a 19-based mathematical code is a magic.

12. There are many other numbers in the Quran and the number 19 has no special place.
13. There are problems in the count of letters or words. For instance, the first verse of the Quran does not have 19 letters; it has 18, 20, 21, or 22 letters, but not 19. For instance, the counts of A.L.M. letters have errors.
14. Part of the numerical claim is based on the Gematria system (ABJAD), a Jewish fabrication and a deceptive tool used by numerologists and astrologists.
15. The pronoun "it" in verse 74:30 is feminine and it refers to Hell not the Quran. Thus verse 74:30-31 is about guardians of hell, not a mathematical proof of authenticity.
16. Even if there is such a code in the Quran it is not important. We need to follow the instruction of the book. We need to focus on how to fight against infidels.
17. The discoverer of Code 19 claimed to be the messenger of God. He deserved divine retribution. Thus, he was killed in early 1990 by an Al-Qaida affiliate American cult, al-Fuqra, as Al-Qaida's first act in the USA.
18. If we believe in code 19, then we would end up rejecting holy teachings of Hadith and Sunna.
19. Code 19 is a Zionist trick.
20. I already believe in the Quran and I do not need miracles.
21. I believe in the Quran because its message is true.
22. I believe in the Quran because it does not contain contradictions.
23. I believe in the Quran on blind faith and I do not need any reason for my belief.
24. And, many more excuses, reasons or lack of them...

I will deal with all these excuses, and God willing, I will respond each of them one by one; but first thing first:

Whatever are your EXCUSES or REASONS to ignore, reject, or ridicule the number 19, this article will expose your true intentions, which you might be trying to hide even from yourself (11:5). If you are claiming to believe in the Quran, and after reading this article still continue ignoring or ridiculing the mathematical code of the Quran, you will be TORMENTED all your life by repeatedly witnessing an exciting fact and losing its sight afterwards, like a person who witnesses succeeding events of lightning in the darkness (2:17-20). You will neither appreciate nor comprehend the miracle, nor will you be satisfied with your denial. You will perpetually oscillate between momentary belief end prolonged disbelief, between private doubt and public denial. You will be doomed to SAQAR here and in the hereafter.

But, if you have acknowledge the truth and gained some goodness in your acknowledgement, then this article, by God's will, may wake you up from ignorance, and may change your paradigm (6:158). You will never be the same; you will be among the progressives (74:30-37). You will be one of the few who are blessed by God to witness one of the greatest miracles. You will be sure about your conviction, not based on self-deceptive claims, on conformity with a religious group, or on blind faith, or wishful thinking; but a faith or more accurately acknowledgement based on knowledge gathered from empirical and rational evidence corroborated by spiritual experience (41:53; 74:31). You will experience God's presence in your life and attain happiness promised to believers and submitters (9:124; 10:64; 16:89). You will dedicate all your life to serve God alone without remorse or fear (2:62; 3:170; 10:62; 46:13). You will understand many Quranic verses that had not much meaning for you (2:1,108). Every time you see an unappreciative disbeliever denying or mocking the 19-based system, your knowledge-based faith will be justified. And the more people do not see what you and few others have witnessed will increase the importance, power and the wonder of the prophetic description of 74:31 in your mind. You will attain certainty (74:31; 27:1-3; 2:260; 13:2; 2:118; 45:20). However, witnessing this miracle will also put some responsibility on you (5:115; 47:25).

Let's start from the translation of verses 21-37 of chapter 74, The Hidden One:

74:21   He looked.
74:22   He frowned and scowled.
74:23   Then he turned away arrogantly.
74:24   He said, "This is but an impressive illusion/magic!"[188]
74:25   "This is human made."
74:26   I will cast him into SAQAR!
74:27   And what will explain to you what the SAQAR is?
74:28   It leaves nothing, it lets nothing (NOT MORE, NOT LESS; PRECISE; PERFECT);
74:29   VISIBLE   (LAWAHATUN)   to   PEOPLE   (BASHAR) (universal)!
74:30   On it is Nineteen.
74:31   As guardians of fire we appointed none except angels/controllers, and we assigned their number (1) to torment the unappreciative disbelievers, (2) to convince People of the Book, (3) to strengthen the acknowledgement of the acknowledger, (4) to remove all traces of doubt from the hearts of People of the Book, as well as the believers, and (5) to expose those who have disease in their hearts, and the unappreciative disbelievers; they will say, "What did God mean by this allegory?" God thus sends astray whomever He wills (or, whoever wills), and guides whomever He wills (or, whoever wills). None knows the soldiers of your Lord except He. IT (HIYA) is a reminder for the people.

74:32   Indeed, by the Moon.
74:33   By the night as it passes.
74:34   And the morning as it shines.
74:35   This (NUMBER) is one of the GREATEST (KUBRA).
74:36   A WARNING (NAZEER) for the PEOPLE (BASHAR).
74:37   For those who want to progress or regress.

Though the function of 19 is listed in Chapter 74, conventionally known *Muddathir* (The Hidden One), its implication and fulfillment was kept hidden according to God's will as the Quran's secret for 19x74 lunar years after its revelation to Muhammad. However, the All-wise God, unveiled this secret via a monotheist scientist in 1974, according to the most commonly used calendar, a calendar allegedly based on the birth of Jesus, which is considered a holy day and the sign of the End (19:15). As a result, the number 19, as the miraculous code of the Quran and the Bible strengthened and continue to strengthen the acknowledgement of believers, removed and continue to remove doubts in the heart of people of the book, and intellectually tormented and continue to torment hypocrites and unappreciative disbelievers.

Now let's first discuss the words written in CAPITAL letters in the translation of the verses above. Then, we will discuss each of the popular excuses used by the unappreciative disbelievers of the miracle 19.

We should understand the meaning of these words by first referring to their usage in the Quran. Their immediate context as well as their use in other verses is usually sufficient to illuminate their meanings. For believers who have been lucky to witness this great miracle, the meaning of the verses above is good news; it gives them hope, enlightens them, informs them, and turns their position from wishful thinking or conjecture to knowledge-based paradigm. Thus, the rhetorical value of these verses is very high for believers:

> 74:27 ---> SAQAR (saqar, to be defined by the following verses)
> 74:28 ---> (NOT MORE, NOT LESS; PRECISE; PERFECT);
>
> 74:29 ---> LAWAHA (obvious; visible; tablet; screen)
> 74:29 ---> BASHAR (humans; people)
> 74:31 ---> HIYA (it; reference to the number 19)
> 74:31 ---> ZIKRA (reminder; message)
> 74:35 ---> HA (it; referring to the number 19)
> 74:35 ---> KUBRA (great miracles)
> 74:36 ---> NEZEER (warner to be embraced and supported)

On the other hand, those who have deprived themselves from witnessing the miracle 19 because of their ill intentions or their dogmatic rejection try hard to render these key words incompatible with the semantic context of the Quran.

They conceive God of the Quran as an angry and despotic God who is not able provide any reasonable argument against those who question the Quran's authenticity, but only resorts to intimidation: "I will burn you in hell!!!" The God they depict has double standard: He asks the disbelievers to bring their evidence for their argument (2:111; 11:17; 21:24; 27:64; 28:75; 35:40) but for His argument He only wants to scare them! The opponents of 19-based miracle, by distorting the meaning of the words in these verses, manage to blind themselves to one of the most profound philosophical and theological arguments and evidences in history. Not only they divert themselves from the right path they try to divert others too (6:25-26; 22:3; 41:83).

Thus, the understanding (more accurately, the misunderstanding) of those who cannot appreciate God as He should be (6:90-91), the argument for Quran's authenticity is scorching, burning, dark, hellish, misfortune, disastrous, and scary. Thus, in the minds of opponents of miracle 19, the rhetorical value of these verses is simply a threat to burn and torture:

> 74:27 ---> SAQAR (hell-fire)
> 74:28 ---> (NEITHER LEAVES THE FLESH NOR THE BONES; DESTROYS CONTINUALLY);
> 74:29 ---> LAWAHA (scorching; burning; shriveling)
> 74:29 ---> BASHAR (skin)
> 74:31 ---> HIYA (it; referring to hell-fire)
> 74:31 ---> ZIKRA (news of disaster)
> 74:35 ---> HA (it; referring to hell-fire
> 74:35 ---> KUBRA (great punishment; gravest misfortune; dire scourge)
> 74:36 ---> NAZEER (warning to be escaped)

Now let's one by one discuss each of these words, which were widely and perhaps JUSTIFIABLY misunderstood by pre-1974 generations, and yet are intentionally distorted by the post-1974 opponents of one of the greatest miracles.

Does "Saqar" In 74:27 Mean Hell OR Something Else?

Though prominent Arabic dictionaries such as Lisan-ul Arab and specialized dictionaries such as Mufradat Fi Gharib-il Quran acknowledge that the word might be of foreign origin with no Arabic derivatives, these and other dictionaries and commentaries of the Quran do not hesitate defining it as hell or heat radiating from Sun. Lisan-ul Arab refers to a Hadith which uses a bizarre derivative of the word Saqar to mean "liars". The word SaQaR is mentioned four times in the Quran, three times in Chapter 74 and once in 54:48. In the later one, the word SaQaR is used in a statement warning that when criminals will be dragged to the fire they will be told: "taste the touch of Saqar". From this verse one might infer that Saqar is another word for fire; but a better inference is that

438

Saqar is a negative feeling or state of mind one tastes after being committed to the divine punishment. In this case, there is no reason to think that this negative state of mind could not be obtained from experiences other than fire.

The Arabic word for hell is GaHyM or GaHaNnaM. The word NAR (Fire), though not a specific name for hell, is also frequently used to denote the same phenomenon. However, the word NAR (fire) is also used in its literal meaning, which is simply fire. For instance, verses 20:10-14 describe God's communication with Moses through fire. Obviously, this fire in the holy land where God spoke through cannot be the Hell. Similarly, the word SaQaR does not necessarily mean hell. In fact, the semantic connection of SaQaR with hell is allegorical, since SaQaR is a descriptive word derived from the verb SaQaRa rather than a noun like GaHYM, GaHaNnaM.

In any case, the verse 74:27 does not ask nor expect us to rush into defining the meaning of this word, which it appears to be its first usage in the Quran. We are warned against rushing to define Quranic words or attempting to preempt the Quranic definition by prematurely assigning a meaning to a verse before considering its immediate or Quranic context or fulfillment (20:114; 75:16-19). Doing so is a sign of pretension and arrogance. Since the word is rarely used in the Quran (total four and three of them is in this chapter) and this verse is most likely the first usage of this rare word, it is more appropriate to wait the Quran explain the word. In brief, rushing to limit/define the meaning of the word Saqar in the verse "Do you know what SaQaR is?" is a disrespectful act against the Quran. When the Quran asks "Do you know what X means?" it does not want us to try to understand the meaning of X in the very question about its meaning! It is a rhetorical question. God wants to pull your attention to its modified or new meaning. The Quran uses this question 13 times either to modify the meaning of an already used word or to add another nuance (See: 69:3; 74:27; 77:14; 82:17-18; 83:8, 19; 86:2; 90:12; 97:2; 101:3, 10; 104:5).

Nevertheless, we see that almost all commentators or translators of the Quran have rushed to translate SaQaR as Hell or Fire:

> **Yusuf Ali**: "Soon I will cast him into Hell-Fire!"
> **Marmaduke Pickthall**: "Him shall I fling unto the burning."
> **T.B. Irving**: "I'll roast him by scorching!"
> **M. H. Shakir**: "I will cast him into Hell."
> **MaulaHUM Muhammad Ali**: "I will cast him into hell."
> **N. J. Dawood**: "I will surely cast him to the fire of Hell. "
> **Muhammad Asad**: "[Hence,] I shall cause him to endure hell-fire [in the life to come]!"
>
> **Rashad Khalifa:** "I will commit him to retribution"

As you see, none leave the word SaQaR as it is. However, Rashad Khalifa, as the one who was chosen to fulfill this great prophecy, renders the word SaQar accurately by translating it with a general word, "retribution." Yasar Nuri Ozturk, a Turkish theology professor, in his post-1974 translation of the Quran, translated the word SaQaR under the light of the descriptive verses and related discoveries as the COMPUTER with succeeding screens manifesting the mathematical miracle of the Quran to all people.

So, we should not prime our minds or blind ourselves with prejudice by assuming SaQaR as HELL-FIRE before reading the following verses (75:16-19; 20:114).

Does "It Leaves Nothing; It Lets Nothing" in 74:28 Mean "Exact, Precise" OR "Destroys Flesh And Bones"?

Though the short verse is not generally mistranslated, but its meaning and implication is distorted. In the light of the context and post-1974 discoveries we should understand it is description of the 19-based mathematical structure that is exact. It does neither leave extra (BaQaYa) nor it let anything necessary go away (WaZaRa); in other words, it is perfect and precise; it is not one more not one less!

However, parroting the pre-1974 commentaries of the Quran, many translations and commentaries still convey the same misunderstanding. Since English translations usually do not comment on this particular verse and leave it to be understood within the context of CORPORAL PUNISHMENT, HELL and FIRE rather than the crucial role of the NUMBER NINETEEN, I will give you a sample of some popular Arabic commentaries of the Quran (which I have easy access in my personal library) in ascending chronological order. If the name of the commentary different than the name of the author his name will be indicated in the parenthesis. The number in parenthesis is the year of the authors' death:

> **Tabari (922)**: Neither kills nor leaves alive; or devours them all and when they are recreated do not leaves them until eating them.
>
> **Tha'alibi (1035)**: Does not leave the dweller of hell alone and burns them.
>
> **Bagawi (1122)**: Neither kills nor leaves alive; eats everything thrown in; does not leave their flesh nor take their bones.
>
> **Nasafi (1143)**: Does not leave the flesh nor does let the bones of its dwellers; destroys everything in it and then restores them back to their starting point.
>
> **Baydawi (1292)**: It does not leave anything thrown in and does not leave it until destroys it.

440

Qurtubi (1272): Does not leave for them neither flesh, nor bone, nor blood, but burns them. Or does not leave anything from them and then does not let them go when they are recreated.

Zad-ul Masir (Ibn Cawzi, 1200): Does not leave but destroys their flesh and does not let them go when they are recreated.

Ibn Kathir (1372): Eat their flesh, sweat, bones, and skin. They do not die in this condition or they live.

Jalalayn (Celaleddin, 1459): Destroys flesh and bones, then starts it again.

Ruh-ul Maani (Alusi 1853): Destroys flesh, bones of everything thrown in.

Interestingly, one can understand the verse as pre-1974 commentators understood. Though they all heavily relied on Hadith for understanding of this verse, and knowing that there were literally thousands competing to fabricate Hadith for various reasons we cannot prove whether Muhammad and his believing friends too understood that way. In fact, since we know that Muhammad and his friends had no clue about the mathematical structure of the Quran but had acknowledged its promise of QURANIC MIRACLES being manifested in the future (10:20; 25:4-6; 29:50-51; 41:53), it is highly conceivable that they understood the fact that these verses were about the importance of the number 19 and that their meaning would be fulfilled in the future. I further assert that Muhammad and those who dedicated their religion to God alone by upholding the Quran as the sole authority in their religion, stopped speculating on these verses as soon as they received the divine instruction in 75:16-19. As we know, after Muslims started following the fabricated Hadiths, Sunna, and man-made teachings of various sects (6:112-145; 6:159; 7:29; 9:31; 16:52; 18:57; 39:2,11;14; 39:29-37; 39:43-45; 40:14,65; 42:21; 98:5), they lost their capacity for understanding of the Quran (6:23-25; 17:46)[189]

However, it is important to remember that the verses 74:26-37 contain many words that can be understood both a description of Hell and a description of a great miracle, though the later is a much better fit. This linguistically marvelous aspect is well appreciated by those who witness the mathematical miracle and understand the original language of the Quran.

Does "Lawaha" In 74:29 Mean Scorching/Burning OR Obvious/Visible?

The derivatives of the word LWH are used in the Quran to mean a surface used for recording information, board, and flat wood; and nowhere is it used to mean scorch or burn. Before the fulfillment of the prophecy, translators and commentators of the Quran had difficulty in understanding the simple meaning of this word and thus, they resorted to external sources and often odd meanings, such as scorch, or burn. In fact, the drive to justify a particular meaning for some "difficult" Quranic words is one of the many reasons for fabricating Hadith.[190]

441

Verse 74:29 is very interesting and crucial in understanding the rest of the chapter. Though it consists of only 2 words, this verse is translated in several different ways. Here are some examples from English Translations:

Yusuf Ali: "darkening and changing the color of man"
Marmaduke Pickthall: "It shrivelleth the man"
T.B. Irving: "as it shrivels human (flesh)."
M. H. Shakir: "It scorches the mortal."
MaulaHUM Muhammad Ali: "It scorches the mortal"
N. J. Dawood: "it burns the skins of men."
Muhammad Asad: "making (all truth) visible to mortal man."

Rashad Khalifa: "obvious to all the people."

Those who do not know Arabic might think that the words are really difficult to understand and translate. In fact, the meaning of these two words, LaWwaHa and BaSHaR is very clear in the Quranic context. The word LaWwaHa, which comes from the root LWH, is the sister of the word LaWH (85:22) and its plural aLWaH. The plural form aLWaH is used in verses 7:145, 150, 154 for the "tablets" given to Moses, and in verse 54:13 for broad planks used by Noah to build his ark. The medieval commentators, not knowing the mathematical implication of the verses, mostly chose an unusual meaning for the word: scorching, burning, shriveling, etc. Ironically, most of them did acknowledge the obvious meaning of the word as "open board, tablet" (See Baydawi, Fakhruddin Er-Razi, etc.) Few preferred the "obvious" to the obscure. For instance, Muhammad Asad, who had no idea of the mathematical code, preferred the most obvious meaning. Rashad Khalifa who fulfilled the prophecy and discovered the implication of the entire chapter reflected the same obvious meaning. That "obvious" meaning, however, was obscured by the smoke of "scorching fire" burning in the imaginations of generations before him.

In 7:145; 7:150; 7:154, the word alwah, the plural of lawha is used to depict the tablets on which the Ten Commandments were inscribed. In 54:13 it is used to describe the structure of the Noah's ship that made of wood panes. In 85:22 the same word is used for the mathematically protected record of the original version of the Quran. As for the lawaha of 74:29, it is the amplified noun-adjective derived from the root of verb LWH, meaning open tablets, succeeding screens, obvious, manifesto, or clearly and perpetually visible.

Ironically, the Quran uses different words to describe burning or scorching. For instance, for burning the derivatives of *haraqa* (2:266; 3:181; 7:5; 20:97; 21:68; 22:9; 22:22; 29:24; 75:10), or for scorching the derivatives of *salaya* (4:10; 4:30; 4:56; 4:115; 14:29; 17:18; 19:70; 27:7; 28:29; 29:31; 36:64; 38:56; 38:59; 38:163; 52:16; 56:94; 58:8; 69:31; 74: 26; 82:15; 83:16; 84:12; 87:12; 88:12; 92:15), or *nadaja* are used (4:56).

Again, we should note that the understanding of pre-1974 commentators was not without basis. Though their understanding did not rely on the Quranic usage of the words, and created some problems (such as explaining the verse 74:31), they had some justifiable excuses to understand the way they understood. The word *lawaha* also meant burn and *bashara* was another word for skin in Arabic language. As I mentioned above, the multiple meaning of these verses allowed the impatient pre-1974 generations to have an understanding, though a temporary and not primarily intended one. In fact, it was better for them to have patient and not rush to speculate on these verses without knowledge (20:114; 75:16-19). It was the computer generation destined to understand their real meaning (10:37-46).

Does "Bashar" in 74:29 Mean Skin OR Human?

The translation of the second word, BaSHaR is also among the distorted one. Many old commentaries translated it as "skin" rather then "human being" or "people" or "humans." For instance, N. J. Dawood parrots such a translation. The meaning of BaSHaR is also obvious in the context of the Quran. The word BASHAR occurs in the Quran 36 times. It is also mentioned as BASHARAYN (two bashars). If we exclude the BASHAR of 74:29 for the sake of the argument, we see that the word BASHAR is used to mean human beings in all 36 verses: 3:47; 3:79; 5:18; 6:91; 11:27; 12:31; 14:10; 14:11; 15:28; 15:33; 16:103; 17:93; 17:94; 18:110; 19:17; 19:20; 19:26; 21:3; 21:34; 23:24; 23:33; 23:34; 25:54; 26:104; 26:186; 30:20; 36:15; 38:71; 41:6; 42:51; 54:24; 64:6; 74:25; 74:29; 74:31; 74:36.

Then, why those who have allergy against the code 19 still insist to translate the word BaSHaR as skin while in its all 36 occurrences the word BaSHaR there is not a single instance where the word BaSHaR is used to mean skin; but always used to mean human beings? Especially, despite the fact that the word BASHAR occurs thrice in the same Chapter: after 74:29, in 74:31 and 74:36, and the fact that the verse 74:36 witnesses for the 36th times for "human beings," and that they were obliged to translate the last two occurrences as "human beings," how could they still insist on translating the BaSHaR of 74:29 as "skin." Since the prophetic verses did not make any sense for them before its fulfillment in 1974, translators and commentators of the Quran had an excuse to translate it differently before the fulfillment of the prophecy. However, after learning the discovery, none has an excuse to still continue parroting the overly stretched meaning.

Furthermore, the Quran uses "GeLD" for skin. This organic wrap that protects our body and provides tactile sense is referred in 13 verses with GLD and its derivatives: 4:56; 4:56; 16:80; 22:20; 24:2; 24:2; 24:4; 24:4; 39:23; 39:23; 41:20; 41:21; 41:22.

In short, while the Quran consistently uses GLD and its derivatives for skin and related words and while it consistently uses BShR for human beings, a convincing reason must be provided for ignoring all these examples and translating the BShR of 74:39 as "skin." The pre-1974 generations can be excused for trying to understand these verses even if it meant accepting some uncommon usages or dialects. As for post-1974 generation, if they are still stuck with hell and fire, then they share the same disease with the disbelievers of the past (2:75; 4:46; 5:13; 5:41).

After the fulfillment of the prophecy and divine clarification of its context, it is distortion to render this two-word verse 74:29 as "shrivels/scorches the skin" or "shrivels/scorches the man" rather than "it is clearly visible for human beings" or "it is a manifesto/successive-screens for human beings." However, the repetitive stretch and distortion committed by the post-1974 translators/commentaries on the many verses of Chapter 74 is bizarre and extraordinary. This pattern is prophetically described by verses 2:18; 3:7; 11:28; 41:44; 17:72; 25:73; 27:81.

Does The Pronoun "Hiya" (She) in the End of 74:31 Refer to the Hell OR to the Number 19?

We know that verse 74:30 does not qualify the reference of 19. It pulls our attention to a NUMBER ALONE. The verse does not say "on it nineteen angles" or "on it nineteen guards" or "on it nineteen this or that." The verse says "on it nineteen." Period. Verse 74:31, after informing us that the number of guardians of hell is 19, isolates this number from hell again describes its role.

Yet, those whose minds stuck in Hell cannot even notice this evident emphasis to the number. Thus, they violate the general grammar rules and universal linguistic logic and identify the reference of HIYA (SHE) in the end of 74:31 as HELL FIRE.

According to the grammar rules and common linguistic logic, the reference of a pronoun should be sought in proximity first. Sure, if there is no compelling empirical or rational reason for skipping a closer noun. For instance, "Yesterday, at Mary's home I saw Lisa. She was very thoughtful." In this sentence grammar and logic leads us to think that the thoughtful person was Lisa not Mary. But, "Yesterday, in Delhi's streets on the back of an elephant I saw Lisa. She was swinging her trunk/hose left and right and walking majestically." (I had given the original example in Turkish and in Turkish the same word is used for both elephant's trunk and hose. For didactic purposes please assume that it is the same in English.) Though grammatically the best candidate for reference of SHE is Lisa, we have an empirical reason to ignore the general rule since the one who would swing her trunk/hose is the elephant. But if these sentences are in a story and if we are told that Lisa was walking in the street with a hose in her hand, then the SHE in the sentence may equally refer to elephant OR Lisa. There will be ambiguity and if it is intentionally done then we wonder the purpose of the ambiguity. But, if the sentences continue, "When she hit the trunk/hose in her hand to a store sign...," then we become sure that it was a hose not trunk. "Your mother had given you a walnut and a book. Have you eat and finished it?" A sound mind can easily deduce that that "it" refers not to the book, but to the walnut. But, if the question were "Your mother had given you a walnut and a book. Have you finished it?" then, an ambiguity will arise. However, if the context of the question is known then we can deduce whether the query is about finishing the book or the walnut or both.

The pronoun HIYA (SHE), based on the rules of grammar, the emphasis of the verse in its context, and based on the rhetorical superiority of its meaning, must be referred to the grammatically feminine closest noun IDDATAHUM (their number, that is Nineteen). How can we explain the act of skipping IDDATAHUM (their number, Nineteen) by ignoring the grammar, context, emphasis, and rhetoric, and insisting to reach the FIRE?

We will see in the miraculously elegant and prophetic expression of the Quran that hypocrites and unappreciative people have deserved the SaQaR penalty both in this world and hereafter. In this world as the 19-based mathematical code of the Quran; they will be intellectually tormented by its powerful evidences. And in the hereafter as the 19 guards of symbolic hell-fire; they will be convicted to eternally face the number 19 in the presence of guarding angles.[191]

Does The "Zikra" (Reminder) In 74:31 Refer To Hell OR The Evidence?

This brings us to the last phrase of verse 74:31 "it/this is a warning/reminder for mankind." Old commentaries and their parroting contemporaries refer "it/this" to the FIRE or HELL.

Those who have difficulty in accepting the possibility of an intellectual argument in The Hidden One (Muddathir), insert a HELL in the translation or the understanding of the last phrase of 74:31:

> "This (HELL) is a warning for people."

This way, they transform the ZiKRa to a warning to be scared, to a penalty to avoid. However, all the derivatives of ZKR, including ZiKRa, are used in the Quran 273 times; and if we include DKR which is mentioned 7 times; this word is mentioned 280 times in the Quran and NOWHERE is it used to describe HELL or FIRE. You may check for yourself all the 21 verses where the word ZiKRa is mentioned: 6:68; 6:69; 6090; 7:2; 11:114; 11:120; 21:84; 26:209;

445

29:51; 38:43; 38:46; 39:21; 40:54; 44:13; 50:8; 50:37; 51:55; 74:31; 80:4; 87:9; 89:23. You may also check the two verses where the word is suffixed with pronouns ZiKRaha and ZiKRahum: 47:18; 79:43.

More interestingly, however, you will find another derivative of the same word "ZiKRa" (reminder) is used in verse 74:49 as "taZKiRa."

"Why do they turn away from this message/reminder (taZKiRa)?"

The disbelievers had ignored the reminder! Obviously, hell cannot be that reminder, since you are not supposed to embrace and face hell while you are alive on this earth. You are expected to turn away from Hell and turn to the message (taZKiRa). Therefore, taZKiRa and ZiKRa cannot be both HELL and the MESSAGE of the Quran. All the derivatives of ZKR are consistently used in the Quran for the divine message that revives and bestows eternal happiness.

Because of the self-ignited and self-inflicted hell fire burning in their minds, the disbelievers and hypocrites ignore the PLEASANT meaning associated to the word 280 times, and fight with us to keep it as HELL. Well, this was exactly what they were promised and what they deserve. Their initial decision, their prejudice, ignorance and arrogance, have led them to bet their faith on hell, a questionable one chance against 280 chances!

How does the Number Nineteen Increase the Faith of Believers and also Remove Doubts From the Minds of People of the Book as Promised in 74:31?

With the exception of Rashad Khalifa, all the translations and commentaries listed above have had big problem with this question. Since they did not accept it as a prophecy left to be fulfilled in the future, and since they rushed to speculate on them without knowledge, they dug a hole for themselves. Surely, they always could deceive themselves and others by claiming that THEIR FAITH was increased because of the association of the number 19 with the guardians of hell. This claim obviously would be a non-falsifiable claim. One can say anything about his or her own faith. However, this claim could not explain why specifically 19 and not another number or another thing. Let's assume they could pretend that their faith was really increased by the nineteen guardians of hell, but how could they explain the other functions of the number nineteen? How could this number nineteen remove the doubts of people of the book? The proponents of HELL-19 just could not make up an answer for this, since the issue involved an OBJECTIVE fact, not a subjective claim.

Interestingly, those who saw the Hell-fire in these prophetic verses claimed that the people of the book would believe in the Quran because they would see that the number of guardians of hell was also nineteen in their own books! What?

446

Please read it again. Yes, this is the explanation of all the prominent Sunni and Shiite scholars of the past and unfortunately it is exactly parroted by the contemporary ones!

First, there is no such a statement in the Bible. Second, even if there was such a statement there would not be anything special about nineteen, since there are many principles, stories of prophets, and instructions mentioned in the Quran that are also in the Bible. In fact, the very existence of similarity had an opposite effect on many people of the book; they claimed and still claim that the Quran was plagiarized from the Bible. Third, none has been persuaded regarding the authenticity of the Quran because the number of guardians of hell is nineteen! I personally communicated and met dozens of Christians or Jews whose doubts about the authenticity of the Quran was removed because of their witnessing the mathematical miracle of the Quran based on the number nineteen. You can find some of these people on Internet forums. This is happening despite the aggressive misinformation and disinformation campaign carried out by numerous Sunni and Shiite groups. Compare the prophetic role of MIRACLE-19 to the role of HELL-19 in their powers of removing doubts from the minds of People of the Book. Two DECADES versus more than 14 CENTURIES, and several THOUSAND people versus more than a BILLION people.

The HELL-19 advocates cannot show a single Christian or Jew who converted to their version of Islam because their doubts were removed after they noticed that the number of guardians of hell is also 19 in their books! This failure alone should be sufficient to wake up those who are still eager to see Hell in these verses. Yet, they still shamelessly repeat this lie to defend their hellish version.

Some opponents of the CODE-19 even tried to use a phrase in verse 74:31 against understanding of the very verse. They quote the fifth function of the number nineteen, "to expose those who have disease in their hearts, and the disbelievers; they will say, 'What did God mean by this allegory?'" and then charge us: "You 19ers are asking this question; therefore, you have disease in your hearts." First, none of us have asked this question, including Rashad Khalifa. We happened to learn the meaning of number nineteen even before asking such a question. We know the meaning of this allegory and we do not challenge that meaning. Furthermore, this question is not a question of a curious person who sincerely wants to learn the meaning of the Quran. This question is the challenge of arrogance and ignorance. It is a question that many still millions of Sunni and Shiite people are asking themselves. They will keep asking this question as long as they follow their ancestors blindly and worship Prophet Muhammad and religious scholars.

Does the "Ha" In 74:35 Refer to Hell OR the Number 19? Does the Word "Kubra" in the Same Verse Refer to "Great Disasters and Calamities" OR to "Great Signs and Miracles"?

447

When we reflect on the context and the usage of the words of verse "This is one of the greatest" we can easily deduce that this refers to the number 19 and its prophetic function as a conclusive evidence for the authenticity of the Quran and a great test for people. Unfortunately, many of those who did not witness the incredible mathematical structure based on the number 19, related this verse to Hell, again.

Let's one by one see several different translations of this verse. (Again, the pre-1974 translations have an excuse in their mistranslations since they did not witness the fulfillment of the prophecy of the mathematical miracle):

> **Yusuf Ali**: "this is but one of the mighty (portents)"
> **Marmaduke Pickthall**: "Lo! This is one of the greatest (portents)"
> **T.B. Irving**: "Surely it is one of the gravest (misfortunes)."
> **M.H. Shakir**: "Surely it (hell) is one of the gravest (misfortunes)."
> **MaulaHUM Muhammad Ali**: "Surely it is one of the gravest (misfortunes)"
> **N. J. Dawood**: "it is a dire scourge."
> **Muhammad Asad**: "Verily, that [hell-fire) is Indeed one of the great [forewarnings]"
> **Rashad Khalifa**: "This is one of the greatest miracles."

I leave for you to assess the contextual reference of the pronoun in 74:35. Here, I will draw your attention to the descriptive word KuBeR, which is the plural of KaBeeR derived from KBR (great). The derivatives of KBR are used in the Quran to describe positive or negative events, people, or things. For instance, in verses 20:23; 44:16; 53:18; 79:20 it is used to describe God's ayaats or miracles. The derivatives of the same word are used for disaster in 79:34 and hell in 87:12.

In other words, if we do not consider the context of the group of verses, we may understand the reference of THIS IS ONE OF THE GREATEST as either HELL FIRE or one of God's greatest MIRACLES. Through this verse alone, one may see flames of fire or signs of a miracle. Nevertheless, considering the context of this verse it becomes clear that the first vision is a man-made hallucination and the later a divine gift.

Does the Word Nazer in 74:36 Refer to the Hell Fire OR to the Devine Evidences?

NAZER is an adjective derived from the root NZR and means "WARNER"
Throughout the Quran the various derivatives of this word occur 130 times.
Here are the verse numbers where the form NaZeR (warner) occurs 44 times:

2:119; 5:19; 5:19; 7:184; 7:188; 11:2; 11:12; 11:25; 15:89; 17:105; 25:1; 25:7; 25:51; 25:56; 26:115; 28:46; 29:50; 32:3; 33:45; 34:28; 34:34; 34:44; 34:46; 35:23; 35:24; 35:24; 35:37; 35:42; 35:42; 38:70; 41:4; 43:23; 46:9; 48:8; 51:50; 51:51; 53:56; 67:8; 67:9; 67:17; 67:26; 71:2; 74:36.

In NONE of these verses the word NaZeR is used for HELL or FIRE. In these verses NaZeR describe God's messengers, books, revelation, and signs.

Then Why Those Who Claim to be Muslims do not Understand or Appreciate the Prophetic Fulfillment of These Ayaat (Revelations/ Signs/ Miracles)? Why They See and Work Hard to See Hell-Fire, Instead of the Precise and Universal Great Miracle?

Surely, previous generations who were not aware the discovery of Code 19 via computer had an excuse to twist the meaning of obvious verses in order to make sense out of them. They could not imagine that the 19 was the code of an elaborate mathematical system. Nevertheless, some early commentators of the Quran who did not limit the understanding of the Quran with Hadith and Sunna sensed something beyond HELL from these verses and discussed them as alternative understanding. For instance, Fakhruddin er-Razi in his famous Tafsir al Kabir, in his 23rd comment on Bismillah, speculates on the 19 letters of Bismillah and lists numerous implications, such as the difference between the number of 5 prayers and the number of hours in a day; the number of physical, intellectual, and emotional faculties that humans are blessed with, etc. Among the modern commentators who lived before 1974, Muhammad Asad is the only one that subscribes to Razi's interpretation of the number nineteen of 74:30.[192] However, Asad too could not avoid but see Hell everywhere.

The opponents of the miracle 19 are no different than those who rejected the entire Quran in the past. The description of these verses fits both groups, which is another miraculous aspect of the Quran:

> 74:21 He looked.
> 74:22 He frowned and scowled.
> 74:23 Then he turned away arrogantly.
> 74:24 He said, "This is but an impressive illusion/magic!" [193]
> 74:25 "This is human made."

In conclusion, those who reject to witness the miracle 19 are insulting the wisdom of God. According to them God's only answer to someone who challenges the authenticity of the Quran is: "Get lost! I will burn you in the hellfire." Depicting God as someone who cannot engage in an intellectual argument with His opponent, but can only employ the cheapest method of persuasion (threat) cannot be the path of believers who are warned by the incredible prophecies of this wonderful chapter, The Secret.

Turning back to the question: Then why those who claim to be Muslims do not understand or appreciate the prophetic fulfillment of these ayaat (revelations/signs/miracles)? Why they see and work hard to see hell-fire, instead of the precise and universal great miracle?

The Quran provides prophetic answers to this question in numerous verses. Please read and reflect on them:

29:1   A1L30M40

29:2   Did the people think that they will be left to say, "We acknowledge" without being put to the test?

29:3   While We had tested those before them, so that **God** would know those who are truthful and so that He would know the liars.

29:4   Or did those who sinned think that they would be ahead of Us? Miserable indeed is their judgment!

2:17   Their example is like one who lights a fire, so when it illuminates what is around him, **God** takes away his light and leaves him in the darkness not seeing.

2:18   Deaf, dumb, and blind, they will not revert.

7:146   I will divert from My signs those who are arrogant on earth unjustly, and if they see every sign they do not acknowledge it, and if they see the path of guidance they do not take it as a path; and if they see the path of straying, they take it as a path. That is because they have denied Our signs and were heedless of them.[194]

29:54   They hasten you for the retribution; while hell surrounds the ingrates. (Please read from 29:48)

3:7   He is the One who sent down to you the book, from which there are definite signs; they are the essence of the book; and others, which are multiple-meaning. As for those who have disease in their hearts, eager to cause confusion and eager to derive their interpretation, they will follow what is multiple-meaning from it. But none knows their meaning except God and those who are well founded in knowledge; they say, "We acknowledge it, all is from our Lord." None will remember except the people of intellect.[195]

25:73   Those who when they are reminded of their Lord's signs, they do not fall on them deaf and blind.

6:158   Do they wait until the controllers will come to them, or your Lord comes, or some signs from your Lord? The day some signs come from your Lord, it will do no good for any person to acknowledge if s/he did not acknowledge before, or s/he gained good through his/her acknowledgement. Say, "Wait, for we too are waiting."

6:25   Among them are those who listen to you; and We have made covers over their hearts to prevent them from understanding it, and deafness in their ears; and if they see every sign they will not acknowledge; even when they come to you they argue, those who reject say, "This is nothing but the tales from the past!"

6:26 They are deterring others from it, and keeping away themselves; but they will only destroy themselves, yet they do not notice.

27:84 Until they have come, He will say, "Have you denied My signs while you had no explicit knowledge of them? What were you doing?"

78:27 They did not expect a reckoning/computation.

78:28 They denied Our signs greatly.

78:29 Everything We have counted in a record.

74:56 None will take heed except if **God** wills. He is the source of righteousness and the source of forgiveness.

A8
Controversies over 9:128-129

Aisha Y. Musa, PhD

The history of the text the Qur'an shows that verses found at the end of Surat al-Tawba (9:128-129) are distinguished from other verses in the Qur'an by the number and variety of conflicting reports regarding their collection and placement in the text.

These reports are related by such well-respected and widely accepted scholars as al-Bukhari and Jalal al-Din alSuyuti, among others. The verses are unique in two important respects. These are classical orthodox Muslim sources, not the works of heterodox, or heretical sects.

Abu Abdullah Muhammad al-Bukhari (d. 256 AH/870 CE) is famous as a collector of Hadiths, or traditions of Muhammad. His most famous work al-Jami' al-Sahih is considered by the majority of traditional Muslims to be the most authentic collection of prophetic Hadiths, and the most important book after the Qur'an.

Jalal al-Din al-Suyuti (d. 1509 CE) was renown as a scholar in a variety of disciplines who wrote many important works. The one which concerns us here is his, al-Itqan fi `Ulumil-Qur'an, one the most extensive works ever written on the various fields of Qur'anic Studies.

Here, we will examine the various reports found in these and other works, related to 9:128-129, and bring out some of the questions these reports raise about the collection of the text and the criteria used to include, or exclude verses. We will consider some of the answers suggested by traditional scholarship, as well as what remains to be addressed and answered.

We will see that the verses are unique in two important respects. First, it is generally agreed upon by Muslims that God determined the arrangement of the Qur'an's verses (al-Suyuti vol. 1, 60). But we will see that several reports indicate the placement of 9:128-129 in the written text was decided by others after Muhammad's death. Second, although other verses required a minimum of two witnesses to be accepted and written in the text, 9:128-129 was reportedly found with only one man.

Accounts differ as to exactly who that man was, and as to the circumstances under which the verses were placed in the Qur'an. But each account shows just one man reporting them.

Two men whose names figure prominently in the reports we will examine are Zaid ibn Thabit and Ubayy ibn Ka'ab. Both of these men were from Medina, and were Muhammad's chief secretaries. They were primarily responsible for writing down the verses of the Qur'an as they were revealed. In his History, al-Tabari reports that Ubayy was the first to write for Muhammad in Medina (vol. 9, 147). Various sources indicate that Zaid ibn Thabit was quite young at the time of the Hijra--Muhammad's emigration from Mecca to Medina in 622 CE— being only about 11. Despite his youth, Zaid's intelligence and language abilities gained him a position as one of Muhammad's most important secretaries. It was Zaid who was given the primary responsibility for collecting and organising the text of the Qur'an after Muhammad's death (EI 1, viii, 1194b-1195a).

The first indication of the uniqueness of 9:128-129 appears in the story related by al-Bukhari about the collection of the Qur'an during the Caliphate of Abu Bakr. After describing how Abu Bakr and 'Umar convinced him to collect the Qur'an, Zaid ibn Thabit says:

> So I pursued collecting the Qur'an from bare palm branches, thin, flat, white stones, and the hearts of men until I found the end of Surat al-Tawba with Abu Khuzaima al-Ansari. I did not find it with anyone other than him: Indeed a messenger has come to you from among yourselves. Your suffering is hard on him... to the conclusion of Bara'a (al-Bukhari, Matn vol. 3, 225).

Three versions of this account are found in al-Bukhari,in his section on the collection of the Qur'an (cited above), in his section on the scribe of the messenger, and in his section on the explanation of *Surat Bara'a [al-Tawba]*. Some versions say the verses were found with Khuzaima al-Ansari rather than Abu Khuzaima (al-Bukhari, *Matn; vol. 3, 140, 226*). Every history of the collection of the Qur'an quotes some version of it, making it perhaps the most repeated story on the subject.

One other verse, 33:21, is the subject of a similar report mentioning Khuzaima al-Ansari. Two versions are included by alBukhari, in the discussion of the collection of the Qur'an under 'Uthman, and in the section on the explanation of Sura 33 (*al-Azhab*). The second of these quotes Zaid ibn Thabit as saying:

> When we copied the pages into volumes, I failed to find a verse from Sura al-Azhab, that I used to hear God's messenger, peace and blessings be upon him, reciting. I did not find it with anyone except Khuzaima al-Ansari, whose testimony God's messenger, peace and blessings be upon him, had made as the testimony of two men... (al- Bukhari, Matn vol. 3, 175).

This account differs significantly from the account about 9:128-129 in that here Zaid says that he used to hear the messenger recite the verse in question. But when in the report regarding the end of *Surat al-Tawba*, he says he found it with no one else.

The story about the verse in *Surat al-Ahzab* is the only account in al-Bukhari that accords special status to Khuzaima's testimony. But this is odd, because Zaid himself says he heard the verse from Muhammad, making him a second witness. A similar account, in the section on the collection of the Qur'an, does not mention such special status. Nor is it mentioned in any of the accounts al-Bukhari relates from Zaid about 9:128-129. It has however, on the strength of Zaid's word in this single report, served to support the inclusion of these two verses in the Qur'an.

Although it is not found in the editions of al-Bukhari consulted here, in *al-Burhan fi 'Ulum al-Qur'an*, al-Zarkashi quotes a variant account of the collection under Abu Bakr, citing al-Bukhari as his source, which says: with Abu Khuzaima alAnsari whose testimony the prophet, peace and blessings be upon him, had made as the testimony of two men (al-Zarkashi vol. 1, 234).

In the *Itqan*, al-Suyuti quotes the collection account from al-Bukhari as it appears in the edition cited here. But in his discussion of the number of witnesses he quotes from Ibn Ashta's *Kitab al-Masahif*:

> The people would come to Zaid ibn Thabit and he would only write a verse
> from two upright witnesses. Even though the end of Surat al-Bara'a was not
> found except with Khuzaima ibn Thabit, he said: Write it, for God's messenger,
> peace and blessings be upon him, made his testimony as the testimony of two
> men. So it was written, even though 'Umar brought the verse of stoning and it
> was not written because he was alone (Ibn Ashta in al-Suyuti vol. 1,58).

Special status allegedly accorded to Khuzaima's (or Abu Khuzaima's) testimony by the Prophet is one way in which the discrepancy in the number witnesses has been addressed. Another argument mentioned by al-Suyuti is that two witnesses meant one written and one remembered. He mentions two views of this argument. One is that writing without memory was not sufficient and the other that memory without writing was not sufficient. So, when Zaid ibn Thabit said, I did not find it with anyone other than him, it meant he did not find it in writing with anyone else (al-Suyuti; vol. 1, 58).

This argument implies that it was memorized by others. But if this was the case, and if memory and writing constituted the two required witnesses, why was there concern that Khuzaima was the only witness? We will see that this discussion of what constituted "two witnesses" takes on added significance in light of other accounts related to 9:128-129.

So far, we have considered only the accounts reported in alBukhari. But what of the series of reports that mention others as the sole witness, reporting these verses under other circumstances? In the reports of Zaid ibn Thabit only Khuzaima or Abu Khuzaima is associated with 9:128-129. But a number of accounts in al-Suyuti and other sources offer quite a different story about these verses and their placement in the text.

By far, the greatest number of varying accounts is found in Kitab al-Masahif by Ibn Abu Dawud al-Sijistani (d. 316 AH), son of the famous Hadith collector Abu Dawud, whose Sunan is one of the six canonical collections of Hadith accepted by the vast majority of traditional Muslims. This important work was discovered and edited by Arthur Jeffery in the first half of this century. His main interest was in Ibn Abu Dawud's detailed listing of a number of variant Qur'an codices, rather than the diverse assortment of traditions regarding the collection of the text.

In addition to sections on the collection's of Abu Bakr and `Uthman, Ibn Abu Dawud also includes a section about a collection done by `Umar ibn al-Khattab and a section devoted specifically to reports about verses 9:128-129. Along with several variants of the accounts recorded in alBukhari Ibn Abu Dawud includes quite a different story:

> On the authority of Ubayy ibn Ka`ab, they were collecting the Qur'an from the volume of Ubayy. Men were writing, while Ubayy ibn Ka`ab was dictating to them. When they reached the end of the verse in surat Bara'a {S. 9 V. 127}: Thus, God has diverted their hearts, for they are people who do not comprehend, they asserted that this verse was the last of what God, the Exalted, revealed of the Qur'an. Then, Ubayy said, "God's messenger, peace and blessings be upon him, had me recite two verses after this: Indeed, a messenger has come to you from among yourselves. Your suffering is hard on him. He is anxious over you, compassionate and merciful to the believers...", to the end of the sura. He said, "So this is the last of what was revealed of the Qur'an" (Ibn Abu Dawud vol.2, 30).

The above is from the section on verses 9:128-129. The same story is included in the section on the collection of Abu Bakr, where it says that this occurred at that time (vol. 1, 9). This story raises some important issues. First, it mentions neither Zaid, nor Khuzaima. Instead, we see Ubayy ibn Ka`ab as the only person who knew the verses in question. The others believed that 9:127 was the end of the sura and of the revelation. It also says that Ubayy was dictating to them from his volume (mashaf). This indicates that Ubayy not only knew the verses, but had them in writing. If Ubayy knew them and had them in his mashaf, how could Zaid find them with only Khuzaima (or Abu Khuzaima)?

It is important to remember that Zaid and Ubayy were Muhammad's chief secretaries and close companions. They were primarily responsible for recording the verses of the Qur'an, as they were revealed. It is unreasonable to think that one of them did not know what the other had recorded.

It could be argued that the dictation mentioned took place based on what Zaid had already collected. But if that was the case, Zaid would have already established the authenticity and placement 9:128-129. Why then, would the writers who were taking dictation think that 9:127 was the end of the revelation?

Further, Ubayy says they were the last of what was revealed. This would mean that they were revealed in Medina. But the traditionally accepted view is that they were revealed in Mecca. Al-Suyuti quotes the same story, claiming Ibn Abu Dawud as his source, with slight, but significant variations:

> On the authority of Ubayy ibn Ka`ab, they were collecting the Qur'an and when they reached the end of the verse in surat Bara'a: Thus, God has diverted their hearts, for they are people who do not comprehend, they thought that this was the last of what had been revealed. Then, Ubayy said, "God's messenger, peace and blessings be upon him, had me recite two verses after this: Indeed, a messenger has come to you from among yourselves..."to the end of the sura, (and he said) "Meccan." (al-Suyuti vol. 1, 61).

In Ibn Abu Dawud's account, both in the section on Abu Bakr's collection, and in the section on 9:128-129, there is no mention of Ubayy saying, "Meccan." The issue of when the verses were revealed is important. If they had been revealed in Mecca, can it be reasonably argued that they were known by only one man—whether Khuzaima or Ubayy—from Medina? Would they not have been memorised, if not written, by some of the Muslims who had migrated from Mecca?

Further questions are raised by two other accounts reported by Ibn Abu Dawud. In the beginning of the section on 9:128-129 he cites:

> Ibn Zubair said, "Al-Harith ibn Khuzaima brought two verses from the end of surat Bara'a: Indeed, a messenger has come to you from among yourselves. Your suffering is hard on him. He is anxious over you, compassionate and merciful to the believers, until His saying, the Lord of the glorious throne, to `Umar. So he [`Umar] said, 'Who is with you in this?' He [Al-Harith] said, 'I only know that I bear witness that I heard them from God's messenger, peace and blessings be upon him.' Then, `Umar said, 'And I bear witness that I heard them from God's messenger, peace and blessings be upon him.' Then he said, 'If it was three verses, I would make them a separate sura. Then, they looked for a sura from the Qur'an and attached them to it. Thus, it was attached at the end of Bara'a" (Vol. 2, 30).

This story adds al-Harith ibn Khuzaima and `Umar to the list of those who reportedly knew verses 9:128-129, with `Umar supporting al-Harith's testimony. If `Umar heard them from the messenger, why did Zaid reportedly find them only with Khuzaima (or Abu Khuzaima)? This again, goes back to al-Suyuti's discussion of what constituted "two witnesses."

It also indicates that they used their own reasoning to decide where the verses would go in the text. In his discussion of this report, al-Suyuti says,

> Ibn Hajar says, "This shows that they were putting together the verses of the suras according to their own reasoning [ijtihad], while the rest of the reports indicate that they did not do any of that except according to what was determined by God [tawqif]" (vol. 1, 61).

The final account Ibn Abu Dawud relates regarding 9:128-129 once again credits Khuzaima ibn Thabit with reporting them, but under very different circumstances than the other accounts involving him:

> So, 'Uthman ibn 'Affan stood up and said, 'Whoever has something from the Book of God, let him bring it to us.' And nothing would be accepted until two witnesses testified to it. Then, Khuzaima ibn Thabit came and said, "I see that you left out two verse that you did not write." They said, "What are they?" He said, "I learned from God's messenger, peace and blessings be upon him, {S. 9 V. 128}: Indeed, a messenger has come to you from among yourselves. Your suffering is hard on him. He is anxious over you, compassionate and merciful to the believers...," to the end of the sura. 'Uthman said, "I bear witness that they are from God. So, where do you think you should put them?" He said, "Conclude the last of what was revealed of the Qur'an with them." So Bara'a was concluded with them (vol. 2, 31).

Again, we are faced with several important issues. First, Khuzaima informs 'Uthman that the two verses had been left out of the Qur'an. This is implies that the collecting and writing had already taken place. Why would Khuzaima go to 'Uthman with the verses if Zaid had already collected them from him? Moreover, if Zaid had collected them already, why would 'Uthman ask Khuzaima to decide where they should go in the text?

Second, there is no question here of Khuzaima as the sole witness, nor any mention of his testimony being equal to that of two men. In fact, here 'Uthman serves as the second witness to their authenticity. If 'Uthman knew the verses and could witness their authenticity, how could Zaid have found them only with Khuzaima?

These various reports related to verses 9:128-129 leave us with a number of important unanswered questions. Who knew these verses? Was it Khuzaima, Abu Khuzaima, Harith Ibn Khuzaima, Ubayy ibn Ka'ab? Were they revealed in Mecca, or Medina? When and how where they placed in the text?

One possible response to the reports and the questions they raise is that most are simply not sound and have, therefore, been rejected. Soundness is traditionally determined by scrutinising the chain of transmitters (isnad) of a given report. Regarding this, Jeffery says in his introduction:

> The greatest difficulty has been with the isnads quoted by the author, and although all available controls were applied to them, there may still be some that will not stand the scrutiny of isnad critics. The assistance of Muslim savants in this matter was not very helpful for we could not overcome the principle that every isnad that led to a statement at variance with orthodoxy was ipso facto condemned (viii).

We have seen that al-Suyuti quotes various reports from Ibn Abu Dawud in his discussion of the collection of the Qur'an. While he states that certain reports are weak because of problems with their isnads, he does not do so with respect to the reports dealing with 9:128-129.

These reports and the questions they raised take on added importance in light of another report related by al-Suyuti in the *Itqan:*

> On the authority of Muhammad ibn Sirin, on the authority of `Ikrima, who said, "After Abu Bakr's inauguration, `Ali ibn Abu Talib stayed in his house. So it was said to Abu Bakr, 'He is averse to swearing allegiance to you.' Then Abu Bakr sent for him and said, 'Are you averse to swearing allegiance to me?' He said, 'No. By God.' He [Abu Bakr] said, 'What makes you upset with me?' He said, 'I think something has been added to the Book of God. So I said to myself that I will not put on my street clothes except for the Friday prayer until it has been resolved.'" (Vol. 1, 57-58).

`Ali does not specify what he thinks was added, but this is a very serious charge. Although many of the Qur'an's verses are the subject of various, often conflicting reports about their meaning, interpretation, or circumstances revelation, no other verses in the Qur'an are the subject of so many diverse reports regarding their collection and placement in the text. Could they be what had made `Ali so upset that he would not leave his house except for prayer?

BIBLIOGRAPHY

Ahmad ibn Hanbal. *Musnad.* vol. 5. Cairo: 1313/1896.

al-Bukhari, Abu `Abdullah Muhammad b. Isma`il. *Matnal-Bukhari.* vol. 3 -4. N.P.: `Isa al-Halabi and Company. 1981

Sahih al-Bukhari. trans. Dr. Musin Khan. vol. 6. Medina: Islamic University. 1981

Ibn Abu Dawud. *Kitab al-Masahif.* ed. Arthur Jeffery. Leiden: E.J. Brill, 1937.

Jeffery, Arthur. *Materials for the History of the Text of the Qur'an: The Old Codices.* Leiden: E.J. Brill, 1937.

The Qur'an as Scripture. New York: Russel F. Moore Company, Inc., 1952.

Two Muqaddimas to the Qur'anic Sciences: The Muqaddima to the 'Kitab al-Mabani' and the Muqaddima of Ibn `Atiyya to his Tafsir. Cairo: The Brothers al-Khanaji, 1954.

Nolin, Kenneth E. The *'Itqan' and Its Sources: A Study of 'alItqan fi `Ulum al-Qur'an' by Jalal al- Din al-Suyuti with reference to 'al-Burhan fi `Ulum al-Qur'an' by Badr al-Din al-Zarkashi.* Ann Arbor: University Microfilm International, Dissertation Services, 1968.

al-Said, Labib. *The Recited Koran: A History of the First Recorded Version.* trans. Bernard Weiss, M.A. Rauf, Monroe Berger. Princeton, N.J.: The Darwin Press, 1975.

al-Saydawi, Yusuf. *Baidat al-Dik: Naqdun li Kitab 'al-Kitab wal-Qur'an'.* NP: ND. Sharur, *Muhammad. al-Kitab wal-Qur'an: Qira'tun Mu`asiratun.* Revised Fifth Edition. Damascus: al-Ahali, 1992.

al-Suyuti, Jalal al-Din. *al-Itqan fi `Ulumil-Qur'an.* Lahore: Suhail Academy, 1980. Von Denffer, Ahmad. *`Ulum al-Qur'an: An Introduction to the Sciences of the Qur'an.* Leicester, U.K.: The Islamic Foundation, 1983.

Watt, W. Montgomery. *Bell's Introduction to the Qur'an.* revised and enlarged. Edinburgh: Edinburgh University Press, 1977.

al-Zarkashi, Badr al-Din Muhammad `Abdullah. *al-Burhan fi `Ulum al-Qur'an.* vol. 1-2. N.P.: `Isa al-Halabi and Company. 1957.

A9
Theometer or Sectometer

(First conducted on the participants of my lectures at Oxford University in November 3-5, 2008)

Edip Yuksel

Name: _____

Email Address: _____

Phone: _____ Age: _____

Occupation: _____

Nationality: _____

Have you read the Manifesto for Islamic Reform? _____

Favorite Books/Authors: _____

Your Sect: (a) Sunni (b) Shiite (c) Salafi (d) Other (d) No sect

Please put a CIRCLE around the letter of your choice:

1. According to the Quran, which one of these is not and cannot be idolized by people?
- a. Prophet Muhammad
- b. Desires or Wishful thinking (Hawa)
- c. Crowds or peers
- d. Ancestors or children
- e. Reasoning (Aql)

2. Which one of these is a true statement?
- a. The Quran is not sufficient to guide us; in addition we need Hadith and Sunna.
- b. The Quran is not sufficient to guide us; we need Hadith, Sunna and follow the teaching of a Sunni sect.
- c. The Quran is not sufficient to guide us; we need Hadith, Sunna and follow the teaching of a Shiite sect.
- d. The Quran is not sufficient to guide us; we need Hadith, Sunna, follow the teaching of a sect and join a religious order.
- e. The Quran is sufficient to guide us when we understand and follow it through the light of reason.

3. Which one of these Hadiths narrated by Bukhari, Muslim and other "authentic" Hadith books, do you think are fabricated:
- a. Muhammad was illiterate until he died.
- b. Muhammad married Aisha at age 54 while she was only 9 or 13 years-old.
- c. Muhammad dispatched a gang of fighters (sariyya) to kill a woman poet secretly during night in her home, for criticizing him publicly through her poems.
- d. Muhammad slaughtered 400 to 900 Jews belonging to Ben Qurayza for violating the treaty.
- e. All of the above.

4. Which one of these laws or rules does not exist in the Quran?
- a. Stone the married adulterers to death
- b. Do not play guitar
- c. Men should not wear silk and gold
- d. Men are superior to women
- e. All of the above

5. The Quran instructs us to follow the messengers. Following the messenger means:
- a. Follow Hadith and Sunna; Bukhari, Muslim, Ibn Hanbal, etc.
- b. Follow his Ahl-al-Bayt.
- c. Follow Hadith, Sunna, consensus of sahaba, ijtihad of imams and fatwas of ulama.
- d. Follow Muhammad.
- e. Follow the message he was sent with, which was Quran alone.

6. The Quran is God's word, because:
- a. There are verses of the Quran stating that it is God's word.
- b. The Quran is a literary miracle. None can bring a sura like it surpassing its literary qualities.

c. I do not need to have a reason. Reason is not reliable. I have faith in the Quran.
d. The moral teaching of the Quran is the best for individual and humanity.
e. The Quranic signs (aya) do not have internal contradiction nor does it contradict the signs in nature. Besides, it is numerically coded book with an extraordinary mathematical structure integrated with its composition and Arabic language.

7. Which one of the following is correct for Muhammad:
a. Muhammad was the final messenger and prophet.
b. Muhammad had the highest rank above all humans.
c. Muhammad demonstrated many miracles such as splitting the moon, healing the sick, and crippling a child
d. All of the above´
e. Muhammad was a human messenger like other messengers.

8. In what year he Bukhari started collecting Hadith for his Hadith collection known as the Sahih Bukhari, the most trusted Sunni Hadith collection?
a. During the life of Muhammad in Medina
b. Ten years after Muhammad's death.
c. 130 years after Muhammad's death.
d. 200 years after Muhammad's death
e. 230 years after Muhammad's death.

9. According to Bukhari himself, he collected the 7,275 Hadith among the 700,000 Hadiths he collected. If each Hadith, together with its *isnad* (the chain of reporters) and *sanad* (the text that was attributed to Muhammad) took about half a book page, how many volumes of books with 500 pages would they take to record all those 700,000 Hadith allegedly collected by Bukhari?
a. 7 volumes
b. 10 volumes
c. 70 volumes
d. 100 volumes
e. 700 volumes

10. What are the last statements in the Farewell Sermon (Khutba al-Wida) which was reportedly witnessed by more than 100,000 sahaba, making it by far the most authentic Hadith among the thousands of Hadiths?
- I leave you Abu Bakr; you should follow him.
- I leave you my sahaba; you may follow any of them.
- I leave you the Quran and Sunna; you should follow both.
- I leave you the Quran and Ahl-al-Bayt (my family); you should follow them.
- I leave you the Quran, you should follow it.

11. According to some "authentic Hadith" found in Bukhari and other Hadith books, there was a verse instructing muslims to stone the married adulterers to death: "Al-shayhu wal-shayhatu iza zanaya farjumuhuma nakalan..." According to Hadith reports, what happened to those verses?
a. After the Prophet Muhammad's death, Umayyad governor Marwan burned the pages where those verses were written.
b. Angle Gebrail came down and deleted it from the scripture.
c. Ibni Abbas forgot it yet Abu Hurayra never forgot it.
d. There is no reference to such a verse in any authentic Hadith books.
e. After the Prophet Muhammad's death, the skin which the verse was written on was protected under Aisha's bed. A hungry goat ate it. Thus, it was abrogated literally yet kept legally.

12. According to both Bukhari and Muslim, when Muhammad was in his death bed, he asked his comrades around to bring him a paper and pen to write something for them so that they would not divert from the right path. According to the same "authentic" Sunni Hadith books, Omar bin Khattab stopped a sahaba who was hurrying for a paper and pen and said the following: "The prophet is sick and has fever. He does not know what he is saying. God's book is sufficient for us." According to the Hadith, all the prominent comrades (sahaba) agreed with Omar and Muhammad passed away without writing down his advice. What do you think about this Hadith?
a. If it is narrated by both Bukhari and Muslim, then it must be true

460

b. If it is true, then, Omar and all other Sahaba must have betrayed Muhammad and committed blasphemy.
c. If it is true, then, Omar and all prominent Sahaba were followers of the Quran alone.
d. If it is false then all other Hadith too should be rejected.
e. C and D must be true

13. Do we need to SAY "sallallahu alayhi wasallam" after Muhammad's name?
a. Yes, every time Muhammad is mentioned we have to praise his name.
b. Yes, but we need to say only once in our lifetime.
c. Yes, the more we say the better.
d. Yes, and those who do not say it after Muhammad's name disrespect him and they will not receive his intercession.
e. No, the Quran does not ask us to say anything after Muhammad's name; muslims were asked (salli ala) to support him, as he was also asked to support them (salli alayhim).

14. What is the correct Testimony (shahada) according to the Quran:
a. I bear witness that there is no god but the God and the Quran is God's word.
b. I bear witness that there is no god but the God and Muhammad is His messenger.
c. I bear witness that there is no god but the God and Muhammad is His messenger and His servant.
d. I bear witness that there is no god but the God and Abraham, Jesus, Moses and Muhammad are His messengers.
e. I bear witness that there is no god but the God.

15. Should Muslims who do not observe daily prayers be beaten in public?
a. Yes.
b. No.

16. Should Muslims who are caught for consuming alcohol for the fourth time be killed?
a. Yes.
b. No.

17. Did the prophet give permission to kill women and children in the war?
a. Yes.
b. No.

18. According to the Quran, are women banned from reading Quran and pray during their menstruation periods?
a. Yes
b. No.

19. In the daily Sala prayers, do you recite "attahiyyatu lillahi wassalawatu .... as salamu alayka ayyuhannabiyyu wa rahmatullahi wa barakatuhu"?
a. Yes
b. No

20. Does the Quran justify taxing Jewish and Christian population under Muslim authority with extra or different taxation called Jizya?
a. Yes
b. No.

21. Does the Quran instruct women to cover their hair?
a. Yes.
b. No.

22. Are woman restricted from leading congregational prayers?
a. Yes.
b. No.

23. Are women mentally and spiritually inferior to men?
a. Yes.
b. No.

24. Does the Quran restrict women from initiating divorce?
a. Yes.
b. No.

25. Is polygamy with previously unmarried women allowed?
a. Yes, up to four women.
b. No, polygamy is allowed only with the widows who have orphans.

26. Do pilgrims need to cast real stones at the devil?
a. Yes.
b. No.

27. Is the black stone near Kaba holy?
a. Yes.
b. No.

28. May a muslim own slaves?
a. Yes.

b. No.

29. Is circumcision a required or encouraged practice in Islam?

Yes.

No.

30. Should converts change their names to Arabic names?

a. Yes.

b. No.

31. How much *zaka* charity one should give away?

a. 2.5%

b. As much as one can afford, without making themselves needy.

32. Are those who break their fast during Ramadan before the sunset required to fast 60 consecutive days as a punishment for not completing the day?

a. Yes.

b. No.

33. Is leadership the right of Quraish tribe?

a. Yes.

b. No.

34. Is drawing pictures or making three dimensional statutes a sin?

a. Yes.

b. No.

35. Are there more dietary prohibitions besides pork, carcass, running blood, and animal dedicated to idolized names?

a. Yes.

b. No.

36. Is displaying Muhammad's name and the names of his closest companions next to God's name in the mosques idol-worship?

a. Yes.

b. No.

37. Did Muhammad advise some sick people to drink camel urine?

a. Yes.

b. No.

38. Did Muhammad gauge people's eyes with hot nails?

a. Yes.

b. No.

39. After following the advice of Moses, did Muhammad, bargain with God about the number of prayers, lowering down from the impossible-to-observe 50 times a day to 5 times a day?

a. Yes.

b. No.

40. Does Muhammad have the power of intercession?

a. Yes.

b. No.

41. Was Muhammad sinless?

a. Yes.

b. No.

42. Did God create the universe for the sake of Muhammad?

a. Yes.

b. No.

43. Did Muhammad have sexual power of 30 males?

a. Yes.

b. No.

44. Was Muhammad bewitched by a Jew?

a. Yes.

b. No.

45. Do some verses of the Quran abrogate other verses?

a. Yes.

b. No.

Here is the story and the answer of this test:

Between November 3 and 10 of 2008, I traveled to UK and Turkey to deliver four lectures; first two at Oxford University, the third at Muslim Institute in London and the fourth one in Istanbul Book Fair. I had prepared a test containing 45 multiple choice questions just the night before my travel. I duplicated them on both sides of a single sheet and I distributed to the audience before the lecture... They were asked to write their name, age, occupation, email address, favorite authors, and their sectarian affiliation. It was a bit awkward to test an audience that consisted of students and professors at one of the world's top universities. The multiple-choice test proved to be a powerful instrument to deliver the message of Islamic Reform under the light of the Quran. The correct answer for each multiple choice question was the E option, and for the Yes or No questions was the B option. So, it would take me a few seconds to evaluate the tests after they were returned to me.

The Sunni or Shiite test-takers found themselves in quagmire of contradiction with their own sectarian teachings. They learned that they were thirty, forty or even more than fifty percent infidels or heretics. Some of those who marked Sunni as their sectarian affiliation contradicted the Sunni teachings on most of the issues. According to their own confessed sects, their lives were worthless; they deserved to be killed! I did not let this mirror or sect-o-meter remain an individual experience; I publicly declared the overall results. Many got all answers correct, including Eric, a monotheist from Unitarian church who already had a copy of the Quran: a Reformist Translation in his possession. Eric knew the original message of islam better than all the mullahs and the so-called "ulama" combined.

If you have chosen the wrong option for any of the questions and you are wondering why you have contradicted the Quran, please visit our site, **www.islamicreform.org** and read the full version of the *Manifesto for Islamic Reform*. If you prefer to have it in a book form, you may order it through online bookstores.

A10
The Blind Watch-Watchers or Smell the Cheese

An Intelligent and Delicious Argument for Intelligent Design in Evolution
(From upcoming, *19 Questions For Atheists*, by Edip Yuksel)

Let's do it backwards. I will start with quoting a sample of reactions I received from people, mostly my close friends, to the draft version of this article. I do not hope they would influence you like those "two-thumbs-up" movie reviews, but I hope that they will confuse you regarding the merits of this article before engaging you in a philosophical and scientific argument. The mixed reaction I received so far tought me this: a great deal of my readers will close their eyes and touch the tail, the trunk or the ear of this elephantine article and they will perceive it as they feel. I wrote this article for the lucky few who will not get distracted by its musings or the side arguments; they will see both the watch and the watch-maker as clearly as they see these letters. Here is a sample from those feedbacks:

> "Very nice and heavily scientific and philosophical as well. You are using simple logic to explain a complex topic and this is a great art." (Ali Bahzadnia, MD., my endocrinologist friend, USA).

> "I loved the cheese!" (Mark Sykes, PhD, J.D., my rocket-scientist lawyer friend, Tucson, Mars and Beyond).

> "Interesting and thought-provoking." (Megan C. PhD, Biochemist, USA, not my friend)

> "Your arguments are against the existence of man and all living, reproducing organisms. Unless we are only God's nightmare without corporal existence, your arguments are foolish. You may want to return to restudy the very simple tenets of evolution. You have a better mind than this paper suggests. Arguing against evolution is not the problem. Your "straw man" argument is... Try again with a little more scholarship... (David Jones, PhD., my psychologist/educator atheist friend, USA).

> "I read the article tonight and enjoyed the article very much... The overall feel of the article for me was that it was a different look at the anthropic principle; and in many ways a restatement of it..." (Oben Candemir, MD., my ophthalmologist friend, Australia).

> "Very ... " (Kristen Lorenz, OD., my physicist friend, USA, who is still reading it).

> "Irrelevant B.S.! Bachelor of Science in philosophy is not the right muscle to dissect or rummage the messy details of fossils, genes, enzymes, and hormones. When lawyers enter a scientific debate, it is time to write its obituary. Irrelevant

B.S.! Jurisdiction denied!" (XYZ PhD, my critic from ABC; or my "The Demon-Haunted" skeptic personality).

"This is not a scientific paper. Because many assertions are flat wrong. Evolution IS falsifiable, for example Static fossil records would falsify it or finding a way that would prevent mutation from accumulating. Marvels of Marble is an extremely bad example. Property of two marbles together is not much different than one, survival of the fittest does not play any part, throwing the marbles down terminates in a finite event of a short period of time. I kind of agree with XYZ." (Fereydoun Taslimi, entrepreneur and philanthropist, a monotheist friend, indeed a good friend, USA)

"I thank and congratulate Edip for taking on." (Mustafa Akyol, a columnist friend expert on evolution versus creation debate, Turkey).

When my older son turned teenager, like others in his age group, his voice and face started mutating. I complimented his evolution from childhood to puberty by jokingly depicting it as devolution. "Yahya, when will you be going to get the kiss that will turn you back into a prince?" He knew well that I was not expecting him to get a kiss from a sweetheart until he graduated from college. Though he did not get that kiss (as far as I know), within a couple of years he started turning into a prince, again.

Please do not spoil your reading of this delicious article by telling yourself, "This guy does not know even the meaning of the words *mutation* and *evolution* in the context of the evolution versus creation." I do not wish to sound arrogant, but I do know this and even more. Though I studied philosophy and received my doctorate degree in law, I took a graduate course entitled "Philosophy of Evolution" just for the fun of it. I am also one of the first people who tried to get some legal inspiration from biology. In the mid 1990's, I wrote articles with bizarre titles, such as, "Biology and Law" or "Biology of Human Rights." (Since they did not possess the characteristics of a "serious" article, such as numerous references, boring language, and lengthy exposition, they were not material for a scholarly journal. Thus, I published them at my personal website: www.yuksel.org). Furthermore, I have read numerous boring and exciting books and articles on this subject matter.

So, I decided to write an essay for the laymen who know that they know very little about the scientific aspect of the debate, yet they feel that they must take sides on this highly controversial issue that has enormous political and theological ramifications. (As for those laymen who do not know that they know very little, even Socrates could not be of any help.) No wonder we see many of those who have no clue about the intricacy of the debate appear to be ready to abort each other on this issue. To them "irreducible complexity" may sound complex, and the sudden appearance of complex life forms in the event called Cambrian Explosion may mean less than Noah's Flood or last year's Emmy's Awards. The argument of one party might be primarily based on the "God of gaps" and of the opposing party on "anything but God." They may not even know more than one or two names besides Darwin. For instance, Empedocles, Cicero, Ibn Sina, Ibn Rushd, Ibn Khaldun, Al-Hazen, Hume, Paley, Mendel, Huxley, Johnson, Dawkins, Gould, Behe, or Dembsky may not spark any ideas in the minds of those who are well versed about fictional characters such as Samson who killed a thousand men with the jaw of an ass and collected foreskins of his enemies as his wedding present. Similarly, those names may not mean much for those who are well versed about fictional characters such as Hamlet who talked with an archaic British accent starting with "Methinks..."

This essay is aimed to reduce the complexity of the debate on the most sensitive point of the controversy. I hope that this will bring the opposing parties in the controversy closer to each other. As the most delicious part of a sandwich is usually its middle, I argue that the truth of this matter is also somewhere in the middle. It is time to start a revolution in the evolution debate and smell the cheese inside the buns.

Let me remind the reader what this article is NOT about. This article is NOT rejecting the theory of evolution; to the contrary it supports the theory of evolution, and its position will not be effected a bit even if we accept that humans are descendants of chimpanzees. I am making this point clear since many pro-evolution zealots tend to demonstrate a knee-jerk reaction to the article without even understanding its argument. My statements regarding some weaknesses of the theory are not used as premises for the conclusion of my arguments, but only to inform the reader about some of the controversial issues between the parties. Even if you smell a bias in my depiction of these issues, even if you think that I am very wrong in those depictions, do not get distracted. Trash those side issues and convict me as "ignorant" or "biased" on them, and get to the main argument, which is:

Evolution of species through mutation and cumulative selection, as subscribed by the modern scientific community, provides sufficient evidences for the existence of immanent intelligent design in nature. The theory of evolution provides evidences about an intelligent designer more than a fingerprint on a canvass could provide clues about the identity of a human painter. Inferring the existence and some attributes of an intelligent designer from nature is as equally scientific as inferring the existence and some attributes of an unknown creature from its footprints left on the sand.

The Genesis

We all started our adventure on this planet as the tiny champions of a vital and brutal competition. Half of all our genetic material was once an individual sperm akin to a tadpole. Hopefully, the events immediately preceding our lives included some laughter and mutually affectionate kisses. After a day-long marathon in a tube not longer than a pen, starting from vagina through the cervix and uterus we finally met our other half and won the award for or condemnation to life. (I am aware that this individual genesis would be told in reverse order if the author of this essay were a woman: "Half of all of our genetic material was once individual eggs waiting...") After reaching the eggs of the chosen female, as the champion sperms, most of us caused the eggs to close their entrances and condemned the other millions of our brothers to death. Whether we like it or not, we started as a selfish gene by causing the demise of millions of viable yet a bit slower or unlucky sperms like us. We are merely the children of murderers who call themselves victors throughout the history. We also started our lives by mass-murdering potential brothers. We are the children of Cane; we are the survivors of ferocious wars, both in macro and micro worlds.

Yes, after our organic rockets hit our organic planets, we became zygotes and we started the 266 daylong evolution, hopefully sans-mutations, in our mother's belly. The approximately six billion bits of DNA program coded in the language of four bases or nucleotide, Adenine, Cytosine, Guanine, and Thiamine create the three-pound jelly, the human brain, whose complexity is beyond our (or, ironically its own) immediate imagination.

There is evolution everywhere: in genes and organs; in stars and planets. Everything, from the smallest organisms to humans... As once a Greek named Heraclitus said, "Everything changes except change itself." You may wish to exclude God, math, or universal laws from this universal statement, but you cannot deny this fact. The mutation of the flu viruses is a well-known fact. The germs are mutating and those that survive antibiotics are now causing a great concern for the health industry. This fact alone is sufficient evidence indicating to at least an intra species evolution.

Though the theory of evolution has produced a brilliant explanation for many questions regarding the origin and diversity of life on this planet, it has also failed in producing explanations for numerous questions. Furthermore, the theory arguably lacks some important characteristics of a good scientific theory since it is not falsifiable. Let's listen to both sides:

- Why did that animal not survive?
- **Because it did not fit the environment.**
- How do you know that it did not fit?
- **Because it did not survive. If they fit, they survive; if they survive they are fit!**
- What? If F then S or if S then F?
- **No, If F then S and if S then F.**
- Wow!

Let's try another one:

- Can you give me an example of a falsifiable claim regarding evolution?

- Of course! For instance, when populations of bacteria A and B are exposed to low levels of toxic substance X, the fraction of the bacteria resistant to X will increase with time.
- So what?
- The experiment is run and the hypothesis correctly predicts the outcome for bacteria A, but not B. Success or failure for evolution?
- Your hypothesis is not falsifiable as you claim.
- Why?
- Because it is circular and the word "low" is too subjective.
- How?
- It is circular since it is no more than saying "those who do not die because of their strength will survive." If none survives, you can easily claim that there were no resistant bacteria. Second, the word "low" is not defined before the event in question. If none survives you will call it high, if some survive you will call it low. Furthermore, the predictive power of your statement regarding the bacteria is close to the predictive power of "Dear Nancy, you will give birth to either a boy or a girl."
- But, what about the Intelligent Design argument? Is it falsifiable?
- No. For any of the 'not-so-intelligent design' examples you bring, the proponent might reject by saying, "In the past, people claimed similar things for this or that, and with time, when we got more information about their purpose and function we learned that they were indeed very intelligent designs. For instance, once scientists thought that the sharp hairs, awns, or bristles were useless and they tried to remove them from spikelets. Guess what? After obtaining grains without those pointy hairs, they learned to their dismay that those sharp appendages were protecting the grains from birds. So, we should investigate the reason behind apparent flaws."
- What about birth defects? Abnormal mutations?
- The proponent of intelligent design might even accept flaws by saying, "Flaws are there to highlight design through contrast. Without the existence of flaws we could not know or appreciate design. The existence of a single example of an intelligent design is sufficient to show the existence of an intelligent designer."

It is also argued that the theory of evolution does not have predictive power on specific events:

- With the humans giving up from hunting in the jungles and turning to sedentary office workers, would this ecological change ultimately select the spherical nerds?
- Spherical nerds?

468

- Yes, brains with horizontally grown bodies!
- **It depends...**
- Will humans finally get wings?
- **It depends...**
- Will the thumbs of the descendants of my X-boxed son finally end up with fast and furiously big thumps the size of hot dogs?
- **It depends...**
- Will cats learn how to use remote control?
- **It depends...**
- Wow!

Some proponents of the theory of evolution argue that the theory of evolution demonstrates all the characteristics of a scientific theory. For instance, proving that dinosaurs and humans co-existed would falsify the theory. Even if the critics of the theory were right regarding their assertion on the falsifiability and predictive power of the theory, the theory of evolution is more scientific than the stories of creation believed by billions of people, since it provides a consistent, parsimonious, progressive and verifiable explanation regarding the diversity and complexity of life forms on this planet. My argument in this paper does not rely on this issue. Regardless of the value of the theory of evolution, I argue that the presence of intelligent design is self-evident.

Methinks it is Like a Blind Watch-watcher

To refute the Creationist's argument of the impossibility of a monkey typing the work of Shakespeare, Richard Dawkins provides probability calculations of a random work on a computer using 26 alphabet letters and a space bar, totaling 27 characters. To randomly type Hamlet's 28-character statement, METHINKS IT IS LIKE A WEASEL, it would take 27 to the power of 28 key strokes, which would be a very small odd, about 1 in 10,000 million million million million million million. Instead of single-step selection of random variation, Dawkins suggests us to program the computer to use *cumulative selection*. The computer generates some random 28 characters and selects the one that most resembles the target phrase, METHINKS...

> "What matters is the difference between the time taken by *cumulative* selection, and the time which the same computer, working flat out at the same rate, would take to reach the target phrase if it were forced to use the other procedure of *single-step selection*: about a million million million million million years. This is more than a million million million times as long as the universe has so far existed. ... Whereas the time taken for a computer working randomly but with the constraint of cumulative selection to perform the same task is of the same order as humans ordinarily can understand, between 11 seconds and the times it takes to have lunch... If evolutionary progress had had to rely on single-step selection, it would have never got anywhere. If, however, there was any

way in which the necessary conditions for cumulative selection could have been set up by the blind forces of nature, strange and wonderful might have been the consequences. As a matter of fact that is exactly what happened on this planet, and we ourselves are among the most recent, if not the strangest and most wonderful, of those consequences." (Richard Dawkins, The Blind Watchmaker, Norton, 1987, p.49).

Though he is a bright and articulate scientist, Dawkins takes too many facts and events for granted without even mentioning them: such as the number of characters, their proportion, the computer programmer and program that selects the right characters, the energy that accomplishes the work, the existence of characters, time and space, the continuity of their existence, etc. In the following page, Dawkins distinguishes his METHINKS example from the live evolutionary process.

"Evolution has no long-term goal. There is no long-distance target, no final perfection to serve as a criterion for selection, although human vanity cherishes the absurd notion that our species is the final goal of evolution. ... The 'watchmaker' that is cumulative natural selection is blind to the future and has no long-term goal." (Id, p.50).

Here Dawkins acknowledges that he added his intelligence and teleological intention by determining a target, criterion for selection. Thus, Dawkins takes for granted many facts and events, and gives an analogy of a computer program in which he interjects his intelligence, a target, and a selection criterion to explain something that according to him has none of them.

Dawkins who depicts human life as the work of a blind process has a much bigger problem: His theory and its conclusion do not have the light of reason. Let me explain with some analogies. If you now feel an urge to seek an immediate refuge in Hume, please be reminded that they are given to explain inferences to the best explanation. (I recommend Elliott Sober's Philosophy of Biology, containing a brief yet sound criticism of Hume's critique of analogies).

The Assembly Line, the Gullible and the Blind

Assume that we have constructed a completely automated assembly line that manufactures automobiles run on fuel-cells. It receives raw materials such as steel and plastic from one end, and after passing through an assembly line run by computers and robots, it spews out automobiles from the other end.

Now assume that we brought two members of a primitive tribe living in an isolated jungle and placed them in front of the exit door. When a car emerges from the exit door, you enter the car and start driving it. You then stop and watch the reaction of the two tribesmen. You see that the one on the right is awed by the moving beast and is thanking God for showing him a miracle by creating such a complex creature in a few seconds.

Let's assume that the other tribesman on the left side is more curious and adventurous. He wonders about the whereabouts of the room behind the exit door. After some trials, he finds an opening somewhere and able to peek into the room. He sees some robots spraying paint on a car. He touches the paint and notices that it is liquid. After that observation, he comes back and shares what he saw with the believing man on the right. "The shiny stuff on this beast is not too thick. In fact, it was liquid before it was sprayed thinly over its solid skin." But, what about the skin, what about the round circle that determines its direction, and what about the power that moves it? The curious man makes numerous trips, entering some other rooms of the assembly line compound, either by forging a key or luckily discovering a peephole... He learns that the raw materials are spilled in molds upon their arrival and the beast is gradually assembled from simple parts. For instance, the doors are attached by robotic hands through hinges. Though he is not able to access some rooms to explain some stages of the assembly line, he gets a good idea how from simple raw building blocks a complex and powerful beast called automobile could emerge. After getting some ideas about the modus operandi of the assembly line, the curious infers what could have happened in the rooms that he could not access. The believing man outside, who is still intoxicated in spiritual awe, is not impressed by the finding of the curious tribesman. He finds problem in the theory of the curious man since he is not able to explain some events in the assembly line. "You see, you cannot ignore the divine mystery and hand in the creation of this beast!"

The believing man declares that an Omniscient and Omnipotent Creator or an Intelligent Designer created the beast in a second or at worst case scenario in six seconds out of steel and plastic. The believing man goes further and declares his friend to be a heretic disbeliever deserving to burn in Hell forever. The curious man, on the other hand, declares that there is no God of gaps, nor an Intelligent Designer or Engineer, since he had seen none in those rooms. Besides, the curious man brags about his knowledge of most of the events in the evolution of the beast and declares that his friend is a delusional lunatic who deserves to be restricted from expressing his opinion on the evolution of the beasts, especially in public places and in front of children.

Why do most believers in God ignore empirical evidences in His creation, while on the other side, most of those who study the empirical evidences ignore intelligent inferences? Parties in the evolution controversy may see each other in these two characters, but perhaps none will identify himself with them. So, let me change my story. Instead of human characters, I will pick some marbles.

Marvels of Marbles

Now let's entertain a thought experiment. We have a gigantic box full of millions of glass marbles. Marbles in different colors, different shapes and sizes... You are an eternal, infinitely patient and curious observer. The box is in a huge empty room and every minute it is tilted by a machine and the marbles

471

are spilled over the clean and smooth surface of the empty floor. Let's assume that you are not interested in the box, machines and the basic laws they follow. You are just interested in the adventure of marbles. Each time, marbles create a particular design randomly and they are filled back to the box to start over the process.

Assume that these events continue for billions of years, trillions of times, without generating anything categorically different. But, in one of the occasions, some of the marbles that were spread over the floor come together and join each other. They then start moving around as a group, slivering through other marbles. Then this gang of marbles start jumping and multiplying. Some even start talking to you. You now may imagine the rest of the story, the marvels of these marbles.

Given an infinite number of trials and years could these happen? If your answer is a "No" then why no? Because they are just made of glasses? What is the difference between glass of marbles and atoms? What is the difference between a cluster of glass marbles and molecules? Well, now you are ready to think on a question and find the answer that somehow eludes some of the brightest scientists. Now, you are ready to see the light of the Intelligent Design in everything, including evolution, including in evolution between species. Do you smell the cheese? Not yet.

The Genius in Hydrogen

Now let's leave the marbles in their box and focus on the simplest atom, Hydrogen. You know that a hydrogen atom has one proton in its nucleus, one electron in its shell, and it does not contain a neutron. Though the structure of each atom is a very complex and precise design, they are somehow seen by the blind watch-watching evolutionists like children see marbles.

The masses of stars are mostly made of Hydrogen atoms. When two hydrogen atoms fuse together they release some energy and particles, and they "mutate" to a Helium atom, a different "species" in periodic table of elements. We know that Hydrogen and Helium atoms have different characteristics and they behave differently and associate with other atoms differently. When you put two pennies or marbles next to each other or fuse them together they do not act differently; they are still what they are. Their mass and gravitational force may increase, but that is it.

When two Hydrogen atoms fuse together, the information about Helium must have been innate or intrinsic in both of them. Since both Hydrogen atoms are the same, they must contain exactly the same information necessary to create the characteristics of Helium. The information might be triggered by the pressure of fusion. Each Hydrogen atom must contain particular information, since two Hydrogen atoms do not create any characteristics, but the particular characteristics of the atom we call Helium. Thus, Helium must be immanent in Hydrogen. Since Helium and Hydrogen fused together may create Lithium, then the information about Lithium too must be immanent in Hydrogen. In fact, based on the same reasoning, we must expect Hydrogen to contain all the information regarding the characteristics of each element in periodical table. It is the change in the quantity of protons that leads to qualitative change.

When two Hydrogen atoms associate with one Oxygen atom they create water, the essential ingredient of life as we know. However, when two Hydrogen atoms associate with two Oxygen atoms they create Hydrogen Peroxide, a powerful oxidizer that kills living organisms. Thus, the Hydrogen and Oxygen atoms must contain the information for both molecules. The information inherent in them must lead to Water when they are combined as H2O and must lead to Hydrogen Peroxide when they are combined as H2O2. Since we know that the information of Oxygen must be immanent in the Hydrogen, all this information must be contained in every Hydrogen atoms.

I hear the voice of my rocket-scientist friend opposing to my Hydrogen example. So, let's side track a bit to deal with his voice. (If you are a prototype layman who thinks that rocket-scientists are a different species, then you may skip this section and go to the paragraph starting with "In sum, ..."):

> "So all of mathematics is immanent in 1 since the combination of 1 and 1 is 2, therefore the properties of 2 must be immanent in one. But also 3.141592654 is obtained by the spatial ordering of different combinations of 1, therefore 3.141592654 must be immanent in 1. I think there is something of a problem here. From 1 alone, one cannot intuit 2 or any other number except by application of rules which (in this example) can be somewhat arbitrary when applied to 1. Are all verbs immanent in the noun? These things are part of a larger context, perhaps indivisible from that context."

What a wonderful refutation, isn't it? My friend just explained the diversity of elements in the periodic table and their millions of off-springs in the nature, by reducing Hydrogen to our poor and ignorant number 1 which is oblivious of even numbers, prime numbers, perfect numbers, Fermat numbers, and infinite of other numbers begotten as a result of numerical polygamy among the clones of the number One! Interestingly, my scientist friend picked two of his examples from IMAGINARY world of human mind: math and human language. Though the language of nature is written in mathematics, as Galileo once articulated, it does not reflect the "properties" of numbers. Yes, "one odd number plus one odd" becomes an even number, but "one odd chair plus one odd chair" does not become "even chairs." In other words, the property of numbers are not reflected in real world. The same is true for our grammar rules. (On this issue, I highly recommend the section in chapter about Pythagoras titled "Where is the Number 2?" in *Lovers of Wisdom* by Daniel Kolak.).

IN SUM, millions of organic and inorganic compounds, including the ones that yet to be discovered, with their distinct chemical and physical characteristics, must be the materialization of the information immanent in the tiniest building block of the universe, that is, Hydrogen. Going backwards, the same qualities must be imputed for the most fundamental subatomic particle. No wonder Heraclitus had brilliantly inferred that intrinsic law permeating the universe, and called it "logos."

Furthermore, when a particular combination of a particular set of elements in particular proportions generates the function we call *life*, the laws or rules of such an event must have existed before the event occurred. In other words, the laws and rules determining how a particular DNA sequence would behave must have preceded the actual occurrence of the event. Why should a particular configuration of particular molecules made of a particular combination of elements lead to a cell or a living organism? Who or what determined such a magical configuration? None, just chance? No, not a chance! *No, not by a chance!* Chance does not lead to laws. In fact, chance itself is subject to the laws of probability. The laws dominating the universe came into existence with the first moment of Big Bang. If you bet your entire wealth in a casino you will most likely lose it and you will deserve the title of "another mathematically challenged person" and you may even receive a silver medal in the next Darwin's Award. But you can bet your entire wealth on a scientific prediction based on natural laws and you will most likely win.

It is because of the natural laws of cause and effect that scientists can employ reason and predict events. Mendeleyev knew that elements were not acting haphazardly, so he discovered the periodical table. Thus, it is irrelevant how many millions or billions of years passed before the first organism came into existence among random and chaotic chain of chemical and physical events. Starting from the first seconds of creation of material particles 13.7 billion years ago, the conditions and laws of life must have come into existence too. What scientists do is not inventing, they merely discover. Scientists do not invent laws of physics or chemistry; they learn those laws bit by bit, after tedious experimentation, and based on the information they acquired they put together the pieces of Legos. The characteristics of each newly discovered shape was coded in their nature since the beginning of the universe.

Thus, when a blind watch-watcher refers to the age of the world and its size to explain the marvels of blind cumulative selection, we should not be blindly accepting his argument. The information or laws of life existed billions years even before the emergence of life. So, we should demand an explanation regarding the a priori information of creating the design of living organisms. Ken Harding, in an article entitled, "Evolution for Beginners," articulates the role of information encoded in genes:

> "One of the most common misunderstandings regards "information". The difference between living and non-living things is that living things have information embedded in them which is used to produce themselves.

Rocks contain *no* instructions on how to be rocks; a fly contains information on how to be a fly.

"Information is not a thing. It, like an idea, is dimensionless. It's simply a comparison between one thing and another, like a list of differences. Information is not a physical property. Information becomes tangible only when it is encoded in sequences of symbols: zeros and ones, letters and spaces, dots and dashes, musical notes, etc. These sequences must then be decoded in order to be useful. For information to be stored or transmitted, it must be put into some physical form- on paper, computer disk, or in DNA- all processes that take energy.

"Life's information (the instructions on how it works) is encoded in genes, which are decoded by biological mechanisms. Then these mechanisms manufacture parts that work together to make a living organism. Like a computer that builds itself, the process follows a loop: information needs machinery, which needs information, which needs machinery, which needs information. This relationship can start very simply, and then over many generations build into something so complicated that some people can't imagine how it ever could have gotten started in the first place. It is important to recognize that the information encoded in DNA is not like a blueprint, which contains a scale model image of the final product, it is like a recipe-- a set of instructions to be followed in a certain order. Life's complexity arises from remarkable simplicity. DNA's message says, "Take this, add this, then add this... stop here. Take this, then add this..." These actions are carried out by a variety of proteins. The result is all the intricacy and diversity of the biological realm.

http://www.evolution.mbdojo.com/evolution-for-beginners.html

The issue, however, gets even more interesting. Not only living *organisms*, but their products too must be the consequence of "blind" evolution.

Just take the beginning of the universe and our modern world. Do not let anyone distract you by the events occurred in between. How can our modern world together with everything in it be the product of a big chaotic explosion? How can such an explosion create the libraries, computer programs and all cars on our streets, in less than 14 billion years? Now, the blind watch-watchers want us to believe that all the books in the Library of Congress, including all the data in our computers, our inventions and technological marvels, yes all of them are the result of marriage between Mr. Drunk Chaos who is unpredictable and Mrs. Blind Evolution who works according to the principle of *cumulative selection*. If the laws of the universe are deterministic, then the immense amount of information and design permeating our libraries, factories and stores must also be the necessary product of the Big Bang. Not only the initial conditions of the universe had the potential for all the subsequent things at the very start, following deterministic laws they were bound to create human intelligence and leading to landing on the Moon and the I-pod. Even a small fraction of products designed by human intelligence cannot fit in a trillion year-old universe, let alone one that aged 13.7 billion years-old, via probability calculations. Nor can they be explained by "random (or not random) mutation" and "cumulative selection."

I hear the voice of my rocket scientist friend, again. I cannot ignore that melodious voice. Let's all listen to it:

> "Rather than close the door on the question, wouldn't it be fun to try and figure it out by trying to understand how things work? Could a religious person approach the universe with an open mind and, regardless of the processes they work to slowly identify and better understand, consider the effort a joy and giving of glory? Or does God need to be put into a box where the outcomes of all such investigations are predetermined by those who find a more limited deity more palatable?"

I do not feel compelled to respond to these rhetorical questions, since I do not have a problem with accepting mysteries. I myself am a mystery. But, I would like to remind my friend that I have no intention to put God in a box. I saw a box and I said that it must have been created by a box-maker. I never claimed that the box-maker was in the box, nor that he/she/it was limited with only making boxes. In fact, I would expect that the box-maker is capable of making cylinders, spheres and many other shapes and things beyond my poor perception and imagination.

Our blind watch-watchers would like us to accept the emergence of human intelligence and its products as a magical moment, as a miracle. A miracle that terminates the application of deterministic laws and guarantees for all its products the immunity from the probability calculations! Because of that miracle or magic, we are asked not to include the probability of authoring millions of books, articles, computer programs, websites, movies, machines, electronic devices, and everything in the Wal-Mart into our equation. The "anything but God" crowd may even talk in quantum language to de-emphasize the deterministic nature of the universe.

All those "Anything but God" people, in fact, believe in many gods!

Ironically, the blind watch-watchers are proud in declaring their disbelief in God or the irrelevancy of God, while they are fanatic believers in infinite number of gods. They are polytheists. Every atom contains all the information necessary for life! Whatever believers in God attribute to the Creator, the blind watch-watchers attribute to atoms, matter, or energy. Though they are proud of depicting their gods as "random," "blind" or "stupid," after some interrogations we learn that is not to be the case. Just replace the word God with the word

476

matter, energy or nature and you will have the tenets of faith of blind watch-watchers.

- God is the first cause.
- God is eternal.
- God is the source of information.
- God created everything.
- God created life.

Accepting a God that is not bound by the laws of this universe is much simpler and reasonable than accepting all atoms having all the attributes of a deistic God, and again much coherent than creating our modern world, together with human intelligence and this article, out of their blind and stupid collisions. I prefer believing in the creation of rabbits popping up from a magician's hat, than a universe coming out of nothing and then blindly creating this planet and the intelligent life on it. So, I assert that if Occam's Razor is sharp for every argument, then it must first shave off the idea of stupid atoms coming into existence out of nothing and billions years later, several billions of them blindly evolving and transforming into Dawkins' mind.

Some atheists might resort to a false argument by pointing at their "undetectable Purple Cow in the sky." Yes, it is a funny example, but far from being persuasive. They craftily wish to equate the argument for an Intelligent Designer to a Purple Cow. This is a cheap rhetoric, since being Purple or Cow has nothing to do with our argument. However, the intelligence and design is in every atom, in every molecule, in every organism of this universe. Besides they are detectable.

We understand why the majority of religious people tend to have problem with science and philosophical inquiry. But, why have many scientists become "anything but God" fanatics? It might be because of the ridiculous claims and arguments of religious zealots who oppose the theory of evolution in the name of God. Atheists have not taken even a small step to answer the fundamental questions related to the issue. What is the cause of the universe or singularity? There is a particular amount of mass in the universe, let's say, N amount; why is it N amount, not more not less? Who or what determined the exact amount of mass or the exact number of atoms/particles/energy in the universe? (We would not have this question, of course, if the entire universe was homogenous). How is the probability of the existence of a universe with fine tuned constants essential to life? Did our universe have infinite time? Are there infinite universes? Is infinity really pregnant to all possibilities? Why is there something rather than nothing? Why is the universe governed by laws? Why do the biological organisms have propensity to mutate? They might believe that answers for these questions are not in the domain of science. Then, how can they claim that the universe and evolution of living beings, from the structure of atoms to the structure of brain and its products, does not need God?

I should again share with you the voice of my scientist friend:

"Actually there are many scientists pondering these questions (but the last), and many or some may be atheists. Does it matter? If an atheist drives a car, does that mean the believer should not? With regards to the last question, are believers afraid that not needing God in the theories formulated to try to explain observations of life and the universe will prove there is no God? I think that is the fear of many anti-evolutionists. It exposes the weakness of their own faith, that they need compelling external evidence that God must exist."

Well said. But, I do not think that it applies to me and many other "rational monotheists," since my acceptance of God is not based on "faith," a euphemism for "joining the band wagon" or "wishful thinking." My acceptance or knowledge of God is based on numerous scientific evidences and philosophical inferences, which I am hoping to share with others in a book titled, "19 Questions for Atheists."

We might be able to duplicate or copy life in the bio-world, but we have not yet been able to imitate the full capabilities of biological assembly line in our technology. We have not yet seen any computer giving birth to other computers. Perhaps, with the progress of our production technology, we may witness it in the future. Assume that a scientist discovered a method for evolving computers or gadgets that could multiply by RANDOM MUTATIONS and CUMULATIVE SELECTION. Wouldn't this SIMPLE task be INCREDIBLY INGENUINE? What if "nature" had created inorganic materials with such a quality? Would you consider such a "creation" lacking intelligent design? Or would you just say that the "the evolving and multiplying computers by random mutations negate God's intelligence and involvement in the creation process completely"? What about your intelligence? Aren't you a product of nature? How come an intelligent person like you was generated by a dumb and stupid process?

Intelligent design is in every moment and point of evolution (71). There is an intelligent power and wisdom that designs incredibly simple assembly lines that can manufacture incredibly complex organisms and creatures, including the intelligent watch-watchers and blind watch-watchers. The signature of the Intelligent Designer in the book of nature is paradoxically as obvious as the number 19 in 74, and as concealed as the number 19 in 74.

Let me give one more chance to the voice of my scientist friend:

"Perhaps the signature is found in our perception of beauty of how things work? Don't know about the numerological references - I think most audiences might scratch their heads and wonder what was up with that?"

Yes, indeed. Let those audiences keep scratching their heads. Who knows, if they are curious enough they will smell the beef after tasting the cheese and learn what was up and down with my numerological references. After all, "On it is nineteen!"

PS:

A delusional cult leader from my country of birth is doing a great disservice to Islam by copying and promoting the works of Evangelical Christians and Discovery Institute. The theory of evolution is supported by many verses of the Quran as I discussed in the endnotes of the *Quran: a Reformist Translation.* (For instance, see: 15:28-29; 24:45; 32:7-9; 71:14-7)

In fact, the theory was first promoted by Muslim scientists. My colleague Dr. T. O. Shanavas, in his book, *Islamic Theory of Evolution: the Missing Link between Darwin and the Origin of Species,* provides references from the works of major Muslim scientists such as Ibn Sina (Avicenna), Ibn Rushd (Averroes), Muhammad Al-Razi, Ibn Khaldun, Abu Bakr bin Tufayl, Muhammad al-Haytham (Alhazen), Al-Biruni, and provides substantial evidence that Darwin got his inspiration from them through his father Erasmus Darwin. In fact, Darwin's contemporary opponents accused him being influenced by "Barbarian Muhammadans."

It is travesty that today Muslims have regressed so much they are now peddling pseudo science against God's system in creation.

A11
Quotes on Religion

The following quotations are a sample from Western scientists, philosophers, authors and statesmen, who expressed the reaction of reasonable people to religions and dogmas that contradict logic and universal laws. Manmade religions have contributed to immense human miseries, tragedies and atrocities throughout history. I think that especially agnostics are closer to God than those who preach fabricated stories on God and pray to idolized humans in churches, mosques, synagogues, and any temple of any religion, sect, or cult. Unfortunately, many opponents of religions are stuck at *La ilaha* (there is no god) of the *La ilaha illa Allah*, that is, *There is no god, but the god*! Acknowledgment and appreciation of God starts with a *La* (no) of atheistic rejection or agnostic skepticism.

Abraham Lincoln: "The Bible is not my book nor Christianity my profession. I could never give assent to the long, complicated statements of Christian dogma."

Aldous Huxley: "You never see animals going through the absurd and often horrible fooleries of magic and religion. Only man behaves with such gratuitous folly. It is the price he has to pay for being intelligent but not, as yet, intelligent enough."

Arthur C. Clarke: "Religion is a byproduct of fear. For much of human history, it may have been a necessary evil, but why was it more evil than necessary? Isn't killing people in the name of God a pretty good definition of insanity?"

Ayn Rand: "Faith is the commitment of one's consciousness to beliefs for which one has no sensory evidence or rational proof. A mystic is a man who treats his feelings as tools of cognition. Faith is the equation of feeling with knowledge. "

Benjamin Franklin: "I have found Christian dogma unintelligible. Early in life, I absented myself from Christian assemblies.... Lighthouses are more helpful then churches."

Bertrand Russell: "Religion is based . . . mainly on fear . . . fear of the mysterious, fear of defeat, fear of death. Fear is the parent of cruelty, and therefore it is no wonder if cruelty and religion have gone hand in hand. . . . My own view on religion is that of Lucretius. I regard it as a disease born of fear and as a source of untold misery to the human race. I cannot, however, deny that it has made some contributions to civilization. It helped in early days to fix the calendar, and it caused Egyptian priests to chronicle eclipses with such care that in time they became able to predict them. These two services I am prepared to acknowledge, but I do not know of any others." ▶ "Fear is the parent of cruelty; therefore it is no wonder if religion and cruelty have gone hand-in-hand."

Billy Joel: "I wasn't raised Catholic, but I used to go to Mass with my friends, and I viewed the whole business as a lot of very enthralling hocus-pocus. There's a guy hanging upon the wall in the church, nailed to a cross and dripping blood, and everybody's blaming themselves for that man's torment, but I said to myself, 'Forget it. I had no hand in that evil. I have no original sin. There's no blood of any sacred martyr on my hands. I pass on all of this."

Carl Sagan: "My view is that if there is no evidence for it, then forget about it. An agnostic is somebody who doesn't believe in something until there is evidence for it, so I'm agnostic." ▶ "Religions are often the state-protected nurseries of pseudoscience, although there's no reason why religions have to play that role."

Charles Darwin: "It appears to me (whether rightly or wrongly) that direct arguments against Christianity and theism produce hardly any effect on the public; and freedom of thought is best promoted by the gradual illumination of men's minds which follows from the advance of science."

Clarence Darrow: "I do not consider it an insult, but rather a compliment, to be called an agnostic. I do not pretend to know where many ignorant men are sure. "

Dainel C. Dennett: Quoting from an anonymous source: "Philosophy is questions that may never be answered. Religion is answers that may never be questioned."

Dave Matthews: "I'm glad some people have that faith. I don't have that faith. If there is a God, a caring God, then we have to figure he's done an extraordinary job of making a very cruel world."

Denis Diderot: "Man will never be free until the last king is strangled with the entrails of the last priest."

Elizabeth Cady-Stanton: "The Bible and the Church have been the greatest stumbling blocks in the way of women's emancipation… The Bible teaches that woman brought sin and death into the world, that she precipitated the fall of the race, that she was arraigned before the judgment seat of Heaven, tried, condemned and sentenced. Marriage for her was to be a condition of bondage, maternity a period of suffering and anguish, and in silence and subjection, she was to play the role of a dependent on man's bounty for all her material wants, and for all the information she might desire...Here is the Bible position of woman briefly summed up."

Ernest Hemingway: "All thinking men are atheists."

Francois Marie Arouet "Voltaire": "Every sensible man, every honorable man, must hold the Christian sect in horror." ▶ "Christianity is the most ridiculous, the most absurd and bloody religion that has ever infected the world." ▶ "Nothing can be more contrary to religion and the clergy than reason and common sense." ▶ "Superstition, born of paganism and adopted by Judaism, invested the Christian Church from earliest times. All the fathers of the Church, without exception, believed in the power of magic. The Church always condemned magic, but she always believed in it: she did not excommunicate sorcerers as madmen who were mistaken, but as men who were really in communication with the devil." ▶ "If we believe absurdities, we shall commit atrocities." ▶ "Doubt is not a pleasant condition, but certainty is absurd."

Frank Lloyd Wright: "I believe in God, only I spell it Nature."

Freidrich Nietzsche: "Faith means not wanting to know what is true." ▶ "So long as the priest, that professional negator, slanderer and poisoner of life, is regarded as a superior type of human being, there cannot be any answer to the question: What is truth?" ▶ "The Christian faith from the beginning, is sacrifice: the sacrifice of all freedom, all pride, all self-confidence of spirit; it is at the same time subjection, a self-derision, and self-mutilation." ▶ "All religions bear traces of the fact that they arose during the intellectual immaturity of the human race— before it had learned the obligations to speak the truth. Not one of them makes it the duty of its God to be truthful and understandable in his communications." ▶ "The most serious parody I have ever heard was this: In the beginning was nonsense, and the nonsense was with God, and the nonsense was God." ▶ "There is no devil and no hell. Thy soul will be dead even sooner than thy body: fear therefore nothing any more."

Galileo Galilei: "I do not feel obliged to believe that the same God who has endowed us with sense, reason, and intellect has intended us to forgo their use."

Gene Roddenberry: "I condemn false prophets, I condemn the effort to take away the power of rational decision, to drain people of their free will--and a hell of a lot of money in the bargain. Religions vary in their degree of idiocy, but I reject them all. For most people, religion is nothing more than a substitute for a malfunctioning brain." ▶ "We must question the story logic of having an all-knowing all-powerful God, who creates faulty Humans, and then blames them for his own mistakes."

George Bernard Shaw: "The fact that a believer is happier than a skeptic is no more to the point than the fact that a drunken man is happier than a sober one." ▶ "At present there is not a single credible established religion in the world."

George Carlin: "Religion is just mind control." ▶"Religion easily—has the best bullshit story of all time. Think about it. Religion has convinced people that there's an invisible man...living in the sky. Who watches everything you do every minute of every day. And the invisible man has a list of ten specific things he doesn't want you to do. And if you do any of these things, he will send you to a special place, of burning and fire and smoke and torture and anguish for you to live forever, and suffer, and burn, and scream, until the end of time. But he loves you. He loves you. He loves you and he needs money." ▶"Thou shalt keep thy religion to thyself."

Gloria Steinam: "It's an incredible con job when you think of it, to believe something now in exchange for life after death. Even corporations with all their reward systems don't try to make it posthumous."

James Madison: "During almost fifteen centuries has the legal establishment of Christianity been on trial. What has been its fruits? More or less, in all places, pride and indolence in the clergy; ignorance and servility in the laity; in both, bigotry, and persecution." ▶ "In no instance have . . . the churches been guardians of the liberties of the people." ▶ "Religious bondage shackles and debilitates the mind and unfits it for every noble enterprise." ▶ "What influence in fact have Christian ecclesiastical establishments had on civil society? In many instances they have been upholding the thrones of political tyranny. In no instance have they been seen as the guardians of the liberties of the people. Rulers who wished to subvert the public liberty have found in the clergy convenient auxiliaries. A just government, instituted to secure and perpetuate liberty, does not need the clergy."

John Adams: "The divinity of Jesus is made a convenient cover for absurdity." ▶ "This would be the best of all possible worlds, if there were no religion in it."

John Stuart Mill: "The time appears to me to have come when it is the duty of all to make their dissent from religion known."

Jonathan Swift: "We have just enough religion to make us hate but not enough religion to make us love one another"

Karl Marx: "The wretchedness of religion is at once an expression and a protest against real wretchedness. Religion is the sigh of the oppressed creature, the feeling of a heartless world, just as it is the spirit of unspiritual conditions. It is the opium of the people." ▶ "The social principles of Christianity preach cowardice, self-contempt, abasement, submission, humility, in a word all the qualities of the canaille."

Kurt Vonnegut: "Say what you will about the sweet miracle of unquestioning faith, I consider a capacity for it terrifying and absolutely vile."

Leo Tolstoy: "To regard Christ as God, and to pray to him, are to my mind the greatest possible sacrilege."

Louis de Bernières: "The primary epiphenomena of any religion's foundation are the production and flourishment of hypocrisy, megalomania and psychopathy, and the first casualties of a religion's establishment are the intentions of its founder."

Mahatma Ghandi: "My belief in the Hindu Scriptures does not require me to accept every word and every verse as divinely inspired... I decline to be bound by any interpretation, however learnet it may be, if it is repugnant to reason and common sense."

Napoleon Bonaparte: "Religion is what keeps the poor from murdering the rich."

Oscar Wilde: "When I think of all the harm the Bible has done, I despair of ever writing anything to equal it."

Robert A. Heinlen: "Any priest or shaman must be presumed guilty until proven innocent."

Robert Frost: "I hold it to be the inalienable right of anybody to go to hell in his own way."

Robert G. Ingersoll: "Ministers say that they teach charity. That is natural. They live on hand-outs. All beggars teach that others should give." ▶ "For the most part we inherit our opinions. We are the heirs of habits and mental customs. Our beliefs, like the fashion of our garments, depend on where we were born. We are molded and fashioned by our surroundings. ▶ "The clergy know that I know that they know that they do not know." ▶ "Why should I allow that same God to tell me how to raise my kids, who had to drown His own?"

Samuel Clemens "Mark Twain": "Faith is believing something you know ain't true." ▶ "If Christ were here now there is one thing he would not be -- a Christian." ▶ "It (the Bible) is full of interest. It has noble poetry in it; and some clever fables; and some blood-drenched history; and some good morals; and a wealth of obscenity; and upwards of a thousand lies." ▶ "A man is accepted into a church for what he believes and he is turned out for what he knows." ▶ "Our Bible reveals to us the character of our god with minute and remorseless exactness... It is perhaps the most damnatory biography that exists in print anywhere. It makes Nero an angel of light ... by contrast." ▶ "I cannot see how a man of any large degree of humorous perception can ever be religious -- unless he purposely shut the eyes of his mind and keep them shut by force." ▶ "It ain't the parts of the Bible that I can't understand that bother me, it is the parts that I do understand." ▶ "Man is a marvelous curiosity . . . he thinks he is the Creator's pet . . . he even believes the Creator loves him; has a passion for him; sits up nights to admire him; yes and watch over him and keep him out of trouble. He prays to him and thinks He listens. Isn't it a quaint idea."

Thomas Edison: "Religion is all bunk."

Thomas Jefferson: "History I believe furnishes no example of a priest-ridden people maintaining a free civil government. This marks the lowest grade of ignorance, of which their political as well as religious leaders will always avail themselves for their own purpose." ▶ "The Christian god can easily be pictured as virtually the same god as the many ancient gods of past civilizations. The Christian god is a three headed monster; cruel, vengeful and capricious. If one wishes to know more of this raging, three headed beast-like god, one only needs to look at the caliber of people who say they serve him. They are always of two classes: fools and hypocrites." ▶ "Millions of innocent men, women and children, since the introduction of Christianity, have been burnt, tortured, fined and imprisoned; yet we have not advanced one inch towards uniformity." ▶ "I can never join Calvin in addressing his god. He was indeed an Atheist, which I can never be; or rather his religion was Daemonism. If ever man worshipped a false god, he did. The being described in his 5. points is not the God whom you and I acknowledge and adore, the Creator and benevolent governor of the world; but a daemon of malignant spirit. It would be more pardonable to believe in no god at all, than to blaspheme him by the atrocious attributes of Calvin. Indeed I think that every Christian sect gives a great handle to Atheism by their general dogma that, without a revelation, there would not be sufficient proof of the being of a god. Now one sixth of mankind only are supposed to be Christians: the other five sixths then, who do not believe in the Jewish and Christian revelation, are without a knowledge of the existence of a god!" ▶ " The truth is that the greatest enemies to the doctrines of Jesus are those calling themselves the expositors of them, who have perverted them for the structure of a system of fancy absolutely incomprehensible, and without any foundation in his genuine words. And the day will come when the mystical generation of Jesus, by the supreme being as his father in the womb of a virgin will be classed with the fable of the generation of Minerva in the brain of Jupiter. But we may hope that the dawn of reason and freedom of thought in these United States will do away with all this artificial scaffolding, and restore to us the primitive and genuine doctrines of this the most venerated reformer of human errors." ▶ "Religions are all alike—founded upon fables and mythologies." ▶ "I do not find in orthodox Christianity one redeeming feature." ▶ "Christianity is the most perverted system that ever shone on man."

Thomas Paine: "The most formidable weapon against errors of every kind is reason. I have never used any other, and I trust I never shall." ▶ "Revelation is a communication of something which the person to whom the thing is revealed did not know before. For if I have done, a thing, or seen it done, it needs no Revelation to tell me, I have done or seen it done nor enable me to tell it or write it. Revelation therefore cannot be applied to anything done upon earth, of which man is himself actor or witness and consequently all the historical part of the Bible which is almost the whole of it, is not within the meaning and compass of the word Revelation and therefore is not the Word of God." ▶ "Whenever we read the obscene stories, the voluptuous debaucheries, the cruel and tortuous executions, the unrelenting vindictiveness with which more than half the Bible is filled, it would be more consistent that we call it the word of a demon than the word of God. It is a history of wickedness that has served to corrupt and brutalize mankind." ▶ "All national institutions of churches, whether Jewish, Christian or Turkish, appear to me no other than human inventions, set up to terrify and enslave mankind, and monopolize power and profit. "

A12
My Normal and Paranormal Adventures in Kazakhstan:

Bukhari's Ghost Dancing with a Hungry Holy Sunni Goat, Misogynistic Dogs Barking at Pigs, Russian Pyrokinesis Burning Holes in Brains and Pockets, Two Extra Letters Correcting Quranic Bismillah, Kazaks Eating Almaty's Apple and Horse Meat...

Edip Yuksel

This is my third country report since 2008. In my first report, *From Tucson to Changsha,* my mission was to discover China educationally, culturally, socially, politically and of course, culinarily. Other than a short visit to an Uygur Mosque, I had no encounters with religious people. In my second report, I shared my experience at Oxford University, Muslim Institute in London, Book Fair and one night in a Turkish jail in Istanbul. During that trip, using my arguments from *Manifesto for Islamic Reform*, I created a multiple choice test, which I called Theometer or Sectometer, and applied it on my distinguished audience in two countries with remarkable success. Now you are reading this report which you might find as delicious as Almaty's apple!

Hoping that your mind is not already polluted by that obnoxious Cohen the Borat, let me first give you a paragraph of dull and boring background information about Kazakhstan, which declared its independence from Russia in 1991 becoming a presidential republic. Though its democracy is confused between bureaucracy and autocracy (as the USA's between corpocracy and oligarchy), we hope that one day it will become a model country for peace, justice and progress. In Kazakhstan, I was told, "men are manly, sheep are nervous and flies are everywhere." It is the worlds 9th largest country, landlocked, and rich with numerous natural resources. Its population of 17 million comprises of about 70% Kazaks and 20% Russians, and its GDP per capita is about 11,000 dollars.

In March of 2007, an elite group of well-educated and well-connected Kazaks discovered my work, especially the Manifesto for Islamic Reform, which they immediately translated into Russian and distributed it in tens of thousands. Before discovering my work, they had adopted the Salafi version of Sunni religion as the product of intense propaganda by regressive forces from Saudi Arabia, the scourge. For instance, they had destroyed their songs and music paraphernalia and had given up many blessings. This unfortunate experience,

485

however, proves their sincerity and commitment. They were lucky, since Kazakhstan did not block the progressive Internet sites and they had not yet traded their brains for good with the volumes of authentic nonsense called Hadith and Sunna. Trashing human brains and deactivating their rational faculties is the ultimate goal of the religious viruses, especially of the Salafi mutation.

The group was the cream of the crop. I had met the leading two members, Aslbek and Aidar, at the home of my Turkish colleague Dr. Caner Taslaman in Istanbul. They were young and restless, curious and humorous, intelligent and knowledgeable, rationalist and monotheist, brave peacemakers and fighters for justice. They were also macho man, according to my standards. They were excited and appreciative of discovering the Message of the Quran, unaltered by fabricated hearsay stories and sectarian jurisprudence. In a short time we became friends, which led me to challenge them to get 1 out of 5 scores in a physical game of power, balance and concentration, which I had mastered while I was in Turkish prisons. They repeated the fate of many young and strong men whom I had challenged: they lost the game, 5 to 0.

The trip lasted about 24 hours from Tucson to Almaty, which has been declared sister cities for a few decades. I was welcomed by Dinmukhamed and Talgat, two young men sent by Aslbek, and taken to an A-Club Hotel, located on a hill in a beautiful section of the city. All streets were lined with rows of trees as well as the median. I have never seen a city as tree-friendly as Almaty. Modern accommodations were combined with fresh air... Everything in the hotel met the Western standards of luxury, except for the bathroom tissues which were coarse and difficult to tear. I could not learn much from their media, since the twenty plus TV channels were broadcast in either Russian or Kazak.

The Intellectual Ambush at Almaty

Aslbek Mussin (30) decided to organize a live debate between me and a Sunni scholar/preacher. He contacted a list of Sunni preachers, including one of the best contemporary Sunni apologists, Zakir Naik. I was told that he was not receiving positive responses to his invitation, which was fully paid by the hosts. However, a popular Sunni imam from the United Kingdom accepted the invitation. He thought that he was going to preach to a Sunni herd, as usual. He was not aware of the exact nature of the event, yet he was treated in the best possible manner. It took him a few days to notice that he did not have a crowd; but a group of critical thinkers, rational monotheists. The exact moment where he realized the real nature of his mission has been recorded on video. My friend Raymond Catton from Canada, whom I first met through Rashad Khalifa in 1988, was our moderator for the first two sessions. Raymond was using the Manifesto for Islamic Reform for his questions. At one point, the Sunni preacher loudly complained about the questions, which were designed as curveballs to expose the manifold contradictions in his Sunni religion.

Several Kazak monotheists acted like Salafi Sunnis and they served him around the clock. Since they were Salafis before, they knew all the relevant jargons and mannerisms. He was allowed to lead the prayers, which he appeared to think was his God-given right because of his black robe and long beard. Anytime the call for prayer was made, he would leap forward and choose himself to lead the prayers. (Those of us who do not mention Muhammad's name besides God in our *Sala* prayers did not join him). The audience was instructed by Aslbek to cheer for both sides. It was a bizarre scene: while we were in a hot debate, our audience was like in the refrigerator clapping for both sides in an orchestrated and reserved fashion. Our moderators did even better. For instance, Arnold Mol, our moderator for the last session, roared like a lion when I interrupted our Sunni imam; for a moment, Arnold's face turned red and declared his authority to cut me off. I was glad that he did, since Abu Eesa would not have any excuse to complain about the Kazak-style intellectual setup: he had the chance to share the teachings and dogmas of his Sunni religion with Muslims in a very friendly and free environment.

Ironically, Sunnis has so far never allowed us to debate with them in their conferences. I wish we were invited by Sunnis to debate with their imams and sheiks. I wish we were set up by them! I do not expect them to pay for my trip, to assign two friendly young men to serve me, or cheer for me so that I would not feel lonely. None of that! A simple invitation, equal opportunity to debate and a promise of not beating us or killing us during the event would be sufficient. My past experience with the Sunnis and Shiite people is just the opposite. For instance, on October 7 of 1989 they kicked me out by force from their conferences in Chicago, when I directed a few questions from my first English book, *19 Questions for Sunni and Shiite scholars,* to the mullahs they ignorantly call *Mawlana* (Our Lord). They had sent an invitation to Dr. Rashad Khalifa to attend their conference; not as a speaker, but as an audience. Rashad knew that their intention was to humiliate him. Upon Rashad's request, I accepted to substitute him at the conference. I flew from Tucson to Chicago to confront the mullahs and their followers. Rashad had printed two hundred copies of a special issue of the Muslim Perspective, addressing the participants of the conference. I had also a draft copy of my upcoming book, 19 Questions for Sunni and Shiite scholars. Asking the speaker a loaded question was sufficient for my excommunication. They banned me from entering their conference rooms, and then they tried to get rid of me from the lobby, where I was surrounded by curious youths, mostly ethnic Pakistanis. Later, they sent two big guys to my hotel room to physically hurt me; but God sent an African American Muslim who sneaked me out of the hotel just seconds before they reached me. Since then, I have had numerous similar experiences. One of them is memorable. In November 23 of 2002, I had a live debate on a popular Turkish TV program with Dr. Süleyman Ateş, the former head of Religious Affairs. Towards the end of the debate, which was full of surprises, I made a surprise announcement. I declared that for the first time I would be participating in a

487

public event since my emigration to the USA. I was going to show up at a book fair to meet my readers. It was a decision I made at that moment. The host of the show advised me not to do such a crazy thing, but I did not listen. Upon my arrival at the huge external yard of the Kocatepe Mosque, I was welcomed by dozens of monotheists. Several of them, especially Hamza Gürer, begged me not to enter the inside the courtyard. They had noticed a Sunni gang gathered in front of an Islamist publishing house's exhibition tables talking about me. They were getting prepared to hurt me. I barely averted their mischief.

When Sunni or Shiite clergymen gain power, they rarely, if ever, allow their sectarian teachings to be challenged by monotheists like me. Though we always open our doors, windows and occasionally our chimneys for them, they rarely allow us in their Internet forums or Paltalk rooms. The moment they realize that we are monotheists, that we do not associate fabricated Hadith to the Quran, that we do not praise Muhammad more than God, that we do not accept verses abrogated by hungry holy goats, that we do not believe that music is prohibited and women should be avoided like a dog, and hundreds of other non-Quranic teachings and practices, they insult us, falsely accuse and sensor us. Their leaders have called me Zionist, Bahai, or the member of the Moon Cult who received a million dollars… They are very good in producing many rabbits from their Hadith-trained imaginations, and ironically they tend to believe the objective reality of their imaginary rabbits. I hope that Abu Eesa appreciates this great difference between monotheists and polytheists. Rational monotheists have nothing to fear, since they have nothing to hide.

Abu Eesa Niamatullah was a smart, articulate and cordial tall man with very long arms that could hug a camel vertically. He was born in the United Kingdom, of Pakistani heritage. With his Arabized title and first name, black robe, kosher beard and short hair contrary to what his Hadith literature describes his fashion idol, he was wearing a strait jacket around his outgoing personality, screaming the troops of contradictions: a former disk-jockey who considered music a sin, a science-educated man who was promoting nonsense, a humorous man who somehow ended up playing the role of a Sunni scholar. Abu Eesa (The Father of Eesa), was a British-educated Pakistani man impersonating the composite Sunni character created by medieval Arab, Persian, and Turkish pagans, Jewish Rabbis and Christian Monks through mishmash stories and norms! Holy concoction! Under the same garb, he was both a mullah and a normal human being. Perhaps we could become close friends if he did not have his second personality, which promoted a cruel, oppressive and repressive religion. But he has hope. As long as he has some sense of humor left in him, as long as he can listen to the opposing voice, he may be able to free himself from the dogma of the master hypnotist. Time will tell.

Like all religious people who follow dogma blindly, he too was convinced that his cloth and grooming was an integral part of his faith. Knowing that faith is a euphemism for wishful thinking or joining a particular bandwagon for petty tribal, social, political and/or economic interests, it was not a surprise to see many of the followers of dogma showing off with their cloth and grooming; a juvenile way of making a point: I am different and holier than you, and I am the center of the universe! I am the missing link between you and heaven! In this regard, Abu Eesa was better than the Catholic priests; at least he did not generate dust and smoke like the Pope with a funny hat who breaks multiple records in <u>Yuksel's Record of Religious Oddities</u>. (I am working on a new book now. I will rank the top 100 religious oddities according to the amount of logical, natural and internal contradictions they cause.)

Sunni Polytheism Exposed

Noticing his talent of smooth-talking and pleasing the crowds, I knew that if I acted softly, brother Abu Eesa would beat around every bush and tree, every pebble and rock, trying his best to window-dress and cover up the devils in the details of Sunni teaching. I applied pressure on him, I provoked him. I had no personal vendetta against him; in fact, I was in admiration of his passion, dedication and zeal. I was tormented by watching him being tormented between his God-given reason and the nonsense he was indoctrinated to follow as a religion. Until the age of 29, I was not much different than him. In other words, I was encountering myself, my ghost from my days of ignorance. I had empathy for him. I knew exactly what my brother Abu Eesa was feeling/thinking, and why he was feeling/thinking that way, and I tried my best to help him to see himself in the mirror. My primary target was not to debase his person but the diabolic teachings he was promoting. I was praying for his freedom. He had chance to accept the truth, so that it could set him free!

At one point, I used the Quranic trap to expose the Sunni polytheism. I read verses 6:145 to 6:150 from the *Reformist Translation*. I gave a few-seconds pause and looked at him after the challenge: "Bring forth your witnesses who bear witness that God has forbidden this." Like many whom I had tested before him, he too fell into the Quranic trap. He responded with one of his idols' names with the usual fabricated phrase: "Muhammad *Sallallahu Alayhi Wasallam*." Then, I continued finishing the verse 6:150 and reminded him of the beginning of the section by reading verses 6:112-6:117. This debate was being recorded live in front of the select Kazak audience. Suddenly, he realized that his polytheism was exposed naked. He appeared to have woken up from a nightmare and complained for not hearing anything I had read to him. Ironically, his answer to the question testified to the opposite. Perhaps, his reception of verses was interrupted with troops of Hadiths bouncing in his head. He was walking with the help of lightning; he would see the truth surrounding him for a few seconds; but would immediately revert back to the darkness of ignorance. I then reminded him and the audience the verses explaining the phenomenon: when you recite God's *aya* to them, they do not hear and do not understand, since there is a wall (*Hijab*) and curtain between them and God's message (17:45).

Abu Eesa was trying to prove his monotheistic zeal by criticizing those who visit graves of saints and ask for their help. At one point he reminded us that ONLY God could be Omnipresent and Omniscient, and condemned the practice as idol-worship. Of course, we were all in agreement with him on this. But, I knew for sure, he had no clue what he was talking about. I knew the nature of Hadith and Sunna, a forest of vertical, horizontal and diagonal contradictions (68:35-38). I knew that he would contradict his own criticism against calling on dead saints and prophets. So, I asked him whether he was commemorating God alone in his *Sala* prayers in accordance with the Quran (20:14; 72:18; 39:45; 3:18). I asked him whether he was addressing Muhammad in the *Tahiyyah* just after addressing God when he was reciting *al-Fatiha* in the standing position. Those who betrayed God and His messenger by associating various sources to the Quran, call on Muhammad while they are in sitting position: "Assalamu alaika ayyuha annabiyyu..." (Peace be upon YOU, O the Prophet...) as if Prophet Muhammad was Omnipresent and Omniscient second person while they pray. At that point, Abu Eesa forgot about his criticism against the worshippers of dead saints and prophets, and declared his polytheistic practice by emphasizing the word AYYUHA, which is a strong indication of the presence of the person. What was his justification for this contradiction? No surprise: HADITH, a word that has been prophetically condemned by the Quran. He used the same justification to continue asking for help from the most popular idol in the world, *al-Hajar al-Aswad*, the black rock in Mecca. (For details of our arguments against Hadith and Sunna, please see the Manifesto for Islamic Reform. It is published by BrainbowPress and also available online in several languages at www.islamicreform.org).

Abu Eesa could not respond to many fatal criticisms to his Sunni position. For instance, his interpretation of the Hadith in which Omar stops a *sahaba* from bringing pen and paper so that Prophet Muhammad in his death bed could write something to help them not deviate from right path. According to that "authentic Hadith," Omar declared "The prophet is sick and has fever. He does not know what he is saying. *Hasbuna Kitab-ulllah* (God's book is sufficient for us)". According to the same Hadith, Omar's reasoning for stopping Muhammad from writing anything in his death bed was accepted by all the prominent sahaba present there. Abu Eesa's attempted defense of this Hadith missed the entire point. He had also hard time to explain the three different versions of the most important statement in the most witnessed Hadith, The Last Sermon, in his "holy Hadith books." According to numerous Hadith books, Prophet Muhammad left people (a) The Quran and Sunna; (b) The Quran and his family; or (c) The Quran. Even a rudimentary knowledge of history would be sufficient to know the reason for these discrepancies and the reasons behind the fabrication of the two versions that contradict the Quran.

Women are in the Company of Dogs, not Pigs!

Abu Eesa was a talented demagogue. He was not a "straw man" that I could punch to death and declare a cheap victory. He was one of the best apologists Sunnis could get. During our discussion on women issues, he took the lead in defense of women. He went even further than me and most of the feminists. He declared women to be superior to men. Yes, this Sunni imam was declaring superiority of women over men! One of the signs for the end of the world! Our Sunni imam's superwoman, however, would not last more than a few seconds. I was not moved by such a hyperbole, since I knew the double talk... If later he were to be interrogated by his misogynist followers, he would defend himself by saying: "I meant mothers; not wives and sisters!" If Abu Eesa were honest about his promotion of Hadith and Sunna, than he should have said exactly the opposite about woman. I did not list dozens of Hadith from his so-called "authentic Hadith books" that discriminate against women, demean, insult, decry, disparage, deprecate, reprehend, reproach, condemn, and accuse women for being the cause of the biggest troubles of ignorant men. I just reminded him of one of his Hadiths from his favorite book, Bukhari (I am not misrepresenting his position regarding Bukhari, since he publicly declared that he believed that some Hadiths abrogated verses of the Quran):

"What do you think Abu Eesa about this Hadith: 'If a donkey, a pig and a woman passes in front of a praying person, the prayer is nullified.'"? After a short pause, our Sunni imam got animated and pointed at my ignorance of his Hadith! He proudly corrected my error. I had misquoted his Hadith; it was a dog not a pig! If you are a pet-loving American, you may find little problem with such a company. But, his Hadith collections condemned dogs, required those touched by a dog to wash themselves seven times in a special way, and instructed the killing of all black dogs... So, there was not much relief for women to be promoted to the level of female dogs, even the white ones. To show off his knowledge of Hadith, our imam inadvertently abrogated his own imaginary Hadith with a dog. The dog in his Hadith books came to life and ate my erroneous pig together with his imaginary Sunni superwoman!

The Extraordinary Powers of Psychokinetic, Telekinetic or Pyrokinetic Energy!

Besides Hadith and Sunna, there was another hoax I had to deal with. I was hearing from my hosts about a Russian guy with paranormal powers. According to many eye-witness testimonies, he was burning holes in things with sheer mental concentration. As a rational monotheist, as a critical thinker, I did not hesitate to reject the claims to be 99.9 percent a hoax. They laughed at me. They had in the past taken extreme skeptics who did not give even a 0.1 percent chance. One of their recent guests was a philosophy professor from Moscow University, who had become a total believer in pyrokinesis. They wanted to take me to a session so that I could witness the paranormal event. I could not pass up the offer.

During the nine days in Almaty, I met three Kazaks who shared the name Serik (from Arabic Sherik, that is Partner or Friend). This Serik was educated in the United States and was a successful businessman and financial advisor. He was in his early thirties. Cool as cucumber. He had two Mercedes cars, one driven by his private driver. He enjoyed trying to scare me by accelerating his new Mercedes G Wagon in Almaty's narrow streets. The Russian guy lived on the fifth floor of a dilapidated apartment building. The door had multiple locks on it. Upon our entry, he gave an envelope to the Russian who called himself Alexander. Later, I learned that he had popped-up 2,000 dollars for the half-an-hour session. Alexander was a skinny man in his forties. He had a very serious demeanor and all-business attitude. I noticed that before leading me to a chair across from him, he rushed to sit at a chair in front of a little desk with a circular top. He started talking in Russian about his talents of collecting energy from nature and focusing on things he wanted to burn. Serik was a fluent translator and experienced disciple. Alexander was claiming connections with Russian military.

Alexander then produced an inflated little balloon and put it between my right hand and his left hand. I was expecting some kind of laser guns hidden somewhere, but nothing appeared suspicious; he wore a simple shirt with short sleeves. He was talking about the special energy he had that would not pop the balloon. The balloon stayed suspended between his palm and mine for about thirty seconds. He was making low humming noises. I started feeling warmth in the middle of my palm. Then the heat increased and I felt as if there was a ball of fire in my palm. I had to let the balloon fall. It was a very unusual experience. I had in the past studied hypnosis and participated in hypnotic sessions, but this had nothing to do with it. I was not even informed beforehand that I would feel heat inside my palm. But, I was open to every scientific and "normal" explanation before believing that all my lost socks were indeed stolen by Martian visitors. Unfortunately, I knew that for many people Martian thieves were the first explanation for the disappearing socks phenomenon!

I was not paying much attention to what was he telling me through Serik. I was carefully watching like James Randi who had exposed Uri Geller, the notorious Israeli fraudster. Alexander moved to his second show. He opened his hand and let me feel it. It was colder than usual. He then pressed against my right hand palm and started doing the same thing: concentrating and humming. I heard a puff sound and felt a burning pain in the back of my hand between my thumb and index finger. I tried not to overreact. I wanted to take the picture of him, but I respected his wish not to be photographed.

Then, Alexander showed me several plastic cups and placed them on the floor next to my feet. He went all the way into another room which was connected to his office. He sat on a chair about 20 feet away. He started humming and I noticed the plastic cup starting to melt from the side facing him. Within a few seconds he carved a hole in the plastic cup. He did a few similar burnings and poking holes in plastic. Noticing that he was burning and poking holes on the same straight line, I grabbed a cup and put it on the floor at another location and asked him to burn it there. He grabbed it and located it somewhere else in an animated fashion and rapid talking. He made me sit on another chair and from behind started concentrating on the cup. He excitedly claimed that he burned it by sending his energy through my eyeglasses or eyes. I then took a dollar bill from my wallet and put it on his desk and asked him to burn a hole in it. He put it inside his palm and pointed his right hand's index finger accompanied with exaggerated concentration and bragging words about his powers. He did poke a little whole in the American dollar that had already been turned to a doughnut by the "robber banks", Wall Street and corporate thieves who stole billions of taxpayers dollars during their recent major heist in American history.

I asked Alexander a few questions about the source of his powers. He talked about his veins, about a special diet of 400 gram of vegetables and 40 gram of nuts, about earth, water, fire, air and ether. Long live Empedocles! I had already witnessed so many red flags that when he started to diagnose my potential health problems and missing the ones I already had, I tried my best to endure his insults to my intelligence. I also wondered about his knowledge about the Randy Foundation, which has been offering 1 million dollars for anyone that could prove paranormal powers. I asked him to go there and claim the money. He made up an excuse: he had a contract with the military for four more months and he would not be able to go out during this period. When I left his office, I was impressed by his talents and showmanship, yet I was sure that he was using some devices to create the burning effect. I suspected two things: laser engravers and chemicals that could have a delayed burning reaction.

The following day, I asked Serik to take me there so that I expose the hoax. I also decided to record my encounter with the fraudster. To make my job easy, Serik arranged this session with Alexander for Aidar, the journalist. At the door, I entered his office with a camcorder. I demanded him to apologize for three things: for insulting my intelligence, for burning my hand and for defrauding thousands of dollars from my friends. I added that he had to give back all the money he received from them. He appeared to be composed and cool. Serik was doing very well in translating our conversation. At a point, I grabbed a plastic cup and put it by the entrance door and challenged him to perform his powers there. He accepted with a condition: he would do it only with the presence of Aidar, the new "recruit." I had no choice but to accept since I had no clear idea what his trick was about and the two of my friends were not sure about my allegations. Serik and I got out and he locked the door behind us. Taking advantage of this period, I decided to climb to the attic from the opening. I climbed the metal stairs on the wall and pushed the square door all the way pulling myself to the attic. It was dark and dirty. I looked for wires and vertically installed laser engravers in the ceiling of his office room. I was disappointed, nothing was there. I came down and asked Serik to call Aidar and learn what was going on. We had to wait a few more minutes. When the door opened I entered, Aidar put his arms on my shoulder with his head down, "Let's get out of here; he is real. I am hundred percent sure, he is genuine." I could not believe my eyes and ears. Aidar appeared pale and shaken. He was very scared. There was big hole on his nylon windbreaker on the right side of his chest. He had not responded to my challenge by poking hole in the cup by the door. Instead, he had chosen to have a new recruit. He had chosen offence. I asked Aidar whether he was injected with some kind of medication. I could not explain his betrayal of me through normal circumstances.

Alexander was now working on Serik, perhaps his best disciple. I had to interrupt. I searched under the desk. I saw sticky stuff under it. I thought they were the secret chemicals he was using; but they were most likely gum pieces as he claimed. Then, I opened the little door under the desk. There I noticed a pedal, exactly as I had predicted. When Serik and Aidar saw it, they were shocked. But, this would not last long. Alexander pointed at a little camera on the corner of the wall and claimed that the pedal is for the camera; he was recording the sessions secretly. I did not buy his explanation. I immediately jumped over the seat by the wall and pulled off the device that looked like a small camera. I suspected it to be a laser, disguised inside a camera cover. But, after a brief inspection I was disappointed in myself. I was wrong in my accusation; indeed it was a camera. But, I was still not convinced that the pedal was for the camera. I suspected a clever cover up. If someone discovered the pedal, then Alexander has a convincing explanation for it. I had promised Aslbek and others that I would surely expose the hoax and now I was nowhere near close to it. The attic had not produced any clue, nor the pedal hidden under his desk. Meanwhile, I noticed that I was losing Serik too. He did not have much faith in my claims to start with. And now, after two failures, he had perhaps no faith at all. I felt the urge to discover the devises the scam artist was surreptitiously utilizing.

I sat down on the chair and held the balloon in my hand and challenged him to do his trick right there. He appeared to accept my challenge. But after a brief moment of concentration, he started telling Serik that he had accumulated too much energy and could blow my hand off. I did not swallow his bluff. I challenged him to blow my hand off and while at it he should also blow my head off. I started timing him, using my watch. I told him that he had only five minutes to unveil his tricks and apologize for his three crimes; otherwise I would call the American embassy and ask them to send police here to ransack his office. He was not giving up. He was trying to influence Serik to ask me to give up. I would not. I informed him about the few minutes left for him to avoid the police.

When the five minutes finished I asked Serik to call the US embassy. I was going to tell them that a Russian scam artist had attempted to defraud me, an American citizen, and I needed police to come to the address. Serik did not respond to me. Losing both of my comrades and my patience, I decided to use some force. I charged the desk which was attached to the floor. I kicked it hard, breaking the jar and spreading some knickknacks to the floor. From the bottom of the table, a bundle of white cables were exposed. They were curving back to the bedroom. Following the lead of the wires, I went to the bedroom across. At that point I heard Serik telling me that he confessed his trick. He was using chemicals. I knew that he was still trying to hide his real trick. So, I continued my search. Behind the bed there was a section covered with blankets. When I removed the blankets, an electronic devise enclosed in two big boxes was exposed. My friends were in shock. They never expected such a professional set up. The devices, according to Alexander, were generating microwaves. He also mentioned using chemicals in combination. I did not pay much attention to his explanations, since I never trusted him. I am not yet sure exactly how it worked, perhaps he was filling the room with microwaves which would activate the chemical that he would secretly attach to things. Perhaps he was sticking the chemical to the back of our hands with his thump when he was shaking our hands. In fact, the location where he burned our hands was exactly corresponding to where the tip of his thump would land. But how could he manage to delay the burning of the back of my hand when he directed heat to my palm? Why he was not able to produce the same effect when I challenged him in different locations? Perhaps, he would not have chance to obtain extra chemicals and attach it under scrutiny. I am not sure. Considering all the locations that he performed his tricks, they were on a straight line across his bed room. Regardless of the details, it was now clear that he was using a high tech device to create the burning effect on his subjects.

I recorded his apology. He apologized for insulting the intelligence of a philosopher, for burning my hand and for defrauding my friends. Later I felt compassion for him and gave him a heart-to-heart advice. I kept my word and did not call police on him. Serik took the envelope containing several thousand dollars. Then, he asked for all the money previously paid by him and his friends. The scam artist told us that he was stashing his money somewhere else. Serik's chauffeur took them; he retrieved about ten thousands dollars.

Two days later, Aslbek wanted Abu Eesa to experience the same show. He was curious about his reaction. I went with Abu Eesa pretending being there for the first time. We recorded his experience and reaction. He was acting like a scientist, but a gullible and confused one. He appeared to trust every word of explanation given by Alexander. Alexander was using natural terminology to explain his powers, but he was also mixing the word spirit with them. Abu Eesa was eager to explain his powers with *jinns* or ghosts. So, he was trying to hear more about the spirit part. I asked Abu Eesa a few short questions so that he

495

could elaborate on his *jinni* theory. I reminded him about the paintings containing Christian figures and symbols. He was convinced that it was jinni power. Before leaving, Abu Eesa advised Alexander to read the Quran. It was refreshing to hear Abu Eesa promoting the Quran. I could not stop myself interjecting: "Brother Abu Eesa, you are peddling Bukhari to us, but I see that you are advising the Quran to outsiders. Why don't you ask him to read Bukhari?" I am sure, Abu Eesa knew that no sound person would accept Islam by starting from Bukhari. None would have any respect or sympathy for the fictional Muhammad depicted by Bukhari. For converts, Bukhari would be inserted into the scene afterwards; to gradually distort the message of the Quran! In other words, Hadith would be introduced in a fashion to induce the effect known "the boiled frog syndrome". (I have been receiving numerous letters from converts complaining about this "bait and switch" method. Dr. Maurice Bucaille was one of the vocal modern tactic of this sophisticated scam of Sunni apologists.)

In Order to Blind Himself to Code 19, the Sunni Imam adds Two More Letters to Bismillah!

The following day, I was asked to give a lecture on Code 19 to a small group of mathematicians and philosophers. I had little time and on top of that the translation slowed me down. I made a philosophical introduction and presented the tip of the iceberg. One of the philosophers, Beket Nurzhanov, invoked Pythagoras's name and dismissed my presentation as numerology. I knew Pythagoras very well and I very much liked him. But, I knew that code 19 was based on a verifiable and falsifiable physical facts and had little to do with Pythagorean esoteric number mysticism.

Hearing that he had company among our distinguished guests, our imam, Ebu Eesa got a second wind. He declared that the frequency of the word Month in the Quran was not 12, and the frequency of the word Day was not 365 as I presented. He obviously had no clue about what he was talking. I wished that we had more time to discuss this issue face to face; but we did not have time. The imam added one more refutation: the number of the letters in the Bismillah (Basmala) was not 19 either; it had 21 letters. He also claimed that he could come up with similar numerical patterns by using the Kazakhstan constitution. I was glad to hear such a concrete statement and I challenged him to do so in three or four months. Later I changed my mind regarding the Kazakh constitution since it is not in the Latin alphabet and he could easily tamper with its letters as he did with the most popular verse of the Quran. So, I challenged him to produce similar patterns from the Constitution of the United States.

Abu Eesa demanded more time and the stage to spew his aversion against the number 19, prophesized in chapter 74 of the Quran as one of the greatest divine signs. I gave him the marker, the board and asked him to show the extra two letters in Bismillah that I had missed! I was glad that the session was recorded by a professional so that the world would witness the kind of ignorance and arrogance the enemies of the prophetic sign have. Interestingly, the former head of the religious affairs in Turkey too had made exactly the same absurd claim in front of millions in a live debate with me, which is now available on the internet. It is such an absurd claim since the number of letters in Bismillah is no secret and it does not require the knowledge of Hadith and so-called (pseudo)science of Hadith to know it. Any student in an elementary school in Arabic speaking countries could easily count its 19 letters. In fact, not a single Sunni or Shiite scholar who happened to mention the number of letters in Bismillah contradicted that simple fact. For instance, famous Molla Jami starts his divan by referring to the 19 letters of Bismillah. Abu Layth Samarqandi in his Quran interpretation refers to a Hadith about the three (not four!) letters of its first word, Bism. Fakhr al-Din al-Razi in his impressive interpretation of the Quran, Tafsir al-Kabir, refers to an interesting connection made between the 19 letters of Bismillah and the guardians of hell, claiming that each letter protects from their harms. Al-Qurtubi in his Al-Jami' li Ahkam il-Quran, reports Hadith about 19 letters of Bismillah. Similarly, the Kurdish Sunni scholar Said Nursi too refers to that simple fact numerous times. Furthermore, millions of Pakistani and Hindu Muslims have the tradition of using 786, the numerical value of the 19 letters, for Bismillah. In sum, our imam neither could verify the simple facts nor was he aware of his own sources.

After the discovery of the code 19 and the fulfillment of its prophecies mentioned in chapter 74, Sunni and Shiite scholars started adding letters to the most repeated verse of the Quran, *BiSMi ALLaH AL-RaḤMaN AL-RaḤYM*. As usual, they could not agree about the number of letters they were hallucinating. Some claimed that it had 21 letters and some claimed 22. Our Pakistani-British imam was hallucinating 21 letters. However, during the few seconds it took him to reach the white board with the marker in his hand, he changed his mind. Instead of adding two *alifs* as he claimed while sitting in his chair, somehow he did just the opposite. He deleted three *alifs* from Bismillah and uttered a few nonsensical claims regarding the ease of coming up with a numerical structure based on its 16 letters! Of course, he did not come up with a single example, except his utter confusion by first claiming two extra *alifs* in Basmala and then when challenged, this time deleting three *alifs* from it! He managed to do both in less than a minute! I should not have expected a better criticism from someone who considered Bukhari a holy book, believed the authority of holy hungry goats in shaping his *sharia law*, and believed that some Hadith reports abrogated the verses of the Quran.

At one point during one of the debates, Imam Abu Eesa made a negative remark regarding the **www.19.org** logo followed by a question mark on my T-shirt. He called it a "cult." I asked him to define "cult" and then check whether I were a cult member. Upon my rebuke and invitation to substantiate his accusation, he gave up. Later, Hasan Mahmud came up with a great line of defense: "No cult would put a question mark under their logo"

The Derrida-loving Philosopher Joins the Sunni Imam in an Imaginary Universe!

While talking against code 19, our imam cleverly reminded the audience his agreement with the great doctor in the room who dismissed the code 19 as a modern version of Pythagorean numerology. He was in complete agreement with Professor Beket Nurzhanov, Head of the Department of History of Philosophy of the Kazakhstan National University named after Al Farabi. Beket was well-groomed and knew how to speak English. His appearance, age and title demanded respect. A few minutes later when the session ended with a tea break, I joined him.

While sipping from my cup of tea, I wondered about Beket's mind and I asked him about his philosophy. He listed the names of his favorite philosophers. Derrida was among them and it was enough for me to get some idea about his modus operandi. I did not find any common philosopher, except for Nietzsche, among our favorites list. I liked Socrates, Leibniz, Wittgenstein, Hume, among many others. I questioned this Derrida-loving professor about the reason of his dismissal of my presentation, without even bothering to study it. He told me this, "According to a mathematician, there could be another universe where 2+2 could be making 3 or 5." Yes, read it again if you wish, without spilling your cup of tea.

I did not ask him the identity of that mathematician. Honestly, I did not care about such a nerd. Our doctor, who dismissed the code 19, was the worst of all relativists. He doubted the reliability of universal mathematical statements. As a constant seeker of truth and servant of the Truth, I could not try to appease his ego or feelings. I had to tell him what he needed to hear: "According to your mathematician, dear professor, these words coming from your mouth too could be nonsense in another universe." I noticed surprise in his face. I corrected myself. "In fact, I do not need to trust your extraterrestrial mathematician. Forget about another universe, your words are nonsense in many languages and countries of this very little planet!" I meant both meanings of the "nonsense"! He was relying on arbitrary human language to deny universal language of the universe.

When the issue became the divine sign in mathematics, our professor was leaving the mathematics of his universe which he relied on without doubt when he counted his money, his children, his socks and fingers. In order to blind himself to one of the greatest signs and reject the most profound facts of this universe, he was seeking refuge in a mathematician from another universe. He was switching universes. At that moment, I felt pity for his students and remembered the Quranic verse 7:146.

By now, you might think that my adventure with Abu Eesa and Beket was the normal one. Honestly, I think my adventure with them was the real paranormal one. The scam that the Russian guy was performing had nothing to do with paranormal; it was based on perfect science and technology. The real paranormal, the real odd events were performed by these two gifted and highly educated individuals. The first had no problem in believing a hungry holy goat abrogating verses from his holy book, thinking that he could value women by equating them to dogs and donkeys, could add letters to Bismillah, and many more religious nonsense, while the second one, seeking refuge in an imaginary universe to blind himself to one of the greatest divine signs. These were the real paranormal beings and events, and you can see their clones everywhere on this planet.

Back to Normal

Aside from confronting theological and scientific hoaxes, among the many memories that I will remember for a long time is my experience in a Russian sauna which, reportedly, had the temperature up to 80 degrees Celsius. For the first time I ate horse meat and drank horse milk (kımız), which was the most disgusting thing after the Durian fruit I had tasted in China a year before. Again, for the first time, I saw young Kazaks juggling not one but two dual cell phones, each phone having two phone numbers. By the way, 2x2=4 phone numbers in our universe!

There I had a great time with Ray Catton, his wife Sophia, and Hasan Mahmud who all joined us from Canada. Tufan Karadere and Gökhan Aycan from Turkey, and Arnold Mol from Holland contributed to the conference with fresh voices and pleasant conversations. I was impressed by Hasan Mahmud who is an activist serving in Muslim Canadian Congress as its Director of Sharia Law since last six years. He was well prepared to expose the so-called Sharia Law. A half-an-hour interview with him by Raymond was recorded, and inshallah it will soon be available on the Internet together with other video recordings.

Unfortunately, several other invitees could not make it there. For instance, Mohammed Jaseer of India had to return from Dubai airport because of miscommunication regarding visa. My colleague Layth al Shaiban planned to join us, but could not make it.

During my brief visit to Almaty, I met many bright Kazaks and enjoyed their company. Aslbek Musin (maverick), Serik Kushenov (entrepreneur) , Yerlan Salmenov (entrepreneur), Aidar Kaipov (journalist), Serik Ryszhanov (thinker/researcher), Serik Kupeishin (lawyer), Damir Almarekov, Berik, DinMukhamed (dusinessman), Abu Walid Khamdi (dentist), Murtaza İzcilik (accountant), Timur, Talgat (lawyer), Ismail, and many others will inshallah be the pioneers in promoting Islamic Reform in Kazakhstan, the surrounding countries and the world. We ended the conference with an evaluation and some decisions, which included the following:

1. Redesign the 19.org and turn it to a multilingual hub of communication and cooperation for monotheists around the world.
2. Start weekly Quranic studies at homes.
3. Include women in philosophical, educational, cultural and social activities. Without women's participation an Islamic reform is not possible.
4. Translate some books into Russian, including the introduction and endnotes of the Reformist Translation of the Quran and the upcoming book, *Nineteen: God's Signature in Nature and Scripture.*
5. Promote critical and creative thinking among secondary school students, and campaign to include critical thinking courses in public school curriculum.
6. Establish a club or foundation to promote culture of innovation through competition among young inventors.
7. Considering the importance of comparative advantage in global economy, focus on a few technologies with great potentials and attract the best minds from around the world to do research on them.
8. Avoid the extravagant life-style and addiction with consumption; focus on charity.
9. Fight corruption and lead Kazakhstan to be a role model for the so-called Muslim world.
10. Without compromising individual freedoms and idiosyncrasies, establish a strong network and cooperation among monotheists.
11. To promote rational monotheism, peace, justice and progress, facilitate global projects and organize the next conference either in London or Istanbul.

Let me finish this report with a remark made by Serik Kushenov in a fancy restaurant in Almaty. When I complained about a fly hovering over our table and bragged about American restaurants having no flies, Serik swatted with a big smile: "We have flies here because our food is natural and organic" Well, I found people of the Kazakhstan as natural and organic! ☺

To see the pictures of our conference in Almaty, you may visit my Picassa at:

http://picasaweb.google.com/edipyuksel

The video recording of the conference will later be shared with public.

A13
To the Factor of 666

(From *Peacemaker's Guide to Warmongers*, by Edip Yuksel)

**If Muslims are Terrorists, then Jews and Christians are
Terrorists to the Factor of 666!**

The verse 9:5 does not encourage Muslims to attack those who associate partners to God, but to attack those who have violated the peace treaty and killed and terrorized people because of their belief and way of life. The Quran does not promote war; but encourages us to stand against aggressors on the side of peace and justice. War is permitted only for self-defense (See: 2:190,192,193,256; 4:91; 5:32; 60:8-9). We are encouraged to work hard to establish peace (47:35; 8:56-61; 2:208). The Quranic precept promoting peace and justice is so fundamental that peace treaty with the enemy is preferred to religious ties.

> 8:72 Those who have acknowledged and emigrated and strived with their money and lives in the cause of God, and those who sheltered and supported; these are the allies of one another. Those who acknowledged but did not emigrate, you do not owe them any allegiance until they emigrate. But if they seek your help in the system, then you must support them, except if it is against a people with whom there is a treaty between you. God is watcher over what you do.*

This verse unequivocally states that the rule of law is above any other affiliation. Islam emphasizes the importance of the rule of law, justice and peace (Also see: 16:91-92).

One of the favorite verses used by warmongers to justify the imperialistic occupations and atrocities against Muslims is 9:29. Unfortunately, it is mistranslated by almost every translator. The correct translation of it should be:

> 9:29 You shall fight (back) against those who do not believe in God, nor in the last day, and they do not prohibit what God and His messenger have prohibited, and do not abide by the system of truth among those who received the scripture, until they pay the COMPANSATION, in humility.

501

You have noticed that I inserted a parenthesis since the context of the verse is about the War of *Hunain*, and fighting is allowed for only self defense. See: 2:190-193, 256; 4:91; and 60:8-9.

Furthermore, note that I suggest COMPENSATION instead of Arabic word Jizya. The meaning of Jizya has been distorted as a perpetual tax on non-Muslims, which was invented long after Muhammad to further the imperialistic agenda of Sultans or Kings. The origin of the word that I translated as Compensation is JaZaYa, which simply means compensation, not tax. Because of their aggression and initiation of a war against muslims and their allies, after the war, the allied community should require their enemies to compensate for the damage they inflicted on the peaceful community. Various derivatives of this word are used in the Quran frequently, and they are translated as COMPANSATION for a particular deed.

Unfortunately, the distortion in the meaning of the verse above and the practice of collecting a special tax from Christians and Jews, contradict the basic principle of the Quran that there should not be compulsion in religion and there should be freedom of belief and expression (2:256; 4:90; 10:99; 18:29; 88:21,22, and 4:137). Since taxation based on religion creates financial duress on people to convert to the privileged religion, it violates this important Quranic principle. Dividing a population that united under a social contract (constitution) into privileged groups based on their religion contradicts many principles of the Quran, including justice, peace, and brotherhood/sisterhood of all humanity.

Some uninformed critics or bigoted enemies of the Quran list verses of the Quran dealing with wars and declare islam to be a religion of violence. Their favorite verses are: 2:191; 3:28; 3:85; 5:10, 34; 9:5; 9:28-29; 9:123; 14:17; 22:9; 25: 52; 47:4 and 66:9. In this article, I refuted their argument against 9:29, and I will discuss each of them later.

Some followers of Sunni or Shiite religions, together with their like-minded modern Crusaders, abuse 9:5 or 9:29 by taking them out of their immediate and Quranic context. Sunnis and Shiites follow many stories and instructions falsely attributed to Muhammad that justify terror and aggression. For instance, in a so-called authentic (or authentically fabricated) Hadith, after arresting the murderers of his shepherd, the prophet and his companions cut their arms and legs off, gauge their eyes with hot nails and leave them dying from thirst in the dessert, a contradiction to the portrayal of Muhammad's mission in the Quran (21:107; 3:159). In another authentically fabricated Hadith, the prophet is claimed to send a gang during night to secretly kill a female poet who criticized him in her poetry, a violation of the teaching of the Quran! (2:256; 4:137; 4:140; 10:99; 18:29; 88:21-22). Despite these un-Quranic teachings, the aggressive elements among Sunni or Shiite population have almost always been a minority.

Six Diabolic Steps to Distort and Discredit

The following six steps are cleverly utilized over and over by the enemies of islam, including Christian missionaries, to discredit the Quran. For the 3rd and 4th steps they find great ammunition inside the volumes of Hadith and sectarian jurisprudence books. (No wonder they like those books very much). For the 5th and 6th steps they find many allies among the followers of Sunni or Shiite sects, who are extremely intoxicated by those anti-islamic sectarian teachings.

Before exposing this unholy alliance let me quote several war related instructions from the so-called authentic Hadith books:

> Narrated As-Sab bin Jaththama: The Prophet passed by me at a place called Al-Abwa or Waddan, and was asked whether it was permissible to attack the pagan warriors at night with the probability of exposing their women and children to danger. The Prophet replied, "They (i.e. women and children) are from them (i.e. pagans)." I also heard the Prophet saying, "The institution of Hima is invalid except for Allah and His Apostle." (Bukhari (Jihad) Volume 4, Book 52, Number 256)

> It is reported on the authority of Sa'b b. Jaththama that the Prophet of Allah (may peace be upon him), when asked about the women and children of the polytheists being killed during the night raid, said: They are from them. (Muslim Book 019, Number 4321)

> It is narrated by Sa'b b. Jaththama that he said (to the Holy Prophet): Messenger of Allah, we kill the children of the polytheists during the night raids. He said: They are from them. (Muslim Book 019, Number 4322)

> Sa'b b. Jaththama has narrated that the Prophet (may peace be upon him) asked: What about the children of polytheists killed by the cavalry during the night raid? He said: They are from them. (Muslim Book 019, Number 4323)

Here are the repeated sixes:

1. Ignore the fact that the Quran is a self-sufficient, self-explaining and detailed book, and destroy its semantic network by deliberately disconnecting its verses. Take a portion of the Quran and ignore all other verses that explain, supplement or bring limitation to that verse. If this is not enough to make it ugly or scary, then;

2. Reduce your reference to a smaller portion; take a Quranic verse or part of it out of its immediate context. If this is not enough to make it ugly or scary, then;

3. Twist the meaning of some words. You may even find a sectarian book or a website that has done that before you. If this is not enough to make it ugly or scary, then;

4. Refer to the mishmash collection of fabrications called Hadith and Sunna; there you will find a treasury of trash to stink an entire city.

Claim that the Quran is useless and unintelligible without these sources. Some Sunni or Shiite people will be confused by your love of those "holy" teachings! That is a good sign. If you cannot convince, you must confuse... But, your goal is to convert as many as possible. So, find as much as garbage out of the Sunni or Shiite sources and introduce it as Islamic. If this is not enough to make it ugly or scary, then;

5. Pick some examples of Sunni or Shiite idiots or terrorists, from among more than a billion Muslims, and generalize it to all Muslims. Especially, choose your examples from traumatized populations that have been abused and oppressed under the occupation of USA, UK, Israel, or Russia, or under the tyranny of a puppet dictator supported by one of these nations. While doing this, you must entirely ignore all the wars, destructions, massacres, tortures, and terrorist acts committed by the Judeo-Christian forces. If this is not enough to make it ugly or scary, then;

6. Exchange words of hatred and bigotry with some intoxicated followers of Sunni or Shiite sects. Then go to your church, sing songs about love and Jesus, and do not forget asking forgiveness for your sins. You will start your next day clean and ready to commit more sins. Your Sunni or Shiite partner (!) will be waiting for you since they do not have confession sessions. If this is not enough to make it ugly and scary, then you have picked a very wrong verse. Choose another verse from the Quran, and go back and start from step one!

Let's apply it to the Bible: "Jesus and His Disciples were a warmongering gang!"

Almost any big size book can be discredited by this dishonest and deceitful method; any book! By following these steps, I could easily depict Jesus, one of the messengers of peace (islam), as a divider and a trouble maker, rather than a peacemaker. Let's take one example from Bible:

> "Suppose ye that I am come to give peace on earth? I tell you, Nay; but rather division: For from henceforth there shall be five in one house divided, three against two, and two against three. The father shall be divided against the son, and the son against the father; the mother against the daughter, and the daughter against the mother; the mother in law against her daughter in law, and the daughter in law against her mother in law." Lu 12:51-53

> "Think not that I am come to send peace on earth: I came not to send peace, but a sword." Matthew 10:34

By using the right-wing Evangelical Christians' own methodology of treating the Quran, I came up with a peace-hating, anti-family, troublemaker called Jesus! All I did was to take the verse out of its context. I did not even resort to twisting its words or adding some trash from secondary sources, or giving some examples from crusades, inquisitions, slavery, or irritate and provoke some crazy people among Evilgelical Crusaders. (To distinguish the militarist Evangelical Christians from the progressive ones, I will heron call this group with one word: Evilgelical)

By using the first two of the six steps, I could claim that the disciple of Jesus were, in fact, a dangerous gang who were planning to shed blood in that peaceful region. They were savages who cut the ears of their opponents:

> "And, behold, one of them which were with Jesus stretched out his hand, and drew his sword, and struck a servant of the high priest's, and smote off his ear." (Mt 26:51. Also see: Mark 14:47 ; Lu 22:50; John 18:10)

I could depict Jesus and his disciples as a gang of blood-thirsty troublemakers, by adding verses justifying violence, blood-shed, massacres and tortures from the Old Testament, which was heavily relied by Jesus and his supporters for their mission. I could even reasonably speculate that Jesus and his few followers were planning a huge massacre in the region, but the Roman Empire stopped them before the cult reached to a dangerous number (Luke 21:24);. Knowing that they were provoked prematurely, Jesus reminded Peter:

> "Then said Jesus unto him, Put up again thy sword into his place: for all they that take the sword shall perish with the sword." (Mt 26:51).

I could reasonably ask a Christian who claims his religion to be the religion of peace: "You will agree that this event happened in the last days of Jesus. Why then did Jesus never tell his disciples not to carry SWORDS before one of them cut off the ear of the servant of the high priest? Or, do you want us to believe that Peter, who was putting his life at risk by trying to defend Jesus, did not give a hoot to the instruction of his leader? Was Peter carrying the sword to peel cucumbers? Obviously, Jesus had seen that his disciple(s) were carrying swords and he did not mind. However, here he knew that tactically using sword would not save them from the Roman army and it would be a futile and premature fight." Perhaps, my argument to depict Jesus as another potential Samson who killed a thousand men with the jaw of an ass (Jg 15:16) would receive cheers from the enemies of Jesus.

To depict Jesus as a rebel who planned a bloody revolution, I could cite Mt 21:12; Mr 11:15; Jo 2:19 and claim that he attacked the temple and destroyed its properties. I might have even continued the attack by quoting him:

> "But those mine enemies, which would not that I should reign over them, bring hither, and slay them before me." (Lu 19:27).

> "Then said he unto them, But now, he that hath a purse, let him take it, and likewise his scrip: and he that hath no sword, let him sell his garment, and buy one." (Luke 22:36)

However, if I had done this it would be unfair to the teaching of Jesus, one of the messengers of islam (peace and submission to God), delivered by the New Testament. It would be unfair because I would be taking them out of their context. Without even mixing them with the verses of the Old Testament that usually published in the same volume and frequently referred by the New Testament.

Modern Crusaders, allied with big corporations are orchestrating a deceptive propaganda and misinformation campaign to promote their bloody cause to colonize new lands and convert more people.

Modern Crusaders distort verses of the Quran, exaggerate the deeds of terrorists and even attribute some events motivated by nationalism or other motives to islam. Their propaganda machine never referred to the Serbs as Christian Rapists and Christian Terrorists. Their propaganda machine never referred to the torturer and murderer Zionist occupying forces as Jewish Terrorists, or Jewish Murderers. Their propaganda machine never acknowledges the Christian faith and zeal behind Nazi crimes. But, they frequently associated any act of terrorism to Islam and Muslims. Furthermore, they cleverly managed to depict the freedom seeking victims of brutal occupying forces as aggressors in conflicts such as Chechnya and Palestine.

They try to depict islam as a violent religion, thereby seeking to justify their own terror, massacres, pre-emptive wars, which are cunningly promoted in a euphemistic language through their propaganda machines. They don't kill and terrorize civilians; they just produce collateral damage by tens of thousands and they just perform colorful shows of "shock and awe." They do not torture prisoners; they either interrogate them or turn them to anecdotal irrelevancies. They do not destroy cities; they do surgical and smart operations. They do not occupy others' lands; they liberate them. They do not take revenge; they take justice to their enemies. Thus, media is cleverly used to hypnotize masses and get their support for neo-colonialism. The ruling class in democracies uses their media to "manufacture consent." In order to plunder the resources of other countries, greedy corporations and their unholy allies replace one dictator after another, create wars and conflicts, undertake covert operations, and if they are bored, they play liberation games for fun and profit, big profit.

Crusaders have directly participated or supported many atrocities and wars in the last millennium; they have killed many more innocent people than their counterpart Sunny or Shiite warmongers. Inquisition, crusades, witch-hunt, World War I and II, holocaust, Hiroshima, Nagasaki, Philippines, Korea, Vietnam, Nicaragua, Argentine, Palestine, Lebanon, Bosnia, Chechnya, Iraq, Afghanistan are just few words in the long list of wars and massacres that are committed or supported by those who call themselves Christians. Nazis used the traditional Christian hatred of Jews as fuel and a twisted Cross (swastika) as the symbol for their racist ambitions. The list of British and American wars, occupations, massacres, slavery, covert operations that were conducted with the approval and support of the Christian church or masses is too long and too gruesome. You can still find many Christians justifying the biggest terrorist attack in the history, the destruction of two big cities with their hundreds of thousands civil population, as a retaliation to the Japanese attack to an American military base. American government has not apologized humanity for this horrific and cowardly act of terror. The mentality of these Crusaders is no different than those of al-Qaeda militants who justified the destruction of the World Trade Center as retaliation to the American support for the Israeli's racist policy of occupation, massacres and terror in Palestine.

Modern Crusaders Use Proxies for their Bloody Cause

Right-wing Christianity, which I call Evilgelicalism, is a growing radical movement in Christendom, officially known as Evangelical Christians. They are also known as Left-behind Rapture Freaks. Here, we will refer them by mutating several letters in their name so that their name will fit their deeds: Evilgelicals. Yes, Evilgelicals have recently mobilized all their sources to launch a campaign against the Quran in order to convert Muhammad-worshipers to Jesus-worshipers. Though there won't be much difference, since both populations are like identical twins, but the plan is to start a new era of colonialism and slavery through holy Trojan horses.

Jomo Kenyatta, the founder of Kenya, once articulated the method of colonialist Evilgelicals in nutshell: "When the missionaries came to Africa, they had the Bible and we had the land. They said: 'Let us pray.' We closed our eyes. When we opened them we had the Bible and they had the land."

But, Crusaders are no more relying on prayers or the closed eyes of their victims to grab their lands. Many people nowadays are no more closing their eyes while praying, especially when there is a priest around. Since public learned that some priests grab other things besides lands, there is more reluctance to close eyes. So, the priests and their followers have mutated since last century and have transformed to modern Evangelicals.

This new strand of crusaders use all kinds of media for propaganda, combining their mesmerizing effect with the devastating impact of smart and dumb bombs and modern weapons. They call themselves pro-lifers, but they are always for increase in military budgets, they chant "God bless America" whenever USA-Inc invades a country and kills tens of thousands of its population, and they are more likely support capital punishment. Though they claim that "it is easier for a camel to go through the eye of a needle, than for a rich man to enter into the kingdom of God" (Mt 19:24; Mr 10:25; Lu 18:25), in reality they support policies that make rich richer and poor poorer.

507

They no more adhere to the highest ethical standards thought by Jesus. To the contrary, for centuries they made a travesty out of it. Before they suck the blood of their victims, they no more use the pain-reducing and sleep-inducing formulas, such as, "right-cheek, left-cheek" or "coat after cloke" (Mt 5:39; Lu 6:29). They claim to bring peace and liberty to barbarians by invading their lands through proxy fighters, such as the armies of corporate-nations. While barbarians terrorize, they do awing and shocking. They destroy their homes, smack their heads, kill their children, torture, rape, and sodomize those they have captured. They further justify their method by comparing their action to the ones committed by the "few thugs" who were ironically their former allies in their previous operations, and they look adamant to outdo those barbarians in the acts of shedding blood and inflicting pain.

Repeating the Old Habits

In the lands they occupy they kill 666 times more innocent people than their counterpart Sunni or Shiite barbarians. They excuse themselves by baptizing those dead and mutilated bodies with the holy word "collateral damage." If one of them or an innocent person is beheaded by Sunni or Shiite radicals by sword, they complain from barbaric nature of this and go on killing spree and shatter their heads together with the heads of many collateral lambs.

Evangelical Christians have last year got a great doze of virtual blood and passion by watching several hours of brutal beating of their idol on the screens. While their mouth uttered peace songs, they dreamed blood and more blood. They drank wine pretending to be the blood of their sacrificial lamb, they ate bread pretending to be the flesh of their idol, but pretence was not satisfying them like actual blood and flesh. They are now determined to direct their anger away from Jews to Arabs. Sucking the blood from Jews is no more feasible since Jews have cleverly taken the top seats almost everywhere. For its unending appetite to suck more Semitic blood, this dangerously mutated strand signed a contract with a newly mutated blood-sucking strand of Children of Israel.

Sure, on the other hand, there are many peacemaking Christians who follow the teaching of Jesus in this regard (Matthew 5:9), such as Unitarian Universalists, Jehovah Witnesses, and Quakers, who have consistently and bravely opposed aggression and unjustified wars. Similarly, among the Jews too there are many peaceful people bravely condemning Israel's fascist policy. Nevertheless, the Old Testament, which is accepted by most Christians as verbatim word of God, is filled with horrific and racist instructions to commit terror, massacres and genocide that cannot be attributed to a Caring and Merciful Lord of all people. It is a great wonder that those Christians and Jews, who take this and few other Quranic verses out of their context in the hopes of misrepresenting the peaceful message of islam, do not see the sword in their own bloody eyes. I do not think that any contextual argument would be able to transform the following blood-sucking beasts to the knights of peace:

508

"And they utterly destroyed all that was in the city, both man and woman, young and old, and ox, and sheep, and ass, with the edge of the sword." (Jos 6:21).

"And Judah went up; and the LORD delivered the Canaanites and the Perizzites into their hand: and they slew of them in Bezek ten thousand men. And they found Adonibezek in Bezek: and they fought against him, and they slew the Canaanites and the Perizzites. But Adonibezek fled; and they pursued after him, and caught him, and cut off his thumbs and his great toes. And Adonibezek said, Threescore and ten kings, having their thumbs and their great toes cut off, gathered their meat under my table: as I have done, so God hath requited me. And they brought him to Jerusalem, and there he died. Now the children of Judah had fought against Jerusalem, and had taken it, and smitten it with the edge of the sword, and set the city on fire. And afterward the children of Judah went down to fight against the Canaanites, that dwelt in the mountain, and in the south, and in the valley. And Judah went against the Canaanites that dwelt in Hebron: (now the name of Hebron before was Kirjatharba:) and they slew Sheshai, and Ahiman, and Talmai.And from thence he went against the inhabitants of Debir: and the name of Debir before was Kirjathsepher: And Caleb said, He that smiteth Kirjathsepher, and taketh it, to him will I give Achsah my daughter to wife." (Jg 1:4-12).

"And the haft also went in after the blade; and the fat closed upon the blade, so that he could not draw the dagger out of his belly; and the dirt came out... And they slew of Moab at that time about ten thousand men, all lusty, and all men of valour; and there escaped not a man." (Jg 3:22,29)

"Then I shall make the heavens shudder, and the earth will be shaken to its foundations at the wrath of the Lord of Hosts, on the day of blazing anger. Like a gazelle pursued by a hunter or like a flock with no shepherd to round it up, every man will head back to his own people, each one will flee to his own land. All who are found will fall by the sword, all who are taken will be thrust through; their babies will be battered to death before their eyes, their houses looted and their wives raped." (Isaiah 13:13-15).

"Now go and smite Amalek, and utterly destroy all that they have, and spare them not; but slay both man and woman, infant and suckling, ox and sheep, camel and ass." (1Sa 15:3).

"But the LORD is the true God, he is the living God, and an everlasting king: at his wrath the earth shall tremble, and the nations shall not be able to abide his indignation." (Jer 10:10).

"Why do the wicked prosper and the treacherous all live at ease?... But you know me, Lord, you see me; you test my devotion to you. Drag them away like sheep to the shambles; set them apart for the day of slaughter." (Jer 12:1-3).

"Then shalt thou say unto them, Thus saith the LORD, Behold, I will fill all the inhabitants of this land, even the kings that sit upon David's throne, and the priests, and the prophets, and all the inhabitants of Jerusalem, with drunkenness. And I will dash them one against another, even the fathers and the sons together, saith the LORD: I will not pity, nor spare, nor have mercy, but destroy them." (Jer 13:13-15)

"They shall die of grievous deaths; they shall not be lamented; neither shall they be buried; but they shall be as dung upon the face of the earth: and they shall be consumed by the sword, and by famine; and their carcases shall be meat for the fowls of heaven, and for the beasts of the earth." (Jer 16:4)

"A curse on all who are slack in doing the Lord's work! A curse on all who withhold their swords from bloodshed!" (Jeremiah 48:10)

"The LORD hath brought forth our righteousness: come, and let us declare in Zion the work of the LORD our God. Make bright the arrows; gather the shields: the LORD hath raised up the spirit of the kings of the Medes: for his device is against Babylon, to destroy it; because it is the vengeance of the LORD, the vengeance of his temple. Set up the standard upon the walls of Babylon, make the watch strong, set up the watchmen, prepare the ambushes: for the LORD hath both devised and done that which he spake against the inhabitants of Babylon. O thou that dwellest upon many waters, abundant in treasures, thine end is come, and the measure of thy covetousness. The LORD of hosts hath sworn by himself, saying, Surely I will fill thee with men, as with caterpillers; and they shall lift up a shout against thee. He hath made the earth by his power, he hath established the world by his wisdom, and hath stretched out the heaven by his understanding. When he uttereth his voice, there is a multitude of waters in the heavens; and he causeth the vapours to ascend from the ends of the earth: he maketh lightnings with rain, and bringeth forth the wind out of his treasures. Every man is brutish by his knowledge; every founder is confounded by the graven image: for his molten image is falsehood, and there is no breath in them. They are vanity, the work of errors: in the time of their visitation they shall perish. The portion of Jacob is not like them; for he is the former of all things: and Israel is the rod of his inheritance: the LORD of hosts is his name. Thou art my battle axe and weapons of war: for with thee will I break in pieces the nations, and with thee will I destroy kingdoms; And with thee will I break in pieces the horse and his rider; and with thee will I break in pieces the chariot and his rider; With thee also will I break in pieces man and woman; and with thee will I break in pieces old and young; and with thee will I break in pieces the young man and the maid; I will also break in pieces with thee the shepherd and his flock; and with thee will I break in pieces the husbandman and his yoke of oxen; and with thee will I break in pieces captains and rulers. And I will render unto Babylon and to all the inhabitants of Chaldea all their evil that they have done in Zion in your sight, saith the LORD." (Jer 51:10-24)

"And to the others he said in mine hearing, Go ye after him through the city, and smite: let not your eye spare, neither have ye pity: Slay utterly old and young, both maids, and little children, and women: but come not near any man upon whom is the mark; and begin at my sanctuary. Then they began at the ancient men which were before the house." (Eze 9:5-6).

"And I will set my jealousy against thee, and they shall deal furiously with thee: they shall take away thy nose and thine ears; and thy remnant shall fall by the sword: they shall take thy sons and thy daughters; and thy residue shall be devoured by the fire." (Eze 23:25).

"Therefore he brought upon them the king of the Chaldees, who slew their young men with the sword in the house of their sanctuary, and had no compassion upon young man or maiden, old man, or him that stooped for age: he gave them all into his hand." (2Ch 36:17).

"Let the high praises of God be in their mouth, and a twoedged sword in their hand; To execute vengeance upon the heathen, and punishments upon the people; To bind their kings with chains, and their nobles with fetters of iron; To execute upon them the judgment written: this honour have all his saints. Praise ye the LORD." (Ps 149:6-9)

"Therefore wait ye upon me, saith the LORD, until the day that I rise up to the prey: for my determination is to gather the nations, that I may assemble the kingdoms, to pour upon them mine indignation, even all my fierce anger: for all the earth shall be devoured with the fire of my jealousy." (Zep 3:8)

Despite their bloody and horrific religious teachings, and despite their practice of colonialism, slavery, discrimination, occupations, destructions, covert operations, productions of weapons of mass destruction, making obscene profits from production and sales of weapons, plunder of natural resources of earth, terrorizing nations, and massacring poor populations, Modern Crusaders and their allies are successful in portraying one billion Muslims as terrorists and themselves as people of peace and freedom!

Terrorists to the Factor of 666!

Why terrorizing an entire nation, destroying their cities, killing, torturing, raping and sadomizing their children and youth in the name of "democracy and liberty" should be treated lightly? Why killing tens of thousands of civilians should be forgiven if the murderers, who are also proven congenial liars, use the magic word "collateral damage?" Why smashing the brains of children with bombs or severing their legs and arms should be considered civilized and treated differently than beheadings? Why destroying an entire neighborhood or city and massacring its population by a push of button from the sky should not be considered equally or more evil than the individual suicide bomber blowing himself or herself among his powerful enemies who snuffed out all their hope? Why surviving to push another button to kill more people should be considered a civilized action not the action of those who gave their own lives while doing the killing? How the smile of a well-fed and well-armed mass murderer be deemed more sympathetic than the pain and anger of a poor person? How can one honestly call an occupying foreign military force to be freedom fighters? How can one call the native population to be terrorists just because they are fighting against an arrogant and lethal occupation army which was mobilized against them through lies and deception? Why the children of poor Americans are used to kill the children of poor countries?

We should not favor one criminal over another because of their religion or nationality. However, state terrorism, regardless of the nationality and religion of the population, is much more cruel, dangerous, and sinister than the group or individual terrorism. In our stand against war, violence, and terrorism we must be consistent and fair. Peacemakers and promoters must also PROTEST and CONDEMN the atrocities conducted by the Evangelical-Zionist coalition in Chechnya, Iraq, Palestine, etc., as they condemn the atrocities committed by Sunni or Shiite radicals in Afghanistan, Sudan, Saudi Arabia, etc.

So, if Muslims are called terrorists because they killed several thousand civilian people in last decade, Christians, Jews and capitalists must be called "terrorists to the factor of 666" since they killed hundreds of thousands in Hiroshima, Nagasaki, Vietnam, and just recently they killed tens of thousands civilians in Iraqi, and wounded even more.

A14
Now What?

If you are among the few who witnessed the prophetic sign of NINETEEN and appreciated it with your intellect and heart, then you are no more a believer, but an eyewitness, a mindwitness. You are a witness to an extraordinary event. You are a witness to the ultimate truth. You are a receiver of a divine message destined for this generation, the message of rational monotheism to which the majority of people are now deaf and blind, and many are hostile...

Every new blessing brings about more responsibilities. As a witness, you have a responsibility to share your knowledge with the world. You are a party of God and you have a mission, the mission to promote critical thinking, rational monotheism, peace, justice, and progress. Nothing can deter you from standing for truth, peace, and justice. Here are some of my suggestions for you:

1. Duplicate and distribute pamphlets in your neighborhood or school. Send an email to 19@19.org to receive two PDF pamphlets summarizing:
    *   Manifesto for Islamic Reform
    *   NINETEEN: God's Signature in Nature and Adventure
2. Campaign for the inclusion of Critical Thinking and/or Philosophy courses in K-12 school curriculum in your state or country.
3. Search, find and meet peacemakers and progressive activists in your town.
4. Volunteer for institutions helping homeless people, children, and victims of domestic violence, hospices, hospitals, and schools.
5. Contact libraries, universities, student clubs, civil rights organizations, and think tanks to organize debates, panels, or lectures on Rational Monotheism, Islamic Reform, Nineteen, World Peace, Human Rights, etc.. For speakers, you may contact us at 19@19.org or through our websites.
6. Ask libraries to order a copy of the *Quran: a Reformist Translation* and other Brainbow Press books. Contact Theology and Near Eastern Studies departments and suggest the use of the *Reformist Translation* as a text book.
7. Send us a hundred-word review on *Code 19* so that we could share it with others. We also invite you to contribute to our upcoming book, *From Blind Faith to Rational Monotheism*, by sending us a 2-5 pages telling us your personal story of discovering and embracing rational monotheism.
8. Record a five/ten-minute video of your testimony about NINETEEN and post it at youtube and other sites, including 19.org.
9. Come up with projects and creative ideas to promote the message.
10. Participate in our annual conference, Critical Thinkers for Islamic Reform.
11. Prepare to join us at our 2014 conference in Mecca, God willing.

Brainbow Press

Quran: A Reformist Translation
Translated and Annotated by: Edip Yuksel; Layth Saleh al-Shaiban; Martha Schulte-Nafeh. Third Edition: Brainbow Press, 2007-2011, 684 pages, $24.70. ISBN 978-0-9796715-0-0. Available also in smaller sizes.

Test Your Quranic Knowledge
Contains six sets of multiple choice questions and their answers. Edip Yuksel, Brainbow Press, 2007-2011, 80 pages, $7.95. ISBN 978-0-9796715-5-5

Manifesto for Islamic Reform
Edip Yuksel, Brainbow Press, 2008-2011, 128 pages, $9.95. ISBN 978-0-9796715-6-2

The Natural Republic
Layth Saleh al-Shaiban (ProgressiveMuslims.org), Brainbow Press, 2008-2011, 198 pages, $14.95, ISBN 978-0-9796715-8-6

Critical Thinkers for Islamic Reform
Editors: Edip Yuksel, Arnold Mol, Farouk A. Peru, Brainbow Press, 2009-2011, 262 pages, $17.95. ISBN 978-0-9796715-7-9

Peacemaker's Guide to Warmongers
Exposing Robert Spencer, Osama bin Laden, David Horowitz, Mullah Omar, Bill Warner, Ali Sina and other Enemies of Peace. Edip Yuksel, Brainbowpress, 2010-2011, 432 pages. $19.95. ISBN: 978-0-9796715-3-1

Islamic Theory of Evolution: The Missing Link between Darwin and the Origin of Species
T.O. Shanavas, Brainbow Press, 2010-2011, 240 pages. $17.95, ISBN 978-0-9825867-0-9

Exploring Islam in a New Light: a View from the Quranic Perspective
Abdur Rab, Second Revised Edition, 2010-2011, 460 pages, $19.95, ISBN: 978-0-9825867-1-6

NINETEEN: God's Signature in Nature and Scripture
A comprehensive demonstration of the prophetic miracle. Edip Yuksel, Brainbow Press, 2011, 620 pages. $24.70. ISBN 9780979671593

Edip Yuksel's Upcoming Books
in years 2011-2014, *inshallah*

Running Like Zebras
   Edip Yüksel's debate with the critics of Code 19
My Journey from Sunni Religion to Islam (Provisional Title)
   An autobiography.
19 Questions for Muslims, Christians, and Atheists
   The first two sections are revisions of old booklets.
Purple Letters
   A selection of correspondence on religion, philosophy, and politics.
From Blind Faith to Rational Monotheism: Inspiring Stories of Forty Converts
   Inspiring stories of converts from Sunni, Shiite, Catholic, Protestant
   religions and Atheism to Islam.
Holy Goat
   You will love this goat!
The Bestest Teacher, Student and Parent:
   57 Rules for Students, Teachers and Parents.
Twelve Hungry Men
   A religious/political/philosophical comedy for a feature film
Edip's Record of Religious Oddities:
   A ranking of the bizarre beliefs and practices of world religions.
USA versus USA: The American Janus
   A political mirror and x-ray of America's best and worst.
Muhammad: A Messenger of Peace and Reason
   A script for an animated feature film about Muhammad's mission.

SELECTED BIBLIOGRAPHY:

Abdulbaqi, Fuad: *al-Mucam ul-Mufahras li-Alfaz al-Quran al-Karim*

Asfahani: *Al-Mufradat fi Gharib al-Quran*

Ateş, Süleyman: *Kuran Ansiklopedisi /Encyclopedia of the Quran*

Baz, Sheikh Ibnul: *El-Edilletün Naqliyyetu vel Hissiyatu Ala Cereyaniş Şamsi ve Sukunil Ardi ve Imkanis Suudi ilal Kavakibi/The Traditional and Empirical Evidences for the Motion of the Sun and Stillness of Earth, and Possibility of Ascending to Planets*, University of Medina, 1975.

Bazargan, Mahdi: *Sayr-i Tahawul-i Quran/Process of Quranic Evolution*, Book Distribution Center, Houston, 1974.

Caldwell, Chris K. and Honaker, G.L. Jr., *Prime Curios! The Dictionary of Prime Number Trivia*, CreateSpace, 2009.

Clifford, A. Pickover, *The Math Book*, Sterling, New Yok, 2009.

Çelakıl, Ömer: *Kuran'ı Kerim Şifresi*, (Kelepir/Düş, Istanbul, 2002-2005)

Dan, Joseph: *Studies In Jewish Mysticism*, Proceedings of Regional Conferences Held at the University ofCalifornia, Los Angeles and McGill University in April, University of California Press, 1978.

Deedat, Ahmad: *Al-Quran: the Ultimate Miracle*, Islamic Propagation Centre, Durban, 1979-1986.

Drosnin, Michael: *The Bible Code*, Simon & Schuster, 1997.

Dudley, Underwood: *Numerology or What Phythagoras Wrought*, Mathematical Association of America, 1997.

Firuzabadi, Muhammad ibn Ya'qub, *Al-Qamus al-Muhit/Comprehensive Dictionary*.

Gardner, Martin: *Scicentific American*, September, 1980.

Guy, Richard K., *Unsolved Problems in Number Theory*, Springer-Verlag, 1994,

Haddad, Yvonne Yazbeck and Smith, Jane Idleman: *Mission to America: Five Islamic Sectarian Communities in North America*, University Press of Florida, 1993

Hamidullah, Muhammad: *Le Saint Coran/The Glorious Quran*.

Ibn Manzur: *Lisan ul-Arab/The Arabic Language*.

Ifrah, Georges: *The Universal History of Numbers*, John Wiley & Son, 2000.

Khalifa, Rashad: *Miracle Of The Quran: Significance Of The Mysterious Alphabets*, Islamic Productions, St. Louis, Missouri, 1973.

Khalifa, Rashad: *The Computer Speaks: God's Message To The World*, Renaissance Productions, Tucson, Arizona, 1981.

Khalifa, Rashad: *Qur'an: The Final Scripture, Islamic Productions*, Tucson, Arizona, 1981.

Khalifa, Rashad: *Quran: Visual Presentation Of The Miracle*, Ibid, 1982.

Khalifa, Rashad: *Qur'an, Hadith and Islam*, Ibid, 1982.

Khalifa, Rashad: *Quran: The Final Testament*, Ibid, 1989.

Livio, Mario: Is God a Mathematician, Simon & Schuster, 2009.

Lucas, Jerry and Wasburn, Del: *Theomatics: God's Best Kept Secret Revealed*. Stein and Day 1977-1986.

Majul, Adib: *The Names of Allah in Relation to the Mathematical Structure of Quran*, Islamic Productions, Tucson, 1982.

Majul, Adib: *Various personal letters to Edip Yuksel*, 1991-1998. Personal collection.

Nawfal, Abdurrazzaq: al-*I'jaz al-'Adadi fi al-Qur'an al-Karim/Numerical Miracles in the Holy Quran*, Dar-ul Kitab-il Arabiy, Beirut, 4th edition, 1983.

Paulos, John Allen: *Innumeracy: Mathematical Illiteracy and its Consequences*, Vintage Books, New York, 1990

Posamentier, Alfred S. and Lehmann, Ingmar, *Mathematical Amazements and Surprizes: Fascinating Figures and Noteworthy Numbers*, Prometheus Books, 2009.

Sagan, Carl: *The Demon-Haunted World: Science as a Candle in the Dark*, Ballantine Books, 1st edition, 1997.

Sagan, Carl: *Contact*, Simon and Schuster. New York: 1985

Shimmel, Annemarie: *The Mystery of Numbers*, Oxford University Press, 1993.

Taslaman, Caner, *The Big Bang, Philosophy and God*, Nettleberry, 206.

Taslaman, Caner: *Kuran Hiç Tükenmeyen Mucize/Quran: Unchallengeable Miracle*, Istanbul Yayinevi, Istanbul, 2002.

Toptaş, Mahmut; Zeyveli, Hikmet; Kutman, Orhan; Yüksel, Sadreddin: 19 Efsanesi/The Myth of 19, Inkilab, Istanbul, 1988-2005

Yuksel, Edip and Deedat, Ahmad: Kuran En Büyük Mucize /Quran, the Greatest Miracle (Inkilab, Fatih-Istanbul, 1983-88, 16 editions, 204 p.)

Yuksel, Edip: *Kuran'da Demirin Kimyasal Esrari/Chemical Secrets of Iron in the Quran*. Timaş, Çağalfoğlu-Istanbul, 1984, 48 p.

Yuksel, Edip: *Kuran Görülen Mucize/Quran: The Visual Miracle*, Timaş, Çağaloğlu -Istanbul, 1985, 308 p.

Yuksel, Edip: Ilginç *Sorular-1/ Interesting Questions-1,* Inkilab, Fatih-Ist., 1985-1987, 8 editions, 214 p. Beyan, Cağaloğlu-Istanbul, 1988, 9th edition, 214 p.

Yuksel, Edip: *Ilginç Sorular-2/ Interesting Questions-2,* Yüzondört, Fatih-Istanbul, 1987, 190 p. Beyan, Cağaloğlu-Istanbul, 1988, 2nd and 3rd editions, 190 p.

Yuksel, Edip: *Üzerinde Ondokuz Var / On It Is Nineteen*, Ay Yayıncılık, 1997, 300p. Ozan, 2005, 320 p.

Yuksel, Edip: *The Prime Argument,* Monotheist Productions Int, Tucson, 1995, 64 p.

Yuksel, Edip: *Running Like Zebras... (74:50): An Internet Debate*, Monotheist Productions Int, Tucson, 1995, 120 p.

Yuksel, Edip: *Mesaj, Kuran Çevirisi/The Message, Translation of the Quran* (Ozan/19.org, 1999-2005).

Yuksel, Edip: *Which one do you See: Hell or Miracle?* (19.org, 2004)

Yuksel, Edip: *Running Like Zebras 2... (74:50),* (19.org, 2005)

Yuksel, Edip, et al: *Quran: a Reformist Translation*, Brainbow Press, 2007-10.

Captions for Selected News Clips starting at page 545

(Identified with their page numbers)

P.545   Rashad Khalifa in Masjid Tucson. A picture taken in 1988 while Rashad was working on the second revision of his translation. On the back of the door of his office, a phrase from verse 18:39, "This is what has God willed. No one possesses power except with God" is hanging. On the front side of his office door, he had posted the question from verse 39:36: "Is God not sufficient for His servant?" .

P.546   Edip Yuksel, Fatemeh Karbassi (Parivash), Rashad Khalifa, Haga from Egypt, and Lisa Spray, in front of Masjid Tucson, 1988.

P.547   Rashad in 1989, Tucson.

P.548   Rashad's work is the cover story of Western Fruit Grower in November 1963. "Growth stimulating citrus auxin discovered by Egyptian graduate student Rashad Khalifah causes oat sprouts to curve when applied to one side. The one at far right is untreated. (See story, page 21.)" Who would know that this scientist would one day be the discoverer of one of the greatest mysteries and would first be celebrated by millions and then would be considered a heretic to be killed for his rejection of Hadith, Sunna and sectarian dogmas and would become the target of false accusations, hate and finally deadly attack? .

P.549-553 Published in the end of year 1973, this book does not contain a single reference to the importance of the number 19 and the prophetic verse in 74:30. It is about the statistical density of the letter combinations in the beginning of 29 chapters. The discovery of code 19 would be fulfilled in the beginning of year 1974. NINETEEN: God's Signature in Nature and Scripture.

P.554   Rashad was the chief editor of the Quarterly journal: Islam, published in 1974.

P.555   An ad promoting Rashad's books and a news about the book: Books Produced in Tucson: Computer divines Koran for the Muslim World, Tucson Citizen, 30 July 1981.

P.556   Computer Highlights the Quran, Hoda Sharabash, Arab News, 13 February 1984.

P.557   In a personal letter dated 9 March 1984, Muhammad Abdul-Rauf, the Rector of International Islamic University at Malaysia, expresses his confusion and quandary regarding the rumors about Rashad's rejection of Hadith. The letter is a typical reaction of many of Rashad's and my friends when they first heard about our "heretic" rejection of sectarian teachings.

P.558   Khalifa warned before killing, Charlotte Lowe and David L. Tiebel, Tucson Citizen, 1 February 1990.

P.559   Computer research led to controversy, Joseph Garcia and Charlotte Lowe, Tucson Citizen, 1 February 1990.

P.560   Mosque leader is found slain, Carmen Duarte, The Arizona Daily Star, 1 February 1990.

P.561   Khalifa investigators considering religious assassination theory, Carmen Duarte, The Arizona Daily Star, 2 February 1990.

P.562   Mathematical study used to show 'miracle of the Koran', Dan Huff, The Arizona Daily Star, 2 February 1990.

P.563   Tucson mosque slaying may be linked to sect, Carmen Duarte and Kristen Cook, The Arizona Daily Star, 12 October 1992.

P.564-566 The No. 19 Murder: Once he proclaimed himself a messenger of Allah, Muslim Rashad Khalifa's number was up, Tim Vanderpool, Tucson Weekly, 19 January 1994.

P.567   Man tied to embassy blasts worked here: Links suggested to bin Laden, Tucson cleric's death, Hipolito R. Corella, The Arizona Daily Star, 30 September 1998.* Second bin Laden aide lived in Tucson, Norma Coilo, The Arizona Daily Star, 4 November 2001.

P.568   Jet plane linked to bin Laden was stored in Tucson, David Wichner, The Arizona Daily Star, 18 November 2001. * Mosque aids group accused of Hamas tie, David Wichner, The Arizona Daily Star, 18 November 2001

P569-576 Married to Alqaida: The American Wife of a bin Laden Operative: A Journey Into Jihad, cover story, Kevin Peraino and Evan Thomas, Newsweek, 14 January 2002.

P.577   The first and last pages of an 8-page pamphlet written by Rashad Khalifa inviting Arabic speaking population to follow Prophet Muhammad and stop associating other authorities to the Quran, since is explained by God, fully detailed and complete.

P.578-579 The widespread Egyptian magazine, *Akher Saa*, in 24 January 1973 (issue:1996), allocated four pages to Rashad's computerized research on the statistical significance of "mysterious letters" initializing 29 chapters of the Quran. There is no mention of the significance of the number 19 and chapter 74, since Rashad would discover it a year later, in 1974, exactly 19x74 lunar years after its revelation. The headline reads: "First time: Quran's Interpretation through Computers. The reporter: Jamil Arif. (*Akher Saa* was later sold to *Akhbar El Yom*)".

P.580   A personal letter to Rashad Khalifa from Abd al-Muhaymen Muhammad al-Faqy the Director of Research and Publication Department of al-Azhar University, Cairo, dated 17 March 1976. The director of research congratulates Rashad for his research unveiling the miracle of the Quran in relation to Bismillah. He prays that God may continuously support Rashad so that his work becomes most successful and effective. Within less than a decade, like other dogmatic Sunni scholars, this prominent scholar too will turn into a Zebra, praying for Rashad's demise and destruction.

P.581-582 *Al Ittihad*, a popular newspaper published in United Arab Emirates, in its 22 February 1977 issue shares the news of the three-year-old discovery with its readers in full page. The reporter: Samir Abd-al-Muttalib.

P.582a   Learning that Rashad had publicly rejected Hadith and Sunna and challenged many of Sunni dogmas, the Saudi religious weekly magazine, Al-*Muslimoon*, in the first page of its 6-12 April 1985 issue, continues the internationally orchestrated Sunni attack against Rashad Khalifa.

P.582b   The title reads: "Game with number 19: It does not support nor negate the universal facts. The perpetrator of the game employed truth to reach falsehood " On the computer screen: "The scholars refute the computer's allegations: the

519

allegations of computer are claims of Bahais." In the fourth title of the article the attackers add "Masons" too to their smear campaign.

P.583a   Al-*Muslimoon* newspaper in 6 April 1985 issue on the top left corner proudly announces a new article by Abd al-Aziz bin Ba'z, Saudi's top cleric, on "Magic and Clairvoyance". Interestingly, the Saudi top cleric's book that argued against a rotating earth and declared those who believe the rotation of earth to be heretics deserving death penalty was already published eighth years before by the University of Medina. Bin Ba'z later would lead Sunni scholars from 38 countries to declare Rashad a heretic, an apostate thereby issuing the fatwa for his death. In this very issue a lengthy article attacking Rashad is also published.

P.583b   Learning that Rashad had publicly rejected Hadith and Sunna and challenged many of Sunni dogmas, the Saudi religious weekly magazine, *Al-Muslimoon*, in the first page of its 6-12 April 1985 issue, continues the internationally orchestrated Sunni attack against Rashad Khalifa. The title of the following page reads: "Game with number 19: It does not support nor negate the universal facts. The perpetrator of the game employed truth to reach falsehood " On the computer screen: "The scholars refute the computer's allegations: the allegations of computer are claims of Bahais." In the fourth title of the article the attackers add "Masons" too to their smear campaign.

P.584   Jamil Arif, reporting from Washington for *Akher Saa*: "In America: They Interpret the Quran with the aid of Electronic Intelligences."

P.585   An Egyptian weekly magazine, *Rose El Youssef* or *Rose al-Yousef*, announces in its cover the public declaration of Mustafa Muhammad al-Hadidi al-Tayr, a scholar member of Islamic Research Academy at Al-Azhar University in its 22 April 1985 issue. The scholar accuses Rashad of heresy and claims that the number 19 has nothing to do with a numerical system. He also takes issue with Rashad's claims regarding the so-called "five unknowns."

P.586   The second page of the Egyptian weekly magazine *Rose al-Yousef* publishing the announcement of Mustafa Muhammad al-Hadidi al-Tayr of Al-Azhar University in its 22 April 1985 issue, where he declares Rashad to be a heretic.

P.587   The third page of the Egyptian weekly magazine Rose al-Yousef publishing the announcement of Mustafa Muhammad al-Hadidi al-Tayr of Al-Azhar University in its 22 April 1985 issue, where he declares Rashad to be a heretic.

P.589   In 6-12 July 1985, the Saudi weekly magazine *Al-Muslimoon* in page 19 published a substantial criticism, rather than the regular ad hominem attack, against Rashad Khalifa's discoveries. The author, Dr. Abd-al-Hamid Muhammad Nada, in the article titled "The Numbers in the Quran," mixes some legitimate criticism with pure ignorance. For instance, he rejects 19 as the number of letters in Bismillah. He produces two extra Alifs from under his turban and argues for a 21-lettered Bismillah.

P.589a The rest of the article published by the Saudi religious weekly magazine, Al-Muslimoon, in the first page of its 6-12 April 1985 issue.

P.589b   In 20-26 April 1985 issue of *al-Muslimoon*, another dogmatic Sunni scholar join the ingrates in rejecting the numerical system of the Quran. The title is interesting: "The Indians and Pharaohs preceded Bahais in Playing with Numbers"

P.590   In the 9 October 1988 issue of Arabic newspaper Houston Times, the furious Dr. Assad Busool of American Islamic College, Chicago, condemns Rashad: "O Rashad Khalifa, may God curse the liars among us. In your response you have no shame. O Rashad Khalifa: you are the only person who is bragging about his ignorance"

P.591   Tempo magazine published in Indonesia provides a one-page summary of the controversy through Sunni clerics' ingrate attitude towards the idea of math employed in the Quran. The common false accusation of Rashad's connection with Bahaism is repeated. The article refers to Saudi chief cleric Abdul Aziz ibn Baz's fatwa against Rashad. Then, the article mentions Bilal Philip's, and hadith allegedly reported from Ibn Abbas, likening the 19-based numerical structure of the Quran to "magic", as exactly prophesized in 74:24.

P.592   My father's statements against me are made headline in Turkish newspapers and magazines, including daily *Zaman* (Time): "The Religious Scholar Sadrettin Yüksel clarified distorted ideas on Islam and wrong interpretations: 'Instead of following the Prophet's companions, they are following heretic missionaries.' Sadrettin Yüksel harshly warned those who abandoned the path of *Ahl al-Sunna*: 'Shame on those who follow Rashad Khalifa instead of following the companions who adhered to the hadiths of Great Prophet!'" *Zaman*, 3 February 1988.

P.593   Zaman newspaper continues the main editorial column from the first page titled, "We Congratulate Sadrettin Yüksel." The lengthy Op-Ed news from the first page too continues with my father's criticism against my controversial book, Interesting Questions-2. Though my father still wished to protect my life used a careful language by not uttering the word "*murtad*" (apostate), a code word for death warrant, the Sunni lynch mobs in the media later attributed such a word to my father. *Zaman*, 3 February 1988.

P.594   My father's first article against my book, Interesting Qusetions-2, was published by monthly *Girişim* (Initiative). Then the monthly magazine *Kitap Dergisi* (Book Magazine) published my response, which they would later regret. In this article published by *Vahdet*, (Unity) in 9 May 1988, my father tries to save the Sunni sect from my criticism. He accuses me of following the "Mason" and "Bahai" Rashad Khalifa.

P.595-603 The cover story of provocative atheist/communist magazine *2000'e Doğru* (Towards 2000), brings the issue of Quran's textual integrity. The title of the cover story: "The fact according to Islamic sources: THE REAL QURAN WAS BURNED." The article was written by Turan Dursun, a former Sunni cleric who became an atheist. The well-written and supported article used Sunnis own sources to refute their claim regarding the perfect preservation of the Quran. Religious scholars and theology professors chose to ignore the arguments. Unfortunately, the only meaningful defense of the Quran would come from no other than the excommunicated heretic, Edip Yüksel.

P.604   The weekly Islamist magazine *Vahdet* (Unity), in its 26 September – 2 October 1988 issue, publishes the controversy in its cover story. Ahmad Deedat joins the fray and harshly condemns Rashad and declares him to be "a liar!" Though Rashad accepted Deedat's invitation and published his response in his bulletin, Muslim Perspective, the Sunni media still propagated the lie that Rashad could not accept Deedat's challenge. Though Deedat was an articulate and experienced debater, I had no doubt that Rashad would win the debate, hands down.

P.605a The cover story of then popular weekly news magazine *Nokta* (Point)—though it was dated April 16, 1989, it appeared in the market a week before as usual— sparks a second wave of attacks against me after the first attack against my highly controversial book, Interesting Questions 2. Zaman newspaper does not waste time reacting to Nokta's story. Reportedly the get the dooming words from my father's mouth: "Whatever Rashad is Edip is the same!" Ironically, even if my father made such a statement, he still subconsciously avoiding to utter the damning word "murtad" (apostate/heretic).

P.605-606 The daily *Türkiye* Newspaper, in 11 April 1989, reports statements from prominent Sunni theologians such as Prof. Salih Tuğ and religious leaders, including my father. The newspaper manages to attribute my father the bloody statement: "*Oğlum mürteddir*" (My son is an apostate/heretic). This is a clear message and incitement for religious zealots and psychopaths to kill me.

P.606 Among those who join the lynch mob were Prof. Salih Tuğ, the dean of Theology Dept. of Marmara University, Prof. Hayrani Altıntaş of Theology Dept. of Ankara Un., Galip Demirel, the vice president of ANAP, the governing political party, Mehmet Kahraman a prominent congressman from the same party. The statement attributed to my father follows the report. They all agree that we are mentally sick and deserve to be killed.

P.607-616 *Nokta* (Point), then the most popular weekly newsmagazine in Turkey, gave the news of Fatwa on Rashad Khalifa and Salman Rushdi as its cover story in 16 April 1989, under the title, "American Khalifa's Attempt to Change the Quran. The Second Salman Rushdi Affair" It also published my pictures with Rashad and an interview with me, creating another wave of Sunni media campaign and death threat against me, which led me to immigrate to the USA.

P.608 The content page of *Nokta* magazine that made the news of death fatwa on Rashad Khalifa and Salman Rushdie as its cover story in 16 April 1989 under the title, "The Second Salman Rushdie Affair."

P.609-615 The weekly news magazine Nokta, in its cover story of 16 April 1989, created a nationwide controversy in Turkey. Sunni Scholars from 38 countries who reportedly met in February 27 in Mecca for the 11th Islamic World *Fiqh* Council organized by Muslim World League (*Rabita*), ended up with a fatwa condemning Rashad Khalifa together with Salman Rushdi to death. The Sunni religious leaders included Bin Baz, Yusuf al-Qaradawi, Mustafa al-Zarqa, and Abul Hasan al-Nadwi.

P.612 An interview made by *Nokta* reporter, Ali Özkaner, via phone with Rashad Khalifa. The reporter asks him about code 19, his claim of messengership, his rejection of 9:128-129 and the fatwa of the Sunni scholars issued at the 11th Islamic World *Fiqh* Council. In the picture taken in Sonora Dessert: Rashad Khalifa, Ramtin, Edip Yuksel, John Spooner, and Muhteşem.

P.613 Nokta's cover story of 16 April 1989 is continued. Dr. Tayyar Altıkulaç, the head of Turkish Religious Affairs supports the fatwa. Mehmet Metiner, the influential Islamist author who was my comrade agreed with the fatwa, knowing it would put my life too at risk. Tayyar says, "If [the theory of nineteen] was sound we would be happy." It is a pathetic statement since he initially published Rashad's discoveries in his book, without verifying them, and he is now similarly rejecting them without doing serious research.

P.614   Dr. Hüseyin Hatemi, a Shiite legal scholar and author, too joins the lynch mob and calls us crazy and computer-worshipers!

P.615   Abdurrahman Dilipak, another influential Islamist columnist/author and my comrade, too supports the Fatwa against our lives. He says that he approves Sadrettin Yüksel's verdict against Rashad for his claim of messengership. Below is Nokta's interview with me.

P.616   Nokta's cover story of 16 April 1989 on the death fatwa issued by the Islamic World *Fiqh* Council against Rashad continues. The second page of the interview with me includes my picture. The cover story ends with quotations from on the interesting "coincidences" in the number of Sunni death squad (19x2) and the name of the British law firm that represented Rushdi during the controversy: Article 19. "These are all a part of a Satanic plot."

P.617   Another Sunni magazine, *Son Mesaj* (The Last Message), three years after I leave Turkey, still continues the attack against me while I struggle to start a new life in the United States. In the same issue, I notice that my younger Brother Müfid Yüksel is a respected columnist of the magazine.

P.618-619. Ruşen Çakır, a prominent Turkish journalist who wrote numerous books on Muslims and Islamic Movements including "Ayet ve Slogan" (Verse and Slogan), in this editorial article of 30 November 1994 *Milliyet* (Nation), discusses my influence on Adnan Oktar, a cult leader who would later assume the pen name Harun Yahya. The cult leader received international notoriety for promoting pseudoscience against the theory of evolution and manipulating the Turkish courts thereby banning many Internet sites, including www.19.org and Word Press blogs in order to censor my article titled "Harun Yahya or Adnan Oktar: The Promised Mahdi?" The caption under my picture taken in the printing house reads: "Edip Yuksel was once the 'Wonder Boy' of the Islamic groups, but later Islamists stole his book from the printing house."

P.620   In mid 1970's Rashad was working for the United Nations and was sent as a United Nations agricultural advisor to Libya where he worked in consultation with Colonel Muammar Qaddafi. Rashad's relationship with the dictator would later deteriorate, after being arrested for a short time he manages to escape further punishment against him. (For more information on Rashad's life and mission, see: Yvonne Yazbeck Haddad and Jane Idleman Smith, Mission to America: Five Islamic Sectarian Communities in North America, University Press of Florida, 1993, pp: 137-168.

ENDNOTES
of NINETEEN: God's Signature in Nature and Scriputure

---

[1] Philip J. Davis & Reuben Hersh, *The Mathematical Experience*, Houghton Mifflin Company, Boston, 1981, 1983, 10th edition, p. 109.

[2] Later, when I was in Tucson, working together with Rashad, I found myself siding with him and condemning Deedat, who by then had cut his relationship with Rashad. Deedat rejected his monotheistic message. However, later I learned that Deedat gradually moved from Sunni teachings towards monotheism. He was too smart to trust Hadith. Even when he was a Sunni, he rarely used Hadith in his books. You will find more details in my upcoming autobiography, God willing.

[3] Carl Sagan, *Contact*, Simon and Schuster. New York: 1985, pp. 418-419

[4] A two-round argument with Carl Sagan on this topic is published toward in the end of this book under the title "The Prime Argument."

[5] Carl Sagan, *Cosmos*, Ballantine, 1985 (Copywrighted in 1980), p. 259.

[6] Carl Sagan, *The Demon-Haunted World: Science as a Candle in the Dark*, First Ballantine Book Edition, 1997, p.69.

[7] David Heller, *Dear God What Religion Were the Dinosaurs*, Bantam Books, New York, 1991

[8] To get a good glimpse of this theory, I recommend Richard Dawkins's *The Blind Watchmaker*, W.W. Norton & Company, 1987. The evolution of species is supported by many scientific facts, and I believe that it is designed by God. The topic is beyond the scope of this book. Here I would like to cite some verses of the Quran, which informs us that the human race evolved from plants and microorganisms that incubated in the layers of clay. See, the Quran: 15:26-28; 24:45; 29:19-20; 71:14-17.

There is a common belief among Jews, Christians and Muslims that God created the first human being from clay; clay as a substance for shaping, as in pottery. According to this understanding, God shaped Adam like a pottery then gave him life. However, this sounds like a mythology, and it appears to be beyond the territory of scientific inquiry. Some believers understood this as the fact that the human body is made up of elements contained in soil and clay.

Interestingly, some modern scientists too are considering clay as the origin of life; sure, for a different reason. They support their claim by scientific research and analysis. Here is a paragraph from the cover article of *Scientific Americana* written by a professor at Harvard Medical School:

"Researchers now think biological evolution began in layers of clay, rather than in the primordial sea. Interestingly, clay is itself a porous network of atoms arranged geodesically within octahedral and tetrahedral forms. But because these octahedra and tetrahedra are not closely packed, they retain the ability to move and slide relative to one another. This flexibility apparently allows clay to catalyze many chemical reactions, including ones that may have produced the first molecular building blocks of organic life." (Donald E. Ingber, M.D., Ph.D., The Architecture of Life, *Scientific American*, January 1998, 48, at 57.)

The Quranic message "the creation of the human being was started from Clay" (32:7) has two meanings: human was made of the substance of clay, or his/her genealogy is linked to the microorganisms that came out of clay. Isn't it interesting that the Old, the New and the Final Testaments provide peoples of all walks and generations with satisfying explanations! For a discussion on evolution, see: this author, *Blind Watch-Watchers or Smell the Cheese: A Delicious Argument for Intelligent Design in Evolution*, by Edip Yuksel.

[9] See my autobiography, which will be published in 2011, God willing.

[10] Marilyn vos Savant & Leonore Fleischer, *Brain* Building, Bantam Books, 1990, p.38.

[11] Rashad Khalifa, *Quran: Visual Presentation of the Miracle*, Islamic Productions, Tucson, Arizona, 1982, Preface.

[12] Charles Pavitt & Ellen Curtis, Gorsuch Scarisbric, *Small Group Discussion: a Theoretical Approach*, Scottsdale, AZ., 1990, p 160-165

[13] Marilyn vos Savant, *Supra* note 10 at 35

[14] *The Book of Mormon, Moroni* 10:4-5

[15] Martin Luther, *Last Sermon in Wittenberg*, 17 January 1546.

[16] Michael Shermer, *The Measure of a Woman: An Interview With Social Scientist Carol Tavris,* Skeptic, Vol. 7, No. 1, 1999. p. 71.

[17] Herold Bloom, *Genius, A Mosaic of One Hundred Exemplary Creative Minds*, Warner Books, 2002, p. 148.

[18] Michael H. Hart, Citadel, *The 100: A Ranking of the Most Influential Persons in History*, Revised edition, 2000, p. 3

[19] Georges Ifrah, *The Universal History of Numbers*, John Wiley & Son, 2000. pp: 513, 515.

[20] There are some critics who argue that *Baca* or *Becca* is different from *Mecca*.

[21] The common belief among Muslims is to the contrary. To distinguish themselves from the Meccan *mushriks*, clerics and scholars fabricated stories about statues. There are dubious narrations that Muhammad broke statutes occupying Kaba. However, the Quran that occasionally refers to the statues of previous communities (see: 6:74; 7:138; 14:35; 21:57; 26:71) never mentions the statues or icons of Meccan *mushriks*. Furthermore, there is no archeological evidence to support the claims of Sunni and Shiite scholars. Besides, the classic book about statues, Al-Kalbi's KITAB UL ASNAM (The Book of Statues) contains many contradictory descriptions of the so-called Arabian statues. Muslim historians who were disturbed by lack of material evidence for the allegedly abundant Arabian statues came up with a "cookie" theory: Meccan idol-worshipers were making their statues from cookies and when they got hungry they used to eat them. That should explain why archeologist cannot find statues in the region for that era! Phew!

[22] *Shirk* is described by the Quran in various contexts. Setting up partners with God, or accepting prophets, clergymen and scholars as *authorities* in God's religion is considered as an unforgivable sin. See 42:21; 9:31; 3:18; 2:48; 6:21; 6:145; 7:17-37; 17:46; 45:6; 16:89; 6:112-115; 19:82; 46:6; 25:30; etc.

23 See this author, *19 Questions for Christians*.

24 The detailed argument on this subject can be found in author's Turkish book, *Kuran Çevirilerindeki Hatalar (Errors in the Translations of the Quran)*, Ozan Yayıncılık.

25 They were originally *Zilhija, Muharram, Safar, Rabi 1*, and later their order was changed by *mushriks*.

26 The purpose and practice of polygamy is another distorted issue in islam (submission). Though the Quran discourage polygamy with two verses (4:3 and 4:129), it allows it as a social and economic institution to take care of orphans in a family environment. The Quran allows polygamy with widows who have children. This permission allowed those who could afford to marry with widows to provide a father figure to their children and take care of their needs. Interestingly, the verse clarifying this limited permission is traditionally mistranslated despite its clear grammatical structure. The correct translation of the verse:

"They consult you concerning women: say, as recited for you in the scripture, God enlightens you regarding the rights of orphans of women whom you deprive of their dowries while seeking to marry them, regarding the disadvantaged children: you shall treat the orphans equitably. Whatever good you do, God is fully aware thereof." (4:127).

Unfortunately, Sunni and Shiite scholars abused this limited permission and justified marrying with four women at a time even without the permission of the first wife who was deprived her right to divorce!

27 The examples of this category are listed in verse 5:3.

28 Many speculations made by Muslims to provide medical reasons for prohibition of *meat* of pig. Though, I consider it as a divine commandment to be followed for just the sake of obeying the Creator of the Universe, I think one of the reasons might lay in the waste of resources and environmental pollution. It is a well-known fact that pigs produce six times more waste than other domestic animals. Pig farms have caused serious environmental problems in some States, such as in North Carolina. Besides emitting disturbing smells, pig waste has contaminated the underground water in many nearby towns.

29 Sunni and Shiite scholars, among many facts, have distorted this one too. They fabricated and narrated stories claiming that Muhammad was an illiterate man and maintained his illiteracy until his death. This claim not only contradicts the Quran and the historical facts, but it is also an insult to Muhammad. Was the prophet who brought a book and dictated it for 23 years not able to recognize the 28 letters of Arabic alphabet? Is it credible that a prophet who brought a scripture, the first revelation of which starts with the word "READ," did not try to learn how to read? Why did a prophet who encouraged his friends to learn how to read and write not practice what he preached to others? If Muhammad was illiterate, then he was either a crook trying to feign that he could not read (which is impossible since there were literally thousands of people who knew him since his childhood) or he did not have the intelligence to learn how to read and write! To support their claim of "Literal Miracle" Sunni and Shiite scholars resorted to this obvious lie and interestingly reached consensus on it! For a detailed argument on this subject see *Quran: a Reformist Translation*.

30 The Meccan Arabs initially called Muhammad and his followers, *Sabeen* meaning

"followers of other religions."

[31] The famous atheist philosopher, Friedrich Nietzsche was so fed up with abuse and exploitation from the Church that he opened a scorching attack on clergymen. He wrote, "As long as the priest is considered a higher type of man—this professional negator, slanderer, and poisoner of life—there is no answer to the question: what is truth? For truth has been stood on its head when the conscious advocate of nothingness and negation is accepted as the representative of "truth." ... In Christianity neither morality nor religion has even a single point of contact with reality.... This world of pure fiction is vastly inferior to the world of dreams insofar as the latter mirrors reality, whereas the former falsifies, devalues, and negates reality. Friedrich Nietzsche, *the Antichrist*, in *the Portable Nietzsche*, ed. and trans. Walter Kaufmann (New York: Viking, 1954).

[32] The following verse, 9:99, makes an exception of this statement.

[33] Nassim Nicholas Taleb, *The Black Swan: The Impact of the Highly Improbable*, Random House, 2007, p 11.

[34] David Hume, *Against Miracles, an Enquiry Concerning Human Understanding*, Oxford: Oxford University Press, 1748.

[35] Harold Bloom, *Supra* note 18 at145-154.

[36] Dr. Maurice Bucaille, *The Bible, the Quran and Science*, American Trust, 1979, pp. 244-248.

[37] David Hume, *An Inquiry Concerning Human Understanding*, ed. by L.A. Selby-Bigge, 2nd ed., Oxford: Oxford University Press, 1920, XII, p. 164.

[38] The Quran repeatedly invites people to be critical thinkers and use their reasoning faculties as individuals. For example, see the following verses. 17:36; 10:100; 39:17-18; 41:53; 42:21; 6:114-116; 10:36; 12:111; 20:114; 21:7; 35:28; 38:29

[39] The person claiming to be the writer of this fabrication would not reveal his name but his address at AOL is suralikeit@aol.com. You may see a lot more suras or verses, claimed to have been written by Quss ibn Saida, an alleged *jaahiliya* (pre-Islamic) poet, available at Jochen Katz homepage at <http://answering-islam.org/Quran/Miracle/>

[40] Dr. Osman Keskioglu, *Nuzulunden Günümüze Kurani Kerim Bilgileri*, Turkiye Diyanet Vakfi, Ankara, 1987.

[41] *Ibid*, p. 193.

[42] *Ibid*, p. 197

[43] An exception of this rule is reported to be the last two verses of Chapter 9, which we will discuss towards the end of this book.

[44] Interestingly, Sunni and Shiite scholars have mistranslated the first word of this Hadith-verse as "married" rather than as "old." The wrong word choice might be considered an indication that the fabricator of this "verse" was not a native Arabic speaker

[45] See the following verses:

They said, "O Shuaib, we do not comprehend many of the things you are telling us, and we see that you are powerless among us. If it were not for your tribe, we would have **stoned** you. You have no value for us." (11:91)

He said, "Have you forsaken my gods, O Abraham? Unless you stop, I will **stone** you. Leave me alone." (19:46)

If they discover you, they will **stone** you, or force you to revert to their religion, then you can never succeed." (18:20)

They said, "Unless you refrain, O Noah, you will be **stoned**." (26:116)

They said (to God's messengers), "We consider you bad omens. Unless you refrain, we will surely **stone** you, or afflict you with painful retribution." (36:18)

[46] These prayers starting with the phrase, "*Allahumma iyyaka na'budu wa iyyaka nastaeen...*" are recited by the followers of Hanafite sect in their extended night prayers.

[47] Abu Dawud, *Sunan*, 40/4557. Allegedly narrated by al-Miqdam Ibn Ma'dikarib.

[48] John Allen Paulos, *Innumeracy: Mathematical Illiteracy and its Consequences*, Vintage Books, New York, 1990, pp. 70, 96.

[49] Annemarie Schimmel, *The Mystery of Numbers*, Oxford University Press, 1993, p.16. This book is one of the best sources on numerology.

[50] Juno Jordan, *Numerology: the Romance in Your Name*, Devorss Publications, Marina del Ray, 1998, 9th printing, p. 6.

[51] Ibid, pp 8-9.

[52] Richard Webster, *Chinese Numerology*, Llewellyn Publications, St. Paul, Minnesota, 1998, p. 5.

[53] John Allen Paulus, *Supra* note 48, at 93-94.

[54] According to CNN USA Today/Gallop Poll, December 16-18, 1994 and Scripps Howard News Service/Ohio University poll, June 1995, 23% of American adults believed in astrology and 16% was not sure. *From Paranormal Phenomena: Opposing Viewpoints*, Greenhaven Press, San Diego, *1997, p. 53.*

[55] Interestingly, two of my books have the number 19 in their titles. I limited my questions for Muslims and Christians to my favorite number 19. Not because I believed in the mystical power of this number, but to remind them the importance of this number in the mathematical structure of the Quran and its theological implications and practical ramifications. The use of this number in *19 Questions for Sunni and Shiite scholars had* another motive: to provoke them to think about the number I knew they hated very much and tried to escape from!

[56] Philip J. Davis & Reuben Hersh, *Supra* note 1 at 98-99.

[57] Adrian Room, *The Guinness Book of Numbers*, Guinness Books, London, 1989, p. 54.

[58] Underwood Dudley, *Numerology or What Pythagoras Wrought*, Mathematical Association of America, 1997. p .45.

[59] Jerry Lucas and Del Washburn, *Theomatics: God's Best Kept Secret Revealed*, a Scarborough Book, Stein and Day, New York, 1986, pp. 89-90. The arbitrariness of the work is acknowledged by the very book. For example, see the authors' definition of the structure of calculations in the second chapter (pp. 29-48).

[60] Searched Theomatics by Del Washburn at Amazon.com on November 22, 2010. The review is titled: Nonsense! http://www.amazon.com/Theomatics-II-Best-Kept-Secret-

Revealed/product-reviews/0812840232/

[61] Jerry Lucas and Del Washburn, *Supra* note 59, at 51-57.

[62] *Ibid*, at 37.

[63] *Ibid*, at 38.

[64] *Ibid*, at 31, 49.

[65] *Ibid*, at 40.

[66] For critical books on Biblical numerology, See John J. Davis, *Biblical Numerology*, Grand Rapids: Baker, 1968; and Oswald Thompson Allis, *Biblical Numerics*, Presbyterian and Reformed, 1974.

[67] Underwood Dudley, *Supra* note 58, at 41-42.

[68] When the Arabic alphabet lost its function as a number system, pedagogues created a new order for the alphabet putting similar looking letters next to each other.

[69] For further information on magic squares please refer to Annemarie Schimmel's *The Mystery of Numbers*. Oxford University Press, 1993, Pp 27-37. Also see, Adrian Room, *The Guinness Book of Numbers*, Guinness Books, U.K., 1989, p.15.

[70] For those who like mathematics, I highly recommend *Mathematical Amazements and Suprises* by Alfred S. Posamentier and Ingmar Lehmann, Prometheus Books, 2009.

[71] Underwood Dudley, *Supra* at note 58, pp. 82-83.

[72] Philip J. Davis & Reuben Hersh, *Supra* at note 1, p.8.

[73] Verse 9:36 relates the number of months to the day of the creation of the earth. Perhaps in early days of the creation, the rotation of moon and earth were synchronized and there were exactly 12 lunar months in a solar year. The increase in the length of the year and the decelerating earth causes problems for modern technology, which is very sensitive to small changes in the measurement of time such as computers, electric grids, GPS systems, and missiles. In the mid-20th century, scientists learned that the rotation of Earth was not sufficiently uniform as a standard of time. Besides solar gravity, there are many minor factors influencing the rotation of the earth such as tides caused by the Moon's gravity which cause deceleration and melting of ice in the North Pole which causes acceleration. To compensate for this deceleration, almost every year we are adding one second to our atomic clocks, which defines and measures a second as *9,192,631,770* electromagnetic radiation or oscillation of Cesium 133. Since 1972, we added 23 leap seconds until 2006. However, the rate of the deceleration does not show a pattern. In recent years, the earth's rotation has been on schedule.

[74] This is the most accurate index of the Quran. Its later editions contain 15 corrections in the introduction section: Fuad Abdulbaqi, *Al Mujamul Mufahras Lialfazil Quranil Kareem*, Darul Hadis, Cairo, 1988.

[75] "Month." *Wikipedia*. Wikimedia Foundation, 08102010. Web. 8 Oct 2010. <http://www.en.wikipedia.org/wiki/Month>.

[76] Time expressed in Ephemeris Time (more precisely Terrestrial Time) with days of 86,400 SI seconds. y is years since the epoch (2000), expressed in Julian years of 365.25 days. Note that for calendrical calculations, one would probably use days measured in the time scale of Universal Time, which follows the somewhat unpredictable rotation of the Earth, and progressively accumulates a difference with

ephemeris time called ΔT.

[77] Caner Taslaman, *The Quran: The Unchallengeable Miracle*, PhD, Nettleberry, USA, 2006.

[78] For further examples please see: Ăbd-ul Razaq Nawfal, *Al-'Ijaz-ul Ădadey L-il Quran-il Kareym*, Dar-ul Kitab-ul Ărabey, Beirut, 1983.

[79] The list provides little flexibility. Contrary to the original list first published in my Turkish book in 1983, here I include Elyasyn of 37:130 since it refers to the Elias and his family. Differing from my earlier list, I now exclude Ezra and *ahmad*. The name Ezra is mentioned only once and it is in negative context. Furthermore, the historical evidence about Ezra's deeds discourages me from considering him as a messenger. The word *ahmad* is not a proper name, but an adjective meaning "more praised". For my arguments on why the word *ahmad* is not a proper name, please see the footnote for verse 61:6 of the *Quran: a Reformist Translation*. The QRT is available online at www.quranix.com

[80] The derivatives of *RaSaLa* appear in about 30 different forms, yet, ignoring the additional letters in some forms, the arrangement of its three letters appear only in three different combinations: *RaSaLa* (274 times), *RaSWL* (235 times) and *ReSAL* (3 times). (The spelling of *ReSAL* in some versions is 7 more while the *RaSaLa* is 7 less.)

[81] The names in bold are expressly stated to be prophets.

[82] See, the Quran 75:9. Hasan Öztürk is one of the more serious researchers, yet I think he lacks mathematical intuition to distinguish anecdotal and arbitrary facts from the patterns or structural components of the system. Unfortunately, this problem is very common among novice enthusiasts. Hasan generously shared with me hundreds of his "discoveries," yet to my disappointment, I found only a few of them to be interesting and a very few worth mentioning. However, it is always a possibility that those disconnected and arbitrary observations might be a part of a bigger pattern that we may not have yet discovered.

[83] *The Quran* 3:59. For more details see Caner Taslaman's book mentioned above.

[84] The word *HeSaaB* is used for the Day of Judgment since on that day our good and bad deeds will be computed.

[85] Traditional commentaries translate it as "When the trumpet is sounded" or "horn is blown," which is an allegorical expression for making a declaration. The root of the word *NaQuuR* as a verb means "strike" or "groove," and as a noun it means "trumpet" or "the smallest matter." Based on our contemporary knowledge of the prophecy mentioned in this chapter, we may translate it as "when the microchips are grooved."

[86] Traditional translations that tend to understand *Saqar* as hellfire, mistranslates the verse *Lawahatun lil bashar* as "scorches the skin." Though this meaning might be obtained by using different dialects of Arabic, the Quranic Arabic is very clear regarding the meaning of the two words making up this verse. The first word *LaWaĤa*, if considered as a noun, literally means "manifold tablets" or "manifestations" and if considered as a verb, it means "making it obvious." The second word *lil* means "for." And the third word *BaŞaR* means "human being" or "people." "For the other derivatives of the first word, *LaWaĤa*, please look at 7:145, 150, 154; 54:13; and 85:22. In all these verses the word means "tablets." For the other

derivatives of the third word, *BaŞaR*, please look at the end of the verse 31 of this chapter and 36 other occurrences, such as, 3:79; 5:18; 14:10; 16:103; 19:17; 36:15, etc. The traditional translation of the verse is entirely different from the usage of the Quran. Previous generations who were not aware of the mathematical structure of the Quran perhaps had an excuse to translate it as a description of hell, but contemporary Muslims have no excuse to mistranslate this verse.

[87] The word "nineteen" occurs in *the Bible* twice: Joshua 19:38 (nineteen cities) and 2 Samuel 2:30 (nineteen men). The word "nineteenth" occurs thrice: 2 King 25:8; 1 Chronicles 24:16, 25:26; and Jeremiah 52:12.

[88] The majority of traditional commentators incline to understand the references of this verse and the ending phrase of verse 31 as "hell fire" instead of "number nineteen." You will find translations of the Quran using parentheses to reflect this traditional exegesis. According to them, "it (the hellfire) is a reminder for the people," and "this (the hellfire) is one of the greatest (troubles)." Their only reason for jumping over two textually closest candidates, that is, "their number" or "nineteen," was their lack of knowledge about Code 19. They did not understand how a number could be a "reminder" or "one of the greatest miracles." Indeed their understanding was in conflict with the obvious context; the topic of the previous verse 31 is the number nineteen, not the hellfire. Finally, the traditional understanding contradicts verse 49. Those who know Arabic may reflect on the word *ZKR* in the ending phrase of verse 31 with verse 49 and reflect on the fact that hellfire is not something the Quran wants us to accept and enjoy!

[89] The Arabic word *inŞaQQa* has been traditionally translated is "being divided in the middle." Hadith books report a "miracle" as the fulfillment of this verse. According to those narrations Muhammad pointed at the Moon and the Moon split. Some of the reports even provide further details about this fabricated "miracle" when half of the Moon fell in Muhammad's cousin, Ali's backyard. The word *ŞaQQa* has a range of dimensions, from splitting into half to simply breaking or cracking as in 80:25-26: "We pour the water generously. Then we split the soil open." If you wonder the usage of past tense for a prophetic statement, it is a well-known Quranic style to indicate the certainty of the upcoming event and the meta-time nature of God's knowledge. (See 39:68; 75:8-9; 25:30; 7:44-48; 6:128; 20:125-126; 23:112-114). For those who know Arabic and wonder about the meaning of *infi'al* form, see 2:60.

[90] For the Quran's position regarding intercession please see 2:48; 6:70,94; 7:5; 9:80; 10:3; 39:44; 43:86; 16:20,21; 78:38.

[91] Caner Taslaman, *Quran, Unchallengeable Miracle*, Nettleberry/Citlembik, 2006

[92] A sample of those discussions is published under the title Running Like Zebras. The book's new edition with additional chapters is published by BrainbowPress.

[93] I do not prefer using the names for chapters, since those names are not part of the original revelation, and they are arbitrarily chosen names that later became conventions. For some chapters, more than one survived, such as *Ghafir* and *Mumin* for chapter 40 or Tawba and Baraa for chapter 9. The names were usually picked from the first words of a chapter or from an important or attention-grabbing word inside the chapter. Such a convention initially had a useful a role in referring to a particular chapter or verse, but after the revelation of the Quran was completed and they were put in their current order by Muhammad as instructed by God, chapters

were expected to be referred according to their numbers of order.

[94] Süleyman Ateş (76), former head of the Department of Religious Affairs in Turkey (1976-1978), theology professor and author, Turkey.

[95] For those who know Arabic, there are more details. This solution provides other parameters to the mathematical system. (1) There are 19 chapters from where a Bismillah is missing to the extra Bismillah. (2) The number of the 19 chapters from the "missing" Bismillah to the "extra" Bismillah
(9+10+11+12+13+14+15+16+17+18+19+20+21+22+23+24+25+26+27) is 342, or 19x18. This is not significant since it is a mathematical property. If you add up any consecutive 19 numbers you will get a number which is divisible by 19. However, the number 342 is equal to the numbers of words sandwiched between the two Bismillah formulas of Chapter 27. A standard method for word count can be deduced from the count of the chronologically first revelation, which is the first five verses of Chapter 96 (Embryo) and the last revealed chapter, Chapter 110 (Aid), each containing 19 words. Dr. Mahdi Bazergan, the Iranian scholar and the first Prime Minister of Islamic Republic of Iran, in his outstanding book, *Sayr-i Tahawul-i Quran* (*The Evolution of the Quran*) confirms the same count. The book was published by Book Distribution Center, Houston, 1977.

[96] Later, I published my debate with Dr. Carl Sagan, which took place between December 1993 and March 1994, in a little pamphlet titled the *Prime Argument*. The booklet is out of print. A copy of this debate is kept at a special section of the University of Arizona's library allocated for student thesis. I have the original letters in my personal collection.

[97] To check our claims, I recommend those who know Arabic to use the classic concordance of the Quran, *Al-Mujamul Mufahras Li Alfazil Quran-il Kareem*. This concordance is the work of Muhammad Fuad Abdulbaqi and was first published in 1938, decades before the discovery of Code 19.

[98] Please note the number 19 in parentheses under the word "*Ism.*" (Luckily, the number 1 and 9 are the only numbers that have a similar form in both Arabic and Latin numeral notations).

[99] Quoted by Philip J. Davis, *The Mathematical Experience*, Houghton Mifflin, Boston, 1982, p.53.

[100] Cesar Adib Majul, Ph.D., *The Names of Allah in Relation to the Mathematical Structure of the Quran*, Islamic Productions, Tucson, 1982, p.6. (ISBN 0-934894-04-3)

[101] Prof. Majul, with whom I had the chance to discuss many issues related to the numerical structure of the Quran, was the founder and former Dean of the Institute of Islamic Studies at the University of Philippines (1974-1979) and visiting professor at Cornell University. He retired and passed away in California.

[102] By "universal" I am not referring to the Platonic versus Positivist definition of mathematics. Whether mathematics is discovered or invented, it is a language of universal convention.

[103] You can find these alphabets and their numerical values in large dictionaries or encyclopedias.

[104] I am using the word "perfect" in the sense of "practically efficient." I also wanted to

allude to the fact that 28 is the second number after 6, called "perfect" in mathematical jargon. A positive number is called "perfect" (sure, an arbitrary nomenclature) if it is equal to sum of all positive integers that are its factors. For instance, 6 is obtained by both the addition and multiplication of 1, 2, and 3.

[105] Here I would like to remind the readers about the need for properly understanding some attributes. For instance one of God's attribute is *ŽuW ÂQAB ALYM* (possessor of painful consequences). Here, the attribute is qualified by the word "consequence" and the word implies the freely made choices that warrant them. Thus, this attribute does not portray God as a "punisher" or "harmer" but as a just judge or educator who assigns negative consequences to wrong choices and evil actions. Another attribute of God may baffle those who are not critical thinkers. For instance, while the Quran uses *JaBaR* (mighty) for God (59:23), it also uses the same word as a negative attribute for cruel people or oppressive tyrants (5:22; 11:59; 14:15; 19:14,32; 26:30; 28:19; 40:35; 50:45). The proverb "power corrupts and absolute power corrupts absolutely" is true for human beings. Therefore, using might and force to implement one's wishes can lead to corruption and injustices on the part of humanity. Thus monarchies, regardless of their initial ideals and leaders, often become tools of corruption and oppression. However might and power will not lead to injustice when it is comes from the caring and loving, the wise and just creator of the universe. So, the attribute *JaBaR* is one of the exceptional attributes that cannot be emulated by us; it befits God alone.

[106] In 1989, despite my grammatically and phonetically handicapped English as a fresh immigrant, I was occasionally asked to deliver the Friday speeches and lead the prayers at Masjid Tucson. My mentor and friend late Dr. Rashad Khalifa, being a revolutionary monotheist and very cautious against the creation of priestly class, was careful not to monopolize the delivery of Friday sermons, the leading of congregational prayers and the weekly Quranic studies. During one of those speeches, I was commemorating God by sharing some of my observation on the prophetic scientific knowledge contained in the Quran. I announced that number of elements should be maximum 114, equal to the number of Chapters of the Quran. Then, the biggest element discovered in labs was 109. The chemists, Dr. Sabbahi and his wife, were present there and Dr. Sabbahi was impressed by my hypothesis because he had read a journal article discussing the issue theoretically. He later gave me a journal article about super heavy elements arguing that 114 was a "magic number" for stable elements. Years later, in 1998, when a couple of scientists discovered the element 114 in lab, I suggested them to name the element, whose temporary name is ununquadium, Quranium. Perhaps they preferred a mythological Greek hero to my suggestion.

[107] Some of Abdullah's observations published in *Beyond Probability* could be seen as arbitrary manipulations or statistically insignificant samples. Nevertheless, his book contains many examples that are undoubtedly components of an extraordinary theomathical design, like the ones I listed here.

[108] I recommend you to read my article, *Blind Watch-Watchers or Smell the Cheese*. The article can be found at www.19.org and as an appendix at the end of the *Quran: a Reformist Translation*.

[109] Rashad Khalifa, *Quran: Visual Presentation of the Miracle*, Ph.D., Islamic Productions, 1982, p. 240.

[110] Rashad Khalifa, *The Computer Speaks: God's Message to the World*, Renaissance Productions, Tucson, Arizona, 1981, Prologue, pp. 2-3.

[111] I met Ahmad Deedat, an intelligent and eloquent debater, in an Islamic Youth Conference and Camp in Çanakkale, Turkey and spent two weeks together. After learning from him the Code 19, I decided to translate his work, which I did along with my additional research and published under the title *Kuran En Büyük Mucize (The Quran, The Greatest Miracle)*, which became an instant best-seller in 1983 and remained as best-seller until 1987, when my rejection of Sunni religion became a public controversy.

[112] Ahmad Deedat, *Al-Quran the Ultimate Miracle*, Islamic Propagation Center, p. 52, 1984

[113] Ibid, 53-55.

[114] Ibn Abu Dawud, *Kitab ul-Masahif*, p. 108; Abu Amr al-Dani, *al-Muqni*, p. 85; Makki b. Ebi Talib, *al-Kashf*, 1, 303.

[115] In his first book where he published his computerized calculations and data analysis in 1973, in Chapter 5 titled "Methods of Calculation," Rashad provided extensive information about the nature of his early studies. In page 31-32 he provides the following details about the computer: "Xerox Data System's Sigma 7 computer, utilizing a teletype terminal (Time-Share Network). All programing was done in FORTRAN IV language. A library program of Com-Share, Inc. entitled "MARS" was used for the arrangement of the final data in ascending order."

[116] Rashad Khalifa, *The Miracle of the Quran: Significance of the Mysterious Alphabets*, Islamic Productions International, Inc., St. Louis, MO, 1973.

[117] The introduction of this out-of-print book contains some Hadith narrations and the remark regarding Muhammad's illiteracy, and his dedication of his book to his father "to the teacher who guided my footsteps along the path: Ăbdulh-Halim Khalifa, Egyptian Sage of Sufism, Founder and Grand Shaykh of Tariqat Al-Rashad Al-Shaziliyya" are clear indications that Rashad was still a Sunni. In fact, in his brief bio, he mentions his "the climax of his Sufi indoctrination took place in Mecca (1391 AH; 1971 AD), where he was officially initiated into the chain of Sufi deputies." (p vii). With the discovery of the code in 1974, soon after the publication of this book, Rashad would experience a paradigm change, which he would share with the world in his historical book, *Quran, Hadith, and Islam*, which was first published in 1980. The book, however, contains some prophetic clues. For instance, the Hadith he quotes as an authority is about preservation of the Quran and mentions the name of a character that emerges again after his discovery about 9:128-129: "... When 'Umar, died, his daughter Hafsa, a widow of the Prophet, kept the original recorded Quran. During the reign of Uthman ibn Ăffan, one of his emissaries to Syria and Iraq, named Huzeife ibn Al-Yaman, came to him and informed him of serious variations in reciting the Qur'an by the Muslims of Syria and Iraq...." The average frequency of letter NuN in the beginning of chapter 68 for each of its verse is given as 2.558, which indicates his count as 133, without his knowledge of 19 and the problem with the spelling of the letter NuN. His count in the letter S is given the total of 153, since the text of the Quran he used contained an extra Sad.

[118] Rashad Khalifa Ph.D., *The Miracle of the Quran: Significance of the Mysterious Alphabets*, Islamic Productions International, Inc., St. Louis, MO, 1973, pp. 69-71

[119] Thus I assert that though the Quran is the most read book in the world, yet it is the least understood and the least followed book as a result of those who follow and promote blind following of dogmas of a particular sect.

[120] In fact, the derivatives of the root *BaSaTa* occurs in the Quran 25 times in various forms and all of them are spelled with the letter س S (Seen). No wonder that Fuad Abdulbaqi in his famous index of the Quran, lists all of them under the correct spelling with س S (Seen), including the commonly mispeled one in 7:69. Here is the list of 25 occurences of the derivatives of the word: 2:245; 2:247; 5:11; 5:28; 5:28; 5:64; 6:93; 7:69; 13:14; 13:26; 17:29; 17:29; 17:30; 18:18; 28:82; 29:62; 30:37; 30:48; 34:9; 34:36; 39:52; 42:12; 42:27; 60:2; 71:19.

[121] Atef Khalifa, *Preserving and Protecting the Quran*, http://www.submission.org/quran/protect.html

[122] For the hadith references see note 122.

[123] Tayyar Altıkulaç, *Yüce Kitabımız Hz. Kuran* (*Our Glorious Book, The Great Quran*), Günaydın, year of publication was not printed but from references it can be inferred, p. 61

[124] Ibn Abu Dawud, *Kitab al-Masahif*, p. 108; Abu Amr al-Dani, *al-Muqni*, p. 85; Makki b. Ebi Talib, *al-Kashf*, 1, 303.

[125] Tayyar Altıkulaç, *Supra* note 123, at 62.

[126] Carl Sagan, *The Varieties of Scientific Experience*, Penguin Press, 2006, p. 167.

[127] I had translated the *Visual Presentation of the Quran* into Turkish and it was published with my additional research on the subject. However, after a fatwa for my death was issued, this book too was entered onto the black list together with me.

[128] Ahmad Deedat, *Al-Quran: The Ultimate Miracle*, Islamic Propagation Centre, Durban, 1979-1984, p. 62

[129] Rashad Khalifa, *The Computer Speaks: God's Message to the World*, Renaissance Productions, USA, 1981, p. 115.

[130] As it seems, I was a critic since my childhood. When I immigrated to the USA to seek freedom and security, I left behind all my belongings. Years later, one of the books published critical of me and my work, *19 Answers to the Muslims of 19: Humans too Slip* contained an excerpt from my high school yearbook. In that yearbook, the senior class students were writing about each other. My desk-mate had written a couple of paragraphs praising my intelligence while complaining about my common sense and habit of criticizing everything. The author of the book, by using my friend's testimony in the yearbook was trying to undermine my criticism levied towards Sunni teachings and practices.

[131] For instance, after consulting and discussing with me, Rashad made minor or major corrections in his early translation of the following verses: 2:1; 2:26; 2:54; 2:106; 2:171; 2:222; 2:224; 3:7; 7:157; 8:35; 10:1; 15:87; 16:44; 17:46; 20:15; 21:87; 22:15; 24:31; 25:5; 33:56; 38:44; 43:61; 56:79; 61:6; 74:29-35.

[132] The day he received a truckload of the second revision of his translation, after noticing an error in it during a Quranic study meeting, he publicly declared it "already obsolete." And soon he started working on the third revision which he did until Chapter 49 before he was stabbed to death by a group of Sunni terrorists when

entering Masjid Tucson for dawn prayer in January 31st 1990.

[133] The Quran has exactly 133 (19x7) verses ending with NUN, that is, NWN.

[134] I would like to thank my Turkish colleague Cemal Aktaş for his help on compiling this list.

[135] Rashad Khalifa, *Quran: The Final Testament*, Islamic Productions, 1989, p. 623.

[136] I would like to share with you a comment made by my colleague Dr. Gazi Alankuş, a computer scientist, on the long numbers in the Quran: "If this big number is a sum of smaller numbers, you don't have to calculate that big number in order to see if it is a multiple of 19. If there is no example that is not a sum of smaller numbers (verse numbers, gematrical numbers etc), the sum having many digits loses its "impossible" status. The title "long numbers" gives an example that is not a sum, so perhaps something like "requires computation of huge numbers" could be added. In general, it might be a nice idea to include a discussion about how one could figure out whether the sum of many small numbers is divisible by 19 using modular arithmetic, which would be possible in Mohammad's time. With that, fixing counts and sums to be multiple of 19 would be possible at Mohammad's time. However concatenating numbers one after the other to form a really long number would not be possible at that time. This distinction would give a better feel of what was possible and what wasn't."

[137] There are other Rabbis who share the name Judah, such as Rabbi Judah the Prince. Our Judah is also called Rabbi-Judah-ben Samuel HaChasid or Jehudah ben Chemouel le Hassid. For the biographical information, see: http://www.chabad.org/library/article_cdo/aid/111829/jewish/Rabbi-Judah-HaChassid.htm. Also see: http://www.danielyharris.com/teaching.shtml

[138] http://en.wikipedia.org/wiki/Judah_ben_Samuel_of_Regensburg

[139] Dan, Joseph. *Studies in Jewish Mysticism, Association for Jewish Studies*. Cambridge, Massachusetts: 1978, p 88.

[140] See the Quran: 37:114-117

[141] First Publication: *Crowning Achievement*, Eliezer Segal, Ha'Atid, the magazine of the Melbourne Hebrew Congregation, Summer 2000. Also see: *In Those Days, At This Time: Holiness and History in the Jewish Calendar*, Eliezer Segal, Calgary Press, 2008.

[142] Kazim Mudir Shanechi, *Some Old Manuscripts of the Holy Qur'an*, Al-Tawhid, translated from Persian by Mujahid Husain, Vol. VIII, No. 4 (Shawwal 1411/May 1991)

[143] Ta'rikh-a Ya'qubi, Persian trans., ii, 15.

[144] *Sahih al-Bukhari*; al-Suyuti's *al -'Itqan*; al-Zarakashi's *al-Burhan*, i, 240; *Ta'rikh al Ya'qubi*, Najaf, ii, 147; Subhi al-Salih, *Mabahithfri'ulum al-Qur'an*, 78.

[145] *Sahih, al-Bukhari* and al-Zarakshi's *al-Burhan*, i, 236:

[146] *Al-Masahif* 24.

[147] *Mabahith fi'ulum al-Qur'an*, 8th edition, 82.

[148] *Al-Masahif* 15; *Tarikh al-Ya'qubi*, ii, 147.

[149] Osman Keskioğlu, *Nüzülünden Günümüze Kuran-ı Kerim Bilgileri*, (Quranic

Knowledge from its Revelation to Our Day), Türkiye Diyanet Vakfı publishing, 1987, p:140. Also see: Dr. Subhi al-Saleh, *Mabahis fi Ulum-al Quran* (Topics in Sciences of the Quran), p. 83 and And numerous books about the history of the Quran.

[150] Rasul Ja'farian, *A Study of Sunni and Shi' Traditions Concerning Tahrif, Al-Tawhid: a Quarterly Journal of Islamic Thought and Culture*, Sazman-e Teblighat-e Islami, Tehran, Shawwal – Dhu al-Hijjah 1409 (May – July 1989), Vol. VI, No. 4. The second part of the article was published in the following issue of the same journal.

[151] Ibn Ashta in *Al-Suyuti* vol. 1,58

[152] *Al-Itqan fi Ulum-il Quran*, Al-Azhar Publishing, Cairo, Egypt, Hijri 1318 (circa 1900 AC), Vol 1, Page 59)

[153] *Bukhari* 6:61:510 (Book 6, Chapter 61, Hadith 510)

[154] "A method of proving this kind of completeness for a set of rules of inference can be found in I. M. Copi, *Symbolic Logic*, 5th Edition. (New York: Macmillian, 1979), chap 8. See also John A. Winnie, "The Completeness of Copi's System of Natural Deduction," *Notre Dame Journal of Formal Logic* 11 (July 1970), 379-382."

[155] *Introduction to Logic*, Irving M. Copi and Carl Cohen, Prentice Hall, Thirteenth Edition, 2009, p. 400.

[156] *Ibid*, at 373.

[157] Remember the number of letters in Bismillah? It contains 9 different letters with 10 repetitions (9+10).

[158] Meldner H. *Realistic Nuclear Single-Particle Hamiltonians and the Proton Shell 114*. Physical Review. 1969;178(4):1815-1826.

[159] Chowdhury PR, Samanta C, Basu DN. *Search for long lived heaviest nuclei beyond the valley of stability*. Physical Review C (Nuclear Physics). 2008;77(4):044603.

[160] Ninov V, Gregorich KE, Loveland W, et al. *Observation of Superheavy Nuclei Produced in the Reaction of 86Kr with 208Pb*. Physical Review Letters. 1999;83:1104-1107.

[161] Dalton R. Misconduct: *The stars who fell to Earth. Nature*. 2002;420(6917):728-729.

[162] Karol PJ, Nakahara H, Petley BW, Vogt E. *On the Claims for Discovery of Elements 110, 111, 112, 114, 116, and 118 (IUPAC Technical Report)*. Pure and Applied Chemistry. 2003;75(10):1601—1611.

[163] Garcia MA. Discovery of Element 118 by Oganessian, *Don't Call it Ununoctium. Chemistry Blog*. 2006. Available at: http://www.chemistry-blog.com/2006/10/16/discovery-of-element-118-by-oganessian-dont-call-it-ununoctium/ [Accessed September 25, 2009].

[164] Stavsetra L, Gregorich KE, Dvorak J, et al. *Independent Verification of Element 114 Production in the [sup 48]Ca+[sup 242]Pu Reaction*. Physical Review Letters. 2009;103(13):132502.

[165] Chowdhury, *Supra* note 159.

[166] Underwood Doodley, Supra note 58, at 91.

[167] Some of the facts listed here have been contested through books and internet sites. For instance, Ataturk's birth certificate number is claimed to be different. However,

our research proved those allegations to be false. Unfortunately, the scope of the book does not allow me to provide evidences for each fact. However, we will publish them in detail in a Turkish book.

[168]   http://www.wired.com/wired/archive/6.08/y2k_pr.html

[169]   http://www.wired.com/thisdayintech/2009/12/1231-y2k/

[170]   Weisstein, Eric W. *Magic Hexagon*. From MathWorld–A Wolfram Web Resource: http://mathworld.wolfram.com/MagicHexagon.html.

The internet site, **http://primes.utm.edu/curios/** has numerous interesting observations on prime numbers. The page on the number 19 contains fascinating mathematical properties and pecularities. The edited content of the site was published as a book in 2009. I highly recommend it to those who love numbers: Chris K.Caldwell and G.L Honaker Jr., *Prime Curios! The Dictionary of Prime Number Trivia*, CreateSpace, 2009. Also see: http://www.virtuescience.com/19.html

[171]   Underwood Doodley, Supra note 58, at 144

[172]   In the Tashkent manuscript the word *Ya ayyuha* is spelled with only two Alifs. Originally there were no *hamzas*; *hamzas* were invented decades after the revelation of the Quran. I have a copy of the Tashkent version; however, it is not complete. It does not contain Chapter 74. There is a possibility that the first word of this chapter was spelled differently.

[173]   Underwood Dudley allocates the Chapter 15 of his book, *Numerology or What Pythagoras Wrought*, (See, *Supra* note 58), on paragrams, statements with numerical values. "In the paragram's finest flowering, an author would take an occasion, attach an appropriate Bible passage to it, and then construct a text appropriate to the occasion. The text would have to have the same gematric sum as the Bible passage." (p. 132). Then the author gives several examples of paragrams made by Johann Friedrich Riederer and Picander (Chirstian Friedrich Henrici). After sharing interesting examples, the author writes: "Paragrams seem to have died out in Germany some time after 1750 and they never caught on elsewhere. Such is the fate of minor art forms. Paragrams were an offshoot of medieval number symbolism that survived long after most other forms disappeared" (p. 134). Then, to show how it is easy to construct such paragrams, the author produces one of his own by using a pocket calculator. "The occasion that it marks is the publication of this book, and the appropriate Biblical passage is from Ecclesiastes 1:1, 8. It was constructed with a little mechanical assistance from a pocket calculator, so if there are any errors in it, they are the calculator's fault." For his paragram, Underwood uses the trigonal scheme of substitution where the "nth letter is replaced by the nth triangular number." He matches 8187, the total numerical value of the verse above with the following translation: "Emptiness, emptiness, says the Speaker, emptiness, all is empty. All things are wearisome; no man can speak of them all." Underwood's numerically equivalent statement is an amusing one: "Finally! Another book by Woody Dudley. I can hardly wait to read it all. I will purchase many copies to give away." In comparison to the Quranic paragram, Woody's calculator-aided silly paragram is extremely primitive and empty... Somehow, Woody managed to match the phrase "emptiness, all is empty" in the Biblical verse. He does match the paragrams made by Picander. However, Woody's paragram lacks a symbolic meaning in the number of its letters; it does not match anything meaningful. Besides, it lacks the prophetic

fulfillment in the numerical value of its words. It also lacks reference to an extraordinary mathematical system.

[174] In some manuscripts, the first word contains one less Alif, thus reducing the number of letters in the statement to 18 and their gematrical values to 1973. This alternative spelling though might provide an excuse for those who do not wish to acknowledge the prophecy. It is still very close to the time of the discovery. Unfortunately, we do not know the exact day of the discovery. If the discovery occurred exactly in the New Year, then the timing could accommodate both dates.

[175] I was the first one who noticed this fact. I was then living in Istanbul communicating with Rashad via snail mail. Witnessing the extraordinary nature of the code and its prophecy, I told myself, "This guy cannot be a random person. He is selected by God to unveil the great secret of the Quran." I decided to look at the concordance of the Quran for his name. It took me a few seconds to learn that the all the frequency of all the derivatives of the word *RaSHaD* was exactly 19. He had not yet declared his messengership. In my next letter to him I informed him about the frequency of his name. Later, when he declared his messengership, he published a section of my letter in the Submitter's Perspective. After my immigration, I was surprised to learn from him that he did not know the frequency of his name in the Quran, which was another evidence indicating that he was initially indeed reluctant to declare his messengership.

[176] For those who claim the infallibility of Dr. Khalifa, I would like to give a sample of verses in his translation that I think carry some minor or important translational problems: 2:114; 2:233; 2:275*; 2:282*; 4:34&*; 4:79*; 7:157; 7:193; 8:64; 10:34!; 11:54; 11:87; 12:37; 14:4; 16:75*; 18:16*; 19:26!; 20:96&*; 20:114; 21:96*; 21:90* x 21:73; 25:30*; 29:12 x 29:13; 32:5!; 34:41; 35:24 x 25:51; 43:11 x 41:12*; 43:36*; 47:11 x 42:15; 49:1 x 38:26&7:3; 56:83-85; 65:12* x 42:29; 73:15!; 75:27; 75:31?; 87:6 (Asterisks are for footnotes and/or subtitles, exclamation marks for missing phrases, and "x" for contradictions.)

Despite clear and numerous evidence to the contrary, some so-called Submitters who left the ranks of Sunni, Shiite, Christian, Hindu polytheism continue their idolization of Rashad by claiming the third revision of his translation to be infallible. In fact, some of them have devolved further and now they claim mathematical miracles for the English translation. Of course the re-re-revised version! I have discussed this issue in length with those who replaced Muhammad's, Ali's or Jesus' idol with of Rashad.

In the last section of this book, you will see some of Rashad's communication and articles published in various magazines and newspapers, both in Arabic and English. In one of the publications, Rashad answers the question regarding the meaning of "Authorized Translation." Those who follow the May 19, 1990 "Doomsday Prophets" who could not wait to fabricate a *hadith* to promote their delusional prophecy, are refuted one more time, with an *authentic hadith* of their own idol. They will soon come up with the so-called "science of hadith" of Rashad in order to reconcile the internal contradictions among the three revised, yet "authorized" versions; articles in the Submitter's Perspective; footnotes, subtitles and Appendices in his translation. In order to explain the contradictions of their "infallible messenger," they will even employ the diabolic Sunni idea of abrogation. They are repeating the history of the past communities who idolized their messengers, in an incredible speed and success.

My previous predictions regarding the backward mutation and devolution of this group have been proven to be true. As it seems, they will continue taking the regressive path of the previous generations.

Rashad never claimed to be infallible, nor did he claim that his translation, with parentheses, footnotes and appendices to be a revelation. He never doubted that the Quran is the last book revealed to the last prophet. However, I agree with him that his translation was authorized by God through discovery of the code and for its clear emphasis on serving God alone and not adding any other sources (including Rashad's) to God's word, which is perfect and fully detailed. Rashad was a student of the Quran, trying to purify his mind from the atmospherics of his traditional past that prevented him from receiving the clear broadcast of the divine message. During my years of mail and face-to-face conversation with him, I found him to be usually humble in acknowledging his errors. For instance, he encouraged us to edit and discuss the second revision of his translation verse by verse. During this intense consultation we had numerous discussions.

We continuously learned from each other according to God's will. During that period, I persuaded him to correct some of the mistakes of the first edition. For example: 2.106; 3:97*; 7.75; 11.87; 11.88; 12.88; 18.83; 21.96; 21.112; 24.35; 27.42; 37.63; 38.44; 39.6; 43.61; 56.79; 72.7; 72.18; 74.31; 96.2. He acknowledged my substantial contribution in the first pages of his translation. Later, when he re-revised his translation, he continued correcting his errors. For example, 4.176; 6.74*; 12.88; 18.83; 30.3; 38.59; 95.5! etc.

Not surprisingly, the gang managed to delete the section where Rashad acknowledged some people, including me for their editorial assistance (My assistance was categorically different, since it was mostly related to the substance rather than grammar or spelling, which was worse during my early years in the USA). The gang wished to purge one of the many evidences indicating that Rashad's translation was not dictated by an angel, but he was consulting and receiving some help from his friends. Of course, the gang also did not wish to see my substantial contribution to Rashad's translation to be known by new comers. Upon protests from first generation of Submitters, the gang's scheme did not last; the acknowledgement section was restored in the following editions of the translation.

Briefly stated, he never claimed to be infallible, as the new idol-carvers among the Submitters claim. The three revised editions of his translations are blatant witnesses to the fact that he was in a continual learning process and that he was open-minded to reasonable criticism. If he were alive, he would surely make many corrections to his third revision. In fact, it is the experience and fate of all translators. Every time I edit my Turkish and English translations of the Quran, I find errors caused by insufficient information, imperfect attention, shortcomings, linguistic problems and unintentional mistakes. Nevertheless, I still believe that both of my translations or Rashad's are good in delivering the message, inshaAllah.

The message, however, will be missed by those who have prejudice and by those who would consider Rashad's or my translation to be infallible. If you have bad intentions or you have tendency to set up idols besides God, the Quran will only increase your deviation from truth. Thank God, we have the original Quran that we can refer to anytime we have a question. In 1995, I warned Submitters that it would be an unfortunate repetition of history if one day some of them would claim that Rashad's translation, Quran the Final Testament, is "equivalent to the original" or "a revelation from God" in itself. But they since then, a growing number of Submitters responded to my warning with bigotry and ignorance. They are passionately adhering to this constant human tendency invoked by the master hypnotist: hero-worship.

[177] Jamar Younger, *Man arrested in 1990 stabbing death of Tucson mosque leader*, Arizona Daily Star, 28 April 2009. Steve Fainaru and Alia Ibrahim, *Mysterious Trip to Flight 77 Cockpit: Suicide Pilot's Conversion to Radical Islam Remains Obscure*, The Washington Post, September 10, 2002; A17. Chris Limberis, *Terrorists in Tiny Town, Tucson Weekly*, September 20, 2001, pp. 4-8. Mark Hosenball, *Another Holy War Waged on American Soil*, Newsweek, February 28, 1994, pp. 30-31. Also see: Tim Vanderpool, *The No. 19 Murder*, Tucson Weekly, January 19, 1994, cover story. Also see: *Tucson Mosque slaying may be linked to sect*, The Arizona Daily Star, October 12, 1992, first page. After September 11, the national media picked up the story. For instance, see: CBS Evening News with Dan Rather, on October 26, 2001; cover story of Newsweek, January 14, 2002, p.44. On March 19, 2002, KPHO-TV at Phoenix, a CBS affiliate, in its evening news, broadcast an interview with me under the headline: *Traces of Al Qaeda Cell in Tucson*. Editorial, *Suspect in 1990 Tucson Mosque Murder Arrested in Calgary 19 Years Later*, Calgary Herald, 29 April 2009. Jamar Younger, *Arrest Made in Mosque Killing*, Arizona Daily Star, April 29, 2009. Jamie Komarnicki, *Calgary's Link to an Arizona Assassination*, Calgary Herald, October 9, 2010.

[178] *Ibid*, p. 78.

[179] Clifford A Pickover, *The Math Book: From Pythagoras to the 57th Dimension, 250 Milestones in the History of Mathematics*, Sterling, New York, 3rd edition, 2009. Pp. 56, 78, 92.

[180] See 3:81; 40:44,78-85; 72:24-28; 74:1-56.

[181] Unlike the creatures made of water (24:45), this one is made from earthly elements. After the discovery of the code and from the context of this verse, this creature (*DaBBah*) can be understood as reference to a computer in the context of this prophetic verse. In traditional books there are many bizarre description of this prophesized creature. Contrary to the Quran's positive depiction of the earth-based creature, Hadith books contain negative descriptions.

Some may object to my interpretation by saying that the word *DaBBah* implies something alive that moves. I think this objection is reasonable. But, I prefer the computer to an animal since I can understand the phrase *dabbatan min al -ardi* not a creature geographically from earth, but a creature made of earth. Thus, I can accept some differences in mobility between the "*dabbah* from water" and "*dabbah* from earth." Since a computer has many moving parts —from its hard disk to the information carried by trillions of electrons— I do not see it a far-fetched understanding of the implication of *DaBBah*.

[182] Yvonne Yazbeck Haddad and Jane Idleman Smith, *Mission to America: Five Islamic Sectarian Communities in North America*, University Press of Florida, 1993. p. 138. (See pp:137-169).

[183] Richard N. Ostling; Michael P. Harris/Armherst and Jon D. Hull/Los Angeles, *Religion: Americans Facing Toward Mecca*, Time Magazine, May 23, 1988. See: http://www.time.com/time/magazine/article/0,9171,967433,00.html#ixzz193kRssO1

[184] *Terrorists Take to Arizona*, CBS News, October 26, 2001
http://www.cbsnews.com/stories/2001/10/26/attack/main316077.shtml (July 2, 2009)

[185] Michael Foucault, *Discipline and Punish: the Birth of the Prison*, Vintage Books, 1979, pp. 233-234. This is one of the best books written on the history and origion of modern prison system.

[186] Title: Soruşturma; Author: Muhammed Tevfik; Translator: Abdullah Şanlı; Publisher: Mücahede Yayınları; Year: 1981.

[187] For a little numerical musing, I would later publish those formulas in my best-selling book, *Kuran En Büyük Mucize*, (Quran the Greatest Miracle), Inkılab Yayınevi, Istanbul, starting with its third edition in 1983.

[188] Magic is not considered an extraordinary, paranormal event by the Quran. Its influence on people is described by its two aspects: illusion and suggestion/bluffs/hypnosis (7:103-120). Magic is an art of influencing gullible people via illusion and hypnosis (7:11; 20:66; 2:102). So, when the unappreciative disbeliever describes the Quran OR the mathematical miracle of the Quran as "influencing magic," what should be understood is that it is just a manipulation and hyperbole.

[189] To see the examples of misunderstanding and distortion of Quranic verses by the followers of Hadith and Sunna, please read the comparative section in the beginning of the Reformist Translation of the Quran.

[190] Soon after Muhammad's death thousands of Hadiths (words attributed to Muhammad) were fabricated and two centuries later compiled in the so-called "authentic" Hadith books, to support the teaching of a particular sect against another (for in-stance, what nullifies ablution; which sea food is prohibited); to flatter or justify the authority and practice of a particular king against dissidents (such as, Mahdy and Dajjal); to promote the interest of a particular tribe or family (such as, favoring Quraysh tribe or Muhammad's family); to justify sexual abuse and misogyny (such as, Aisha's age; barring women from leading Sala prayers); to justify violence, op-pression and tyranny (such as, torturing members of Urayna and Uqayla tribes, massacring Jewish population in Medina, assassinating a female poet for her critical poems); to exhort more rituals and righteousness (such as, *nawafil* prayers); to validate superstitions (such as, magic; worshiping the black stone near *Kaba*); to prohibit certain things and actions (such as, prohibiting drawing animal and human figures, playing musical instruments, chess); to import Jewish and Christian beliefs and practices (such as, circumcision, head scarf, hermitic, using rosary); to resurrect pre-islamic beliefs and practices common among Meccans (such as, intercession; slavery;); to please crowds with stories (such as the story of Mirage and bargaining for prayers); to idolize Muhammad and claim his superiority to other messengers (such as, numerous miracles, including splitting the moon); to defend Hadith fabrication against monotheists (such as, condemning those who find the Quran alone sufficient); and even to advertise a particular fruit or vegetables (such as, the benefits of date grown in Ajwa farm). In addition to the abovementioned reasons, many Hadiths were fabricated to explain the meaning of the "difficult" Quranic words or phrases, or to distort the meaning of verses that contradicted to fabricated Hadiths, or to pro-vide trivial information not mentioned in the Quran (such as, Saqar, 2:187; 8:35...)

[191] For an article titled *Eternal Hell and Merciful God*, visit www.yuksel.org OR

www.19.org.

After translating the verse 74:30 as "Over it are nineteen (powers)" Muhammad Asad explains his parenthetical comment with the following footnote:

"Whereas most of the classical commentators are of the opinion that the "nine-teen'" are the controllers that act as keepers or guardians of hell, Razi advances the view that we may have here a reference to the physical, intellectual and emotional powers within man himself: powers which raise man potentially far above any other creature, but which, if used wrongly, bring about a deterioration of his whole personality and, hence, intense suffering in the life to come. According to Razi, the philosophers (*arbab al-hikmah*) identify these powers or faculties with, firstly, the seven organic functions of the animal - and therefore also human - body (gravitation, cohesion, repulsion of noxious foreign matter, absorption of beneficent external matter, assimilation of nutrients, growth, and reproduction); secondly, the five "external" or physical senses (sight, hearing, touch, smell and taste); thirdly, the five "internal" or intellectual senses., de-fined by Ibn Sina - on whom Razi apparently relies - as (1) perception of isolated sense-images, (2) conscious apperception of ideas, (3) memory of sense-images, (4) memory of conscious apperceptions, and (5) the ability to correlate sense-images and higher apperceptions; and, lastly, the emotions of desire or aversion (resp. fear or anger), which have their roots in both the "external" and "internal" sense-categories - thus bringing the total of the powers and faculties which preside over man's spiritual fate to nineteen. In their aggregate, it is these powers that confer upon man the ability to think conceptually, and place him, in this respect, even above the controllers (cf. 2:30 ff. and the corresponding notes; see also the following note)."

193 "Whereas most of the classical commentators are of the opinion that the "nine-teen'" are the controllers that act as keepers or guardians of hell, Razi advances the view that we may have here a reference to the physical, intellectual and emotional powers within man himself: powers which raise man potentially far above any other creature, but which, if used wrongly, bring about a deterioration of his whole personality and, hence, intense suffering in the life to come. According to Razi, the philosophers (*arbab al-hikmah*) identify these powers or faculties with, firstly, the seven organic functions of the animal - and therefore also human - body (gravitation, cohesion, repulsion of noxious foreign matter, absorption of beneficent external matter, assimilation of nutrients, growth, and reproduction); secondly, the five "external" or physical senses (sight, hearing, touch, smell and taste); thirdly, the five "internal" or intellectual senses., de-fined by Ibn Sina - on whom Razi apparently relies - as (1) perception of isolated sense-images, (2) conscious apperception of ideas, (3) memory of sense-images, (4) memory of conscious apperceptions, and (5) the ability to correlate sense-images and higher apperceptions; and, lastly, the emotions of desire or aversion (resp. fear or anger), which have their roots in both the "external" and "internal" sense-categories - thus bringing the total of the powers and faculties which preside over man's spiritual fate to nineteen. In their aggregate, it is these powers that confer upon man the ability to think conceptually, and place him, in this respect, even above the controllers (cf. 2:30 ff. and the corresponding notes; see also the following note)."

194 The plural word *AYAAT* means revelation, sign, evidence, or miracle. However, its singular form *AYAT* is mentioned in the Quran 84 times and in all its occurrences it

means sings, evidence or miracles, not literary revelation of the Quran.

[195] This verse is a crucial verse in understanding the Quran and ironically this very verse is one of the most commonly misunderstood verses in the Quran. For a detailed argument on this verse please visit: www.yuksel.org or www.19.org.

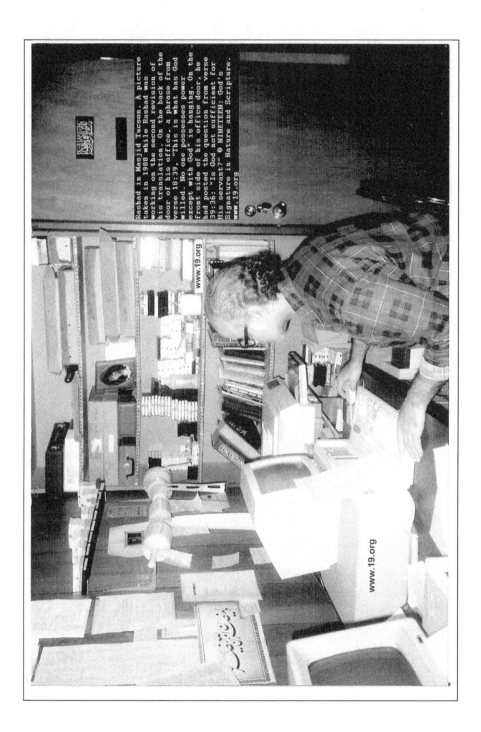

Rashad in Masjid Tucson. A picture taken in 1988 while Rashad was working on the second revision of this translation. On the back of the door of his office, a phrase from verse 18:39, "This is what has God willed. No one possesses power except with God" is hanging. On the front side of his office door, he had posted the question from verse 39:36: "Is God not sufficient for His servant?" © NINETEEN: God's Signature in Nature and Scripture. www.19.org

www.19.org

www.19.org

545

Edip Yuksel, Fatemeh Karbassi (Parivash), Rashad Khalifa, Haga from Egypt, and Lisa Spray. In front of Masjid Tucson on Euclid and 6th Street ,1988. www.19.org

19.org. Dr. Rashad Khalifa, 1989.

NUMBER 11 NOVEMBER, 1963

WESTERN *fruit* GROWER

Rashad's work is the cover story of Western Fruit Grower in November 1963. "Growth stimulating citrus auxin discovered by Egyptian graduate student Rashad Khalifah causes oat sprouts to curve when applied to one side. The one at far right is untreated. (See story, page 21.)" Who would know that this scientist would one day be the discoverer of one of the greatest mysteries and would first be celebrated by millions and then would be considered a heretic to be killed for his rejection of Hadith, Sunna and sectarian dogmas and would become the target of false accusations, hate and finally deadly attack? © NINETEEN: God's Signature in Nature and Scripture. www.19.org

Growth stimulating citrus auxin discovered by Egyptian graduate student Rashad Khalifah causes oat sprouts to curve when applied to one side. The one at far right is untreated. (See story, page 21.)

Chapter 5

METHODS OF CALCULATION

The only calculations carried out manually were the initial determinations of the frequency of occurrence of each letter in each sura. A special form was prepared as shown in Figure 1 to facilitate the counting process. As shown in Figure 1, the name of the sura, the number of verses in that sura, its chronological number in the sequence of revelation, and its number in the sequence of recording were listed at the top of the form. The 28 alphabetic letters were listed on the right-hand side of the form on a vertical line. The counting was carried out by reading the sura while placing a short vertical line in front of each letter read. Thus, as

was read, a vertical mark was placed in front of the letter Bā, then in front of the letter Sīn, then in front of the letter Mīm, then in front of the letter Alif, then two marks were placed in front of the letter Lām, and so forth. Every fifth mark was a slash across the previous four marks. When a sura was completed, the number of each letter was obtained by counting the marks in front of it, and the total number of alphabetic letters was calculated by adding up the numbers of all 28 letters. The final result for sura Al-Fātiḥa (no. 1) is illustrated in Figure 2. All subsequent calculations were carried out by means of a Xerox Data System's Sigma 7 electronic computer, utilizing a teletype terminal (Time-Share

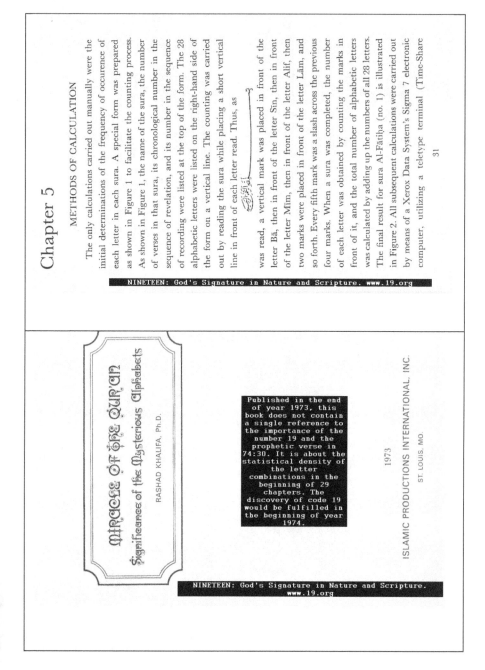

MIRACLE OF THE QUR'AN

Significance of the Mysterious Alphabets

RASHAD KHALIFA, Ph.D.

Published in the end of year 1973, this book does not contain a single reference to the importance of the number 19 and the prophetic verse in 74:30. It is about the statistical density of the letter combinations in the beginning of 29 chapters. The discovery of code 19 would be fulfilled in the beginning of year 1974.

1973

ISLAMIC PRODUCTIONS INTERNATIONAL, INC.

ST. LOUIS, MO.

Network). All programing was done in FORTRAN IV language. A library program of Com-Share, Inc. entitled "MARS" was used for the arrangement of the final data in ascending order.

For each of the 14 letters which participate in the Qur'anic initials, the following three values were determined:

1. *The Absolute Frequency:* This was simply the number of occurrences of each letter in each sura.

2. *The Percentage of Frequency:* This value was calculated by dividing the frequency of occurrence of each letter by the total number of letters in the sura, then multiplying the product by 100.

3. *The Average Per Verse Value:* This was determined by dividing the absolute frequency of a given letter by the number of verses which constitute the sura.

For a multi-lettered set of Qur'anic initials, these three values were determined by adding up the corresponding values of all the constituent letters. Thus, the absolute frequency values were added together, the percentage frequency values were added together, and the average per verse values were added together. To illustrate, let us consider sura Al-Baqara. This sura is made up of 286 verses, with the first verse consisting of three alphabetic letters, Alif Lām Mīm (A.L.M.). The total number of letters in this sura is 25,717. The absolute frequency of occurrence of the letter Alif (A) is 4,329. This makes the percentage value of the letter Alif (A) in sura Al-Baqara = $(4,329/25,717) \times 100 = 16.8\%$. The average per verse

34

occurrence of the letter Alif (A) in sura Al-Baqara would be $4,329/286 = 15.14$. The corresponding values for the letter Lām (L) are 2,941, 11.4%, and 10.28. For the letter Mīm (M), the three values were determined as 2,195, 8.5%, and 7.67, respectively. Thus, the absolute frequency value for the set of initials Alif Lām Mīm (A.L.M.) was determined by adding $4,329 + 2,941 + 2,195 = 9,465$. Similarly, the percentage value of ALM in sura Al-Baqara was determined by adding $16.8 + 11.4 + 8.5 = 36.7\%$. The average per verse value of ALM in Al-Baqara was calculated as $15.14 + 10.28 + 7.67 = 33.09$. Of course, all these computations were carried out by the computer. The three values for each one of the Qur'anic initials in each one of the 114 suras were thus determined.

The reason for following this particular method for calculation of the multi-lettered Qur'anic initials is the assertion by Prophet Muhammad (peace be upon him) that their constituent letters are independent of each other. This was in a hadith reported by Al-Bukhāry, Al-Baydawy, and Al-Suyūty. The Prophet said, "I do not say that Alif Lām Mīm (A.L.M.) constitutes one entity. I say that Alif (A) is an independent letter, Lām (L) is an independent letter, and Mīm (M) is an independent letter."

The following data were fed into the computer:

1. The absolute frequency of occurrence of each letter which participates in Qur'anic initials, in each sura. These letters are Alif (A), Hā (Ḥ), Rā (R), Sīn (S),

35

550

Şād (Ş), Ţā (Ţ), 'Ayn ('A), Qāf (Q), Kāf (K), Lām (L), Mīm (M), Nūn (N), Hā (H), and Yā (Y). The computer print-out of these values is shown in Table 8.

TABLE 8

The Absolute Frequency of Occurrence of the Letters Alif (A), Hā (Y), Rā (R), Sīn (S), Şād (Ş), Ţā (Ţ), 'Ayn ('A), Qāf (Q), Kāf (K), Lām (L), Mīm (M), Nūn (N), Hā (H), and Yā (Y), in Each Sura.

```
I:21:5,8:2;2;6:1;3;22;15;11;5;14
II:459;8:330;876;451;156;99;795;553;838;3204;2195;2018;1412;1847
III:2576;173;512;288;89;50;385;306;484;1885;1251;1235;768;1134
IV:2291;173;491;260;182;70;402;255;583;1965;1305;1333;880;1280
V:2237;173;380;215;74;58;335;246;335;1401;1053;977;615;936
VI:2169;169;505;811;69;52;369;272;466;1401;1042;1013;671;966
VII:2563;167;534;899;98;50;400;356;467;1583;1165;1303;734;993
VIII:905;54;187;71;29;22;162;109;200;653;456;440;286;450
IX:1804;143;414;199;68;33;314;216;299;1351;963;878;741;801
X:1402;88;324;113;60;89;243;180;255;785;591;693;369;623
XII:1335;103;250;167;61;19;216;191;812;491;634;361;542
XIII:625;44;137;71;20;12;100;85;104;479;260;289;202;278
XIV:594;35;160;76;23;11;80;53;65;384;268;320;114;214
XV:450;49;90;23;11;11;80;63;65;384;260;320;114;214
XVI:1804;133;425;193;60;35;289;187;115;569;445;508;366;476
XVII:1029;890;301;145;32;289;187;115;255;541;401;512;399;335
XVIII:1195;106;276;125;45;39;206;151;174;661;495;504;366;476
XIX:784;33;178;108;19;9;215;117;88;137;401;292;340;169;341
XX:920;78;212;120;35;28;173;163;179;568;380;397;315;500
XXI:582;75;199;33;15;15;103;91;103;155;341;401;512;498;335
XXII:747;63;182;67;80;17;129;108;11;475;427;247;289
XXIII:1348;32;91;35;20;61;63;31;69;298;177;153;127;170
XXIV:934;85;177;90;33;24;160;161;161;720;486;439;358;489
XXV:737;46;194;82;18;11;108;90;162;442;247;880;160;300
XXVI:932;61;281;99;42;30;251;111;111;197;713;481;507;310;454
XXVII:815;54;190;94;66;27;134;120;140;564;410;406;269;363
XXVIII:1139;108;291;49;176;147;176;562;459;564;314;512
XXIX:764;32;173;118;109;19;176;318;218;278;317
XXX:547;45;142;71;16;59;47;77;120;396;318;238;181;86
XXXI:348;33;91;35;20;61;63;31;69;298;177;153;127;170
XXXII:582;51;127;54;29;20;98;74;65;332;210;255;144;189
XXXIII:744;63;172;95;42;11;81;111;80;95;445;317;434;182;275
XXXIV:562;53;140;72;17;12;181;81;115;374;387;326;205;254
XXXV:430;45;133;72;17;12;181;81;115;374;387;326;205;254
XL:249;163;83;47;35;50;141;149;155;67;121
XLV:355;31;63;40;9;3;60;36;65;248;200;150;109;179
XLVI:504;209;99;33;12;14;81;87;619;389;404;227;401
XLVII:417;61;37;12;37;574;287;812;133;214
XLVIII:404;33;98;55;19;53;47;85;327;210;150;195
XLIX:290;22;46;30;13;64;32;39;198;135;81;23;66;120
L:282;28;54;28;12;15;17;38;86;41;113;155;118;71;93
LII:247;19;67;37;9;7;39;46;39;163;147;143;71;114
LIII:285;18;47;30;3;7;34;17;33;151;12;115;83;130
```

TABLE 8 (Continued)

```
LIV:234;42;108;3;13;3;53;48;57;12;1;112;120;67;84
LV:417;15;87;30;7;10;18;22;85;142;131;143;44;99
LVI:288;44;82;24;7;7;44;35;49;19;92;208;59;105
LVII:348;11;91;53;39;18;54;47;48;46;118;137;67;118
LIX:348;42;79;35;19;4;38;44;275;153;153;128;143
LXI:181;28;52;24;6;3;33;27;66;174;142;135;65;185
LXII:155;1;44;28;9;4;19;28;12;86;80;77;56;92
LXIII:157;19;42;44;9;3;12;24;24;49;43;66
LXIV:183;16;46;2;20;11;43;3;14;33;16;49;43;66
LXV:197;25;52;25;3;4;44;28;85;116;79;95;88;83
LXVI:189;18;50;11;42;33;17;38;128;87;199;63;89
LXVII:224;17;72;38;16;6;37;47;46;112;100;60;118
LXIX:196;22;48;52;31;4;24;18;48;133;133;55;96
LXX:145;18;38;11;11;3;28;16;20;102;102;91;55;93
LXXI:200;5;62;21;4;5;25;81;30;110;80;61;35;56
LXXII:231;18;50;27;8;8;37;28;20;119;74;113;40;64
LXXIII:179;7;49;18;8;5;20;28;24;107;58;58;45;67
LXXIV:190;7;49;18;8;5;20;28;24;107;58;58;45;67
LXXV:128;7;30;24;6;9;18;18;35;30;66;14;81
LXXVII:136;5;38;15;8;8;3;38;80;61;71;28;73
LXXX:187;9;36;20;8;9;27;39;82;7;11;16
LXXXI:186;5;34;9;24;5;8;61;41;49;25;35
LXXXIII:165;6;33;9;11;5;3;28;39;14;33;39;55;20;44
LXXXIV:103;8;20;11;7;11;3;32;11;18;30;41;89;25;35
XC:66;11;12;8;6;1;7;10;25;15;3;39;9;39;0
XCI:62;5;19;12;8;0;1;3;23;12;29;9;10;10
XCV:29;6;6;7;1;1;3;4;10;3;29;6;19
XCVI:42;19;3;5;3;2;10;42;16;85;13;31
XCVII:72;7;2;19;4;1;7;4;15;49;32;35;32;37
XCVIII:89;5;13;6;3;14;21;10;3;4;22;14;7;1;13
XCIX:19;3;5;7;2;0;1;5;3;6;19
CI:34;3;10;2;0;0;7;5;6;3;15
CII:18;4;7;4;0;0;7;3;5;23;14;5;6;13
CIII:13;4;7;5;0;2;10;14;5;6;13
CIV:34;3;5;8;4;8;16;0;3;20;12;5;6;13
CV:42;7;3;4;5;0;2;10;14;5;6;13
CVI:35;3;6;1;1;1;0;4;8;13;6;3
CVII:80;3;4;3;8;16;0;3;20;12;5;18
CVIII:11;3;3;6;1;1;3;0;4;8;13
CIX:28;2;3;6;1;0;0;8;1;3;18;12;10;2;6
CX:15;5;5;5;1;0;3;0;2;11;4;6;5
CXI:19;4;2;4;1;1;0;0;1;10;5;4;8
CXII:4;2;3;4;2;1;0;5;18
CXIII:21;8;1;0;1;2;1;0;5;6;10;3;4
CXIV:21;2;8;11;1;0;1;0;6;16;10;3;4
```

---

2. The total number of letters in each sura.

3. The number of verses in each sura.

The computer was programmed to perform the following functions:

1. Compute the percentage value for each one of the 14 letters in each of the 114 suras.

2. Compute the average frequency of occurrence of each one of the 14 letters in each verse of each sura.

3. Compute the absolute frequency of occurrence of the multi-lettered Qur'anic initials, namely Tā Hā (T.H.), Tā Sīn (T.S.), Yā Sīn (Y.S.), Hā Mīm (H.M.), Alif Lām Mīm (A.L.M.), Alif Lām Rā (A.L.R.), Tā Sīn Mīm (T.S.M.), Alif Lām Mīm Sād (A.L.M.S.), Alif Lām Mīm Rā (A.L.M.R.), Kāf Hā Yā 'Ayn Sād (K.H.Y.'A.S.), and Hā Mīm 'Ayn Sīn Qāf (H.M.'A.S.Q). Table 9 is a computer printout listing the absolute frequency of occurrence of the Qur'anic initials in each sura.

4. Compute the percentage of frequency value for each of the multi-lettered initials in each of the 114 suras. Table 10 is a computer printout of the percentage frequency values of all the Qur'anic initials throughout the Qur'an.

5. Compute the average occurrence per verse for each of the multi-lettered Qur'anic initials in each sura. These data are presented in Table 11 which is a computer printout of the average per verse values for each of 14 Qur'anic initials in each one of the Qur'an's 114 suras.

6. Arrange all the suras of Qur'an in ascending order with regard to the absolute frequency of occurrence of each Qur'anic initial. Thus, for each one of the Qur'anic initials, the sura which contains the lowest frequency of occurrence appears at the top of the list, and the sura containing the highest frequency appears at the bottom of the list. It was initially intended to have the computer list the suras in a 'descending' order, to have the sura with the highest value at the top, rather than the bottom of the list. However, due to a programming error, this particular command to the computer became reversed. This of course does not affect the results or the conclusions in the least.

7. Arrange the 114 suras of Qur'an in ascending order with regard to the percent frequency of occurrence for each of the 14 sets of Qur'anic initials.

8. Arrange all suras of the Qur'an in ascending order with regard to the average occurrence in each verse of each sura. The computer printouts of all the lists are shown within the text, and will be referred to as required.

In searching for a single value which will represent each one of the Qur'anic initials most accurately, the percentage value stands out as the best possible choice. Certainly, we cannot use the absolute frequency of occurrence of a given letter, or a set of letters, as a representative measure or as a basis for comparing the various suras. For example, we cannot compare a long sura such as Al-Baqara (286 verses, 25,717 alphabetic letters), with a short sura such as Al-Nās (3 verses, 99 alphabetic letters) on the basis of absolute frequency of occurrence. Similarly, the average per verse value cannot be used as a truly representative measure of the frequency of occurrence of the Qur'anic initials. The percentage value, therefore, appears to be the only value which can be used as a basis for comparison. However, we will have to take into consideration that the percentage value does not ALWAYS offer a good representation of the frequency value. It can be distorted by such factors as the lack of sufficient component units (statistically known as observations). To illustrate this point, let us take the extreme example of a chapter which consists of only the two letters A and B. The percent of each of these letters would be 50%, an extraordinarily high percentage value. If we compare the letter A in each chapter of the book, the hypothetical two-lettered chapter undoubtedly will have the highest percentage value (50%). But we cannot honestly conclude from this comparison that this two-lettered chapter "has the highest frequency of the letter A." In this study, we will come across instances where the percentage value is obviously distorted by the extreme shortness of certain suras. Whenever the percentage value is questionable (as a true representative of the frequency), we will have to consider carefully all three values of the Qur'anic initial under study (the absolute number, the percentage, and the average per verse value). These instances and the computations involved in them will be discussed in detail wherever the occasion arises in the text.

40

Additionally, since different letters make up different sets of Qur'anic initials, we do not expect all the initials to exhibit one and the same phenomenon (e.g. the frequency of occurrence). Thus all three values may be needed under certain circumstances as we study the Qur'anic initials.

41

بسم الله الرحمن الرحيم

VOLUME 1 ● Rabī' I, 1394
April, 1974 ● **NUMBER 1**

ISLAM

An International Journal Expressing the Islamic Point of View

EDITORS

Dr. Muhammad 'Abdul-Rauf (Washington, D.C., U.S.A.)

Dr. Mujāhid Al-Sawwāf (Mecca, Saudi Arabia)

Dr. Sherif El-Hakım (St. Louis, Missouri, U.S.A.)

Dr. Rashād Khalīfa (St. Louis, Missouri, U.S.A.)

S. Shāhid Mufassir (Palmer Park, Maryland, U.S.A.)

Dr. Hārūn Nasution (Jakarta, Indonesia)

Dr. Altan Necioğlu (Ankara, Turkey)

Dr. Ahmad H. Saqr (Lombard, Illinois U.S.A.)

Muhammad Sirājuddīn (Hyderabad, India)

Dr. Yūsuf Amīn Wālī (Cairo, Egypt)

PUBLISHED QUARTERLY *by*
Islamic Productions International, Inc.

COPYRIGHT 1974 ISLAMIC PRODUCTIONS INTERNATIONAL, INC
PRINTED IN THE UNITED STATES OF AMERICA

554

Thursday, July 30, 1981   Tucson Citizen

Books produced in Tucson

Computer divines Koran for the Muslim world

Two books of interest to Muslims have been published here recently: "The Computer Speaks: God's Message to the World" and "Quran: The Final Scripture (Authorized English Version)".

Islamic Productions, 739 E. Sixth St., at the Islamic Mosque of Tucson, has produced both books, written by Imam Rashad Khalifa.

Using a computer, Khalifa has been analyzing the Koran for 10 years.

He has discovered what he calls physical, scientific proof of meanings of the Koran's mysterious alphabets with "verse by verse details of the Quran's (his preferred spelling) miraculous numerical code."

The number 19 appears in the Koran in such complex ways that no person could have decoded it without the electronic aid, he says. It is a proof that God is the author of the book Muslims call the Latest Testament.

The prologue states that the entire book is written by a Hewlett-Packard HP-1000, E-series computer.

"The work is based on a coded message that arrived to this world, from the creator of the world. It is the decoding of this message that uncovered a plethora of evidence, so overwhelming that you will know you are dealing with proven truth," it reads.

Khalifa's 600-page English version of the holy book is the first translation by a Muslim whose mother tongue is Arabic, he said. Now an American citizen, he was born in Egypt.

He calls his an "authorized" version because it is the first and only translation "blessed" with his computer discoveries. Khalifa, who holds a doctorate in chemistry, says, "This code, which remained a divinely guarded secret for 1,400 years, presents to the world the first physical, touchable, and utterly indisputable proof that this Quran is a divine scripture."

555

Computer highlights figures in Qur'an

Arab News, 13 February 1984

By Hoda Sharabash
Riyadh Bureau

www.19.org

RIYADH — Everyone enjoys a good healthy argument or discussion. It provides the perfect arena in which we can exercise otherwise dormant recesses of our minds. Two of the most popular topics for a discussion are politics and religion. But whereas it is somewhat easy to take a logical stand on one's political tendencies and beliefs, religion is an area in which all our defenses and rebuttals must be based on pure faith.

In a day and age where we are skeptical of anything that can not be analyzed in black and white, even religion has been put to the test and for once came out with flying colors.

The Qur'an was written into a General Electric Time-sharing terminal connected to a central computer. Each Arabic letter was given an English equivalent. The computer was then programmed to count and report the frequency of occurrence of each letter in each chapter. It was found that a highly sophisticated mathematical code does exist which focuses around the number 19.

The Qur'an consists of 114 chapters in total and this number equals 19x6. The first Qur'anic verse, Bism Allah Alrahman Alraheem consists of 19 Arabic letters and each of these four words appear in the whole Qur'an a number of times which is also a multiple of 19. All of the 114 chapters in the Qur'an begin with this verse with the exception of Al-Tawbah. This would make the number of times that this verse appears in the Qur'an 113 which is not a multiple of 19. But strangely enough the missing verse is found in chapter, or Sura, Al-Naml. By using Al-Tawbah as a starting point, this sura with the two verses falls as the 19th chapter. The number of words between the two repeated verses is 342 (19x18).

The first sura ever revealed, Al-'Alaq is chapter number 19 from the end of the Qur'an and consists of 19 verses. The whole sura contains 285 letters (19x15). This sura was revealed in stages. The first five verses to be revealed by the angel Gabriel is made up of exactly 19 words. These 19 words are made up of 76 letters (19x4). When the angel Gabriel came down for the second, third, fourth, and fifth time, the revelations made followed the same mathematical pattern.

The Qur'an contains many numbers such as "We summoned Moses for 40 nights." "We created the seven skies", etc. It was found that there are 285 numerals (19x15) mentioned throughout the Qur'an. The sum total of all these numbers is 174,591 (19x9,189). Taking all the numbers mentioned only once and adding them with no repetition gives us a sum of 162,146 (19x8,543).

A feature unique to the Qur'an is that 29 of its chapters are prefixed by letters or Qur'anic initials which have no apparent meaning. The sura entitled Qaf (Q) contains 57 Q letters (19x3). The only other sura initialed Q also contains 57 Q letters. An example of how this occurrence cannot be deemed coincidence is seen in verse 13 of sura Qaf. This verse says, "Ad, Pharaoh, and the brethren of Lot." The word brethren is translated Qawm throughout the Qur'an with the exception of this verse where the synonym Ikhwan is used. To have used the word Qawm would have meant using an additional letter Q and would have disrupted the coding.

The only Noon (N) initialed sura, Al-Qalam, contains 133 letter Ns (19x7) and the three Sad (S) initialed suras contain a total of 152 letters S (19x8). In the 13 suras which are initialed Lam (L) there are 11,780 letter Ls (19x620), and in the 17 suras which are initialed Meem (M) there exists 8,683 letter Ms (19x457).

The same code holds true for the suras which are initialed with combinations of these Qur'anic letters, as in sura Ya Seen where the total of Yas and Seens is 285 (19x15).

There are many more examples of how this system holds true for all these letters and a great deal of the principal verses. Further proof that this is no coincidence is found in sura Muddath-Thir, verse 25, where God states that any person who claims that the Qur'an is human-made will be disproved. He will show us this by means of the number 19 (verse 30.)

While fabricating a book with the same mathematical characteristics as the Qur'an is not a physical impossibility in our age of computers, it was most certainly impossible in the dark ages of 610 A.D. The Qur'an was revealed through an illiterate man and judging from the handwriting of the few scribes who wrote the Qur'an as it was revealed (a photocopy of the original is kept in the Library of Congress), these men were barely literate — certainly not mathematically sophisticated. Coincidence is ruled out by the laws of statistics.

Thus the only explanation to this phenomena we have left, according to Dr. Rashad Khalifa, imam of the Tuscon Mosque, is that the Qur'an is beyond doubt divinely inspired. Dr. Khalifa in his book *The Computer Speaks: God's Message to the World* also concludes that should a human hand have had any part in this "miracle", this genius would have long since claimed credit for a book which manages to maintain this code without ruining the lyrical, poetical, and linguistic beauty that the Qur'an is famous for.

556

Rujukan Kami IIU.R/1.1/
Our Reference

Tarikh 9th March 1984
Date

Dr. Rashad Khalifa,
737 E. 6th Street,
Tucson,
Arizona 85719,
United States of America.

السلام عليكم ورحمة الله وبركاته

My dear Dr. Rashad,

In recent months, I have been hearing a great deal about you,
your new publications and also about an attitude you are said
to uphold about the position and the authority of Al-Hadith.
Of course I have been defending you since I have known you
very closely and I did not think that you would go to the extend
of rejecting Al-Hadith authority altogether.

For some time, I have been thinking of writing to you just to assure
myself about this rumour and also to know about how you and your
family are.

We shall be interested to secure copies of your publications. If
you could kindly let me know the best way of getting them, we shall
be happy to order one set for our library.

With best wishes to you and members of your distinguished family.

Sincerely yours,

M.A. Rauf

MUHAMMAD ABDUL-RAUF
Rector

Khalifa warned before killing

By CHARLOTTE LOWE
and DAVID L. TEIBEL

NINETEEN: God's Signature in Nature and Scripture. www.19.org

Police uncovered an apparent murder conspiracy three days before the Tucson stabbing death of internationally known Moslem leader Rashad Khalifa, his successor said yesterday.

Police said Khalifa, 54, was stabbed in the chest several hours before dawn yesterday.

The weapon used was not found, but police said they did find a handgun under Khalifa's body.

The case may have international implications. The FBI and a police special investigations unit that monitors some Mideast affairs here have been called into the investigation.

Abdullah Arik was Khalifa's assistant and now replaces him as leader of a controversial moderate Moslem sect based at the Masjid (Mosque) of Tucson, 739 E. Sixth St., near the University of Arizona.

Arik said the most recent of many death threats against Khalifa was uncovered three days ago in Salt Lake City.

Warned to be careful

"They found someone with a picture of the mosque and evidence of some intention to do harm, to blow the mosque up. I believe they arrested the person and they warned Dr. Khalifa to be careful," Arik said.

The Islamic leader's controversial religious beliefs and "the way he rewrote the Koran" made him "a Salman Rushdie" to many other more conservative sects, Detective Sgt. Charles Arnold said yesterday.

Rushdie wrote the controversial book "The Satanic Verses" and a year ago, Iranian leader Ayatollah Ruhollah Khomeini urged his followers to hunt down Rushdie and kill him. Rushdie has remained in hiding since then.

Not afraid of being killed

Last year, Khalifa said he was not afraid of being killed. "God promises to guide and protect his messengers. No one kills. The time comes and God takes."

Arik said that as new leader of the group, his own safety does not concern him. "I'm more worried about pulling these people out of this situation and delivering the message he (Kha

KHALIFA continued 2A

MELANIE ROOK/Tucson Citizen

Grieving followers of Rashad Khalifa gathered outside his mosque yesterday.

1989 Tucson Citizen photo

Khalifa praying in the mosque where he died

> 'God promises to guide and protect his messengers. No one kills. The time comes and God takes.'
> — Rashad Khalifa
> In interview a year before his slaying

TUCSON CITIZEN

Computer research led to controversy

**By JOSEPH GARCIA
and CHARLOTTE LOWE**
Citizen Staff Writers

Traffic slowed along North Euclid Avenue at the Islamic Mosque of Tucson yesterday as curious motorists tried to catch a glimpse past the yellow plastic tape used by police to cordon off the area.

The mosque, at 739 E. Sixth Ave., with its "Happiness Is Submission To God" message painted on the side of the building, was the site of a homicide.

Khalifa

Other than two dozen pairs of shoes left at the complex's doorstep, there was not much to see yesterday that was out of the ordinary.

While adults grieved inside, children played outside. Tears streamed from a youngster's eyes only after falling off the swing set. Two police officers standing nearby rushed to the child, handing him over to the parents, who then quickly went back inside, avoiding reporters.

Rashad Khalifa was dead.

Khalifa's followers, known as the "True Moslems," considered him the Messenger of God — the man who used a computer to decipher ancient codes of the Koran, the Moslem holy book.

The Arizona license plate of a car parked behind the mosque yesterday read, "ON IT 19," in reference to the numeral Khalifa said he used as the common denominator throughout his two decades of internationally known research.

The number 19 appeared too many times in the Koran to be a coincidence, he said. Through use of technology, he soon found patterns.

Khalifa, 54, said that without his Hewlett-Packard HP-1000,

COMPUTER, continued/6C

NINETEEN: God's Signature in Nature and Scripture. www.19.org

Tucson Citizen, Feb 1, 1990

Continued from 1C

Computer research led to controversy

E-series computer, he — as countless others before him — would have lacked the essential tools in proving the Koran's authenticity.

"The code shows that the Koran was written by God, not man," he said in a Tucson Citizen interview last year. "It is beyond human ability. It is His way of saying, 'I created this.' It is like a combination to a safe. It is a way to make contact with God."

He called himself "the Messenger of the Covenant," noting that his root name appears 19 times in the Koran and also is mentioned in Malachi, the last book of the Old Testament of the Bible.

The book Khalifa wrote, "The Computer Speaks: God's Message to the World," was printed by his own publishing company, Islamic Productions.

He also wrote "Quran: The Final Scripture (Authorized English Version)," said to be the first such translation of the Koran — or Quran, as he preferred — by a Muslim whose mother tongue is Arabic.

He said his 600-page English version is the only "authorized" one because it is "blessed" with his computer discoveries that broke the ancient code.

"This code," he said, "which re-mained a divinely guarded secret for 1,400 years, presents to the world the first physical, touchable and utterly indisputable proof that this Quran is a divine scripture."

The 1968 discovery earned him much notoriety in newspapers and magazines throughout the Middle East. His views also appeared in the September 1980 edition of the magazine Scientific American.

Khalifa's views were controversial. In 1978, when he was vice president of the Universty of Arizona's Islamic Center, he was physically removed from the congregation after voicing his opposition to stoning as punishment for adultery. He said stoning was tradition and not scripture-based.

That same year, he founded his own mosque in a converted house, with mostly University of Arizona students as his followers. The mosque later was remodeled and expanded to include five two-bedroom apartments, with rent helping the mosque become financially independent.

Throughout the years, Khalifa continued to espouse the idea that the majority of Moslems in the world were following customs and traditions — not the actual teachings of the Koran.

"The code proved that many Moslems were following satanic guidance," Khalifa said in an interview last year. "They were distorting the religion by following prophets that were men instead of God."

Khalifa was a naturalized American citizen who came to the United States from Egypt in 1959. He was the son of a major Sufi leader who gave religious instruction and later became his father's deputy.

Former Minnesota Vikings receiver and current NBC sports broadcaster Ahmad Rashad, known formerly as Bobby Joe Moore before he adopted Khalifa's first name, was one of his father's students.

Khalifa believed that women are equal to men. His sect did not adhere to the Moslem traditional head coverings and cloaks for women, instead opting for what he said the Koran called for — modesty, covering only of the female's chest and arms in a lengthy dress.

Khalifa, who earned a doctorate in chemistry from the University of California, also believed that violence should be avoided at all costs, other than for self-defense.

The Arizona Daily Star

© 1990 The Arizona Daily Star

Vol. 149   No. 32 *   Final Edition, Tucson, Thursday, February 1, 1990

Mosque leader is found slain

Tucsonan was focus of religious uproar

By Carmen Duarte
The Arizona Daily Star

An internationally renowned and controversial Islamic leader was killed early yesterday morning in a Tucson mosque.

Imam Rashad Khalifa, 54, the founder and spiritual leader of the Mosjid, or Mosque, of Tucson, 739 E. Sixth St., was found "in a kitchen area" by the mosque's secretary, authorities said.

Officials said Khalifa had received death threats because of his interpretation of the Koran, the sacred book of Moslems.

Khalifa, according to friends and associates, caused anger and hatred in the Islamic community because of his interpretation of the scriptures.

And a police homicide sergeant said there is a possibility his death may be connected to political or religious problems.

FBI involvement

The FBI was called in to help the Tucson Police Department because of the possibility Khalifa was slain because of political or religious beliefs.

Police responded to the mosque at 5:45 a.m. after a report of a shooting, authorities said.

Police would not confirm if Khalifa, who once was a science adviser to Libyan leader Col. Moammar Gadhafi, was shot or say what type of wounds Khalifa suffered.

Authorities said Khalifa died a violent death.

The body was taken to the Pima County Medical Examiner's Office, where an autopsy was scheduled for today.

'Number of avenues'

There is a possibility that motives for the slaying may include political and religious problems, said homicide Sgt. Charles Armijo of the Tucson Police Department.

"There are a number of avenues we're pursuing," Armijo said. "We are not limiting ourselves to any one specific lead or area at this point."

FBI Special Agent Larry Bagley, supervisor of the Tucson office, said agents will coordinate out-of-state leads and that the agency has offered police its laboratory services.

"Khalifa is a moderate Moslem who's made interpretations of the Koran that has angered many Mideastern Moslems," said a law enforcement official who asked not to be identified.

"He's been a high-profile person who has received death threats in the past," the official said.

Khalifa, an imam, or spiritual leader of the mosque, made a computer analysis of the Koran and wrote books about his findings.

See SLAYING, Page 4A

Slaying

Continued from Page One

friends and associates said.

Edip Yuksel, who was an assistant to Khalifa, said Khalifa arrived at the mosque at about 2 or 3 a.m. every day to work on his religious writings and translations of the Koran.

He and Khalifa founded the mosque, was well-known among Moslems because of a computer analysis of the Koran that showed a mathematical formula that Khalifa said proved that the Koran is divine.

Khalifa wrote books about his findings, and also published a translation of the Koran in which he omitted two "satanic verses," said a friend of Khalifa's who asked not to be identified.

Khalifa accused other Moslems of following a satanic Koran, an action that caused anger and hatred of him, said the friend.

Khalifa also claimed to be a messenger of God, and mainstream Moslems believe that Mohammad was the last messenger, the friend said.

Khalifa continually preached that Moslems should not idolize Mohammad, Jesus Christ or saints, rather let people only worship God, said Yuksel.

Yuksel said Khalifa was "controversial from Turkey to Morocco and from Saudi Arabia to Iran."

Yuksel said about 80 percent were "that Khalifa's slaying was the work of a religious fanatic.

"I can't believe that it would be so soon," Yuksel said.

"He received a death threat a few days ago," Yuksel said of Khalifa. He did not release further information on the threat, but said police knew about it. Police would not talk about the threat.

The controversial Imam Rashad Khalifa died violently

"We're all sorry about his death," Yuksel said. "We believe in the resurrection. We believe he went to heaven."

A few followers gathered yesterday afternoon and mourned at the mosque, which had a message on one of its walls that read "Happy 1990," Yuksel said.

Khalifa's death pains the sectarian spirit of submission to God.

"He did not recognize sectarian differences. He felt that all Moslems are Moslems," said Betteridge.

Anne Betteridge, a University of Arizona Middle Eastern studies professor, said Khalifa wasn't a mainstream Moslem.

Yuksel said there were about 300 followers who worshiped at the mosque.

1989 Star photo

then 20 years. He moved to Tucson from Tunis, Egypt, to attend the University of Arizona. He received a doctorate in biochemistry from the University of California, where he taught for two years before spending six years in industrial research.

Khalifa was married. The survivors include a son and daughter.

Officer John Leavitt stands in front of the Tucson police barricade outside the mosque

David Sanders, The Arizona Daily Star

In 1976, he was a science adviser to Gadhafi, and later, was imprisoned by the Libyan leader, Yuksel said.

Yuksel said some of Khalifa's friends said the reason why Rashad was a pupil of Khalifa's until Rashad had freed him from prison. Rashad was imprisoned from 1978 to 1981 and returned to Tucson as a technical expert for the United Nations Industrial Development Organization, which promotes industrialization of developing countries.

Rashad has a weekly, nationally syndicated 30-minute television program called "Is Sport," described by its NFL spokesman yesterday as a show with a magazine format that focuses on sports entertainment. Khalifa was formerly a player with the NFL.

Khalifa, who formerly was known as Bobby Moore, played for the San Francisco 49ers, the Buffalo Bills and the St. Louis Cardinals, the Buffalo Bills and for the Minnesota Vikings. He ended his career as a wide receiver in 1982.

His son, Sammy, was an infielder in the Pittsburgh Pirates organization from 1982 until November, when the Pirates dropped him from their 40-man roster.

560

The Arizona Daily Star

©1990 The Arizona Daily Star

Final Edition, Tucson, Friday, February 2, 1990

35¢

Khalifa investigators considering religious assassination theory

By Carmen Duarte
The Arizona Daily Star

A homicide detective said yesterday that police are "leaning toward the possibility" that the slaying of Islamic leader Rashad Khalifa was a religious assassination.

Khalifa, founder and spiritual leader of the Masjid, or Mosque, of Tucson was stabbed numerous times, and a .22-caliber gun was found under his body Wednesday, officials said.

"We're leaning toward the possibility that it may have been a religious assassination," said homicide Sgt. Charles Armijo.

He refused to elaborate.

But Khalifa, 54, had received death threats because of his interpretation of the Koran — the sacred book of Moslems.

He was found lying "in a kitchen area" of the mosque by the mosque's secretary at about 5:45 a.m. Wednesday.

An autopsy by the Pima County Medical Examiner's Office began yesterday at 8:30 a.m. and had not been completed.

Armijo refused to comment on the stab wounds.

He said investigators believe the gun found belonged to Khalifa. Armijo would not say if the gun had been fired.

On Wednesday, investigators re-

moved several of Khalifa's computers, files and documents from the mosque.

Yesterday afternoon, followers hugged each other and expressed their sorrow near where Khalifa's body was found in the mosque, 739 E. Sixth St.

Followers gathered to pray.

Before the prayers began, Abdullah Arik, an assistant to Khalifa, said Khalifa began receiving threats more than 20 years ago when he began preaching that people must worship God and not Mohammed, Jesus Christ, or saints.

Khalifa accused other Moslems of

See KHALIFA, Page 2A

Khalifa

Continued from Page One

following a satanic Koran, an accusation that directed anger and hatred at him, said his friend.

Khalifa also claimed to be a messenger of God, and mainstream Moslems believe that Mohammed was the last messenger, the friend said.

According to friends and associates, Khalifa, who received a doctorate in biochemistry from the University of California, gained international attention after he made a computer analysis of the Koran and wrote books about his findings.

He used a computer to find a numerical code in the Koran based on the number 19 to show that the Koran is a divine scripture and God's message to the world, said Edil Yuksel, an associate of Khalifa's.

Khalifa's research began more than 20 years ago.

Khalifa's message will continue to be spread around the world according to God's will, read a prepared statement from worshipers at the mosque.

Khalifa, who moved to Tucson from Tanta, Egypt, more than 20 years ago, was a science adviser to Libyan leader Col. Moammar Gadhafi, according to a friend.

Arik said the FBI contacted the Tucson Police Department about three days before the killing about a murder plot.

Arik said the plot to kill Khalifa

originated in Salt Lake City and that he believed someone was arrested. He said police warned Khalifa about the plot.

Armijo denied that police told Khalifa about a plot.

Yesterday, FBI Special Agent James Screen of Salt Lake City and officers of other law enforcement agencies there denied knowing about a plot to kill Khalifa.

FBI Special Agent Larry Bagley, supervisor of the Tucson office, also denied knowing about the plot.

"We have not contacted the Police Department or Khalifa about any recent threats," Bagley said.

A law enforcement official, who did not want to be identified, said that several years ago, a plot to kill Khalifa was discovered. But the plot did not originate in Salt Lake City, the official added.

The official said that "some other agencies" knew about the plot, and that the Tucson Police Department was given the information.

"It may or may not be related to what happened now," the official said. "We will be looking into it."

Bagley said FBI agents will conduct out-of-state interviews on the case for the Tucson Police Department. He would not comment further.

Tucson police Lt. Anthony Daykin, community services division commander, said police are "working with the FBI in gathering intelligence on reports of (death) threats."

He said because of the "possible international implications the investigation will take some time."

Mathematical study used to show 'miracle of the Kor:

"In the name of God, most gracious, most merciful."

— The Holy Koran, Sura 1, Verse 1

By Dan Huff
The Arizona Daily Star

Rashad Khalifa preached what he called the "miracle of the Koran," which, he maintained, is evident in the first verse of the scripture holy to Moslems.

Khalifa applied the rigors of computer analysis to the Koran to discover his "miracle."

He maintained that the first verse contains exactly 19 letters in Arabic, the language in which the Koran was written 1,400 years ago and is still spoken today.

Khalifa said his computer analysis found complex patterns based on the number 19 throughout the Koran. The complexity is of

such a magnitude that only God could have put it there, he believed.

Critics in the Middle East disputed Khalifa's assertion that the first verse contains 19 Arabic letters. Others say that Khalifa, for all his years of research — he began the project in 1976 — only managed to state numerically the natural rhythm inherent in Arabic.

In an appendix to his translation of the Koran, Khalifa seemed to anticipate this criticism. "The Arabic code used in the Koran . . . was of such complex and rhythmic pattern that no human being was or is capable of composing it," he wrote.

"This code, which remained a divinely guarded secret for 1,400 years," he wrote, "presents the world the first physical, touchable, and utterly indisputable proof

that this Koran is a divine scripture."

In a 1983 interview with The Arizona Daily Star, Khalifa explained that before the invention of Arabic numerals — the numbers we use today — people in the Middle East used the Arabic alphabet to express numbers.

Using this system, Khalifa assigned numerical values of 1 to 10 to the first 10 letters in the Arabic alphabet. He then added the numbers represented in the Arabic word for "one," as in one God.

The four characters, with their values of 6, 1, 8 and 4, equal 19, which symbolizes the message of the Koran, Khalifa said in 1983.

"The theme of the Koran is that we shall worship one God, the one God alone, and never idolize anyone or anything else. The whole message of Koran centers around the

one God, and it was discovered that 19 equals one."

Among other items Khalifa cited to support his belief:
● Every word in Sura 1, Verse 1, is mentioned throughout the Koran a number of times that is consistently a multiple of 19.

"Of the millions of books in existence," Khalifa asked, "how many will exhibit this elaborate phenomenon: that the opening statement consists of an X number of letters, and every word in the statement is mentioned throughout the book a multiple of X?"
● The Koran consists of 114 suras (19 times 6).
● The first sura ever revealed, Sura 96, is placed in the Koran in position No. 19 from the end.
● The first Koranic revelation, namely

the first five verses of Sura 9(
words.
● The 19 words of the first
lation contain 76 letters (19 ti
● The last Koranic revela
consists of 19 words.
● In suras 42 and 50, which
Q, there are 57 Q's (19 times 3

● Sura 68 is initialed with
and there are 133 N's (19 tim

Before his murder Jan. 31,
up with dozens of such obser

He said he believed God
based code in the Koran to
veal His presence, but to the
would add unauthorized v
claimed to have found two
both, he said, erroneously a
hammed, Islam's prophet, ar
alone.

Lone assassin

Killing wasn't the work of any group, Islamic scholar s

By Dan Huff
The Arizona Daily Star

It is doubtful that any organized Islamic faction such as the shadowy Moslem Brotherhood was responsible for Rashad Khalifa's murder, a leading Islamic scholar says.

Secretive, and organized by "cells" so its ultimate leaders are protected, it was the Moslem Brotherhood that engineered the 1981 assassination of Egyptian President Anwar Sadat for his peacemaking overtures to Israel, according to some authorities.

The Brotherhood was formed in Egypt in the 1930s and has an estimated 1,000 members in the United States.

But Mohammad T. Mehdi, spokesman for the National Council on Islamic Affairs, based in New York City, says he believes Khalifa's murder was more than likely the act of an individual.

"The stupid person who did this will give him (Khalifa) more credit," Mehdi says. "Over time he could become a martyr, even if he was not able to obtain any meaningful standing within the Is-

> "The stupid person who did this will give him (Khalifa) more credit. Over time he could become a martyr, even if he was not able to obtain any meaningful standing within the Islamic world during his lifetime."
>
> **Mohammad T. Mehdi**
> National Council of Islamic Affairs

lamic world during his lifetime."

Mehdi has written extensively about Sirhan Sirhan, the Palestinian-born assassin of Robert Kennedy. He recently compiled a book attacking the Ayatollah Ruhollah Khomeini's call for the death of "Satanic Verses" author Salman Rushdie.

Mehdi says Moslems should have ignored Rushdie, Khalifa and other critics of Islam. Death sentences and assassinations give undue publicity to their victims' views, says Mehdi, who describes himself as a moderate Mos-

lem troubled by the intolerance a
that has gripped the Middle East.

Although Khalifa's murder ma
horrible — and rendered even mo
because it occurred on American so
dom of speech and religion are gua
under the First Amendment to the l
tion — Mehdi pleads for understandi
of Turtunous in particular and Chr
cans in general.

"Intolerance and violence hav
part in Christianity, too," Mehdi poi

He notes that such deplorabl
not begin to abate in the West u
Europe entered its modern era sor
since, 400 years ago. Mehdi mark
Arab modernism with World War I.

"American Moslems are the m
Moslems in the world, because here
freedom to think, to re-evaluate o
and to judge their validity," Mehdi
when we put our act together, Mos
lead Moslems in the old country i
century."

Khalifa

Continued from Page One

political and religious leaders.

While Khalifa was a tenaciously devout Moslem, according to his followers, he did not accept Islamic traditions and doctrines common to his Egyptian homeland and throughout the Middle East.

Because these all but-inviolate traditions are handed down from father to son in the Islamic world, Khalifa apparently felt it necessary at some point in his spiritual development to renounce his father, according to one follower. "He referred to his father as his ex-father."

Computer study of Koran

Khalifa's initial notoriety was due to the fact that between 1968 and 1981, using a computer to study the original Arabic Koran, he developed what he maintained was cold, clear mathematical proof that the scriptures were written by God.

According to critics and supporters, the discovery at first was well accepted throughout the Moslem world, where it was taught briefly in some religious universities. It even merited a passing mention in that bastion of logical Western thinking, Scientific American. However, with the publication of his second major work, "Koran, Hadith, and Islam," in 1982, Khalifa became more controversial among Moslem faithful.

Khalifa strongly rejected "hadith," generally defined as that body of Moslem writings that detail the earthly practices of the Prophet Mohammed. He wrote and published a book slamming hadith.

The book was "slanderous," according to Ihsan Bagby, acting secretary general of the Islamic Society of North America, which claims about 50,000 members in the United States and Canada.

"Slanderous beliefs"

"Khalifa denigrated the prophet, and he denigrated the beliefs of Moslems in general," Bagby said, adding such an act alone "would have been enough to endanger his life from somebody fanatical enough to respond to his slanderous beliefs."

The final straw, according to Bagby, came about 1½ years ago, when Khalifa claimed in his newsletter to be the messenger of God mentioned in the Koran.

"This enraged many people," Bagby said. "None of us have any sympathy for what he was doing. Basically he even claimed to have ascended into heaven and to have walked in heaven. Obviously somebody took it in his own hands to stop him."

Khalifa's followers say the Koran defines a messenger as one who comes after a great prophet, such as Moses, Jesus or Mohammed. A prophet gives us God's word containing God's word, they say, while a messenger purifies that message, blowing away the impurities put there over the centuries by impure human beings.

Translated Koran

Khalifa, they add, never made up things, but based all that he said on the Koran alone. He was the first native speaker of Arabic — the language in which the Koran was written — to translate the book into English, his followers add. They

While his believers say Khalifa preached peace, love and understanding, his critics cite a 1979 rape charge and subsequent fraud conviction to cast doubt on his practices.

praise the work for its clarity and simplicity. Critics say they haven't read it.

Who was Rashad Khalifa?

"He was very gentle, most kind, super-good to children, super-nice to his wife," Ersien said. "He was kind to everybody, kind to strangers. Words cannot describe his kindness. He had no ego."

The record shows Khalifa was born in a small village in Egypt.

As he was later to reject hadith, he reportedly rejected the teaching of his father, whom followers have heard him describe as a Sufi master. Sufism, the mystical form of Islam, teaches that ultimately there is no reality but God.

After coming to the United States in 1959, Khalifa received a doctorate in biochemistry from the University of California at Riverside in

"Rashad knew that he
delivered the message — h
purified the message of Go
And he knew that once a m
delivered, it is time for the
messenger to move on."

Khalif

Arizona Commission on Agriculture
1976.

After he resigned in 1986, Khal
state, claiming he had been denied
because of his Moslem beliefs and
gin.

but U.S. District Court Judge (
found no evidence of discriminati
ruled that Khalifa failed to get the
he could not get along with his super

Khalifa accused one of his boss
ciation of "devious attempts" to destro
ity, of "devilish schemes" and of a "
court records show.

Khalifa's "dark side"

More recently, Khalifa was invo
pute that some say shows he had a da
Linda Abih, a 27-year-old man
thought Khalifa was a kind and con
when she and her husband began fr
his apartments next to the mosque in

But she and her 3-year-old son c
Khalifa's sect and went into hiding.

Abih won a court order of protect
husband, but said in a recent interv
fears "not only a violent husband, b
religious cult. That's what he (Khali
ning."

His followers deny the accusation
gion is one of peace and love, they mo

Abih said Khalifa endorsed the tr
obedient wives — something Khalifa
deny.

Karima Omarr, an American-bor
ician who later left the religion becau
it oppressive to women, said Khalifa
treat women as equals.

"He was a very sweet man," she s
eccentric, but sweet."

Khalifa's followers — there are an estimated 50 in Tucson, perhaps several thousand worldwide — say their leader knew why, and how, and perhaps even when, he would die. It was ordained, they say, by Allah.

1989 Star photo

The Arizona Daily Star

Vol. 151   No. 286 *

©1992 The Arizona Daily Star

Final Edition, Tucson, Monday, October 12, 1992

35¢ U.S./50¢ in Mexico   48 Pages *

Tucson mosque slaying may be linked to sect

By Carmen Duarte
and Kristen Cook
The Arizona Daily Star

Colorado authorities are investigating a possible link between an Islamic fundamentalist sect and the slaying of an internationally renowned Islamic leader here more than two years ago.

Officers raided a 101-acre compound owned by the sect in Colorado last week, seizing attack weapons.-In other raids, four men were arrested.

The compound had been used for military training, an investigator said.

Law enforcement authorities say they may have evidence that could implicate members of the FUQRA sect in the Jan. 31, 1990, stabbing death of the controversial

leader Rashad Khalifa, the Rocky Mountain News reported yesterday.

Khalifa, 54, was the founder and spiritual leader of the Masjid, or Mosque, of Tucson, 739 E. Sixth St.

The mosque's secretary found Khalifa's body shortly before 6 a.m. in the kitchen area of the building, located across the street from Tucson High School.

"We have been aware of the possibility of the FUQRA involvement in the homicide since shortly after the incident," said homicide Sgt. Charles Armijo of the Tucson Police Department.

"We are currently unaware of what's happened in Colorado, although we have been working with the FBI since the homicide occurred," he said.

"We will be in contact with the FBI and Colorado authorities to see what they have retrieved and what information they have implicating FUQRA in the homicide," he added.

"We are not aware of any FUQRA activity in this state apart from one incident with Khalifa," he said.

Armijo confirmed that not much is known about the group, whose members law enforcement authorities have tied to terrorist activities.

Joe Reyes, head of the FBI's Tucson office, said yesterday that he is unable to comment on the Colorado investigation or give any details of the case.

Sheriff George Chavez of Chaffee County, Colo., said the group apparently is made up

of Black Muslims who were all born in the United States.

Chavez added that other law enforcement officials said some of FUQRA's activities may be bankrolled by people in Pakistan and Afghanistan.

The organization was said to be responsible for a 1983 bombing of a Portland, Ore., hotel owned by followers of Indian guru Bhagwan Shree Rajneesh. A man with ties to FUQRA was convicted in the case, according to a Rocky Mountain News article.

The raid at the compound last Thursday occurred after a yearlong investigation into the bilking of $335,000 from the state workers' compensation fund, Chavez said, noting that the FBI had initially conducted Colorado officials about a possible problem

with FUQRA.

He said five men were indicted on federal racketeering charges related to the bilking. They are Chris Childs, James D. Williams, Vicente Rafael Pierre, James L. Upshur and Edward Ivan McGhee, he said.

Four are in custody, and authorities are searching for the fifth, Chavez said.

They were arrested during raids at homes in Colorado Springs and a home in Lycoming County, Pa., Chavez said.

No ages or hometowns of the men were available yesterday.

About 60 federal, state and local law enforcement authorities took part in the raid at the compound, which is near Trout Creek Pass, a rugged and remote area in the Pike

See KHALIFA, Page 5A

TUCSON WEEKLY

Volume 10, Number 46 • January 19-January 25, 1994 • FREE

SMITH: Developers Are The Bad Guys

NINETEEN: God's Signature in Nature and Scripture. www.19.org

The No. 19 Murder

HAPPINESS IS SUBMISSION TO GOD

Once he proclaimed himself a messenger of Allah, Muslim Rashad Khalifa's number was up.

BY TIM VANDERPOOL

THE SKINNY: Bad Blood Drenches Our Legislators

DANEHY: Golf Is Nature's Way Of Making It Rain

NEWS EXTRA: Tucson's Own Nuclear Testing Nightmare

Small-Time Hack Or Annointed Messenger Of Allah? Either Way, Rashad Khalifa Had To Die. But Who Killed Him?

MUSLIM

MURDER

MYSTERY

 ATWA IN ARABIC means a published decision regarding religious law. It can also mean punishment—as in death—for flouting that law.

Fatwa is not a pretty word. Just ask Salman Rushdie.

Or Rashad Khalifa.

On January 31, 1990, the balding, cherubic, 54-year-old imam, or teacher, was found lying in a pool of blood, stabbed several times and left to die on the kitchen floor of his Tucson mosque. His gun was tucked, unfired, beneath his body.

The case languished until October, 1992 when a battalion of Colorado state police and federal agents swept down upon a 101-acre Black Muslim stronghold southwest of Denver. Members of the fundamentalist Fuqra sect were suspected of running a worker's compensation scam. But cops also found maps and photos of Khalifa's mosque. Included were notes detailing an assassination plot.

In February, 1993 seven Fuqra members were charged with conspiring to kill the imam. None has been charged with the actual homicide.

Khalifa's death was no great surprise. To many Muslims, he was a small-time hack with a big-time computer, hungry mostly for power and self-glorification. Others thought him a brilliant theological guerilla who, armed with modern technology, had set out to overthrow corrupt Islamic traditions.

Using a beefy Hewlett-Packard machine, Khalifa mapped what he claimed to be numerical patterns in the Muslim bible, or *Qur'an*. Based on the prime number 19,

he said their complexity pointed directly to divine creation. They also revealed his own role as a "Messenger of God." (The Christian equivalent would land someone just a few notches beneath Jesus).

His followers called themselves "Submitters," believing that salvation lay in complete submission to God, and only God. That meant sanctifying the Prophet Mohammed, as most Muslims do, is a big mistake. Khalifa then referred to these misguided souls as "sinners and idol worshipers."

That's when all hell broke loose. Muslims tend to take their religion seriously. Fundamentalists in particular viewed this attack on Hadith and Sunna—Mohammedan worship traditions—as a direct hit at Islam. Soon they blasted middle-eastern propaganda mills into high-gear, commencing a nasty media campaign that peaked in 1985, when a top Turkish

Rashid Khalifa was slain in his Tucson mosque in 1990.

rag accused Khalifa of collaborating with fellow pariah Salman Rushdie.

Muslim clerics were no less blunt, calling Khalifa, among other things, a tainted infidel and CIA stoolie. His answering machine was regularly glutted with snarling death threats.

By 1989, the fight was purely vicious. Khalifa countered vitriolic critics through his monthly newsletter, *Submitters Perspective*, hurling slurs back as quick as they came in.

Finally, Ibnul Baz, a powerful Saudi Arabian cleric, halted the commotion with a fatwa. Now the verdict was in: Rashad Khalifa had become a dead man.

"God promises to guide and protect his messengers," he bravely told the *Tucson Citizen* in 1989. "No one kills. The time comes and God takes."

But Khalifa refused to rush the process along. He bought a pistol and began working long hours, furiously finishing a revision of his 1981 *Qur'an: The Final Scripture.*

He almost made it.

For their part, allegedly plotting to ice the imam certainly wasn't Fuqra's first infraction. The paramilitary-style sect had long been under the federal gun, linked to numerous terrorist attacks, including the 1984 bombing of a Hare Krishna temple in Denver.

Neither was it the first concrete threat against Khalifa. Months before his death, Colorado Springs police had stumbled across a similar scheme while on a burglary investigation. Their findings went to the FBI, who in turn warned the imam.

This didn't herald a new line of work for the FBI, either. Ever since Khomeini's dour countenance started adorning Tehran billboards, they've been chasing imported muslim conspirators, real or perceived. Now they were definitely on to the real thing.

Add to that Tucson's reputation as a hotbed of fundamentalist activity, and you have an irresistible mix. Just how Khalifa added to the stew, at least in FBI eyes, remains a mystery. But if they were curious about the messenger and his little flock, they sure had their mitts on one well-placed snitch.

Cathlene Clarke had already scored high marks by cavorting with members of the environmental group Earth First! while strapped into a body mike. She dutifully transmitted overheard conversations to her FBI cohorts. Then at night, the Tucson nurse would drive home to her little shotgun apartment, nestled just behind Khalifa's mosque.

In 1989, four of the environmental activists—including charismatic leader Dave Foreman—were popped on federal conspiracy charges. Clarke was among a small cabal of informants who'd gathered

HAPPINESS IS
SUBMISSION TO GOD

details on activists' alleged plans to sabotage a handful of nuclear facilities, including the Palo Verde Nuclear Generating Station near Phoenix.

At the time, Clarke had become Khalifa's right hand gal, helping him run the 70-member mosque, or masjid, and spread his word through videos and *Submitters Perspective.* She also fancied herself his bodyguard.

When asked whether shielding her boss meant swapping info with the bureau, Clarke says, "Let me tell you this. I protected Rashad with my life all the time that I was at the mosque, by any means I had to."

Though her methods remained a secret, her shadow life did not. "Rashad already knew she had a relationship with the FBI," says Edip Yuksel, another former Khalifa aide "He told me that. But he didn't know."

Yuksel claims Clarke's bizarre behavior did become a hassle. "She's a mentally sick person," he says, "a troublemaker personality. She would sometimes get hysterical, yelling, breaking windows at the mosque. Rashad called the police several times. Then she would hide somewhere, until the police would leave.

"He asked her to go many times. But he was trying to be gentle. Many times he said to me, 'Is this a test from God? What should I do?'"

Clarke was ultimately given the boot, one month before Khalifa's murder.

Phoenix FBI Special Agent Jack Callahan refuses to comment, either about Khalifa's death or the agency's dealings with Clarke. "The case is still open," he says, "And it doesn't make much sense, if we're trying to recruit informants, to reveal their identities."

According to James Abourezk, a former U.S. senator from South Dakota and chairman of the American-Arab Anti-Discrimination Committee, it figures Clarke was working both sides of the fence. He describes FBI surveillance of mosques—including infiltration—as ongoing.

> On January 31, 1990, the balding, cherubic, 54-year-old imam, or teacher, was found lying in a pool of blood, stabbed several times and left to die on the kitchen floor of his Tucson mosque. His gun was tucked, unfired, beneath his body.

"They've been doing it for years," he says. "All I can judge from is the number of complaints we get, and sometimes they're heavy. When we first started ADC I suppose there had been a build-up for years. God, we had hundreds of affidavits in 1980 and '81. I went up and turned them all in to (then FBI-chief) William Webster. But I don't think they've ever stopped."

Others question Khalifa's own role. William Wilson, associate professor of Middle Eastern History at the University of Arizona, says the imam may have unknowingly become a government lackey.

"People like Khalifa, they introduce all these strange notions that aren't a part of Islam," he says. "It's divisive, and just leads to violence."

He then suggests darker possibilities: "Some might view it as another western plot to undermine Islam. In a sense, whether unwittingly or not, Khalifa was kind of an agent of western powers."

Like all previous miracles, the Qur'an's miracle is perfectly suited for its contemporary generation; it is a mathematical, computer-age miracle. Through mathematical coding, God has named Rashad Khalifa, by name, as His messenger...whose mission is to confirm all previous messengers and restore their messages to their original pristine purity.
—From "Certificate Of Proof That Rashad Khalifa Is A Messenger Of God," a pamphlet published by the Masjid of Tucson.

IT'S A FRIDAY night near the end of Ramadan, the Muslim holy month. This is a time when the faithful world-wide spend their days fasting, their nights eating, talking and praying.

On a busy corner next to the University of Arizona, the hungry Masjid of Tucson members fill the porch, gazing intently westward. They're waiting for the sun's last sliver to slide beneath the purple-tinged mountains.

A heaping feast lines the parapet's broad perimeter, breads, salads and casseroles in big aluminum tins, all covered against the chilly March air. Children dart impatiently between legs, most too young to grasp the moment's symbolism. A burr-headed boy climbs towards a plastic bowl of hummus, before his mother gently tugs him down.

Tucsonans notice the mosque mostly because they're meant to. "Happiness Is Submission To God," spreads boldly along the street side in tall, blue letters. During Clarke's reign, "Submission," was changed to "Devotion," maybe illuminating some feminist sentiment. Today, the original is back. Otherwise, the house is just another sadly aging, nondescript local landmark.

Five-laned Sixth Street, just a few feet away, is silent. Rush-hour has ebbed to nothing, and only an occasional honk breaks the subdued porch conversation.

Pre-chow talk continues, with everyone waiting for The Moment. When it arrives, sunset and a food line explode in tandem. "Kids first," someone says. A chunky woman in the back leans over an ice chest. "Sodas, anybody?" she hollers.

Just then, Abdul Arik strides out the front door toting paper plates. Tall, with salt-and-pepper hair, Arik comes from Turkey. He traveled here to study under Khalifa and learn computer programming. As part of the mosque's five-member leadership council, Arik is now in the upper ranks of the hierarchy. He peels apart the stack of plates and queues up.

Soon they're all inside, gathering on blankets spread around the floor. A

Amerikalı Halife'nin Kuran'ı değiştirme çabası

İKİNCİ SALMAN RÜŞDİ OLAYI

coffee maker perks loudly near the kitchen. The mosque's guts are plain as its skin, a simple meeting place, reminiscent of church basements. Walls are white. The floor is a mauve-colored shag carpet, broken in the middle by two columns, with a shelf centered between them. On the shelf is a miniature four-spired mosque made of wood.

The diners are also plain old folks; a smattering of Arabs and many anglos, with no frothing, turban-topped radicals in sight.

Arik leans against a wall, eating. Between bites, he says Khalifa's message lives on. "We've tried to continue his work. He was revising his translation on the *Qur'an,* and since then we've published it."

Sitting at the edge of a blanket, Lisa Spray gingerly finishes her meal, dabbing her mouth with a napkin. Spray was unlucky enough to find Khalifa's

body on that cold January morning. "I don't care about the criticism of his work," she says. "I just know what he meant to me. This is where I really learned what being a Muslim was all about."

The eating subsides and everyone slides into position for prayers, always facing east towards Mecca. Kneeling in rows, they simultaneously lean forward, touching their heads to the carpet. A man in front begins a monotone chant, which is repeated by a choir of voices.

When rituals are complete, the crowd scatters through the room, digging out turquoise-colored copies of *The Final Testament.* Jason, a meaty college kid sporting a Rangers jersey, starts reading a passage, Sura 97. The sura relates to Ramadan. Jason is allowed to offer his own interpretation. "To me, it's mystical,"

continued on page 10

By Tim Vanderpool

The Arizona Daily Star

Serving Tucson and Southern Arizona

© 1998 Final Edition, Tucson, Wednesday, September 30

7   No. 273 ★

50¢ U.S./$1.00 in Mexico   54 P

NINETEEN: God's Signature in Nature and Scripture. www.19.org

Man tied to embassy blasts worked here

Links suggested to bin Laden, Tucson cleric's death

By Hipolite R. Corella
The Arizona Daily Star

A man linked to the U.S. embassy bombings last month in Africa spent time in Tucson during the 1980s working as a janitor and a driver.

A New York prosecutor hinted in a court hearing last week that Wadih El-Hage also took part in surveillance of a Tucson mosque before its cleric was found slain in 1990.

And although the suspect's Tucson employment appears to have been limited, it had a profound effect on one Tucsonan. He was paralyzed in a collision with a Van Tran vehicle. El-Hage was driving.

Federal authorities in New York say they believe El-Hage is a leader in the Kenyan branch of Al Qaeda, a terrorist organization run by Osama bin Laden — the suspected mastermind of the embassy bombings in Kenya and Tanzania.

The blasts killed hundreds of people, including a dozen Americans.

Although El-Hage, 38, hasn't been charged in connection with the bombings, he was indicted last week in Manhattan on several counts of lying to authorities about his relationship to members of the bin Laden organization.

He pleaded not guilty.

Prosecutors say they believe El-Hage, an American citizen who was most recently managing a Texas tire store, served as personal secretary to

bin Laden

During last week's bail hearing in New prosecutors also said El-Hage bought gun Mahmud Abouhalima, who was convicted of ing and transporting the chemicals used to the World Trade Center in 1993.

Furthermore, prosecutors said he was to El-Sayyid Nosair, who helped plan the Trade Center attack and killed Jewish leader Meir Kahane in 1990.

U.S. Assistant Attorney Patrick Fitzgera there is also evidence El-Hage helped a ma was conducting surveillance on an Arizona leader who was later found slain, wire repor

In January 1990, Muslim Sheik U Khalifa, 54, was killed at the Masjid of Tu small mosque then located on East Sixth

See EL-HAGE, Pag

Arizona Daily Star
4 November 2001,
NINETEEN: God's Signature
in Nature and Scripture
www.19.org

Second bin Laden aide lived in Tucson

By Norma Coile
ARIZONA DAILY STAR

A man U.S. authorities believe is Osama bin-Laden's chief of logistics lived in Tucson in the mid-1980s and was active in the Islamic Center here.

Wa'el Hamza Jalaidan, who is also described by the U.S. government as one of the founders of the al-Qaida terror network with bin Laden in the late 1980s, was on the Islamic Center of Tucson's executive committee.

"Yes, he was here in the mid-'80s," an Islamic Center spokesman, Muhammad As'ad, confirmed last night.

"He left school and Tucson around 1985 and went to Afghanistan to fight against the Russians," said As'ad, who is on the center's executive committee. "When the Russians left Afghanistan, he returned to Saudi Arabia, and no one (at the Tucson center) has heard of him since."

Jalaidan is the second of bin Laden's top associates known to have lived in Tucson. As the Arizona Daily Star reported last Sunday, Wadih El-Hage, who also lived here in the 1980s, is believed to be bin Laden's personal secretary.

In addition, one of the suspected hijackers of ... ... that hit the Pentagon on Sept. 11, Hani

AIDE
Mosque leader not aware of Tucson ties

Continued from Page A1

viduals and organizations suspected of conducting or financing terror.

The Los Angeles Times reported in today's edition that the Treasury Department is gathering information about the Tucson Islamic Center. The Times said Jalaidan was president of the center, citing state incorporation records.

As'ad, who was not affiliated with the center in the 1980s, called a founding member last night when told of the Times report. He was told Jalaidan was not the president and was not particularly memorable, he said.

"He was just a kid, a student, an undergraduate," said As'ad, who was not sure where Jalaidan was study-

ing.

"At that time, nobody ever heard of Osama bin Laden," he added.

Imam Omar Shahin, the spiritual leader of Tucson's Islamic Center, said he had not heard of Jalaidan or his Tucson ties.

Shahin pointed out that the U.S. government supported bin Laden and the Afghans' fight against the Soviets in the 1980s.

Shahin said no U.S. authorities have contacted him about Jalaidan. "We are comfortable telling them everything about the Islamic Center," he said. "We have nothing to hide."

As'ad added: "This one's a very cold, dead-end trail. We have nothing to do with people like this. Violence against defenseless citizens is against the teachings of the Quran and the teachings and traditions of the prophet. This is something we roundly condemn."

▶ *Contact Norma Coile at 573-4102 or at ncoile@azstarnet.com.*

567

Jet plane linked to bin Laden was stored in Tucson

By David Wichner
ARIZONA DAILY STAR

A surplus U.S. Air Force training jet that wound up in the hands of Osama bin Laden had been mothballed at an Air Force storage center in Tucson before it was sold through a private dealer.

The plane's origins had been the subject of speculation since February, when a Tucson connection was revealed by a witness in the case of the 1998 terrorist bombings of U.S. embassies in Kenya and Tanzania.

Egyptian-born pilot Essam Al-Ridi testified that he purchased a T-39A Sabreliner training jet on behalf of bin Laden from a Tucson-area aircraft "bone yard." Bin Laden is the suspected mastermind of the Sept. 11 terrorist attacks on the World Trade Center and the Pentagon.

Officials at Davis-Monthan Air Force Base had said it was impossible that the 1960s-era jet came from the thousands of old aircraft stored at the base's Aerospace Maintenance and Regeneration Center.

But arms-control advocates say the mere fact that a former Air Force plane fell into bin Laden's hands shows that surplus sales should be restricted.

While the plane did not come directly from AMARC, records show the jet was decommissioned and stored there in 1985.

In January 1990, the plane was traded to a California aircraft broker, along with five other T-39As, in a swap for a historic biplane sought by an Air Force museum in Ohio.

The plane was transferred to Western International Aviation, a private aircraft maintenance and storage yard adjacent to Davis-Monthan, and languished there until it was sold to Al-Ridi in September 1992.

An AMARC official said the command had no role in the sale to bin Laden, and neither the transfer of the plane to the private dealer nor the eventual sale to bin Laden's agent broke any laws.

"We don't sell aircraft to the general public," AMARC spokeswoman Terry Vanden-Heuvel said.

The Air Force and other AMARC clients are allowed to sell noncombat planes to dealers, but even then they are stripped of any combat-related equipment in a process known as "demilitarization," she said.

AMARC stores about 4,600 planes, including 22 T-39A Sabreliners and 31 later versions of the T-39, Vanden-Heuvel said.

SEE TRAINER / A15

NINETEEN: God's Signature in Nature and Scripture
www.19.org

Mosque aids group accused of Hamas tie

Islamic Center says charity's hands are clean

By David Wichner
ARIZONA DAILY STAR

Tucson's major Islamic center collects money for a relief group that is barred from receiving federal aid and is accused by Jewish groups of having ties to the Palestinian terrorist group Hamas.

But the leader of the Islamic Cen-

leader of the Islamic Center of Tucson, said he is monitoring Holy Land's status but will continue to periodically collect money for the group unless it is officially shut down.

"If they are licensed here in America, we allow them to collect funds. Otherwise nobody is allowed to collect any funds," Shahin said.

Shahin said the center collected about $7,000 last week and sent it to the Holy Land Foundation for needy Afghans.

He said he has collected for the group in the past, in annual driv-

568

ECONOMY 2002: IS THE WORST OVER?

Newsweek

January 14, 2002 : $3.95

Married to Al Qaeda

EXCLUSIVE

The American Wife of
A bin Laden Operative:
A Journey Into Jihad

NINETEEN: God's Signature in Nature and Scripture.
www.19.org

April Ray, spouse of convicted terror conspirator Wadih El-Hage   newsweek.msnbc.com

April Ray's husband became bin Laden's
secretary. Now he's behind bars. Her brush
with the shadowy world of Al Qaeda.

BY KEVIN PERAINO AND EVAN THOMAS

Odyssey Into Jihad

S HE DRIVES A DARK GREEN MINIVAN WITH A "MY CHILD IS AN
HONOR STUDENT ..." bumper sticker on the back. She scrimps
and saves in discount shopping malls. Her kids like to watch
"The Simpsons" and the WWF. (Her oldest son recently shaved
the heads of his three little brothers to make them more closely
resemble his favorite wrestler, Stone Cold Steve Austin.) Looking determined if a bit worn out at 34, April Ray might be just another
struggling young American mother, except for the fact that her husband
was, for a couple of years, the personal secretary of terrorist mastermind

Osama bin Laden. How did a
suburban Dallas housewife
become a bride of the mon-
strous Al Qaeda?

April Ray's husband, Wadih
El-Hage, is now serving a life
sentence in a maximum-secu-
rity prison for conspiracy to
commit terrorism in the August 1998 bombings of two
American Embassies in East
Africa. Within Al Qaeda, El-
Hage was nicknamed "the
Manager," according to federal prosecutors.
For several years during the 1990s, the U.S.
government alleges, El-Hage performed ne-
farious chores for his terrorist boss, like pur-
chasing a jet plane in order to deliver Stinger

BUSTED: Wadih El-Hage

missiles (El-Hage personally
handed the keys to bin Laden
at a dinner party). Before the
embassy bombings, federal
wiretaps picked up El-Hage
talking about "fixing papers"
and preparing "notebooks"—
code, the prosecutors said, for
creating false passports for
Qaeda operatives. The prosecutors did not prove that El-
Hage formally swore alle-
giance to bin Laden with an
oath, or bayat. But as a federal prosecutor
told the jury: "The evidence showed that
Wadih El-Hage led a double life, a secret
criminal life on behalf of Al Qaeda, and that
he performed logistical services for Al Qae-

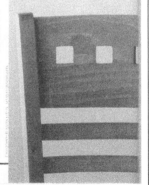

Newsweek 14 January 2002.
www.19.org

ANHAR TRADING

Wadih El-Hage
Director

U.S.A	GERMANY
400 DARLENE LN	UHLENHORSTER WEG 34
ARLINGTON TX 76010	2000 HAMBURG 76
Phone (817) [REDACTED]	Phone 49-40-2277536
Fax (817)	Fax 49-40-2278810

THE FIXER: El-Hage charging the judge in 1999 hearing (top left); bin Laden plane (above) procured by El-Hage; FBI mug shots; El-Hage acquaintance Sheik Rahman (left)

April Brightsky (pronounced "bright sky," as it was on the morning of her birth) Ray came by her wanderlust naturally. Her mother, who has been married five times, was a spiritual searcher called "Crusader Rabbit" by an ex-husband for her propensity to hop from cause to cause (Ray says she didn't have much of a father figure growing up). Brown, raised by Roman Catholic and Congregationalist parents, dabbled in Judaism and Buddhism before settling—finally, at 40—on Islam. As a young teen, Ray says that she briefly rebelled against her mother's faith. But then, at 16, Ray was almost kidnapped from high school by a boy on a motorcycle. "He was whacked out, and he thought he could take me somewhere so he could have some fun and I wouldn't go for it." Ray told her mother, who "freaked out" and pulled her daughter out of her Arizona high school.

Tucson in the 1980s was "wide open" and "scary," says Brown. Ray says her mother wanted her to have a safe Islamic marriage, and "not screw around" and turn into a "statistic." Brown took the direct approach. One day, as she attended the local mosque, 18-year-old Ray heard the PA system squawk: "Marion Brown is announcing that her daughter is at the age of marriage." Says Ray; "I was set up." Her name was put on "what we call the Arab grapevine," she says, and pretty soon proposals were arriving in the afternoon mail. Ray was presented with the photograph of the man she was to marry. Wadih El-Hage, 25, was slight, dark and squinting. "I said, 'This man's going to beat me'," Ray recalled. "My mom's saying, 'Shut up, he's not going to beat you'." In fact, she was soothed by the man's soft, warm voice. "He was just really nice, really sweet, and we clicked," Ray recalls.

Ray and El-Hage, a Lebanese-born Kuwaiti who was attending college in Louisiana, were married within a few weeks. The bride wore what she described as a kind of "froufrou" cowboy hat with pearls on top. Ray by then had come around to Islam as a haven from her chaotic upbringing. "It's complete," she now says of the Quran. "All the answers are there. There's no mystery to this, mystery to that, trust in this, trust in that, you've got all the answers. Everything is right there." In 1986, they moved to Pakistan to join the holy war in Afghanistan against the Soviet occupation. Born with a withered arm, El-Hage was not able to be a frontline warrior. But, carrying a gun and riding a motorcycle, he smuggled money, supplies and what Ray vaguely described as "stuff" over the Pakistan border. After one monthlong disappearance El-Hage returned bald. He told his wife that he had shaved his head to keep the bugs out while he slept in caves.

Ray says that she knew nothing about terrorism. She cannot, or will not, see Wadih as a criminal: 'Everybody loves him.'

Married to Jihad
Newsweek 14 January 2002.
www.19.org

Private Lives

A convert to Islam in her teens, April Ray married
Wadih el-Hage in Tucson, Ariz. The couple went to
Pakistan in 1986 and later back to Texas. In 1992
El-Hage was hired by Osama bin Laden, and the
family moved to Sudan. In 1994 they went to Kenya.

SEARCHING FOR ORDER:
April Ray at 11 (left); as
a young wife in
Nairobi, Kenya (above);
posing with infant son
Abdullah in Quetta,
Pakistan (right)

Pregnant and almost always nauseated at
the time, Ray says she was "shocked ... It
was scary." Just going outside was dangerous. "You're a walking target. You've got
these weirdos who attack tourists all the
time." But, as an American, she felt relatively protected. America at that time was
backing the jihad; the CIA was supplying
the mujahedin with Stinger missiles.
"Everybody loved Americans," recalls
Brown, who had also moved to Pakistan to
support the jihad.

Often traveling to the United States,
Ray's husband worked for the shadowy
Services Office, a forerunner of Al Qaeda
which raised money and men for jihad. He
became close to Mustafa Shalabi, a 39-year-
old Egyptian who ran the Al-Kifah Refugee
Center, a Services Office affiliate in Brooklyn, N.Y. In 1991, Shalabi was found murdered; he had been stabbed and shot. Devastated, El-Hage called Ray. "He was
crying," she says. In 1990, El-Hage had
been touched by an equally mysterious
murder. He admitted that he had met with
a man who investigators believe was spying

on Rashad Khalifa, an unorthodox imam
who allowed men and women to pray together in his Tucson mosque. Several
months after El-Hage and the man met,
Khalifa was murdered. El-Hage had also
been jolted when his mentor Abdullah Az-
zam, a fiery jihadist who had founded and
ran the Services Office in Pakistan, was
killed by a car bomb.

Despite the carnage around her husband, Ray willed herself to be calm. "You
do worry. But then you've got to stop—no,
don't really dwell on that. God willing, he'll
be fine. He'll come home." She was reassured when El-Hage got a good-paying
job in 1992: from Osama bin Laden, the
wealthy holy warrior who had moved to Sudan after the Russians were defeated in
Afghanistan. El-Hage and Ray were living
back in Texas at the time. Bin Laden flew

El-Hage to Sudan for an interview. "He's really nice," El-
Hage reported back to his
wife. El-Hage would make $1,200 a
month—a fortune in their new home city of
Khartoum.

El-Hage was working for bin Laden's legitimate business enterprises, which included farming and chemical manufactur-
ing. One of El-Hage's titles was "Director
of International Marketing and Purchas-
ing" for one of bin Laden's companies. But
investigators believe that many of bin
Laden's businesses are mere fronts for
moving money and supplies around the
globe, and that in any case any profits are
plowed into bin Laden's terror network.
Bin Laden is known to own as many as 20
ships (the better to smuggle arms and,
since his disappearance from Afghani-

Ray used to go to bin Laden's picnics. 'He was a great boss,' she says. 'He's not the monster people make him out to be.'

FAMILY MATTERS: Like any doting father, El-Hage posed for snapshots with his seven children as the family traveled the globe

stan, possibly bin Laden himself). The used T-36 Sabre jet that El-Hage bought for bin Laden in 1993 was intended to carry shoulder-fired surface-to-air missiles. (But just one year later its brakes failed and it crashed on landing.)

Ray says she was oblivious to her husband's peripatetic work. She was "busy busy busy. House house house, kids, kids, kids, house," she says. There were few amenities in Khartoum and Ray was afraid to drive. On the other hand, she could look forward to recreation at bin Laden's version of a company picnic—parties of 30 to 40 of his followers invited to grill shish kebab at his farm outside the capital city. The women would gather in a tent a safe distance from the men, who would congregate round bin Laden and hear him rant about the evils of the corrupt Saudi regime. As their children played and swam in the Nile, the women would talk about families—but never about their husbands' work. Ray says this discretion was partly to avoid jealousy. It may also have been because the Qaeda terrorist training manual forbids operatives from discussing their work with the wives.

Ray says she never met bin Laden himself. "I don't meet the men," she says, "My husband could bring home the president of the United States and if he didn't want me to know, I wouldn't know they were there. The women don't sit with the men ... You don't look at the men." She did, however, feel bin Laden's influence on her husband. In 1993, El-Hage told Ray that he was going to take a second wife. He explained that bin Laden was encouraging the men to have more than one wife "because," Ray explained, "there are so many women who don't have husbands." Ray was not buying. She reminded him that, in their original marriage contract, he had promised not to take a second wife. She couldn't force him to divorce the new wife (who was already under contract) because, she said, "that's un-Islamic." In-

stead, she says, "I made his life hell ... I was becoming a real b----." After six months, El-Hage relented. He decided not to go through with his second marriage after all.

Ray complained about the fierce dust storms in Sudan, which were aggravating her asthma. After two years in Sudan, "I couldn't wait to get out of there," says Ray. El-Hage accommodated her wish, quitting the bin Laden organization and moving to Nairobi in Kenya in 1994 to go out on his own as a trader, dealing in jewels and other commodities.

He was "bad at it," says Ray. His business dragged. Ray urged him to go back to work for bin Laden. Actually, federal prosecutors believe, he never stopped working secretly for the terrorist mastermind. Among the documents seized by investigators is one called "The New Policy," directing Qaeda members to revive their activities in Somalia. The first point in the document is "the return of Wadih" to Kenya after a visit with bin Laden. El-Hage, prosecutors say, is sometimes re-

573

Married to Jihad

Married to Jihad

Newsweek, 14 January 2002

© NINETEEN: God's Signature in Nature and Scripture. www.19.org

THE BOSS: Wadih told his wife that Osama bin Laden, shown here in 1998, was 'really nice'

busy with her household chores to notice the news reports that bin Laden had issued a deadly *fatwa*—proclaiming that it was the duty of Muslims to kill Americans. But when, on the morning of Aug. 7, 1998, she heard the news of the embassy bombings in Africa, she was overcome by a sense of dread. "Oh my God," she says she thought to herself. "This is really bad. We were there. They're going to think my husband did it."

Panicking, she called her husband at the Ft. Worth tire dealership where he worked, but he brushed her off. He was busy, he said. A little after midnight on Aug. 12, Ray's mother called her daughter to say that the FBI had come around asking questions. This was not Brown's first run-in with the bureau: 33 years earlier, she told her daughter, she was involved with some far-right-wing "Minute Men" who were setting up camps and training exercises to fight against communism. The FBI shut down the group. The G-men back then were "nasty," said Brown. The FBI agents these days were "very nice, very polite," said Ray. In the transcripts of the FBI wiretaps, the two women sound at once wary and savvy. In between gushing—somewhat artificially perhaps—about what a "good man" El-Hage is, they talk about how to handle the FBI. "You know," says Brown, "if they [the FBI agents] were smart they would have tried to enlist El-Hage's help. If they were smart." Replies Ray: "I figured they already got what they wanted. They know what we are up to. They have our phone bugged and everything. But they probably think— ... My hypothesis ... [She pauses] ... is they want to see what you would say to us and act on what we would say back to you ..."

At one point, Brown refers to bin Laden as "Abu," an Arab diminutive that means father and is also a common alias for Al Qaeda recruits. Ray corrects her: "He is Osama bin Laden." "Whatever," says Brown. El-Hage gets on the line and the women tell him the FBI may question him. "So what," he replies. "I told them before, everybody knows bin Laden. They all know him. The man is on TV and in the newspapers." Brown interjects, "Yeah, but you are probably the only one who had dinner with him."

ferred to by a pseudonym, Abdel Sabbur, and called an "engineer."

In fact, court evidence showed, El-Hage was a fixer. He traveled around the world opening bank accounts and arranging documents to support Al Qaeda's terror cells, prosecutors said. And he maintained relationships with a wide array of people who wound up convicted of terrorist activities. He acknowledged to investigators that he bought guns at the request of a man later imprisoned for mixing and transporting chemicals for the 1993 World Trade Center bombing. A bit of a pack rat, El-Hage collected address books, diaries and business cards that would later provide investigators with a kind of terrorist road map. For instance, one of his contacts was a Hamburg, Germany, businessman named Mamoun Darkanzali, who denies terrorist ties but has reportedly admitted to being in at least casual contact with members of the Hamburg-based Qaeda cell that carried out the September 11 hijackings. Among the documents arranged by El-Hage are ID cards for a charity he set up called Help Africa People. One card identifies Fazul Mohamed as a computer-software specialist for the charity. The FBI believes that Fazul is actually Haroun Fazil, the man suspected of masterminding the truck-bomb attack that blew up the U.S. Embassy in Nairobi.

Transcripts of El-Hage's phone conversations, which were being secretly wiretapped by the Feds in 1997 and introduced as evidence at trial, show him speaking guardedly and sometimes in code. In one conversation with Ray, El-Hage asks his wife to send "ten green papers." "Green papers?" she asks. "You mean money." El-Hage replied sarcastically, "Thank you very much." He adds, "That's only for you. Nobody else is listening." But Ray suspected that her phone was being tapped. Investigators would later obtain a Qaeda "security memo" proposing that certain of El-Hage's files be destroyed lest they be discovered. In this memo, which was retrieved from a computer in El-Hage's house in Nairobi, the author complains that Ray has heard English voices coming out of the TV set. "This is it. This is the line," Ray says she hears the voices saying. "Is he Arab or English?" She apparently thought she had stumbled over a sloppy wiretap.

Ray's suspicions turned to outright fear in 1997 when a group of Kenyan police and FBI men knocked on her door. "We believe El-Hage's life is in danger," the G-man told her, Ray recalls. "Somebody might try to kill him. Do you know who would want to do that?" Ray said she didn't know. She asked if her children were in danger. "We don't think so, but we can't really be sure," an FBI man said. "If you want us to take you in right now, we can." But Ray said, "I'm not leaving without my husband," who was in Pakistan on business.

Shortly thereafter, the family moved back to Texas. Ray claims that she was too

Called 'the Manager,' El-Hage bought bin Laden a T-36 Sabre jet to carry Stingers, handing him the keys at a dinner party

El-Hage tries to be sarcastic: "Yeah, I had the last supper with him." Ray interrupts, "I don't see anything humorous about that." Agrees Brown: "I don't either."

It's doubtful that El-Hage was making jokes a few days later when he was arrested by the FBI and charged with conspiracy and perjury. (He was not accused of taking a direct role in carrying out the embassy bombings, but rather of conspiring to kill Americans at the embassies and around the world.) For two years he languished in a federal prison in Manhattan, awaiting trial. In November 2000, one of his codefendants stabbed a prison guard in the eye. When Ray and her kids visited El-Hage in February 2001, the month his trial began, he seemed broken and bewildered. "He didn't recognize us," she says. "He was totally out of it." Prison psychiatrists determined that El-Hage was faking amnesia. He subsequently snapped out of it and began writing Ray again, although she says the two have not spoken over the phone or in person since September 11.

Ray says she learned of the attack on the World Trade Center and Pentagon when a friend phoned her and asked: Are you safe? She turned on the TV and saw the devastation. "I literally called everyone that I knew and I told them, 'Go get your shopping done right now. The next few days are going to be pretty rough for people.'" Sure enough, in the grocery store, one of her Muslim friends, who was handicapped, received a death threat. In the post office, when Ray complained of a bad smell because it hurt her breathing, another woman sneered, "You people should stop complaining ... go back where you came from." Ray says she shot back, "Excuse me? I'm 100 percent American and I have a lineage that would put yours to shame ... I'm not letting anyone walk over me."

Ray says she is struggling to make ends meet, living off donations from the mosque and welfare. Her children miss their father (whom they call "Bubba"); they cry for no reason and cling to her. But she is defiant. Like many true believers, she won't accept that bin Laden ordered the September 11 attacks. She suspects they were plotted by the CIA or Israeli intelligence. She is opposed to killing civilians, but if the jihad against the enemies and corrupters of Islam goes on, and her 15-year-old son, the WWF fan, wants to fight, then she'd consider letting him join when he comes of age. She says she puts her faith in the will of Allah. "As Muslims, we accept death," she says. "We know it's part of life." But just in case, she says she wants to buy a gun.

With GRETEL C. KOVACH in New York and MARK HOSENBALL in Washington

The deeply ambivalent role women play in bin Laden's world. BY CHRISTOPHER DICKEY AND GRETEL C. KOVACH

Revered—And Yet Repressed

IN THE COSMOS AS DEFINED BY OSAMA bin Laden, men and women have very clear roles. Men are the warriors, and the foremost among them become martyrs. For their sacrifice, they are promised 72 virgins in the afterlife. It's up to their mothers, wives and sisters to help guide them toward jihad, and then to mourn for them when they're gone. The men in turn should fight for the "honor" of the women. On page five of the Qaeda training manual, recruits are encouraged to take a pledge to "the sister believer whose clothes the criminals have stripped off" and "whose body has been abused." The men must "retaliate for you against every dog who touches you even with a bad word."

Testosterone has always had a lot to do with terrorism, even among secular bombers and kidnappers like Italy's Red Brigades and Germany's Baader-Meinhof gang. As Andreas Baader himself once declared, "F----ing and shooting are the same thing." The rise of radical Islam in the 1970s and '80s saw a change in that pattern. Fundamentalist groups like Islamic Jihad in Egypt, Hizbullah in Lebanon and Hamas in Palestine made women central symbols of their struggle, a measure of both male righteousness and machismo. But as April Ray's story shows, the woman behind the veil is not always submissive. And the male need to dominate and "protect," more often than not, is a reflection of weakness, not strength.

The West is regarded a a threat, in part because o its potential influence on Muslim women. Bin Lad in his declaration of holy war against Americans in the Arabian Peninsula took particular offense that Washington "brought forces o Christian wome to help defend M ca. The Covena the Palestinian f damentalist mo ment Hamas ex plicitly regards " Muslim woman as an object of th struggle. The "e mies ... consider that if they are al to direct and bri her up the way t wish, far from Is lam, they would have won the ba tle," the Covena

TALIBAN RULE: An Afghan man beats a woman in Kabul last October

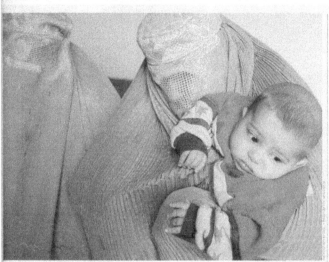

BABIES AND BURQAS:
Fariba, holding her
infant son, is married to
a member of Al Qaeda

states. "That is why you find them giving these attempts constant attention through information campaigns, films, and the school curriculum."

The Taliban and Al Qaeda, of course, made sure that women saw none of that in Afghanistan. Women became virtual prisoners of their husbands' or fathers' homes, unable to work or study. But while pledging to protect their "sister believers," the fundamentalists often abused them. Some Afghan girls were sold into marriages with local and foreign Taliban; others were kidnapped. "There were a lot of forced marriages during this time because it made life easier for the [Qaeda] Arabs," says Anisa Mahmood Omar, director of an aid program for Afghan women in Kabul. Outside Afghanistan,

Qaeda wives had a role in the organization similar to Mafia wives—to take care of the family and remain ignorant of "business" details.

The stereotype of the abusive Qaeda husband doesn't always apply. Fariba, a 20-year-old Afghan woman, was forced to marry a Saudi Qaeda member against her will—a man she saw for the first time at 6 p.m. on her wedding day. But she insists now that she fell in love with him, despite the severe restrictions he put on her. "He was a good man," she says. Lawyers for convicted Qaeda member Mohamed Sadeek Odeh included in their case tapes of tender phone conversations between him and his wife. In one taped message, he begged her to write to him. "Tell me every-

thing," he said. "Everything you feel, whether it is big or small. I wouldn't get bored listening to your voice."

Many leaders of Al Qaeda, however, haven't waited for Paradise to claim their reward in virgins. Although four wives are allowed according to the Quran, polygamy is not generally encouraged by Muslim thinkers. The Prophet himself, who improved rights for women in seventh-century Arabia, set the standard for multiple wives very high—some say impossibly high—by insisting that a husband treat each wife equally. But Qaeda radicals, like some of the corrupt Saudi royals they say they are fighting, have embraced polygamy as the reward for their fundamentalist faith. Bin Laden himself has four

wives; according to some reports, one of his elder wives became estranged from him after he wedded a 17-year-old Yemeni more than a year ago. At one point, bin Laden also encouraged the practice known by some Arabs as *al mutuaa* marriages, short-term sexual liaisons over a fixed time, often for a fixed price. He and 35 followers had shown up in the remote Teerah Valley of Pakistan in 1996, and bin Laden told the villagers that under Islam, men were entitled to "temporary marriages." "There was fighting for two days between Arabs and locals," says Sayeed Hussain, a local journalist. "Then

they were kicked out."

Hundreds of wives and children of Qaeda fighters are now caught in the turmoil of Afghanistan. Up to 300 Qaeda warriors brought dependents with them when they retreated to the caves of Tora Bora in November, according to Afghan sources in Jalalabad. In late November, anti-Taliban Afghan fighters reported seeing a child yelling "Allahu Akbar" as adult Qaeda fighters fired mortars near the front line. Arab kids were also seen playing outside one of the caves, only to be grabbed up and carried inside the hideout by adults at the sound of approaching U.S. aircraft.

Human Rights Watch has appealed for international protection for Qaeda dependents. So have Qaeda fighters themselves, in a different fashion. In an open letter circulating in Pakistan and Afghanistan, the fighters ask locals to provide shelter to their wives and kids. "If you look at how we are separated from the 'meat of our hearts' the tears will flow from your eyes," the letter says. Then it continues: "We don't worry that [the Americans] will kill our women and children. But America is the enemy of Islam ... If they find our children alive, these Jews and Christians will try to convert them." For bin Laden's boys, that paranoid vision represents the ultimate humiliation.

With BABAK DEHGHANPISHEH in Kabul, SCOTT JOHNSON and ZAHID HUSSAIN in Islamabad, SAMI YOUSAFZAI in Peshawar, MARK HOSENBALL, ROY GUTMAN and DANIEL KLAIDMAN in Washington and JEFFREY BARTHOLET

576

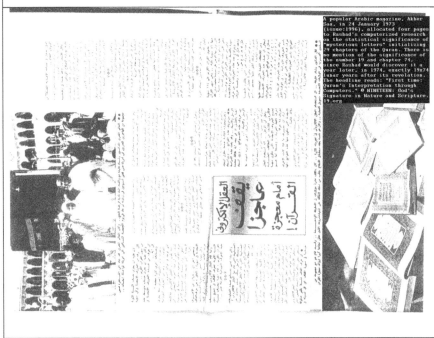

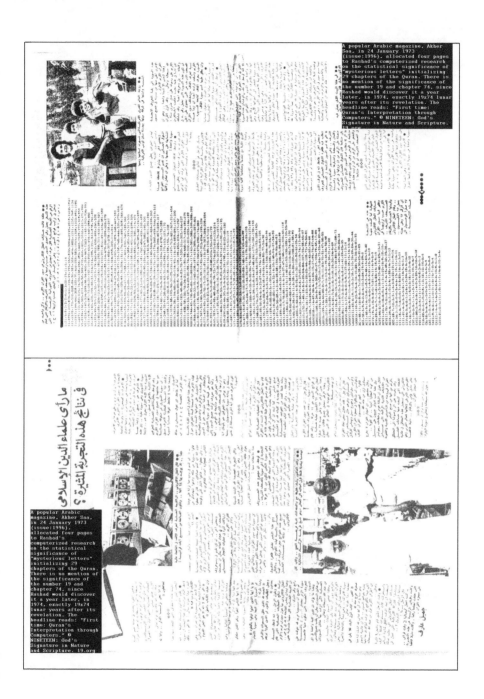

بسم الله الرحمن الرحيم

AL AZHAR

Academy of Islamic Research

(Research & Publication Dept.)

Cairo, R. E. A.

الأزهـر

الأمانة العامة أمين البحوث الإسلامية

إدارة البحوث والنشر

تحريراً فى ١٦ / ٣ / ١٣٩٦ هـ الموافق ١٧ / ٣ / ١٩٧٦ م رقم

السيد الدكتور / رشاد خليفه رئيس جمعية الدعوة الاسلاميه بأمريكا

السـلام عليـكم ورحمـة اللـه وبركاتـه   " وبعــــد "

فانه قد تبين من بحثكم القيم حـول " البسـمله " وما جاء بهـا مـن

اعجاز ٠ ان بحثكم هذا محاولة طيبه لكشف اسرار القـرآن الكـريم

غير أنه لم يصـل بعد الـى الحقائق العلميـه ٠

واملنا أن يزيدكم اللـه عونـا وتوفيقـا لعمـل اكـثر نفعـا واعظم أثـرا ٠

والسـلام عليـكم ورحمـة اللـه وبركاتـه

مـديـر

ادارة البحـــوث والنشـو

عبدالمهيمن محمد الفقـــى

١٩٧٦/٤/١٧

تحريرا فى ١٦ ربيع أول ١٣٩٦ هـ

١٧ مـــارس ١٩٧٦ م

عبدالنبى

الرقم ١٩ آخر فضائح الحركة البهائيّة

علماء الدين: هدف اللعبة شغل المسلمين عن مشاكلهم الحقيقية !

ندوة الأدب الإسلامي
تبدأ اليوم بالرياض

شدا اليوم بالرياض أكبر ندوة أكاديمية عن الأدب الإسلامي ومنهجه نظام الندوة بكلية اللغة العربية بجامعة الإمام محمد بن سعود. ويشترك فيها عدد كبير من رجال الأدب الإسلامي بالمملكة العربية السعودية، مصر، والعراق، والمغرب، والكويت، وتركيا.

وصرح الشيخ ساصر العبد الله الغريم رئيس الندوة بأنه ساصر مسئم خلال الجلسات التي تستمر ثلاثة أيام بحث تحديد مفهوم الأدب الإسلامي، والتعرف على سماته، ورسم الخطوط العربية لمنهج إسلامي جديد في القصة والرواية والمسرحية والتمثيلية.

من بين المشتركين في الندوة الدكتورة أحمد عبد الباسط، وصالح أم، ومحمد سعد الشويعر، وعبد الرحمن الباشا من المملكة العربية السعودية، ومحمد مصطفى هدارة، ومحمد حرب، من مصر، ومحمد المنصر الريحاني من المغرب، وأحمد صنعي فرات من تركيا، وأحمد شوقي العمري من الكويت.

(الصفحة ٥)

ملامح ذكريات الشيخ الباقوري

... نافر، نصعيد مصر جاء هذا الرجل، لينطأ ٨١ عاما على ساحة العمل العام، وتحت دائرة الضوء.

ألقي علي بعض أعبائه تسميت كثيرة، حليفة صانت، الرجعة لصيد بمصر البارد، وأحمانا أخرى يرجل الدين الحلودي، وأحمانا ثالثة رجل كل مصر الشيخ الباقوري، هو نصف الصفحات... إلى بعلي الآن تراجعه عن أشياء ومنها، وعن أخرى، لم يفعلها وكان...

وهو بعمر بصداقاته وصلاته الشديدة بزعماء مصر واحدا بعد آخر، فقد مشاركة مصر السادات... إلى آخر ما يخبر به كما يقول بمشاركته الحركات الثلاث التي حاولت تعمير مصر وهي فترة الإخوان...

(ملامح ذكريات ــ الصفحة ٧ ، ٦)

ماضر غدا، العبي بفهم الكسبير... إلى أم في قدرة على النهار من رجيعه يوم العلم، الكسبير، وعوك سقوط العبت.

نفير أن اللعبة بهائية الأصل، وأن المقصود منها التشويش، إلى فضايا وشاغل المسلمين الحقيقية

إلى الدكتور طهارة مصرب مصار عمد بكلية أصول الدين إن رشاد حليفة صانت... اللعبة مصر من عناصر الحملة البهائية وأن كل ما ذكره لا يصبل بالعقيدة العلمي بأي صلة، وأنه تستهدف أمور قد أثر لا لطيل.

وقال الدكتور محمد حليم الدار برئيس جامعة الأزهر السابق إن أبة «وعلقم في الأرقام» له تفيد إن القرآن باها معرفة الدكتوراه والأدونة أكانوا تتناولوا ما سيكون بلده الضمن في المستقبل.

وأكد الشيخ عطية صقر مجمع البحوث الإسلامية الأزهر كت مهندس الكسبير، لا مسألة معرفة بيوم الساعة وقال: إن النوع الدقيق لا يعلمه إلا الله، حتى أنه من شانه لم يطلع النبي «صلى الله عليه وسلم» نفسه فعندما سأل جبريل النبي عن الساعة قال له ما المسئول عنها بأعلم من السائل.

وأما الدكتور يحيى الدين السادق عميد كلية أصول الدين بالقاهرة إن الكسبير مجرد مصيد لا يستطيع التفكير إلا بما يضخه الإنسان من معلومات تفيد تحقيق هدفه.

وذكر الدكتور الحسيني أبو فرحة العميد السابق لكلية الدعوة الإسلامية بالقاهرة في تقديم اسم الله في قوله «إن الله عنده علم الساعة» ويفيد الذكر بأنه يفيد القصر، وتقديم الظرف، وأن «عنده علم الساعة» بهذه الاختصاص، ولفظ عنده كذلك يفيد حفظ الموعد عنده العجب، بقدر منا لله الصدمة، قهر لا ترك أن نؤكد أن رقم بعتبه حقيقة علمية لا تولية، وأن أي رقم له ثلاث دلالات في القرآن الكريم.

علماء المسلمين يفندون مزاعم الكمبيوتر ــ الصفحة ٨ ، ٩

المسلمون
AL-MUSLIMOON
جريدة المسلمين الدولية

Volume 1 - Issue No: 9 - Sat 16 Rajab 1405/ 6 April 1985

سماحة الشيخ
عبد العزيز بن باز
يكتب لـ «المسلمون»
عن السحر والكهانة
(الصفحة ١٦)

شيخ الأزهر يخص «المسلمون» بحمل رسالته إلى المؤتمر الإسلامى:
العالم الإسلامى مسئول عما يحدث فى بلغاريا
تصفية الأقليات المسلمة عار وإثم يلحق بالعالم الإسلامى

القاهرة ـ المسلمون ـ من محمد الزرقانى ...

رسالة من الناشر

(نص المقال بالعربية)

اتحاد إسلامى رياضى عالمى
المؤتمر التأسيسى بعد الشهر القادم بالرياض

الرياض ـ المسلمون ـ من كمال شاهين ...

الدول الإسلامية تنتج مالا تستهلكه
وتستهلك مالا تنتجه !!

اللعب بالرقم ١٩
لا يؤكد ولا ينفى الحقائق الكونية

مزاعم الكمبيوتر
ادعاءات بهائية

صاحب اللعبة استخدم الحق ليصل إلى الباطل

(نص المقال بالعربية)

هذه مؤامرة بهائية ـ ماسونية للتشويش على قضايا المسلم

مؤامرة بهائية - ماسونية للتشويش على قضايا المسلـ

الأخفاء عبارات علامات له
مطلقة شاملة لكل الزمان ..
ويزكد الشيخ عطية صقر
..اكابده في اللغة العربية
ويسؤل لنافه مثلا كلمة إذا
لم اكتب .. ويقول .. هل مد
أنه لم يمهم مع أبو بصر
أحفاها .. والقرآن لا يخاطب

يقول الدكتور في مد
الجاب من عند التفسير فا
أخفاء الساعة من .. الميتايا
الغرب من ذلك أنهي لعدم وجهم
في الآية أنه ..
..أحدها .. أنه أكاد مد تعالى ..
ذكره كانة لتوصف، ا..
كذلك كما هنالك ..
الكريم .. وإن كان هناك من
.. يرابعها .. إن المعنى ..
لفرط إرادة إخفاء إجفاءه
الأعمال الصالحة وقط د ا
.. والحكمة في أخفاء قا
بعفادرنا وعد .. الموت لن الا
بعثادرنا وحده حافيا ..

الثلاث غيبات الأولى من الخمس غيبات
المذكورة .. عنده علم وإنه قيام الساعة ولا يعلمه أحد
سواه .. وإن مبيح نزول الآية أن الحارث بن
عمرو أني النبي صلى الله عليه وسلم
فقال .. متى قيام الساعة ؟ .. ويزكد عمد
كلية أصول الدين أن التلاث الأول في ما
إن الله عنده علم الساعة ويمزل الغيث
ويعلم ما في الأرحام .. تلك الثلاث الأول
أسرها أعظم وأقعم فضمت بالاضافة إليه
تعالي والأخيرات من صفات العباد فضمت
بالاضافة اليهم سواء أنه ؟ إذا تواها سيم
طهمها كأن انتفاء علم ما تداهما عن الخمس
أولى .. ؟ أما قوله تعالى (وما أدرك ما نفس ..)

الثلاث غيبات الأولى من الخمس غيبات
المذكورة .. وما أدري نفس ماذا تكسب
غدا .. وما أدري نفس بأي أرض تموت ..
أن الخمسة سواء في اختصاص الله تعالى
بعلمها واستقاء علم العباد بها .. ويزكد عمد
أن أصول الدين .. معني تتمم الساعة ؟ وما
إن الله عنده علم الساعة ؟ وما أعمل غدا ؟ وأين
أموت ؟ .. ولذلك ترلت نأت القرآن الكريم

ليس في الشرع دليل

يقول الدكتور عبد الغاء الشيخ عميد
كلية الشريعة والقانون بجامعة الأزهر إن
موعد قيام الساعة علمه عند ربي فقط ولا
يعلم إلا الله وقد سئل النبي صلى الله عليه
وسلم عن موعد قيام الساعة فقال .. «علمها
عند ربي .. أما إن كان بإمكاننا أو قيامها
بشكل دقيق وإعداد .. وليس في الشرع ما يبن
بقواعدها وبواطنها

في مناقشة تفسيره لثلاثة ٣٤٠ من سورة لقمان .. (إن الله عنده علم
الساعة وينزل الغيث ويعلم ما في الأرحام وما تدري نفس ماذا تكسب غدا وما تدري بأي
أرض تموت إن الله عليم خبير) .. إن الله عليم خبير
ة الساعة أو موعد نزول الغيث ومكانه .. وأضاف .. إنما الآن فنحما
رل الغيث كما أننا نعرف بالضبط ما في الأرحام .. ونضع نذكر أو أنثى .. ونحدد
د موعد قيام الساعة باستخدام الكومبيوتر ..

ويضيف .. ونحن نعلم مثلا بمعدنة الرياح
والعواصف .. ولكن العلماء يضعون ذلك الشيخ
دائما موضع الاحتمال ..

مجرد تجديد

ويذكر الدكتور محي الدين الصافي عميد
كلية أصول الدين .. جامعة الأزهر بالقاهرة إن
الكومبيوتر مجرد تجديد .. ولا يستطيع التفكير
إلا بما يحشوه الانسان من معلومات يقوم
بتسليمها بعد ذلك ولو أم يضع بها الله تعالى
المعلومات ما استطاع الكومبيوتر التوصل إلى
شيء

ويزكد إن كل المفسرين يقولون إن الله
عنده علم وإنه قيام الساعة ولا يعلمه أحد
سواه .. وإن مبيح نزول الآية أن الحارث بن
عمرو أني النبي صلى الله عليه وسلم
فقال .. متى قيام الساعة ؟ .. ويزكد عمد

أما عبد قيام الساعة فإنه بكل شيء عليم
فيقول .. إن الله تعالى لا خص أيا علم
الأخيرة المذكورة في قوله (وأن الله عنده علم
الساعة) .. ذلك أنه عبد مختص بها من أية بايم
الغيب إلا .. وهذا الرزق .. من مستطيع الرجم لأن علم
باسمائه النشو مذاك من

وقول الله عز وجل .. ويعلم ما في الأرحام
أي من ذكر أو أنثى .. سعيدة أم شقية

الشيخ الأمينة الأزهرية
من الجامعة الأزهرية
لا نفسيم ما توصل اليه
قول الله تعالى .. عنده علم
.. بالساعة إلا لانه سماه ه
وقت نزول المطر .. لأن الآية
الذي في يوحيه القاسمين
رؤية بمحدد أو لم شتمات
.. تلك التنوبات ..
رز النجار أما كلمة .. ويعلم
بقيدها القرآن الكريم بأنها
لأنه لكنها تتناول العلم
اليمن .. في حياة المستقبلية
.. ميسائم على الساعة
لا أو ه .. فلت أن السموات
بكم إلا يغتنا بسألونك

لا أعدها

عطية صقر عمم محمـ
في بالزعم الشريف .. فقد بدأ
.. بالدعوات وقفة .. لتقسيم
القرآن الكريم مجموعة
.. بنسبائم علي الساعة
لا أو ه .. فلت أن السموات
بكم إلا يغتنا بسألونك

الشيخ عطية صقر .. النطرق في هذا البحث إلى البحث الذي لا علم لأحد بالحافة
(١٩) يشير إلى أنه عنده سماه من المهانية
إلا الله.

الدكتور محمد الطيب النجار

The rest of the article published by the Saudi religious weekly magazine, Al-Muslimoon, in the first page of its 6–12 April 1985 issue. © NINETEEN: God's Signature in Nature and Scripture. www.19.org

---

Jamil Arif, reporting from Washington for Akher Saa: "In America: They Interpret the Quran with the aid of Electronic Intelligences." © NINETEEN: God's Signature in Nature and Scripture. www.19.org

جميل عارف يكتب من واشنطن

مرة أخرى استخدم عالم الكيمياء المصري الذي يعيش في أمريكا العقول الالكترونية
لتأكيد اعجاز القرآن الكريم .. وكان العالم المصري واسمه الدكتور رشاد خليفة ، قد قام
باستخدام هذه العقول الالكترونية في محاولة نشرت ((آخر ساعة)) تفاصيلها
لتفسير معنى بعض الحروف الأبجدية التي تسبق بعض سور القرآن الكريم وهي التي
يطلقون عليها اسم فواتح السور ،وأثارت هذه المحاولات ضجة في أوساط الكثيرين من
علماء المسلمين .. ولكن العالم المصري لم يتوقف عن ابحاثه وظل يواصل دراسة القرآن
الكريم بواسطة العقول الالكترونية .. واستطاع بعد عمل استمر أكثر من سنة
كاملة أن يخرج للعالم بنتائج مذهلة لم يسبق اليها فكر بشري عن معجزة القرآن هذه
الكريم .. ماذا كشفت عنه العقول الالكترونية لهذا القرآن الكريم هذه
المرة ؟ .. ولماذا يقول عالم الكيمياء المصري أن الذين يتشاءمون بالرقم ١٣ عليهم
أن يعرفوا أن هناك رقما بركة كله هو الرقم ١٩ .. وعلى المسلمين في كافة انحاء العالم
أن يتفاءلوا بهذا الرقم الجديد ؟

في أمريكا: بالعقول الألكترونية
يفسرون القرآن الكريم

ROSE ELYOUSSEF
NO.2967-22 - 4 - 1985

الاثنين ٢٢ أبريل ١٩٨٥ ـ العدد ٢٩٦٧ ـ السنة الستون ـ الثمن ٢٥ قرشا

مواجهة صريحة مع وزير الداخلية:

أحكام القضاء وتجاوزات الأمن!

بيان من الأزهر:

بعُدتَ عن الرشاد يادكتور رشاد!

ـ ٣٩ ـ

بيان من الأزهر حول مزاعم الكمبيوتر

بعيداً عن الرشاد

● الله جعل الكشف عن موعد نهاية العالم مستحيلا

● الرقم ١٩ يبين حقيقة عدد الملائكة الذين يعذبون أهل النار

● معرفة الجنين في بطن أمه ليس علماً بالغيب .

نشرت مجلة روز اليوسف بحثاً للدكتور/رشاد خليفة إمام مسجد (توسان) بالولايات المتحدة عن الاعجاز الذى ظهوره فى الحروف التى افتتح بها بعض سور القرآن ، ونغالى فى ذلك ، حتى حدد بها عمر الاسلام ، ووقت قيام الساعة ، فاقتضى الأمر بيان خروجه عن دائرة الحق وتجاوزه وجه الصواب ، وجرأته على الله تعالى ، ومعارضته لصريح القرآن ، واليكم البيان .

جاء بصدر المقال قوله تعالى : " إن الله عنده علم الساعة وينزل الغيث ويعلم ما فى الارحام وما تدرى نفس ماذا تكسب غدا وما تدرى نفس باى أرض تمــوت ان الله عليم خبير " .

وعقب على هذه الآية بقوله : تعلمنا هذه الآية أن الله سبحانه قد اخفى عن كل نفس العلم بما تكسب غدا ، واخفى عن كل نفس العـلم باى أرض تموت ، ولكنه سبحانه لم ينف امكان معرفة موعد الساعة ، ولم ينف امكان معرفة مكان ومكان نزول الغيث '، ولم ينف امكان معرفة ما فى الارحام .

وعقب ذلك بقوله : ونحن الآن نتطبأ بموعد ومكان نزول الغيث ، كما اننا نعرف بالضبط ما فى الارحام من ذكر أو أنثى ، بل ونعرف ان كان الجنين صحيحا او مريضا وباى مرض ...... كذلك قال .

والواقع ان هذه الامور الخمسة مما استأثر الله بعلمه ازلا ، وقبيل ان تكون ، ولا سبيل الى علم بعضها الا بتعليم الله وابراز اماراتها عند ظهورها او قبله .

وحينئذ يخرج عن نطاق الغيب ، ويبقى قصر معرفة الغيب على الله تعالى معرفة ذاتية بما به هذه الخمسة ، روى الامام البخارى بسنده فى كتاب الاستسقاء من صحيحه ، عن عبد الله بن عمر قال : قال رسول الله صلى الله عليه وسلم مفاتيح الغيب خمس ، ثم قرأ " ان الله عنده علم الساعة وينزل الغيث .. " الى آخر الآية .

● اما قول د.. رشاد : ان الله لم ينف امكان معرفة موعد الساعة ، فهو قول واضح الخطأ من عدة وجوه :

اولا : ان تقديم الخبر على المبتدأ يفيد الحصر ــ كما هو معروف عند أهل العلم ــ وقد تقدم فى الآية لفظ (عنده) وهو خبر على لفظ

(علم الساعة) وهو مبتدأ فالمعنى : ما علم الساعة الا عند الله تعالى .

ثانيا : ان الله تعالى قال فى سورة الاعراف " يسألونك عن الساعة أيان مرساها قل انما علمها عند ربى لا يجليها لوقتها الا هو ثقلت فى السموات والارض لا تأتيكم الا بغته يسألونك كأنك حفى عنها قل انما علمها عند الله ولكن اكثر الناس لا يعلمون " ١٨٧ .

مصطفى محمد الحديدى الطير
عضو مجمع البحوث الاسلامية

اى يسألونك يا محمد عن الساعة متى تجىء؟ قل للسائلين : ما علمها الا عند الله تعالى ، لا يظهرها لوقتها ولا ينبى بها الا الله ، لا يأتكم الساعة الا بغته دون سابق علم ــ يسألونك عنها كأنك عليم بها ، وهم مخطئون فى تقدير ذلك محيط بوصفها ، قل انما مرة اخرى ما علمها الا عند الله ، ولكن اكثر الناس لا يعلمون ، انها مما استأثر الله بعلمه ، فلذلك سألونك

عنها .

وبقول سبحانه فى سورة الاحزاب : " يسألك الناس عن الساعة قل انما علمها عند الله وما يدريك لعل الساعة تكون قريبا " اى قل للسائلك : ما علم الساعة الا عند الله ، وما يدريك ايها الرسول لعل الساعة تكون قريبا ، ماتت مع قربها لا تعلمها ، لانك لا سبيل لك الى درايتها .

والغرب الذى يشير اليه الآية ، انما هو بالنسبة الى عمر البشر فى الدنيا ، وهو بلايين من السنين لا يعلمها سوى الله تعالى ، واذا كان الامر كذلك ، فان من تجاوز الحق حدد هذا الدكتور بتلمانه وسمع بسين ، كما جمع الله الدكتور رشاد ، وسحبن عما يلى صاد استنباطه مما شاء ان شاء الله تعالى :

● وبقول سبحانه فى سورة فصلت " الله وما تخرج من ثمرات من اكمامها وما يحمل من أنثى ولا تضع الا بعلمه ... " من الآية ٤٧ . اى الى الله وحده يرجع علم الساعة ، وما يخرج من ثمرات من أوعيتها وظروفها (وما يحمل من أنثى ولا تضع الا

The third page of the Egyptian weekly magazine Rose al-Yousef publishing the announcement of Mustafa Muhammad al-Hadidi al-Tayr of Al-Azhar University in its 22 April 1985 issue, where he declares Rashad to be a heretic. © NINETEEN: God's Signature in Nature and Scripture. www.19.org

يا دكتور رشاد!

جاد الحق على جاد الحق

الله تعالى لها ، أما قبل ذلك فانهم لا يعرفون متى ينزل آ مهم يعتمدون على امارات تفيد الظن وقد تخلف آثارها ، ولهذا نراهم ذ أحيان كثيرة يخطئون ، اذا أخلف الله الاتجاهات نجاة نبرود صحو مكان الغيم ، أو غيم بدون المطر المنظر ، لكن الله تعالى يعلم الغيب علما ذاتيا وبحدثه لعباده بمقتضى تدبيره فيعرفونه بمعاينته ، أو بتوقعونه قبل حدوثه بامارته ، رئيس لهم به علم ذاتي ، مهم متعلمين من الامارات وليسوا بعالمين ، ومتعرفون وليسوا بعارفين .

((معرفة الجنين))

● وكذلك معرفة الجنين ونوعه حين يكُون ذ بطن أمه وقد نخلق ، باستعمال الاشعة أو بالامارات ، فليست من باب علم الغيب ذاتيا ، ولذلك لا يستطيعون الاخبار به قبل حدوثه ولا قبل نخلقه ذ بطن أمه ، أما الله تعالى فيعلم أزلا ماذا سيكون ، لانه مدبر وخالقه ، وهذا العلم الذاتي هو الذي اختص الله به ، أما النعرف بالامارات أو بالاشعة لجنين نخلق مهو نعرف لامر موجود ، باسباب من صنع الله وتمكينه ، وبهذا علم وجه استثنار الله تعالى بعلم نزول الغيث وعلم ما ذ الارحام .

((جرأة الدكتور رشاد على الباطل))

● وانك لتجد الدكتور رشاد متناقضا مع نفسه ومع الحق وجريئا على الباطل اذ يقول : (وبدل النعبير القرآني على أن الله سبحانه قد جعل الكشف عن موعد نهاية العالم صعبا بل مستحيلا على أجيال ما قبل الكمبيوتر ، الى أن بحين الموعد المحدد الذي بشاء الله سبحانه أن يكتشف فيه عن موعد نهاية العالم ، وقد تضافرت مجموعة كبرة من البراهين للكشف عن نهاية العالم ، بحث لا يبقى اى شك أو ريبة ذ قلب أي انسان) .

هذا كلامه ● وهو يعترف فيه بان الله قد جعل الكشف عن موعد نهاية العالم مستحيلا . وبنقض اعترافه هذا بالكذب على الله وعلى القرآن اذ يقول : ان هذه الاستحالة موقوفة بما قبل أجيال الكمبيوتر ، فاين نجد هذا التوقيت ذ كتاب الله أو ذ سنة رسوله ، ان الله يقول « يسألونك عن

عنده علم الساعة .. » الآية .

وقال ابن عباس : هذه لا يعلمها الا الله تعالى ، ولا يعلمها ملك مقرب ولا نبي مرسل ، ومن ادعى أنه يعلم شيئا من هذه فقد كفر بالقرآن لانه خالفه .

● ثم انا نسأل الدكتور رشاد : هل من الحكمة أن يعلم الله أحدا من الناس متى يخرب العالم وبجرى وقف الحساب ، وهل سياسة نكون العليا على البشر أن يعرضوها ، هذا خطأ ذ التفكير ، ونزعة غير مستقيمة ذ معرفة أهم سر من أسرار النكون لا يصح أن يعرفه سوى مدبنه جل وعلا .

((متى يكون نزول الغيث من الغيبيات))

● يقول الدكتور رشاد : انه أمكن معرفة مكان وموعد نزول الغيث ، ونحن نقول : ان الغيث يكون غيبا قبل أن يوجد أو نظهر أماراته ، وأما ما يحدث من توقعات خبراء الارصاد من نزول المطر ، فذلك لا يكون منهم الا بعد رصد الرياح وحركة السحب نحو انجاهات شتاها

بعلمه .

ثالثا : أن السنة بينت أن هذه الخمسة هي مفاتيح الغيب ولا يعلمها الا هو سبحانه ، فقد جاء ذ شأن الساعة أن جبريل سأل رسول الله — صلى الله عليه وسلم — قائلا : يا رسول الله متى الساعة ؟ قال : ما المسئول عنها باعلم من السائل ، ولكن سأحدثك عن أماراتها : اذا ولدت الامة ربنها مذاك من أشراطها ، واذا كان الحفاة العراة رؤوس الناس ، مذاك من أشراطها ، ذ خمس لا يعلمهن الا الله « ان الله عنده علم الساعة وينزل الغيث .. » الآية ، رواه البخاري بسنده ذ تفسير سورة لقمان كما رواه أصحاب السنن .

● فها هو ذا رسول الله — صلى الله عليه وسلم— يقول بصراحة : أنه لا يعلم الساعة لا هو ولا من سأله عنها ، وهو جبريل عليه السلام ، وانها ذ جمله خمس لا يعلمها الا الله ولا الآية .

● وقال ابن مسعود : كل ني، أوسى نبيئم صلى الله عليه وسلم ، غير خمس « ان الله

دراسة

الأرقام
في القرآن الكريم

دعانا الله تبارك وتعالى إلى تعلم الأعداد والحسابات الرياضية حتى نستطيع تنظيم حياتنا بدقة وانضباط . فقال تعالى : لتعلموا عدد السنين والحساب . وأورد القرآن الكريم كثيراً من الأعداد الصحيحة والكسرية

دراسة أجراها
د. عبد الحميد محمد ندا
أستاذ الثقافة الإسلامية - جدة

تحديد نوع الجنين لا يعني معرفة ما فى الأرحام

الرقم ١٩ وسر القرآن

حلقة فى السلسلة الطويلة للتآمر على الإسلام

الدكتور التهامى الوكيلى :

الهنود والفراعنة سبقوا البهائيين فى اللعب بالأرقام

د. التهامى الوكيلى يدعو المسلمين الاطلاع على تلك الحسابات التى قيل إن بها يتم معرفة موعد الساعة

هذا هو الشكل الالحادى

الاتفاق مع السحرة والدجالين

In the 9 October 1988 issue of Arabic newspaper Houston Times, the furious Dr. Assad Busool of American Islamic College, Chicago, screams at Rashad: "O Rashad Khalifa, may God curse the liars among us. In your response you have no shame. O Rashad Khalifa: you are the only person who is bragging about his ignorance" © NINETEEN: God's Signature in Nature and Scripture. www.19.org

لعن الله الكاذب فينا يا رشاد خليفة ••وردودك لا حياء فيها ولا خجل

يا رشاد خليفـــة : انت الشخص الوحيد الذي يفخـــر بجهلـــــه

لقد ضحكت اليوم كما لم أضحك من مدة طويلة عندما قرأت في العدد الأخير من "هيوستن تايمز" رد رشاد خليفة على مقالي الذي فندت فيه ادعاءاته الباطلة بأنه "رسول الله" والعياذ بالله .هذا المقال الذي نشرته "هيوستن تايمز" في عددين سابقين.

أمّا لماذا ضحكت ؟ لأنني وجدت في ردّه ما توقعته منه بالضبط.فأنا أعرف رشاد خليفة معرفة جيدة دون أن أقابله بالمرة .عرفته من كتاباته وردوده البذيئة على كل الذين فندوا ادعاءه الباطل بالرسالة من علماء المسلمين في الشرق والغرب. كذلك ضحكت لما أبداه رشاد خليفة في ردّه علي من الضعف والخور وقلة الحيلة لأنه لم يستطع أن ينقض علميا ولو كلمة واحدة مما كتبته .وأين ردود رشاد خليفة الهزيلة على خصومه من ردود خاتم الأنبياء والمرسلين سيدنا محمد صلى الله عليه وسلم البليغة المفحمة والتي قهرت خصومه الى الأبد ؟ شتان ما بين الثرى والثريا .

ان رشاد خليفة يدعي في رده علي :"بأنه يؤمن بالقرآن وأن القرآن هو خاتم الرسالات جاء به محمد خاتم النبيين."

أي قرآن يا رشاد خليفة ؟ القرآن الذي تدعي أنّ فيه آيتين زائدتين في آخر (سورة التوبة ٩) زادهما الخليفة الراشد ذو النورين عثمان بن عفان رضي الله عنه وأرضاه كما كتبت في عدد شهر آذار/مارس ١٩٨٥ وعدد شهر أيار/مايو ١٩٨٧ من نشرتك (Muslim Perspective) (أنظر الصفحات المرفقة)

انّ الانسان يا رشاد خليفة يتهم بالكذب عندما يدّعي ما لا يستطيع اثباته .أمّا اذا اثبت ما يقول بالدليل الحسي والعلمي الملموس فمن الفجور أن يقال عنه انه كاذب.وأنا لم أدّع في مقالي أي شيء بدون دليل حسي وعلمي ملموس .فمقالتي مملوءة بالاقتباسات من كتاباتك وردي على تلك الاقتباسات موثق توثيقا علميا لم تستطع الرد عليه ولو بكلمة علمية واحدة .فكل ما كتبته في ردك علي هو بذاءات لا داعي ولا مبرر لها.على أية حال اني اعتبر كل كلمة بذيئة وجهتها الي في ردك علي وسام شرف أعلقه على صدري حتى ألقى الحق عزّ وجل "يوم لا ينفع مال ولا بنون الا من أتى الله بقلب سليم" .لأنني كتبت ما كتبته دفاعا عن كتابه ودينه .

أمّا علمك بالعربية أو عدم علمك بها .فهو لا يعنيني بكثير ولا قليل.ولا يمكنك بأيّ حال من الأحوال أن تفرض جهلك على الناس . فأنت الشخص الوحيد الذي يفخر بجهله ويحاول أن يفرضه على العلماء ببذاءاته وطول لسانه .انّ بذاءة اللسان يا رشاد لا تنفي حقّا ولا تثبت باطلا. وهي كذلك ليست من أخلاق الأنبياء والرسل وقد وصف الله سبحانه وتعالى رسوله الكريم محمّد صلى الله عليه وسلم بقوله :"وانك لعلى خلق عظيم" . ولما سئلت عائشة أم المؤمنين رضي الله تعالى عنها عن خلق سيدنا محمّد صلى الله عليه وسلم أجابت :"كان خلقه القرآن". كذلك وصف في كتب السيرة :"ما كان بذيئا ولا فحّاشا ولا متفحّشا ولا صخّابا في الأسواق".

شيكاغو في ١٥/٩/١٩٨٨

الأخ العزيز أسامة فوزي حفظه الله

اشكرك جزيل الشكر على نشرك ردّي على رشاد خليفة في جريدتكم "هيوستن تايمز" بالأمس وعلمي العدد الأخير من "هيوستن تايمز" وقرأت رد رشاد خليفة المضحك على مقالتي وتحدوني عرفت في هذه الصحافة ردّا على ردّه أرجو أن تنشروه بأكمله في عدد قادم. ولكم الشكر سلفا.

مع أطيب التمنيات لكم بالنجاح

أخوكم

الدكتور أسعد بصول

Dr. Assad J. Busool

الكلية الأمريكية الإسلامية

American Islamic College

640 W. Irving Park Road, Chicago, Illinois 60613 U.S.A.

MUSLIM PERSPECTIVE

Published Monthly by Masjid Tucson

March 1985 — Jumada II 1405

WHO ARE WE?

★BULLETIN★ ★ ★BULLETIN★ ★ ★BULLETIN★

THE COMPUTER EXPOSES AN HISTORICAL CRIME

TAMPERING WITH THE WORD OF GOD

TWO FALSE VERSES UNVEILED IN QUR'AN

AN INVITATION TO ALL MUSLIMS TO EXAMINE THE EVIDENCE BEFORE REMOVING THE FALSEHOOD

"Surely, we have sent down this message, and surely, we will preserve it." (15:9)

In the 9 October 1988 issue of Arabic newspaper Houston Times, the furious Dr. Assad Busool of American Islamic College, Chicago, screams at Rashad: "O Rashad Khalifa, may God curse the liars among us. In your response you have no shame. O Rashad Khalifa: you are the only person who is bragging about his ignorance". This is the continuation of the open letter. © NINETEEN: God's Signature in Nature and Scripture. www.19.org

(. 28) ISSN 0890-6831

MUSLIM PERSPECTIVE

Published Monthly by MASJID TUCSON

May 1987 — Ramadan 1407

Editor: Rashad Khalifa, Ph.D.

THE RESTORATION OF AN IMPORTANT ISLAMIC TRUTH

IMAM ALI & IMAM HUSSEIN DID NOT FIGHT FOR POWER

They Were Martyred Trying To Protect Qur'an

صور عن منشورات رشاد خليفة زودنا بها الدكتور بصول

كذلك قال تعالى في كتابه الكريم :"قل هل يستوي الذين يعلمون والذين لا يعلمون".

أمّا فيما يتعلق بكلمة "محمّد" لو قطعناها حرفا حرفا حسب أصول اللغة العربية لظهرت هكذا : "مححمد" لانّ الشدّة في اللغة العربية اذا كتبت فوق أي حرف فهي تعني انّ الحرف مضعّف أي أنّه مكرّر.وهذه بديهية يعرفها من له أدنى المام باللغة العربية وقواعدها. ولو أننا اتبعنا جهلك بالعربية وقواعدها وقسنا عليه لاضطررنا أن نقلب اللغة رأسا على عقب .

خذ مثلا : لو وضعنا خمس قطع نقدية متساوية في القيمة والحجم فوق بعضها وشددناها بشدّة وطلبنا منك ان تنظر اليها وتعدّها .فانك والحالة هذه ستراها وتعدّها واحدة فقط.

ثم اذا رجعت الى أوزان الأفعال في العربية لوجدت وزن (فَعَل) ووزن (فَعَّل) فهل هما نفس الشيء يا رشاد ؟. كذلك كلمة (صَلَى) و (صَلَّى) والأمثلة على ذلك أكثر من أن تحصى . زيادة على ذلك فانك في كل نشراتك بالانكليزية تكتب اسم "محمّد" كالتالي "Muhammad" فما الذي جعلك تكتب حرف الـ "m" مرتين في وسط الاسم لولا انّه مضعّف بالعربية؟ ولكنك كما يقول المثل العربي القديم :"عنزة ولو طارت".فارجع عن غيّك وضلالك فالرجوع عن الخطأ فضيلة يا رشاد.

انك تتباكى في ردّك علي وتقول:"ما هي المصلحة التي يخدمها الاستاذ والتي دفعته الى هذه الأكاذيب البائسة الواضحة ؟؟؟" علامة سؤال واحدة تكفي يا رشاد.

أوّلا يا رشاد انا لم ألجأ الى الأكاذيب في ردّي عليك وقد علّقت على هذا في بدء ردي عليك فلا حاجة للتكرار.

ثانيا .ليس وراء ما كتبته يا رشاد خليفة سوى مصلحة الاسلام والمسلمين .

فانا لم أحذف من الأذان عبارة "وأشهد أنّ محمدا رسول الله" كما فعلت أنت.

وأنا لم أطالب المسلمين بطرح السنة النبوية المطهرة والحديث الشريف جملة وتفصيلا كما فعلت أنت.

وأنا لم أسمح لزوجتي أو أية امرأة أخرى أن تؤمّ الرجال في الصلاة كما فعلت أنت مخالفا لكل سنّة وشريعة اسلامية .

فهل أفعالك هذه أفعال شخص يؤمن بالقرآن والاسلام ؟ انك آخر من يتباكى على مصلحة الاسلام. ادعاءاتك هذه الجوفاء ما هي الا كلمة حق يراد بها باطل يا رشاد.

ثم تدعي في ردّك دون حياء أو خجل :"

لقد اكتشف الاستاذ بصول أن القرآن الكريم يخبرنا فى سورة ٣ آل عمران ، الآية ٨١ أنه بعد أن يبعث الله جميع الأنبياء ، ويختمهم بخاتم النبيين محمد ، فانه سوف يرسل رسولا مؤكدا لرسالات جميع الأنبياء وليصحح جميع الانحرافات التى حدثت، ويعلمنا القرآن الكريم فى الآية ٧ من سورة الاحزاب أن هذا الرسول المؤكد ليس محمد ، وانما يأتي بعد محمد •• ولقد شاء المولى عز وجل أن يمد العالم بالبراهين القرآنية التى لاتقبل الشك أو الجدال على أن رشاد خليفة هو هذا الرسول المؤكد ••

هذا كلامك انت والذي نشرته في نشرتك Muslim Perspictive عدد أيار/مايو ١٩٨٨ أليس من العار عليك أن تنسب أقوالك الى الآخرين ؟ هذا الأسلوب الرخيص في الكذب معروف عنك عند القاصي والداني . مرة أخرى لعن الله الكاذب فينا يا رشاد خليفة .

انني اتحدّاك يا "مسيلمة" ان تثبت ادعاءك بالبرهان الملموس .فلا عجب فمن يفتري على الله الكذب فلا بد وأن يكذب على عبيد الله ايضا .

على أية حال يا "خليفة مسيلمة" لقد كتبت نقضا لادعاءاتك الجوفاء باللغة الانكليزية يبلغ ٤٥ صفحة وحال الانتهاء من طباعته ستملك نسخة منه وحاول أن تفنده علميا ان استطعته أرجو من القراء الكرام الاتصال بي على العنوان التالي ان احبّوا ان يحصلوا على نسخة من ردي الشامل على ادعاءات رشاد خليفة الجوفاء : Dr. Assad Busool, American Islamic College, 640 W. Irving Park Rd., Chicago, Ill. 60613

Rabithah Menggugat Rashad Khalifah

Komputer mengutik angka 19 "mukjizat Quran" buatan imam Masjid Tucson, AS. "Haram salat makmum di belakangnya," seru Rabithah Alam Islami di Mekah.

RASHAD Khalifah namanya. Sarjana pertanian asal Mesir ini juga "bunyi" di Indonesia. Di kalangan Islam 'terpelajar, ia tidak asing. Kini, sebuah organisasi ulama terkemuka di dunia, yang berpusat di Mekah, Rabithah Alam Islami (Liga Islam Sedunia) "mengafirkan" dia. Siapa yang tidak terhenyak?

Cuma, imam salat di Masjid Tucson, Arizona, itu tidak peduli. Ia masih menganggap dirinya pemuka Islam di AS. Padahal, sejak setahun lalu ia sudah disebut murtad. Dan baru-baru ini, kedua kalinya, Sekjen Rabithah Dr. Abdullah Umar Nasif mengeluarkan beleid pengafiran untuk Rashad. Dan dalam *Akhbar al-'Alam Seduniaj* diumumkan: "Ia mencemarkan akidah Islam suci".

Nasif juga merujuk keputusan Majelis Fikih Islam Rabithah yang bersidang di Mekah, 19-26 Februari 1989 — khusus "mengadili" Rashad. Kata majelis, "Rashad mengingkari sebagian ayat Quran, inkar Sunnah, menyamakan salat kaum muslim dengan sembahyangnya kaum musyrik, dan menobatkan diri menjadi nabi baru".

Kesepakatan (*ijma'*) ulama, "keempat pengakuan itu mengarah murtad, sehingga peserta majelis menetapkan Rashad kafir, dan keluar dari Islam". Kepalsuan Rashad lalu dibeber, supaya umat mengucilkannya. Tapi tertuduh bandel dan tetap imam di Masjid Tucson. Padahal, pengkafiran kedua yang keluar di koran tadi ada pula tambahan: "haram salat makmum di belakangnya".

Rashad memamerkan penelitiannya tentang Quran mulai 1976 di London. Komputer, katanya, "Membuktikan mushaf Quran Usmani asli." Malah, ia menguak angka 19 sebagai "mukjizat Quran". Bilangan prima dalam matematika itu mendasari hitungan huruf, kalimat, ayat, dan surat Quran. Selain tak habis dibagi (kecuali dengan sendirinya), bilangan itu terdiri angka 1 terkecil serta 9 terbesar.

Dan sedikitnya, menurut Rashad, ada 31 bukti yang menjelaskan mukjizat Quran dalam angka 19. Misalnya, kalimat *Bismi Allah al-Rahman al-Rahim* tersusun dari 19 huruf. Dalam kalimat itu ada empat kata. Juga, setiap kata disebut di Quran berkelipatan ulang 19. Kata *ismi* (19 × 1), Allah (19 × 142), al-Rahman (19 × 3), dan al-Rahim diulang 114 kali atau 19 × 6. "Ini bukan kebetulan," kata Rashad. Dan kalimat *basmalah*, yang mengawali surat-surat Quran, juga disebut 114 kali. Lha, bukankah ada satu surat (nomor 9, al-Tawbah) yang tidak dibuka dengan *bas-*

malah? Allah Sang Penghitung ternyata memasangnya di tempat lain, di tengah surat 27 (al-Naml), ayat nomor 30. "Saksikanlah bagaimana Allah menyelesaikannya, seperti ahli matematik merampungkan soal adirumit," ujarnya. Menurut dia, teori-19 itu ditarik dari ayat 30 surat al-Muddatstsir: *Yang atasnya ada 19.*

Tentu, ulama menentang Rashad. Dr. Abdurrahman bint al-Syathi', ahli tafsir

TEORI 19 RASHAD KHALIFAH DAN GUGATANNYA

Mesir, menuduh Rashad menyerap teori-19 itu dari Yahudi. Maulana Abdul Quddus Hashimi dari Pakistan mengingatkan tentang pemujaan angka 19 dalam sekte Syiah Qaramithah. Malah sempalan Syiah, yaitu Kaum Bahaiyah, mengagungkan angka 19 sebagai angka pusat alam semesta. Dan rupanya pendiri Bahaiyah, Ali Muhammad Bab, lahir pada 1819 (1 + 8 + 1 + 9 = 19).

Sarjana Arab terkemuka, Syeikh Abdullah ibn Abdul Aziz ibn Baz, menulis fatwa mengenai klaim bidaah Rashad. Dinilainya ia sesat. Sejak itu, Rashad menanggalkan kebangsaan Mesir. Ia jadi penduduk Amerika. Dibantu istrinya, ia menyebar gratis terbitan bulanannya dari Tucson ke pusat-pusat Islam di AS dan Kanada. Ia giat membina pengikut baru. Wanita bebas pilih pakaian dan membolehkan salat jamaah di

samping lelaki.

Gawat? Temuan Rashad tidak melulu ditolak. Misalnya, Fahmi Basya dari Fakultas MIPA Universitas Indonesia, menyebarkan ide "19"- dalam bukunya *One Million Phenomena* (kini edisi 1989). Ahmad Deedat, debator Durban di Afrika Selatan, menyebar paham Rashad ke pelosok dunia lewat ceramah dan buku *Al-Quran: The Ultimate Miracle* (sudah diterjemahkan dalam bahasa Indonesia, 1984). Deedat cerai dengan Rashad yang meramal Hari Kiamat itu pecah 1709 tahun setelah wahyu Quran. Ini ditafsir dari ayat 87 surat al-Hijr.

Abu Ameenah Bilal Philip, dosen di al-Manara, Riyadh, Arab Saudi, bersama mahasiswanya pada 1987 malah menelitinya. Ia menemukan banyak salah tafsir pada Rashad, karena tak punya program baku penghitungan huruf atau kata dalam Quran. Kata *Qawm*, misalnya, ia ratakan artinya kaum Nabi Luth, sesuai kelipatan 19. Padahal, di ayat lain menunjuk arti baru. Dan bagi Rashad, 19 itu kode numerik Quran. Artinya: *Wahid*, Allah Esa. "Ini dasar sistem numerologi. Hukum Islam menolaknya," kata Abu Ameenah. Menurut Ibn Abbas, numerologi adalah cabang sihir.

Pada 1970-an, numerologi asal ajaran bangsa Babilonia dan Yunani kuno itu dikembangkan oleh Isa Abdullah, pendiri sekte Ansaru Allah di Brooklyn, New York. Dengan teori-19 juga, Louis Farrakhan mengganti nabi palsu Elijah Muhammad mengembangkan sekte "Negara Islam". Rabithah menganggap Rashad mengikuti jejak mereka.

Rashad juga "sengaja" mengingkari Quran dengan menghitung jumlah kata *al-Rahim* di Quran alias 19 × 6. Seharusnya 115. Dengan demikian, ia menyangkal kata *Rahim* di ayat terakhir surat al-Tawbah. Dan alasannya: Zaid ibn Tsabit, pengumpul Quran suruhan Abu Bakar, tidak menemukan naskah ayat itu di tangan sahabat lain. Adanya cuma dalam hafalan.

Padahal, menurut Quraisy Shihab, dosen tafsir IAIN Jakarta, usaha pencarian naskah tersebut tidak pernah terhenti, sampai belakangan ditemukan ada pada seorang sahabat, Abu Khuzaimah al-Anshari. Jelas, Rashad memang sengaja menyangkal Quran.

"Ini fatal. Ulama lampau pun sepakat mengafirkan orang yang mengingkari sebagian Quran," kata Quraisy. Ketua Majelis Ulama Indonesia itu sekata dengan keputusan Rabithah.

Ahmadie Thaha

591

Zaman

200 TL.
3 Şubat 1988 ÇARŞAMBA
Hicri CAHIR 15 1408
SAYI: 845B

● Din bilgini Sadrettin Yüksel, İslâm ile ilgili bozuk fikirlere, yanlış yorumlara açıklık getirdi

"Sahabeye değil, zındık misyonerlere uyuyorlar"

Yorum
Sadrettin Yüksel'i tebrik ediyoruz

DEVAMI 11. SAYFADA

Rajiv Gandi yönetimi baskı yaptıkça, muhalefet lideri "daha fazlasını" istiyor

Müslümanlara Hindu zulmü

...al vahşetine BD desteği

oskoca ABD yahudilerin sömürgesi...

Önce İslam'ı seçtiler

Sahabeye değil, zındık misyonerlere uyuyorlar

• BAŞTARAFI 1. SAYFADA •

cihdir. Hal böyle olunca
adir:
cumünist Çin'deki uygu-
övmekte midir?
: bile uygulanan müsa-
huriyeti'ni yermekte mi-

da bekleme hakkına sa-
n okuyucunuz..

Hasan ERDEM

Isi ve atelst bir düzeni ör-
ılamaz. Ancak Mao'dan
la Şarki Türkistan'da bir
ju hava içinde Türkistan-
refes almışlardır. Bir de,
vese edilmek gerekirse, bi-
tim:lin eski yazı yasağın-
sırtılü öğrencileri okula-
srci bir hâdisedir. Türkî-
nî'yoruz: bozuk düzeni ye-
mi_anmızia.

kapıyı tamamen kapatmıştır.
Tartışırken de o tezi savunuyor.
İstersenîz "İlginç Sorular-2" pa-
çavrasından 156'ncı sahifesini ve
onu takip eden sahifelere dikkat-
le bakın, okuyun. Eminim ki bu
gerçeği çok bariz bir şekilde ora-
larda müşahede edeceksiniz.
Böyle bir anlayış İslâm peygam-
berine karşı korkunç bir cinayet-
tir. Sankî Allah karafından Hz.
Peygambere Kur'an'ın manala-
rını beyat etmek yetkisi verilmemiştir! Bu ne biçim ilim ve bu ne
biçim iman! Oysa ki o yetki ve
selahiyet Cenab-ı Hak tarafından
son derece açık bir biçimde Nahl
Süresi'nin 44. ayeti ile Hz. Peygambere verilmiştir.
Ayet meâlen şöyledir:
"Sana zikri (Kur'anı) indirdik

ki insanlara kendine indirileni
açıklayasın. Ta ki düşünüp ögüt
alsınlar."

Demek ki, Hz. Peygamber
hem Kur'anın lafızlarını iletmek-
le görevlidir, hem de beyan ve
açıklamaya muhtaç yerleri de beyan etmekle. Evet, tebliğ ayrı,
tebyin de ayrıdır.

Mesela, Kur'an-ı Kerim namaz kılmayı, zekat vermeyi,
hacca gitmeyi emretmiştir. Fakat
namazın kaç rekat olduğunu, verilen zekatın miktarını ve haccın
ibadetlerini beyan etmemiştir.
Yani bu hususdaki ayetler müc-
meldir. Allah'ın resûlü ameli ve
sözlü sünnetleri ile bu gibi ayetleri tefsir ve beyanda bulunmuştur. Mesela Cenab-ı Hak mücmel
olarak alışverişi helal, faizi haram kılmıştır. Bu kadarı ayetle
sabittir. Fakat hangi alışverişi sahih ve hangi alışverişi fasit ve haram, faizin çeşitleri nelerdir? İş-
te bütün bunları ancak efendimi-
zin sünneti beyan buyurmuştur.

Evet, Hz. Peygamberin hadis-
lerine bu derecede önem ve
ehemmiyet veren sahabe-i kira-
mın emek almaya da Reşad Halife gibi zındık misyonerlerin pe-
şinde koşanlara bin defa yazık-
lar olsun!. Onlarla beraber haşr
olacaklardır haberleri olsun.
Edip'in bir-iki saçmasına son ver-
timası etmeden yazma son ver-
meyeceğin.

İlginç Sorular 2 adlı paçavra-
sının 72. ve 73. sayfalarında ne
herzeler vermiştir:

Hz. Peygamberin sabit ve sahih olan sözlerine iman edip pe-
nan bütün islâm müfessirlerine
ve Bediüzzamana karşı çıkıyor,
dil uzatıyor. Hatta orada sahabe
müfessirlere değil açıkça Hz.
Peygambere bile karşı çıkıyor.
İslâma hiç inanmayan kişilere
karşı büyük bir değişük duygu-
su içinde bulunan Edip Yüksel
mezkür kitabının 73. sayfasında
Lokman suresinin sonundaki
ayetten bahsederken "Gayb ben
değil, bildir" diye yazıyor. Bu
suretle açıkça Peygamberin sözünü reddetmiş oluyor: Gaybı beş-
ten ikiye indiriyor!

Demek cеninin durumu da Allah'ın ilmine bas olan o beş gayb
maddesinden birisidir. Edip bu
saçmalarsa saçmalasın bu böyledir değişmez.

Not: (1) okumamış diyorum,
çünkü İmam-Hatip Okulunda
iken Arapça olarak sadece "El
Kuraatü'l-Arabiyye" adlı küçük
bir kitabı okumuştur. Bundan
başka hiç bir şey okumamış.
lâmî kaynaklardan kopma bir
varsa Türkçe olarak yazılmış kitap, dergi ve ansiklopedilerden
alınmadır. Asıl İslâmî kaynaklardan tamamen habersizdir.
Onun için haklı olarak
"okumamış" diyorum.

(2) Münasebet almışken şunu
da ilmas etmek yerinde olur:
Amerika'da yaşıyan misyoner
Reşad Halife, İngilizce olarak ba-
zim Edip'i yazdığı bir mektupta şöyle yazıyordu: "Eti'ur-
Resüle'deki 'Resûl' deki mesaj masumdır. Yani Kur'an-
dır, Muhammed değildir. Yani
Muhammed'e değil Kur'an'a il-

Sadrettin Yüksel'i tebrik ediyoruz

• BAŞTARAFI 1. SAYFADA •

hidliğî yayarak gençlerimiz arasında taraftar toplamağa çalışmaktadırlar. Amerika'-
da yuvalanmış bir sapık olan Reşad Halife
adlı adam da, bu bozuk akımlardan en bet-
likesinin başındadır. Bu akımların, bu adam-
ların ortaya attıkları bozuk fikirler müsli-
manlar arasında yayıldıkça, ehl-i İslâm'ın
birlik ve beraberliği sarsılmakta; nifak, şi-
kak, tefrika, fitne, fesat, düşmanlık yangın-

ları çıkmaktadır. Ülkemizdeki bütün din bil-
ginlerinin ve ümmet liderlerinin ehlisünnet
prensiplerini korumak, sapık akımlara karşı bilhassa gençleri uyarmak için bir irşad
seferberliğine girişmelerinin zamanı artık
gelmiş ve hatta geçmektedir. Muhterem Sadreddin Yüksel Hoca'yı, kaleme aldığı ten-
kid yazısından dolayı tebrik ediyoruz.

Zaman

"Halkımız kültür

Recep ERDOĞAN

Refah Partisi Genel Başkan Yardımcısı Bahri Zengin Zaman'a
yaptığı açıklamada "Hıristiyanlaşan Türkler" ile ilgili olarak "Birkaç tane insanın Hıristiyan inancını
kabullenmiş olması halkımızın
kültür emperyalizmine karşı gösterdiği direnci ortadan kaldırmaz"
dedi. Zengin'e yönelttiğimiz sorular ve aldığımız cevaplar şöyle:

ZAMAN - Hıristiyanlaşan
Türkler hakkında ne düşünüyor-
sunuz?

CEVAP - Tabii bir sonuç. Bir gibi kaide yıllardan beri bazı kültürü
eğitim kurumlarında işlenmekte-
dir. 150-200 yıllık süredir bu durum devam ediyor. Halkımızın bu

emperyalist güce direncini gösteriyor.

Lozan anlaşması ve diğer
uluslararası anlaşmalarda ülkemizde Hıristiyan konularının işlenme-
sinde çeşitli kurallar uygulanıyor.
Halkımız bundan habersiz. Bu
maddede kişisel ve medenî hukuk
alanlarında azınlıkların dini inanç
ve düşüncelerine aykırı yasalar çı-
karılamaz deniliyor. Bu alanda ya-
pılacak bir düzenleme azınlıkların
inançlarına uymaktır. Yıllardan beri çeşitli propagandalar sο-
nucu birkaç tane insanın Hıristiyan
inancını kabullenmiş olması başlangıçta da söylediğim gibi, halkımızın içen içe büyük direncini et-
kilemez..."

Öğretmenlere dinsizlik

• BAŞTARAFI 1. SAYFADA •

"12 Eylül'den sonra TÖB-
DER gibi ileri örgütler kapatıldı.
TÖB-DER kapatılmasaydı Yüksek İslâm Enstitüsü ve İlahiyat
mezunları bütün okullara tayin
edilebilir miydi? Okul müdürle-

ZAMAN - TBMM'deki sürtüş-
me olaylarını nasıl değerlendiriyorsunuz?

CEVAP - Meriste şimdiye kadar süren tartışmalar bundan sonra da sürecek. Bir tek düzenlik
meclise görülüyordu. Meclise al-
mamaya çalışıyorum. Meclise al-
lerde daha da renklendirilecek.
hınların Türkiye'nin meseleleri ile
yakından uzaktan ilişkileri yok. İn-
san ve ülke olarak geleceğimiz
ipotekli, hakkı, zulüm ve sömürü
devam ediyor. İmrime hukku en sabil hak nihassına rağmen yok, bu
temel meseleleri ele alarda yok,
saçikli kırfi akan mehrim ürünlerine
görünürde bir tek işeği temizliği
bir devşirme görüyorum. Sorun-
ların kaynağına inen yok.

Türkiye'nin Bizanslaştırılması
projeleri uygulama safhasında ve
bunlar sinsi sinsi bu projeler yü-
rütüyor. Bütün bunlar kamuoyunun
gündeminden uzak tutuluyor. Oysa Türkiye'nin Avrupa Topluluğu
projesinin Bizans oyununa ve yoksul-
luğu tartışmalı, bir avuç hatılın

Öğretmenler

Lozan anlaşması...

rail vahşetine ABD desteği

TARAFI 1. SAYFADA •

LEŞMİŞ MİLLETLER—
srail işgali altındaki toprak-
ısında BM Güvenlik Kon-
arından hazırlanan karar
anı veto ettil. Tasarıya Gü-
Konseyi'nin ABD dışındaki
ısi ise lehte oy kullandı. An-
ısimi üyelerden olan ABD'.
tosu, tasarının esasın dipu-
ı engelledil
D'nin BM Temsilcisi Büyük-
erbert Okun, Ortadoğu ko-
da BM gözetiminde barış gö-
leri düzenlenmesini öngören
tarasınınin, ABD'nin diplo-
girişimine müdahale niteli-
idiğini söyledi.
un, "Tasarı, tu anda dip-
tik kanallardan ele alınabi-
bir konuya Güvenlik Kon-
nin dahil edilmesi yönünde
abadır" dedi.
ail ve ABD, doğrudan görüş-
: yerine, BM gözetiminde bir
toplantısın düzenlenmesi fik-
karşı çıkıyorlar.
ail'in BM Temsilcisi Büyü-
Johanan Bein de Konsey'-
pluğu konuşmada, ülkesin ta
a ABD vetosundan memnun-
uyduğunu ve ABD'nin Ürdün
tur'ın doğrudan görüşmeler-
dunmasını sağlamasını ümit
ni belirtti.
ASARIDA NE VARDI?
rar tasarısı, İsrail'i işgal al-

tında tuttuğu topraklara insan hak-
larını ihlal etmekle suçluyor ve bu
ihlallere bir son verilmesi, ayrıca
İsrail'in Filistinlilere 4. Cenevre
Sözleşmesi'nde yer alan hakları
vermesi çağrısında bulunuyor.

İran Yanlısı Şîî Müslüman Is-
lâmî Direniş Cephesi Örgütü, İs-
rail'in Batı Şeria ve Gazze Şeri-
di'nde gösterilen düzenleyen Filistinlilere karşı uyguladığı şiddetin
yöntemine devam etmesi halinde
elindeki İsrail'li rehineyi öldürme
tehdidinde bulundu

Örgüt tarafından Batı Beyrut'ta-
ki Batılı bir haber ajansına gönde-
rilen mektupta. "siyonistler Filis-
tin'deki vahşinin insan edip yeni-
ıle vahşi önlemleri durdurmadı-
ğı takdirde, elimizdeki tutuklu
İsrailli'nin kaderinin tehlikeli
bölgeye göreceğini ilan ediyoruz"
ifadesini kullandı.

RABİN'İN SÖZLERİ

İsrail Savunma Bakanı İzak Ra-
bin, işgal altındaki topraklardaki
şiddet olaylarına neden olan gös-
tericileri engellemek için ordunun
kuvvet kullanmaya devam edece-
ğini söyledi.

İsrail radyosunda konuşan Ra-
bin, "Batı Şeria ve Gazze'de şid-
deti önlemek amacıyla başlattı-
ğımız kuvvet kullanma politika-
sını aynen sürdüreceğiz" dedi.

Tahtakale'de korkulu

• BAŞTARAFI 1. SAYFADA •

ABD Doları başta olmak üzere, yabancı para birimlerinin.
ıhtakale olarak bilinen İstanbul serbest döviz piyasasındaki de-
er kayıpları sürüyor.
A. A muhabirinin gözlemlerine göre, yabancı paraların Tah-
kale'deki önceki günkü değer kaybı, dünkü işlemleri de etki-
adı. Piyasada dün, alandan çok satan vardı. Tasarruf sahipleri
ie döviz satıcılarının "döviz elden çıkartma" gayretleri, ön-
eki gün olduğu gibi dün de Türk Lirası'nı
Tahtakale piyasasında alım işlemlerinin küçük, satışların ise
büyük miktarlarda olduğu dikkat çekiyor. Piyasa çevreleri, hü-
kümetin yeni ekonomik tedbirler paketi açıklamasını
"muhtemel" bulduklarını, "beklenen" paketin açıklanması ha-
inde de, döviz fiyatlarını rekor düzeylerde düşeceğini
öylüyorlar.

YAYA TRAFİĞİ DE AKSADI

A. A muhabirinin sorularını cevaplandıran Tahtakale piyasa-
ı olarak bilinen çevrenin güvenliğinden sorumlu çarşı karakolu
u yetkilileri, ara sokaklarda zaman zaman trafiğin yaratıcak
lüzeyde kalabalık oluştuğunu belirtiyorlar.
Ayaklı borsada hareketin giderek arttığını, bunun da sokak-
arın yaya trafiğini engellediğine işaret eden polis yetkilileri, za-
nun zaman yapılan müdahalenin, piyasayla ilgili olmadığını.
"Yaya trafiğinin açılmaya çalışıldığını" kaydettiler. (A. A)

Önce İslâm'ı

• BAŞTARAFI 1. SAYFADA •

Eylül'den sonra anarşinin kaynağı
p olarak gösterildiğine dikkat çekerek öğretmenlerin önündeki ör-
gütsüzlük engelinin kaldırılması
gerektiğini söyledi:

İslâm ve müslümanlara karşı
kin koyan İsmail Hakkı Bayram
da 12 Mart'ın kararları günlerinde
örgütlenmenin onurlu (?) mücadelesini TÖB-DER'e borçlu olduk-
larını ifade etti. TÖB-DER'in mi-
ting, seminer ve birçok yayınıyla
onur duyacaklarını belirtti.

Kuruluşundan, kapanışına kadar
mektupları okuyucularla daha
ağlatan Cumhuriyet gazetesi yazarı
Mustafa Ekmekçi ise, öğretmen-
lerle birlikte bütün memurların ör-
gütlenme özgürlüğünü savundu.

Konuşmasında yer yer anılarını
başlayan Hasan Fehmi Güneş,
örgütlenmenin ve müslümanların
demokrasinin vazgeçilmez
gerekleri olduğunu ileri sürdü ve
"Örgüt dışında kalmış insan,
yalnızdır, çözüsüzdür" dedi.

Konuşmasında yer yer anılarını
başlayan Hasan Fehmi Güneş,
örgütlenmenin ve müslümanların
demokratik anlayışların kopartıp
rağk müslümanların ikinci emir bir
vatandaş durumuna indirgeniştir.
İngiliz sömürge döneminde bile
müsaade edilen ve okularda müslümanlara eğitim lisan dilleri olan
belli erden Urduca, merkezi hüki-
met tarafından yasaklanmıştır.

Alikari islâm Üniversitesi'nin
özerkliği ve hürriyeti almaırak
okulda gayrî İslâmî uygulamalar
zorunlu hale getirilmiştir. Geçtiği-
miz günlerde Alikari Üniversitesi-
ni, üniversite müdürünün inicgiy-
le "Gençlik Gecesi" düzenlen-
mesinin ve bu gecede okul idaresi diverir-
sitenin kuruluşuna ters düşen ey-
lemleri teşvik etmiş; dansöz oyna-
tılmış, bunun üzerine gayrî İslâmî

My father's first article against my book, Interesting Questions-2, was published by monthly Girisim. Then the monthly magazine Kitap Dergisi published my response, which they would later regret. My father, here tries to save the Sunni sect from my criticism. He accuses me of following the "Mason" and "Bahai" Rashad Khalifa. Vahdet, 9-15 May 1988. NINETEEN: God's Signature in Nature and Scripture. www.19.org

Edib'in Cevabi Yazısına Bir Bakış:

Sadreddin YÜKSEL

Evvela şuradan başlayalım: Bizim Edip, onun inancına dair "Girişim" dergisinde çıkan yazıma karşı "kitap" dergisinde cevap verirken diyor ki: (Amerika'da ikamet eden Mısırlı Dr. Reşad Halife'nin müridi olduğunu iddia ediyorsunuz. Yanılıyorsunuz. Bu makaleyi okuyan gençler benim kimin ve neyin müridi olduğumu anlamışlardır.)

Yani Edip, meşhur mason Reşad Halife'ye olan bağlılığını kat'i surette inkar ediyor. Ama ben şimdi onu bu iddiasında tekzip eden cerh edilmez bir sahidi huzurunuza çıkaracağım. İşte size, Edib'in, bir taraftan mason, bir taraftan da mürted Bahaiye tarikatının lideri bulunan Reşad Halife'ye kendi eliyle yazmış olduğu sadakat ve bağlılık mektubu:

Yani Edip, meşhur mason Reşad Halife'ye olan bağlılığını kat'i surette inkar ediyor. Ama ben şimdi onu bu iddiasında tekzip eden cerh edilmez bir şahidi huzurunuza çıkaracağım. İşte size, Edib'in, bir taraftan mason, bir taraftan da mürted Bahaiye tarikatının lideri bulunan Reşad Halife'ye kendi eliyle yazmış olduğu sadakat ve bağlılık mektubu:

Tercümesi şöyledir:

Değerli İmam, Değerli ve Sevgili Mürşid

[handwritten]
Your comments on Mehdi, Imam was very well and UNEXPECTED! You have solved your and our Problem! And you have enlightened (Inshallah US) about Mehdi, Imam came. I can't go on writing now. Please admit me, as the first member of UIN from Turkey.
Edib Yüksel

29 MAYIS 1988/YIL:2/SAYI:23/1500 TL

2000
İKİBİN'E DOĞRU

İslâm kaynaklarındaki gerçek:

ASIL KUR'AN YAKILDI

The cover story of provocative atheist/communist magazine 2000'e Dogru, brings the issue of Quran's textual integrity. The title of the cover story: "The fact according to Islamic sources: THE REAL QURAN WAS BURNED." The article was written by Turan Dursun, a former Sunni cleric who became an atheist. The well-written and supported article used Sunnis own sources to refute their claim regarding the perfect preservation of the Quran. Religious scholars and theology professors chose to ignore the arguments. Unfortunately, the only meaningful defense of the Quran would come from no other than the excommunicated heretic, Edip Yüksel.

© NINETEEN: God's Signature in Nature and Scripture. www.19.org

2000 Polor

595

İSLAM KAYNAKLARINDAKİ GERÇEK

Asıl Kur'an yakıldı

Kur'an ın orjinali Hz. Hafsa'ya emanet edilmişti. Hz. Hafsa yaşadığı sürece emaneti sakladı. Onun ölümü üzerine Emevi halifesi Birinci Mervan, "Yakılıp yok edilmeseydi zamanla kuşkulara yol açabilirdi" diyerek Kur'an ın aslını yaktırdı. Bugün İslam dünyasında bilinen ve elde bulunan Kur'an Peygamberin "vahy katiplerine yazdırdığı" söylenen Kur'an dan farklı.

Emevi halifesi Mervan İbni Hakem, orijinal nüshayı Hafsa'nın sandığından alıp yaktırıyor. (Dr. Suphi e's-Salih, Mebahis fı ulûm-il Kur'an s.83)

Yakılsın! dedi. Birinci Mervan. Emevi halifesinin bu buyruğu yerine getiriliyor ve *Kur'an'ın* aslı yakılıyordu. Aslında Mervan'ın bu konuda daha önce de girişimleri olmuştu.

Kur'an'ın orijinali Hz. Ömer'in kızı ve Peygamberin karısı olan Hafsa'da bulunuyordu. Halife bu sayfaları alıp yakmak istemişti. Ama Hafsa her seferinde karşı koymuş, elinde bulunan mushafı teslim etmemişti. Bu mushaf Hz. Hafsa tarafından bin bir zahmet ve özenle bir araya getirilmiş, kendisinden de titizlikle korunması istenmişti. Hafsa yaşadığı sürece bu emaneti sandığında sakladı. Kimse elinden alamadı. Birinci Mervan, Hz. Hafsa'nın ölüm haberini duyunca çok sevindi. Önündeki en büyük engel ortadan kalkmış oluyordu. İstediğini yapabilirdi artık. Yaptı

Orijinal Kur'an, ölene dek Hz. Ebubekir'in yanındaydı, sonra Hz. Ömer'de kaldı, o da ölünce, kızı Hafsa'ya verildi.

da...

Halife Mervan kendi gerekçesini şöyle açıklar; "Onda yazılı olanlar, Osman tarafından yazdırılan mushaflara geçmişti. Artık ona gerek kalmamıştır. Yakılıp yok edilmeseydi, zamanla kuşkulara yol açılabilir, ondan alınarak yazılan mushaflar çevresindeki kuşkuları önlenemeyebilirdi. Bundan korktum o nedenle yaktırdım." (Kaynak: İbni Ebu Davud, Leiden 1937, yay., s. 243- Suphi e's-Salih Mebahis Fi ulûm-il Kur'an)

Halife Mervan'ın *Kur'an'ı* neden yaktırdığı Buharî E's-Sahih'te de aynen geçiyor.

İslam kaynaklarında bu ilk yazımın yakılma olayı üzerinde fazla durulmaz. Hz. Osman zamanındaki ikinci yazıma önem verilir. Hafsa'da bulunan ilk orijinalin ve o günlerde ortalıkta dolaşan başka mushafların bir karışıklığa yol açmaması için ortadan kaldırıldığı söylenir.

Ebubekir döneminde yazılan *Kur'an* Hafsa'ya teslim edilmişti. Hz. Osman da onu Hafsa'dan isteyerek karışıklıkları önlemek amacıyla yeniden derledi. Esas alınan ilk mushafta yazılı olanlarla yeni derlenen **mushaftakiler** arasında fark olmadığı **söyleniyordu.** Ama o ki iki resmi nüsha içerik yönünden farksızdı, neden kuşkulara karışıklıklara yol açılabileceğinden söz ediliyordu? Hali-

596

fe Mervan ilk mushafı yaktırırken neden korkmuştu?

Öte yandan Hz. Hafsa kendisine emanet edilen asıl nüshayı neden önce titizlikle sakladı ve ona el sürdürmedi?

KUR'AN NASIL YAZILDI

Kur'an ayetleri bugünkü biçimiyle yazılıp bir araya getirilmiş değildi. Hadislerde peygambere vahy olan ayetler çeşitli nesneler üzerinde yazılıydı; hepsi de dağınık durumdaydı. Ayetler ''Lihaf'' (küçük taşlar), ''Rıka'' (deri, ağaç yaprağı, bir çeşit kâğıt), ''Ektaf'' (deve ve koyun kemikleri), ''Üsub'' (ağaç parçası) gibi nesnelere yazılmıştı.

''Yitip gitmesin'' diye tümünü bir araya getirme çabasına ilk kez Halife Ebubekir döneminde gerek duyuldu ve bu çabalar gerçekleştirildi.

Bir aktarma da ''bunların tümünün peygamberin evinde, bir arada bulunduğu ve dağınıkken bir araya getirip, içinden eksilen olmasın dive ortasından iple bağlanmış olduğu''da açıklanır.

Buhari'nin yer verdiği bir hadise göre; ''Dinden dönüş (''ridde'') olayları ve bu olaylar nedeniyle savaş hali vardı. *Kur'an*'ı ezber etmiş kişilerin bir bölüğü ölmüştü. Ölenlerin sayısı artabilirdi, bunların tümü ölüp gitmeden *Kur'an*'ın orada burada yazılı ayetleri derlenmeli, tümü bir kitap durumuna ge-

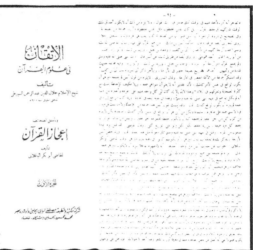

Kur'an'ın ilk derlemesi Hz. Ebubekir döneminde gerçekleşiyor. (Suyuti'nin El İtkam fi ulûm-il Kur'an, c.1, s.94)

■

Hadislerde Peygambere vahy olan ayetler çeşitli nesneler üzerine yazılıydı. Hepsi de dağınık durumdaydı. Ayetler küçük taşlara, deri, ağaç parçası ve deve, koyun kemiklerinin üzerine yazılıyordu.

■

tirilmeliydi. Hattaboğlu Ömer durumu ve konunun önemini Halife Ebubekir'e anlattı. Ayetlerin derlenmesini önerdi. Halife başlangıçta pek doğru bulmamıştı bu görüşü.

''Peygamberin yapmadığı şeyi yapmak nasıl doğru olabilirdi?'' diye düşünüyordu. Ömer direndi ve önerisini kabul ettirdi. İşin gerçekleşmesi için de Zeyd İbn Sabit'e görev verildi. Zeyd ''Ebubekir bana: 'Sen akıllı bir gençsin. Peygambere vahy de yazdığın için senin başaracağına güveniyorum. Araştır ve topla Kur'an ayetlerini!' dedi. Tanrıya ant içerek söylerim ki, dağlardan bir dağı yükleyip taşımayı önerseydi, buyurup verdiği görev kadar bana ağır gelmeyecekti. Yani *Kur'an*'ı derlemek kadar'' diyor, ama sonunda

HZ. MUHAMMED HUTBE OKURKEN
(Siyer-i Nebi Üçüncü cilt s.448 b)

görevi kabul ettiğini söylüyor ve işi nasıl yaptığını şöyle dile getiriyor:

''*Kur'an* (ayetlerini) derlemeye koyuldum. Hurma dallarından, küçük taşlardan ve kişilerin ezberlerinden izleyip derledim. İşin sonunda, Tevbe (Bera-

et) Suresinin sonunu, Ebu Huzeymetu'l - Ensari'de buldum. Ki, başkasında da bulamamıştım bu parçayı''. Zeyd, bu parçanın Tevbe Suresinin sonundaki ayetleri (128 ve 129. ayetleri) oluşturduğunu açıklıyordu.

Böylece Zeyd, *Kur'an* ayetlerini derleme işini yaparken iki kaynağa başvurmaktaydı: Ayetlerin yazılı bulunduğu nesneler (ağaçlar, taşlar...) ve ezber bilenlerin bellekleri.

Ebubekir döneminde yazılan *Kur'an* için başvurulan ezbercilerin başka deyişle hafızların sayısı Müslümanlar arasında tartışmalıdır. O döneme ilişkin önemli kaynaklardan Buhari'nin *'e's-Sahihi''*nde yer alan üç hadisten anlaşıldığı kadarıyla *Kur'an*'ın tümünü ezberleyenlerin en iyimser rakamla 7 kişi olduğu kabul edilebilir. Aynı zamanda Peygamber dönemindeki ''hafız''ların, yani *Kur'an*'ı tümüyle ezberlemiş olanların sayısı pek azdı.

Buhari'nin *''e's-Sahih''*inde geçen 3 hadis şöyle:

Birinci hadis: Amr İbnu'l-Ass anlatıyor: Peygamberin ''*Kur'an*'ı dört kişiden alın, Abdullah İbn Mes'ud'dan, Salim'den, Muaz'dan ve Übeyy İbn Ka'b'den'' dediğini işittim. (Buhari, Fadailu'l-Kur'an: 8

İkinci hadis: Enes anlatıyor: ''Peygamber öldüğünde, dört kişiden başka *Kur'an*'ı tümüyle ezberlemiş olan yoktu. Ebu'd-Derdâ, Muâz İbn Cebel, Zeyd

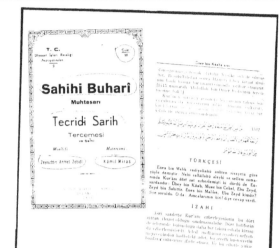

Celaleddin Suyuti El itkan fi ulûm-il Kur'an, Mısır 1978 4. baskı

Muhammed öldüğü zaman Kur'an'ı bütünüyle ezberlemiş olan dört kişi vardı. (Buharî, Kitab-ı menakıb-ul Ensar s.229)

ci, ikinci, üçüncü, hadiste)

İslam dinbilirleri bu hadislerdeki açıklamaların "dinsizlerin işine yaradığı"nı ileri sürerler. Suyuti, El İtkan, Mısır 1978, c. 1. s. 94, satır 13.)

İtkan'da daha başkalarının da 'Kur'an'ı ezberlemiş oldukları adlarıyla açıklanıyor. Ama aktarmayı yapan, bu adları sayılanlardan kimilerinin, Kur'an'ın tümünü ezberleme işini Peygamberin ölümünden sonra bitirdiklerini açıklamaktadır. İtkan, c. ls. 95-96.)

Zeyd İbn Sabit, herhangi bir parçayı Kur'an'a geçirmek için 'iki tanık' koşulu koymuştu. Ancak bir tanıkla Kur'an'ı alma gereği duyduğu ve geçirdiği parçalar da vardı. Örneğin, Ebu Huzeyme'de bulduğu ve Tevbe Suresinin son iki ayeniti oluşturan parça böyleydi.

Kur'an'ı derleme ve yazma işi bir yıl sürer. Bu işe girişildiğinde Ömer'le Zeyd, mescidin kapısında oturmuşlar, 'Herkesin peygamberden ayet olarak elde ettiği ne varsa getirmesini' istemişlerdi.

Başarılan iş kaynaklarda şöyle tanımlanır: 'Kur'an ayetlerinin, surelerinin bulunduğu iki kapaklı bir kitap!

Zeyd, 'Derlenip yazılan sayfalar, ölene dek Ebubekir'in yanında kaldı, sonra (halife) Ömer'in yanında bulundu.

İbn Sâbit ve Ebû Zeyd". (Buhari'nin Menâkıbu'l-Ensar'ının 17. bölümü.)

Üçüncü hadis: Katade'den aktarılıyor: Malik oğlu Enes'e; "Peygamber döneminde, Kur'an'ı tümüyle ezberleyenler kimlerdir?" diye sordum. Şu karşılığı verdi:

'Dört kişi. Tümü de Medineli Übeyy İbn Ka'b, Muâz İbn Cebel, Zeyd İbn Sabit ve Ebu Zeyd (Buhari hadis no: 1785, Müslim 2465. hadis.)

Bu hadislerde adları yazılanları topladığımız zaman Peygamber döneminde Kur'an'ı tümüyle ezberlemiş olanların sayısı, yediyti demek gerekiyor.

İbn Mesud (birinci hadiste), Salim (birinci hadiste) Muâz İbn Cebel (birin-

Yaşamı boyunca. O da ölünce, kızı Hafsa'ya verildi.

KUR'AN İKİNCİ KEZ YAZILIYOR

Buhari'de yer alan bir hadis şöyle; Ermeniyye ve Azerbeycan'ı ele geçirmek için savaşıyordu. Huzeyfe İbnu'l-Yemân, Halife Osman'a geldi. Müslümanların okudukları Kur'anlardaki birbirini tutmamazlıktan yakındı, "Emîre'l-Mü'minin! Bu ümmet, kendisinden önceki Yahudiler ve Hıristiyanların içine düştükleri birbirini tutmazlıklar gibi bir duruma düştü! "Bunun üzerine Osman, Hafsa'ya adam gönderdi, başka Kur'an nüshaları yazıp almak için kendisinde bulunan 'sayfalar'ı (yani

598

Ebubekir döneminde oluşturulmuş olan kitabı) göndermesini istedi. "İş bitince, geri sana gönderirim" dedi. Hafsa da gönderdi o sayfaları Osman'a. Osman, hemen Zeyd İbn Sabit'e Abdullah İbn Zübeyre, Sa'd İbnu'l-Âs'a ve Hişam oğlu Haris oğlu Abdurrahman'a buyruğunu verdi. Onlar da Hafsa'dan getirilenden alıp *Kur'an* nüshalarını oluşturdular. Osman kuruldaki üç kişiye şunu söyledi: "(Medineli) olan Zeyd'le, *Kur'an*'dan herhangi bir kesimde ters düştüğünüz zaman, tartışma konusu olan parçayı Kureyş diliyle yazın. Çünkü *Kur'an* yalnızca Kureyş diliyle inmiştir."

Onlar da buyruğu yerine getirdiler. Sonunda (esas) sayfalardan *Kur'an* nüshaları oluşturup işi bitince: Osman söz

■   ■

Hz. Osman kuruldaki üç kişiye şunu söyledi: Medineli Zeyd'le "Kur'an'dan herhangi bir kesimde ters düştüğünüz zaman, tartışma konusu olan parçayı Kureyş diliyle yazın! Çünkü Kur'an yalnızca Kureyş diliyle inmiştir."

■   ■

konusu sayfaları (Hafsa'dan getirileni) geri gönderdi. Alınan nüshaların da her bir kesime gönderilmesini buyurdu. Ve bunların dışında kalan her bir *Kur'an* sayfasını ya da Mushafı buyurup yaktırdı. (Buhari, Kitabu'l-Fadailu'lKur'an)

Buhari'nin hadiste anlatılan çabalardan ve 'Kureyşli olanlarla olmayanlar arasında belirecek anlaşmazlığın çözüm biçiminden anlaşıldığına göre, Kur'an nüshalarını ortaya çıkarırken, Hafsa'daki Mushaftan aynen kopya etmek söz konusu değildi.

Aynen kopya etmenin gerekçesi ise "ağız farkı"ıyla diye açıklanmaktadır. Ancak (Dr. Suphi e's-Sâlih, *Mebâhis Fi Ulumi'l-Kur'an, Beyrut*) 1979 adlı eserinin 80, 84, 85, sayfalarında bu gerekçenin inandırıcı olmadığını belirtiyor. Dr. Suphi'ye göre, o zaman, aynı metni, aynı sözcükleri değişik okunacak nitelikte yazıp yansıtabilmek için gerekli işaret ve noktalama yoktu. O zamanki yazı, harflerinin dışında işaretsiz harfler de noktasızdı. Kısacası Halife Ebubekir döneminde oluşturulan "Mushaf", istenseydi bile, çeşitli kabile ağızlarını (şiveleri) içerir nitelikte yazılmış olamazdı.

Durum böyle olunca şu sorular karşılıksız kalıyor: Ebubekir döneminde hazırlanan ve Hafsa'dan alınarak getirilen "Mushaf"la, Osman döneminde

Cebrail Hz. Muhammed'e Âl-i İmran suresinden ayetler getirir. (Siyer-i Nebi, üçüncü cilt s.4576).

■   ■

Aişe: Osman döneminde Kur'an tahrif edilmeden önce Âl-i İmran Suresi iki ayetti diyor, daha sonra bu ayetlerin nasıl iki yüze çıktığını anlamadığını belirtiyor.

■   ■

meydana getirilen "nüshalar, mushaflar" arasındaki fark neydi? Yeni çalışmayla gerçekleştirilen nedir?

Yukarıda anlamı sunulan hadiste bu açıklanmamakta. Ancak, hadisin devamı niteliğindeki bir açıklamada, yapılan işin yalnızca "bir temel nüshadan alınıp başka mushaflara aktarma" olmadığını anlatır niteliktedir.

Dörtlü kuruda yer alan Zeyd İbn Sâbit, şöyle diyor: "Mushaf oluşturma işini yaparken, Azhab Suresinin sonundan bir ayet yitirdim ('fakat tu'). Ki, Peygamberin onu Kur'an'dan bir parça olarak okuduğunu işitip tanık olmuştum. Aradık bu ayeti. Ve Sabit oğlu Huzeyme el Ensâri'de bulduk: (Azhab/23.) Suresine ekledik Mushaf'ta." (Itkan, Mısır, 1978, C. 1, s. 79.)

599

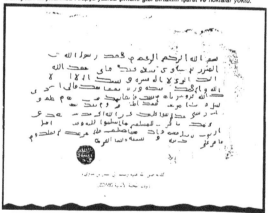

Hz. Osman döneminde Kur'an yeniden derleniyor. Kur'an nüshaları oluşturulup bitince, bunların dışında kalan her bir Kur'an sayfasını ya da mushafı buyurup yaktırdı. (Buhari, Kitabu'l-Fadâil-ül Kur'an c.4. s.99)

Eldeki resmi Kur'an içerik yönünden farklı. İbn Mesud'un Mushafında, Fatiha Suresi, Felak ve Nâs Sureleri yok. Ali'nin Mushafındaki sureler, Resmi Kur'an'daki sıraya uymuyor. Dr. Suphi e's-Salih: Hz. Osman döneminde hazırlanmış resmi nüsha şimdi nerededir?" sorusunu ortaya atıyor. Kahire Kütüphanesi'nde olduğu söylenen nüshanın Osman döneminden kalamayacağını belirtiyor. Çünkü bu kitapta birtakım işaret ve noktalar vardır. Bu işaret ve noktaların İslamiyetin ilk yıllarında bulunmadığı bilinmektedir.

HZ. AİŞE: "KUR'AN'DA TAHRİFAT YAPILDI"

Bugün elde bulunan resmi nüshaların Peygamberin "vahiy kâtiplerine" yazdırdığı nüsha ile aynı olduğu da, eldeki bazı bilgi ve bulgulara göre tartışmalıdır. O günlerden zamanımıza kalan bütün önemli İslam kaynaklarında kuşkuları doğrulayacak hadisler vardır. Suyuti'nin İtkan adlı eserinde, Buhari'nin eserlerinde bazı önemli mushaflardan ve bu mushafların içindeki surelerin listelerinden söz edilir. Örneğin, Hz. Muhammed'in en yakınlarından biri bilinen ve Peygamberin, Kur'an için ezberine başvurulacak dört kişiden biri olarak belirttiği İbn Mesud'un mushafı, yine Hz. Muhammed'in danışılması gereken dört kişiden biri olarak söz ettiği Übeyy İbn Ka'b'ın mushafı, Abdullah İbn Abbas'ın mushafı, Muhammed'in karısı Aişe'nin mushafı, Ali'nin mushafı bunların başlıcaları.

Ayrıca bugün Alevilerin, Ali'nin mushafı olarak sözünü ettikleri bir mushaf ve Hindistan'da saklanan ayrı bir mushaf daha var.

Suyuti'in ve Buharî'nin kitaplarında belirtilen mushaflardan hiçbiri günümüze gelememiş. Ancak bunların içerik listeleri yazılmıştır. Ayrıca bazı din kitaplarında, bunlarda bulunduğu söylenen ayet ve surelerden parçalar günümüze kadar gelmiştir. Eldeki resmi nüshadan içerik yönünden farklı oldukları bu listelere bakınca hemen anlaşılıyor. Örneğin İbn Mesud'un "Mushaf"ında Fatiha Suresi gibi çok temel bir sure yok. Felak ve Nâs sureleri de. Ali'nin surelerinin sırası bugünküne uymuyor. Suyuti, kitabında, Bakara Suresinin Azhab Suresiyle aynı uzunlukta olduğunu söyler. Oysa resmi Kur'an'da ikisinin uzunluğu çok farklı. Yine İbn Mesud'un "Mushaf"ında bulunduğu bildirilen iki duanın da resmi nüshada bulunmadığını görüyoruz.

Muhammed'in eşi Aişe'nin Suyuti'nin İtkan kitabında sözü edilen düşünceleri ve kuşkuları artırır yöndedir. Aişe, Osman döneminde Kur'an tahrif edilmeden önce Al-i İmran Suresi iki ayetti diyor ve daha sonra bu ayetlerin sayılarının nasıl iki yüze çıktığını anlamadığını belirtiyor. Muhammed'in eşi açıkça bir tahrifattan bahsediyor, Suyuti gibi çok önemli bir İslam kaynağı da bu sözleri aktarıyor.

İslamiyetin ilk yıllarında Arapça yazıda şimdiki gibi birtakım işaret ve noktalar yoktu.

600

CEDVEL II

Kur'an-ı Kerim'lerde farklılık yoktur. İbn-i Mesut veya birkaç sahabinin kendi derledikleri Kur'an-ı Kerim'in tertip bakımından birbirinden farklı olduğu içerik olarak aynı olduğu kesindir. (Prof.Dr. İsmail Cerrahoğlu Tefsir Usûlü. İkinci Baskı, 1976. Ankara Üniv. İlâhiyat Fak. yayını S.84-85)

PROF. MEHMET SAİT HATİPOĞLU

'Yakmak istediğini sanmıyorum'

Hz. Peygamber zamanında çeşitli maddeler üzerinde yazılı olarak ve ezberlenmiş halde bulunan Kur'an-ı Kerim ilk halife Hz. Ebubekir zamanında isimleri bilinen bir heyet tarafından bir kitap haline getirilmiş, bu nüshayı Hz. Peygamber'in hanımı Hz. Hafsa'ya muhafazasına teslim etmiştir. Bu doğrudur, ama Mervan İbn-i Hakem'in Kur'an-ı Kerim'i yakmak için istediğini sanmıyorum. Mervan İbn-i Hakem, Mervani kolunun başıdır, Ashabidir. O ilk nüshaya sahip olmak ister tabii. Yakmak için değil, saklamak için istemektedir.

İlk halifenin zamanındaki Hz. Hafsa'ya verilen nüshanın yakıldığına dair bir bilgim yok. İmha hadisesi ilk nüshaya kaynak teşkil eden malzeme üzerinedir. Hz. Osman ilk nüshanın kopyalarını çıkartarak çoğalttı, başka birşeyi değil.

Müslümanların inandığı ve Batılı ilim adamlarının da kabul ettiği üzere Kur'an-ı Kerim ilk yazıldığı şekliyle günümüze kadar hiçbir değişikliğe uğramadan yazılı ve hafızların ezberlemesi yoluyla günümüze kadar ulaşmıştır.

İlk Kur'an kaynaklarının bugüne ulaşılmamış, imha edilmiş olması kötü bir şey. Ama bu bugünkü Kur'an-ı Kerim'in'aslına uygun" anlamına gelmez.

İKİBİNE DOĞRU • 29 MAYIS-4 HAZİRAN 1988 • 13

Yararlanılan İslami kaynaklar:

Buhari E's-Sahih (Arapça): Kitabu-ı Fedail-ül Kur'an Menakıbu'l Ensar.
Sahihi Buhari Mustasarı. Tecridi Sarih Tercemesi.
Dr. Suphi E's-Salih: İslam dünyasında son yüzyılın ileri gelen ve birçok eserleri olan araştırmacı. Mebahis fi ulûm-il Kur'an adlı eseri.
Celalettin Suyuti: Kur'an yorumcusu, Hadis uzmanı olarak İslam dünyasında en güvenilir din bilirlerinden birisi.
El İtkan Fi ulûmi-l-Kur'an adlı eseri.
Müslim E's-Sahih (Arapça)
Ebu Davud.

Üçüncü halife Osman döneminde bir heyet tarafından yeniden derlenip yazılan Kur'anların kaç adet olduğu ve şu anda nerede bulundukları da tartışmalıdır.

Kimilerine göre dört, kimisine göre beş ya da yedi adet yazılmıştır. Dörttür diyenlere göre, Osman bir nüshasını kendisine alıkoymuş, diğerlerini Kûfe'ye, Basra'ya ve Şam'a göndermiştir. Mekke'ye, Yemen'e ve Bahreyn'e gönderilenlerden de söz ediliyor.

Bazı kitaplardaki bilgilere göre, bu nüshalardan kopya edilip çoğaltılmasına izin verilmiş, yeni kişiler kendileri için "mushaf"lar meydana getirmişlerdir. Ancak, o zaman bu mushaflarda bulunduğu söylenen ve örnekler aktarılan bazı Kur'an parçalarının resmi Kur'an'da bulunmaması ne demeli?

Bazı İslam kaynaklarında, Osman döneminde çoğaltılan nüshaların bir kısmının bugün elde bulunduğu iddia edilir. Örneğin bir kopyanın Taşkent'te olduğundan söz eden çok sayıda kitap vardır. Yine bazı İslami Türk kaynaklarında Topkapı Müzesi'ndeki Kur'an'ın da Osman zamanından kaldığı söylenir.

Konunun araştırmacılarından Dr. Suphi e's-Salih, kitabında, "Pekiy, Osman döneminde hazırlanmış resmi nüsha şimdi nerededir?" sorusunu ortaya atar ve doyurucu bir cevap bulamadığını açıklar. Kahire Kütüphanesi'nde olduğu söylenen nüshanın Osman döneminden kalmış olamayacağını belirtir. Çünkü bu kitapta birtakım işaret ve noktalar vardır, böyle işaret ve noktaların İslamiyetin ilk yıllarında bulunmadığı bilinmektedir.

Müslümanların kutsal kitabının resmi nüshasının her yerde aynı olduğu doğrudur. Ancak, bugün İslam dünyasında bilinen ve elde bulunan Kur'an, Peygamberin "vahy kâtiplerine yazdırdığı" söylenen Kur'an'dan farklı.

The cover story of provocative atheist/communist
magazine 2000'e Doğru, brings the issue of Quran's
textual integrity. The title of the cover story:
"The fact according to Islamic sources: THE REAL
QURAN WAS BURNED." The article was written by Turan
Dursun, a former Sunni cleric who became an atheist.
The well-written and supported article used Sunnis
own sources to refute their claim regarding the
perfect preservation of the Quran. Religious
scholars and theology professors chose to ignore the
arguments. Unfortunately, the only meaningful
defense of the Quran would come from no other than
the excommunicated heretic, Edip Yüksel. @NINETEEN:
God's Signature in Nature and Scripture. www.19.org

EDİP YÜKSEL

Kuran, Allah tarafından korunmuştur

Kuran'dan başka dini kaynak tanımayan ve hidayetimiz için Allah'ın son Mesajını yeterli gören bir Müslüman olarak tam bir fikir özgürlüğünden yanayım. Kuran'a inanan bir kimse fikrini açıklamakta ne kadar hürse, inanmayan birisinin de Kuran'a inanmama konusundaki inancını, hakarete varmadan ifade etmesi serbest olmalıdır. Kuran, dinde zorlama olmadığını beyan eder (2: 256; 10:99; 88:21-22).

"Dinden dönen mürted öldürülür, namaz kılmayan Müslüman hapsedilir, yahut öldürülür." gibi Kuran'a tamamıyla aykırı teo-faşist hükümlerin yer aldığı kitapları, Kuran'a tercih edenlerin Kuran adına yaygara koparmalarını anlamak bir hayli zordur.

Peygamberimizden çok sonraları derlenen, doğruların yanında yalanlar da içeren hadis kitaplarını ve bunların türevleri olan çelişkili fıkıh ve usul kitaplarını dinlerinin "sahih" kaynakları olarak belleyen insanların sıkıntılarını çok iyi anlıyorum.

Zamanla kutsallaştırılan bu kitaplarda yer alan "ayıpların" arada bir "kafirler" tarafından ortaya çıkarılması ve yüzlerine vurulması çileden çıkarıcıdır. Birbirlerini körükörüne taklid etmekten öteye geçmeyen inançlarını sarsan bu tür yayınlara cevap vermeye çalışırlarken sürekli şu sıkıntıyı yaşamışlardır: Yukarı tükürse bıyık, aşağı tükürse sakal!

YEPYENİ BİR ÇAĞIN ARİFESİ

Yaklaşık 1200 senedir, Kuran'ı yetersiz görerek Kuran'a eş yüzlerce cilt kitap oluşturan ve böylece mezhep mezhep, tarikat tarikat tefrikaya düşen suçlu bir ümmetin (23:52-56) tek kurtuluş yolu Kuran'a dönmektir.

Nitekim hicri 15. yüzyıl, Müslümanların, Kuran'ı, tüm Kuran'ı, başka şeyi değil sadece Kuran'ı rehber edinecekleri bir yüzyıl olacaktır. Kuran'daki gaybi haberlerin ve mucizelerin bir gerçekleşmesi, İslam'ın tüm dünya sistemleri üzerine egemen olacağının açık işaretleridir (9:33; 48:28; 61:9).

Artık dost düşman herkes Kuran'ı konuşacaktır. Böyle bir dönemde, 2000'e Doğru dergisinin İslam ve Kuran hakkındaki yayınları, amaçlarının tam zıddına sebep olacaktır. (2:216; 61:8). Müslümanların Kuran'ı daha iyi tanımalarına ve körükörüne olan inançlarını bırakıp akıl ve bilim üzere iman etmelerine yol açacaktır (17:36; 10:100). Yepyeni bir çağın arifesini yaşıyoruz (74:33-34).

ASIL KURAN'IN YAKILMASI

Peygamberimizin döneminde tedvin edilen Kuran'ı gözbebeği gibi koruyan Hafsa'nın vefatından sonra, Emevi halifesi Mervan'ın onu alıp yakması olayı, tarihî bir gerçektir. Nitekim şu anda, peygamberimiz ve ilk üç halife dönemindeki orijinal nüshalar elimizde yoktur. Hatta Osman'a nisbet edilen nüshaların orijinalliği bile kuşkuludur.

Kuran tarihiyle ilgili kitapları ve Sunnî Şiî hadis kaynaklarını okuyanlar, Kuran hakkında bir sürü iddiaların çok şiddetli tartışmalara neden olduğunu bilirler. Mervan'ın orijinal mushafı yakması olayını nakleden rivayetlerde bu yakma olayının sebebi olarak "yeni tartışmalara sebep olması"gösteriliyor. Bu her iki "sebep" de düşündürücüdür. Nitekim ikinci sebebi tehlikeli bulanlar, Mervan'ın peygamberimiz döneminedeki nüshayı yakmasına başka bahaneler yakıştırmaya çalışmışlardır. Örneğin, ilk nüshanın harekesiz ve noktasız olduğunu, böylece karışıklığa sebep olabileceğini ileri sürenler bile çıkmıştır. Harekesiz ve noktalı ben-zer nüshayla çelişmesi mümkün değildi. Ayrıca bu bahane, böyle bir nüshanın yakılmasını meşru kılamaz. Zira rahatlıkla hareke ve noktalarla donatılabilirdi. Kaldı ki 8. yüzyıldan kalma deri nüshaların bir çoğu harekesiz ve noktasızdır. Bunlar neden imha edilmedi?

Bu konudaki rivayetler, Dr. Osman Keskioğlu'nun da kafasını karıştırmış ve "Nüzulünden Günümüze Kur'an-ı Kerim Bilgileri" adlı kitabının 140. sahifesinde şunları yazmıştır:

"Görüyoruz, muhtelif eski nüshalar, Sahabe devrinden kalma Mushaflar bugün de elde mevcuttur. Ancak burada mühim bir meseleyi sormak hatırımıza geliyor:

Peygamberin huzurunda Vahiy kâtipleri tarafından yazılan o Kur'an sahifeleri acaba ne oldu, nerede kaldı? Ebubekir zamanında Kur'an cem'olunurken o sahifeleri behemehal heyete getirip gösteriyorlardı. Kur'an bir yere toplanarak tedvin ve tespit edildikten sonra onları ne yaptılar? Vakıa artık onlara lüzum yok. Fakat bunların eserî ve tarihî emsalsiz bir değeri var. O bakımdan Ashab bunları alıkoymadı mı? İlk Vahiy bunlara tespit edildi. Resulüllah'ın gözleri gördü, elleri değdi diyerek onları hıfzetmediler mi? Resulullah'ın saçını, sakalını teberrüken alan Ashab, bu sahifeleri en kudsî bir eser gibi saklamadılar mı? Sakladılarsa bu sahifeler sonraları ne oldu? Bu hususta hiçbir kayda rastlayamadım. Kime sordumsa bu sorum cevapsız kaldı.

Diğer bir mesele daha var: Hazreti Osman zamanında istinsah edilen nüshalardan bahisler rastlıyoruz, hem bol bol. Fakat Ebubekir zamanında cem'edilip ondan istinsah edilen asıl nüsha ne oldu? Bu hususta şunu biliyoruz: Hazreti Osman istinsah ettikten sonra o nüshayı yine Hazreti Ömer'in kızı Hafsa'ya iade etti. Nüsha Hafsa'da durmaktadır. Taberanî'nin sahih bir senetle Salim'den rivayet ettiğine göre: "Mervan, Hafsa'ya adam göndererek Kur'an'ın istinsah edildiği bu Mushafı ondan istiyordu. Hafsa da vermekten çekiniyordu. Hafsa'yı defnettikten sonra Mervan, İbni Ömer'e (Hafsa'nın kardeşine) adam göndererek "bu Mushafı bana gönder" dedi, o da Mushafı gönderdi." "Mecmuaz-Zevaid, Mısır tab'ı".

Böylelikle bu nüshanın Emevilere geçtiğini anlıyoruz. Hafsa, H. 41 veya 45 senesinde öldüğüne göre Mushaf o tarihte Emevilere intikal etmiştir. Acaba sonra ne oldu, nerede kaldı? Yine bir kayda rastlayamıyoruz. ∎

602

Abdül-Azim Zürkanî *"Menahilül-İrfan"* ında (1940 tab'ı) şu tuhaf malûmatı veriyor: "Medine Valisi Mervan, Hafsa'nın cenazesine iştirak etti. Abdullah ibni Ömer'den o Mushafı aldı.Hafsa'dan istemişti, vermemişti. İbni Ebi Davud bunları yaktı diyor. Bir rivayette yıkadı, diğerinde ise yırttı. Şüpheye düşmesinler diye böyle yapmış. Çünkü dağınık sahifeler halinde imiş." *"Mecmauz-Zev'aid"* in rivayetinde öyle bir şey yok. Bunu nereden ve nasıl çıkarıyorlar bilmem!"

KURAN'I ALLAH KORUMUŞTUR

"Zikri biz indirdik, onu yine biz koruyacağız" (15:9) ayeti, Kuran'ın, alemlerin Rabbinin garantisi altında olduğunu belirtiyor. Kuran'ın Allah Kelamı olup olmadığı ve gerekse koruma garantisi veren bu ayetin sonradan Kuran'a sokulmuş olup olamayacağı gibi konular tartışılmalıdır.

Kuran, 17:36 ayetinde,körü körüne bir imanı reddeder. Kuran'ın bizzat kendisini soruşturmadan, kritik etmeden, çevrenin etkisiyle kabul edenler, Kuran'ın istediği mümin tipi değildir. Kuran, kalabalıklara ve atalarına körü körüne kapılan insanların bu davranışlarını sürekli eleştirir. (5: 104; 31:21; 43:22-24). Atalarının ve çevrelerinin etkisiyle Kuran'ı kabul edenler, aslında Kuran'a değil, kalabalıklara ve geçmişlerine bağlanmışlardır. Kuran'a ters düşen geleneksel hurafeleri ve yanlışları eleştiremezler. Aksine Kuran ayetlerini lastik gibi çekerek atalarıyla, çevreleriyle ters düşmemeye gayret ederler.

Rabbimiz, büyük lütuf sahibidir. Gerek Kuran'a inanmıyanlara ve gerekse tüm müminlere önemli belgeler ve kanıtlar bağışlamıştır. Kuran'ın birçok ayetinde ileride gerçekleşecek bir mucizeden söz edilir. (10:20; 25:4-6; 41:53).

Nitekim son yıllarda bilgisayar yardımıyla Kuran üzerinde yapılan çalışmalar, Kuran'ın Allah Kelamı olduğunu ve mükemmel biçimde *Allah tarafından* korunduğunu ortaya çıkarmıştır. Görsel ve matematiksel bir nitelik arz eden bu yeni çalışmaları, Kur'an Görülen Mucize ve Kur'an En Büyük Mucize adlı kitaplarda yayımladık. Her geçen gün gittikçe gelişen bu Kuranî belgelere birkaç örnek vereyim:

Kuran'daki birçok kelimenin tekrar sayıları ilginç mesajlar vermektedir. Meselâ, *şehr* (ay) kelimesi, tüm Kuran'da tam 12 kere, *yevm* (gün) kelimesi tam 365 kere geçmektedir. *Dünya* ve *ahiret* kelimeleri birbirine eşit

tam 115'er kere, *şeytan* ve *melek* kelimeleri de birbirine eşit tam 88'er kere, *şems* (güneş) ve *nur* (ışık) kelimeleri birbirine eşit 33'er kere tekrarlanmaktadır.Buna benzer yüzlerce örnek Kuran'da ikişerli bir sistemin varlığını ortaya koymakta ve Rabbimizin her şeyi bir bir saydığıyla ilgili sözünün (72:28) bir tecellisi olmaktadır.

MATEMATİKSEL MUCİZE

Kuran, her bir haberin gerçekleşeceği bir zamanı olduğunu bildirir (6:67; 13:38; 38:88; 27:93). Nitekim, 74. sure olan Müddessir (gizlenen) adlı surede 1400 yıl boyunca gizlenmiş olan 19 mucizesi, Kuran'ın kompüterle incelenmesi sonunda Dr. Reşat Halife tarafından "rastlantı sonucu" fark edildi. Kuran'ı baştan başa saran bu 19 kodu, bir matematiksel örgü ve koruma zırhı işlevini görmektedir. Kuran'ın bir insan ürünü olamayacağını ayrıca harfi harfine, kelimesi kelimesine ilahî korunma altına alındığını, evrensel bir dil olan matematiksel bize kanıtlayan Rabbimiz, 19 kelimelik Nasr (Yardım) suresindeki vadini yerine getirmektedir.

Kuran hakkındaki tüm şüpheleri ortadan kaldıran bu mucizeyi özetlemeden önce, bu matematiksel mucizenin adeta kılavuzu, belki de bir sağlaması olduğunu gösteren örneklerden birisini vereyim:

HARFİ HARFİNE KORUMA

"Sad" harfi ile başlayan üç suredeki "sad" harfinin tekrarlanma sayısı elimizdeki Kuran nüshalarında 153'tür. Ne var ki bu sayı 19 sistemini tahrip etmektedir. Çünkü 19'un tam katı değildir.Kuran'daki 19 sisteminin rastlantı sınırlarını ve beşer gücünü çoktan aştığını iddet bizler, hemen araştırmaya koyulduk. Fazla olan "sad" harfinin nerede olabileceğini araştırdık. Sonunda, "sad" harfi ile başlayan 7. surenin 69. ayetindeki bir kelimeye takıldık. Bu ayette geçen

Yukarıda, Araf suresinin 69. ayetinin yeraldığı iki Kuran nüshasını görüyorsunuz. Sekizinci yüzyıla ait Taşkent nüshası ile bugün yaygın olan Kuran nüshaları arasındaki "sad" ve "sin" farkı dikkat çekicidir. 19 sistemi, Taşkent nüshasını doğruluyor.

'Bastatan' kelimesi "sad" ile yazıldığı halde üstünde veya altında küçük bir "sin" harfi mevcut... Bu enteresan yazım biçimi, bu kelimenin "sad". ile yazıldığı ancak "sin" ile okunması gerektiği biçiminde yorumlanıyordu. Hatta, Tayyar Altıkulaç'ın Tercüman gazetesinin 21 Mart 88 sayısındaki yazısında kaynak olarak gösterdiği bazı kitaplarda bu kelimeyle ilgili hadis rivayet ediliyordu. Altıkulaç, bu hadislere dayanarak 19 mucizesinin yanlış olduğunu iddia ediyordu. Hadise göre, Cebrail, bu kelimenin "sad" harfiyle yazılmasını emretmişti.

Ne var ki, Süleymaniye Kütüphanesi'ndeki Kufî nüshalar ve ünlü Taşkent nüshasının kopyaları üzerinde yaptığımız araştırma sonunda bu kelimenin yüzyıllardır yanlış yazılmakta olduğu ve söz konusu hadisin de uydurma olduğu ortaya çıktı. Böylece, 19 sistemiyle çelişen bir "sad" harfi iyot gibi açığa çıkmıştı. Tabii bu arada "sad" üstündeki küçük "sin" harfinin varlık hikmeti de anlaşılıyordu. Demek ki, ilk orijinallerden kopya eden kâtiplerden birisi 7:69'daki "bastatan" kelimesini yanlışlıkla "sad" ile yazıyor. Daha sonra bu nüshayı kontrol eden bir hafız, bunun "sin" ile yazılması gerektiğini belirtmek için üzerine bir "sin" harfi yazıyor.Bu tashihli nüshayı daha sonra kopya edenler bu küçük "sin" harfinin bir düzeltme olduğunu düşünemeyip "sad" üzeri"sin" diye kopya edip duruyorlar.

Biraz düşünürseniz söz konusu hadisin uydurulma sebebini de tahmin edebilirsiniz:"sin"'li ve "sad"'lı nüshalar üzerinde tartışmalar yoğunlaşınca o günün modası olan hadis uydurmacılığı devreye girmişti. "Sad"'çılar hadis uydurmada daha ağır davranınca galip gelmişlerdir. Şu anda dünyada yaygın olan Kuran nüshaları, bu uydurma hadise göre yazılmış oldukları için bir fazla "sad" harfi ihtiva etmektedir!

603

Peygamberliğini İlan Eden Yalancı: Reşad Halife

Ahmed Deedat,
Açıklıyor...

İfşa Ediyoruz...

Açık Oturum Çağrımız Cevapsız Kaldı

Güney Afrikalı ilim adamlarından Ahmed Deedat "Kur'an En Büyük Mucize" adlı bir eser kaleme almış, adı geçen eser İngilizce olarak basılmış, daha sonra ise bu eser çeşitli dillere çevrilerek dünyada satış rekorları kırmıştır. Türkçeye de çevrilen eserin Türkiyeli müslümanlar tarafından ilgiyle karşılandığı ve defalarca baskı yaptığı biliniyor.

Ahmed Deedat, bu eserinin yanısıra bir çok eser daha kaleme almış, özellikle "Kitab-ı Mukaddes" üzerine pek çok broşür, kitap ve eserler vermiş, gene bu konularla ilgili olarak çeşitli yerlerde konferanslar, seminerler ve açıkoturumlar tertip etmiştir.

"Kur'an En Büyük Mucize" adlı eserinde işlediği Kur'an'ın 19 mucizesi Reşad Halife ... ... saptırılmış, buna dayanarak kendisini sapık fikri akımların içinde bulmuştur. Hatta bunun üzerine, bu tür sapkınlıklara kaynak gösterildiği için de Ahmed Deedat bu eserini yayından kaldırmış ve yayınlanmasını yasaklamıştır.

Reşad Halife ise giderek sapkınlığını artırmış, bilahare kendisinin peygamber olduğunu, kendisine vahiy geldiğini iddia edecek kadar sapkınlığa düşmüştür. O'nun bu sapkınlığı karşısında ve Kur'an ayetlerinin bir kısmını inkarına kadar dayanan seyri içinde, Ahmed Deedat kendisini açık oturuma davet etmiş, bu konuları topluluğun önünde tartışmaları gerektiğini, insanları aldatmağa devam edemeyeceğini açıklamıştır. Fakat Ahmed Deedat'ın yeni yaptığı açıklamada da belirttiği gibi, Reşad Halife Deedat'ın bu çağrısını olumsuz bulmuş ve oturuma katılmayacağını açıklamıştır.

Bu gelişmelerden sonra ise Ahmed Deedat, Reşad Halifenin bir yalancı olduğunu, yalancı olmasaydı kendisinin bu davetine icabet etmesi gerektiğini bildirmiştir.

Sizlere bu konuyla ilgili olarak, Ahmed Deedat'ın çağrı mektubunu, adı geçen isimlerin kısa kimliklerini, ve gene Ahmed Deedat'ın konu ile ilgili açıklamasını sunuyor, Reşad Halifeyi Ahmed Deedat'ın tespitleri ışığında gerçek yüzünü açıklıyoruz.

The weekly Islamist magazine Vahdet, in its 26 September ‖ 2 October 1988 issue, publishes the controversy in its cover story. Ahmad Deedat joins the fray and harshly condemns Rashad and declares him to be "a liar!" Though Rashad accepted Deedat's invitation and published his response in his bulletin, Muslim Perspective, the Sunni media still propagated the lie that Rashad could not accept Deedat's challenge. Though Deedat was an articulate and experienced debater, I had no doubt that Rashad would win the debate, hands down.
NINETEEN: God's Signature in Nature and Scripture. www.19.org

Ahmed Deedat, hayatını İslamı doğruları insanlara anlatmaya.adamış bir müslüman ilim adamı... İslami konuları dünyanın dört bir yanında anlatmaya, insanlara duyurmaya gayret gösteriyor. Yukarıdaki resimde Ahmed Deedat'ın bir konferansı...

İPCİ-Uluslararası İslâm Propaganda Merkezi Başkanı Ahmed Deedat'ın Açıklaması

Ahmed Deedat Kimdir

1919'da Hindistanda doğmuş. Sonradan Güney Afrika'ya doğmuştur. Daha sonra Güney Afrika'da "İslâm Propaganda Merkezi"ni kurmuştur. Hristiyan misyonerlere karşı, İslamiyeti yaymak için çalışma yapmaktadır. Kitab-ı Mukaddes üzerine bir çok broşür, kitap ve video kaseti neşretmiştir.

Kur'anda 19 sayı sistemi konusunda "Kur'an En Büyük Mucize" kitabını kaleme almıştır. Ancak bu sayı sistemini doğru olmadığı, ve Reşad Halife'nin bunu bahane ederek emellerine hizmet ettirmek gayesiyle uydurduğu ortaya çıkınca, bu kitabının yayın ve dağıtımını durdurmuştur.

Biz İslâm Propaganda Merkezi olarak ABD, Arizona eyaleti Tuscon şehrinde bulunan Dr.Reşad Halife'nin Allah'ın Resulü olduğuna dair alçakça ve uydurma iddialarını red ve ifşa ediyoruz.

Bu Reşad Halife aynı zamanda hadisleri ve sevgili Peygamberimizin (s.a.s) sünnet-i seniyyesini de red etmektedir. Bu suretle, ümmet-i Muhammed'in ictimai ve siyasi bünyesinde tefrika ve bölünmelere yol açmak istemektedir. O bilgisayar hesaplamalarını da Kur'an-ı Azimuşşan hakkındaki saçma teorisine (19 mucizesi) destek olacak mahiyette ayarlamıştır. Reşad Halife'den önce, Lanetli Mirza Gulam Ahmed ve İranlı Ruhaullah gibi peygamberlik iddiasıyla çıkan diğer sahtekârlar da aynı iddialarla emperyalist efendilerine hizmet ettiler. Bu sahtekârlık hususu ulaşamamıştır. Reşad Halife denen sahtekâr da Allah'ın izniyle başarıya ulaşamayacaktır.

Ben şahsen, Reşad Halife'yi Kızında, ... na iddialarından dolayı ilk defalarımda açık görüşmek için "Madison Square Garden" da açık tartışmaya çağırdım.

Ben daha önce de, 1987'de onu, hadisler Sünnet-i seniye ve Kur'an-ı azimüşşan hakkındaki bilgisayara dayalı teorilerine karşı açık tartışmaya davet etmiştim.

Şu anda da, bu Allah'ın hakir kulu ile "Madison Square Garden"da karşılaşması için

Reşad Halife'ye nasibin olsurmu.

Allah bizi tüm bela ve tehlikelerden muhafaza buyursun. Amin.

AHMED DEEDAT
(İSLAM HADİMİ)
20-5-1988

M. Yüksel

Ahmed Deedat'ın yoğun çalışmalarından bir başka kesit. Kendisinin çalışmalarını insanlara duyurmak için yollara asılan afişler ve pankartlar...

Sun'i gündem oluşturmak için bir dergide "2. Selman Rüşdü Olayı"nı ortaya atan Edip Yüksel'e babasından cevap:

"Reşat Halife neyse Edip odur"

Haber Merkezi

Türkiye'nin tanınmış alimlerinden ve Reşat Halife'nin iddiaları konusunda çeşitli makaleler yazan Sadreddin Yüksel Reşat Halife ne ise oğlu Edip Yüksel'in de o olduğunu belirtti.

Sadreddin Yüksel'in Orhan Kuntman'ın, Tayyar Altıkulaç'ın, Celal Yıldırım ve Salih Akdemir'in konuyu her yönüyle incelemesine ve dünyada da konunun kapanmasına rağmen Reşat Halife'nin iddialarını yeniden şüphe ve tereddüt uyandıran ifadelerle gündeme getirilmesi mazide karşılandı. Gözlemciler ve ilmi çevreler bu yayınların Reşat Halife ve benzerlerinin reklamı...

Devamı 8. sayfada

Zaman 10 Nisan 1989

The popular weekly news magazine Nokta's cover story (shown) it was dated April 16, 1989, it appeared in the market a week before as usual) starts a second wave of attacks against me after the first attack against my highly controversial book, Interesting Questions 2. Zaman newspaper does not waste time reacting to Nokta's story. Reportedly the get the dooming words from my father's mouth: "whatever Rashad is Edip is the same". Ironically, even if my father made such a statement, he still subconsciously avoiding to utter the naming word murtadd (apostate/heretic). www.19.org @NINETEEN: God's Signature in Nature and Scripture.

süren okul var mı?" diye sormuş. İşte aldığı cevap: "İrticai faaliyetlere karıştıkları gerekçesiyle bugüne kadar 95 askeri okul öğrencisinin okullarla ilişkisi kesilmiştir. Bugün askeri okullarda böyle bir soruşturma söz konusu değildir."

Genelkurmay başkanları öyle hergün gazetecileri karşısına alıp görüşen kişiler olmadıkları için, Sayın Torumtay'ın muhabirle görüşmesi başlı başına ilginç bir olay. Genelkurmay Başkanı'nın muhabirin kendisine yönelttiği, nükleer silahların modernizasyonu, askerlik süreleri gibi teknik soruları cevaplamayıp daha çok siyasi mahiyette açıklamalar yapması da ayrıca dikkat çekti.

"İrticai faaliyetlere katıldıkları gerekçesiyle" okullarıyla ilişkisi kesilen askeri öğrenci sayısını, Sayın Torumtay 95 olarak ve...

Devamı 8. sayfada
FEHMİ KORU

The Türkiye Newspaper, in 11 April 1989, reports from prominent Sunni theologians such as Prof. Salih Tuğ and religious authorities, including my father. The newspaper manages to attribute my father the bloody statement: "Oğlum mürteddir." (MY son is an apostate/heretic). This is a clear message and incitement for religious zealots and psychopaths to kill me. @NINETEEN: God's Signature in Nature and Scripture.

rkiye
11 NİSAN 1989 SALI
YASI GAZETE
Santral: 513 99 00 (20 hat) • TELEKS: 22000 Yuas Tr • FAKS: 519 05 46

solcular başkaldırdı

muhtıra

ekili, Deniz Baykal'ın tüzük değişikliğine karşı çıkıyor

Ültimatomu diğer milletvekilleriyle birlikte İnönü'ye verirken konuşan eski DİSK Genel Sekreteri ve Bursa Milletvekili Fehmi Işıklar, kurultayın yetkisinde bulunan bazı tasarrufların bir başka organa devredilmesini faydalı bulmadıklarını belirterek, "Kurultayın yetkisi yine kurultayca kullanılmalıdır" dedi ve Başbakan Özal ile dışa yönelik meselelere yönelinerek, parti içi meselelerin asgariye indirilmesini istedi. **9. Sayfada**

plantısında konuşan Genel Başkan Erdal İnönü, "İktiseçimin gereğini anlayacaktır" dedi.

İlahiyatçılar ve siyasilerden sapık Mısırlıya sert tepki

Reşat Halife şarlatandır

İlahiyat Fakültesi Dekanı Prof. Dr. Salih Tuğ, Reşat Halife tarafından ortaya atılan tutarsızlıkların ilmi bir tarafı bulunmadığını belirtirken, İstanbul Müftü Vekili Fikri Gültekin, "İslam'a ve Kur'an'a saldırılar her dönemde olmuştur. Bundan böyle de olacaktır. Müslümanlar, dinimizi temel kitaplardan öğrenmeli, bu tür saldırılara kulak asmamalıdır" dedi.

Sadreddin Yüksel, Reşat Halife'nin Türkiye temsilcisi oğlu Edip Yüksel için konuştu:
Oğlum mürteddir
Seyfullah Türksoy-Sayıt Aydoğan **9. Sayfada**

M.Ü. İlahiyat Fakültesi Dekanı Prof. Dr. Salih Tuğ

● Sapık Mısırlıya, İlâhiyatçı ve siyasetçilerden sert tepki

"Reşat Halife şarlatandır"

● SEYFULLAH TÜRKSOY
● SEYİT AYDOĞAN

İSTANBUL/ANKARA — ABD'li sapık Reşat Halife'ye tepkiler artarak devam ediyor.

Sırf, ortaya attığı 19 teorisine uymadığı için, Kur'ân-ı Kerim'de fazlalık olduğunu ileri süren, daha da ileri giderek peygamberlik iddia eden 53 yaşındaki Reşat Halife'nin, İslâmiyeti içten yıkmak için faaliyet gösteren bir İslâm düşmanı olduğu belirtildi.

Konuyla ilgili görüşlerini aldığımız Marmara Üniversitesi İlâhiyat Fakültesi Dekanı Prof. Salih Tuğ, Reşat Halife tarafından ortaya atılan 19 teorisinin hiçbir ilmî tarafının olmadığını belirterek, "Reşat Halife, kendi şahsî görüşlerini, düşüncelerini İslâma maletmeye çalışıyor. 19 meselesiyle ilgili iddialar tefsir ilminden uzaktır. Tamamen şahsîdir" dedi.

Bu tür uyduruk ve ilim dışı görüşlerin zaman zaman ortaya atıldığını; bundaki esas gayenin müslümanları bölmek, İslâmiyeti yıkmak olduğunu kaydeden Prof. Salih Tuğ, "Bu tür sapık cereyanlar her devirde görülmüştür. Yüce Peygamberimizden hemen sonra ortaya çıkan İbn-i Sebe, Müseylemetü-l Kezzâb, Behaullah, Salman Rüşdi ve Reşat Halife bu sapıklardan

Kamuoyunu uzun süre meşgul eden Salman Rüşdi olayından sonra ortaya çıkan Reşat Halife olayı, gündemdeki yerini korurken, konuya Ankara'daki İlahiyatçılar da tepki gösterdiler.

Ankara Üniversitesi İlahiyat Fakültesi öğretim üyelerinden Prof. Dr. Hayrani Altıntaş, konu ile ilgili olarak yaptığı açıklamada, son peygamber olduğunu iddia eden Reşat Halife'nin "sapık biri" olduğunu söyledi. Hayrani Altıntaş, "Hazret-i Peygamber'den sonra peygamber gelmeyeceği, bütün İslâm kaynaklarında bulunur ve bilinirken, böyle bir safsatanın ortaya atılması gülünç. Bu kişinin sapık biri olduğu kesin. Yahut da satın alınıp bu işin içine sokuluyorlar. Yapılan sansasyonel reklamlar

ile, İslâm âleminin dikkatini başka başka yerlere çekip, boş şeyler ile meşgul etmek istiyorlar. Bu gibi işler ile vakit kaybetmeye gerek yok. İtibar etmemek lâzım." dedi.

MÜSLÜMAN, BU SAPIĞA İTİBAR ETMEZ

ANAP Genel Başkan Yardımcısı Galip Demirel, Reşat Halife'nin Kur'ân-ı Kerîm ile ilgili ortaya attığı iddialara tepki göstererek, "İddiaları saçma, Reşat Halife de sapıktır" dedi.

Anavatan Partisi'nin Basın ve Halkla İlişkilerden sorumlu Başkan Yardımcısı Erzurum Milletvekili Mehmet Kahraman da Reşat Halife'nin ortaya attığı iddiaları mantıksız bularak, "Bu adam şizofrenidir. Ruh hastasıdır acımacak bir zavallı mürteddir" dedi.

"Oğlum mürteddir"

● SEYFULLAH TÜRKSOY

İSTANBUL — Yüce kitabımız Kur'ân-ı kerîm'de fazlalık olduğu hezeyanını ortaya atarak peygamber olduğunu ileri süren ABD'li sapık Reşat Halife'nin Türk yandaşlarından olan Edip Yüksel, babası Sadrettin Yüksel tarafından sert bir dille eleştirildi.

ABD'li sapık Reşat Halife ve yandaşlarının sapık yazar Salman Rüşdi gibi, İslâma iftira attıklarını ve müslümanların şüpheye düşmelerini istediklerini söyleyen Sadreddin Yüksel, oğlu Edip Yüksel için, "Oğlum ne yazık ki mürteddir. İslam dışıdır. Allah kendisine hidayet nasip etsin" şeklinde cevap veriyor.

Müslümanlar tarafından sevilen ve zaman

zaman İslâmî konularda bilgisine başvurulan Sadreddin Yüksel, İslam dışı düşünceleri Reşat Halife'nin etkisiyle aldığını ve böylece, dünya ve ahiretini mahvettiğini belirtti.

Oğlu ile görüşmediğini anlatan Sadreddin Yüksel "Ne o bizi arıyor, soruyor, yanımıza geliyor. Ne de biz onu kabul ediyoruz. O artık mürteddir. Bir zamanlar İslâm mücahidi idi, şimdi İslâm dışına çıkmıştır" şeklinde konuştu.

Reşad Halife neyse

Baştarafı 7. sayfada

İslamını yapmaktan öte bir niyet taşımadığını ve dergi ve yayınlarla Müslümanların duygularını rencide ettiğini belirtiyorlar. Edip Yüksel'in Müslümanlar tarafından dışlanmasına ve kimse tarafından dinlenmemesine rağmen dini derginin ısrarla konu üzerine gitmesi din, duygu ve merak sömürüsü olarak nitelendirildi.

Tiraj kaygısıyla veya konu bulamamaktan olacak yine bazı haftalık dergiler konuyu döndürüp dolaştırıp İslam'la ve Kur'an-ı Kerim'le uğraşmaya getiriyorlar. Birkaç peygamber birini muhakkak irticaî faaliyetlere (!) ayrıan bir dergi, son sayısında ve hem de Ramazan'ın üçüncü gününde Müslümanların kutsal değerleri üzerinde münakaşa başlatmak suretiyle dikkatleri kendi üzerinde toplamaya gayret ediyor.

Dergi bu hafta okurlarına ikinci Salman Rüşdü Amerikalı Deedat'ında Halife'nin sapıkkları zannında kendisine sırt çevirdiğini ve onu Medison Square Garden'de münazaraya davet ettiğini belirttiği gibi yaptığı gibi

Sözü edilen dergi, Ahmed Deedat'ında Halife'nin sapıkkları tanıtıyor. Edip Yüksel'in Kur'an-ı Kerim'i de görüşlerini savunduğu için sardan Reşad Halife'nin Kur'an'ın doğrusunu yayınlayacağını ifade eden derginin Reşad Halife'nin Amerika'nın korunması altında olup olmadığına ilişkin sorusuna Edip Yüksel, "Reşad Halife'nin Allah'ın korumasında olduğu" şeklinde cevap veriyor.

Dergide Edip Yüksel'le ve Reşad Halife ile yapılan görüşmelerden her ikisi de görüşürlüğü halinde Peygamberimiz Hz. Muhammed'in son nebi, Reşad Halife'nin ise son Resul olduğunu iddia ediyorlar. Bu konuda görüşlerine başvurduğumuz Edip Yüksel'in babası ve değerli alim Sadreddin Yüksel, kendisinin bu konuda çok sayıda, Girişim dergisinde ve diğer yayın organlarında makaleler yazdığını ve bunlardan bir kısmının İnkılap Yayınları arasında çıkan "Kur'an ve 19 Efsanesi" adlı kitapta yeraldığını hatırlattı. Edip Yüksel'in ve Reşad Halife'nin Tevbe Suresi ve hadisler konusundaki ileri sürdükleri iddiaları değerlendiren Sadreddin Yüksel şunları söyledi: "Bunlar birtakım insanların ağzından sakız haline geldi. Edip'te Reşad Halife gibi mürteddir. Reşad Halife ne ise Edip'te odur. Bunların ilmî bir tarafı yok. Bunlar mücerred inkâr örnekleri. Bunlar Bahailerin, Kadıyanilerin ve Babilerin devamıdır."

Sadreddin Hoca: "Bunu ne cesaretle söylüyorsa" diyerek hayretini dile getirdi. Reşad Halife'nin ve Reşad Halife'nin konusundaki İslâm Peygamberlik iddia etmesini gülünç bulan Sadreddin Yüksel: "Allah onlara iman ve hidayet nasip etsin" diyerek sözlerine son verdi.

606

16 NİSAN 1989   YIL:7 SAYI:15   2000 TL. (KDV dahil)

ÜÇ BÜYÜK İLİN
BELEDİYE PRENSLERİNİ
AÇIKLIYORUZ

Nokta, then the most popular weekly newsmagazine
in Turkey, gave the news of Fatwa on Rashad
Khalifa and Salman Rushdi as its cover story in
16 April 1989, under the title, "American
Khalifa's Attempt to Change the Quran. The
Second Salman Rushdi Affair" It also published
my pictures with Rashad and an interview with
me, creating another wave of Sunni media
campaign and death threat against me, which led
me to immigrate to the USA. Nokta 16 April 1989.

®NINETEEN: God's Signature in Nature and
Scripture. www.19.org

Amerikalı Halife'nin Kuran'ı değiştirme çabası

İKİNCİ SALMAN RÜŞDİ OLAYI

607

İkinci Salman Rüşdi olayı

Amerika'da yaşayan ve kendisini peygamber ilan eden Reşat Halife'ye göre Kuran'da fazlalıklar mevcut... Buna karşın Dünya Fıkıh Konseyi'nin fetvası açık: Halife kâfirdir... İslam dünyası ikinci bir Salman Rüşdi olayı ile karşı karşıya. **Nokta**, Halife'nin Türkiye temsilcisi Edip Yüksel ile görüştü, olayın tüm boyutlarını açığa çıkardı.
(Sayfa 14)

Adnan Hoca'nın son çengeli

Adnan Hoca'nın sağ kolu Ahmet Uçan, din dersi öğretmeni olarak İstanbul Erkek Lisesi'ne atanınca veliler ayaklandı.
(Sayfa 37)

Meclis'te Demirel formülü

Özal'ı erken seçime zorlamak için Demirel'in bir formül geliştirdiği ileri sürülüyor. Formüle göre, ANAP'tan kopacak milletvekilleri hülle partisi kuracak, Necmettin Karaduman cumhurbaşkanı seçilecek ve erken seçime gidilecek. Bu arada Erbakan da ANAP'tan kendilerine geri dönecek 20 kadar arkadaşları olduğunu söylüyor.
(Sayfa 24)

Çukurova Holding'te ayrılık rüzgârı

Grubun tek ve tartışmasız hâkimi diye bilinen Mehmet Emin Karamehmet'le "anlaşmazlığa" düşen Hasan Karamehmet ve ailesi Çukurova Grubu'ndan ayrılma kararı verdi.
(Sayfa 56)

Fotoğraf 150 yaşında

İmgelerden kurulu bir dünya... Bugün bize çok doğal gelen dünya kavrayışımızın sadece 150 yıllık bir geçmişi var. İki Fransız, buluşlarıyla 1839'da gerçek bir devrime açtılar.
(Sayfa 80)

NOKTA 16 NİSAN 1989 **3**

KAPAK

İKİNCİ SALMAN RÜŞDİ OLAYI

"KURAN-ı KERİM'DE FAZLALIK VAR"

İslam dünyası yeni bir Salman Rüşdi olayıyla karşı karşıya. Kuran'ın 19 rakamı üzerine kurulu olduğunu iddia eden Reşat Halife, iki ayetin de fazla olduğunu söylüyor. Kendini peygamber ilan eden Halife, Kuran'ı iddiasına göre düzeltmeye hazırlanıyor

"Konseyimize gönderdiği çağrıda, bazı ayetlerin Kuran-ı Kerim'e sonradan eklendiğini savunan ve vahyi on dokuz sayısı ile sınırlamaya çalışan Mısırlı Ziraat Mühendisi Reşat Halife; hadis-i şerifleri ve sünneti de inkâr 14 NOKTA 16 NİSAN 1989 etmektedir. Halife'nin bu tavrı Salman Rüşdi'nin kitabında da olduğu gibi ilme ve nasslara aykırıdır. Halen ABD'de yaşayan Reşat Halife'nin peygamberlik iddiası ise doğrudan doğruya küfürdür. Konseyimiz, Reşat Halife ve Salman Rüşdi'ye hitaben bir bildiri yayınlayarak, sapık fikirlerinden dönmeleri ve tövbe etmeleri çağrısında bulunmaktadır. İddialarında ısrar ettikleri takdirde her ikisi de bütün İslam dünyasınca kâfir kabul edilecektir. Bu karar oybirliği ile alın-

609

The weekly news magazine Nokta's cover story of 16 April 1989. Sunni Scholars from 38 countries who met in February 27 in Mecca for the 11th Islamic World Fiqh Council organized by Muslim World League (Rabita), ended up with a fatwa condemning Rashad Khalifa together with Salman Rushdi to death. The Sunni religious leaders included Ben Baz, Yusuf al-Qaradawi, Mustafa al-Zarqa, and Abul Hasan al-Nadwi. ®NINETEEN: God's Signature in Nature and Scripture. www.19.org

ABD'de yaşayan Mısırlı Reşat Halife'nin iddiaları İslam dünyasını karıştırırken, Dünya Fıkıh Konseyi Rüşdi ile birlikte Halife'yi de ''kâfir'' ilan etti

mıştır...''

Tarih 27 Şubat 1989. Yer, Müslümanların kutsal beldesi Mekke. Aralarında Prof. Yusuf Kardavi, Mustafa Zerka, Nedvi gibi ünlü isimlerin de yer aldığı 11. Dünya Fıkıh Konseyi'nin kararı, yukarıdaki cümlelerle sona eriyor. Böylece Salman Rüşdi olayı ile birlikte ayağa kalkan İslam dünyası, Reşat Halife'nin ''kâfir''liğinin onaylanmasıyla yeni bir çalkantının daha eşiğine geliyor. Salman Rüşdi, ''alt tarafı'' bir roman yazmıştı ama Reşat Halife'nin durduğu çizgi çok tehlikeliydi... Çünkü hem Tevbe Suresi'nin son iki ayetinin Kuran'a sonradan eklendiğini savunuyor ve hem de şöyle diyordu: ''Ben Kuran-ı Kerim'de bildirilen son peygamberim...''

Kuyuya atılan taş. Salman Rüşdi ile Reşat Halife arasında bazılarının tesadüfle, bazılarının da komplo teorileriyle açıkladıkları önemli benzerlikler var. Bir kez "Rüşdi" ile "Reşat" aynı kökten türemiş iki isim. Sonra, Reşat Halife 1987 yılında "Muslim Perspective" dergisinde, Tevbe Suresi'nin son iki ayetinin şeytana ait olduğunu yazıyor. Bilindiği gibi, Rüşdi'nin kıyametler koparan kitabının adı da "Şeytan Ayetleri." Reşat Halife'nin Türkiye şubesi olarak çalışan Edip Yüksel, bütün bunlara dikkat çekerek şu yorumu yapıyor: "Rüşdi için koparılan yaygaranın bir benzeri de Reşat için koparılacak... Konsey kararında ikisinin adının birden zikredilmesinin anlamı bu..." Yani, dünya "ikinci Salman Rüşdi" olayının eşiğinde... Çünkü, Halife bir süre sonra piyasaya bu iki ayetin yer almadığı bir Kuran sürecek...

Salman Rüşdi ile Reşat Halife arasında bağlantı kuran isimlerden birisi de Prof. Hüseyin Hatemi. Prof. Hatemi şöyle konuşuyor: "Akıl hastalığında çok ileri dereceye varanlar, Salman Rüşdi gibi Reşat Halife'yi de 'takdis' edeceklerdir. 'Deccal' kelimesinin 'ebced' değeri de (38) olduğuna göre, iki 'İns Şeytanı' toplamının Deccal'e eşitolduğunu da düşünebilir ve bunun üzerine de kuramlar geliştirebilirler..."

Peki ama bu Reşat Halife kimdi? Tevbe Suresi'nin son iki ayetinin Kuran'a şeytan tarafından eklendiğini iddia ederken, ne gibi kanıtlar gösteriyordu? Bu on dokuz hikâyesi de neydi?

Mısır-Libya-ABD üçgeni. Halen ABD'nin Arizona eyaletinin Tucson kentinde yaşayan Reşat Halife Mısır doğumlu. Amerika'ya gelmeden önce de iki yıl Libya lideri Muammer Kaddafi'nin danışmanlığını yapmış. Şimdilerde ise İslam dünyasının yeni boy hedeflerinden biri. Onu boy hedefi haline getiren yaşamöyküsünün en önemli olayı da bilgisayarla tanışması. Bilgisayara büyük bir tutkuyla bağlanan Halife, Kuran-ı Kerim'i de bu alete yükleyip Kuran'ın sırlarını çözmeye çalışıyordu.

Günlerden bir gün Müddesir Suresi'nin 30. ayeti dikkatini çekti. Ayette "Onun üstünde on dokuz vardır" deniliyordu. Uzun süre bu sözün üzerinde düşünen Halife'nin beyninde şimşekler çakmakta gecikmedi. Bu sayının Kuran'da yer almasının bir nedeni olmalıydı. Bir

Alpaslan Yasa, "kâfir" fetvasına karşı çıkıyor

süre sonra Kuran'ın on dokuz sayısına göre biçimlendiğini savunmaya başladı Reşat Halife. Hem de örnekler vererek: Besmele on dokuz harften meydana geliyordu, Kuran'da 114 sure vardı ve bu da on dokuzun altı katıydı vs. Arkasından da ilgiyle karşılanan tezini bütün dünyaya ilan ediyordu: Kuran matematiksel olarak yazılmış bir kitaptır ve on dokuz sayısı, bu matematiksel yöntemin kilit unsurudur...

Reşat Halife, dünyanın dört bucağındaki Müslüman âlimlere mektuplar yazarak bu "büyük buluş"-undan söz eder ve örneklerini de alt alta sıralar. Hemen hemen hiç kimse Halife'ye ve buluşuna ilgisiz kalmaz. Güney Afrikalı vaiz Ahmet Deedat'ın yazdığı "Kuran: En Büyük Mucize" adlı kitap dilden dile çevrilir. İslam dünyasında Kuran'ı bilgisayarlara doğrulattıran Reşat Halife'ye karşı bir hayranlık fırtınası esmektedir. Bu arada tezini destekleyecek örnekleri artırmak için harıl harıl çalışan Halife'nin karşısına bazı problemler çıkmaktadır.

Türkiye'deki tepkiler. Reşat Halife ve tezleri biraz geç de olsa Türkiye'de de duyulur. Dönemin Diyanet İşleri Başkanı Dr. Tayyar Altıkulaç, 1981 yılında Cezayir'de katıldığı bir konferansta tanışır Halife'yle. Konferansa davet edilen Halife, büyük buluşunu içeren tebliğini okur ve dinleyenler tarafından büyük bir ilgiyle karşılanır. Teksir edilerek dinleyicilere dağıtılan bu tebliğe ilgi gösterenlerden birisi de Altıkulaç'tır.

Altıkulaç, Türkiye'ye döndükten

Reşat Halife'nin ABD'nin Arizona eyaletindeki çalışma merkezi olan çiftliği

"Beni Allah görevlendirdi..."

Elli üç yaşında Mısırlı bir Ziraat Mühendisi olan Reşat Halife, kendi ifadesiyle, "Amerikalı eşine ve Amerika'da doğan iki çocuğuna Müslümanlığı öğretmek kaygısıyla Kuran'ı incelemeye başlamış." Bu incelemeleri esnasında, birdenbire Allah'ın kendisini elçi seçtiğini ve bunun da Kuran'da yer aldığını "fark eden" Halife, "gerçek Müslümanlığı" dünyaya yaymak için kolları sıvamış. Amerika'nın Arizona eyaletinde çalışmalarını sürdüren ve kendisince doğru kabul ettiği "Yeni Kuran"ın yayımına hazırlanan Reşat Halife, Nokta'dan Ali Özkaner'in sorularını yanıtladı.

Nokta: Kuran'ın şifresi olarak kabul ettiğiniz on dokuz sayısını nasıl tespit ettiniz?

Halife: Müddesir Suresi'nin 30. ayetinde "Üzerinde on dokuz var" deniliyor. Devamında, bu rakamın inananların imanını artıracağı, kitap verilenlerin şüphelerini kaldıracağı belirtiliyor. Bu noktadan hareket ettiğimizde besmelenin on dokuz harf olmasından, Kuran'ın bütün harflerinin toplamının on dokuzun katları olmasına kadar istisnasız her yerde on dokuz şifresinin olduğunu gördük.

Nokta: Kendinizi "Allah'ın elçisi" olarak nitelendiriyorsunuz, bu peygamberlik iddiası değil mi?

Halife: Allah'ın beni haberci seç-

tiğine dair kanıtlar bulunuyor. Bu kanıtlar Kuran'ın üçüncü sure, seksen birinci ayetinde mevcuttur. Bu ayette, "Sizde olanı tasdik edecek bir peygamber gelecek" deniliyor. Ayrıca bunu gösteren fiziksel kanıtlar da var...

Nokta: Ama Kuran'a göre son peygamber Hz. Muhammed'dir ve ondan başka peygamber de gönderilmeyecektir...

Halife: Evet, ancak Hz. Muhammed Nebilerin sonuncusudur deniliyor, Resullerin sonuncusu değildir. Aksine yeni Resullerin geleceği açıkça belirtiliyor.

Nokta: Ama dünyanın değişik yerlerindeki Müslümanlar size sert tepkiler gösteriyor, hatta Ahmet Deedat bile sizi suçluyor...

Halife: Bu onlara kalmış bir şey değil. Onların dedikleri, güneş doğudan doğmaz demeye benziyor. Konunun tartışılacak bir tarafı yok. Bu çaba, milyonlarca Müslüman'a hizmet edecektir. Onların dinle ilgili olarak yaptıkları her şey yanlış. İslam'ın beş temel şartını yerine getirirken bile hata yapıyorlar. Mil-

yonlarca Müslüman bunların doğrusunu bilmiyor. İslamiyet'in buyrukları, şeytan tarafından saptırılmış bulunuyor. Allah bunlara doğrusunu öğretmek istiyor, beni de bu işle görevlendirdi. Bu tehlikeli yola, Allah'ın emriyle çıktım...

Nokta: Tevbe Suresi'nin son iki ayetinin Kuran'a sonradan eklendiği şeklindeki iddianız konusunda ne diyeceksiniz?

Halife: Bu konuda kanıtlarımız var. Bu iki ayetin Kuran'a konulması sırasında gerekli şartlar yerine getirilmemiş. En az iki tanık olması gerekirken, bir tek kişinin tanıklığına itibar edilmiş. Oysa, Kuran'da her ayetin pek çok kişi tarafından desteklenmesi hayati bir meseledir. On dokuz mucizesi, şüphe götürmez bir biçimde bu iki ayetin Allah'a ait olmadığını ortaya koyuyor...

Nokta: Peki Fıkıh Konseyi'nin sizi "kâfir" ilan etmesini nasıl karşılıyorsunuz?

Halife: Konsey, şeytana uymuştur. Bu iddiamın kanıtlarını yakında yayımlayacağım...

NOKTA 16 NİSAN 1989 17

Metiner, Fıkıh Konseyi'nin kararını
destekliyor

Dr. Haluk Nurbaki, Reşat Halife'nin
çok bunaltıldığını düşünüyor

"Tutsaydı sevinecektik..."

Reşat Halife'nin on dokuz tezini önceleri destekleyip "Hz. Kuran" adlı kitabına alan, yükselen eleştiriler üzerine Tercüman gazetesinde yayımladığı bir yazı dizisiyle "hatadan döndüğünü" itiraf eden ve her iki davranışıyla da çeşitli suçlamalarla karşı karşıya kalan Diyanet İşleri eski Başkanı Tayyar Altıkulaç, sorularımızı yanıtladı.

Nokta: Reşat Halife'nin kendisini Allah'ın elçisi olarak ilan etmesini nasıl değerlendiriyorsunuz?

Altıkulaç: Hemen belirteyim, Reşat Halife sapıkların ne ilki, ne de sonuncusudur. İddia, üzerinde durmaya değmeyecek kadar gülünçtür. Söz konusu ayetteki "Resul"den maksat da Hz. Mu-

hammed'dir.

Nokta: On dokuz tezi Kuran'ın bazı yerlerine uyuyor, bu bir tesadüf mü?

Altıkulaç: Reşat Halife, on dokuzla ilgili olarak ortaya bir iddia atmış, ama tutmamıştır. Tutsaydı sevinecektik. Nitekim işin başında sevinmiştik...

Nokta: Fıkıh Konseyi, Reşat Halife'nin "kâfir" olduğunu ilan etti. Siz ne diyorsunuz?

Altıkulaç: Kuran'ın bir kısmına inanıp, bir kısmını inkâr etmek elbette insanı küfre götürür. Kimseyi zorla Müslüman göstermek gibi bir mecburiyetimiz yoktur. Dileyen inanır, dileyen inkâr eder. Bu bir nasip meselesidir.

Nokta: Reşat Halife, kendi görüşleri doğrultusundaki bir Kuran yayımlayacağını söylüyor. İslami açıdan böyle bir suçun cezası nedir?

Altıkulaç: Sapıklığın sonu yoktur, eh fikir hürriyeti de var, herkes dilediğini yazmakta özgürdür. Bilhassa bilim açısından bu böyledir. Reşat Halife de, kanaatimce bir sapıktır. Onun ötesinde bir değerlendirmem yoktur. Halife, on dokuz saplantısından kurtulamadığı için sapıklık noktasına gelmiştir. İslamiyet'e Kuran'ı bu şekli ile kabul etmek esastır. Kuran'ın şu kadarına inanırım, işime gelmeyene inanmam demek Müslümanlık'la bağdaşmaz. Kuran'ı bütünüyle benimseyen ve bütününe inanan kişi Müslüman'dır.

tabı, Edip Yüksel tarafından "Kuran: Görülen Mucize" diye tercüme edilerek, 1983 yılında Türk okurlara sunulur. Kitap, büyük bir ilgiyle karşılanır ve kısa sürede tam on altı baskı yapar. Müslüman çevreler, bu tezi gündemlerine alırlar. Nurcu kesimin tanınmış isimlerinden Dr. Haluk Nurbaki "on dokuz mucizesi"ni televizyondan bütün Türkiye'ye anlatır...

İlk çatlak sesler. "On dokuz mucizesi"ne ilk tepki emekli müftülerden Celal Yıldırım ve Ankara Üniversitesi İlahiyat Fakültesi öğretim üyesi Doç. Salih Akdemir'den gelirse de, o atmosfer içinde pek ciddiye alınmazlar. Her iki isim de, Reşat Halife'nin dayandığı esasların çürük olduğunu ve örneklerde tutarsızlıklar bulunduğunu söylemektedirler.

Orhan Kuntman adındaki bir doktor da bu mucizeyi iş edinmiştir kendisine. Kuntman, Reşat Halife'yle mektuplaşma kadar uzanan bir çizgi üzerinde sürdürür mücadelesini. Ancak asıl kıyamet Diyanet İşleri Başkanlığı'ndan emekli olan Tayyar Altıkulaç'ın Tercüman gazetesinde yayımlanan "Hatadan Dönmek..." başlıklı iki günlük yazısı üzerine kopar. Altıkulaç bu yazısında, Reşat Halife'nin tebliğini yayımlamakla hata ettiğini, hatta "maksatlı bir teşebbüsün yayılmasına vasıta olduğunu" kabullenerek Halife'nin tutarsızlıklarını sergiler.

Artık rüzgârlar ters yönden esmeye başlamış ve Reşat Halife gözden düşme sınırına gelmiştir. Ancak "Reşat Halife mütercimi" olarak tanınan Edip Yüksel, sonuna kadar direnecek ve tanınmış din bilgini babası Sadreddin Yüksel tarafından evlatlıktan reddedilecektir.

Bugün ne oluyor? Ancak Halife

613

"Nebi olmayan Resul olmaz..."

Son olarak, piyasaya çıkan yeni kitabı "Şeytan Rivayetleri" ile ilgi toplayan Prof. Dr. Hüseyin Hatemi, konuyla ilgili sorularımızı yanıtladı.

Nokta: On dokuz sayısıyla Kuran-ı Kerim'in ilgisi nedir?

Hatemi: Kuran-ı Kerim, "ahiret" âlemindeki belirli görevlilerin sayısını on dokuz olarak bildirir (74/30). Hemen sonraki ayette de, bu rakamın saplantı haline getirilerek, akıl nimetinin yitirilmemesi için insanlık uyarılır. Kuran'ın bütün haberleri gibi bu da elbette doğru çıkmış, bu yüzden pek çok kişi ya aklını yitirmiş yahut, Kuran'daki her kelimenin on dokuz sayısı veya on dokuzun katı kadar geçtiği hezeyanını ortaya atarak, bu hesaba uymayan ve kendi işine gelmeyen ayetleri Kuran'dan çıkartmaya kalkışmıştır.

Nokta: Reşat Halife nasıl başlıyor bu işe?

Hatemi: Bahailik yolu ile İslam'ı ortadan kaldıramayacağını anlayan on dokuzcular, bu kez de başlangıçta bir "Müslüman bilgini" olarak ortaya çıkan, fakat kitaplarından buram buram Resul-i Ekrem'e (S.A.) düşmanlık kokusu yükselen ABD'de yuvalanmış Reşat Halife; Ahmet Deedat ve Türkiye'de de Edip Yüksel gibi iyi niyetli kişileri kandırmaya muvaffak olarak, bir tür batıl din, yir-

minci yüzyıl putçuluğu, "kompüterperestlik" kurmuştur.

Nokta: Bu aşamadan sonra Halife'den kopmalar oluyor galiba...

Hatemi: Reşat Halife, Kuran ve Sünnet gibi "iki ağır emanet"in yerine, kendi keyfine göre yüklediği ve programladığı "kompüter"i koymuş, Tevbe Suresi'nin son iki ayetini Kuran-ı Kerim'den (hesaplara uymadığı gerekçesi ile!) çıkartmaya kalkışmıştır. Arkasından da kendisinin peygamberliğini ilan etmiştir... Bunun üzerine Ahmet Deedat ve birçok kişi Kuran'ın Müddessir 74/31'de belirtilen tehlikeyi görerek kendi-

lerini uçurumdan kurtarmışlar, ama maalesef Edip Yüksel kurtaramamıştır.

Nokta: Reşat Halife, "Nebi değil, "Resul olduğunu iddia ediyor...

Hatemi: Bir insanın "Nebi" olmayıp da "Resul" olması imkânsızdır. "Nebi", Allah'tan vahiy alan zattır. Nebilerden bazılarına, aldığı vahyi insanlığa tebliğ görevi verilir. Bu Nebiler aynı zamanda Resul diye adlandırılır. Yani, Nebi olmayan Resul olmaz. Şu halde, ilahi elçilik görevi (vahiy) kapandığına ve sadece "şeytanı ilham" devam ettiğine göre, bir kişinin "Nebi" değil "elçi" olduğunu ileri sürmek, şeytani ilhamın aracısı olduğunu itiraf etmek demektir. Reşat Halife maalesef bu durumdadır.

Nokta: Selman Rüşdi ile Reşat Halife arasında bir bağlantı kurulabilir mi?

Hatemi: Reşat ile Selman Rüşdi'nin adı arasında kök birliği vardır. Herhalde akıl hastalığında çok ileri dereceye varanlar, Reşat Halife gibi Selman Rüşdi'yi de "takdis" edeceklerdir. "Deccal" kelimesinin "ebced" değeri de (38) olduğuna göre, iki "İns Şeytanı" toplamının Deccal'e eşit olduğunu da düşünebilir ve bunun üzerine de kuramlar geliştirebilirler! Allah imandan ve akıldan ayırmasın!

pes etmeyecektir. İslam dünyasını bugün Salman Rüşdi olayındakinden çok daha büyük çalkantılara gebe bırakacak bir adım atmaya hazırlanmaktadır Reşat Halife.

"... Bu mektubu aldığınızdan itibaren size dört aylık bir mühlet tanınacaktır. Bu mühlet sona erdiğinde eğer siz Allah'ın sonsuz hükümranlığına girmeyi reddederseniz otomatik olarak şeytanın hükmü altına girmiş olursunuz... İmza: Reşat Halife-Allah'ın elçisi..."

Bu satırlara, son aylarda Halife'nin kendisiyle şu ya da bu biçimde temas kuran herkese gönderdiği "Allah'ın Dünyaya Bildirisi" başlıklı yazıda yer alıyordu. Mucizeden efsaneye dönüşen on dokuz tezinin

çatırdaması Halife'yi çileden çıkartmıştı. Halife'ye göre, tezine uymayan Tevbe Suresi'nin son iki ayeti Kuran'a sonradan eklenmişti. Kuran dünyası varlığı Kuran'a iman ediyordu. Kendisi de doğru Kuran'ın yazımı için kolları sıvamıştı zaten... On dokuz rakamına uymayan son iki ayet Kuran'dan çıkarılmalıydı. O ayetler Kuran'a sonradan muhtemelen şeytan tarafından sokulmuştu.

Bütün bu iddialarla büyük tepkilere neden olan Reşat Halife, bir adım daha atıyor ve peygamberliğe soyunuyordu. "Allah kendisini dünyaya mesaj sunmakla görevlendirmişti ve bilgisayarlar kendisinin Allah'ın elçisi olduğunu açıkça or-

taya koyuyor ve on dokuz mucizesiyle destekliyordu."

Reşat Halife'yi ilk terk eden, ününün yayılmasında büyük emeği geçenlerden Ahmet Deedat olacaktı. Deedat, "Kuran: En Büyük Mucize" kitabının da basım ve yayınını durduruyor, hatta bununla da yetinmeyerek Halife'ye cephe alıyordu. Uluslararası İslami Propaganda Merkezi adına açıklama yapan Deedat, Halife'yi sapıklık ve sahtekârlıkla suçlayacak ve kendisini Madison Square Garden'da "münazara"ya davet edecekti...

Türkiye'deki durum. "Reşat Halife, kelimenin tam anlamıyla sapkın bir eğilimin temsilcisidir. On dokuz mucizesi bir mucize değil,

614

peygamber olduğunu iddia eden Halife'nin 'bilimsel amentüsü' niteliğindedir. Bu 'amentü'nün ne denli çelişkilerle ve tutarsızlıklarla dolu olduğu bir bir gösterilmiştir. Ancak Halife, 'bilimsel amentüsü'nü bir mucizeymiş gibi sunmak için Kuran ayetleri üzerinde keyfince oynamalarda bulunmuştur..." İslamcı Girişim dergisi Genel Yayın Yönetmeni gazeteci-yazar Mehmet Metiner, Reşat Halife'nin peygamberlik iddiasını ve on dokuz tezini bu sözlerle değerlendiriyordu. Dünya Fıkıh Konseyi'nin kararını desteklediğini de açıklayan Metiner, şöyle sürdürüyordu sözlerini:

"Reşat Halife, on dokuz olarak adlandırılan 'bilimsel amentüsü' için değil, asıl peygamber olduğunu iddia ettiği için bütünüyle mahkûm edilmeyi hak etmektedir. Güvenilir İslam âlimleri- Türkiye'de Sadreddin Yüksel, mesela-Halife'yi peygamberlik rolüne soyunduğu için 'mürted' olarak değerlendirmişlerdir. Bu hüküm, dediğim gibi on dokuz araştırması için değil, Halife'nin peygamberlik iddiası için verilmiştir. Bu hükmü onaylıyorum..."

İslamcı kesimin bir diğer ismi Abdurrahman Dilipak ise "Reşat

Dilipak'a göre olay suni bir gündem oluşturuyor

Halife ve on dokuz olayı, Müslümanlar için suni birer gündem maddesidir" diyordu. Dilipak'a göre, "Bu tür marjinal akımlar, öteden beri vardı ve var olmaya da devam edecekti. Teknoloji karşısında yalnızlaşan insanın dramı burada yatıyordu. On dokuz olayı da, bil-

giyi eşyalaştıran iletişim teknolojisinin yansımasından ibaretti." "Ümmet için fitne." Reşat Halife'nin on dokuz tezinin peşine düşüp daha sonra günah çıkartanlardan birisi de on altı baskı yapan "Kuran: En Büyük Mucize" kitabını yayımlayan İnkılâb Yayınevi'ydi. Kitabın yayınını durdurmanın kendilerini kurtarmayacağını anlayan yayınevi "Kuran ve 19 Efsanesi" adlı bir karşı-kitap yayınlayarak hatasını "itiraf" ediyordu:

"...bu 'sistemin' mucidi Reşat Halife, yine kurduğu 'sistemiyle' Allah'ın elçisi olduğuna dair düzme iddialarda bulunmakta ve Kuran'dan bazı ayetleri ayıklama hezeyanlarına mesnet hazırlamaktadır. Mesele, kısaca istismar noktasındadır ve ümmet için fitne olmaktadır."

On dokuz tezine televizyon aracılığıyla katkıda bulunan Dr. Haluk Nurbaki ise hâlâ kararsızlar safında yer alıyordu. Nurbaki'ye göre, "...'On dokuz'da esprisi olduğu muhakkaktı, ama Reşat Halife bunu tam olarak çözememişti. Halife, Kuran ayetlerini reddetmek yerine, çözümü yine Kuran'da arasaydı çok daha iyi olurdu. Herkes birden üzerine gidince şaşırmıştı.

Abdurrahman Dilipak, another influential Islamist columnist/author and my comrade, too supports the Fatwa against our lives. He says that he approves Sadrettin Yüksel's verdict against Rashad for his claim of messengership. Below is Nokta's interview with me.
◉NINETEEN: God's Signature in Nature and Scripture. www.19.org

"Muhammed Peygamber putlaştırıldı..."

ODTÜ Makine ve Boğaziçi Üniversitesi İdari Bilimler Fakültesi'ni terk ederek öğrenim hayatını yarıda bırakan Edip Yüksel, 163. maddeden dört yıl içeride yatmış. İngilizce, Arapça ve Farsça bilen Yüksel, sorularımızı yanıtladı.

Nokta: On dokuz sayısının üzerinde bu kadar çok durulmasının sebepleri nelerdir?

Yüksel: Reşat Halife'nin bulduğu bu mucize, Kuran'ın kesinlikle Hz. Muhammed'in sözü olamayacağını ve harfi harfine Allah tarafından korunduğunu ortaya koyuyor. Bu mucize yardımıyla, mevcut Kuran'larda hatalar bulunduğunu tespit ettik. Tevbe Suresi'nin son iki cümlesinin -ki ayet deniliyor ona- Kuran'a ilave olduğunu ortaya koydu bu mucize. İslam dininin Hz. Muhammed'den sonra Kuran dışında oluşturulan kaynaklarla dejenerasyona uğradığı da böylece ortaya

çıktı.

Nokta: Nedir bu Kuran dışındaki kaynaklar?

Yüksel: Hadis, fıkıh, tefsir kitapları... Kuran'a göre İslam'da bunların yeri yoktur. Peygamberimiz döneminde hadis kitapları yazılmamış, Hz. Muhammed'in vefatından iki yüz yıl sonra yani en az yedi nesil sonra Buhari yazılmıştır. Bunlarda bir sürü yalan mevcuttur.

Nokta: Yani siz hadisleri kabul etmiyorsunuz?

Yüksel: Kesinlikle reddediyoruz. On dokuz mucizesini kavrayanların hiçbirisi bunu kabul etmiyor. Çünkü hadis, Peygamber'e iftiralardan ibarettir. Zaten Peygamber de sağlığında hadis yazımına karşı çıkmıştır. Hem unutmamak gerekir ki, on dokuz mucizesi her şeyden önce rasyonel düşünmeyi getiriyor. Hadis kitaplarında çeşitli çelişkiler, hurafeler vardır.

Nokta: Peki Kuran'ın anlaşılması

için böyle bir mucizeye gerek var mı?

Yüksel: Gerek var mı, yok mu onu bilemiyorum, ama bu mucizeyi Allah 1400 senedir gizledi ve şu dönemde nasip kıldı. Allah sözde Müslümanların bunu anlayamayacağını da bildiriyor.

Nokta: Bu mucizenin bilgisayarla bulunması mı önemini artırıyor?

Yüksel: Bu bilgisayara nasip oldu. Nitekim kıyamet alametlerinden birisi de budur. Tesadüfen bilgisayar uyoyla bulunan bu mucize, İslam ümmetinin Kuran'a inanmadığını ortaya çıkartıyor. Misal mi? Kuran kadına boşama hakkı verirken mevcut mezhepler vermiyor. Kuran'a göre zinanın cezası yüz kırbaç iken bugün recm cezası uygulanıyor.

Nokta: Hz. Muhammed'e ilişkin ne söyleyeceksiniz?

Yüksel: Muhammed Peygamber putlaştırıldı İslam dünyasında. Hiç

Adamı çok bunaltmışlar ve netice itibariyle de çıldırtmışlardı..."

Tabii bir de hem Reşat Halife'yi, hem de ona karşı çıkanları eleştirenler vardı. "Yesevizade" lakabıyla tanınan Alpaslan Yasa da bunlardan birisiydi. "Tarih ve Sosyoloji Açısından Kuran'ın Sorgulaması" adlı kitabının hazırlıklarını sürdüren Yasa, giriş bölümünde "On dokuz ve Reşat Halife" olayının Türkiye'de takip ettiği seyri de özetliyordu. Yasa, Ahmet Deedat'ın kitabını okuduğu zaman karşı çıkmıştı on dokuz tezine. "Ama" diyordu Yasa, "Reşat Halife'nin fikrinde yanıldığını düşünüp bu yanlışlığı ortaya koymak başka, yobazca bir tavırla onu hemen tekfir, tahkir etmek, 'zındık, misyoner' falan gibi çirkin yaftalar yapıştırmak başkadır..." Alpaslan Yasa, işin mantığının sakat olduğunu da şu sözleriyle ortaya koyuyordu: "Halife, kendi kendine 'on dokuz şifresi' diye tamamen subjektif bir kıstas tespit etmiş, sonra Kitab'ın buna uymayan yerlerini uydurma ilan etmeye kalkışmıştır..."

Atatürk'süz olur mu hiç? Reşat Halife'nin Türkiye şubesi görevini tek başına da olsa sürdürmekte kararlı olan ise Edip Yüksel'di. Dananın kuyruğunun peygamberlik

hata etmez dediler, halbuki Kuran'da Peygamber'in birçok hatası zikredilir.

Nokta: Peki Reşat Halife'nin resul olduğunu nasıl iddia ediyorsunuz?

Yüksel: Allah bütün elçilerine mucizeler verdiğini söylüyor. Reşat on dokuz mucizesini kendisi bulmuştur. Kuran bu mucizelere ina-

iddialarından sonra koptuğunu fark eden Yüksel, önce bu konuyu açıklığa kavuşturmaya çalışıyordu: "Reşat Halife Nebi olduğunu değil, Resul olduğunu söylüyor. Hz. Muhammed Nebilerin sonuncusudur fakat Resullerin sonuncusu değildir. Bu Kuran'da açıkça belirtiliyor." Peki ne fark vardı arada? Yüksel'in yanıtı şöyle: "Nebi, kendisine kitap verilen elçidir. Resule ise kitap verilmemiştir..."

Edip Yüksel, Halife'nin tezlerinin doğruluğunu kanıtlamak için Türkiye'de sıkça başvurulan bir yöntemi de deniyordu: "Allah yeni bir dönemi başlatmak için eski dönemi son vermiş ve bunu da Mustafa Kemal aracılığıyla gerçekleştirmişti..."

Burada, eskiden sıkı bir Atatürk karşıtı olduğunu, hatta Atatürk'e hakaretten yargılandığını vurgulayan Yüksel'in Atatürk'e bakış açısı da yüzde yüz değişmişti. Yüksel'e göre, "Atatürk, İslam'ı çekilmez, yaşanmaz bir din haline getiren, tümüyle despot, hatta faşist denilebilecek bir döneme son vermişti. Bunun hikmeti de gayet açıktı, çünkü Atatürk'ü de Allah görevlendirmişti. Kanıt mı? Atatürk'ün hayatındaki on dokuzlar ne güne duruyordu. Doğumundan ölümüne, aldığı ma-

dalya sayısından nüfus cüzdanı numarasına kadar bir on dokuzlar yumağıydı Atatürk. Hatta Mustafa Kemal Atatürk bile on dokuz harften meydana geliyordu. İnanmayan sayar bakardı..."

Edip Yüksel, Reşat Halife için de tıpkı Salman Rüşdi meselesinde olduğu gibi "ölüm fetvası" verileceğine kesin gözüyle bakıyordu. Ama bu kez fermanı Humeyni değil, Suudiler verecekti. Zaten bir süre önce Suudi dini lider İbnul Baz, kanının helal olduğunu söylemişti. Dünya Fıkıh Konseyi'nin Halife'yi kafir ilan etmesiyle de ilk adım atılmıştı. Halife'nin, Salman Rüşdi ile birlikte mahkûm edilmesi bu açıdan ilgi çekiciydi.

Yüksel, konsey kararını da on dokuz teziyle değerlendirmekten geri kalmıyordu. "Halife'yle Rüşdi'yi kafir ilan edenler otuz kişiydi yani on dokuzun iki katı... İngiltere'de Salman Rüşdi'yi savunan bir insan hakları örgütü var. Bu örgütün ismi de 'Article On dokuz.' Bu sayı Rüşdi'ye de çoktan bulaştı." Yüksel'in genel durum değerlendirmesi şu sözlerle noktalanıyor: "Tüm bunlar şeytanın provokasyonu.."

Sefa KAPLAN — Can KARAKAŞ

nilmayacağını ve efsane olarak nitelendirileceğini söylüyor. Bakın, bu kitabın da adı "Kuran-ı Kerim ve 19 Efsanesi." Aynen Allah'ın dedikleri gerçekleşiyor.

Nokta: Salman Rüşdi, ile Reşat Halife arasında bir bağlantı var mı?

Yüksel: Biliyorsunuz, şeytan bir hayli bilgiye sahip. Şeytan, on dokuz mücizesinin ileride Kuran'da çıkacağını da biliyor. Bildiği için de Bahailiği kullanarak bu mucizeyi dejenere etmek istiyor. Bunun için de Rüşdi ile Reşat arasında çok acayip benzerlikler oluşturuyor. İsimleri aynı kelimeden türüyor, Reşat'ın söylediği şeyler Rüşdi'nin kitabının adı oluyor. Şeytan ikisinin birbirine karıştırılmasını istiyor. Fıkıh Konseyi'nin ikisini de aynı kefeye koyması bunu doğruluyor. Önümüzdeki aylarda Reşat yeni Kuran'ı neşrettiği zaman aleyhinde büyük bir kampanya oluşturulacak ve bunun öncülüğünü Suudi Arabistan üstlenecek. Suud'un muhalefette bulunduğu bir kişi-

ye İran geri planda kalacaktır.

Nokta: Ama Suudi Arabistan'la ABD'nin arasından su sızmıyor. İstese Reşat Halife'nin sesini kesmez mi?

Yüksel: Bu öyle görünüyor, ama öyle değil. Şu anda Rabıta bu konuda alabildiğine para yağdırıyor. Reşat'ın aleyhinde neşredilen birkaç kitap da Suudlular tarafından bedava dağıtılıyor.

Nokta: Peki bu size garip gelmiyor mu? Hem ABD'nin arası Suudilerle çok iyi, hem de Halife'ye ses çıkarmıyorlar?..

Yüksel: Tabii ama ben Allah'ın koruması altında olduğuna inanıyorum Reşat'ın. Yani öyle bir şey yapmaya kalkışsalar bile başaramayacaklardır. Şu anda Nokta'nın bunu haber yapması da Allah'ın takdiri...

Nokta: İkinci bir Salman Rüşdi olayı mı yaşanacak diyorsunuz?

Yüksel: Tabii, ben Reşat'a bu konuda ne düşündüğünü sordum. Dedi ki Allah onların enerjilerini böylece sarf ettiriyor.

616

Bir sahte peygamberin ehl-i sünnet düşmanlığı

İKİNCİ SALMAN RÜŞDİ OLAYI

Amerikalı Halife'nin Kuran'ı değiştirme çabası

● Allah'a karşı yalan yere iftira düzenden veya kendisine hiç bir şey vahyolunmamışken bana da "Vahiy geldi" diyen ve "Allah'ın indirdiğinin bir benzerini de ben indireceğim" diyenden daha zalim kimdir? Bu zalimleri ölümün şiddetli sarsıntıları sırasında meleklerin ellerini uzatarak onlara: "Canlarını çıkarın, bugün Allah'a karşı haksız olanı söylediğiniz ve O'nun ayetlerinden büyüklenmeniz dolayısıyla alçaltıcı bir azapla karşılık göreceksiniz" dediklerinde bir görsen. (En'am 93)

Reşat Halife'ni İslam'ı bozma gayretleri basına da yansımıştı. Reşat Halife'nin Türkiye'deki vekili Edip Yüksel (sağda).

İslamiyet'in 14 asırdır aslına sadık kalınarak bugüne ulaştırılması, fitne ve bozgunculuk hareketlerinin bertaraf edilmesi büyük mücadeleleri gerektirmiştir. Allah-ü Teala (cc) müceddidleri, gerçek din alimlerini vesile ederek ümmetin sapmasına mani olmuştur. Bu noktada **ehl-i sünnet itikadının önemi** daha iyi anlaşılmaktadır. Çünkü sapkın görüşlere, yalancı peygamberlere karşı mücadele edenler **sünni din büyükleri** olmuştur.

Fitne ve bozgunculuk hareketlerinin bir diğer çeşidi de yalancı peygamberlerdir. Burada dikkati çeken bir husus daha peygamberimiz hayattayken yalancı peygamberlerin faaliyete başlamış olmalarıdır. Kur'an Kerim ve hadisi şeriflerde açıkça Hz. Muhammed (s.a.v.)'in son peygamber olduğu bildirilmesine rağmen, çeşitli tevillerle her devirde yalancı peygamberler ve sahte din alimleri türemiştir. Bunların ortak özelliği bölücülük yaparak, ümmeti parçalamaya çalışmalarıdır.

Reşat Halife

Hz. Peygamber (s.a.v.) devrinin sahte peygamberi **Müseyleme**'nin günümüzdeki benzerlerinden biri de **Reşad Halife**'ydi. Peygamberliğin ilan ederek sapkın bir yol tutan Halife'nin görüşleri taraftar da topladı. Ülkemizde de **Edip Yüksel** başta olmak üzere Reşad Halife'nin propagandasını yapanlar oldu. Bunu yapanlar ehl-i sünnet itikadına açıkça cephe aldılar, yazılarıyla pervasızca saldırdılar.

Reşad Halife ve taraftarları, Kuran-ı Kerim'in tamamının 19 sayısı üzerine kurulu olduğunu iddia ettiler. Kuran'da 19 sayısıyla muta-

bık pek çok matematiksel mucize olmakla birlikte sahte peygamber ve havarileri bu düşünceyle Kuran'ın tümünü bir matematiksel şifreler kitabı olarak görmüşler ve kendi sistemlerine uymadığı gerekçesiyle Tevbe suresinin son iki ayetini Kuran'dan çıkartacak kadar ileri gitmişlerdir. Ehl-i sünnet alimi bir kardeşimiz konuyla ilgili ayrıntılı açıklamayı yazdığı kitabında yapmıştır. Allah(c.c) Kuran-ı Kerim'e sapkın mantıkla bakanları şöyle tehdit ediyor:

"Çünkü o, düşündü ve bir ölçü tespit etti. Kahrolası, nasıl bir ölçü koydu? Yine kahrolası nasıl bir ölçü koydu?" (Müddessir, 18-20)

Ancak ehl-i sünnet alimlerinin zamanında müdahalesi ve sünni müslüman cemaatlerin sağduyusuyla Kur'an'ı Kerim ve ehl-i sünnet aleyhinde ortaya atılan her fitne gibi Reşad Halife'nin fitnesinin de yayılması engellendi.

Peygamber efendimiz bir hadisi şerifinde: 'Ümmetim yetmiş üç fırkaya ayrılacak. Bunlardan yetmişikisi cehenneme gidip

yalnız bir fırkası kurtulacak (Fırka-i Naciye)' buyurmuştur. Alimler kurtuluşu olan ehl-i sünnet ve'l cemaat olduğu hususunda ittifak etmişlerdir. Sünni mezhepler İslam'ı aslına uygun şekilde yorumlayarak milyonlara mal olmuşlar. ehl-i sünnet alimleri Allah'ın Peygamberin'in yolunu kitaplara geçirerek değiştirmekten ve bozulmaktan korumuşlardır. Din düşmanlarının mezhepleri hedef seçmesi bu yüzendir. Ehl-i sünnet alimlerinin bundan sonra da Kur'an'ı Kerim ve Peygamber'in sünnetine bağlılıklarından aldıkları güçle sapkın akımlara ve bölücülüğe karşı tavrını sürdüreceklerine kuşku yoktur.

Some PROFOUND STATEMENTS by Sheikh Abdul Aziz Bin Baz Grand Mufti of Saudi Arabia.

(1) The World is flat.

(2) Music is Haraam (Sinful).

(3) Taking pictures of living things is Haraam.

(4) The Basmalah does NOT consist of 19 letters.

(5) The Qur'an does NOT consist of 114 Suras.

(6) Those who believe in and follow the Qur'an are Kaafirs (pagans).

(7) Rashad Khalifa is Kaafir.

(8) Those who go to MASJID TUCSON are Kaafirs.

THE NEW YORK TIMES, MONDAY, DECEMBER 17, 1984

The Saudi, Sheik Bin Baz, who also recently repeated his view that the world is flat, was quoted in the leaflets as having ruled that the intermingling of sexes in educational centers in Kuwait was anti-Islamic and corrupted morals.

Music and Singing Criticized

The ruling also lashed out against those who taught or listened to music, against singing in public and against taking photographs of living things.

İSLAMCILAR VE ATATÜRK

Ruşen ÇAKIR yazdı

Adnan Hoca'nın mucizevi Atatürkçülüğü!

Atatürk'ü, söyleyip yaptıklarıyla bir bütün olarak değil, doğruluğu şüpheli birtakım yönlerini öne çıkartıp severmiş gibi yapan İslamcılar bir taşla birkaç kuş vurma hesabı yapıyor

SOSYOLOG Doç. Dr. Nilüfer Göle, Türkiye'de son dönemde tırmanan Atatürk'e yönelik ilgiyi "Atatürkçülük" değil "Atatürk perverlik", "Atatürksever lik" olarak adlandırıyor.

Atatürk'ü, söyleyip yaptıkları ve bir bütün olarak değil, doğruluğu şüpheli birtakım yönlerini öne çıkartıp severmiş gibi yapan İslamcılar bir taşla birkaç kuş vurma hesabı yapıyor.

Herşeyden önce içinde yer almayan, merkezine yerleşimek isteyen politik sistemin etkili güçlerine duvarlı oldukları bir konuda teminat veriliyor. İkinci olarak, RP'li mili Rize Belediye Başkanı Şevki Yılmaz'ın bile sahiplenebileceği bir iddiayla "düşman" kendi silahıyla vurulmak isteniyor: "İslamı Atatürk dersi veririz."

İstanbul Büyükşehir Belediye Başkanı Recep Tayyip Erdoğan'ın "Atatürk, Türkiye'den mazlum milletlere önder çevresine ulaşan bu eğitimin İslamcı tabandan tepki görme riski de pek az. Çünkü asıl Atatürk'ün

bu tabanın antipatisine neden olan yönleri ön plana çıkartılmıyor.

Erdoğan bu hayli spekülatif sözleri Adnan Hoca (Oktar)'dan ö dünü aldı. Erdoğan, 27 Mart yerel seçimleri kampanyası sırasında Hoca'dan, önce sohbetum yanıklı, helleri silahlı, elitri telefonlu, jaguarlı yakışıklı müridlerini, ardından müridlerin saflarına dahil ettiği tövbekar manken Gülay Pinarbaşı'yı da ödünç almıştı.

ÖNCE EDİP YÜKSEL VARDI

Aslına bakılırsa Adnan Hoca

miklleşmiş sünni İslamcı yaklaşımları sorgulayan cüretkar yorumlara girişti.

Türkiye içinde giderek yalnızlaşan Yüksel, dünya çapında bir başka yalnızlığa sürüklenen, Arizona'da Birleşik İslam Ulusu adlı bir kuruluş çerçevesinde faaliyete bulunan Halife ile bütünleşti. Halife'nin yeni İslami yorumlarına öfkelenen uluslararası İslamcı çevreler 19 sayısında mucizevi bir yön olmadığını kanıtlamak için kolları sıvadı. Sonunda Tevbe Suresi'nin son iki ayetinin "matematiksel mucize"yi geçersiz kıldığı ortaya çıktı.

Halife ise, daha sonra Salman Rüşdü'nün "Şeytan Ayetleri" romanına da konu olan eski iddiaya vardır: "Tevbe Suresi'nin ayet denilen son iki cümlesi Kuran'a sonradan ilave edilmiştir. Biz yakında "hakiki" Kuran'ı neşredeceğiz."

Türkiye'de de, "19 kitaplarıyla" kişeyi dönen yayınevleri bu kez "mucizeyi çürüten" kitaplar basmaya, Yüksel'in kendi olanaklarıyla bastırdığı kitapları matbaadan çalıp yakılmaya başlamıştı. Bu süreç içinde Yüksel bir zamanlar kendisine hakaretten hapis yattığı Atatürk'ü keşfetti. Ona göre Atatürk, "İslam'ı çekilmez, yaşanmaz bir din haline getiren, tümüyle despot, hatta faşist denilebilecek bir döneme son veren, Allah tarafından görevlendirilmiş bir kişiydi.

Yüksel, Atatürk'de de "19 mucizesi" bulmuştu. Doğum tarihi 1881, yani 19x19, ölüm tarihi 1938, yani 19x102, Samsun'a ayak basışı 19 Mayıs 1919.

Bir tek Adnan Hoca, Yüksel'e, daha doğrusu onun görüşlerine sahip çıktı. Önce örtünme gayri koşulları kızlar açıldı; müridler, sonradan aldıkları "İslami" isimleri bırakıp gerçek "şık" isimlerine döndü.

Bundan böyle İslam'da hırsızlara verilen ceza el kesme değil el çirme idi; ayhası halinde kadınlar namaz kılabilir di; günde beş vakit değil, ikindi ve akşamın da görevleriyle birleştirilmesi suretiyle vakit namaz kılınmalıydı; müslümanlar hadislere itibar etmemeliydi...

En önemlisi Atatürk, Adnan Hoca'nın, "tavşanım, civcivim" diye hitap ettiği müridlerinin başlangıçta kulaklarına fısıldadığı gibi "Deccal" olmaktançıkmıştı.

Bir zamanlar yayınlanan ve Genel Yayın Koordinatörlüğü'nü yaptığı "Rönesans" isimli dergide, Adnan Hoca kendi kendini yazdığı

PROF. DR. İSMET GİRİTLİ
Atatürk, Laiklik ve Din

RÖNESANS

ŞUBAT-NİSAN 1991 3000 TL.

Ruşen Çakır, a prominent Turkish journalist, who wrote numerous books on Muslims and Islamic Movements, including "Ayet ve Slogan" (Verse and Slogan), in this editorial article of 30 November 1994 Milliyet, discusses my influence on Adnan Oktar, a cult leader who would later assume the pen name Harun Yahya. The cult leader received international notoriety for promoting pseudoscience against the theory of evolution and manipulating the Turkish courts thereby banning many Internet sites, including 19.org and Word Press in order to censor my article titled "Harun Yahya or Adnan Oktar: The Promised Mahdi?"

The caption under my picture taken in the printing house reads: "Edip Yüksel was once the 'Wonder Boy' of the Islamic groups, but later Islamists stole his book from the printing house." NINETEEN: God's Signature in Nature and Scripture. www.19.org

Adnan Oktar: GERÇEK ATATÜRKÇÜLER GÖREVE

Adnan Hoca, "geçmişte hakkında yanlış fikirlere sahip bulunduğum Büyük Önder Atatürk'e ve Atatürk ilkelerine bağlılığımı derlikle vurgulyorum" diyor.

HOCA DA KAYIP YÜKSEL DE

Gerçek düşüncelerini açıklamaktan kaçınan ve çekinmeden yalan söyleyen (takiyye yapan) Adnan Hoca'nın Atatürkçülüğüne Edip Yüksel erken doğum yaptırmış

görüşlerini tekrarlayıp Hoca'nın bunlara katıldığını bir kez daha kanıtladı. Ardından kaseti, kendisini aforoz etmiş olmakla birlikte "Adnanizm"e öldürücü bir darbe vurmak için sabırsızlanan İslamcı yayın organlarına teslim etti. Bu kasetin birkaç İslamcı dergide yayınlanmasıyla İslam'dan "saptığı"

lamcı tarafından öldürüldü. Uzun bir süredir ortalıkta görünmeyen Edip Yüksel'in Halife'nin Arizona'nın Tucson kentinde kurduğu merkezde yaşadığı biliniyor.

Adnan Hoca da uzun zamandır kayıp, ancak müridleri boş durmuyor.

Artistlerin, mankenlerin, gaze

ne duyarlı oldukları bir konuda teminat veriliyor. İkinci olarak, RP'li ünlü Rize Belediye Başkanı Şevki Yılmaz'ın bile sahiplenebileceği bir iddiayla "düşman" kendi silahıyla vurulmak isteniyor: "İsteyene Atatürk dersi veririz."

İstanbul Büyükşehir Belediye Başkanı Recep Tayyip Erdoğan'ın "Atatürk, Türkiye'den maşonları kovmuş liderdir" sözleriyle zirvesine ulaşan bu eğilimin İslamcı tabandan tepki görme riski de pek az. Çünkü asla Atatürk'ün

Edip Yüksel, bir dönem İslami kesimin "harika çocuğu"ydu. Sonra İslamcılar kitaplarını matbaadan çaldılar.

Adnan Oktar:
GERÇEK ATATÜRKÇÜLER GÖREVE

Adnan Hoca, "geçmişte hakkında yanlış fikirlere sahip bulunduğum Büyük Önder Atatürk'e ve Atatürk ilkelerine bağlılığımı özellikle vurguluyorum" diyor...

bu tabanın antipatisine neden olan yönleri ön plana çıkartılmıyor.

Erdoğan bu bayii spekülatif sözleri Adnan Hoca (Oktar)'dan ödünç aldı. Erdoğan, 27 Mart yerel seçimleri kampanyası sırasında Hoca'dan, önce solarium yanıklı, belleri silahlı, elleri telefonlu, jaguarlı yakışıklı müridlerini, ardından müridlerin saflarına dahil ettiği tövbekar manken Gülay Pınarbaşı'yı da ödünç almıştı.

ÖNCE EDİP YÜKSEL VARDI

Aslına bakılırsa Adnan Hoca da "gerçek" sıfatını yakıştırdığı Atatürkçülüğünü bir başkasından ödünç aldı: Edip Yüksel.

Yüksel bild dönem İslami kesimin "harika çocuğu"ydu. Şimdi ise görüşlerini, babası ve kardeşleri başta olmak üzere İslami camiada uyandırdığı hiddet yüzünden Türkiye'ye pek gelemiyor.

Parlak bir zekaya sahip olan Yüksel ilk olarak Güney Afrikalı müslüman usta Ahmet Deedat'ın "Kuran En Büyük Mucize" adlı kitabını çevirdi. Ardından Deedat'ın üstadı Mısırlı Reşat Halife'nin "Kuran Görünen Mucize" adlı kitabını piyasaya sürdü.

Aslen ziraat mühendisi olan Halife bilgisayar başında yaptığı çalışmalar sonucu Kuran'ın "19" sayısı üzerine kurulu bir mucize olduğunu kanıtlamış: Besmele 19 harfli, Kuran'da 114 (19x6) sure var...

1980 ortalarında "İslami best - seller" olan bu kitaplar değişik cemaatler tarafından tebliğ amacıyla kullanıldı. Yüksel, modern bilimler ve yeniliklerle kafası karışanlar için "İlginç Sorular" adlı iki cilt kitap yazdı. İslam'ı hayli spekülatif ve "bilimsel" yerlerle kanıtladı. "Bilimsel cihad"da hızını artıran Yüksel, temas kurduğu ilk Halife'nin de etkisiyle ke-

manına da konu olan eski iddiaya sarıldı: "Tevbe Suresi'nin ayet değillen son iki cümlesi Kuran'a sonradan ilave edilmiştir. Biz yakında 'hakiki' Kuran'ı neşredeceğiz."

Türkiye'de de, "19 kitaplarıyla" köşeyi dönen yayınevleri bu kez "mucizeyi çürüten" kitaplar basmaya. Yüksel'in kendi olanaklarıyla bastırdığı kitapları matbaadan çalınıp yakılmaya başlamıştı. Bu süreç içinde Yüksel bir zamanlar kendisine hakaretten hapis yattığı Atatürk'ü keşfetti. Ona göre Atatürk, "İslam'ı çekilmez, yaşanmaz bir din haline getiren, tümüyle despot, hatta faşist denebilecek bir döneme son veren, Allah tarafından görevlendirilmiş" bir kişiydi.

Yüksel, Atatürk'de de "19 mucizesi" bulmuştu: Doğum tarihi 1881, yani 19x19, ölüm tarihi 1938, yani 19x102, Samsun'a ayak basışı 19 Mayıs 1919...

Bir tek Adnan Hoca, Yüksel'e, daha doğrusu onun görüşlerine sahip çıktı. Önce örtünme şartı koşulan kızlar açıldı; müridler, sonradan aldıkları "İslami" isimleri bırakıp gerçek "şık" isimlerine döndü.

Bundan böyle İslam'da hırsızlara verilen ceza el kesme değil el çizme idi; aybaşı halinde kadınlar namaz kılabilirdi; günde beş vakit değil, ikindi ve yatsının gerleriyle birleştirilmesi sonucu üç vakit namaz kılınmalıydı: müslümanlar hadislere itibar etmemeliydi...

En önemlisi Atatürk, Adnan Hoca'nın, "tavşanım, civcivim" diye hitap ettiği müridlerinin başlangıçta kulaklarına fısıladığı gibi "Deccal" olmaktan çıkmıştı.

Bir zamanlar yayınlanan ve Genel Yayın Koordinatörlüğü'nü yaptığı "Rönesans" isimli dergide, Adnan Hoca kendi kendine yaptığı veya müridlerine yaptırdığı söyleşinin bir yerinde şöyle diyor: "Geçmişte hakkında yanlış fikirlere sahip bulunduğum Büyük Önder Atatürk'e ve Atatürk ilkelerine bağlılığımı özellikle vurguluyorum."

HOCA DA KAYIP YÜKSEL DE

Gerçek düşüncelerini açıklamaktan kaçınan ve çekinmeden yalan söyleyen (takiyye yapan) Adnan Hoca'nın Atatürkçülüğüne Edip Yüksel erken doğum yaptırmıştı. Hoca'nın aksine açıkcaölü ve cesur olan Yüksel, onun genellikle kendisinden aşardığı aykırı fikirlerini açıkça söylemekte inat etmesine çok kızıyordu.

Bir gün Hoca'nın evine gitti, aralarındaki samimi konuşmayı gizlice teybe kaydetti. Kendi aykırı

görüşlerini tekrarlayıp Hoca'nın bunlara katıldığını bir kez daha kanıtladı. Ardından kaseti, kendisini aforoz etmiş olmakla birlikte "Adnanizm"e öldürücü bir darbe vurmak için sabırsızlanan İslamcı yayın organlarına teslim etti. Bu kasetin birkaç İslamcı dergide yayınlanmasıyla İslam'dan "saptığı" tescillenen Adnan Hoca da kendini iyice Atatürkçülüğe verdi.

27 Şubat 1989'da Mekke'de toplanan 11. Dünya Fıkıh Konseyi Selman Rüşdü ile birlikte Reşat Halife'yi de kafir ilan etti. Bu kararadan yaklaşık altı ay sonra Halife bir İslamcı tarafından öldürüldü. Uzun bir süredir ortalıkta görünmeyen Edip Yüksel'in Halife'nin Arizona'nın Tucson kentinde kurduğu merkezde yaşadığı biliniyor.

Adnan Hoca da uzun zamandır kayıp, ancak müridleri boş durmuyor.

Artistlerin, mankenlerin, gazetecilerin özel hayatlarına en son teknoloji ürünü kamera ve dinleme cihazlarıyla füturusuzca giren müridler, santaşları boş kalan zamanlarında Atatürkçülük yapmayı da ihmal etmiyorlar. Hem de Refah Partisi saflarında.

YARIN: BİTMEYEN SORU: ATATÜRK DİNDAR MIYDI?

19 Bayrağını Cenk Koray devraldı

"**19** Mucizesi"nin itibarını Cenk Koray iade etti. Ünlü sunucunun "Kuran, İslamiyet, Atatürk ve 19 Mucizesi" adlı kitabı tıpkı bir zamanlar Edip Yüksel'in çevirdiği ya da yazdığı kitap-

"Atatürk için can alabilecek" olan Cenk Koray yazdığı kitap

lar gibi çok satıyor. Aradaki fark, Koray'ın kitabının, Yüksel'in kitaplarının aksine İslamcı olmayan bir yayınevi, Altın Kitaplar tarafından basılmış olması. İşe kitabında da "Atatürk için adamın canını alır" diye tanıtılan Koray'ın uğruna bıçaklandığı kitaptan bazı örnekler:

"Q harfiyle başlayan iki sure var: Şura ve Kaf sureleri. Her iki surede de Q harfi 57'şer kere geçmektedir. İkisinin toplamı 114 yapar (19x6: 114)

Nun harfiyle başlayan sure Kalem suresidir. Bu harf bu surede 133 defa geçer (19x7: 133).

Sad harfi, Araf, Meryem ve Sad surelerinde geçmektedir. Araf'ta 97, Meryem'de 26 ve Sad'da 29 kere. Bu üçünün toplamı 152'dir (19x8: 152).

Y ve S harfleri Yasin suresinde bulunur. Bu surede Y 237, S ise 48 kere kullanılmıştır. İkisinin toplamı 285 olur (19x15: 285)."

BİRAZ DA ATATÜRK

"Mustafa Kemal bizim gibi raslantıyla

Türkiye'de doğup yaşamışa bir insan değildir. O Allah katından görevli olarak Türkiye'ye yollanmış, belli bir misyonu yerine getirdikten sonra da Hakkın rahmetine kavuşmuştur.

Görevli olduğuna nereden hükmediyoruz? Ata'nın hayatında da 19'lar egemendir. Hayatta hiçbir şeyin raslantıyla olamayacağını biliniyor. Allah'ın izni olmadan sineğin kanadı kıpırdayamıyor. O zaman Atatürk'ün hayatındaki 19 olayı da yine Allah'ın bilgisi içinde oluşmuştur.

Nedir Atatürk'ün hayatındaki 19'lar?

Atatürk, 19. yüzyılda 19 yıl yaşamıştır.

Atatürk, 19. yüzyılın bitmesine 19 yıl kala doğmuştur.

Atatürk'ün ilk askeri görevi 19. Kolordu komutanlığıdır.

Mustafa Kemal Atatürk adına mada kavuşmuştur. Fakat ilginç raslantı daki harf sayısının 19 olmasıdır.

Bandırma vapurunda yolc 19'dur."

Telephone (319) 362-3711
Telex 464 434 MAMAR AAL CDR

NIXON TO IRAN NEXT

According to reliable sources close to the former President, Richard M. Nixon will visit Iran this spring as a "private citizen." Although Nixon has just returned from a controversial trip to China, Iranian Ambassador Ardeshin Zahedi acknowledged last week that "the door is open" for such a trip.

Ambassador Zahedi stated that "after President Nixon resigned, I told him that whenever he wanted to go to Iran as a private citizen, he is welcomed." Zahedi says that the former President has not told him when he wants to go, but other sources close to Nixon say that the trip will be arranged in late April or early May.

The Iranian Ambassador did say that his friendship with Nixon goes back some 22 years when the ex-President was Vice President and visited Iran. He, also, confirmed reports that he has visited Nixon a number of times in San Clemente since Nixon resigned from the Presidency.

Islamic Items

AN INDEPENDENT NEWSLETTER ON MODERN ISLAMIC THOUGHT

PUBLISHED FROM THE **HEART** OF AMERICA BY UNITY PUBLISHING COMPANY

Vol. 4, No. 46   Editor: Muhammad Tahir   Friday, March 12, 1976

P. O. BOX 521 CEDAR RAPIDS, IOWA 52406

WE HAVE MORE IMPORTANT THINGS

LET US NOT QUARREL

Because your newsletter has had several letters regarding the use of English in Islam, I am making a replay.

One letter said a little knowledge is a dangerous thing, which is true in this case. I correspond rather regularly with the editor of *Islamic Items*, and have since its beginning. The editor was born near my home, and therefore, I have always felt we can understand each other better. The comments that were published were made in an off the cuff letter I sent him regarding an entirely different matter. A significant part of my letter was omitted. I said, "although I do intend to learn Arabic, don't you think, etc. - only the part after the etc. was published.

I certainly would not remark to an Arab that I thought part of the problem was nationalism--that is unkind. Those Arab readers who were offended could not possibly know how much I admire their culture, and like them as a group. I have published numerous letters in the *Kansas City Star* supporting the Palestine viewpoint, when no one else did and received no small amount of abuse for it. During the Six Day War I offered a free copy of Dr. Alfred Lilienthal's *The Other Side of the Coin*. The response cost me hundreds of dollars.

Nevertheless, I do not recant. I did learn the prayers in Arabic from an Egyptian, and when I received the records from the Islamic Center (Washington, D. C.), the dialects made the two versions sound differently. I feel so false reciting the prayers when I am alone, just parroting phrases which mean much more to me in my own language.

"There are no Muslim names" someone said. Likewise, I feel God has no special language. All languages are translatable into all other languages because all humans are capable of having the same

(Cont'd on page 2)

Dr. Rashid Khalifa meets Colonel Qaddafi during the Islamic/Chrisitan Dialogue in Tripoli last month. Dr. Khalifa, an American, has just completed a modern English translation of the Holy Quran. During the translation he used computers, which according to Dr. Khalifa proves scientifically that the Quran is the Word of God. He feels that his translation will be a special gift to the scientific minded American people. (ARNA Photo)

CPSIA information can be obtained
at www.ICGtesting.com
Printed in the USA
BVHW030439201021
619266BV00010B/2